# *THE*

# TRIAL MASTERS

## A Handbook of Strategies and Tactics That Win Cases

### Bertram G. Warshaw, Editor

PRENTICE-HALL, INC. • ENGLEWOOD CLIFFS, NEW JERSEY

Prentice-Hall International, Inc., *London*
Prentice-Hall of Australia, Pty. Ltd., *Sydney*
Prentice-Hall of Canada, Inc., *Toronto*
Prentice-Hall of India Private Ltd., *New Delhi*
Prentice-Hall of Japan, Inc., *Tokyo*
Prentice-Hall of Southeast Asia Pte. Ltd., *Singapore*
Whitehall Books, Ltd., Wellington, *New Zealand*
Editora Prentice-Hall do Brasil Ltda., *Rio de Janeiro*

10   9   8   7   6   5   4

**Library of Congress Cataloging in Publication Data**
Main entry under title:

The trial masters.

    An anthology of articles from Trial diplomacy journal.
Includes index.
    1. Trial practice--United States--Addresses, essays,
lectures.   I. Warshaw, Bertram G.   II. Trial diplomacy
journal
KF8915 . A2T735   1984    347.73'7    84-11575
                          347.3077

ISBN 0-13-930892-X

Printed in the United States of America

# Foreword

The significant role being played by America's trial lawyers in the cause of justice for the "Little Guy" is one of America's best-kept secrets. This information gap, unfortunately, has done little to enhance the image in this country of lawyers in general, and trial lawyers in particular. Certainly, more should be known about the outstanding job being done by America's trial bar, day-in and day-out. Just consider for a moment the awesome responsibilities that are placed upon the shoulders of trial lawyers under the American system. By comparison, the British barrister's responsibilities are relatively light; after all, his case is prepared for him by his solicitor. The American trial lawyer, on the other hand, bears total responsibility for his case from the time his client walks through his door.

The burgeoning caseload now making its way through America's judicial system mandates the need for many more qualified, competent trial lawyers in the near future than ever before in our history. Our reputation as a litigious society is being bolstered by an explosion of activity in our judicial system. What is being done to develop the corps of skilled trial lawyers that will be required in the near future?

Unlike the British system, where trial practitioners (barristers) are carefully selected, then rigorously trained in the Inns of Court, we have no similar training system in this country. Again, under the British system, only the highly trained barristers are entrusted with the authority to try cases in the courts (except in the lowest Magistrate courts where solicitors can also practice). The American system permits virtually any licensed lawyer, with or without previous trial training or experience, to represent clients at the bar of justice.

Historically, American law schools have been notoriously opposed to the idea of teaching law students the skills of trial advocacy. The prevailing wisdom in the biggest and most highly regarded law schools dictates that law students are taught to *think* like lawyers; rarely, if ever, do they address the question of teaching law students to *behave* like lawyers in court. In recent years, a trend toward advocacy training has surfaced in some law schools, particularly the smaller independent ones. For the most part, however, new law school graduates must face an indisputable fact of life: They are ill-prepared to effectively represent a client in the courtrooms of America until they have been adequately trained in trial skills and techniques. How can these skills be acquired?

Doubtless, the best way to acquire trial skills is the tried and true method of working closely with skilled practitioners. Virtually all of the great trial lawyers of past generations, Clarence Darrow, for example, honed their trial skills in this manner, many without the benefit of having attended law school. Regretably, the opportunities for such "on-the-job" training today are quite limited, certainly insufficient to meet our future requirement for well-trained, effective trial lawyers. For those who can afford them, trial advocacy seminars provide an excellent opportunity to develop trial skills and these seminars have become big business; the problem for most young lawyers, however, is the expense involved, not to mention the time required to take advantage of them.

Another important factor in the drive toward excellence in trial advocacy, and the one with which this writer has had the most experience, is that of print materials. As publisher and executive editor of *Trial Diplomacy Journal*, I have been amazed and gratified by the willingness of America's Trial Masters to share their expertise, yes, the secrets of their successful techniques with their fellow members of the trial bar. Frankly, this has been a revelation to me! Since the magazine's inception, more than one hundred original articles written by the Trial Masters specifically for *Trial Diplomacy Journal* have appeared; literally a treasure trove of invaluable information! Many of these articles have been used as source material in the seminars previously alluded to and many, too numerous to mention, have been quoted in books and articles on the subject of trial advocacy.

*The Trial Masters,* a tightly woven compilation of many of these articles, is an invaluable working tool for the trial lawyer who seeks to improve his trial skills. Its emphasis is on "How-to-Win" oriented materials; specific, practical, successful suggestions from America's Trial Masters. Make no mistake about it, the adversarial nature of the American Justice system makes every trial potentially a hard-fought contest, a battle, if you will, with a winner and (unfortunately) a loser. The *effective* trial lawyer is a *winning* trial lawyer! The only meaningful measure of success for the trial lawyer is his *winning* record in the courtroom. Your clients *expect* you to win their cases for them. The Trial Masters can help you win. They have opened the door for you by developing innovative courtroom techniques and strategies that have proven to be successful for them time after time. They explain and demonstrate these techniques and strategies in an easy-to-follow, step-by-step manner. The total thrust of this book is on *winning in the courtroom.*

*The Trial Masters* is divided into ten chapters, each dealing with a specific phase of a trial. Within each chapter are grouped the articles dealing with that subject. A brief introduction is presented at the beginning of each chapter, highlighting some of the key features and helping the reader to tie the various chapters together. For example, Chapter One is titled "How to Prepare a Winning Case." After a brief introduction to the subject of preparation, the first Trial Master that the reader will meet is the dean of today's eminent trial lawyers, **Louis Nizer.** Who could be more qualified than Mr. Nizer to tell the reader how to prepare a winning case? In the chapter on "Picking Juries," Trial Master **Herald Price Fahringer**, considered by many of his contemporaries to be today's premier criminal defense lawyer, discloses his successful techniques for selecting a jury. In the chapter on "Final Argument" no one could possibly be better qualified to tell the reader about successful techniques than Trial Master **Melvin Belli**, whose innovative contributions to the field of trial advocacy are legend. The chapter titled "Secrets of Courtroom Psychology" leads off with Trial Master **Harry H. Lipsig**, who stresses the importance of continuing sensitivity to what's happening in the jury box. The chapter "A Treasury of Courtroom Tactics," features Trial Masters **Harry M. Philo, Philip H. Corboy**, and the inimitable **Gerry Spence**, whose latest courtroom victory at the time of this writing was a $52-Million jury award in a commercial breach of contract case in Chicago, Illinois. These are but a few of the famous Trial Masters the reader will meet.

*The Trial Masters* has been a labor of love to me, as its publisher and executive editor. I'm confident that trial lawyers will find it to be an invaluable working tool.

Bertram G. Warshaw

# The Editor

Bertram G. Warshaw received AB and JD degrees from the University of Chicago Law School, where he served on the Editorial Board of the *University of Chicago Law Review*. He is a former editor for a law publishing company specializing in tax and governmental regulations. He is also a former attorney for the Federal Government and had a general law practice in the city of Chicago. Warshaw is currently Publisher and Executive Editor of *Trial Diplomacy Journal*, a periodical published quarterly that is dedicated to helping trial lawyers to improve their trial skills. The *Journal* is widely recognized among trial lawyers nationwide as the premier publication of its type in the field.

# CONTENTS

# Chapter One

# *How to Prepare a Winning Case*

The Trial Masters you will meet in the following pages, each in his own way, bring fresh new insight to one of the oldest principles of trial practice: *Most cases are won or lost before you even set foot in the courtroom.*

In other words, the name of the game is preparation. Whether you are prosecuting or defending a criminal case, whether you are representing the plaintiff or the defendant in a civil action, the attorney who prepares best, usually is also the attorney who wins.

But how much preparation is enough? Exactly what steps should you take before trying your next case? You will find the answers to these crucial questions spelled out half a dozen different ways in this first chapter of *The Trial Masters,* as six distinguished practitioners reveal the preparation methods that have delivered winning results in the courtroom in case after case, from medical malpractice to murder one.

In the illuminating interview that begins the chapter, **Louis Nizer** remarks that thorough preparation is the "be-all and end-all of trial work." Indeed, the facts upon which you must build your entire case "never fly in through the window," Mr. Nizer observes, "they have to be dragged in by the heel." And to help you accomplish this task, he outlines his unique Rule of Probability, the "magical instrument" that leads you straight to the facts, the documents, the witnesses you need to win at trial. Using the very same process by which the jury decides the case, Nizer's Rule of Probability lets you fit all the different pieces of evidence together into a picture so compelling that a favorable verdict for your client is the only logical outcome.

Having enjoyed remarkable success both as prosecutor and defense attorney, Vincent T. Bugliosi addresses the question of trial preparation with a double-edged authority. As you will soon discover, his own secret weapon for winning at trial—the Yellow Pad Technique—is as simple as it is powerful. It costs you next to nothing, but it gives you the big advantage of having your case organized, digested, polished and perfected long before you have to face the jury. You will see how Mr. Bugliosi "orchestrates" each phase of the case, from voir dire to final argument, directly from his yellow pad. "The trial," he says, "is merely the acting out of the scenario or script you've already written."

One issue of particular concern to defense counsel in criminal cases is whether or not the defendant should testify. An error of judgment here could very well cost you the verdict in a close trial. To help you make the right decision, Henry B. Rothblatt has developed a detailed five-point checklist for determining if your client should take the stand. In addition, he provides six valuable pointers for preparing and presenting your client for an effective appearance in court.

The final three Trial Masters to share their expertise focus on the civil side, spotlighting the specific preparation techniques that work best in such actions as personal injury, medical malpractice, and product liability

For starters, noted defense counsel John P. Ewart takes you step-by-step through the pre-trial procedures he has used with consistently successful results, from reviewing the complaint and drafting interrogatories to creating a winning strategy for investigation and discovery. Next, **David S. Shrager** explains the key points you should know about the preparation and trial of medical malpractice claims, including what is perhaps the most important step of all: How to give the jury the essence of your case in just a few dramatic sentences.

Finally, to close out the chapter, Robert L. Habush discusses three of his landmark personal injury cases and how he won multi-million dollar awards for his clients—thanks to some innovative preparation methods you will want to adopt in your own practice.

# Preparing for Trial

## An interview with Louis Nizer

Louis Nizer, New York, N.Y., graduated from Columbia University Law School, LL.B., 1924. He is senior partner of the law firm Phillips, Nizer, Benjamin, Krim & Ballon in New York; counsel to the Motion Picture Association of America; and author of nine best-selling books, including *Reflections Without Mirrors, My Life in Court,* and *The Jury Returns,* as well as numerous articles. He has been portrayed on television and Broadway by George C. Scott, and Ed Asner, among others.

*During this interview, Mr. Nizer refers several times to the "rule of probability." He explained this rule in the Prologue to My Life in Court, as follows:*

*From experience, we can anticipate with reasonable certainty how people will react under a given set of circumstances. We can use this "knowledge" in two ways.*

*First, we can determine what a person probably would have done as a reaction to certain stimuli, and this will tell us what facts to seek; it will lead us to witnesses and documents we didn't know existed.*

*Second, if the conduct described is implausible, "it must be rejected as untrue no matter what assurances the client or witness gives of his recollection. It points out the vulnerable area of a hostile witness's testimony and suggests cross-examination."*

*"The rule of probability rarely misleads [when] applied by one who has good insight into the motivations and reactions of people."*

### Thorough Preparation the Nizer Way

EDITOR: Briefly, what constitutes thorough preparation for trial?

NIZER: Preparation cannot be too thorough. Consequently, it involves in every case a different approach to exhuming the facts, as if the lawyer were an archaeologist. But the thoroughness, relentlessness, perseverance, is essential and limitless. Therefore, the lawyer should not only obtain all facts from the client—relevant and irrelevant, because what may appear irrelevant at some point may throw a light on what is relevant—but also, he has an opportunity to learn from that personal contact with the client some psychological insights: why is the client over-defensive about a certain fact? Why is he going off on a torrent of irrelevancy to justify what he did? This gives him a clue that there are vulnerabilities here and there which he ought to examine. And those often lead him to other witnesses and other documents, under the rule of probability, which I've written about.

Every witness should be thoroughly, thoroughly examined. There should be no impatience to keep him only to what the lawyer thinks is highly relevant. The more the witness talks, the more one learns of aspects which might otherwise be lost in memory, and also one learns how to treat such a witness when you get him on the stand. If he's voluble he may need restraint, if he's shy he may need encouragement. So the personal contact with the witness, or the client, gives information concerning trial tactics which cannot be obtained in any other way.

Every document should be examined thoroughly, and indexed, because the rule of probability leads from one piece of evidence to another. And the rule of probability, I have explained in some of my writings, is a magical instrument. If a thing sounds improbable, it probably didn't happen that way. And if you stick to it long enough and govern yourself by what is more likely to be probable, you ultimately find that that's the truth. So it leads you to evidence, and I've illustrated many times the magic of the rule of probability, where the client denies something, and you find out from the rule of probability that he's wrong, and he's denied something against his own interest. Time and again I've found documents which the client insisted did not exist; he never wrote a letter at that time; he never had a conversation with a man at that time. The rule of probability tells me he must have, or the letter written one month later wouldn't have been written the way it was.

And so thorough preparation is an unending search—it is the be-all and end-all of trial work. All the other qualities—improvisation, ebullience, resourceful thinking, felicity on your feet, and facility of expression—all these are satellites, and they all revolve around the sun; and the sun is thorough preparation.

## Budgeting Your Time

EDITOR: You say preparation is an unending search. Doesn't a lawyer have to budget his time somewhat?

NIZER: If he's thinking in terms of economics, and budgeting his time, he is not doing justice to the case, and he will not have the successes which will raise him to the pinnacle where he can receive huge fees because he has the reputation of winning cases. The lawyer who wants to be a good, successful trial lawyer cannot afford to think in those terms. He must prepare the cases as thoroughly as he can.

One of the sequelae of this proposition is also interesting. A good case can be lost and a bad case won not because justice is confused, or bad, or the process of justice is unfair; it's because a jury or judge can only react to the stimuli to which they or he are subjected. And those stimuli come from evidence. If the lawyer doesn't drag the evidence into the courtroom, the wrong side may win because it has a preponderance of evidence which hasn't been answered or contradicted. The facts never fly in through the window; they have to be dragged in by the heel. And the person who drags them in is the lawyer. That is the reason why you can have a terrible result in a very good case, and win a bad case—it's because the other side hasn't brought in all the facts resulting from thorough preparation. That's how important thorough preparation is. The lack of it may cause an injustice.

### How to Prepare Effective Witnesses

EDITOR: Does a busy lawyer like yourself take the time to interview and get to know all important witnesses?

NIZER: Yes, it is absolutely essential. And let me mention one other thing, which is rarely done, and even rarely asked—you haven't asked it, and I don't think you will. What is just as important is that each witness and the client be prepared for *cross*-examination. The lawyer has a pretty good idea, if he is thoroughly, thoroughly prepared, as to the attack that will be made by a skillful cross-examiner. And after the witness has been thoroughly prepared to tell the truth—and I'll go to the truth in a moment in this matter, because a false impression is created that thorough preparation means imposing upon the witness some fancy story; that's the best way to disserve the case, practically speaking; I'll come to that—but getting back to the mainstream: if the lawyer has thoroughly prepared his client to tell a story in which he has reconstructed maybe three years, five years, ten years of events, no memory is good enough for that. It's the lawyer's duty, by reading every document and talking to witnesses, to tell his own client the sequence of events, what really happened. Where the client has no recollection, show him the document which proves it. Show the sequence which makes it inevitable.

Now after the witness has been so thoroughly prepared, the next question is, is he prepared for a skillful cross-examiner? And I will spend hours with that witness, subjecting him to an attack. And the attack again is to elicit the truth. For example, I know that the other side, let's say, is going to present him with a letter which has a damaging paragraph. But if that letter is read carefully, the next to the last paragraph explains the language of that [damaging] paragraph—at least it ameliorates the contradiction; it shows how the ambiguity arose. If the witness is simply faced with that letter without advanced preparation, he may fall  The cross-examiner hammers him, "Now  that paragraph shows, that letter that you wrote shows, that what you said here wasn't the truth, doesn't it?"

"No, uh. . . . " You know, he begins to waver, he doesn't know what to say, he looks for help.

And then you cross-examine him. And don't let him step out of character. The moment he begins to ask you, you say, "No, no. You're a witness, and I'm your enemy. Now what do you say when I face you with that paragraph?"

"Well," he says, if he's thoroughly prepared, "Mr. Cross-Examiner, you haven't read the entire letter. If you read the next to last paragraph, you'll see the true meaning of that paragraph. Or, if you will look at a letter I wrote one month later you'll see that I couldn't have meant what you say that letter means."

Now that is essential. The cross-examination drill, which is part of thorough preparation, is not often utilized, I'm afraid. And it is essential to thorough preparation.

Now let me make one observation here about a common misconception by the public, sometimes even by lawyers. The thorough preparation of a witness is the only way in which you can approximate the truth. If you don't thoroughly prepare him, he will inadvertently lie, and often against his own interest. And if the facts require him to make an admission against his interest, he should be encouraged to do so. And you should bring it out as his lawyer, bring it out before the cross-examiner does.

No case is perfect. In every case there are contradictory facts. But if the jury and the judge get the feeling that the witness has been honest, and he's told the whole truth, even some facts which are adverse to him, then it is fair to sum up and say the *preponderance* of evidence is in your favor. Notice the word preponderance. It doesn't mean the facts are unanimously in your favor, ever. To win a case, all you need is a preponderance of evidence; which assumes that there is a good deal of evidence on the other side. Which is the fact of life when there is a dispute.

So I have always, in lectures at law universities, made the point that entirely apart from honor, and I've never found an outstanding trial lawyer who wasn't a man of character and honor, but entirely apart from honor, the only practical way to win a lawsuit is to be thoroughly honest, even with adverse facts. The witness or the client who tries to hide a letter, or change a truth and a fact, sooner or later must fall, if he is skillfully cross-examined. But if he concedes it, and says, "Nevertheless, look at everything else that happened. I was still right," he will win by preponderanace.

So I make the point that it so happens that ethics and honor are parallel with successful trial work, even as a pragmatic matter.

EDITOR: And you take the time to explain that to each witness?

NIZER: Yes. Every young lawyer will find that some witness says, "Well, can't you tear that letter up, they haven't got it?" That's the time for character to adduce itself, and say, "I'm not going to tear up anything. I'm not going to dishonor you and myself; but more than that my friend, that's the best way to lose this case, because you never know when the other side hasn't heard of that letter. And as a practical thing it's the most dangerous thing to do. We're going to produce this letter. And this is the best explanation you can make for it, because that's the fact, isn't it?"

And then the blow is lessened. In a long trial, in a complicated set of facts, the fact that the witness has made admissions against his interest doesn't hurt you at all, if the main preponderance of evidence is in his favor. And woe to the witness on the other side who practices differently. That man must fall—if the lawyer is thoroughly prepared.

### Nizer's "Rule of Probability" in Action

EDITOR: You mentioned the rule of probability, and I know you wrote about it in My Life in Court. I'll state the question as you did yourself. With respect to finding evidence, how does a lawyer know where to search, and for what?

NIZER: Well, he is guided by the rule of probability, and that's how he knows. I have illustrations in the Charlie Chaplin case, which I once tried, of how we discovered that a certain witness had asked Chaplin to star in a picture, the issue being whether Chaplin had stolen the property of this story written by Konrad Bercovici, which he had taken, as we claimed. And I showed how the rule of probability led me to it. It happens to me at every trial.

A short time ago, I insisted that there must have been some other transaction that caused an English company, involved with a bank, to give relief to our client. Why would they give him relief, when there was a dispute between them in which the bank claimed it hadn't received enough money; why would they suddenly give him relief? It violated the rule of probability.

So I said to my client, "There must have been some other transaction."

"No, Mr. Nizer, we searched the records, we've done everything we can."

"Well, go back to London and search again." Went back, searched, couldn't find it.

So we went to trial. In the midst of the trial I got an excited cable. "We've found the letter, and another which accounts for this relief"— which I couldn't explain, which embarrassed me in the case.

"And how did you know?" they asked.

And I say, the rule of probability told me so. It's unlikely that this would have happened unless some other transaction had taken place.

Now this happens dozens of times every trial. That's how you know what to look for. You go by what the rule of probability is. Which incidentally isn't as mysterious as it sounds. How do you decide when you're seated at a dinner table that your partner next to you is not to be trusted? You never met him before, you talked to him for an hour or two at the dinner table, and yet you go home and you say, "You know, that fellow next to me, I wouldn't trust him as far as I could throw a piano." What made you do that?

It's the same thing. You didn't like the way he looked at somebody else while he was talking to you, the way he flirted artificially with someone, the way he laughed too raucously, there was a lack of sincerity. The rule of probability told you something about his personality was untrustworthy.

Or vice-versa; you go home, you say, "The fellow next to me, you know, is a marvelous fellow. I only met him for an hour—"

The rule of probability is after all what makes a jury decide a case. How does a jury decide between A and B, which is constantly happening in every trial, given opposite testimony concerning a fact? The fact is so probable that I don't believe the fellow who told the *other* story. You go by the rule of probability. When you accept one version as against another, as a juror, you apply the rule of probability.

EDITOR: Can I substitute the word "instinct" for "probability"?

NIZER: No, because it isn't instinct. It's a logical process. When you say instinct, you're making it a mysterious thing like a woman's intuition. I don't think it's that at all. I think there's a logic behind it.

If you told me that you had gotten all A-pluses in your courses, I would have no reason to know that it isn't so, but I'd be skeptical of it. And if I started to investigate and I found you'd gotten a B in some courses, I'd mark you down as a fellow who exaggerates. It's the rule of probability that led me to it. It isn't instinct. Nor is it even intuition, though some people insist it is; I don't believe them.

### Making the Most of Your Witnesses and Opening Statement

EDITOR: In general, in a jury trial do you schedule your strongest witness first, or last; or how do you otherwise determine your schedule?

NIZER: It is the general rule, always subject to some special reason for exceptions, to start with a very strong witness, and end with a strong witness. The weaker witnesses, if you think they're not as important or weaker, should be in the middle. But chronological sequence sometimes forces you to revise that. But generally, that's the best way to do it. A very strong witness begins with a good impression. And a very strong ending witness.

Now, that's even true of the opening statement. It gives you a wonderful head start in the trial to have a very, very thorough opening statement. You have carefully thought it out; and you don't give away too much—you leave holes for your opponent to step into, you even cover them with some leaves. But the statement is so skillfully devised, and so sincerely presented, without notes, that the jury immediately gets the impression that your client is probably right. That's an awfully good head start. That's why I'm for very thorough openings.

There is a school of thought that you can make your opening very brief, and you can hear it from the witness; the jury will be more impressed. I belong to the other school. And if the jury recognizes the testimony already told to it, it may even appreciate it and pride itself on recognizing it—in the way that you like music that you are more familiar with. I'm not afraid that repetition by the witness, of what you told the jury you're going to prove, will diminish the impact.

On the other hand, it gives you the chance in the opening statement to anticipate what the argument on the other side will be, and tell them what you're going to prove with respect to that. It's part of the opening statement, and you've already taken the wind out of the sail of the other fellow's argument, and almost given your answer.

Now the reason I go to the opening statement is, it's part of the answer to the same question. The opening witness, probably your client, should be strong. The opening statement should be strong, so that the jury begins with an impression that your side is right. That's very important.

### Preparing and Presenting Final Argument

EDITOR: And the closing argument should be strong as well?

NIZER: Obviously. In closing argument, I have a technique that I follow. And incidentally, I'm not saying it's right or wrong to do it any other way, I can only say this is my personality and my experience. I have my associates, my partners who are assisting me, get the minutes—I'm talking of an important trial where it's long, and you get the minutes late at night delivered to your home—and you sit up for hours, three o'clock or four o'clock in the morning, and the important admissions or contradictions are noted on the outside of the minutes, on the envelope.

When the time for summation comes, I make sufficient notes in which I am able to refer to the volume of the minutes, based upon those notes. And my own technique is, each folder, each package of minutes delivered every night, is marked with a number. Very simple, one, two, three, four, five, and so forth. The page is 469, and A, B, and C—top of the page, middle of the page, end of the page, so you don't have to be searching for it; it's underlined, of course, on top of that.

Now when I'm summing up I'm able to say, "I'm going to prove to you, not merely out of the mouths of our witnesses but out of the mouths of our very adversaries, the witnesses on the other side, how right we are." And as you go along, you quote *them*: "They admitted this. Do you recall the picture of the witness?" They've forgotten him. It was three weeks ago, let's say, in a long trial. "Remember that young man with blond hair, who was so nervous; he admitted this fact. If you don't recall it, let me read from the official stenographic minutes.

"Question. 'Did you meet him on the night of so and so and tell him that you agreed?'

" 'I'm not sure it was that night, but I agreed.'

"Well, whether it was that night or two nights later, you did meet him and agree.'

" 'Yes, sir.' "

Now the impact of reading admissions from the other side, which are always obtained if you're thoroughly prepared, is very great upon a jury. You don't just make a speech at them. You read admissions. And also you read the way your witness answered a cross-examination question. Because he was thoroughly prepared, he destroyed the cross-examiner: "Do you remember this attack upon him? Mr. Jones asked my client so and so and so and so. Let me read his answer again to you."

Now that's a technique for summation that I use. And the rule of summation in my judgment is juries decide issues on fact. You must have a thorough foundation of fact. After that you can superimpose all the emotion and oratory you want. And you should. The impact of your deep feeling that your client is right is very good, very persuasive. A righteous indignation is very persuasive. But you cannot win with righteous indignation or declaiming. People who think that a lawyer is a mouthpiece, that terrible expression, just an eloquent orator, is a fellow who loses cases. You don't win cases as an orator. You win cases because you have established the facts in your favor. Now after you have established that, you can ring all the bells you want on what an outrage this is to your client, and why there should be punitive damages in a libel case, or whatever you wish; or in an antitrust suit, why treble damages, why does the law *give* treble damages. And isn't it deserved in this case more than any other that ever was tried in this court? That's different. But the facts must be established first. A careful building, brick by brick, of the facts, quoting the record, and then superimposed on that your emotional excitation, can be effective.

EDITOR: At what point do you begin preparing the final argument?

NIZER: Towards the very end, because there is too much happening every day. And that means very often being up all night preparing the final argument. If we finished at four o'clock or five o'clock on Wednesday and the judge says we will have summation on Thursday, I may not go to sleep. I am working all night, going through the process I just described in preparing my argument.

The trial of a case is a great test of vitality. Anybody who isn't in very good health shouldn't be a trial lawyer. And I have once written, it may be somewhat exaggerated, that no decent trial lawyer ever goes through a trial without losing at least six to ten pounds.

# Tactics and Techniques for Handling Each Phase of a Criminal Trial

## Vincent T. Bugliosi

Vincent T. Bugliosi received his law degree in 1964 from UCLA law school, where he was president of his graduating class. In his eight-year career as a prosecutor for the Los Angeles District Attorney's Office, he tried close to 1,000 felony and misdemeanor court and jury trials. Of 106 felony jury trials, he lost only one case. His most famous trial was, of course, the Manson case, which became the basis of his best-selling book *Helter Skelter*. He is also co-author of *Till Death Us Do Part*, and *Shadow of Cain*. Both *Helter Skelter* and *Till Death Us Do Part*, in their respective years, (1974 and 1979) won the Edgar Allan Poe award as the best true crime story of the year. Bugliosi is a member of the National Advisory Board of National Victims of Crime; he has served on the Board of Editors for Trial Diplomacy Journal; and is a member of the faculty for the Association of Trial Lawyers of America. He has also lectured at Law Schools and Bar Associations throughout the nation on the subject, "Tactics and Techniques in the Trial of a Criminal Case." F. Lee Bailey has called Bugliosi "The Quintessential Prosecutor."

Before I discuss the first phase of a trial, the selection of a jury, I want to discuss at some length something that is applicable to every phase of a trial, be it cross-examination or final argument, something that, to me, is the *sine qua non*, the single most important factor in the successful prosecution or defense of any lawsuit, this thing called preparation.

As Hamlet says, "The readiness is all." The term "tactics and techniques" carries with it the connotation of almost descending, as it were, to feints and maneuvers calculated to gain an advantage over one's opposition. But permeating all these tactics and techniques is a more elegant notion, that of preparation, which is more attitudinal in nature than that which it faithfully begets, the steps one employs to win a lawsuit. Much of this article is an effort to bring about this attitudinal change in those who may not be adequately preparing their cases.

Perhaps the most shocking thing to me when I first became a trial lawyer was discovering the abysmal lack of preparation on the part of trial lawyers in general. Even many lawyers with whom I went to law school, who were conscientious and burned the midnight oil, came to court shooting from the hip. Believe it or not, I have prosecuted first degree murder cases where the defense attorney had not even read the preliminary examination transcript.

The paradox is that while all lawyers agree there is no substitute for preparation, many lawyers sincerely and genuinely believe they have prepared their case, when in point of fact, at least in my opinion, they have not.

Let me tell you what preparation means to me. It means more than just going to the scene of a crime, interviewing witnesses, reading police reports, listening to tape-recorded conversations, employing experts to examine parts of your case, and so forth. That is the fun part, the part so many lawyers confuse as constituting thorough preparation.

To me, thorough preparation means not just those things, but in addition thereto—and this is the main point I want to make—reducing virtually everything you know about a case, number one, and number two, the manner in which you intend to present it in court, to a yellow pad. This is where most lawyers, in my opinion, fall down. Either they use hardly any notes at all, which is becoming more and more fashionable among many trial lawyers today, including some prominent ones, or much more commonly, their notes are woefully sketchy and inadequate. They are not nearly comprehensive enough. For instance, in a complex case, instead of having two or three hundred pages of notes, they will have twenty or twenty-five.

It is really a curious phenomenon how, when these same lawyers were in law school, they took extensive notes. But when they get out and start trying cases, they simply do not. And this reality is the precise reason why I feel impelled to spend so much time, as I am going to, on what would appear to be such an obvious point.

Why is there this dichotomy in note-taking between the law student and the practicing lawyer? This has always puzzled me, and I do not have the answer. But here is one possible explanation. In law school, you write down what the professor is saying. This does not require any thinking on one's part—at the most, merely some interpretation. But when you try a lawsuit, the great bulk of what you write down is your own ideas, your own questions, your own articulations.

So what we are trained to do in law school is different from what we have to do on the outside, which is considerably more difficult. Most people are almost allergic to reducing their thoughts to writing, be it in a letter, a book, or what have you. It is very taxing. That may be the answer.

Whatever the reason, I believe that lawyers trying cases have grossly inadequate notes, and therefore, are inadequately prepared. There are hundreds of pieces of information in their head, but because they are human beings, not computers, of necessity the information is disorganized and undigested, and a dangerously high percentage of it is ineffectively presented when it leaves the lawyer's lips in court.

The sequence should not be from the lawyer's mind to the jury. It should be from the mind to the yellow pad—for organization, digestion, polishing and review—and then to the jury.

When the information in one's mind has not been reduced to the yellow pad, not only is it almost by definition usually disorganized, but the potential such information has in being a fertile source for the sprouting of new ideas is appreciably hampered. However, working on a yellow pad and contemplating the wallpaper in the study of your home, you will come up with all types of questions, ideas and articulations. It is rather amazing the impressive heights you can reach if you just sit down and work with pad and pencil. I have come up with thoughts and articulations I did not think my alleged mind was capable of.

I do not have to tell you that reducing what is in your mind to writing is extremely tedious and time-consuming. It is pure drudgery and sweat, sometimes agony. It is very hard work. It is not fun. *To me, it is the hardest part of trying a case.*

But in my opinion, it is the only way to try a complex lawsuit, and the only way to make a superior presentation of your case, as opposed to a good or merely adequate one.

For instance, in preparing your cross-examination, you might know, in your mind, what point you want to make, but it might take you a half-hour of sweat on a yellow pad to work out the very best way of establishing this one point on cross-examination. Before you ask your key question, you might decide you have to ask ten preliminary questions, and in a particular sequence. Some of these preliminary questions you may rewrite three or four times, because when you examine them closely you will see that the witness might be able to discern the direction in which you are taking him.

In final argument, you might know what point you want to make, but when you try to articulate the point on a yellow pad, all of a sudden your pencil comes to a stop. It is at this point that you realize you did not quite understand your point as well as you thought you did, or even if you did, you certainly realize you were unable to extemporaneously articulate the point with the clarity and power you want. To verbalize this point in the best way possible—the right words, yes, even the right pauses—takes time.

Moreover, many ideas, thoughts and concepts simply do not lend themselves to easy articulation. But they can be mastered if you will invest the proper time. Is it not much better for your pencil to come to a stop in the privacy of your home than for you to sound incoherent to a jury?

I have not mentioned the most obvious danger of not reducing everything to a yellow pad. Almost invariably during cross-examination or final summation in a complex case, since a lawyer has virtually no time in court to pause and cogitate, he is going to simply omit many points, some of which may very well have been crucial to his client's cause. How many lawyers walk out of court every day muttering "Gee, I forgot to ask this question. I forgot to argue this point," and so forth?

When every point you want to make is on that yellow pad, this will not happen. I have always subscribed to an old Chinese proverb that the palest ink is better than the best memory. For example, when I am on the freeway in Los Angeles and I think of something pertaining to a case I am trying, I will have my wife jot it down on any scrap of paper available. If she is not with me, I have been known to take the next offramp and jot it down. For me, the times have been numerous where an important thought has come into my mind, and one second later, not five minutes or an hour later, but one second later, to save my life, I cannot remember what it is.

Incidentally, when I talk about reducing everything to writing, I am not suggesting, for example, that on cross-examination you read your questions. That, of course, would be very amateurish and ineffective. But if your questions have been written down, you can review them over and over to the point where they are so firmly in your mind that when you commence cross-examination you can stand up, leave your notepad, and fire your questions at the witness.

It is my view that a substantial portion of the trial can literally be orchestrated before you ever enter the courtroom. Arguments, counterarguments, questions, objections, the whole gamut, can take place on a yellow pad before the trial even starts. The trial is merely the acting out of the scenario or script you have already written. Granted, unpredictable things happen at a trial, but if you have done your homework, even many of these otherwise unpredictable occurrences can be anticipated and prepared for.

I had lunch with a reporter from Newsweek a few years ago in New York. He told me he liked my book *Helter Skelter*, with one exception. I did not indicate in the book that I had made any significant errors during the Manson trial and he found this to be unrealistic. He asked me flat out if I did make any significant errors. I told him that to my knowledge I did not. Before he could throw his glass of water at me for my apparent pomposity, I hastened to add that I had made many errors in the Manson case, but they were made outside of court. I had already spotted and eliminated them from my yellow pad before I walked into court.

The standard cop-out of lawyers who religiously avoid the pain and agony of the yellow pad is this: they make the anemic argument that if a lawyer does all that preparation and has everything written down, he cannot be flexible, and cannot think on his feet when something not covered by his notes occurs.

If that is not a classic non-sequitur, I do not know what is. Who said that just because you are prepared in writing, you cannot also be flexible? Is instant improvisation and flexibility the domain only of those who are unprepared? That is pure moonshine and so transparent an argument a blind man could see through it.

On the issue of preparation, my method of trying a lawsuit is relentlessly simple. I sit down and determine what testimony and evidence I need to win the lawsuit. I then dedicate myself with a total immersion to going out and finding the facts upon which the testimony and evidence will be based, and then, with the help of a yellow pad, getting these facts before the jury by way of direct examination, cross-examination and final argument, and each one in the most powerful, effective way possible, i.e., I bleed my case white. That way, if I lose, I do not have to kick myself in the derriere for not doing the best job possible. That is what I mean by preparation.

There may be a lawyer somewhere in this country who is so brilliant, that even in a complex case he can give an A+ performance in court without extensive written notes, but I have never met him and I do not believe he exists. If he does, I want to meet him and get his autograph. In my opinion, in a complex case, without extensive notes you might give a C performance, maybe a C+. If you are particularly brilliant, and lucky, maybe even a B or B+. But not an A. For whatever it is worth, that is my opinion.

### Voir Dire

With respect to the selection of a jury, I think most lawyers have been disabused of the notion we may have once had, fresh out of law school, that we could pick jurors who would be favorable to our client's cause simply by evaluating the answers they give on voir dire, or by noting the prospective juror's demeanor or outward appearance.

Although you still hear joking about the fact that prosecutors are always looking for the conservative, crewcut Nordic types, defense lawyers for long-haired fellows with wide red ties, I think most lawyers agree that the greatly limited scope of allowable questions on voir dire reduces jury selection to one-third art and skill, and two-thirds guesswork.

Even in the area of art and skill, however, I have never felt particularly adequate, having never been a terribly good judge of people early on. But again, in this area of art and skill, preparation is the main ingredient—sitting down and deciding what type of juror would be the best for your client under the facts of the case, and what questions you should ask to ascertain whether a prospective juror is the type whom you are looking for.

Although you obviously want to excuse jurors who have prejudices which will work against your side, ironically, to ask a juror that very question, i.e., if he is "prejudiced" against something, a question trial lawyers frequently ask, is almost pointless, since a juror will rarely admit he is prejudiced against anything. Phrases like "lean towards," "preference for," or even "like" or "dislike" have to be employed to expose the bias.

Another point: jurors usually sit wooden in the jury box during a trial, believing they are never supposed to change their expression, almost as if they are participants in a black tie poker game. This extreme decorum on their part while amidst an atmosphere of officialdom completely foreign to them starts with voir dire, making them hesitant to speak their mind.

I always make it a practice to urge the jury to relax. And I tell them that if they disagree with any of the rules of law I refer to, now is the time to speak up, not later on in the jury room. If they do not disagree, I get a commitment under oath from each juror—a commitment I remind them of during my summation—that if the facts so warrant, they will faithfully apply these rules of law during their deliberations back in the jury room.

In this regard, during voir dire, it is always good tactics to try to educate and instruct the jury on those *specific* rules of law which you feel, under the facts of the case, will apply favorably to your client, and also seek to find out the jury's state of mind with respect to those rules of law.

Unfortunately, many judges, during voir dire, will not permit you to examine on the *specific* law of the case. With the exception of a few questions on reasonable doubt and circumstantial evidence, on matters of law, they will only permit you to ask the jury the general question whether they will follow the law given them by the court at the conclusion of the evidence.

This restriction, I feel, is incorrect. How assured can you be by a juror's telling you he will abide by the law given to him by the court, when at the time he is telling you this, he does not even know what that law is going to be?

Therefore, in selecting a jury, it is highly important that you make every effort to explain to the jury what the specific law of the case is, and find out whether they understand that law and agree with it.

For instance, as a prosecutor, it was my experience from questioning jurors that some people are disinclined to assign equal guilt and/or punishment to the co-conspirator who does not actually perpetrate the crime. With this in mind, I always went into depth with the jury on the conspiracy rule of vicarious liability. I could not afford to have some juror at the end of the case back in the jury room saying "Oh, I cannot convict this person of first degree murder. He wasn't even present at the scene of the murder."

If the trial judge offers resistance to your inquiring into the specific law of the case, which has happened to me on many occasions, you might appeal to his logic with this type of argument: A juror with a fixed opinion against a particular rule of law cannot always act in the impartial manner required of him under the law, despite his conscious desire to follow the law given him by the Court. It is human nature to be swayed, even if unconsciously, by one's sentiments. Moreover, even if the juror does follow the law given him by the Court, he might be swayed against finding those facts present which give rise to the rule of law, and thereby avoid having to apply it.

Although the right to inquire into a juror's understanding and sentiments concerning specific rules of law has not found its way into the hornbooks, there are several cases which specifically authorize it. In California, the cases are: *People v Tuthill*, 31 C. 2d 92, 98 (1947); *People v Wolff*, 182 C. 728, 736 (1920); and *People v Bennett*, 79 C.A. 76, 90 (1926).

## Opening Statement

In a complex case, as where the case is fragmented and scattered in its times, places and events, and elliptical in its evidential architecture, I usually make an opening statement to enable the jury to better follow the evidence as it comes from the witness stand.

But if my case is *not* complex, although obviously there are distinct advantages to making an opening statement—perhaps the most important of which is that it gives you an extra opportunity to sell your case to the jury and predispose them at the beginning of the trial to your side—as a basic proposition, I usually waive opening statement. I have two principal reasons for doing this: One, when you make an opening statement, you are divulging to your opposition, right at the start of the case—a case that might last a few weeks or even a few months—the heart of your case, sometimes even the intricacies of it. And this, of course, gives him so much more time than he would normally have had to work up an effective response.

My second reason for waiving opening statement is that I feel it takes the edge off my witnesses' testimony when the jury has already heard the story from me. When my key witnesses testify to important points, I want their testimony to have as much dramatic impact as possible with the jury, and if the jury has already heard the story from me, I feel it might diminish that impact. I do not feel strong about my position on opening statement. I am well aware I could be making a tactical error in not making an opening statement in a non-complex case. It is just a personal preference on my part.

If you do decide to make an opening statement, make sure you do not bite off more than you can chew, that you do not promise the jury you will prove something you may be unable to prove. You must be careful in your statement so you do not have to contradict yourself or retract by trial's end. It is very effective for opposing counsel to point out to the jury at the conclusion of the case that in your opening statement you said you were going to prove something and you failed to do so. It hurts your credibility in the eyes of the jury and can adversely affect their perception of your entire case.

## Direct Examination

On direct examination, for the most part I stay at the counsel table with my yellow pad, containing hundreds of questions, doggedly trying to get into the trial record—literally trying to force into the record—the facts and evidence upon which my case is based.

On cross-examination and final summation, however, I am apt to roam every inch of the courtroom floor.

A trial tactic I frequently employ on direct examination is that if I know the opposition is going to elicit, on cross-examination of my witness, evidence damaging to my side, I try to introduce the evidence myself. This achieves two objectives: number one, it conveys to the jury your willingness to see that all evidence, unfavorable to your cause as well as favorable, comes out—that you are not trying to suppress it in open court or back in the judge's chambers. This helps to establish your credibility with the jury. Secondly, it frequently converts a left hook by your opposition into a left jab. If it does not do that, it will almost always at least shave a few decibels off the opposition's trumpets. It indicates to the jury that the evidence really cannot be all that bad if it was matter-of-factly and almost cavalierly brought out by you on direct examination of your own witness.

This tactic I have referred to can be implemented not just by asking questions of your own witness which you anticipate the opposition is going to ask on cross-examination, but in some situations, by actually calling an opposition witness as your own witness.

A few years ago, in a celebrated murder case in Fort Worth which was tried on a change of venue in Amarillo, the multimillionaire defendant did not testify, nor as I understand it did he present much of a defense at all. Most of the defense was devoted not directly to the murder charge, but to making the defendant's wife, the star witness for the prosecution, look like the cheapest, most tawdry Jezebel ever to come down the plank. The defense allegations, though essentially legally irrelevant, were for the most part true. And the up-tight, Bible Belt jury, aghast at the revelations of immorality on the part of the defendant's wife, in effect convicted her and almost as an incidental by-product thereof, found her husband not guilty. The defense attorney reportedly later told the press he knew he had won the case the moment the last red-neck was seated on the jury.

I cannot help but wonder what the result would have been in that case if the prosecutor, whom I have since spoken to, had matter-of-factly presented all of this negative, depreciating evidence on direct examination. Maybe, just maybe, they at least would have had a murder trial in Amarillo.

## Cross-Examination

As old and venerable as the history of jurisprudence, cross-examination has been the principal weapon known to the law, as one legal scholar wrote, for separating truth from falsehood, actual knowledge from hearsay, fact from imagination and opinion—the best technique for reducing exaggerated statements to their true dimensions.

Professor Henry Wigmore called cross-examination "beyond any doubt the greatest legal engine ever invented for the discovery of truth."

The famed trial lawyer of a few years back, Jake Ehrlich, bemoaned "the lost art of cross-examination."

Cross-examination takes on more importance than direct examination because juries listen to it more closely. First of all, they realize that unlike direct examination, there has been no dry-run in a lawyer's office, and secondly, they find it far more interesting because of its adversary nature.

As with all other facets of a trial, the keynote to successful cross-examination is thorough preparation.

One point I would like to briefly touch upon. Before you prepare your cross-examination, always try to interview the opposition witnesses. As a prosecutor, I was always amazed to see so many fellow prosecutors never making any effort to ascertain the identity of the defense witnesses, and then seek to interview them. I was likewise amazed that so many defense attorneys rely on what they are given by way of discovery and make no effort to interview the prosecution witnesses themselves.

When you attempt to interview the opposition witnesses, there is really no way you can lose. If they give you a statement, you obviously can use it as a basis for impeachment at the trial if it differs from their trial testimony or from any other statement they have made. Even if they are unwilling to give you a statement, as is frequently the case, this too can work to your advantage. On cross-examination, this refusal to give a statement can be brought out to show the bias of the subject witness.

Entire books have been devoted to cross-examination alone. I am only going to discuss here two hallowed maxims of cross-examination, both of which I have never understood nor followed.

The first maxim which I reject out of hand, and whose genesis is unknown, is this: "Never ask a witness a question unless you know what the answer is going to be." Although this legal caveat is valid for direct examination of one's own witness, it is my belief, for whatever it is worth, that the overwhelming majority of experienced trial lawyers will tell you it simply is not always valid for cross-examination.

Although the ideal situation clearly would be to know in advance what the adverse witness's answers are going to be to all of your questions, the reality is that, inasmuch as you frequently have not had an opportunity to interview the witness, of necessity, cross-examination oftentimes is a trek through new terrain, and experience, caution and instinct sometimes are one's only guide.

I would only accept this antiquated commandment if it were amended to read: "Never ask a question concerning a matter *critical* to your case without being reasonably sure what the answer is going to be."

The second maxim, and one about which I want to spend some time, is this: Books on cross-examination all advocate never asking an adverse witness "why" he did something implausible.

Trial lawyers are equally insistent against the use of the "why" question. A few years ago, a speaker at a trial lawyers' convention in Los Angeles, said: "Now, the last thing I want to call your attention to is that you should never ask a hostile witness 'why.' This is the question that will really murder you."

Louis Nizer, a very respected cross-examiner, in his highly acclaimed book *My Life In Court* says: "One can quickly spot a bad cross-examiner if he asks 'Why.' This opens the door, and the witness may buttress whatever weakness has developed in his story."

I might say at this point that virtually all human beings, from children on up regularly cross-examine those with whom they interact. And the main, principal technique they employ is to ask "why," or "how come?" The wife to the husband: "If your meeting ended at eight last night, why did you get home at ten-thirty?" Girl to boy: "You say you like me so much, how come you didn't ask me to the dance?"

Yet ironically, this most natural, instinctive and practiced of all cross-examination techniques is frowned upon by the very people who need it the most—trial lawyers.

Why is the "why" question frowned upon? As Francis L. Wellman says in his book *The Art of Cross-Examination*, "If you allow the witness a chance to give his reasons or explanations, you may be sure they will be damaging to you, not to him."

In writing my second non-fiction book *Till Death Us Do Part*, a book in which I include many pages of my cross-examination wherein I frequently asked the frowned upon "why" question, I decided I had better scrutinize my cross-examination in several of my prior cases and try to ascertain how, although my cross-examination was not always homicidal, it had never yet been suicidal, even though I was consistently violating this well-recognized maxim of cross-examination.

Upon examining my earlier cross-examinations, I found a very consistent pattern emerging surrounding the use of the "why" question—a pattern that instinctively developed when I was preparing my cross-examination.

If I feel a witness is lying, I just about know, in advance, that he would not have acted—in a given, related area—the way a person telling the truth would have acted. Sometimes, I already have evidence he did not act this way. To expose the fact he is an untruthful witness, I frequently employ the following technique. I first elicit answers from the witness on preliminary matters, answers which, when totalled up, show he would be expected to take a certain course of action, i.e., *expected to act in a certain way*. The witness having committed himself by his answers, I then ask him what course he in fact took, and follow this up with the "why" question.

If time after time a witness is unable to satisfactorily justify conduct of his which is incompatible with what would be expected of a reasonable person, the jury will usually conclude that his testimony is suspect.

Note that there is at least one common denominator between the approach I have just mentioned, and other approaches—you have to first get the witness to commit himself. F. Lee Bailey, in his best-selling book *The Defense Never Rests* makes this excellent observation. It applies whether you use the "why" question technique I have referred to, or some other approach. He said: "The most common error lawyers make on cross-examination is that of immediately attacking a witness who has not been sufficiently pinioned. The result is that the witness escapes."

And witnesses do have a remarkable proclivity for escaping. Unlike their fictional counterparts in novels and on the screen, who cave in under the pressure of the first or second good question, real witnesses simply do not do this. They are as doughty and elusive as all hell. When all but trapped, and at the brink of a public, courtroom humiliation, human beings seem to secrete a type of mental adrenalin that gets their minds working almost as fast as Houdini's hands probably worked in a trunk at the bottom of the Hudson River.

Textbooks on the art of cross-examination, wherein classic, courtroom cross-examinations compiled throughout the years are presented, reveal that contrary to popular belief, even the most piercing cross-examination rarely, if ever, completely destroys a witness. At best, the witness is only hurt, not demolished.

So the witness you are facing on the stand, for some inexplicable reason, is almost inherently formidable. But just as no one, not even an Houdini, can pull a rabbit out of the hat when there isn't any rabbit in the hat, a witness cannot go somewhere when he has nowhere to go.

So if you use the "why" question technique, you have to first sit down with your yellow pad and block off all possible and anticipated escape hatches.

Let's take a few examples: In the case I prosecuted and wrote about in *Till Death Us Do Part*, there were two murders. In the second murder, I was alleging that the male defendant, Alan, was responsible for the murder of his wife, Judy. But the defense presented evidence that on the night before Judy's murder, two friends of Alan's and Judy's, Mr. and Mrs. Daryl Lott, had stopped by Alan's and Judy's apartment, that Judy was alone, and she was in deathly fear of some other man, a former boyfriend from New York, the implication being that this other man was the true murderer.

Using the "why" question approach of first eliciting answers from the witness on preliminary matters (each of which is designed to block off a possible escape hatch) which, when totaled up, show he would be expected to take a certain course of action, then asking what course he in fact took, and then asking "why," I started in on the issue of whether Mr. and Mrs. Lott had ever even stopped by the victim's apartment on the night in question, as they claimed they did.

Q: How did you happen to stop by Alan's and Judy's apartment, as you claim you did, around 11 p.m. Friday night, April 19, Mr. Lott?

A: I don't know. I do a lot of things on the spur of the moment. Just decided to stop in, say hello.

Q: I understand you were a closer friend of Alan's then you were of Judy's, is that true?

A: Well, I knew Alan longer. Let's put it that way.

Q: Is there any question in your mind that you were much closer to Alan than Judy?

A: No. I was. You're right.

Q: You had been to Alan's Grand Duke Bar on previous Friday nights, had you not?

A: Yes.

Q: About what time did Alan normally close the bar on these Friday nights?

A: Two o'clock in the morning.

Q: Did you think that this particular Friday night Alan would be home instead of at the Grand Duke?

A: I had no idea.

Q: The Grand Duke is pretty close to their apartment, is it not?

A: Sure is.

Q: Would it have been out of your way to *first* stop at the Grand Duke?

A: No.

Q: *Did* you first stop at the Grand Duke to see if Alan was there before you went to Judy's apartment?

A: No, I don't believe we did.

Now the "why" question:

Q: Any particular reason why you didn't, Mr. Lott?

A: Uh (pause) (and if you look at the transcript, there is a dash, indicating a pause) no reason at all.

Since the witness's conduct was implausible, and he had no satisfactory explanation for his conduct, the cross-examination raised the inference that he and his wife had not, as they claimed, stopped by the victim's apartment at all.

As you can see, this is all very simple stuff. I am not suggesting there is anything esoteric here, but no matter how bright you are, if you do not sit down with that yellow pad, here and there you are going to fail to block off an escape hatch, and I guarantee you, if the witness is a typical witness, he will find it.

Later on in my cross-examination, on the same issue of whether Mr. and Mrs. Lott had stopped by the victim's apartment, but taking it a step further—if they had, whether Judy had in fact been in fear of some other person on the night before she was murdered, I first wrested from Daryl Lott an admission that he felt the police in this case were genuinely interested in finding out the true identity of Judy's killer. I then asked:

Q: So Judy left this boyfriend from New York more than a year ago, but the night you came to the door, she was armed with a gun, right?

A: That's right.

Q: And she led you to believe she was in constant, everyday fear of this man killing her, is that correct?

A: Yes, she led me to believe that.

Q: Then you learned that the very next day, Judy was murdered?

A: Right.

Q: And in your mind, Alan Palliko, the defendant in this case, was innocent, isn't that true?

A: Yes.

Q: I take it the thought must have entered your mind that maybe this man from New York was the one who did it?

A: Yes, it did.

Q: Did you ever contact the police in any way whatsoever, by phone, letter, or by going down to the station, and tell them what you knew?

A: No, I didn't tell the police.

Q: Why not sir?

Now the Houdini routine:

A: Well, I believe I told Alan and I figured that was enough.

Q: But you believed Alan was innocent and you knew he was being charged with murder. Didn't you want to help your friend Alan by telling the police that someone else probably murdered Judy?

A continuing Houdini routine:

> A: That's why I'm testifying here right now.
>
> Q: You decided to wait until now, a year later, to tell your story? Is that right sir?
>
> A: No.
>
> Q: Why didn't you call the police then, Mr. Lott?
>
> A: I don't know. I just didn't call them. I don't really know.

I agree with the authorities that a "why" question can end up burying you, but I feel that as a general proposition, this is only true if you have not first closed off all escape hatches. And you can only close them off by thinking about them and anticipating them on a yellow pad. Incidentally, I have no fetish about the color yellow. You can use any color pad you wish.

I believe that the primary purpose of cross-examination is to destroy credibility, seeking and eliciting new information normally being a secondary purpose. When you are trying to destroy credibility, although you do not necessarily have to be aggressive, and although some of your questions may be velvety in nature and tone, I maintain that most of your questions necessarily have to have a cutting edge to them.

And I feel that the "why" question is one of the very best techniques—perhaps *the* best technique, if you know how to use it—to destroy credibility.

The greatly overused question "Isn't it true, sir, that . . ." ( . . . being a statement of an alleged fact, e.g., "Isn't it true sir that you told Frank you intended to lie at this trial to protect Bill?") may be a good way for a lawyer to testify before a jury without being under oath, but it is also one of the very most ineffective questions. You know the almost invariable answer: "No, it is not true." What do you think the witness is going to say: "Well, yes, it is true. You got me there." You only see that type of thing on television.

I might add, and there are many cases that so hold, that the question "Isn't it true sir that . . . " is a highly improper and highly unethical question unless the questioner, after getting his "no" answer from the witness, is prepared to present evidence proving the point alleged in the question.

One footnote to the "why" question. When a witness has done something which you feel is implausible—for instance, Mr. Lott not going to the police—even if you do not ask the why question, on redirect, the lawyer who called the witness, if alert, will. The witness has then often had a court recess or perhaps overnight to think up the very best answer to the "why" question. I would much rather force the witness to answer the "why" question on cross, not giving him extra time to fabricate.

Of course, both lawyers can avoid asking the "why" question and, as in some other situations, save for final argument the implications of the witness's testimony, but by that late point in the trial, the witness's reason for his improbable act is a matter for competing speculations by the lawyers, not court record.

## Final Summation

In my opinion, final summation is the most important part of the trial for the lawyer. Let me qualify this. If your case is extremely weak, chances are you will not be able to save it by your summation. Conversely, if your case is extremely strong, chances are your summation will not play that significant a part in the usually favorable verdict. It is the close case where summation tips the scales one way or the other.

Usually the first thing I think about when I get on a case and begin to learn the facts is, what am I going to argue? Given the facts I am aware of, how can I best argue them to obtain a favorable verdict?

I frequently work backwards from the summation. Since summation has to be based on the evidence, many of my questions on direct and cross examination—some of which, when asked, may have seemed completely irrelevant—are asked for the specific purpose of getting testimony into the record which will enable me to make an argument I feel I must make in a certain area of the case.

In fact, I often prepare at least half of my closing argument before the first witness at a trial has even been called. As soon as I learn the strengths and weaknesses of my case, I begin almost immediately to work on how I'm going to argue these strengths, and what I'm going to say in response to the opposition's attacks on the weaknesses. Getting an early start on the summation, and continuing to expand and modify it during the trial, gives me up to weeks and sometimes even months to develop arguments and articulations.

A great number of trial lawyers do not feel that final summation is the most important part of the trial.* I have never really understood why. In life, if one applies for a job, or asks for a raise, isn't what he says and how he says it all-important? If someone accuses you of wrongdoing, what are

---

*Somehow I have the feeling that many of these lawyers may realize that summation is the most important part of the trial, but they cannot admit this, even to themselves, much less to others, because if they did, they would have to justify not spending hundreds of hours preparing it, hours which they are unwilling to invest.

you going to say? And how are you going to say it? If you are proposing marriage to someone, what is your pitch? If a salesman wants to sell a product, or an advertiser is trying to sell something over TV, what is he going to say? Isn't what you are going to say almost always the bottom line?

Is a trial any different? As in every other area of life, aren't you trying to convince someone, in this case a jury, of the rightness of your cause? Therefore, shouldn't most of your preparation and your efforts be directed toward this final appeal to the jury?

Not so, say many experts. Louis Heller, a Justice of the New York Supreme Court and formerly a very prominent trial lawyer, in his book *Do You Solemnly Swear*, writes, "An address to the jury should be extemporaneous and reflect spontaneity." I have read almost identical statements in many other books.

Even some experts who agree that final summation is all-important speak in terms of an extemporaneous argument to the jury, relying on one's memory. The late, eminent trial lawyer, Lloyd Paul Stryker, who defended Alger Hiss in his first perjury trial and lectured regularly at Yale Law School, in his book *The Art of Advocacy*, advises lawyers: "If your *memory* has been well trained, you will *remember* the main parts of the evidence, and many expressions of the witnesses will stick there in verbatim form."

In my opinion, a summation must either be written out or put into a comprehensive outline. The problem with even a comprehensive outline is that all the points you want to make may be there, but you do not have the articulations. And if you think you can stand up in front of a jury and effectively and powerfully articulate, say, a hundred points without prior written preparation, well, I think you will find out you simply cannot do this. But whether one should write out one's summation or put it into an outline, it has been my experience that the majority of trial lawyers—even many high-priced ones in major, nationally publicized criminal trials—do neither, addressing the jury almost off the top of their heads after scandalously little preparation. Far too often this results in their delivering arguments which are disjointed, at times difficult to understand, and which, most injurious of all to their clients, omit a number of salient facts and inferences. I am aware that what I am saying here is difficult to believe. The only problem is that it happens to be the truth, and there is much documentary evidence to support this.

I realize I have almost an obsession about the preparation of a final summation. For instance, in the *Manson* case, I put in around 600 hours working on my opening and closing arguments. Of course, we were dealing with 28,000 pages of transcript. Conceding that I probably go to an unnecessary extreme, I still feel it cannot be wise to go to the other extreme and wait until the last second.

I do not know of any lawyer in America who has been quoted more on the issue of preparation than Louis Nizer. Nizer always says "Preparation is the be-all and end-all" in the trial of a lawsuit.

Yet even Nizer apparently short-changes final summation, relegating it to a relatively minor role in the trial of his cases. I say that because in his most famous trial, in which he represented Quentin Reynolds in a libel suit against Westbrook Pegler— a case that Nizer was involved in for over a year and into which he put a tremendous amount of preparation—he apparently waited until one second before midnight to prepare his summation. On page 153 of his book *My Life in Court,* he describes the night following the last day of testimony, the night before final summation: "With my assistants, I culled the citations from the record and *organized* a summation that would predigest the enormous amount of testimony, without sacrificing emotion or lucidity . . . a few of my associates found themselves in grotesque postures of slumber on the edge of a sofa or on the carpet before the sun rose."

In a complex trial involving upwards of a hundred witnesses and thousands of pages of transcript, I feel that an enormous amount of *written* preparation is required to discuss the highlights and nuances of the case, draw the necessary inferences, and in the most telling sequence, always seek simplicity and clarity of expression.

There is only one advantage I can see in arguing extemporaneously, and that is in being able to talk to the jury eye to eye, with the candor of spontaneity. But if a trial lawyer is willing to put in the hours, he can have such a grasp of his written or outlined argument that, like an actor on a stage whose lines flow naturally, he can deliver it to the jury giving the appearance of spontaneity. When I give my summation, my preparation is such that I only have to glance at my notes sparingly. I can look at one word on a page, and the whole page is vivid in my mind.

Final argument is nothing more than a speech, and I know of no generally accepted great speech in history that was not prepared before it was spoken. Lincoln's Gettysburg Address consisted of only ten sentences. Of his 271 words, 202 of them were just one syllable. But these historic words were the result of two weeks preparation on Lincoln's part and were handwritten by him on two pages which were in front of him while he spoke.

I don't know what my IQ is. I suspect it is not particularly high. But I will say this. Whether my role is as a prosecutor or a defense attorney, if you give me a yellow pad, a pencil and one or two hundred hours, I don't care how bright my opposition is; I don't care if he was Editor-in-Chief of the Harvard Law Review; I don't even care if, in addition, he was the winner of the National Moot Court competition; if he puts merely a modicum of preparation into his final argument in a *complex* case, although I'm not a gambling man, I will give you ten-to-one odds I will dominate him in final summation. And very obviously, you could do the same.

If this sounds boastful, let me just say it is confidence. When delivering a summation, a trial lawyer has to be confident before a jury, or at least appear confident. It is one of the most essential ingredients of a successful trial lawyer. If he is not confident, the jury will pick it up immediately—in the way he talks, the way he walks, the expression on his face, the inflection in his voice. And a lawyer cannot expect a jury to buy his cause if they detect that he does not believe in it completely himself. A lawyer must be very careful, however, that he does not trespass beyond the permissible margins of confidence into the area of arrogance or condescension. That can only hurt him with the jury.

Throughout your summation, your tone should be affirmative in nature. So many *defense* attorneys take their title too seriously, assuming a defensive posture. Is there any other way to convey to the jury the confidence you have in your own case than by speaking in a positive, affirmative manner?

In making your summation, you should address yourself to the weak parts of your case first. If you do not, while you are arguing your strengths, the jury will inevitably be thinking "Well, that may be true, but what about ...," and this can only serve to dilute the force of your argument.

One final point about closing argument. They say it is difficult to keep a jury's attention for more than an hour. I do not agree. It is very easy. In fact, it is not difficult to keep their attention for an entire day if you can deliver a powerful, exciting summation to them which is sprinkled with example, metaphor and humor; and particularly when you make it very obvious to them that you have a lot of very important observations to make about the case, and they can only fulfil the oath they took to reach a proper verdict if they listen closely to you, i.e., if you convince them they need you.

An illustration of humor tied in to the facts of the Palliko-Stockton murder case, upon which the book *Till Death Us Do Part* was based: One of the defense witnesses had changed his testimony several times on the witness stand. I told the jury that this witness's flip-flops reminded me of a story people tell about a civil case years ago.

The plaintiff, I recalled to the jury, sued his neighbor, alleging that while he was walking on the sidewalk past his neighbor's home, the neighbor's dog had run out and bitten him, causing injury. The neighbor filed an answer to the complaint in which he set forth three contentions.

Number one, he said, "My dog was chained to the house and the chain does not extend out to the sidewalk, so there was no way for my dog to bite the plaintiff." Number two, "My dog is an old dog, he doesn't have any teeth, so even if he did bite the plaintiff, he couldn't possibly have hurt him." And number three, "I don't even *own* a dog."

The use of example coupled with metaphor is always advantageous. For instance, in the Palliko-Stockton case the defense made the old argument about circumstantial evidence being like a chain; that if one link breaks, the chain is broken. They argued that there were several missing or broken links in the prosecution's case.

This was my response: "I think that counsel's problem is that they misconceive what circumstantial evidence is all about. Circumstantial evidence is not, as they claim, like a chain. You could have a chain extending the span of the Atlantic Ocean from Nova Scotia to Bordeaux, France, consisting of millions of links, and with one weak link, that chain is broken. Circumstantial evidence, to the contrary, is like a rope. Each fact is a strand of that rope. And as the prosecution piles one fact upon another, we add strands and we add strength to that rope. If one strand breaks—and I am not conceding for a moment that any strand has broken in this case—but if one strand does break, the rope is not broken. The strength of the rope is barely diminished. Why? Because there are so many other strands of almost steel-like strength that the rope is still more than strong enough to bind these two defendants to justice. That is what circumstantial evidence is all about."

## Instructions

Getting into instructions, to bring this article to a close, I am only going to mention one of them.

Although legal scholars have openly confessed that the term "beyond a reasonable doubt" does not lend itself to a good definition, and the attempt to define it only confuses further,* one all-important principle,

---

*It is generally accepted that the doctrine of reasonable doubt whose first recorded appearance was in the high-treason cases tried in Dublin in 1798, (as reported by MacNally in RULES OF EVIDENCE ON PLEAS OF THE CROWN, DUBLIN, (1802) is, as Sir Winston Churchill once described Soviet Russia, "an enigma wrapped up in a mystery." Legal scholars and authorities say it simply cannot be satisfactorily defined. *See* CLEARY, MCCORMICK ON EVIDENCE § 341, at 798-800 (2d ed. 1972); ILLINOIS JUDICIAL CONFERENCE COMMITTEE ON PATTERN INSTRUCTIONS, ILLINOIS PATTERN JURY INSTRUCTIONS-CRIMINAL, § 2.05 (1968): "We have so frequently discussed the futility of attempting to define reasonable doubt that we might expect the practice to be discontinued."; J. WIGMORE, WIGMORE ON EVIDENCE § 2497, at 317 (3d ed. 1940): "[t]his elusive and undefinable state of mind."; E. Morgan, *Instructing the Jury Upon Presumptions and Burden of Proof,* 47 HARV. L. REV. 59, 63 (1933): "It is coming to be recognized that all attempts to define reasonable doubt by paraphrase or circumlocution tend to obfuscate rather than clarify the concept." Many courts, in abject surrender, e.g., the United States Seventh Circuit, do not even attempt to define reasonable doubt in any way whatsoever to the jury.

though damaging to the prosecution, is implicit* in the term—namely, that a jury does not have to believe in a defendant's innocence in order to return a verdict of not guilty. Even their belief in his guilt, if only a moderately held one, should result in a not guilty verdict. To convict, their belief in his guilt has to be beyond a reasonable doubt.

In every federal court in this country, the judge properly instructs the jury that to convict the defendant they must conclude that his guilt has been proven beyond a reasonable doubt. But unbelievably, in the very same instruction, No. 11.06 of the *Federal Criminal Jury Instructions*, and as if he were merely stating the same thing in a different way, he tells the jurors, "You are here to determine the guilt or innocence of the accused."

This added instruction is simply not consistent with the first, and does not belong under existing law.

Yet, even the United States Supreme court, in case after case, e.g., *Jackson v. Denno*, "There must be a new trial on guilt or innocence," continues to loosely and erroneously define the jury's function in a criminal

---

*Why is such a notion implicit? The articulation of the answer is not an easy one, but I make this effort: if the judge were to merely instruct the jury that to convict the defendant, they had to be "convinced of the defendant's guilt," the issue for the jury to resolve would seem to be guilt *as opposed to what?* The inference is innocence, i.e., the opposite side of guilt is innocence. So the question would be that of *guilt or innocence.* But the judge does not give this truncated instruction. To the words "convinced of the defendant's guilt" he appends the words "beyond a reasonable doubt." It would seem we have now jettisoned the previously inferential "innocence," at least to the extent that it no longer is a *sine qua non* in the legal equation necessary for a verdict of not guilty. Now the issue seems to be guilt *as opposed to what?* Guilt beyond a reasonable doubt. The new comparison seems to be between believing in guilt on one hand, and believing in guilt beyond a reasonable doubt on the other. In other words, when the judge tells the jury that to convict, they have to be convinced *not only* of guilt, but guilt beyond a reasonable doubt, he clearly is telling them that *a mere belief in guilt is not enough to convict.* And if a mere belief in guilt is not enough to convict, and has to result in a not guilty verdict, *a fortiori, a belief in innocence is not necessary* in order to result in a not guilty verdict.

As if the concept of reasonable doubt does not have enough indigenous semantic problems, I might add that the word "beyond" in the term "beyond a reasonable doubt" is an unnecessary element of a concept already mired in metaphysical confusion. During my years as a prosecutor, I noted how defense counsel, in discussing the term "beyond a reasonable doubt," emphasized the word "beyond" as if the prosecution had to go beyond the horizon and to the ends of the earth to prove guilt. Because of the confusing, misleading context in which it was used, I developed a line of thought to explain to the jury the word "beyond." I pointed out to the jury that in "beyond a reasonable doubt," "beyond" is a needless appendage which is not even used in its principle sense of "further," "more than." (If it were, the prosecution would have to prove there is *more than* a reasonable doubt of a defendant's guilt, when obviously, they have to prove just the opposite–that there is *less than* a reasonable doubt.) Instead, "beyond" is used in the sense of "to the exclusion of," i.e., the prosecutor has the burden of proving the defendant's guilt to the exclusion of all reasonable doubt. Excising the word "beyond: from the term "beyond a reasonable doubt," I would proceed to tell the jury the much more simple: "If you do not have a reasonable doubt of guilt, convict. If you do have a reasonable doubt, acquit." I then went on to define reasonable doubt as a sound, sensible, logical doubt reasonably based upon the evidence in the case.

trial. Needless to say, far less insightful state, country and municipal courts throughout the land make this same mistake. And a great number of prosecutors and defense attorneys also erroneously use the two terms—proving guilt beyond a reasonable doubt, and determining guilt or innocence—interchangeably.

While the defendant's guilt or innocence obviously is the most important *moral* issue at every criminal trial, and could not possibly be more legally relevant (since if a jury believes a defendant is innocent, the verdict has to be not guilty), the *ultimate legal* issue for the jury to determine is not the defendant's guilt or innocence, i.e., it is not to determine whether or not the defendent committed the crime. Their function is to determine whether or not the prosecution has met its legal burden of proving guilt beyond a reasonable doubt.

These two issues are simply not the same.

Stated another way: To say one is guilty is to say he committed the crime; to say one is innocent is to say he did not commit the crime. In American criminal jurisprudence, however, the legal term "Not Guilty" is not synonymous with innocence. "Not Guilty", of course, is a legal finding by the jury that the prosecution has not met its burden of proof. A "Not Guilty" verdict based on the insufficiency of the evidence can result from one of two states of mind on the part of the jury: that they believe the defendant is innocent and did not commit the crime; or, although they do not believe he is innocent and *tend* to believe that he did commit the crime, the prosecution's case was not sufficiently strong to convince them of his guilt beyond a reasonable doubt.

As long as the terms "Not Guilty" and "Innocent" are used interchangeably in courts of law, thousands of defendants throughout the nation will continue to be tried before juries who are misinformed and misinstructed on the most fundamental issue at a criminal trial.

Under present law, although this instruction is never given, I firmly believe that defense attorneys are entitled to request that the judge instruct the jury—and the judge should instruct the jury—that "Innocent" and "Not Guilty" are not synonymous, and they do not have to believe the defendant is innocent to return a verdict of Not Guilty. Perhaps the issue for the jury to determine should be the defendant's guilt or innocence. But since it is not, jurors should not be misinstructed on existing law.

In the 1981 Criminal Justice Journal of Western State University Law School in San Diego, California, I wrote about this entire issue in considerable depth in an article titled "Not Guilty and Innocent—the problem children of Reasonable Doubt." It is nothing short of incredible that with legal treatises having been written on virtually every point of law imaginable, prior to this article, apparently none had ever been written on this subject before in America. At least, I have never come across such an article or treatise and none is listed in the "Index to Legal Periodicals," or the "Criminal Justice Periodical Index."

With respect to final argument on this last point, the way in which a defense attorney argues to a jury the critical distinction between "Not Guilty" and "Innocent", without thereby implying to the jury that he has conceded the fact that his client is not innocent, is in my opinion usually the single most important issue for the defense attorney to deal with in his summation, and is an article all by itself. For the purposes of this article, suffice it to say that it is obviously advisable, and in fact nearly always essential, for defense counsel to argue his client's innocence, but never in the context of "guilt or innocence" being the issue for the jury to decide. The approach almost necessarily has to be broken down into two levels. At the first level, counsel can argue that the evidence proves, or at least points to, his client's innocence, i.e., he did not commit the crime. Defense counsel can then go on to the second level and argue that the prosecution's case against his client was so weak that even if one or more of the jurors nonetheless believes that he did commit the crime, they certainly should not believe in his guilt beyond a reasonable doubt. And therefore, under the law, they *still* are duty-bound to return a verdict of not guilty.

## Conclusion

In closing, if there is one message I would want to leave with you, it is to prepare your cases. You owe it to yourself, to your client and to your noble profession.

---

*If the thought which is uppermost in the jury's mind when they retire to deliberate is "did he do it or did he not do it," as opposed to "did the prosecution meet their burden of proof or did they not meet their burden of proof," even if the evidence against the defendent is only moderately strong (as opposed to the requisite very strong) the jury will probably be psychologically attuned to a conviction. But a defense attorney has a serious dilemma when he argues to the jury that the prosecution has not met its legal burden of proving guilt beyond a reasonable doubt. The baggage of such an argument can be the implication that he has conceded his client is not innocent. In other words, if his client had absolutely nothing to do with the crime, and is completely innocent, how is it appropriate to argue that *his guilt* has not been proven beyond a reasonable doubt? Though there is no *legal* implication of guilt in a reasonable doubt argument, as a practical matter it tends to go in that direction, though by analogy, not as conspicuously as a plea of "Not Guilty By Reason of Insanity." While there is likewise no legal concession of guilt in the insanity plea, that is the precise effect of such a plea. Again, if a defendant had absolutely nothing to do with the commission of the crime, a plea of "Not Guilty By Reason of Insanity" is completely inappropriate. The plea in effect tells the jury, "I'm guilty, but give me a break because I'm crazy."

# The Defendant—Should He Testify?

## Henry B. Rothblatt

Henry B. Rothblatt has been actively engaged in the practice of
criminal law for over four decades as a member of the New York,
California, Florida and District of Columbia Bars, and the Bar of
the Supreme Court of the United States.

He is currently adjunct professor of law at New York Law
School. He was Chairman of the Penal Reform Committee, and
past Chairman of the Criminal Law Section of the Association of
Trial Lawyers of America; and also Chairman of the Criminal Law
and Procedure Section of the New York State Trial Lawyers
Association.

In association with F. Lee Baily, he has written many books
which deal with various facets of criminal trials and procedure,
including *Investigation and Preparation in Criminal Cases*; and
*Cross Examination in Criminal Cases*.

Rothblatt is the author of *That Damned Lawyer*, a book
about his well publicized cases.

The decision of whether or not to allow a client to testify on his own behalf in a criminal case can be the most important decision of the case.
Your client has the absolute right not to testify. The Fifth Amendment of
the Constitution states: "No person shall be compelled in any criminal
case to be a witness against himself...." The courts have ruled that the
Fifth Amendment prohibits both the prosecution and the court from com-
menting on a defendant declining to testify.[1]

However, most jurors deem a defendant's "failure" to testify as a failure. The prosecutor might further this feeling by using comments of a

general nature[2] in his closing argument, that no one's testimony rebutted or denied the prosecution's case.[3]

The court is permitted to, and usually will, instruct the jury that they are to draw no inferences from the defendant's silence.[4] In spite of any instructions, the majority of jurors will assume that a defendant has something to hide, if he does not take the witness stand on his own behalf. Therefore, a defendant should generally testify, unless there are compelling reasons against it.

After giving this fact serious consideration, several other points must be weighed before permitting your client to take the stand, and be subjected to cross-examination by the prosecutor:

### Checklist for Determining If Your Client Should Take the Stand

**1. Will your client's testimony support the defense theory you intend to present?** Although this question and the appropriate response are self-evident, they can be easily overlooked because of their obviousness. A client who superficially might appear to be an impressive witness, but whose testimony is either actually incredible or might factually contradict better defense witnesses, is one who should not take the stand.

**2. Will your client's testimony reveal information not covered by the testimony of other witnesses?** After outlining the points covered by other witnesses and assessing their credibility in the minds of the jury, omitted evidence of an essential nature may necessitate the testimony of your client. Conversely, if credible witnesses have attested to all relevant information, there may be no benefit in your client testifying. However, confidence in your client's ability to convey an image of honesty creates its own usefulness. You may want his testimony even if he has nothing to add beyond declarations of innocence.

**3. Does your client have a prior record which may impeach his credibility?** In most jurisdictions previous recent convictions of a defendant may be used for impeachment, if he takes the stand.[5]

The benefits of the testimony versus any detrimental effect of prior convictions must be carefully evaluated. Should you decide that your client's testimony is necessary, bring out all prior admissible convictions in your direct examination. Do not leave it for the prosecutor to reveal in cross-examination

**4. What is the actual strength of the prosecution's case?** If the prosecution's case is weak, exposing your client to cross-examination may be an unnecessary risk. Conversely, if the prosecution's case is unusually strong, then the risk may be minimal compared with the possible positive effect of his testimony.

**5. Will incriminating evidence become admissible because of your client's testimony?** Will your client's testimony open up any areas which would be better left unexamined? For example, your client may on cross-examination, without being aware of it, furnish sufficient facts to undermine any attack on an arrest or search.

Will your client's testimony be impeached on rebuttal by the prosecution's use of prior statements or evidence, which was not used in the prosecution's direct case? The prosecution may withhold the use of a second confession, believing that the defendant will testify—the expectation being that if the defendant manages to explain the confession already in evidence, later producing a second confession will reinforce the first.

You should not permit your client to testify unless he can explain all statements he may have made to the authorities. In some jurisdictions, the prosecution can use an admission which has been suppressed as involuntary for impeachment of the defendant.

The most important consideration is, of course, whether the defendant is a credible witness. Will *the jury* (judge, in a non-jury situation) *find your client's testimony credible*? A positive, favorable demeanor on your client's part is essential to his testimony. Dress, voice and speech patterns, physical characteristics, and body language can all either antagonize a juror or establish good rapport.

### Grooming Your Client for an Effective Appearance in Court

Physically attractive individuals are found to have more credibility in this society, and likewise with jurors.[6] Your client's physical appearance should be carefully scrutinized and, if necessary, you must advise needed changes. The more respectable and dignified your client appears, the more credible he will be found.[7] However, your client's style of dress should not deviate from his usual mode to the extent that he is uncomfortable and projects an unnatural, uneasy appearance.

**1. Clothing.** A criminal defendant who is incarcerated has a constitutional right to wear civilian clothes at his trial.[8] Insist upon this. Make certain that your male client shaves every morning before appearing in court. Arrange that he have his hair cut, if needed. A female client should be advised to use a minimum of make-up and style her hair conservatively. Obviously, alluring styled clothing should be prohibited.

**2. Preparation.** Preparation is essential, in order that your client appear as articulate as possible. He should be instructed to speak in a clear, unhalting manner. A direct quality is vital in establishing credibility. Increased intonation and added volume of voice can enhance your client's persuasive ability. Jurors tend to acquire doubts when testimony is given containing hesitations, spoken in monotone, or at an unusually soft level. Although it may appear obvious to you, warn your client against shouting at the jury, which can produce a negative effect.

Intelligence and articulateness are important factors to your client's general credibility as a witness. The less intelligent or articulate your client, the greater the possibility that the prosecutor can confuse him during cross-examination. Nervousness also can transform an articulate individual into a hesitant-speaking incredible witness.

If your client is going to testify, carefully prepare him for taking the witness stand. Scrutinize his testimony with extreme precision, since it is essential that he convince the jury of his innocence. Explain to him in detail the theory of the defense. Review all the facts and the role of each witness in the building of his case. Familiarize your client with all the procedures of a trial and what should be anticipated at each stage. This should be done in a manner which will make your client feel at ease when he takes the stand. If possible, have your client observe various parts of another trial, if he is not familiar with a courtroom surrounding.

Explain to your client the purposes of direct and cross-examinations. Go over his direct testimony, which should be given in narrative form, as much as possible. Inadequate preparation can often result in a client omitting essential facts from his testimony. Should this happen, the testimony may be cleared up by the asking of appropriate questions in a manner that does not appear to be leading.

Subject your client to an intensive mock cross-examination. Make sure to eliminate any inconsistencies in his testimony.

**3. Eye contact.** When testifying, your client should be advised to maintain eye contact with the jury.[9] When eye contact is not established, jurors are likely to believe that your client is ashamed of or hiding something. However, eye contact should not be excessive, making jurors feel uncomfortable or under scrutiny.

**4. Smile.** A smile can have a very positive effect upon jurors, and your client should be instructed to smile briefly at the jury (or judge, in a non-jury situation). It should be a small, friendly smile—a smile of pleas· ant recognition or acknowledgement rather than a broad smile of happiness.

**5. Body language.** The body language keys to successful testimony should be discussed with your client. For example, he should be instructed to lean slightly towards the jury (or judge, if there is no jury). A small, sideways lean in the jury's direction projects a message that your client believes they can be trusted—a feeling of closeness and rapport. He should also be advised that an exaggerated movement in the jury's direction can create an uneasy feeling. It may be interpreted as a calculated attempt at closeness or to win them over.

An open, as opposed to a tight-closed, body position implies a positive, I-have-nothing-to-hide attitude. In order that your client maintain an open posture, you may wish to instruct him to keep his arms on either side of his body. The equally effective position of keeping palms upward resting in front of him, may be more comfortable. The open palms also convey a message of truthfulness and sincerity.[10]

**6. Defendant testifies last.** Your client should be the last witness called to testify. Explain to him why he is being called last. There is a great benefit when a defendant has become accustomed to the courtroom, prosecutor, and the prosecutor's technique of cross-examining other witnesses, prior to testifying. A great deal may be gained simply by observing others on the witness stand. There is considerably less danger of mistakes in your client's testimony, when he has had the opportunity to hear the testimony of his supporting witnesses. As the final witness, your client has the chance to explain any inconsistencies that might have arisen in the presentation of the defendant's case.

In the final analysis, the decision of whether or not to testify rests with your client. Occasionally, a reluctant client will refuse to testify under any circumstances. Conversely, a client may insist upon testifying, knowing it is against your best judgment. Should this occur, consider getting a written statement from him acknowledging that he is proceeding with his testimony against your advice. If he should refuse to sign a statement, weigh stating for the record, in camera or certainly out of the jury's hearing, your disagreement with the defendant's offering testimony. However, in most situations, your client will be guided by your advice and experience, if you act appropriately.

# Notes

1. See *Griffin v. California,* 380 U.S. 609, 616 (1965).

2. Amsterdam, Segal & Miller, Trial Manual 3 for the Defense of Criminal Cases, §390 (1976).

3. Id.

4. See *Griffin v. California,* 380 U.S. 609, 615 (1965).

5. *United States v. Palumbo,* 401 F.2d 270 (2d Cir. 1968); Feinberg, J. Held, trial judge must balance all relevant factors to determine whether probative value of evidence of other crimes is outweighed by its prejudicial effect.

"In short, we hold that a trial judge may prevent such use, if he finds that a prior conviction negates credibility only if slightly but creates a substantial chance of unfair prejudice, taking into account such factors as the nature of the conviction, its bearing on veracity, its age, and its propensity to influence the jurors improperly.": *at p. 273.*

Court cites its traditional holding that with any prejudicial evidence, the trial judge must balance all relevant factors to determine whether its probative value is outweighed by the prejudicial effect . . . See *United States v. Johnson,* 382 F.2d 280 (2d Cir. 1967); *United States v. Deaton,* 381 F.2d 114 (2d Cir. 1967).

The District of Columbia Circuit in interpreting the D.C. Code has strictly upheld this discretionary power of the trial judge. See, *Brown v. United States,* 370 F.2d 242 (1966); Luck v. United States, 384 F.2d 763 (1965).

6. Bergman, P., *Trial Advocacy in a Nutshell,* p. 25–26 (1978).

7. See *Bentley v. Crist,* 469 F.2d 854 (9th Cir. 1972).

8. *Trial Manual* 3 at §281.

9. See *Mehrabion & Williams, Nonverbal Concomitants of Perceived and Intended Persuasiveness,* 13 Journal of Personality and Social Psychology, 37 (1969).

10. Nierenberg & Calero, *How to Read A Person Like A Book,* p. 44–45.

# Preparing for the Defense of a Civil Action

## John P. Ewart

John P. Ewart graduated from the University of Illinois School of Law in 1960. He is a member of the following: Illinois State Bar Association (Chairman of Fire & Casualty Committee and Member of Insurance Law Section Council, 1970-1972; Legal, Medical & Dental Cooperation Committee, 1972-1973; Civil Practice & Procedure Section Council, 1975-1978); American Bar Association; Illinois Defense Counsel (Director, 1971-1979 and President 1978-1979); Appellate Lawyers Association (Director 1980-1983); National Association of Railroad Trial Counsel; American Bar Foundation; and American College of Trial Lawyers.

The trial of a civil action is, for the most part, an execution on pre-trial preparation. Therefore, the success or failure of the defense in such an action depends in large measure on the effort that is devoted to the preparation by the attorney representing the defendant. The better the preparation, the better are the chances for a good result. Over the years, I have noted that experienced defense lawyers utilize similar methods, with some minor variations, in preparing for the trial. The similarity in their methods is not accidental—it is the result of years of experience.

Once the defense attorney has completed his preparation in an organized manner, he knows he can go to trial with only a minimum risk of surprise. He has seen all the documents that will be offered in evidence and has statements or depositions from all witnesses who will testify. Also, he will have had an opportunity to plan his response to all of the Plaintiff's evidence.

## Checklist for Reviewing the Complaint

As you know, a lawsuit starts with a Complaint or similar pleading. Ini
tially, one should determine if there are any defects in the Complaint o⸱
its filing. I believe that, to avoid overlooking a defect, it is wise to have a
checklist when reviewing the Complaint. The checklist should be an
open-ended document to which additions can be made as experience
dictates. While the checklist will vary from jurisdiction to jurisdiction, the
following matters are common to most jurisdictions:

 **1. Is the court of filing a proper venue?** Normally, this question can
be answered by reviewing the applicable statute on venue. Sometimes research will be required.

 **2. Does the court have jurisdiction over the parties and subject mat-
ter?** This question is usually more complex than the venue question.
While a review of the statute on jurisdiction may suffice, research is frequently required.

 **3. Has the filing been within the applicable statute of limitations?** A
review of the Statute of Limitations will, in most instances, answer this
question.

 **4. Have all the necessary notice requirements been satisfied?** Many
causes of action require the giving of a Notice to perfect the cause of action. For instance, in the State of Illinois, a Notice of claim must be served
within a specified period of time after the cause of action accrues against
a Governmental Unit. To effectively answer this question, one must carefully apprise himself of the various Notice requirements through research.

 **5. Is the plaintiff qualified to file the lawsuit?** There are many aspects to this question. Is the Plaintiff a minor and, if he or she is, must the
suit be filed by a guardian or "next of kin"? Is the Plaintiff under a
conservatorship? If so, then the Conservator should probably be named as
the Party Plaintiff. Is the Plaintiff a foreign corporation which is not au-
thorized to do business in the State? If that be the case, then state law may
prohibit the filing of a suit under those circumstances. Again research is
required for complete control over this question.

 **6. Does the Complaint state a cause of action under the law?** Of all
the questions presented, this is the most comprehensive. It requires a
knowledge of the causes of action that are recognized in your jurisdiction

and the elements that must be alleged to state those causes of action. Only careful research can answer those questions. Even the most experienced practitioner must continue to supplement his research in this area. This includes constant review of recent decisions in the Courts of Review.

**7. Is there a jury demand and, if not, do you want to make such a demand?** Of all the questions, this is the easiest to answer and yet the one that is most often overlooked. Because of concentration on the other questions, attorneys frequently miss this question. As a result, they get Bench Trials when they would have preferred Jury Trials.

**8. If the case is filed in the State Court, is it removable to the Federal Court, and, assuming it is, do you want to remove?** In most instances, this question is covered by the Federal Statute on diversity of citizenship jurisdiction. If the Federal Court does have jurisdiction then you must make a decision as to whether you do or do not want to remove to that Court. That decision must be based on your judgment as to whether you feel the defense of a particular lawsuit can be best prosecuted in the Federal Court or the State Court. That, in turn, will depend on your experience in those Courts when trying similar cases.

If any defects are found in the Complaint or its filing, then that defect should be contested in some fashion. Normally, this will be done by a Motion. Even if the lawsuit is not dismissed with prejudice, you may force the Plaintiff to take some corrective action which, in turn, will eliminate whatever advantage he would have gained by the defect having gone unchallenged.

In the event there are not defects or the defects have been cured, and you have filed an Answer to the Complaint, then you are ready to proceed with discovery. So as to avoid disorganized and unproductive discovery, I recommend you proceed in an orderly fashion.

### Interrogatories Step-by-Step

Initially, Interrogatories should be served on the Plaintiff. The Interrogatories should be for the purpose of obtaining preliminary information which will enable you to formulate a complete investigation and discovery program. Of course, the Interrogatories will vary from case to case, but inquiries on the subjects hereinafter described are common in most cases.

First, background information about the Plaintiff should be obtained. Where the Plaintiff is an individual, this may include the following:

1. His or her full name and address.
2. His or her age at the time of the occurrence alleged in the Complaint.
3. His or her marital status at the time of the occurrence alleged in the Complaint and at the time the Interrogatories are served.
4. The members of his or her family at the time of the occurrence alleged in the Complaint and at the time the Interrogatories are served.
5. Whether he or she has ever been convicted of a felony.

In the event the Plaintiff is a corporation, this background information may include the following:

1. The names and addresses of the officers of the corporation.
2. The names and addresses of the directors of the corporation.
3. The state of incorporation.
4. The principal place of business.

Most of the time, the Answers to the inquiries are utilized in preparing for the discovery deposition of the Plaintiff or, in the case of a corporation, its representative. However, on some occasions, the Answers will reveal a fact that can be most helpful in the defense of a lawsuit. For instance, a positive response to the question about conviction of a felony may lead to some evidence which can be utilized at the trial by way of impeachment.

Next, get the names and addresses of all persons who have knowledge about relevant facts. For instance, in a personal injury case arising out of an automobile accident, you might frame your Interrogatories as follows:

1. "State the names and addresses of all persons known to you or your agents, servants, attorneys, or other persons associated with you or engaged in any investigation activities in your behalf, who have knowledge concerning:
   "a. The conduct or any utterances, pertaining to the alleged occurrence, of the parties or their agents, at the time of, immediately before, or immediately after the occurrence.
   "b. Any statements made by the Defendant, John Doe, or his agents, concerning the occurrence at any time since the occurrence.
   "c. Any statements made by any person at the scene of the occurrence at the time of, immediately before, or immediately after the occurrence.

"d. The condition of the place of the occurrence at the time of, immediately before, or immediately after the occurrence.

"e. The condition of the automobiles involved in the occurrence at the time of, immediately before, or immediately after the occurrence.

"f. The nature and extent of the alleged damages and injuries."

2. "Give the names and addresses of any and all doctors, dentists, etc., who have treated you or who have examined you incident to this occurrence."

In a malpractice case involving the death of a patient, the Interrogatories might vary as follows:

1. "State the names and addresses of all persons known to you or your agents, servants, attorneys, or other persons associated with you or engaged in any investigation activities in your behalf, who have knowledge concerning:

"a. The conduct or any statements made by this Defendant during the time he was treating the Plaintiff.

"b. Any statement made by this Defendant since the treatment of the Plaintiff.

"c. The physical condition of the Deceased while she was being treated by the Defendant.

"d. The cause of death of the Deceased.

"e. The nature and extent of the alleged pecuniary damages sustained by the next of kin."

2. "State the names and addresses of all physicians or doctors who purport to know that the Defendant, in his treatment of the Decedent, failed to follow the acceptable standards of medical and surgical care in the locality of _____, or similar localities.

These Interrogatories will continue to vary depending on the type of case. However, the drafting of these variations are quite simple once you have a standard form which meets your needs on the subject.

Where pertinent, information on damages should be obtained. In personal injury and wrongful death actions, this will include information on wages and special damages. Illustrative Interrogatories in a personal injury action on this subject are as follows:

1. "Were you employed at the the time of the occurrence alleged in the Complaint? If you were, answer the following:

"a. Name of your employer.

"b. Date you went to work for said employer.

"c. Rate of pay.

"d. Total amount of time allegedly lost, together with total income, wages or salary allegedly lost."

2. "List, by itemization, all special damages, including hospital bills and doctor bills and other types of special money loss incident to this occurrence, giving the names and addresses of the persons paid or to whom the amounts are owing and the reasons for each such amount."

In a wrongful death action, the first Interrogatory might vary as follows:

"Was the deceased employed or engaged in any occupation for which she received remuneration at the time of the occurrence? If your answer is 'yes,' answer the following:

"a. What was the employment or occupation?

"b. When did the deceased first enter into the employment or occupation?

"c. If the deceased was paid a salary or wage, state the amount of his or her wages or salary by the hour, day, week, or month."

The Answers to Interrogatories on damages will put you in a position where you have definitive information on the subject and do not have to speculate on what the Plaintiff will offer as evidence on the subject at the trial. Also, if any of the Answers are suspect, you will have ample time to conduct additional discovery on the subject. This may include depositions of the Plaintiff's employer or individuals who provided services to the Plaintiff.

Inquiries should be made about the existence and location of all documents that may be relevant in the case. In personal injury and wrongful death actions, this may include Income Tax Returns, Doctors' Reports, Hospital Records, Statements of Witnesses, and photographs. Information on this area will enable you to frame your Request for Production of Documents with specificity. Some typical Interrogatories on this subject are:

1. "Did you file Federal Income Tax Returns for the years 19___, 19___, 19___, and 19___? If you did, who has custody of copies of same?"

2. "Have you or your agents, servants, or other persons associated with you or engaged in any investigation activities in your behalf

obtained medical reports from doctors or hospitals? If you have, answer the following as to each such report:

"a. A general description of the report.

"b. The name of the individual preparing the report.

"c. The date of the report.

"d. The name of the individual having custody of same."

3. "State whether any photographs were taken of any such matter of fact pertaining to the occurrence alleged in the Complaint. If there were, then answer the following:

"a. When, where, and by whom such photographs were taken and who was present at the time, if you know?

"b. Will you produce these photographs for the inspection of the Defendant?"

4. "Are there in existence, any statements from witnesses or documents or memorandums pertaining to witnesses with respect to the subject matter involved in this action? If such statements, documents, or memorandums do exist, give the description, nature, custody, and location of same."

Next, in cases involving damages, inquire about payments from other sources incident to those damages. A good Interrogatory on that subject is as follows:

"Have you received any payments from any person or persons incident to the damages sustained by you in the occurrence involved herein? If you have, give the names and addresses of such persons and the amount of such payments and the reasons same were made to you, together with a statement of the circumstances."

Information on this subject will apprise you of whether there might be other individuals who have an interest in the controversy and whether there might be a set-off available.

### Devising a Winning Strategy for Investigation and Discovery

Once the Plaintiff has filed his Answers to Interrogatories, the Defendant's attorney is in a position to formulate an investigation and discovery program. This should include the following:

1. A Request for Production of Documents which have been listed in the Answers.

2. Obtain Statements or Depositions of all witnesses listed in the Answers.

Generally, depositions will be taken of the Plaintiff and all witnesses who have some special relationship to him. Statements can and should be taken from the other witnesses. When taking those statements, I recommend that they be in a question-and-answer form before a Court Reporter whenever possible. This will commit the witness to his version of the transaction prior to trial and, in the event he should change his version at trial, impeachment is assured by the existence of the Court Reporter Statement.

When taking depositions, I suggest that one work from a checklist. This will help avoid omitting questions on relevant subjects. Over the years, I have prepared checklists for all the common civil actions. My sources have been a combination of checklists published in various legal articles and my own experience. While it takes some time to formulate such a checklist, the time it saves and the confidence it instills when taking the deposition more than compensates for that effort.

One area where caution should be exercised in preparation is the independent physical examination in personal injury actions. Frequently, such an examination will only buttress the Plaintiff's claims. Therefore, one should request such an examination only when there is doubt about the accuracy of the treating physician's testimony. This necessarily will cause you to defer a final decision on the subject until you have taken the depositions of the Plaintiff and his or her treating physicians.

There is a most important part of preparation that is frequently neglected by attorneys who receive the employment from some individual or entity other than the named Defendant, viz, a conference with the named Defendant in the early stages of the litigation. This conference serves two purposes. First, it demonstrates to the Defendant your interest in his welfare and, in most instances, will result in a cooperative attitude throughout the litigation. Moreover, it frequently enables you to get information which cannot be obtained from any other source.

When participating in such a conference, I attempt to cover the same subjects that I would cover if I were the Plaintiff's attorney taking the Defendant's deposition but, at the same time, avoiding the appearance of an "inquisitor".

Once the conference has been concluded, immediate attention should be given to completing any investigation that might be indicated. Otherwise, the "leads" obtained at the conference may grow stale and be unavailable at the time of trial.

As one nears the trial date, he should give attention to what I call the "final trial preparation". The purpose of this preparation is to give attention to all matters that can be completed prior to trial so that you can then concentrate on those matters which can only receive attention in the courtroom. This final trial preparation will include the following:

## Master Checklist for Final Preparation

1. A review of all statements and depositions for the purpose of preparing for cross-examination. I recommend that an outline be prepared from the statements and depositions for the cross-examination of each witness, with cross-references to the portion of the statement or deposition that will support each question in your cross-examination.

2. The preparation of a questionnaire outline for the jury in those jurisdictions where you are permitted to question the prospective jurors. The questionnaire outline should be designed for the specific case you will be trying. For instance, in a personal injury action where the Defendant is a Corporation, the outline might include the following:

   a. Is the juror acquainted with any of the parties?
   b. Is the juror acquainted with any of the attorneys?
   c. Is the juror acquainted with any major witnesses, such as treating physicians?
   d. Has the juror ever heard of the event?
   e. Has the juror or any immediate member of his or her family ever been a party to a lawsuit?
   f. Has the juror had previous jury service?
   g. Will the juror give a corporation the same treatment as he or she would an individual?

3. Prepare your stock jury instructions and motions for directed verdict. There is nothing more frustrating than to defer this project until the time of trial and then attempt to work it in with all the other demands on your time. In the event there should be an unexpected development at the trial which requires that you change or prepare a new instruction, that task can usually be completed with little difficulty.

4. Prepare and have available forms for keeping records on typical trial activities. This can include forms on exhibits and jury instructions conference. The headings for an exhibit form may be as follows:

| No. | Description | Obj. | Ruling Reserved | Obj. Sustained (S) or Overruled (O) | Admitted |
|-----|-------------|------|-----------------|-------------------------------------|----------|
|     |             |      |                 |                                     |          |

The headings for a jury instructions conference may be as follows:

| No. | Obj. | Withdrawn | Ruling | | |
|-----|------|-----------|--------|--------|------|
|     |      |           | Given  | Refused | Res. |

5. Have a final conference with the Defendant. The purpose of this conference is two-fold. First, it permits you to review his testimony in advance of the trial. This, in turn, will assist you in framing your questions so as to elicit all relevant and material evidence on the subject of the lawsuit. Next, it will enable you to apprise the Defendant about trial matters in general. This is particularly helpful when the Defendant is involved in his first lawsuit. Some of the subjects that should be covered are:

   a. A description of the Courtroom, with explanations of where all participants will sit. (A photograph of a typical Courtroom is helpful when reviewing this subject.)

   b. Describe the circumstances under which he may be called to testify and the manner in which the oath will be administered.

   c. Describe the demeanor that is expected while giving testimony.

   d. Explain the manner in which objections are made and ruled upon.

   e. Explain the subject of impeachment and how it might arise.

   f. Make suggestions on attire that is appropriate for the occasion.

The importance of this final conference with the Defendant cannot be overemphasized. It is easy to recognize the Defendant who has not had the benefit of such a conference. He stumbles and falters which, in many cases, can be the difference between a good result and a bad result.

# The Preparation and Trial of the Medical Malpractice Case

## David S. Shrager

David S. Shrager is a partner of the Philadelphia law firm of Shrager, McDaid & Loftus. He currently serves as President of the Association of Trial Lawyers of America. He is past President of the Pennsylvania Trial Lawyers Association, and a past Chairman of the Civil Litigation Section of the Pennsylvania Bar Association. He has served as a member of the Board of Governors and Director of Continuing Legal Education for the Association of Trial Lawyers of America, and is a Trustee of the Roscoe Pound Foundation. Mr. Shrager has lectured extensively throughout the country on medical negligence and products liability, as well as on other facets of trial advocacy. He completed a four-year tenure as an adjunct professor of medicine at Hahnemann Medical College and Hospital in Philadelphia.

An attorney assumes significant professional responsibility when he agrees to undertake a client's representation in a medical negligence claim. He has an obligation to his client, to the physician (or other health care provider) and to himself to vigorously screen and evaluate these cases at the outset and, once accepted, to press a claim with skill and determination. I am convinced that quite often this is not the case, and that it is the major reason for the tremendous mortality rate in medical negligence claims.

### Developing a Theory of Liability

At the stage when counsel is prepared to launch formal litigation, he should already have developed a theory of the case. This theory should be the common theme in counsel's mind in pre-trial discovery and other preparation, and must be the liability theme at trial. Except in very isolated circumstances, the theory of course will require the imprimatur of a competent expert witness.

The basic bifurcation in theories of liability is between negligent treatment and negligent diagnosis. Wherever possible, counsel should attempt to explain the case on the basis of a *specific* error in medical management (treatment). Such a theory is easier to visualize and be understood by a jury. Negligent diagnosis, on the other hand, involves larger issues of proof in terms of "errors in judgment" (a legally exculpatory notion) and causation. Except in cases in which the patient was totally ignored, counsel must have a refined theory of liability concerning a specific event which can readily explain the catastrophe to which the patient was subject as opposed to painting with broad brush a series of questionable treatment judgments by the attending medical personnel. It is always a good trial strategy for counsel to assume the most modest burden of proof in order to get the job done.

And now a word of caution about yet a separate theory of liability—informed consent. This theory has a role in a narrow category of cases. It is probably being bandied about in litigation much more than it should be. It is a theory which is almost universally misunderstood by the medical community as being a "Sword of Damocles" over their heads, and is even supposed by some plaintiffs' counsel as being a species of "strict liability" in the medical negligence area. It is not. Counsel should remember that under the consensus view which establishes a legal obligation upon the attending physician to make reasonable disclosure of risks associated with the proposed course of treatment and the reasonable alternatives thereto, there must be a showing that "the reasonable patient" would have made a different choice had the warning in fact been given which allegedly was withheld. This, then, is the causation issue in the informed consent cases. The plaintiff's subjective judgment will not control. The main issue, in short, is one of creditibilty. A patient who is about to undergo major surgery to avoid an impending medical disaster can hardly be heard to claim that had he known of a one-in-one-thousand chance of paralysis, he would have declined the surgery and then faced a one-in-ten chance of death or other crippling disease or injury. The theory of informed consent should probably be reserved for cases which can satisfy all four of the following: elective surgery; significant injury of the type generally understood within the medical community to be among the classic risks of morbidity or mortality associated with the treatment in question; lack of a specific theory of negligence which crisply explains the events; and an arguable claim of lack of informed consent from the medical records *as well* as from what the patient or the family says. If a case can satisfy these criteria, there should be no hesitation to mount a legal attack, particularly in circumstances in which an expert witness is not available. But again, counsel should know that the courtrooms are riddled with defense verdicts in cases which smack of retrospective ignorance of what was ahead for the patient, or where it appears that the patient was not in the mood to hear or listen.

## Making the Most of Pre-trial Discovery

The importance of the generous use of the discovery armament is central to every piece of litigation. Certain facets of discovery are especially vital to the proper pre-trial preparation of the medical negligence case. In any case in which a hospital is a defendant, or where records possessed by a hospital may be important, a deposition of the Administrator or Medical Director of the hospital is mandatory. In our practice, we include an extensive list of the documents to be produced in the Notice of Deposition, or alternatively, file a Request for Production coincidental with the deposition notice (and for good measure often incorporate by reference the content of the Request into the Notice). Where the hospital is not a named party, the same result may be achieved by the filing of a deposition notice with a subpoena duces tecum. In any case in which there can be a dispute as to the authenticity of records, an appropriate request for admission of authenticity is filed. Once the theory of the case has been established in counsel's mind and the strategic format for trial is well set, Requests for Admissions can be an effective tool.

## Attorney's Deposition Checklist

But the key ingredient in discovery in the medical negligence claim is the thorough and thoughtful conducting of the deposition of any defendant physician and of any other medical care provider witness. The deposition of the physician-defendant must at least accomplish the following:

1. The doctor's education, experience and training should be covered in detail, with particular reference to the procedure, treatment and disease in question. Counsel must be able to conclude from the testimony either that the physician knew how to handle the problem in question and failed to do so, or really didn't have the requisite training and experience to deal with the medical issues in the case and was wandering around.

**2.** The entire sequence and content of the medical treatment offered must be identified so that when the deposition has been concluded, counsel may feel comfortable in having available the entire predicate for the evaluation or further evaluation of the case. Equally important, he must feel assured that at trial there will be no surprises in terms of testimony on defendant's behalf which offers the "real" explanation for what happened.

**3.** All conversations including advice, instructions, warnings and the like to the patient and any member of his family should be disclosed. Such testimony may include admissions and significant medical facts. It is of course critical in any informed consent case.

**4.** The final diagnosis together with any tentative diagnoses and any differential diagnosis should be explored. As to each diagnosis, on the basis of what medically germane facts it was confirmed or ruled out; and where the validity of the final diagnosis is in issue, the doctor should be asked retrospectively why and how the true diagnosis was missed. So too, in any case involving a particular course of treatment, inquiry must be made in detail into the course and purpose of the treatment rendered, whether it was properly executed and what alternatives were considered. Again, where the course of treatment did not work out, a retrospective analysis of the reasons therefore is in order.

**5.** In every case, counsel must learn from the physician, so far as he can, why things went wrong; did someone else do something wrong; what could have avoided the tragedy.

Many counsel are hesitant to aggressively seek out the physician's retrospective analysis of the case. This is wrong. Particularly in jurisdictions where there are discovery restrictions based upon "opinion" evidence, information learned "in anticipation of litigation" or "attorney's work product," plaintiff and defense counsel often misconstrue the limits of discovery. In any event, plaintiff's counsel must not hesitate to ask pertinent and ultimate questions and to pursue by appropriate motion improper failures to respond or directions by counsel not to answer. Of course the diagnosis, prognosis and etiology of a condition are "opinions," but they are as well historic medical "facts" in evaluating the case. The conclusions of the attending physician, the rationale and merit of his judgment are always in issue, and any of these subjects on which he is expected to testify at trial are the fit subject matter for pre-trial deposition inquiry.

If a good deposition has been conducted, in a surprisingly large number of instances, counsel will have developed the basis for liability already tentatively outlined by his pre-trial investigation and consultation with his expert witness. In several instances we have seen the defendant establish his own liability, and he is one expert who will not deprecate his own credentials at trial! In other instances, the deposition will at least have achieved a limitation of the issues and permit counsel to zero in on the narrow grounds which will determine the outcome. This is especially true in cases in which the etiology of the patient's condition is in issue or where the plan of treatment did not work out. There may be multiple explanations for this, but surely the interrogation of the doctor should have disclosed which variables can be ruled out as competent explanations and thus narrows the ground of controversy. In yet other instances, significant new wisdom will be obtained by counsel in questioning the doctor and a tentative theory of the case may be undermined.

It is never too late to reassess one's position in a medical negligence claim and indeed, to terminate the case if that be indicated. In several instances, I have used the deposition as a testing ground for exploration of a theory of liability in a claim which otherwise warranted the commencement of litigation. I want to be able to judge from having seen the doctor under questioning and on the basis of the content of his testimony, whether I think there is a fair shot at persuading the jury of his culpability. The deposition is also the time for setting up crisp inconsistencies between the doctor's recollection and other historic facts of the case which may be important. As with every other witness whose conduct is in question, the physician often cannot resist the temptation to have a self-serving recollection. He may present a scenario, which, with textbook clarity and precision, recounts a clinical picture or sequence of medical facts which will validate the course of conduct he in fact pursued. The jury will expect the physician to tell the truth, and he will be penalized if he lacks candor. The physician who lies or ignores a central fact in the case is mortally wounded at trial.

I am always interested in identifying the physician's style of deposition. Should he be handled with "kid gloves" and apparent full measure of deferential respect? Or is he a quarrelsome and even arrogant type who can readily be baited and who should be the object of some "heavy hitting" on the witness stand? I want to know whether I can afford to call the doctor as an adverse witness—as on cross-examination—at trial.

## Obtaining and Selecting Your Expert Witness

Before the final arrangements for trial are set, counsel must complete his development of the case in terms of the theory of liability with his expert witnesses and any other health care providers who will be offering expert testimony. "But where and how do I obtain the expert?" It takes some years to develop a coterie of potential expert witnesses in various specialties who are prepared to evaluate and testify in these cases. I personally avoid professional witness types who have been "on tour" through the courtrooms of the country unless they are highly qualified and will wear well at trial against cross-examination on their credentials, background and experience. I like to know that any such expert has testified for the *defendant* as well as plaintiff in medical negligence claims. But generally, I look for medical staff members who have both strong academic credentials and active clinical experience. Full-time staff members are an excellent source of expert witnesses, since they are more likely to be concerned academically about poor medical practice and more immune to peer group pressure than their colleagues who are engaged in active private office practice.

I make it a practice to have my file evaluated by a competent physician who will *not* testify, and I strongly encourage this practice at an early stage of the screening and preparation of the file. I have found that in a surprising number of instances, when I present a carefully prepared narrative statement with accompanying medical records and even appropriate excerpts from the medical literature, disclosing that I have conscientiously screened and evaluated the case *before* the material has been submitted to a potential witness, there is very often a favorable reaction from the potential expert who *will* testify. My witnesses are satisfied that an effort has been made responsibly to consider the case; that I am not simply fishing for a case and that I am sensitive to the proposition that a case of questionable merit should not be lodged. I recommend this approach to every attorney. I do not mean to criticize every single "medical malpractice advisory service." Some of these groups have excellent physicians available, but counsel should find out up front about the quality of the expert witness who will be available, assuming the case is otherwise meritorious, and in addition, what the cost considerations will be through trial. Even in cases where such a service is employed, simply dumping hospital charts with a cover letter generally and briefly identifying the case is not the thing to do. The potential claim should already have been generally thought out, and the areas of inquiry should be raised with specificity. Physicians understand medical vernacular and the medical significance of the facts in the case, but counsel's common sense in terms of raising the right questions is every bit as good as the doctor's. I insist upon delineating the areas of concern to me as well as inviting any other input from the proposed witness. It's too easy for a physician to say that "overall" the case was satisfactorily handled or "on balance" the otherwise negligent event can be excused. I want to hear the answer to specific questions, and oblige the doctor to face up to the issues in his report. It goes without saying that it is astute business practice to recognize the value of a physician's time and to avoid compromising the quality of the evaluation by trying to save dollars. It is well to pay for the evaluation in advance.

Wherever possible, the family physician, even though a general practitioner, should be sought out to testify in the plaintiff's case—even though he will not be offering expert testimony against the defendant. I look for any basis on which the family physician can testify comfortably in the plaintiff's case. This testimony may be limited simply to the pre-existing medical status of the plaintiff or, more significantly, he may testify to the presenting symptoms which occasioned the referral to a specialist and then, the post-treatment medical situation. In the typical instance in which there is antipathy on the part of the family physician toward the negligence aspects of the case and he doesn't want to "get involved", I make it a practice to meet personally with the doctor to explain in detail the reasons for the litigation, to emphasize that he will not be imposed upon to offer expert testimony, and to make certain that at a minimum, he remain a "neutral" on the liability issues. If he is prepared to remain neutral, I will routinely call him as a witness. If he is prepared as well to testify on liability on some issue which arguably is within his area of expertise, I will of course attempt to take advantage of that testimony even though I am mindful of the fact that an objection in certain cases and in certain jurisdictions to his qualifications to offer expert testimony may be sustained. Again, the important point to me is that he is in court at some stage "on the patient's side" so far as the jury is concerned. It is of course dangerous business to rely upon the family physician as the sole expert, unless the area of medical-legal inquiry comfortably falls within that physician's area of professional competence or, under the law of the particular jurisdiction, a general practitioner has been held to be qualified to offer expert testimony and counsel simply has no other expert.

## How to Prepare Your Expert for Trial

The key to preparing the lead expert witness is a thorough understanding by counsel and a decision between counsel and the expert as to the theory of liability which will be argued at trial. The expert must be encouraged to explain at length the medical chronology and significance of the medical events in plain English to the jury. They must understand what happened—what went wrong—how it could have been avoided through reasonable medical management. Sophisticated or esoteric medical points of view described and articulated in medical vernacular may be very neat for the medical journals, but it doesn't work in the courtroom. The style of the expert should be professional. He must not appear to have a hatchet out for a colleague. He can even appear to be disappointed at his need to testify in court against a colleague. Obviously he must be tutored in the legal implications of his testimony, with particular reference to the causation issue on the defendant's negligence and the favorable prognosis had appropriate medical attention been pursued. So too, he must understand the requirement in most jursidictions that his opinion on ultimate issues be styled "with reasonable medical certainty." It is not inappropriate to assist the expert by supplying the expert with material from the medical literature which buttresses his own opinion. This may be particularly useful on cross-examination or on redirect examination when the witness's opinion is challenged by contrary views also appearing in the literature.

### How to Capture the Essence of Your Entire Case in a Few Dramatic Sentences

The starting and finishing points of the trial must be a readily understandable theory of the case, drawn as narrowly as possible, which convincingly imposes fault on the medical care provider defendant, with significant damages resulting which are plainly attributable to that fault. The theory of the case should permeate every stage of the trial, starting with voir dire examination of the jury. Any proof or arguments which are not supportive of the theory of liability are surplusage and more important, generate the risk of a case being sidetracked on collateral issues. I challenge myself on this strategy by attempting, prior to trial, to articulate the entire case in a few plain English sentences. I try out those few sentences on my wife and friends to see whether I have succeeded in quickly communicating both the thrust and flavor of the claim. It is the one part of the preparation of the case which I want down pat. With those few sentences I will begin the voir dire examination and the opening statement to the jury. If I cannot neatly summarize the case in this fashion, I am not ready for trial. I recommend this exercise to every attorney, if not as a matter of style in presenting the case, then at least as a check to determine whether the case is ready for presentation to a jury. Let's see how it can work in practice.

"My client, Mrs. Janet Martino, was a patient of Dr. Robert Johnson, a specialist in gynecology, for 20 years, relying upon and trusting him to treat her properly for any medical condition involving any disease of the reproductive or genital systems. In November, 1973, then a young woman in her 40s, Mrs. Martino, complaining only of an occasional feeling of pressure in the lower portion of her stomach, was told by Dr. Johnson that she should have her entire uterus removed by surgery—a hysterectomy. In fact, this major surgical procedure was not necessary, but relying upon him, she agreed. During the course of the surgery, Dr. Johnson mistakingly cut through the bladder, the organ of the body where urine is stored, and as a result, despite two attempts to repair this problem, Mrs. Martino has and will for the rest of her life, suffer from the uncontrollable loss of urine. This condition, known as urinary incontinence, has largely destroyed Mrs. Martino's ability to pursue a normal life. In short, this case involves a hasty and unnecessary hysterectomy which has inflicted severe and lifelong injuries for which Mrs. Martino asks you to award a substantial verdict of money damages."

• • •

"My client, Mr. Ralph Byrd, is 35 years old. Before March, 1972, he was the manager of a successful wholesale hardware business in Philadelphia, the father of three young children, deeply involved in community affairs, and engaged in an active and happy personal and social life with his wife. On March 15, 1972, low back surgery close to the spinal cord was performed on Mr. Byrd by the defendant in this case, Dr. Richardson, and from that day to this and for the rest of his life, Mr. Byrd will suffer from almost total paralysis of his left leg, numbness of a portion of the leg and in the groin area, and severe back pain. He is unable properly to work, or engage in normal leisure activities with his children, wife and friends. He does not have a normal married life. He is a permanent partial cripple, and as a result of all this has and will suffer tremendous financial losses. Dr. Richardson is a skilled, highly qualified and experienced back surgeon who knew that with this type of surgery, one patient in 25 can end up with a worse problem after surgery than he had before the surgery. Mr. Byrd was entitled to know the risks, but the doctor didn't tell him. In short, this is a case in which a generally healthy young man trusted the recommendation of an experienced surgeon that he should undergo major surgery without knowing what was ahead of him, because the doctor didn't properly explain things beforehand."

• • •

"The tragedy which you are about to consider involves the death of my client's young husband who was taken to the Rockbridge Hospital emergency room on August 20, 1975 after being involved in an automobile accident. He was suffering from all sorts of cuts and bruises of his head, face and chest. He was seen by a young intern for about 5 minutes and then was left alone for 3 hours—to die unattended."

• • •

"Mrs. Simon was just 35 years old when she was sent by her family physician to Dr. Masterson, a specialist, because she had a lump in her right breast. Dr. Masterson felt the lump, assured her that everything was O.K.; that she had nothing to worry about. No other tests or examinations were conducted or ordered by the doctor who simply told her to come back in a year. Within that year Mrs. Simon died because the lump, which Dr. Masterson said was O.K., was in fact cancerous. If he had conducted further examinations and tests, he would have found that out, and he could have spared this patient, who relied on and trusted in him for good medical attention, from the diastrous spread of that cancer from the breast to almost every portion of her body. Her husband, Robert Simon, is here today, asking on behalf of their 4 children and himself that the family be made whole for this unnecessary and tragic loss . . . When you consider the evidence that even if Dr. Masterson had properly treated Mrs. Simon, her life expectancy would have been limited to 5 to 10 years, I know you will consider too that for Mrs. Simon, it was the whole rest of her life, and for her husband and young children, the whole rest of their time with a wife and mother. They feel they were entitled to have her during that period."

• • •

What common threads emerge from these several examples in terms of the presentation of the case at trial?

1. First and foremost, the jury has been told simply what the claim is about. The more detailed explanation of the case which of course will follow in the opening statement and in the presentation of the testimony should comfortably fall under the cover of the basic theory. The jury does not need to fish around for where counsel is heading.

2. The flavor of the case has been set. Note that particularly in the first example, the concepts of trust, confidence and reliance have been inserted. This is important to the chemistry of a medical negligence claim. Patients tend to rely upon the doctor. They trust him to make them better. The jury will understand this.

3. Note that the issues were narrowed and articulated as generously as possible and without heavy reference to medical vernaculars or em-

phasis on details which will of course be presented in the testimony—the unnecessary hysterectomy (fistula from mechanical trauma during surgery with urethral dehiscence after two unsuccessful attempts at surgical repair); the patient's right to know (cauda equina syndrome following lumbar laminectomy in the absence of crisp clinical indications for the procedure); the abandoned patient in the emergency room (death from unsuspected adult respiratory distress syndrome despite evidence of significant chest trauma); misdiagnosis of breast cancer (arguably non-adherent and soft lump on palpation but without follow-up x-ray examination or frozen section biopsy or timely direction for follow-up examination).

4. Note that where possible an attempt is made to immediately preempt defense issues. Thus, in the informed consent example, involving a distinguished neurosurgeon who made an excellent appearance, the style of counsel's approach was to attempt to take advantage of the defendant's distinguished background; to treat him "softly" and to argue simply that he knew better. The case went to the jury simply on the basis that a fine doctor could not take things into his own hands, however well intended he was, without letting the patient know the downside risks. A better example still is the breast cancer case in which, in a disputed liability situation, it was elected to preempt the causation issue by conceding out-front a limited life expectancy.

## What to Look For During Voir Dire Examination

In any jurisdiction in which voir dire examination of the jury panel is permitted, plaintiff's counsel must secure the opportunity not only to explore prejudices for purposes of preemptory challenges or challenges for cause, but in addition to commence in earnest the adversary process in presenting the plaintiff's case. Any mindset on the part of a member of the jury panel in terms of "medical malpractice" cases must be identified. The panel must be presented with the concept that the claim is simply for negligence on the part of a professional whose general expertise and conduct as a physician is not in issue (at least in the typical case). The theory of the case should of course be presented at the outset. Frankly, I am hesitant to ask the jury panel's reaction to the short presentation of the theory of the claim or about any negative medical treatment experience which they or any member of their families have suffered. Some years back, I participated in an interdisciplinary survey under a federal grant of a representative population sample, which dealt in part with the issue of negative medical treatment experiences. Over 50% of the sample were involved with or were aware of a medical treatment experience which was characterized as "negative." Prior to that experience I had asked jury panel members about any negative medical experiences. Too many members of the jury panel raised their hands, and of course this led either to challenges for cause or a more careful delineation of the judicious use of preemptory strikes by my opponent. It is better to leave this subject matter to defense counsel who, while he may gain a certain benefit in terms of the intelligent use of his strikes, will himself run the risk of establishing a good mindset in terms of receptivity to the plaintiff's claim—yet another negative medical experience for which the jury can do something by its verdict.

### How to Present Testimony the Jury Will Understand

The medical negligence claim is particularly challenging to counsel in terms of the art of communication. Terminology and concepts beyond the ken of the average juror are involved. Plaintiff's witnesses should be ready to translate such concepts into plain English. Whenever possible, counsel should either avoid the use of medical vernacular, or parenthetically add to the question or comment a several-word explanation following the use of a medical term. Sometimes a formal glossary on a chart will be in order.

  The use of demonstrative evidence can be critical. Pertinent pages of a hospital record should be enlarged and placed before the jury. Anatomic charts, well and plainly labeled, should be generously used. A good and thorough pre-trial deposition will typically include one or more admissions, or at least testimony that foreseeably a witness will attempt to explain away. I have found it useful in such circumstances to have several of the deposition pages enlarged to chart size to be readily available for display in conjunction with cross-examination of the defendant physician.

  The order of presenting the witnesses is of some significance in the respect that it is important to get the factual basis for the claim in front of the jury as promptly as possible. It is a must to have the medical records as trial exhibits at the outset, an issue which should always be handled pre-trial and if not then resolved, then as the first order of business before the trial commences. The plaintiff, or in the case of a decedent a reliable and knowledgeable member of the family, should be the lead witness on the stand. There may be a few exceptions to this. If the plaintiff is a particularly poor witness, counsel should not hesitate to start off with the strongest fact witness he has. *If* the defendant physician is known to be a poor witness *and* counsel has a thorough and good deposition transcript, he may elect to call that defendant as on cross-examination, checking first as to what the evidentiary implications are under the law of the particular jurisdiction concerning the extent to which the plaintiff is bound by the testimony offered in his own case. There is a further exception in terms of calling a defendant as a witness in the plaintiff's case, where it is known from the deposition that certain issues are conceded by the defendant and counsel is prepared to limit the interrogation to those issues. Such a decision should be taken with knowledge of the fact that defense counsel may elect to cross-examine his own client on *all* issues as is proper in the case of a *party* under cross-examination. Interestingly, defense counsel rarely exercise this option, either because the witness and/or counsel are not really ready to present the full spectrum of testimony, or because of a conscious decision not to expose the entire defense in the plaintiff's case. In any case in which the family physician is a cooperative witness, his testimony should be offered at a prominent point in the case—if not as the lead-off witness, then immediately following; or alternatively, as the last witness in the plaintiff's case.

Wherever possible, the sequence of the substantive testimony should highlight at the outset the injuries suffered, followed by that same witness's description of his knowledge of the pertinent facts relating to liability. The concluding witness in the plaintiff's case should generally be a damage witness.

### Cross-Examination of the Defendant's Experts

All litigation counsel are familiar with standard maxims with respect to cross-examination. They are all relevant here including in particular limiting the examination to questions to which counsel has good reason to believe he can get an appropriate response, or where he is indifferent to the response and is asking the question to make a point. An attack on the witness's bias or lack of proper expertise should virtually never be made unless counsel has the ammunition. It is dangerous business to make the result of a medical negligence claim hinge upon assessing the relevant credibility or expertise of witnesses. It is evident that in general there is not a parity of access to expert testimony between plaintiff and defendant in a medical negligence claim.

However, there are some areas of inquiry on cross-examination which can be fruitful. If the plaintiff's expert witness is a generally well-thought-of physician, the defendant's expert will concede that he is a qualified physician who is entitled to his point of view. Most defense experts will concede that they have made mistakes in medical management of the case and that the defendant is capable of making a mistake as well. Once I heard an expert witness say he had never made a mistake of any significance in his medical care. Several members of the jury laughed out loud.

If there is an item in a reputable source in the medical literature which contradicts a point, counsel should confront the witness with such material. But special care must be taken that within the four corners of the article in question, the contradictory point is well established. It is of course fundamental that every possible relevant contribution to the medical literature by the witness must be obtained and carefully examined pre-trial—an obvious potential for cross-examination of the author on the stand.

Finally, in a certain few cases where plaintiff's counsel is convinced that the expert witness is basically an honest and academically sound physician, there can be some probing on the underlying merits of the claim. Thus, in negligent diagnosis cases, such a witness may be asked, "Although you've indicated that Dr. Defendant conformed with reasonable medical practice when he mistakenly diagnosed Mrs. Plaintiff's chest pain as gastric distress, would you not agree with Dr. Plaintiff's Expert that a differential diagnosis with heart disease would have represented good medical management?" In a negligent treatment case, if the expert has indicated that the same type of result (as was experienced at the hands of the defendant) had never occurred in his practice, that fact should of course be highlighted.

On balance, it remains good advice to err on the side of under- rather than over-cross-examination. This fundamental precept was brought home to me recently when I asked a defense medical expert, who at several times testified on behalf of physicians in medical negligence claims, whether I could not safely assume that he would not be willing to evaluate a file on behalf of a patient and come to court to testify against a colleague of his. Without hesitation the doctor said he would be pleased to evaluate any file of mine and to testify. Because I was convinced that the plaintiff's claim was not mortally wounded by his testimony, I elected to proceed further. "Are you testifying under oath that if I sent you a file next Monday morning for evaluation with a check to cover your services, you will objectively evaluate the case, and if you are satisfied there has been medical error, that you will testify on behalf of my client?" The answer was simply, "That's right." I did and he did!

# "Hey, Manufacturer, You Blew It"

## An Interview with Robert L. Habush

Robert L. Habush graduated from the University of Wisconsin (J.D., 1961). He is a member of the American Bar Association; Milwaukee Bar Association; State Bar of Wisconsin (Board of Governors 1980-present); Wisconsin Academy of Trial Lawyers (President 1968-69 and 1970-71); the Association of Trial Lawyers of America (Board of Governors, 1969-70, 1983-present; National Parliamentarian, 1971-72; National Secretary, 1972-73); International Academy of Trial Lawyers (Board of Governors, 1983-85); Inner Circle of Advocates; International Society of Barristers; Diplomat in the National Board of Trial Advocacy; board certified in civil trial advocacy by the National Board of Trial Advocacy. Habush is the author of several articles including "Wisconsin General Attempt Statute," and "The Puhl Case and Prenatal Injuries," and the book *Cross Examination of Non-Medical Experts* (Matthew Bender & Company, Inc., 1981). He has lectured on trial advocacy at the University of Wisconsin Law School for the past 14 years.

*Robert L. Habush won what is believed to be the largest personal injury verdict in the history of Wisconsin in 1975, when a jury returned an award of $1,860,995. According to the* Milwaukee Journal:

> "His client, Lawrence Totsky, was paralyzed from his chest down after his Volkswagen crashed when the steering mechanism failed.
>
> "In 1977 Habush won another $1.5 million in a jury trial against Chrysler Corp. His client was totally disabled when she struck her head on a mirror in an automobile."

*In fact, in the last five years Habush has been awarded jury verdicts of approximately $6 million dollars, most of which were products liability cases.*

*In November of 1979, Habush won an out-of-court settlement for his
clients that could amount to nearly $5 million, in a case in which a girl was
seriously burned when her pajamas caught fire. Habush told us that this
case is a classical teaching example of the products liability case. According to the* Milwaukee Sentinel:

> "The accident occurred when [Michelle Stich, then four years old] was
> playing with a cigaret lighter while wearing 100% cotton flannel pajamas. It
> was alleged that the pajamas had not been treated with a flame retardant
> and should have been.
>
> "Under the settelement, Michelle will receive $1,000 a month com-
> pounded at 4% annually for life, with payments guaranteed for the first 20
> years. With a lifetime expectancy of 70 years, the potential settlement is
> $4,371,485. Other elements of the settlement brought the potential award to
> $4,721,485.
>
> "The defendants were K-Mart Apparel of Wisconsin Corp., S. S. Kresge
> Co., which is the parent company, and Ganis Bros., Inc., which manufac-
> tured the pajamas. The pajamas were bought at a store in Milwaukee in
> 1973."

*In the following interview, Robert Habush discusses the techniques used in
the three cases mentioned above.*

### A Classic Products Liability Case

HABUSH: *Stich v. K-Mart, et al.* is a classical teaching example of a products
liability case. In the typical situation people come into your office not
knowing whether they have a case. Frequently they don't have all the evidence. This little girl was burned in February of 1975 while wearing pajamas that were purchsed by her grandmother in December, 1973. The clients had saved the remnants of the pajamas that had been burned, but
after the fire, out of anger, threw away companion pajamas that hadn't
been burned.

Of the several lighters owned by the family, one leaked very badly,
and therefore, the question of which lighter the child was using turned
out to be a very important question.

The next problem was proving where the grandmother bought the
pajamas, because like most people the grandmother didn't use a check,
she paid with cash. It was the grandmother's word against K-Mart.
K-Mart's people took the position originally that they never sold the
goods, that they never handled pajamas with that style or fabric. But we
sued them anyway, based upon the grandmother's word.

We then asked them through interrogatories who their suppliers were; that is, who were the manufacturers of children's sleepwear. They gave us a list of five or six. We sued all of them. After extensive discovery and affidavits the defendants convinced us that these particular manufacturers did not manufacture this type of pajama at this particular time.

However, during the course of that discovery we picked up the name of Randolph Mills in North Carolina who supplied a great deal of cloth and cotton flannelette for children's sleepwear. We went down and took the depositions at the mill. They provided us the name of a company called Ganis Bros. of New York, with whom they said they did substantially all of their children's sleepwear business, and that the yardage we had looked like the type of yardage that they produced and shipped to Ganis. Randolph Mills had a curious invoice which showed that Ganis apparently drop-shipped to a place called Buehler Warehouse, which was in Cookeville, Tennessee. We sued Ganis. Ganis said, "Never saw the stuff, wouldn't touch it; don't like the seams, don't like the buttons, don't like the pattern, never produced it."

At this point K-Mart Apparel, which is a subsidiary of S. S. Kresge, changed their interrogatory answers and stated that a re-check of records indicated that Ganis did produce and supply the subject pajamas. Ganis persisted in denying that they manufactured the sleepwear right up to the end.

I sent an investigator down to Tennessee. I said, "Go down to Cookeville, and don't come back until you turn something up." He found a plant in Cookeville, Tennessee, where the Ganis Bros., using *aliases*, operated a corporation called the Appalachian Corporation. Appalachian Corporation made these pajamas. And for reasons I'm still not certain of, the Ganis Bros. not only failed to reveal that they owned all the stock in that Appalachian Corporation down in Tennessee, but when they went down there to visit the plant they used aliases—they never used their real names in their dealings with the supervisor and the manager of the plant. We found the former manager of the plant, who had taken some records with him when he was fired, and we were able to prove that this particular pajama was manufactured there in 1973 in an appropriate period of time before the sale.

EDITOR: How long did it take you to reach this point?

HABUSH: Discovery took two and a half years to put together and cost a great deal. I'd say that we probably had about $80,000 of our firm's money invested in the whole procedure all the way up to the end. It was an extraordinary effort, but not that atypical, in terms of gathering the evidence in a products case. The ultimate settlement was borne chiefly by Ganis the manufacturer, and to a lesser extent by K-Mart.

But isn't it curious how initially we were up against that stone wall—everyone was denying that they either sold or manufactured the product. It takes a great deal of persistence and tenacity to keep pressing ahead. You've got to be stubborn as hell, that's the bottom line. And I must tell you, as a matter of economics, you have to have a substantial injury. If the kid had been hurt to a very minor degree I probably would have said the hell with it; I can't spend twenty-five, thirty thousand dollars for a case that's maybe worth five or ten thousand.

EDITOR: Do you have your own investigator?

HABUSH: I have had a full-time investigator for the last fifteen years. I think that's essential for any trial lawyer who does any kind of volume in substantial cases.

EDITOR: If the case had gone to trial, would you have included K-Mart and Ganis both as defendants?

HABUSH: Oh, yes, I would definitely have included both of them. I felt I had separate allegations of negligence against each of them, that were independent of each other. I felt that the time frame involved here, which was July of 1973, lent some credibility to the allegation that K-Mart shouldn't have sold this stuff. Without getting into too much detail, after July 1 of 1973 it was illegal to manufacturer cotton flannelette pajamas that did not have flame retardant chemicals in them. From July 1, 1972, to July 1, 1973, a year earlier, there was a kind of moratorium where manufacturers could still manufacture untreated pajamas, but had to attach warning labels. The pajamas the Stiches bought were manufactured in the moratorium year, so they should have had a label on them; there was a question of whether they did. But there were a lot of manufacturers who were refusing to manufacture this flammable sleepwear even during that period of time, and there were a lot of retailers who were not selling it. For instance, in the Fall of 1973 when these goods were sold by K-Mart, J. C. Penney was selling flame-retardant pajamas. Moreover, there were other fabrics safer than cotton to pick from, and there were chemically treated pajamas available. A retailer had to make a deliberate choice to sell these more dangerous products. It wasn't illegal to do it, but it was, I submit, at their risk. By the same token, the manufacturer did not have to accept flammable cotton to put into pajamas. They could have insisted on either material treated with the flame retardant chemicals or another type of fabric which inherently was flame retardant.

So I thought they both breached a duty. To me it was a negligence case, a straight case of negligence. Both of them, I think, would have gotten stuck.

EDITOR: Was the large settlement due to the fact that you might have sued for punitive damages?

HABUSH: We didn't have a punitive damage count. Punitive damages have not yet been adopted in a products case in Wisconsin. Thus, the state of the law was very uncertain. And I thought that the punitive aspect of the case was sufficient to have given me a sizable verdict *absent* punitive damages. In other words, as you correctly detect, in order to get punitive damages you have to have some kind of outrageous conduct. And I'm sure that their outrageous conduct in manufacturing and selling the pajamas was as provocative as the way they handled themselves after the case was started.

EDITOR: Could you have introduced evidence to a jury about the manufacture using aliases?

HABUSH: Yes. Although that was a hotly disputed point. As a matter of fact, the defendants brought a motion *in limine* a few days before the trial was to start, to exclude that evidence. The judge ruled that because they were denying that they had manufactured the goods, we were entitled to go behind the denial to prove that the pajamas were in fact manufactured in Tennessee; and when we proved that they were manufactured in Tennessee we were then obliged to show the connection between the Tennessee operation and Ganis in New York. That could only be done by showing stock ownership. Moreover, the fact that they were using aliases when they came down there would be revealed.

If there was one single thing that caused them to say let's get the hell out of this lawsuit, I think it was losing the preliminary motion. I don't have to tell you how a jury would have viewed their conduct.

EDITOR: Are you reluctant to sue a local retailer that may be popular in the community? Or does that apply only to small towns? Would you ever dismiss the local retailer before the trial starts?

HABUSH: Yes, I am. Well, let me qualify it in this way. K-Mart is the fourth largest retail outlet in the country. If you've got them as defendants, you shouldn't have to be concerned about the size of the town or whether the public loves them. However, if you've got a ma and pa hardware store, some local retail outlet, and it's even in a small town, which makes it worse, and you don't need them, it is foolish to keep them in the lawsuit even though the strict liability law allows you to bring in the entire chain of distribution.

I believe that in products liability cases, once you find your target defendant, and there is sufficient coverage, that's all you'll need. I like to go after the target defendant and concentrate my effort on that particular defendant and dump all over that defendant. You must avoid being distracted by peripheral, less negligent parties. Of course, this advice is dependent on the fact that your target has sufficient coverage to pay you any anticipated judgment.

Sometimes you must keep a retailer in when you can't get jurisdiction over the manufacturer, or the manufacturer has gone bankrupt, or the manufacturer has inadequate insurance coverage and inadequate assets to cover a judgment.

Sometimes retailers have *independent* duties with respect to products. For instance, a retailer may assemble a snowmobile or a motorcycle or a lawnmower before they sell it, in which case there may be some question about negligence in the assembly of the product. For example, a car dealership who has had something to do with the maintenance of the car may be implicated in a products case against a car manufacturer. Moreover, a dealer may have gotten a warning from the car manufacturer about the defect, and when the car was brought in, they didn't fix it properly.

Let me give you another example of evidence accumulation which I think you might find really interesting. I had a $1.5 million verdict against Chrysler in Menominee, Wisconsin, a couple of years ago. This was a little town of 5,000 people. My client had been a passenger in a 1961 Plymouth Belvedere, and in what was characterized as an ordinary highway crash was thrown against the interior mirror. The mirror stem penetrated her skull and she received a brain stem injury, and never recovered from a coma. She is still in a coma today; I think she's been in a coma six or seven years. She had been a gorgeous girl.

In order to determine if we had a case I had to find out what the state of the art was with respect to rear view interior mirrors. The accident happened in 1971, so the car was ten years old. I sent my investigator out into the countryside to search for mirrors in the junkyards, and he came up with at least two dozen rear view interior mirrors from cars of the same vintage, 1961, and even a couple of earlier models that had mirrors that were flexible. Our contention was that this mirror was fixed onto the header, or the dash, with no ability to flex if someone struck it. The mirror of course would deflect where it was attached to the stem—because that is where one adjusts it. But the state of the art at that time required that the stem *bottom,* where it's attached to the dashboard or to the header, should also deflect by a ball joint. The Belvedere didn't have it; it had a fixed, inflexible mirror. We were able to show several mirrors from a number of cars manufactured around 1961 that had the deflecting mirror, which was safer. As a matter of fact, Chrysler had the deflecting mirror in their top of the line, the New Yorker, but they didn't put it in the Belvedere.

These mirrors, hung on a huge board, were one of the more significant pieces of evidence presented during the trial.

EDITOR: I've heard of state of the art used as a defense, but rarely used on the offense.

HABUSH: It's usually used by the defendant as a shield. They rarely have it asserted against them as a sword—it blows their minds when that happens. They never thought they would lose this case in a million years. They never offered a dime before trial. It may be the only interior rear view mirror case in the country that's been successful at trial. They started offering money during the trial. They offered a structured settlement for life. For *life!* I didn't know whether the lady was going to live for five minutes! She almost died a week before trial. I was constantly expecting someone to run into the courtroom during the trial and say Julie died. That's how tenuous her life was, and still is. I told them to shove it.

But anyway, I just wanted to give you that as an example of evidence accumulation which made the case, and that's just plain hard work.

### Explaining Products Liability to the Jury

EDITOR: In the trial, at what point and how do you explain to the jury what products liability is? I imagine most jurors you have in a case have either never heard of products liability or don't understand it. Is that true?

HABUSH: I think that practically everybody has read about product defects. I think that practically everybody has experienced, at some time in their life, something that went wrong with a product. Housewives experience it more than any other group. Moreover, they've read about the Ford Pinto cases, and they've read about General Motors, and they've read about Ralph Nader, and they're really quite familiar with products being defective.

When I first started trying cases in this area, and that was about fifteen years ago, juries at that point were very unfamiliar with products liability, and they still had that feeling that these great big companies had such sophistication that they could do no wrong; it really took a hell of a lot to win those cases at that time. This was before Ralph Nader. I cite Ralph Nader because despite his critics, I still feel that he has been a substantial contributor to product safety. From a trial lawyer's point of view he's conditioned my jurors; he's given them the impression that these big companies are fallible, and so I've got fertile ground to sow my seeds in. Consequently, I don't believe that I have to convince them to the same degree that I did years ago that a manufacturer can be negligent and that he could do things wrong.

Also, you have to convince jurors that they, as just ordinary folks, can criticize the manufacturer. There used to be the feeling that, "My God, here I am, I'm a retired person, I'm a housewife, I'm an auto mechanic," you know, or "I'm a school teacher, how in the hell can I sit and say that General Motors' engineers blew it?" Well, in time these people had less reluctance to find fault with the manufacturers of defective products, and they didn't feel the same kind of restraint. They were comfortable in saying, "Hey G. M., you just blew it."

In addition, the lawyers have gotten better. The number of lawyers today who are really good enough to take on the major manufacturers in a serious products liability case is many times greater than the number of lawyers who were good enough fifteen years ago to do that.

There are better experts available. Years ago most of the experts were highly suspect.

EDITOR: Would you hire an expert who is what they call a whore, who'd sell himself to you?

HABUSH: Never. And I'll give you two reasons. I'll give you the practical reason first. I want to know whether I really have a case. For me to get stroked and to spend thousands of dollars, only to find out thousands of dollars and years later that I really don't have a case, blows my mind. I mean that's pretty stupid.

Number two, I think it's important for a trial lawyer to maintain a level of morality and ethics. You acquire a reputation very quickly in this business, and good or bad it stays with you a long time. You are sometimes judged as a trial lawyer by the quality of the witnesses that you present in cases.

Moreover, the defense lawyers who are generally very capable in this area usually have a book on these "pros." I tried a case against Volkswagen in 1975 where they used two experts, their "dynamic duo" who had testified dozens of times together as a team for Volkswagen. I was able to show that, and I believe they lost their entire effectiveness in front of a jury. When you can show that most of his professional life he's been "experting," if I can coin an expression, for one particular group, whether it's plaintiff lawyers or automobile manufacturers, his effectiveness in front of a jury is reduced; not necessarily eliminated, but reduced.

EDITOR: At what point would you bring that out? Cross-examination?

HABUSH: Yes, that's how it would be done at trial. Usually I would discover that in deposition before trial. Then I would circulate their names amongst my friends around the country and make sure I have all the cases they've testified in. What I frequently do is acquire depositions or trial transcripts from cases they've testified in around the country. In that particular case I told you about, the Totsky case, which ended up with a $1.8 million verdict against VW, I impeached one Volkswagen expert with testimony he had given in a case in California. He was surprised as hell that I'd gone to the trouble to pick up that trial transcript. I don't think that's so unique. I think most of the trial lawyers who try cases in this area make the same kind of effort to acquire potentially impeaching testimony, either from depositions or trials that the experts had been involved in.

EDITOR: Getting back to the question I asked before, explaining to the jury at some point in the trial what products liability is. Is there a point where you discuss exactly what products liability is, and how it evolved? Do you *call* it products liability?

HABUSH: Having in mind what I just told you a few moments ago about people's increased awareness of defective products and the people who make them, I want to let the jury know right away that they're in a products liability case. I do it during voir dire when I introduce them to the case. I say, "Ladies and gentlemen, this is a products liability case, also known as a *consumer* liability case." I let them know that I think this is a significantly important case, and I use that as a preliminary comment. "And therefore I want you to be candid with me in answering your questions, and let me know whether or not you can sit on the case for two or three weeks, because this is a very important case."

So they're starting to get the impression, "Ah, it's one of these products liability cases we read about in the newspaper." And of course they don't read about $5,000 cases in the newspaper, they read about the million dollar cases in the newspaper.

From time to time I also ask on voir dire whether they could follow the law on strict liability. Why do I do that? There are some people who feel that you shouldn't be able to recover unless you can prove negligence or fault. In other words, even absent negligence, if the product's found to be defective, you recover under strict liability. Some people have trouble with that concept, and so I think it's a legitimate area of inquiry on voir dire; I will tell the jury, "At the end of the case, the judge is going to instruct you under a doctrine called strict liability. Now, this allows the plaintiff to recover without proving negligence, without proving fault, if we meet certain conditions. Some are that the product was defective when it left the plant, and it hasn't been altered or changed, and was used properly. Now is there anyone on the jury who would have any difficulty holding Chrysler Corporation responsible even if I don't prove that they did anything negligently?"

In the Chrysler case, as it turns out, I had a good negligence case, so I went on that theory. In most states you can plead warranty and strict liability. Some states require you to elect remedies. In Wisconsin, for instance, I can go to the jury on two theories, negligence and strict liability. There are different obstacles to overcome in order to recover under the respective theories. I feel personally that it's easier to get a jury to answer the negligence question "yes" than the strict liability question "yes." The strict liability question in Wisconsin, "Was the product defective and unreasonably dangerous?" is harder to get an affirmative response to than "Was Chrysler negligent with respect to the way they designed the mirror?"

On final arguments, I really lay the consumer business on the jury. Number one, I remind them that the corporation is as fallible as a human being. Number two, I remind them that the corporation has the same duties and the same responsibilities as an ordinary human being. I remind them that the corporation is responsible for all acts of its employees and its agents. I remind them of what the law is on products liability; I give them a little short course of what the law is. I remind them that in this country the poorest, most insignificant of injured victims has the same standing in this courtroom as the largest and most significant of corporations, and that they as twelve consumers have the ultimate right and responsibility to say to the manufacturer, "Hey, manufacturer, you blew it, you know, you were wrong and now you've got to pay the piper."

EDITOR: You think jurors enjoy having that power, or do you think they're nervous about it?

HABUSH: They love it.

## How to Hurt the Defense with Your Opening Statement

EDITOR: What issues do you address yourself to in opening statement?

HABUSH: Generally, I believe in a strong opening statement. I believe in hurting the defense on opening statement. My opening statements have all guns blazing. I don't hold *anything* back. My opening statement may take an hour and a half in a major case. I detail my evidence, I bring out the weakest parts of their case. Where I have an opportunity to ridicule their positions, I will do so. For instance, in that Chrysler case I referred to, we knew there were inconsistent answers in their interrogatories. Some of the answers to interrogatories were completely untrue. Some of the written material we had obtained—memoranda, testimony from other witnesses, sales materials—contradicted many answers to interrogatories. On opening statement I laid it all out. My objective was to try to make that jury angry at Chrysler before the evidence started.

And so to answer your question, the opening statement is a time when I try to influence the jury, without being too argumentative, on the case. There have been studies which found that a high percentage of jurors stated that the impression they got from opening statement was consistent with their final determination in the case. Therefore I think the lawyers who feel that opening statement is not important, to be very sketchy, are making a very serious mistake.

## Demonstrative Evidence and How to Use It Effectively

EDITOR: When and for what purposes do you use demonstrative evidence?

HABUSH: Demonstrative evidence in my judgment is the most important part of a products liability case. The reason I say that is, you are an educator. Sometimes you've got to teach these people a very complex subject. You've got to make these people into design engineers, into chemical engineers, into metallurgical engineers. You have to teach them the science of biomechanics, that is, the movements of the body under certain stresses and under different accident environments. And you have to be a good teacher. It has to be done in a way that is not patronizing, and that's not insulting. The use of photographs, blowups, charts, makes this task easier. Demonstrative evidence is very consistent with our visual society. Many of our jurors grew up in a TV environment from the time they were old enough to walk.

Consequently, I spend a *tremendous* amount of time and money getting exhibits together like the ones you took pictures of, for the

Chrysler case. I frequently blow up pages from hospital records that have significant statements on them for use during a trial. I blow up photographs on six-by-eight foot boards for the trial, for the jury. The use of these exhibits is very effective during the testimony of the experts. For instance, you ask the court for permission to approach the jury. You then have the expert stand down and talk to the jury using the exhibits.

Blown-up exhibits on cross-examination can be very effective. For instance, if you have a prior statement that contains a contradiction and you want the jury to see it in all its glory, take the statement, have it blown up on a big board, and when you're impeaching the witness you can show the jury and the witness that statement simultaneously. It has a much greater impact on the jury.

Finally, on final argument you can use these exhibits effectively. Some lawyers use exhibits excessively on final argument, to the point where the jury isn't listening to them. It becomes a visual show. This is a mistake because persuasion is still the basis of advocacy. If you've wrapped yourself in a damned carnival of photographs and exhibits, the jury may do little listening.

If you put all this stuff up on boards and tripods *behind* you, they're going to be sitting there looking over your shoulder. It's like having a conversation with someone who never looks at you, but is always looking around the room over your shoulder. That's very disconcerting. They're not really listening to you. Consequently, it's really somewhat of an art to learn how to use exhibits properly, not only during the course of the trial but on final argument.

## Should You Settle Or Not?

EDITOR: Do you tell your clients whether to take a settlement, or does the client decide?

HABUSH: There have been times when I have **had** difficulty with clients. Any lawyer who hasn't doesn't have any clients. But for the most part I'm able to maintain control over them and they'll follow my advice.

Trust has to be established early with the client. If it's your own client, that's fairly easy. The difficulty arises when you get a client from a referral. Where you haven't had that initial rapport with the client, this frequently can cause problems. If you recommend a settlement to a client and they don't take it, you're under an obligation to continue through with the case and try to be professional about it. More often you don't want to take the settlement, and the client does because he is either terrified over the prospect of trial, or the prospect of losing, or both. Many times these people are economically deprived and cannot walk away from a $500,000 offer, which completely boggles their mind. You may know in your heart that it's a million dollar case and you want to try it; you've worked on it for two years, you've got your heart and soul in the damned case and you know you've got them on the ropes, and the client says, "Please, you've got to take it, you've got to take it," and that just tears you up.

I'll tell you something honestly. We trial lawyers are people who have highs and lows emotionally. Our highs are fantastic and our lows are just awful; and some of my lowest lows have been when I have had to take a settlement in a case that I was in trial with, and I wanted to finish. You get yourself into a fever pitch; it's like preparing for the Superbowl and the other team doesn't show up. Consequently, the kicks aren't there in a settlement. The only true exhilaration in this business is the "verdict". Even "winning" in a less than spectacular fashion is somewhat of a downer, and the problem is maintaining some sort of balance about yourself and your cases, so that you don't set your expectations so high that you're never satisfied and never happy—and there are people like that. You can get in a great deal of difficulty, mentally, with that kind of attitude.

EDITOR: Takes a little discipline?

HABUSH: Yeah, exactly, you can't let yourself get so caught up in your juices that your judgment is impaired. There was a case recently in California where a lawyer got a sizable offer in a malpractice case and didn't communicate it to the client, because he obviously wanted to go ahead with the case and was afraid that the client would accept it. He lost the case, and the client sued the lawyer for malpractice and punitive damages, and recovered both. So I guess the bottom line is you can't say, "This is *my* case," although sometimes you start to feel that way. It's the client's case.

## Small Towns and Big Verdicts

EDITOR: Is there any particular way you can go after a large verdict in a small town?

HABUSH: Yes. And I think the fact that I had this million-five in Menominee, Wisconsin, a town of 5,000 people, lends some credibility to my answer. Obviously, the small town folks are not used to dealing in numbers that size. Obviously, too, the small town people tend to identify that kind of large money with big city folk, who they might have some deep seated bias and prejudice against. So it's important to establish right from the start on voir dire whether anyone on the jury would have any reluctance in rewarding damages in excess of a million dollars if the evidence could justify it. Sometimes I get eyes rolling back in jurors' heads, and sometimes I get the gasps and sometimes I get no facial expression at all but I want to smoke feelings out. Then I discuss the big damages on opening statement. I don't tell them what I'm going to ask for at the end of the case, but I give them everything I've got on past medical, future medical, reduced earning capacity; so on opening statement they may hear of damages of several hundred thousand.

Although I don't think economists are particularly persuasive on small town juries, the economist aids me in laying out the big dollars before the jury. Repetition conditions the jury until the small town conservatism gives way to the wish to do something very exciting.

Finally, let me say this about small towns. In Menominee, this trial was voted the number one news story of 1977. They had radio there every day, they had newspaper coverage every day. The point is, they're involved in probably one of the most exciting experiences that they have ever been involved in. That helps you. In Milwaukee the juror would be more sophisticated, and he'd be less excited. Paradoxically, small town juries may be capable of giving you larger verdicts than people in the large cities who are more attuned to big dollars, because they get excited with their job and want to be a part of a big verdict that makes the paper. Defeating the plaintiff may not even make the newspaper. Interesting psychology.

EDITOR: In a small town or a big town, I don't know if there's a distinction here, but instead of bringing in a mechanical engineer, or in addition to bringing in a mechanical engineer, is it also effective to have a local mechanic, just some kind of humble person who doesn't talk very well?

HABUSH: Yes, if you can. You don't put some dummy up there just to give a home town touch. But if you have someone local you should use him. For instance, a local doctor is frequently used; a local engineer would be nice, too. I tried a case in LaCrosse ten years ago involving a sawmill accident, and I used a sawmill inspector expert from the area. He was a far more effective witness than the super-duper design engineer that I brought in—in fact, I'm convinced he sold my case for me. And so you're right, there are different considerations in selecting which expert you're going to go with if you're in a small town.

## The Ideal Products Liability Juror

EDITOR: Is there an ideal juror for a products liability case?

HABUSH: Yes, housewives. They are the best. They are the ultimate consumers. They're the consumers who are the most frequently victimized by defective products, they're generally the purchasers in the house, and they are sensitive to the drug cases, as well as others, **and** I think they're the best.

I think in the category of age, a younger person will be more critical than an older person. A highly educated person, if you have a good case, would be excellent on liability, but I wouldn't want to try the case in front of an engineer, because there's no way in hell that you're going to get an engineer to be a good juror for a plaintiff in a products liability case.

EDITOR: He might say to himself, "This could be me some day getting sued."

HABUSH: Of course. Moreover, he'd be an "expert" in the jury room and likely to dominate the rest.

EDITOR: What would be the best kind of juror for the defense?

HABUSH: Someone who could identify with the defendant: a businessman such as the man who owns his own company, an engineer, a man who has had association with the insurance industry; basically anyone who feels they could be sued someday or would be adversely affected by a products liability judgment.

EDITOR: Do you try to excite the jurors by telling them that they have a chance here to set standards, that they're the watchdogs for society and consumer affairs?

HABUSH: One of the subjects we discussed up to now is the conditioning of the jury in a products liability case. Conditioning to the point where they feel that they're competent to criticize a sophisticated manufacturer. The second conditioning we talked about was how to condition them into thinking of large dollars, even in a small town. The next thing we discussed was in a small town in particular, where jurors feel they're involved in something big, something significant and exciting. Finally, as you've just suggested, if the jury feels that the verdict is going to receive notoriety elsewhere, this can be helpful. So the answer to your question is basically yes, I do suggest to the jury that their verdict will be heard in Detroit or elsewhere, and that the effect of their verdict will not be lost on the people who should be affected by it; and that yes, they can do a great deal for the safety of the consumer in finding that the particular defendant in this case was negligent with respect to design or producing a defective product.

One has to be very careful in this area, because there are some fine lines between appropriate and inappropriate final argument. Asking the jury to consider extraneous factors in coming to a verdict might be grounds for a mistrial. The last thing in the world you want after a four to six week products liability case is a mistrial on final argument, or grounds for a new trial if you should win the case.

EDITOR: For example, what could you say that would cause a mistrial?

HABUSH: I'll give you an example. "General Motors can well afford to pay this poor litigant." In other words, comparing relative wealth is grounds for a mistrial. Suggesting to the jury that the verdict should punish them, absent punitive damages, would be an improper argument. Asking the jury to put themselves in the place of the plaintiff—"how would *you* feel if this happened to *you* or one of your loved ones"—is clearly inappropriate final argument; that would be grounds for a mistrial.

You'd be shocked at how many lawyers don't even know all the prohibited arguments. They learn how to *do* final argument, but they don't learn what the inappropriate comments to avoid are. It's a whole area of instruction.

Sometimes you get so caught up in the case that you're tired and you haven't slept well for months; you can hardly think straight, and in the heat of the moment, you over-reach. There is the tendency to be excessive, and you have to constantly control yourself, discipline yourself not to let yourself cross over that line from propriety to impropriety, and not to let your anger and frustration manifest themselves in an outrageous final argument that would allow you to lose the credibility of the jury or get yourself a mistrial.

EDITOR: Where did you say a lawyer can look for these improprieties?

HABUSH: American Law Review and digest contain the prohibited comments. When I instruct law students on final arguments I will always include this area as part of the instruction.

*Chapter Two*

# *What You Should Know About Jury Selection*

Having thoroughly prepared your case before trial, you are already well on your way to victory in court. Now it is time to press your advantage even further by picking a jury that will see the facts from *your* point of view rather than from your opponent's.

Here to join you for this make-or-break phase of trial are five leading trial masters, who will show you in the following chapter the art—as well as the science—of jury selection. You will discover not only how to pick the right jurors, but also how to ask the right questions and make the right impression during this crucial first contact with the individuals who hold your client's fate in their hands.

Heading this list of experts is California psychiatrist and attorney **Marvin Blinder, M.D.,** a leading authority on psychiatry and the practice of law. Dr. Blinder shares his insights and experience concerning key social, psychological and ethnic characteristics of prospective jurors that should be considered during the selection process. He pinpoints those areas—occupation, age, religion, dress and body language, among others—that can provide vital clues to a prospective juror's true personality and whether he or she will be sympathetic to a client's case.

Next to share his views is the Honorable Walter Jordan of Texas. In his characteristically direct and colorful style, he cuts to the heart of the issue, summing up volumes of tactical information in just 23 do's and don'ts for a successful voir dire examination.

Judge Jordan points out that a "good trial lawyer must be, among other things, a good salesman. He must make a strong but favorable impression on as many of the panel members as possible." To this end, the Judge gives you the winning elements of voir dire technique that he has gleaned from his 20 years' experience on the bench. You will discover, for example, why it pays to level with the panel about any weaknesses in your case . . . how to forewarn panel members diplomatically that you will need to ask some personal questions . . . and the one last question you should ask to help assure a totally fair and impartial juror. You even get sample statements for explaining clearly what the burden of proof is in the case, be it reasonable doubt or preponderance of evidence.

Echoing Judge Jordan's point that there is no more important phase of trial than jury selection, Herald Price Fahringer goes on to note that in a criminal trial particularly, "the defendant's fate is fixed after the jury is chosen." Indeed, regardless of how well you present your case, a biased jury could easily doom your client to an undeserved "Guilty" verdict. To avoid such an outcome, Mr. Fahringer has developed—and here reveals—a step-by-step jury selection procedure for rooting out the hidden prejudices that certain jurors bring with them to court.

Featured among Mr. Fahringer's working tools are a master checklist for examining prospective jurors inside out and top to bottom . . . pointers on how to read the many unspoken signals that can tell you more about a juror's real feelings than words alone could do . . . and a simple yet ingenious system that lets you focus on the jurors themselves (instead of on your notes) as you conduct your examination.

To conclude the chapter, forensic psychologist Thomas Sannito and attorney Edward Burke Arnolds spell out the results of an intriguing study they conducted in order to "dispel or confirm the legendary myths" surrounding the jury selection process.

"Trial attorneys," they remark, "are too frequently put in the position of picking jurors according to folk lore and desperate hunches." Here, at last, are some straight facts—scientifically proven—that will sometimes surprise you and always enrich your understanding of those potential allies in the jury box. So if you want to reduce the guesswork in jury selection once and for all, this study should prove to be an invaluable help in everything from picking out the likely foreperson ahead of time to predicting a prospective juror's final vote.

# Picking Juries:

## Social, Psychological and Behavioral Factors to Consider

### Martin Blinder, M.D.

Dr. Blinder, who is both a professor of psychiatry and a professor of law, as well as author of a popular text on voir dire and other aspects of psychiatry in the practice of law, here offers practical insights for the attorney who wants to take jury selection seriously.

However much help in picking jurors an attorney may expect from consultants such as myself, the primary burden must still rest with him. He has to face the jurors day after day and he best knows the kinds of people with whom he generally has rapport and those with whom he generally does not. He has come to know his client and many of the witnesses, and has begun to form a solid notion of how they come across as human beings. He may have seen opposing counsel in action several times and knows, perhaps better than his opponent himself, just how the latter strikes other people.

Thus, the attorney would do well to listen to his consultant, but then integrate his recommendations into the approach and intuitive style with which he feels most comfortable. If the verdict comes out against his client, it is the attorney who bears the responsibility—not his consultant. Accordingly, the first bit of advice I give attorneys beginning selection process is to feel free to ignore all subsequent recommendations.

That said, I advise beginning with scrutiny of the professionals and laymen on the litigation team itself, who will be assisting in the selection process, for their probable strengths, blind spots, and biases.

## Helpful Questions to Ask at the Outset

Next, we assess and make explicit the psychological nature, appeal, and unattractiveness of the attorney's case and his opponent's; of the key litigants; of principal witnesses; and of the respective attorneys' personalities. I find it helpful at this point to ask:

> What kinds of people will be sympathetic/hostile to my client (or to the image of my client that I will present)?
>
> What kinds of people are likely to be sympathetic/hostile to my client's position (or to the position I shall fashion for him at trial)?
>
> What kind of person will be sympathetic/hostile to the circumstances in my client's life which bring him to court?
>
> What kind of person will be sympathetic/hostile to key witnesses?
>
> Which kinds of people are likely to prefer me, and which likely to prefer my opponent?
>
> How do I recognize the ideal juror if and when I find him?

## Develop a Checklist of Critical Juror Characteristics

The next step is to develop a checklist of critical desirable and undesirable characteristics accessible to scrutiny in prospective jurors ("blue collar" workers, former policemen, participants in two defense verdicts in the past, etc.). We can then construct the hypothetical ideal composite juror for the case at hand, e.g., cigar-smoking male chauvinist with classy address, expensively dressed, middle-aged, Republican, carrying *U.S. News and World Report,* has many children most of whom are beginning professional careers; or, welfare mother carrying old, tattered *New Republic,* splinter party registration, and emitting warm, possibly seductive smile at attorney.

Fortunately, there is a wealth of information readily obtained which will enable the attorney to begin making useful assumptions as to a prospective juror's biases. No single generalization is the valid basis for a conclusion, but a number of them together can be invaluable in making judgments about a questionable juror.

**1. Occupation.** An area most reliably interpreted is that of a man's work. Businessmen, particularly shopowners and bankers, invariably good defense jurors in civil cases, in the criminal courts often show prosecution bias, especially in instances of crime against property. People in "liberal arts" fields such as teaching, or in the helping professions (nurses, social workers), are usually willing to look past the hard facts and into mitigating circumstances associated with them, and thus may be well-attuned to defense arguments.

An overriding consideration, however, when evaluating prospective jurors by occupation, is the vocational identities of key witnesses and litigants themselves. Workers in the same field usually "talk the same language"; a "hard hat" juror is likely to be attuned and sympathetic to a "hard hat" witness, and a geneticist to another geneticist, regardless of which side his testimony may fall.

Individuals whose occupations involve fine, detailed work, and who, in the criminal court, respond better to the orderly laying down, piece by piece, of the prosecutor's evidence than to the defense attorney's broad brush work, will also tend to focus on the inevitable flaws in the plaintiff's case, rather than see it in the overview. Accountants and "engineering types" particularly will be preoccupied with cognitive detail and are proportionately insensitive to the human/emotional factors. Retired military men have a strong authority/law-and-order bias, identify with the state in criminal cases, and can be relied upon in personal injury litigation to be strict, ungenerous and impatient with free-wheeling, emotional plaintiff attorneys. Athletes also tend to lack sympathy for the fragile plaintiff. Cabbies, by contrast, are generally good plaintiff jurors, although they have an abiding dislike of pedestrians, injured or not.

**2. Age.** Age enables the attorney to make another kind of fairly reliable generalization about the prospective juror which may have bearing on his desirability in a particular case. Young people, though they tend to see things in black and white, have had less time to "fix" their ideas, and thus are more susceptible to new information, as may be provided them in court, than are their elders; they can be expected to be open to and comprehending of the latest scientific/psychiatric evidence. There are many elderly people, however, whose skins have aged faster than their cerebral arteries, witness the minds of some of the Warren Court Justices of the 1960s; such individuals, besides bringing a susceptibility to new ideas, may now have patience for a consideration of and a tolerance for ambiguities, a quality lacking in their youth.

In personal injury litigation, young jurors, suffused as they are with a sense of immortality, may not identify well with the injured party; while the very old may envy his receiving a large settlement. Both are thus potential defense jurors. The ideal plaintiff juror is probably a middle-aged individual who carefully and cautiously takes his or her seat, sits stiffly without leaning back and then rises very gingerly—sure signs of a chronic bad back, ie, "pain behavior".

**3. Sex.** All other things being equal, men are disposed favorably, and women unfavorably, to the words of an attractive woman (defendant, witness, etc.). Women tend to be swayed by an attractive man (whose good looks rarely put him at a compensatory disadvantage with his fellows), but may be harsher in penalty phases of criminal trials unless maternally aroused. Because of this innate attraction between the sexes, and the initial, instinctual distrust between women, women are surprisingly good defense jurors in rape trials, and men, good prosecution jurors.

**4. Religion.** Catholics, fundamental Protestant sects, and orthodox Jews tend to lean to the prosecution (in civil cases, to the defense); liberal Protestant sects and most Jews tend to favor the defense (in civil cases, the plaintiff).

**5. Ethnic group.** Ethnic minority groups usually will favor the "underdog"—individuals rather than business firms, insurance companies, or the state. Yet, a "White Establishment" juror may be more forgiving of a defendant in a criminal case when both offender and victim are members of the same minority group, dismissing their conflict and the resultant offense as "just two animals having a Saturday night brawl".

Although racism is not as overtly fashionable among whites as it once was, recently it has found considerable favor with minorities. As with occupation, the strong unconscious identification between members of the same ethnic/racial group may override all other considerations, a factor which must be weighed heavily in a context of the cultural background of litigants, the key witnesses, and the attorneys themselves.

### Preparing Questions for the Voir Dire

The litigation team reviews all material thus far available regarding each venireman for evidence of potential bias and draws up a preliminary retain/reject list, based on resemblance or dissimilarity to the aforementioned ideal juror construct. The team then decides what additional information would be helpful and prepares questions to be used during voir dire most likely to elicit that data. Unfortunately, the principal determinant of the answers veniremen give to the kind of questions most lawyers traditionally ask on voir dire is the way the questions are phrased, rather than what is really in the veniremen's heart, eg, "Given that a man's life is at stake here, would you make every effort to be fair and impartial as you listen to the evidence?" (How difficult it would be for a prospective juror to think of himself as willing to precipitantly destroy a man's life, even if it be that of a man to whom he has already taken an innate dislike.) Therefore, to improve the voir dire process, wherever possible questions should be the sort that require a narrative, rather than a "yes" or "no" response. A question such as "Are you prejudiced against people who drink from time to time?" in this day and age will get a flat "no" from all but an occasional Seventh Day Adventist, irrespective of the responder's deep biases. How much more useful is likely to be the answer to "What is your attitude toward (or opinion of) people who drink from time to time?" Or, compare: "The prayer of the complainant in this case is $200,000; do you believe anybody can be so injured that he should be awarded that sum?" with "How do you feel about awarding a sum as large as $200,000 in a suit like this?"

Thus, questions should be prepared as broadly as the court is likely to permit, irrespective of whether or not the attorney puts the questions to the prospective juror, or whether he operates in a jurisdiction where that remains a function of the court. The attorney should also prepare a series of alternative, more conveniently phrased questions covering the same areas—though more narrowly and in language closer to the usual formulas—in the event that some of the first questions are not permissible.

Now the attorney is ready to face his prospective jurors for the purpose of ferreting out their prejudices. He is armed with the knowledge that no prospective juror is comfortable with the notion that he is prejudiced. He knows that the prospective jurors all like to think of themselves as people totally free of bias, judicious, fair-minded—not unlike the attorney himself. The veniremen will be reluctant to reveal their biases to others because *they* prefer not to know about them. Thus, these prejudices must be exposed and defined indirectly, and by deduction, in such a way as to circumvent defenses and obviate the necessity for fibs or half-truthful replies.

For example, an attorney would never ask a venireman straight out if he is prejudiced against the poor. Instead, he might inquire if he does much business in a certain (ghetto) part of town, and then evaluate his response according to the favor, disfavor, or ignorance it reveals, (e.g., "No." "Yes. I find it a principal source of income." "Goodness, no!" "Where is that? Don't believe I know where that neighborhood is." "It's convenient, but I can only shop in the evening, so I don't shop there." etc.)

The prospective juror is most likely to give himself away at unguarded moments—when he doesn't know by what criteria he is being judged, or when he doesn't believe he is being judged at all. To these ends, the attorney keeps the prosective juror at ease. If the attorney's technique produces anxiety, the prospective juror will erect defenses that keep true feelings from view. The attorney pays particular attention to the prospective juror's reactions to questions being put to *other* prospective jurors. He watches, and if possible, eavesdrops on the prospective juror during those informal moments at court recess. Each of these moments may provide a glimpse into the sort of man the prospective juror really is.

Throughout the process of peering past the prospective juror's conscious facade, the attorney must not lose touch with his own subconscious likes and dislikes, for if he can pick a juror whose likes match his, he probably will have picked a juror who likes him as well. Neither must he forget that the trial has already begun, and that voir dire provides him a good opportunity to start persuading the juror (by dint of establishing rapport, by careful choice of words, by sensitivity to the juror's bias, etc.) as to the merits of his case.

### Look Beyond What the Juror Says to How He Says It

Of even greater importance than *what* our prospective juror tells the attorney during voir dire is *how* he says it. Even when limited to yes/no responses to questioning (further limited in those jurisdictions where voir dire is the responsibility of the court rather than counsel), much can still be learned by looking for covert phrasing, expressions, and movement which will negate the manifest response. For example, a juror who *says* "yes" while subtly shaking his head in a horizontal plane, or who says "I think so", or who suddenly looks away or laughs when he answers, is *telling* you "no". His paramessages serve to disqualify or contradict his apparent or primary message.

The attorney must be on the alert for signs in the prospective juror's manner of speech which point to emotionally charged areas that may be the repository for bias. For example, if, when asked if he can be impartial, the prospective juror hesitates before answering in the affirmative, or says that he "thinks" or "hopes" or "will try" to be impartial, or doesn't seem to comprehend the question (as indicated by a nonresponsive answer), it is a safe assumption that he is already emotionally committed to one side or the other. Slips of the tongue, spontaneous statements volunteered by the prospective juror (as opposed to answers to structured questions), and particularly the behavioral messages to be discussed below, are the richest source of clues as to which side this bias lies.

### Appearance and Behavior: Vital Clues to the Juror's True Personality

The prospective juror is perhaps most revealing through his appearance and behavior. A man can successfully watch and control what he *says* so that it conforms to his idealized self-image, but modifying *who he is*, even for the few minutes of voir dire, is an infinitely more difficult maneuver.

First, the attorney notes the prospective juror's manner of dress. Clothes may not always make the man but they can often provide compensation for inner deficiencies. Thus, the frigid, child-like hysteric, fearful of adult sexuality (and aspects of it which might be presented at trial), compensates with seductive clothes and makeup. The slight, bookish accountant sartorially may put aside his occupation and instead dress like the athletes with whom he really identifies. Immaculately dressed, compulsive individuals tend to be sensitive to cognitive detail at the expense of human/emotional factors, and thus are more likely "prosecutor's jurors" ("defense jurors" in personal injury litigation). Expensively dressed individuals are also good defense jurors in civil cases, as they tend to be parsimonious. A short juror may dress flamboyantly denoting an inner inferiority complex, or quite possibly a spiting of authority. In short, the attorney would be remiss if he failed to make special note of dress inappropriate for the occasion, or inconsistent with the prospective juror's known background.

The attorney also studies the prospective juror's manner and movements for clues as to emotionally-charged areas in his makeup. Sighs, the licking of lips suddenly dry, blushing, the covering of the face and mouth with the hands, visible swallowing, a sudden restlessness, all suggest that the attorney has touched a sensitive area.

The attorney should determine what it is that sets the prospective juror off. Is it when he raises the issue of the innocent being punished, or that of the guilty going free? The victim's injury or the need for reparation? Property rights or individual rights?

The attorney watches closely to determine the prospective juror's non-verbal *attitude toward counsel* (e.g., "I'm bored by/hostile to what this guy has to say." "I'm open to and enthusiastic about this fellow.") and *toward the concepts* each attorney presents (e.g., "Hearing this makes me angry." "I don't want to hear this—I'd like to get away from this." "This is what turns me on.").

The attorney ascertains how the prospective juror's responses to him differ from his reaction to opposing counsel. Which attorney seems most successful at commanding his attention? Toward which does he literally lean his body? Conversely, whose words does he shut off by leaning back with a swift crossing of arms and legs?

Finally, if the attorney observes the prospective juror smiling benignly at opposing counsel, he does not want him on the jury.*

The venireman who leans forward and sits on the edge of his chair, head cocked, is actively and conscientiously listening to what is being said. An unbuttoned jacket, open hands with fingers relaxed, and a direct gaze suggest he is open to the ideas being presented, or at least to the attorney as an individual. If he uncrosses his legs, turns to face the attorney directly, leans further forward, smiles, and perhaps unconsciously even echoes the attorney's posture and gestures he has given evidence of excellent rapport; one may presume bias for the concepts being presented at that moment.

By contrast, the venireman who is "turned off", will lean back, or partially turn away (so that his side rather than his front faces the speaker); he may keep his coat or jacket buttoned and thrust his hands inside his pockets; he may drum his fingers, cross his arms and legs and rock his ankle, or glance repeatedly at the ceiling, his watch, or the front door.

The juror whose response to a question is accompanied by hands hidden behind the back or in the pockets, or moved upward to cover the throat or mouth, who scratches, blinks and swallows, and who repeatedly licks his lips, is uncomfortable with his answer, probably because it simply is not a true one. If he says "yes", he *can* theoretically accept such and such position, that he *is* open to considering such a proposition fairly, but you observe that arms and legs cross as he speaks, lips turn down, brow furrows, hands go into his pockets and some parts of the body—perhaps just the foot—rocks from side to side, one may be sure that he won't buy any of it. If fists clench, heels lock, and arms pull tightly across the chest, or in the case of a woman the hands come up as if to protect the breasts, then one may be sure that the instant exchange has made the prospective juror quite defensive. If one hand goes back to grasp the back of the neck and the other clenches into a tight fist, the venireman has become downright angry.

---

*Quite the opposite is true once the trial is underway. While jurors will often smile at witnesses with whom they concur, they usually turn stony-faced or look away from the attorney whose position they favor. The reason is that they wish to believe they have decided for him impartially, on the basis of the evidence, and not because they like him. They act so as to convince others and themselves that this is so—that they are not being led by emotions—that they are not playing favorites. By the same token, they will smile pleasantly at the attorney whose position they will soon assault in the jury room, so as to demonstrate that they are not guilty of any hostility toward him personally, and that they wish him no harm, even though ("judging from the evidence") he is dead wrong.

The juror who says that he has a "completely open mind", but sits in what I call the "John Mitchell position" (simply because every picture I've seen of him has him looking this way—sitting back, head resting on hands clasped behind the head, fingers intertwinded, legs crossed with one an-kle resting on the other thigh, or the feet resting on or over the chair in front, perhaps a slight, superior smile on the lips) is lying about being open and fair. He already "knows what's right", has made up his mind, and is not about to change it.

By contrast, the venireman who strokes, scratches, or rubs some part of the face, or pinches the bridge of his nose, is in considerable conflict or doubt. If he actually picks at himself, tugs his ear, pulls at his cuticles, slumps in the chair, and clears his throat continually he has become quite insecure about what is transpiring.

It should be noted that in personal injury cases involving psychic trauma or "traumatic neurosis", a juror's receptivity to psychiatric testi-mony depends as much upon his reaction to a particular psychiatrist as it does upon the nature of the medical evidence presented. Usually, how-ever, college-educated, politically liberal, or irreligious people, those who have had training in psychology or personal experience with psychother-apy, and women in general tend to be more accepting of psychiatric testi-mony and may give it great weight in reaching a verdict.

Once having decided which venireman he would like excused, the attorney exercises his challenges. If opposing counsel is psychologically unsophisticated, the attorney may be able to put questions to prospective jurors he deems dangerous which will elicit answers likely to provoke a challenge from opposing counsel, in effect, granting the attorney addi-tional challenges (his own plus those of opposing counsel, now the attor-ney's unwitting agent).

## Remember: Juries Are Resistant to Rational Selection

Fortunately for the American judicial system, the process of jury selection is easier to describe than to effect. Human motivation is quite complex. A juror may possess one characteristic which creates a favorable bias at one level, but which prejudices him against another aspect of the attorney's case. The juror himself may not be aware of how he really feels, or why. He may be preoccupied with a small, conscious element of his beliefs while the larger and more powerful unconscious elements may, unbeknownst to him, bias him in quite another direction. And even if the attorney by chance knows a great deal more about a prospective juror and his psy-chological makeup than ordinarily can be learned during *voir dire*, it may still be impossible to predict how he will react when thrust into a group. If individual psychodynamics are complex, the dynamics of a group of 12 jurors are 12 times more so.

For these reasons, juries are extremely resistant to rational selection by even the most diligent and insightful of attorneys. Perhaps that is why the jury system works so well.

Even so, the attorney who takes jury selection seriously and is diligent about the psychodynamics involved, though perhaps unable to ensure 12 ideal jurors, at least completes the process far better informed about the jury he has finally obtained than the attorney who flies through the voir dire process by the seat of his pants. The knowing and informed attorney is thus in the best possible position to determine the strategy appropriate to the jury actually drawn.

## Reference

Blinder, M: "Psychiatry in the Everyday Practice of Law"; Lawyers Co-Operative Publishing Co., Rochester, NY; Bancroft-Whitney, San Francisco, CA; 1973

# Rules for a Successful Voir Dire Examination

## The Honorable Walter E. Jordan

Walter E. Jordan was appointed as Judge of the 48th Judicial District of Texas in 1963. He practiced law in Grand Prairie and Fort Worth, Texas from 1947 to 1963, almost exclusively in the trial of civil lawsuits. Since 1982 he has been a Justice on the Court of Appeals for the Second Supreme Judicial District of Texas. Judge Jordan is the author of *Modern Texas Discovery* (Bancroft-Whitney, published in 1974); *Trial Handbook for Texas Lawyers* (Bancroft-Whitney, 2nd Edition published in 1981); and *Jury Selection* (Shepards, Inc./McGraw-Hill, published in 1980).

There is no one phase of any jury trial which is more important than the voir dire examination. It is the engine that starts the vehicle. It is the act, if you will, that gets the show off the ground. It is the first, and best, opportunity for the lawyer to perform and to sell himself and his product.

A lawyer trying a lawsuit to a jury is like a salesman. To be successful in any jury case, he must sell himself and his product, i.e., his side of the case. This doesn't mean that any good salesman can win a jury case, or that there is no difference between selling goods or merchandise and trying jury cases. But the fact remains that a good trial lawyer must be, among other things, a good salesman. He must make a strong but favorable impression on as many of the panel members as possible. Remember, the lawyer is on display before the panel. He must be personable and persuasive and avoid irritating or aggravating the potential jurors. To this end, I recommend the following do's and dont's.

**1. Do not be a hot dog.** Never put on a show to indicate how smart or brilliant you are. I have seen some lawyers flaunt themselves in a rather embarrassing manner during voir dire. They try to paint the opponent and his counsel as ignorant louts. Such conduct may convince the jury panel of that lawyer's brilliance, but it may also create considerable sympathy for his opponent. This will turn the opponent into an underdog and may lead to one of those jury verdicts which from time to time confound and confuse court attachés, lawyers and others. Don't be a hot dog.

**2. Never embarrass a prospective juror.** Questions which could in any way embarrass or humiliate a prospective juror should be avoided. Never ask a question which would, in any way, bring out a juror's lack of training, education or sophistication or which would highlight a juror's ignorance, inexperience or lack of general understanding. Such questions can anger the juror involved, as well as some other members of the panel. Even if the embarrassed juror is eliminated by a peremptory challenge, the remaining jurors will remember the slight. Counsel is dealing not with machines, but with emotional human beings who have feelings.

Also, avoid at all costs using sarcasm or puns at a juror's expense. Some lawyers can't seem to resist making a wisecrack about a juror's name or something a juror said in reply to a question. Such tactics will inevitably hurt that lawyer's cause.

Counsel should not embarrass a prospective juror by flippantly asking questions in a tone that indicates disbelief of that juror's replies. It will always be detrimental.

During a voir dire examination it is often impossible to avoid an area or subject which is potentially embarrassing to one or more of the panel members. Sometimes a potentially embarrassing question cannot be avoided if the lawyer is to probe for possible prejudice or disqualifying matter. When these situations occur, proceed with caution: reluctantly and apologetically delve into the matter, always being careful to assure the panel that it is not your intent to embarrass anyone.

**3. Avoid unfairness.** Trial counsel should always carefully avoid any hint of unfairness to an opponent. Without giving any ground to the opponent, counsel should always seek to maintain an attitude and create an impression of fairness. For instance, if it becomes obvious that one juror is for some reason disqualified and subject to a successful challenge for cause, the other counsel could demonstrate his fairness by stipulating that the juror may be excused. Any time a lawyer has a chance to demonstrate his sense of fair play he should do so. The average juror is usually impressed by a display of fairness on the part of trial counsel, and is irritated and sometimes actually angered by a demonstration of unfairness.

**4. Say please and thank you.** It is a wise lawyer who uses "please" and "thank you" liberally throughout his examination of a jury panel. Use the manners your mama taught you. This is not only a proper display of common courtesy and politeness, but leaves the panel with a better impression of you. Of course, you should not fawn or be too solicitious.

**5. Use jurors' names.** Counsel should always have a list of the names and addresses of the panel members. It is a good idea to use jurors' names during the course of the voir dire questioning. Everyone likes to have his or her name used and pronounced correctly. Of course, you should always address jurors as Mr., Mrs., or Miss, and should never use only the first or last name of a jury. I shudder whenever I hear lawyers address jurors by their first or last names.

Some defendant's lawyers in civil cases memorize the jurors' names while the plaintiff's attorney is conducting voir dire. The defense lawyer then begins voir dire, addressing jurors by their correct names, often skipping from row to row and from seat to seat, out of seating order. The idea behind this tactic is to impress the jury with the keen mind and memory of counsel—while it is doubtful whether this method ever actually sways or influences jury verdicts, it is impressive and often intriguing to panel members.

**6. Prepare your questions.** Unless you are a seasoned veteran of the trial wars, it is a good idea to prepare voir dire questions before the voir dire. Thus, you will cover all important matters and not overlook questions that should be asked. It also frees your mind to study and evaluate the jurors. Preparation of questions in advance is particularly helpful in the federal courts, where the judge, after questioning the jury panel, may ask counsel to submit any additional questions quickly.

It is important, though, to listen carefully to the answers given by the jurors (that sounds obvious, but how many lawyers really do it?) and be flexible enough to react to the answers spontaneously with creative questions. In other words, don't limit yourself to your prepared list of questions.

**7. Don't bore the jury.** Many voir dire examinations are of necessity long and somewhat boring, at least to those veniremen not being questioned at the time. After an hour or more of listening to repetitious questioning of different jurors, some members of the panel become restless, nervous, and possibly irritated. To avoid this reaction, you should, whenever possible, put questions to the panel as a whole. I am well aware that most experienced trial counsel like to talk to individual jurors, but I also know that too much individual talking is boring. Routine questions should never be repeated to each juror. If it is necessary to ask some questions individually of each juror, you should ask the question of one, and then ask the others (in groups if necessary) if their answers would be the same. This saves time and should make a good impression on the panel.

**8. Avoid legalese and other complex language.** Use simple, everyday English. The point is not to show off one's vocabulary. Avoid legal terms and words which are not familiar to the average person. Remember that each jury panel probably contains some people who do not have the benefit of a college education or legal training.

**9. Stay away from personal exploits.** Some lawyers can't seem to refrain from telling the jury "war stories" or tales of personal adventure. The fact is, the jury panel is not interested in your previous successes in trial or in any other area, and such storytelling is a waste of the court's and jury's time. The jury panel is comprised of people who are giving their time and energy to try your lawsuit, and they want you to get to the heart of the matter and not waste their time. I know of some lawyers who, in every case they try, insist on telling the jury panel about their experiences as college football players. Whereas it may impress some jurors, it doesn't impress me, and it probably embarrasses and irritates more jurors than it impresses.

**10. Advise jurors about personal questions.** It is always advisable for trial counsel to advise jury panel members that in order to properly represent his client and get fair and impartial jurors to try his case, he will need to ask questions that may delve to some extent into their personal business or affairs. They should understand the need for background information about their experiences, occupations, beliefs, or feelings about any person or subject related to the case to be tried. Emphasize that you are not trying to meddle or be nosy.

**11. Explain trial procedure.** If the judge does not do so, you should explain trial procedure to the panel. Counsel should briefly tell them that the plaintiff, because he has the burden of proof, will commence every phase of the proceeding, and that counsel for the defense will follow in each of those phases.

Counsel should also advise the panel that after both sides have put on their cases-in-chief, the plaintiff is entitled to offer rebuttal evidence, and that depending on the procedure followed in the particular jurisdiction, then either the court delivers its charge on the law to the jury after which attorneys for both sides make their closing arguments, or vice versa.

**12. Mention trial objections.** The panel should be advised that objections to evidence or procedure are bound to be made during the trial. Explain that there are certain rules of evidence, promulgated over the years by courts and legislatures, which must be followed by all parties and their lawyers in trial. Explain that there will be times when one of the lawyers, feeling that some rule of evidence or of trial procedure is being violated, will make an objection which the judge will rule on.

The panel must understand that it should not view such action as an attempt on the part of either lawyer to slow down the trial or to hide anything from the jurors. It should be made clear that once an objection has been made, the judge will rule on it. If the judge agrees with the lawyer making the objection he will sustain the objection. If the judge disagrees with the objection, he will overrule it, which means that the evidence is proper and may be admitted for the consideration of the jury.

**13. Explain the burden of proof.** It is important that counsel clarify for the jury panel what the burden of proof is in the case. For instance, in a criminal case, the panel should be told that the state's burden is to prove the guilt of the accused beyond a reasonable doubt. There should also be an explanation or example of what reasonable doubt entails. Reasonable doubt ordinarily will not be defined by the court and it is not a particularly easy term to define. For the purpose of illustration or example, assume the trial of a rape case in which Mr. Jones is accused of raping Mrs. Smith. The following statement by way of explanation of reasonable doubt may be made to the jury:

> When this trial is over you may or may not like either Mr. Jones or Mrs. Smith personally. However, that is not the issue in this trial. The central issue for your decision is, regardless of whether you like or dislike either of these persons, or would prefer to take either of them home for dinner, would each of you be willing to decide only one issue—and that is whether or not the State has proved beyond a reasonable doubt that Mr. Jones had intercourse with Mrs. Smith without her consent? This decision, of course, must be based on believable and credible evidence beyond a reasonable doubt. In all probability the court will not define reasonable doubt for you. Reasonable doubt does not mean proof of guilt beyond any doubt whatsoever, but simply refers to any serious doubt that could be held by a reasonable person. In some cases, it has been defined as that doubt which is held by a juror beyond a moral certainty, and in others it has been said that a reasonable doubt is a doubt which would cause a reasonable person to hes-

itate in the conduct of his or her own personal affairs. All I want to get across to this jury is that if any juror, at the conclusion of this trial, has any real or serious doubt concerning the guilt of this defendant, that juror should vote for acquittal.

In civil cases, the panel should understand that the burden to prove the case as a whole by a preponderance of the evidence is on the plaintiff. Preponderance of the evidence should be explained as the greater weight and degree of the credible or believable testimony and evidence admitted in the trial. For example:

> The greater weight and degree of the credible evidence means only that the evidence should preponderate or lean in one direction or another, or in favor of one side or the other. For instance, if the evidence as a whole in this case is weighted to an extent of even 51% in favor of one side or the other in this case, then that side should prevail. For a further example, we lawyers usually like to refer to the scales of justice which are usually displayed someplace in the courtroom. Consider that those scales (up on the judge's bench or behind the judge) are tipped by placing a coin or some other object on one side of the scale. Suppose that that is the evidence in this case, and if that evidence would tip the scales, as the coin does, then the side introducing that evidence which tipped the scales should prevail in the lawsuit.

It is important to explore the differences between these two types of burdens, emphasizing that the burden of proof in a criminal case is an extremely heavy and onerous burden, while the burden of proof in a civil case is much lighter.

**14. Admit the weaknesses of your case.** If there are weaknesses in your case, as there are in most cases, they should be brought to the jury panel's attention early in the examination. It is important to give the jurors an impression of honesty and fairness. This tends to lessen the impact of problems which might otherwise be disclosed for the first time during the trial, with perhaps a more devastating effect.

Suppose, for example, you are representing a client who has had a previous criminal conviction, which is not so remote as to be inadmissible in evidence. If this is the case, counsel should reveal that criminal record, in its most favorable light, and get the matter right out in the open before the jury panel, hopefully lessening the sting or the impact of the criminal conviction. Or, as another example, assume that counsel has a client who has had a history of excessive consumption of alcoholic beverages, and that evidence will be admissible during trial. If that harmful knowledge is going to be disclosed by the other side, it is much better for counsel representing that drinking individual to bring it out on voir dire, level with the panel, acknowledging the client's problem, and hope that your honesty and openness will reduce the harmful effect of the evidence of drinking.

**15. Discuss handicaps of client or witness.** Some people, clients and witnesses alike, have speech, language, physical or other defects, which they can't help. These should be anticipated, recognized and made known to the jury panel during voir dire in order to avoid shock and surprise during trial. For instance, if counsel plans to introduce a witness who stutters, tell the panel, and ask for a commitment by panel members not to let the impediment influence their consideration of that witness's testimony.

**16. Do not make side bar remarks.** This particular piece of advice should not have to be given to experienced trial counsel, but unfortunately it is necessary. Anyone who has tried lawsuits, either as a lawyer or a judge, can well understand that during the heat of battle and in the zealous protection of the client's rights, tempers can become frayed and a lawyer can snap and growl a little at his opponent. *Don't do it.* If you yield to the temptation to swat that fellow across the bar from you, you will only irritate "the old grouch on the bench" and make the jury panel impatient and intolerant. If your opponent gets to be overbearing during voir dire, or if he oversteps the lines, appeal to the judge, who, if he is doing his job, will put a rein on your obstreperous antagonist.

**17. Don't argue with the judge.** If you want to start off on the wrong foot in your voir dire examination, try arguing with the judge. Or, better still, make some cutting remark toward him. Remember that while you may not have a high opinion of that judge, the jury panel respects him. After all, the judge, with his robe and his austere and dignified manner, is cloaked with authority. That jury panel has an ingrained respect for the law and the courts. A lawyer who does not show that same respect, or who argues with the court's rulings, usually pays a high price.

**18. Commit jurors to the law as given by the court.** In most jurisdictions, counsel is not permitted to discuss the law with the jury panel, either on voir dire examination or later in argument. Most judges quickly sustain objections to any attempt on the part of lawyers to discuss the law of the case with the jury. The jury, of course, is primarily concerned with the facts of the case, and is bound to follow the law as given by the court. Counsel, therefore, should always commit all prospective jurors to follow the law as given them by the court in the instructions. They should be advised that it is their duty not to substitute their own opinions of the law, or their own versions of the law, for the instructions of the court in charge.

Counsel should not ask whether a juror will take the law from the court or follow a personal conception of the law if such juror's idea differs from the one given by the court. This will only embarrass the juror who happens to first announce the intent to follow a personal conception of the law. The preferred method is to explain that even though individual members of the panel might disagree with the law, it is their duty to strictly and conscientiously follow and apply the law as explained by the court in its charge. Then you should ask the panel as a group if they will make a commitment to do so.

**19. Avoid the "one-person jury."** Sometimes there will be one strong, articulate individual who may have some expertise in the field or area with which the lawsuit is concerned. For instance, in a products liability case, there could be an engineer on the panel who is somewhat knowledgeable about the very product involved in the case. If that person happens to be a strong-willed, independent sort, and is articulate, he may pull the rest of the jury with him. If he happens to disagree with your particular position or version of the lawsuit, the lawsuit may well be lost.

It is not always possible to avoid placing these people on the jury. In many cases, a lawyer wants a juror with some knowledge and experience in the area involved. At other times it is hard to keep such a juror off because of the necessity to make other strikes. If a "knowledgeable" person is on the jury, you should often remind the jurors to be independent and to make up their own minds from the evidence, and not be unduly swayed or influenced by one individual on the jury.

**20. Don't take the first twelve jurors.** Occasionally, I will see a lawyer who, soon after the jury is seated, will announce to the court, "Your Honor, all of the jurors look good to me; I'll just take the first twelve." That gesture, in my opinion, is usually a grandstand play, and I don't think it is a very smart one. Unless the lawyer knows intimately all of the jurors on the panel, which he might in a small town, he should never just accept the first twelve. By doing so he risks having an adverse juror, such as a relative or close friend of his opponent, on the panel. Use your peremptory strikes; that's what they are for.

However, if your opponent grandly announces that he will take the first twelve, you are placed at a disadvantage. You simply cannot afford to go along and also agree to take the first twelve. For all you know, he may have a ringer among that first twelve. In other words, your opponent may have a very good reason for his display of confidence. Placed in this position, the best thing to do is smile sweetly at the panel and tell them that while you know all of them are fair-minded and qualified, you must, in fulfilling your obligations to your client, ask them a few questions.

**21. Have voir dire reported.** The voir dire should be taken down by the court reporter in many civil cases. If the entire examination is reported, any error of opposing counsel in asking improper questions, or making prejudicial remarks to the panel, as well as any error of the trial judge during voir dire, will be preserved for appeal.

Suppose the trial judge refused to excuse a juror challenged for cause, and you were forced to accept an unfavorable juror who eventually proved to be harmful to your case. If the voir dire was reported, the complete record is before the appellate court, and if you are able to show that your case was prejudiced by the action of the trial court in refusing the challenge for cause, you might obtain a new trial.

Also, the record will show any false answers of jurors to voir dire questions, and it will disclose failure on the part of some jurors to answer up when asked about past experiences or prejudice which could affect their verdict.

It will cost the client a little extra money, but it could be well worth it.

**22. One last question.** Counsel should conclude voir dire by emphasizing that the purpose of voir dire has been to obtain a fair and impartial jury. Then ask one last question: Is there any reason, whether or not it concerns something which has already been discussed during voir dire, why any of you could not sit as a totally fair and impartial juror?

This general question covers a lot of ground and gives a juror a last chance to bring up something which might disqualify him on points not previously mentioned. Most jurors are very conscientious and will take this opportunity to speak up if there is any doubt whatsoever in their minds as to their ability to be a fair and independent juror.

**23. Be yourself.** The best advice that can be given is act naturally and normally. Don't emulate some prominent trial lawyer. You can't copy someone else's style or characteristics without looking foolish. This does not mean that you can't or shouldn't learn from other, more experienced and successful trial lawyers, but you should develop a style and courtroom demeanor with which you feel comfortable.

# Jury Selection in a Criminal Case

## Herald Price Fahringer

Herald Price Fahringer graduated from the University of Buffalo Law School and is a partner in the law firm of Lipsitz, Green, Fahringer, Roll, Schuller and James, with offices in New York City and Buffalo. He is a Fellow of the American College of Trial Lawyers; a Fellow of the International Society of Barristers; General Counsel to the First Amendment Lawyers Association; and author of numerous articles on various legal subjects. He lectures frequently on trial advocacy at Continuing Legal Education seminars throughout the country.

The selection of a jury is the most important part of any criminal trial. In most cases the defendant's fate is fixed after the jury is chosen. Consequently, counsel's ability to select a favorable jury in a criminal case is of paramount importance.

At the outset, it must be conceded that jury selection in a criminal case (or for that matter a civil case) involves some guile. Lawyers regularly announce to the panel that they only want jurors who will decide the case impartially. In fact, they want partisan jurors. Counsel is obligated to pick people who, by reason of their background, personality or attitudes, can be reasonably expected to find in their client's favor. This insincerity is quickly detected by the jurors. We lie to them and they in turn lie to us.

Most jurors come to court burdened with prejudices that can easily wreck the defense of a criminal case or the prosecution of a civil complaint.[1] They are reluctant for these symptoms of their own bias to be publicly confirmed. Thus, the unmasking of bigotry is frustrated by a regrettable lack of candor on the part of most jurors. Impelled by a desire to be selected, they tend to shape their answers into what they believe to be socially acceptable responses. Anyone who has ever selected a jury in a highly celebrated case, where the whole community has been drenched in publicity adverse to the defendant and who has listened to one juror after another disavow any knowledge of the case, knows how disheartening that can be.

A study done by John Murray and John Eckman, concerning the trial of the "Camden 28," revealed that a considerable portion of the jurors interviewed gave substantially different answers in private interviews, conducted after the trial, than those furnished during voir dire.[2] A carefully conducted survey in the 1976 Joan Chesimar murder prosecution, in Middlesex, New Jersey, disclosed that 71% of the community eligible for jury service had fixed opinions about her guilt. And yet, during a searching and skillfully conducted voir dire by counsel, only 15% of the jurors admitted any form of predisposition. This gaping disparity between the survey results and the uncovering of bias during the voir dire can only be explained by a sad lack of honesty on the jurors' part.

The simple truth is that prejudice is a staple in the jury box and most lawyers are without the necessary equipment to adequately deal with it. The uprooting of intolerance among this unique constituency lies beyond the appliances of the legal profession. There is no antidote for this form of social infection. Although in most cases these explosive forces cannot be defused by counsel, they must be located and identified. Lawyers must learn to pick the lock of these deep-seated prejudices if they are to secure a relatively impartial jury. Consequently, jury selection in a criminal case taxes the talents of a trial lawyer enormously. No undertaking requires deeper professional commitment or greater preparation.

### How to Zero In on the Kind of Jury You Want

Any sensible approach to choosing a jury requires a plan. Common sense dictates that the lawyer should have an idea of precisely what type of jury he wants for his case before jury selection begins. This "profile" will vary from one law suit to another. Factors which must be considered in deciding what kind of a juror is needed can range from the client's personality, to the makeup of the prosecution's witnesses, to the nature of the charge. A trial is a human enterprise and the jury tends to identify with certain people who populate the case. Thus, jurors should be selected who will empathize with either the defendant, his witnesses, or even his attorney.

However, surface identities can be misleading. A middle-class black may be embarrassed by the actions of a black narcotics dealer. An Italian banker may despise a person of his own nationality who is accused of membership in that elusive group labeled "organized crime." A high-ranking executive may wish to make an example of the broker who is charged with securities fraud. Accordingly, counsel must be sensitive to the crosscurrents that sweep through any large city seething with antagonism. Ask the defendant how he feels about blacks, Italians, Jews or any other minority group that will make up a significant segment of the jury panel. His feelings may be representative of his minority and can be helpful in making important choices. Where possible, ask members of other minority groups how they feel about the class to which your client belongs.

Make a list of the prosecution's witnesses, if known, and analyze their race, nationality, age and other social traits. If a particular prosecution witness is going to play an important part in the case, jurors who identify with that witness should be avoided. The realization that two impressive black police officers will testify against a black defendant may have some influence upon the type of black jurors selected. An elderly complainant in a robbery case will appeal more to older jurors. Consideration must be given to these separate components.

Do not lose sight of your adversary's background and nationality. Irish jurors may yield more to an Irish prosecutor's arguments. A young, inexperienced prosecutor may have more appeal to young jurors who can sympathize with his failings, whereas a brash and aggressive prosecutor may offend jurors who are soft-spoken and genteel. These human features and many more must be considered.

The nature of the case has a significant impact upon certain members of the community. Religious persons must be avoided in obscenity prosecutions; wage earners are dangerous in income tax prosecutions; blacks who have seen the ravages of the drug trade in their community must be considered carefully in a narcotics prosecution; and young, idealistic jurors, or "limousine liberals" may be unacceptable in a political corruption case.

List all the favorable features sought in the ideal juror on one side of a sheet of paper, and all the unfavorable features on the other side. Grade these factors in the order of importance. An adequate inventory should include ten to fifteen features on each side. After the catalog is complete, study it diligently. If nothing else, this exercise will compel counsel to think clearly about what kind of a jury is desired. Knowing exactly what type of a juror is sought will improve the chances of achieving that objective.

To better organize the recording of the jurors' names and addresses, draw a diagram of the jury box with a square for each seat. An abundant supply of these sheets can be kept in the lawyer's office and used when needed.

## Your Key Objectives in Voir Dire

The voir dire has two objectives. The first is to enable counsel to gather sufficient knowledge to make well-informed judgments about jurors whose biases may interfere with a fair consideration of the evidence. The second is to familiarize the jurors with certain legal concepts and gain from them assurances of fairness. The latitude allowed in discussing the law with jurors varies from state to state. More and more this critical area of inquiry is being fenced off by our courts.[3] Equally frightening is the clamor coming from some sectors of our profession that the voir dire should be taken from counsel and conducted by the court, as in the federal system. This practice renders jury selection virtually meaningless.[4]

The chemistry that reveals a juror's true feelings can be generated only by confrontation. Without face-to-face inquiry, an intelligent choice of a juror is severely impaired. Furthermore, a juror's answer to one question may prompt inquiry into another important area which can only be conceived of by the singlemindedness of counsel. A judicial officer who is "presumably" disinterested cannot effectively conduct such an investigation.

Most members of the Bar do not object to a trial judge's insistence that the selection process be conducted expeditiously. Needless repetition of questions and dragging out the examination of jurors not only alienates them, but endangers this privilege for all of us. Thus, in those communities where the privilege of speaking with jurors still exists, a sense of responsibility and good judgment among the Bar should be encouraged.

In those places where the court conducts the voir dire, a motion should be made for an examination of the jurors by trial counsel. Explain in detail why an interrogation of the jury panel by counsel will improve the chances of obtaining a fair trial. A respectable body of law supports the advisability of lawyers conducting the examination in an unfettered fashion.[5] Provide the trial judge with sample questions that will dramatize the need for an individual inquest of the jurors. Ask for a hearing which will permit a full judicial investigation of your complaint.[6] The court may accede to the defendant's application; but if it is rejected, an important issue will be preserved for appellate review if necessary.

Recently, the science of survey research has been harnessed by defense lawyers in cases where the client can afford that service. The survey firm will produce a "jury profile" which can be used to guide the trial lawyer through the treacherous shallows of jury selection in a controversial case. Such a scientific investigation is usually initiated by designing a questionnaire which measures attitudes associated with the important trial issues and the personality characteristics of people who are sympathetic to the defendant's claims. Interviewers use these questionnaires to collect information from a random sample of the juror population. The interviewers do not approach any of the prospective jurors. Through correlating the background characteristics with the behavior measures, it is possible to detect the important variables that predict the population's attitudes. It may be discovered, for example, that men are more favorable to the defense than women; young people more than the aged; liberal people more than authoritarians; readers of the *New York Times* more than readers of the *New York Daily News*; blacks more than whites; Protestants more than Catholics; or that the level of education, introversion, age, political affiliation, and many other features are not related to the decisive opinions.[7]

The major benefit of obtaining demographic correlates of attitudes is that, although jurors may color their answers to specific questions during a voir dire, they cannot conceal their pedigree and background. Armed with this information counsel can better plan his questions for the prospective jurors. The National Jury Project is, by far, the most prominent organization specializing in surveys of this type. However, other individuals and firms have entered this expanding field and may be consulted.[8] The cost of a survey can range from $5,000 to $20,000, and up.

If the client cannot afford a professional survey, counsel can conduct a less comprehensive investigation. In virtually every jurisdiction, each juror has a corresponding ballot or card which bears his name, address and occupation. When a panel of 50 jurors is sent to a particular courtroom, the jurors' ballots are transferred to the court clerk. The clerk places them in a draw from which the jurors' names are randomly drawn for placement in the jury box. Defense counsel should request to examine the jurors' cards *before* they are dispatched to the courtroom. This application is based upon a need to examine all the jurors so that counsel can be adequately prepared for their selection. Furthermore, in most jurisdictions, any complaint that the panel is not representative of the community at large must be made before the selection process begins.

After receiving the ballots, counsel should make up a list of the jurors with their names, addresses and occupations. This will provide a better portrait of the jury. The analysis will reveal how many men, women, blacks, Italians, or other groups make up the jury. Accordingly, counsel can better estimate the probability of getting certain kinds of jurors.

In some jurisdictions the list of prospective trial jurors is published and distributed in advance of their term of service. A copy of this list should be obtained in advance of trial and carefully studied. With more time available, a detailed breakdown of jurors' occupations, sex, nationality and race can be plotted. These vital statistics help the trial lawyer better plan the choice of jurors he will ultimately make. Sometimes a particular strain of an ethnic group will, by circumstance, dominate a pool. The discovery of a high ratio of Germans or Hispanics in the panel is valuable in planning the approach to jury selection.

## Why and How to Move for Extra Peremptory Challenges

All convention conspires against the defendant in a criminal case. Two-thirds of most jury panels are unsympathetic to the defendant. The National Jury Project has done the most authoritative research in the field of jury dynamics ever uncovered by any such scientific expedition. Their findings show that 25% of the people selected for jury duty believe that an accused person is guilty, otherwise he would not have been charged. Thirty-six percent believe that it is the defendant's responsibility to prove his innocence, rather than the state's duty to prove him guilty.[9]

In light of this disadvantage, it is imperative that counsel make a motion for additional peremptory challenges. In most jurisdictions the judge has authority to grant this relief. If this crucial imbalance in the panel is not corrected, the defendant is placed at a distinct disadvantage.[10] Express in detail the need for extra challenges by identifying the sectors of bias the defendant will encounter among jurors. A survey of the community showing a high level of aversion toward the defendant will lend force to this application. Most courts are sympathetic to the defendant's handicap in this area and will grant some relief.[11]

## Master Checklist for Examining Prospective Jurors

A thorough examination of the jurors must include every relevant topic of inquiry in order to gain the necessary knowledge to make an enlightened choice. A checklist of the areas of interrogation should be used. A catalog of subjects to be covered ought to include:

1) Family status
   a. Number of children, ages and sex?
   b. Wife's employment, if any?
   c. Reside with parents?

2) Residence
   a. Do you own your home, or rent?
   b. How long have you lived at your present address?
   c. How many places have you lived in the past 10 years?
   d. Do you own any other real estate?
3) Occupation
   a. What kind of work do you do?
   b. If you have a job title, what is it?
   c. In your job, do you have the authority to—promote people, hire people, fire people?
   d. How many people do you supervise, or how many people report directly to you in your job?
   e. How many different employers have you worked for in the past 10 years—name them?
   f. If your wife works outside the home, what does she do?
4) Education
   a. How far did you go in school?
   b. Have you done any post-graduate work?
   c. If so, at what school and what degree did you acquire?
   d. What subjects did you major in while in college?
   e. Did you participate in any athletics or extracurricular activities?
5) Prior jury service
   a. Civil?
   b. Criminal?
   c. Was juror foreman?
   d. If verdict reached, what was it?*
   e. Grand jury service?
   f. Membership in Grand Jury Association?
6) Relationship with law enforcement agencies
   a. City, state, federal police?
   b. Prosecutors?
   c. Internal Revenue Service, Immigration, and other quasi-law enforcement agencies?
   d. Military police?
   e. Know any lawyers?
7) Victim of crime
   a. Appearance before grand jury?
   b. Meetings with District Attorney?
   c. Testified at trial?

---

*Editor's note—in many jurisdictions this is an improper question.

8) Experience with justice system
   a. Ever been a witness?
   b. Ever been an investigator?
   c. Ever a party to litigation?
9) Publicity
   a. Newspapers or magazine subscribed to?
   b. Have you read anything about this case?
   c. Do you know anything about this case?
   d. Know anyone connected with this case?
10) Military service
    a. What branch?
    b. Rank?
    c. Ever in combat?
    d. Military police?
11) Organizations
    a. Civic?
    b. Religious?
    c. Political?
    d. Social?
    e. Union?
    f. Scouting, PTA, CYO, YMCA, YWCA, etc.?
    g. Ever held office in organizations?
12) Leisure time
    a. Hobbies?
    b. Favorite television show?
    c. Drink alcoholic beverages, or visit night clubs?
    d. What is the last book you've read?
13) Special issues
    a. Alibi
    b. Self defense
    c. Lack of intent
    d. Involuntary statement
    e. Insanity
    f. Intoxication
    g. Entrapment
    h. Recantation
    i. Justification
    j. Duress
    k. Renunciation
14) Legal principles
    a. Presumption of innocence
    b. Proof beyond a reasonable doubt

  c. Circumstantial evidence
  d. Separate verdicts for each defendant
  e. Elements of crime charged
  f. Character evidence

Although this list is extensive, it is by no means complete.[12]

  Unless counsel is endowed with an infallible memory, the list of questions to be asked of prospective jurors must be outlined on a legal pad so that those topics can be reviewed periodically. Failure to ask one important question, such as, "Do you know any police officers?" can be ruinous. Jurors are only obliged to answer those questions put to them.

  On the other hand, to be effective with the jurors, counsel should avoid the use of notes as much as possible. Being "pad bound" is distracting to the jury. A good trial lawyer wants to establish eye contact with the jurors in the early stages of the trial. A helpful memory technique called the "Link System" which is best explained in *The Memory Book*.[13] Arranging your questions in an order that follows a daily routine helps you to remember them. For example, if you think of getting up in the morning and meeting your family for breakfast, that will remind you to ask the juror about his family. The following table illustrates how the system works.

### The "Link System" in Action

| *"Links"* | *Question To Be Asked Of Juror* |
|---|---|
| Breakfast with family | —Ask about family |
| Leaves for work and drops children off at school | —Inquiry about educational background |
| Stops at work | —Ask about occupation, union, number of people supervised |
| Stops at newsstand on way to courthouse | —Ask about publicity and reading habits |
| Meets police officer outside courthouse | —Questions about law enforcement officers, prosecutors, victim of crime |
| Passes grand jury room in courthouse | —Ask about prior grand jury service |
| Passes jury pool | —Ask about prior jury service |

| *"Links"* | *Question To Be Asked Of Juror* |
|---|---|
| Enters courtroom | —Ask about experience as witness or investigator |
| Commences service as juror | —Ask about all legal propositions |
| Goes home at end of day and plays with children | —Ask about hobbies |

This simplified version of the Link System can be expanded to cover a variety of special situations. Despite the use of such memory aids, keep a written list of questions available so that in moments of confusion, the more reliable source can be checked to make sure that every subject is covered.

The lawyer's greatest enemy is habit. Each trial involves different considerations. The selection of a jury cannot be followed by rote. Each case must be thought out. Every jury must be chosen differently. Thus, many questions should be added to the foregoing list in order to meet the special needs of a given case. For instance, in a perjury case, concepts of truthfulness must be discussed. The defense of a lawyer mandates an intensive inquiry into feelings about the legal profession and a juror's experiences with lawyers. The trial of a public figure requires asking about political involvements and attitudes toward politicians. These special areas of inquiry are only limited by the boundaries of an attorney's imagination.

### Picking Up Helpful Clues from the Jurors

Jury selection begins the moment counsel enters the courthouse. He must be observant. Jurors usually stand out because of their apparent unfamiliarity with the courthouse. Watch what they do and try to remember their faces. What they say in the lobby of the courthouse, how they behave, and what newspapers they buy, will reveal in a small way what they are like. When the jury panel is brought into the courtroom, study them. Search for clues that may be helpful in making important choices. A *Wall Street Journal* tucked under an arm, a sexy paperback book protruding from a purse, or a best seller in a juror's hands, can be meaningful.

Remember those jurors who are friendly and talking to others. Make a note of those who stay to themselves and talk to no one. If you listen closely, sometimes complaints about the jury selection system can be overheard. Their lives show in their faces and bodies. Rounded shoulders, thin tight lips, cruel eyes, faces that are unable to smile, a bowed head, a stiff posture, and voices weakened by a life of subservience can be significant. Counsel must learn to read these signs. You must never tire of looking into faces.

During this important stage of the proceedings, a client must be reminded that while in the courthouse he is "on camera" all the time. Jurors are inquisitive about him, as well as his lawyer, and he cannot escape their curious eyes. One thoughtless, rude act can make a bad impression that may damage his case immeasurably.

### How to Make Use of the Judge's Remarks to the Jury

In many jurisdictions, the judge will introduce the case to the jury by explaining its nature and presenting the participants. He will usually welcome help in describing the nature of the litigation to the jury. This is particularly true in a controversial prosecution. If the case has some very unattractive aspects, from the public's viewpoint, it may be well to have the judge emphasize those bad features. Prepare a statement of the case from the defendant's viewpoint and ask the judge to read it to the jury: Suggest, in an effort to save time, that the court ask whether any jurors, with reservations about a special aspect of the case, would prefer to be excused. This invitation, coming from a judicial officer, may inspire some jurors to exempt themselves from service who would not be prone to do so under counsel's examination and after they have become more self righteous.

The court's suggestion that the trial may last four or five weeks will have the effect of eliminating many young working jurors who cannot afford such a large investment of time. Whereas, older jurors who are retired can endure a longer tenure of service. This action will decimate the jury and leave the old, the jobless, and the poor. Unless counsel finds this class of jurors attractive, an objection must be raised immediately to avoid this special purge.

### A Simple System for Tracking Juror Information

Make certain the voir dire is transcribed. In most courts jury selection is not recorded. Without a record, important issues raised during this critical stage of the trial may be lost.

After the twelve jurors are placed in the jury box, the prosecutor usually speaks to them first. While he is talking to the jurors, counsel should study them carefully. Don't hesitate to move your chair close to the jury box so you can hear the prosecutor's questions and the juror's responses. Make careful notes of *how* each of the jurors answers the District Attorney's questions.

It is helpful to use a shorthand system of recording essential information supplied by the juror. Defense lawyers have the advantage of listening to the prosecutor ask the jurors about their occupation, marital status, number of children, prior jury service, and a number of other topics dealing with the juror's pedigree. The following abbreviations may be useful:

Married—M
Children—Ch
Boy—B
Girl—G
Prior jury service—J
Civil—C
Criminal—Cr
Participated in verdict—V
Wife—W
Husband—H
Divorced—D
Separated—Sep
Single—S
Widow—Wid
Work—Wk
Military—Mil

A juror who is married, with two boys and one girl, whose ages are 14, 12, and 8, should be recorded:

M, 2B—14, 12, G—8

A juror who has previously sat on one civil case in which no verdict was reached, and two criminal cases resulting in a verdict, will appear as:

1C; 2Cr—2V

A juror who has worked as a machinist for 12 years at the A. W. Bolt Co., and is a supervisor will read:

Wk—Mach.—A. W. Bolt—Super. 12

If the juror's wife does not work outside the home, she can be listed as "Hw" for housewife. If she has worked as a receptionist at a doctor's office for 5 years, it will be recorded:

W—Wk—Recp. Dr. Off—5

Developing a shorthand system will enable counsel to record information quickly and accurately. While transcribing this information, give the juror an acceptability grade based upon your first reaction. This crucial entry must be made in code because of the risk that it may be inadvertently observed by the district attorney.

This recorded information should not be squeezed into the jury chart which is designed to simply hold the names and addresses of the jurors seated in the jury box. Use a standard legal pad and allocate a separate page for information on each juror. This technique will allow sufficient room for additional comments or information. If a juror is excused you can remove that page and place it in a separate file. Be sure to keep a careful record of your challenges. As the prosecution nears the point of exhausting his challenges, check with the court clerk to make certain the final count is accurate.

Chances are when the district attorney finishes his inquiry, counsel will know which jurors he wants to excuse. A few marginal jurors will require further examination. However, each juror must be examined carefully to confirm or alter the original impression.

## What to Say in Your Opening Remarks to the Jury

Defense counsel's opening remarks to the jurors should not be made from behind a podium. Get close to the jurors. Do not allow anything to come between you and them. If the defendant's family is in the courtroom, counsel may wish to introduce them to the jury in order to find out whether any of the jurors know them. Then address the twelve jurors and collectively impress upon them the importance of this phase of the trial. Explain to them that they are going to be called upon to make the most important decision that they will render in this case (with the exception of their final verdict, if chosen). That decision is whether they can sit on the case and be completely fair and impartial. Advise them that your task is to help them make that choice by bringing to their attention possible experiences that could unduly influence their judgment. Point out to them, as an example, that a close relationship with a police officer may make it difficult for them to be impartial, since members of that department will testify for the prosecution. Stress that there are no "right" or "wrong" answers and that frankness is the key to succeeding in this part of the trial.

Tell them that the term "voir dire" means "to speak the truth," and you ask no more of them than that. Once the tone of jury selection has been set, begin with an examination of the individual jurors.

Picking a jury can be expedited without sacrificing thoroughness by asking a number of questions of the entire panel. Such inquiries can cover unique experiences; for example, an inquiry concerning prior grand jury service, experience as a witness, or military service. A juror who acknowledges that he has served on a grand jury or was in the military service can be examined on that subject more thoroughly during his individual voir dire. Remember, the longer you talk to the jurors, the greater the risk of forfeiting their good will. Although the risk of some impatience must be assumed, everything should be done to minimize their boredom.

### How to Get the Jurors to Talk

Once you begin speaking *with* the individual jurors (and not *to* them), it is important that the juror be encouraged to talk as much as possible. Begin with nonthreatening questions, concerning the juror's occupation, marital status, children, and education; that will relax the juror. Someone said that the primary index of a person's intelligence is his diction. The more a juror talks the better you will come to know him. A series of "yes" or "no" answers are of little help. Ask "open ended" questions, rather than "closed" questions. For example, ask, "How far did you go in school?" rather than "Did you attend college?" Ask, "What is your marital status?" rather than "Are you married?" Where permitted, ask "How do you feel about the presumption of innocence?" rather than "Do you agree with the proposition that a defendant should be presumed to be innocent?" The latter question usually gains little more than a straight-faced assurance that is of no value; whereas, the former question should unlatch the juror's thinking on this critical subject.

In the same fashion, ask "What does the concept of proof beyond a reasonable doubt mean to you?" rather than "Do you agree that the prosecution must prove the case beyond a reasonable doubt?" The so-called "How do you feel" questions are limitless. For instance you may want to ask:

How do you feel about Billy Williams as he sits here in this courtroom right now?

Do you have any feelings about him at all?
How do you feel about police officers?
How do you feel about citizens being allowed to own guns?
What does the phrase mean to you, "My Government right or wrong"?
How do you feel about lawyers?

Try to start as many of your questions with "How" and "What" rather than "Do you agree," or "Do you believe." There are occasions when you must ask, "Do you believe the actions taken by the FBI are always right?" or "Do you believe that police officers can make mistakes?" Obviously, a "yes" or "no" answer to these questions can be instructive. But the majority of the questions should be of the "How do you feel" brand.

Ask the jurors in great detail about their occupations by inquiring, "Tell me, Mr. Jones, specifically what do you do as a salesman?" If the answer to that question is not expansive enough, ask, "Can you tell me on a given day what you do from the time you start work until the time you finish?" Every question should be structured to prompt as complete an answer as possible.

## How to Tell the Real Meaning of a Juror's Responses

Despite the emphasis placed upon candor, many jurors strive to give the answers they think are correct or more pleasing. Consequently, the *way* they answer the questions is often more important than *what* they say. Study their reactions carefully. Questions should be developed that will explore their feelings rather than their words. For instance, when inquiring about the presumption of innocence, consider this technique:

Q. How do you feel about the presumption of innocence?

A. I think it's a good rule, and it should be followed.

Q. Mr. Jones, I'm going to ask you to do me a favor. Will you look at my client, Billy Williams right now and tell me whether you can honestly think of him as being innocent?

At that very instant, concentrate on the juror's face. If he has difficulty looking at your client, or when he glances at him he drops or narrows his eyes, rejection is evident. The expression on the juror's face at that moment will tell you more than all the words in the world.

Beware of the juror who gives qualified answers. For instance, the juror who is asked whether she could follow the rule of proof beyond a reasonable doubt and answers, "I will, if the judge tells me that's the law," is obviously distrustful of counsel's version of the rule. The juror who is asked whether he could vote not guilty if the prosecution failed to prove the case beyond a reasonable doubt and answers, "I would have to hear all the evidence before I could say," is resisting an affirmative response. Qualifying words such as—"I think so"—"I guess I could"—"I'll try"—are indications of "No". Weak speech is exemplified by the use of "hedges," such as "It seems like"—"Kinda"—"Sort of."[14]

After responding some jurors will unconsciously look to the district attorney or the judge, for either approval or reassurance. Other jurors will find it hard to look at you or the defendant. This "gazing behavior" can be informative.

These movements of a juror replace speech. On occasion, gestural information can speak more eloquently than words.[15] The jury must be mined for these meaningful human traits. Questions must be sharpened like a scalpel to cut through the jurors' callous pretenses and affectations in order to reach the core of their personalities.

Behavioral engineers tell us that communicative conduct among people can be classified in terms of three dimensions: verbal, paralinguistic, and kinesic.[16] For instance, social researchers find that people tend to talk longer with those toward whom they have positive emotions.[17] Thus, keeping track of the amount of time a prospective juror spends speaking with the district attorney, or defense counsel, may tell with which side he feels more at ease. Excessive movement of the hands, such as tapping the fingers on a thigh, intertwining them, or excessive activity, reflects a juror's anxiety. This may indicate discomfort with the attorney examining the juror. The large body of research in this area should be read by trial lawyers.

### What You Can Learn from a Juror's Hobby

Another effective method of gaining insight into the true personality of jurors is to ask them what they like to do in their spare time. A person who belongs to a gun club and likes to shoot animals, tells us one thing. A person who collects stamps or coins, tell us something else. Engineers, scientists, accountants, and bookkeepers are for the most part unemotional.[18] They are trained to be objective and reach conclusions based upon facts. They would be unsuitable in a case where the defense relies upon a heavy emotional appeal, but might be acceptable in a case where the prosecution depends upon sheer circumstantial evidence unattested to by any hard facts. However, because of stereotypes, a bank teller who plays in a rock band on weekends may be more acceptable than his occupation would imply. Learning about a juror's favorite TV program can be telling. Inquiries of this type are designed to slip by the juror's defenses and reach his true feelings.

### How to Involve the Jurors in Your Case

Try to convert jurors to your cause by simplifying the issues and discussing them in terms they will understand. In an identification case, ask whether a juror has ever had the experience of seeing someone he thought he knew and then later learned it was the wrong person. In a "bad-check" case, ask a housewife whether she has had the unhappy experience of innocently issuing a check and later learning there were insufficient funds in her account. In a perjury trial, ask a businessman whether or not he has recalled an event differently than his secretary. Then ask him, when he told someone else that the meeting occurred on the wrong day, whether he intended to deliberately mislead them. In this way jurors become directly involved in the defense and can better understand it.

Do not be afraid to reveal the unattractive features of your case to the jury. A confession or criminal record that is bound to be received in evidence must be discussed. Present the issue as gracefully as possible and ask each juror if he can follow the law relating to that question. Where only one witness will condemn your client and he or she has received immunity, develop the "deal" with the jury. Explain to them the benefits the witness has received and tell them of his obvious motive to incriminate your client. This can be accomplished by asking them whether they would be willing to apply the law as it relates to credibility of witnesses.

Defense lawyers differ in their views about whether to disclose to the jury that the defendant will not take the stand. Most lay people misinterpret the invocation of the privilege against self-incrimination as an admission of guilt. Thus, this revelation at the very beginning of the trial involves grave risks. First impressions are important. If the trial begins with the jury believing that the defendant will not testify, you may lose and never regain their confidence. Another approach is to speak of the presumption of innocence and the principle that a defendant in a criminal case does not have to prove anything. Inquire of the jurors whether or not they can follow that precept. In this way, the foundation is laid for the defendant resting at the end of the prosecution's case. This somewhat surprising event will come after the defense has already done a great deal of damage to the prosecution's case through cross-examination. The disappointment experienced by the jury in not hearing the defendant is more easily handled later in the trial.

Finally, ask one last question of each juror that protects the defendant against harmful information possessed by the juror which may have been left uncovered. Ask, "Are there any reasons, which I may not have touched upon, why you could not sit on this case and give us the benefit of your judgment?"

## Exercising Your Challenges Wisely

The final choice concerning which jurors will be kept is the most agonizing part of jury selection. There are those jurors, who bear extreme characteristics, that both sides know will be removed. The police officer's brother and the flower child will be among the first casualties in the striking process. The remaining jurors possess features appealing to the state and the defense. These are the hard choices. Thus, the "alpha" factor is an element that must be carefully considered.

The alpha factor has emerged as an important symbol in the psychodynamics of jury selection. The alpha factor (which may also be called the "authority quotient") describes those strong human qualities which cause certain jurors to succeed in establishing their own territorial imperatives (rank, dominance, influence) in the jury room. Counsel should strive to have at least one juror with a high alpha factor who he is certain will be on his side. Whereas a juror favorable to the defense with a high alpha factor may ensure success, a juror antipathetic to your client with a similarly high alpha factor may guarantee defeat.

Age, gender, education, social status and the number of persons a juror supervises are all features that contribute to the juror's alpha factor.[19] For example, a bank executive with 50 employees under his supervision is bound to have a higher alpha rating than a maintenance man who sweeps classrooms in a public school. The maintenance worker will probably defect to the stronger side, whereas the bank executive may convert a majority of the jury to his view. Thus the alpha rating is one of the most important considerations in deciding whether or not to retain a juror. Counsel can afford to "pad" the jury with weak people because they will not exercise much influence in the jury room. However, a juror with a high alpha factor whom one is unsure of should be excused, because of the risk that such a person may exercise a disproportionate amount of authority in the debating process. On the other hand, a benign juror whom one is uncertain of may be left on the jury with safety.

Leadership qualities are obvious to most of us. Jurors who have occupied an office in a garden club, union, service club, or fraternal organization are accustomed to exercising authority and, therefore, usually have a higher caliber alpha factor. A person who has held a rank in the military, as master sergeant or captain, is used to giving orders and is a good candidate for the office of jury foreman. Questions should search for experiences that disclose a juror's exercise of control over others. Perhaps the most important question that can be asked during jury selection to detect this quality is, "How many people do you supervise?"

A person who answers with "Yes, sir" or "No, sir" is usually deferential to authority and may yield more to the power wielded by the prosecutor. Normally, softness of voice and shyness normally indicate that the juror will play a modest role in the jury's ultimate verdict.

Although it is risky to generalize, in most criminal cases the defense is looking for jurors with fewer social ties. Someone once said that the average defendant wants a juror who is unemployed, unattached, and unintelligent. That may be an exaggeration, but certainly the surveys conducted by such groups as the National Jury Project reveal that young people who are single and not deeply rooted in the community are best for the defense. Older people, entrenched in the establishment, will quickly identify with the prosecutor and normally find in his favor. They feel more threatened by the defendant than the young do.

Be wary of veteran jurors. It is easier for people to convict when they have done it before. On the other hand, jurors who have acquitted in the past are sometimes told unfavorable things about the defendant by the prosecutor which were not developed during the trial. This form of contamination will spoil a juror for the future.

Although instincts are sometimes unreliable, bear in mind the advice given by an experienced trial lawyer who said, "If you don't like a juror's face, chances are he doesn't like yours either—and you'd better get rid of him." If you have an uneasy feeling after talking with a prospective juror, excuse him.

## How to Bolster Your Challenges for Cause

Do not give up too easily on challenges for cause. Where a juror has a clearly defined bias but continues to protest that he can be fair, seek a hearing before the judge. Carry with you to court a brief prepared on the law governing challenges for cause. In New York, the case of *People* v. *Culhane* is most useful.[20] In *Culhane*, the New York Court of Appeals said, in unmistakable language, that it is better for a court to err by excusing the juror, where there is doubt, rather than letting the juror sit with the risk of affecting the integrity of the verdict in the event a conviction follows. The common sense of this argument would seem to apply in any jurisdiction.

# Notes

1. Bennett, Cathy E., "Psychological Methods of Jury Selection in the Typical Criminal Case," *Criminal Defense*, March-April, 1977. Vol. 4, No. 2, National College of Public Defenders and Criminal Defense Lawyers.

2. John Murray and John Eckman, *A Followup Study of Jury Selection*, a paper presented to the annual meeting of The American Psychological Association, September, 1974, in Montreal, Canada.

3. Under Rule 24(a) of the Federal Rules of Criminal Procedure, the judge decides who will conduct the *voir dire*. In 85 judicial districts, the judge conducts the *voir dire* in 51; the judge and the parties in 22; and the litigants alone in 12. *The Jury System in the Federal Courts*, 26 FRD 409, 466. In most state courts the parties are permitted to participate in the selection of a jury. Statistics show that in 22 states, the judge and the parties conduct the *voir dire*; in 10 states, the judge selects the jury; in 8 states, it is done exclusively by the parties; and in 10 states, it is discretionary with the judge. Annotation, 73 AL R2d 1187; Comment to *ABA Standards, Trial by Jury*, Standard 2.4.

4. One study conducted by the well known psychologist, Alice Padawer-Singer, showed that juries selected by lawyers, as compared to those that were not subjected to any *voir dire*, were less easily swayed and more resistant to group pressure. They were, also, "more aware of the importance of legal procedures and admissible evidence". Padawer-Singer, Alice, *Voir Dire by Two Lawyers: An Essential Safeguard*, 57 Judicature 386, April, 1974.

5. Our courts have always acknowledged the importance of a *voir dire* conducted by counsel. *Swain v. Alabama*, 380 U.S. 202 (1965); *United States v. Dellinger*, 472 F.2d 340 (7th Cir. 1972); *United States v. Blount*, 479 F.2d 650 (6th Cir. 1973); *Bailey v. United States*, 53 F.2d 982 (5th Cir. 1931); *Lurding v. United States*, 179 F.2d 419 (6th Cir. 1950); *United States v. Lewis*, 467 F.2d 1131 (7th Cir. 1972). See generally, *Jury* 46 AM. Jur.2d 789 § 201. 1. Busch, *Law and Tactics in Jury Trials*, § § 81, 84, 93. Bush, *The Case For Expansive Voir Dire*, 2 Law and Psychology 9 (1978). But see *Ham* v. *South Carolina*, 409 U.S. 524 (1973) (holding that the Fourteenth Amendment required questions about race but not about facial hair). *United States* v. *Oscar Bear Runner*, 502 F.2d 908, 910, 911, 912, (8th Cir. 1974). See also, *Nebraska Press Association* v. *Stuart*, 427 U.S. 539 (1976), where the Supreme Court suggested an indepth *voir dire* conducted by counsel to locate prejudice generated by adverse publicity.

6. *United States* v. *McNeil*, No. Cr. 73-0098-OJC, N.D. Cal. 1973.

7. Saks, Michael J., *Social Scientists Can't Rig Juries*, Psychology Today, January, 1976.

8. Dr. Charles Winick, 160 Riverside Drive, New York, New York, 10024; Roger Seasonwein Associates, 2 West 45th Street, New York, New York, 10036; and Dr. Alice Padawer-Singer, 130 East 67th Street, New York, New York, 10021.

9. Statistics obtained from the National Jury Project, 853 Broadway, New York, New York, 10003.

10. Significantly, the defendant in a criminal proceeding is given more challenges than the prosecutor in the Federal jurisdiction, and in 20 states. The states which allow more challenges to the defendant than the district attorney are: Alabama, Georgia, Minnesota, New Mexico, North Carolina, Oregon, West Virginia, Alaska, Arkansas, Kentucky, Maryland, Missouri, South Carolina, Tennessee (in all felony and capital cases, but not in misdemeanor trial); Michigan, Nebraska (in cases with a penalty of death or life imprisonment); Delaware, Maine, New Hampshire, New Jersey (in capital trial only). J. Van Dyke, *Jury Selection Procedures*, 282-3 (Ballinger, 1977).

11. Extra peremptory challenges were granted to the defense in the following cases, *United States v. Ahmed, et al*, MD Pa, 1971, (18); *United States v. Anderson, et al*, No. 602-71, D NJ, Camden Division 1973, (15); *United States v. Means and Banks*, 3rd Division of Minnesota (St. Paul), (10); *United States v. Mitchell and Stans*, No. 73 cr. 439, SDNY, 1974, (10); *United States v. Means and Poor Bear*, 409 F. Supp 115 (D ND 1976), (16); *United States v. Mitchell, et al*, 559 F2d 31, 1976, (5); *United States v. Ehrlichman*, 546 F2d 910 (DC Cir. 1976), (5); *United States v. Goldfarb, et al*, No. 8-80-572, ED Mich, Southern Division, January 1979, (14); *State v. Russell Means and David Hill*, 7th Judicial Circuit, Clay County (South Dakota), 1976, (10); *Commonwealth v. Susan Sare*, No. 51775, Suffolk County (Massachusetts) Superior Court, 1976, (16); *People v. Hill and Pernesalice*, Erie County (New York) Supreme Court, 1975, (10); *United States v. Sturman, et al*, ND Ohio No. 1976, (14); *United States v. Olin, et al*, No. cr. 78-38, WDNY, 1979, (2).

12. For a more expansive index of subjects to be covered in a variety of criminal prosecutions see, Ann Fagan Ginger, *Jury Selection in a Criminal Trial*, Lawpress, 1975, see also, *Jury Work: Systematic Techniques*, National Jury Project in cooperation with the National Lawyers Guild and the National Conference of Black Lawyers.

13. Harry Lorayne and Jerry Lucas, *The Memory Book*, Stein and Day, 1974.

14. Bodin, *Civil Litigation and Trial Techniques*, New York: Practicing Law Institute (1976, P. 258); *The Power of Language Presentational Style in the Courtroom*, John M. Connolly, William M. O'Barr, and E. Allan Lind, Duke Law Journal, Vol. 1978.

15. See, M. LaFrance and C. Mayo, *Moving Bodies: Nonverbal Communications in Social Relationships*, Monterey, C. A. Brooks Cole, 1978; N. Henley, *Body Politics*, Englewood Cliffs, N.J., Prentice-Hall, 1977; Fast, *Body Language*, New York: Pocketbooks, Inc., 1970.

16. Howeler and Vrolijk, *Verbal Communications as an Index of Interpersonal Attraction*, 34 ACTA Psychologia, 511, 514 (1970); Pope and Siegman, supra, Note 12 at 296; Wiens, Jackson, Manaugh and Matarazzo, *Communications as an Index of Communicator Attitude: A Replication*, 53 J. Applied Psych. 264-65 (1969).

Paralinguistics is defined as that aspect of speech dealing with breathing, pauses, pitch and tone of voice, as well as speech disturbances. Kinesic behavior or body language, consists of such physical activity as facial expressions, body movements, body orientation, eye contact and hand movement.

**17.** See David Suggs and Bruce Dennis Sales, *Using Communication Cues to Evaluate Prospective Jurors During the Voir Dire*, Arizona L. Rev. 20, 1978; see also, Pittenger and Smith, *A Basis for Some Contributions of Linguistics to Psychiatry*, 20 Psych. 61, 69-74 (1957).

**18.** Blinder, *Psychiatry in the Everyday Practice of Law*, Rochester: The Lawyers' Cooperative Publishing Co. (1973), § 27 (Supp., P. 52); Kennelly, *Jury Selection in a Civil Case*, 9 Tr. Law Guide 87 (1975).

**19.** "Authoritarian Personality"—Brown, R., *Social Psychology*, New York: Free Press, 1965; Robinson and Shavers, *Measure of Social Psychological Attitudes*, Survey Research Center, Institute for Social Research, University of Michigan, Ann Arbor, Michigan, 1969.

**20.** *People* v. *Culhane*, 33 N.Y.2d 381, 350 N.Y.S.2d 397 (1973).

# Jury Study Results: How to Reduce the Guesswork in Jury Selection

## Thomas Sannito, Ph.D., and Edward Burke Arnolds

Thomas Sannito is professor of Psychology at Loras College, Dubuque, Iowa. He specializes in Forensic Psychology. He is a lecturer and consultant to trial attorneys on the applications of psychology to the courtroom. Dr. Sannito is on the Board of Editors of *Trial Diplomacy Journal*. He is also co-Director of *TDJ*'s jury study.

Edward Burke Arnolds is Associate Professor of Law and Director of Trial Advocacy Training at John Marshall Law School in Chicago, Il. Mr. Arnolds is on the Board of Editors of *Trial Diplomacy Journal* and co-Director of *TDJ*'s jury study.

The person who was later to be named foreman of the jury looked at the two plaintiffs' attorneys and smiled. They smiled back and then grinned at each other. The case had gone their way, they just knew it. Liability seemed clear for they had brought out their clients' damages skillfully and dramatically. But the jury took only 3 hours and 15 minutes to determine zero damages and exonerate the defendants. The leader of the jury had smiled at them because he had known he was going to give them nothing.

In a rape case tried in the Midwest, the prosecution loaded the jury with women. For a highly publicized case of violent sexual assault, they reasoned that women would certainly be eager to convict. The defense theory of mistaken identify wouldn't wash with women. They would feel the pain of the victim and be ready to strike back; whereas, men might be calloused and let the defendant go. The jury, composed mostly of women stalemated in a hung jury.

The same defendant was tried on a second rape charge and was convicted by a jury, composed mainly of men. Through this trial and error experimentation, the prosecutors were able to discover the fallacy of their hypothesis about male and female stereotypes in rape cases. How many attorneys have the luxury of two trials, in which they use the first as a "pilot" study to test out their theories about jurors?

Trial attorneys are too frequently put in the position of picking jurors according to folklore and desperate hunches. Hard-nosed scientific data, of which there is a dearth, are sorely needed to dispel or confirm the legendary myths and to reveal the relationships that operate between juror characteristics and verdicts.

## Reducing the Guesswork in Jury Selection

In the Fall of 1979, we launched an all-out effort to reduce the guesswork in jury selection. Since our jury project began, more than 6,000 questionnaires have been mailed to 215 judges in 33 states and Canada. To date, over 600 completed *Jury Questionnaires* have been returned by judges, who administered them to jurors at the conclusion of each trial. An analysis has been conducted of the responses of 323 jurors to 74 questions about the foreperson, attorneys, witnesses, and the jurors' personal backgrounds, experiences, and preferences. Of the cases tested, 55 percent of the jurors convicted. Conclusions have been reached in a wide variety of criminal cases concerning the significant factors that influence juror verdicts and the characteristics that jurors pay attention to in choosing the foreperson.

The jurors who filled out and returned the questionnaires were between the ages of 18 and 81, with a mean age of 46.24. Ninety-two percent of the nationwide sample were white and 7.6 percent were from a racial minority; 55 percent were male and 45 percent were females. Their educational level ranged from 2 to 22 years of school, with the average juror having 13.99 years of school [2 years of college]. Only 9.4 percent of the jurors had less than a 12th-grade education; 31 percent had 12 years of education; 18.8 percent had a college education; and 11 percent had postgraduate training. Sixty-three percent of the jurors had degrees above high school. Birth order data showed that 27 percent were first-borns, 27 percent were second-borns, 16 percent were third-borns and 13 percent were born in position four or later. The average family yearly income of jurors was between $20,000 and $23,000, with 8 percent below $12,499, 25 percent between $12,500 and $19,999, 18 percent between $20,000 and $24,999, and 41 percent between $25,000 and $49,999.

## How to Predict the Foreperson

Since we know that the leader of the jury will direct and dominate the decision process and will be responsible for about 25 percent of the total acts of participation during deliberation, scientific findings that would assist the attorney in predicting the foreperson seem long overdue.

What are the characteristics to which jurors respond in picking a foreperson? Psychology has enjoyed an abundance of studies dealing with traits of effective leaders. An exhaustive literature survey has shown that leaders are taller, fastidious, buoyant, intelligent, self-confident, dominant, decisive, and sensitive.[1] But, since a trial is a relatively brief period in which to discover leadership qualities, which of these traits will have the greatest bearing on the foreperson selection?

Jurors were asked to rate the foreperson of their jury for height, attractiveness, verbosity, intelligence, dominance, confidence, and warmth. In making their judgments, jurors were instructed to compare the foreperson with others on the jury. Also, those jurors who had previous jury service were asked to indicate their observations of the previous foreperson. From the juror perceptions of the elected leaders, it is possible to provide a foreperson profile.

The most prominent trait perceived by jurors in the 62 forepersons who were studied (30 percent females and 70 percent males) was *verbal productivity*. Seventy-nine percent of the 550 jurors saw the foreperson as either "talkative" (37 percent), "one of the most talkative" (36 percent), or "the most talkative" (5 percent) person compared with the others.

Also, 79 percent of those questioned said the foreperson was either the first, second, or third person to speak at the start of the selection process. It is even more remarkable that 36 percent of the jurors indicated that the foreperson was the *first* person to speak, and 50 percent of the forepersons themselves thought they spoke first.

This finding is consistent with another study of 588 jurors, in which the authors reported that in one-third of the 49 deliberations studied, the man who opened the discussion became the foreman.[2] It may be that most jurors are looking for someone willing to take the "heat" for their decision, and the person bold enough to speak first may seem like the obvious choice.

In our study, the leader who typically talked the most was not necessarily the one with the best vocabulary. Only two percent of the jurors perceived the leader to have "the best use of words" on the jury, and only five percent of the forepersons said they themselves had "the best use of words." In fact, in one instance, a female juror took exception with her leader's word choice by stating "he tried to impress us with his 'foul language.' " Hence, loquacity did not always mean eloquence in forepersons, although the leaders were at least average or better than average in word usage. The bulk of jurors (67 percent) said the leader was "about the same as everyone else" in word usage.

It has been said that prosecutors dream of having a cold-blooded authoritarian as foreperson. But this type was rarely chosen as leader. Not one juror saw any foreperson as "a *very cold* person," and less than 1 percent of the jurors indicated that the leader was "a *cold* person."

Quite the contrary, 60 percent perceived the foreperson to be "a *warm* person," and another 10 percent described the jury head as "a *very warm* person."

One possibility is that defense attorneys strike "cold" people, which would account for the virtual absence of the trait of *coldness* from the 62 forepersons. However, it would not explain the substantially high percentage of jurors who characterized the jury leader as a *warm* or *very warm* person. A better interpretation of the data collected is that likability is a strong factor in short-term leadership. The warmer the individual, the greater was his chance of being elected foreperson.

Studies have shown that bishops are taller than priests, university presidents are taller than college presidents, and insurance executives are taller than policy holders.[3]

But it is *not* true that forepersons are taller than other jurors. In fact, they're probably shorter. Sixty-nine percent of the jurors thought the jury leader was "shorter than average height." It may be that stature is not as prominent during jury duty, since people are usually seated. Perhaps the only time height variances are noticed is when jurors are engaged in irrelevant activities such as going to the bathroom, and are not given much importance.

Leaders of the juries also tended to be more sure of themselves. Over one-half of all jurors depicted the foreperson as "the *most confident* group member" or "*one of the most confident* group members," and 76 percent of the forepersons used these statements to describe themselves. This finding is not surprising, since jurors have a need to be sure of their decisions. A person who exudes confidence would help them feel comfortable with their verdict.

A disconcerting finding is that only one-third of the jurors thought the foreperson was more intelligent than the rest. About two-thirds of them felt their leader was "about average compared with the others." Also, the leaders were rated just barely more dominant than the others. Perhaps jurors feel threatened by intelligent, dominant types who wield much influence in deciding a verdict.

## A Simple Checklist for Picking Out the Foreperson

In summary, the foreperson jurors choose was abundantly talkative, exceptionally warm and very confident. Also, he (she) was slightly above average in IQ, dominance and word usage and less than average in height.

Psychologically, it seems that this individual takes pressure off fellow jurors by initiating discussion, eases their tension by his sanguinity, and reduces their uncertainty with his confidence.

Moreover, jurors may derive these psychological benefits without having to surrender their free choice, since the foreperson does not overwhelm them with his size, dominance and IQ. If he were physically imposing, intensely dominant and awesomely bright, they might feel compelled to capitulate. As it is, he gets them off the griddle, soothes their feelings, and reassures them without threatening their freedom.

In addition to the psychological profile of the jury leaders, we gleaned demographic information from the responses provided by the forepersons. Extrapolating from our demographic data, the odds are that the foreperson will be a man (7 times out of 10), white (95 percent), age 47, with about 2½ years of college, who is earning about $35,000 per year (31 percent were between $12,500-$25,999; 58 percent were between $25,000-$49,000; and 10 percent were $50,000 and over), and neither conservative nor liberal in political orientation.

When the foreperson was a woman, her average age was 33; she averaged two years of college, had a family income of about $30,000, and tended to be politically "slightly liberal." Both male and female forepersons were usually white-collar professionals, such as professors, managers, supervisors, executives, foremen, administrators, etc.

Identifying the foreperson during jury selection is like a medical diagnosis, in that the emphasis should be on the *syndrome* or collective pattern rather than on one isolated *symptom*. The person who best approximates the profile above has the greatest chance of being selected. With a simple checklist of the salient characteristics (_____talkative, _____ warm, _____ confident, _____ educated, _____ middle aged, _____ male, and _____ white-collar occupation), you can usually narrow the probable foreperson down to one or two persons. The venireman with the most checkmarks most likely will be chosen as foreperson.

## Predicting a Prospective Juror's Final Vote

Most good trial lawyers think about "deselecting" juries rather than about selecting them. The number of veniremen is limited. So, more importantly, is the number of peremptory challenges. The lawyer who selects only "good" jurors will normally use up all of his challenges long before he has selected a panel. The idea, therefore, is to deselect those prospective jurors who are prejudiced against one's self, one's client or one's case, and those who are biased towards the other side.

Let us assume a trial lawyer is deselecting a jury in a criminal case and he wishes to make use of the findings of the study. Are there single items of information about a juror that can predict his/her final vote in a case? How many questions that attorneys ask during voir dire actually measure an attitude that will influence a juror's decision to convict or acquit? Does it really help to know a juror's age, sex, religion, ancestry, politics, etc.? Do so-called warm-blooded jurors, such as Irish and Italians, actually acquit more than jurors of German and Scandinavian ancestry? Should defense attorneys really hold their breath and search for black women to hear their case? To answer these and other questions, we examined the relationship of each questionnaire item with a) the final verdict and b) the feelings of jurors ("definitely guilty," "probably guilty," "undecided," "probably innocent," or "definitely innocent") at the start of deliberations.

Each of the 72 items of information about juror and foreperson background, characteristics, and attitudes was statistically correlated with what jurors remembered to be their pre-deliberation feelings about innocence or guilt and their final verdicts. This correlational technique allows us to measure the degree to which a relationship exists between the sex, occupation, age, education, birth order, income, politics, etc. of a juror and his/her tendency to acquit or convict. Through this analysis, we were able to identify the items that make the difference and to isolate those characteristics that have little or no effect.

### The Importance of Attorney Characteristics

The best predictors of the jurors' individual feelings about the innocence or guilt of the defendant and their final verdicts were their perceptions of the attorneys.

*Skill* and *likeability* were the most important attorney qualities, while attorney *dress* was an insignificant predictor of outcome. When jurors thought the prosecutor was "well prepared, knowledgeable, persuasive, and likeable," they were substantially influenced to believe the defendant was guilty before deliberations and to convict him after deliberations. Hence, it's not what you wear but what you say that influences jurors most.

### The Victim vs. the Defendant

How the victim came across influences the jury's decision about the defendant. When the jury liked the complaining witness, the defendant's chances of going free were substantially reduced; conversely, when the jurors strongly disliked the victim, they tended to acquit the defendant. Similarly, jurors who had close friends or admired relatives that were victims of violent crimes, were disposed to convict and to feel the defendant was guilty before deliberations started. Since a trial involves choosing one side or the other, it makes sense that if jurors are attracted to the victim, they may be against the defendant.

While dressing up a defendant won't overcome strong evidence, it may make a difference in closer cases. There was a significant correlation between the attractiveness of the defendant and the verdict. When jurors were esthetically impressed, they were more prone to acquit, and the more their eyes were offended, the greater was their tendency to convict. Also, the more they agreed "the defendant was likeable," the more they voted to free him and the more certain they were that he was innocent.

### How A Juror's Occupation Affects His Verdict

We related several juror characteristics to their pre-deliberation conclusion and their final verdict. One of the most critical items of information to know about prospective jurors is their *occupation*. We tabulated the independent feelings before deliberation and the final verdict of jurors of 25 different occupations. Our analysis of the frequency with which different groups decided "guilt" or "innocence" showed that *secretaries* and *managers* convict with alarming frequency.

Also there is a significant conviction rate for the combination of female *teachers* and *secretaries*, occupations concerned with control, precision, and organization. Furthermore, the pre-deliberation feelings of secretaries and managers were significantly on the side of "guilty". Only 1 secretary in 16 and 3 managers in 16 felt any defendant was innocent. Statistically, these findings have 99 chances out of 100 of representing a true tendency. All of the foregoing groups are trained to avoid mistakes and may overreact to any form of deviancy.

Others whose jobs demand precision, such as engineers, machinists, programmers, bankers and accountants, often at first felt the defendants were guilty, but changed their minds after deliberations. The frequency with which these groups, taken together as *precision* occupations, initially reported feeling the defendants were guilty was highly significant.

However, they did not convict the defendant significantly more than they acquitted him. Because they are in jobs of exactitude, they may feel uncertain convicting after hearing the dissonance that is produced by group discussion. Also, they might demand stringent levels of proof to be convinced.

The occupations which did not lean towards guilt or not guilty were *nurses, factory workers, professors, clerks, social workers*, and *truckers.* Their votes were not significantly skewed on either side, and the frequencies obtained in many cases were too small to draw a final conclusion.

### The Danger of Courtroom Stereotypes

One of the juror characteristics that has been of greatest concern to old craftsmen of the courtroom has been ethnic background. The older attorneys have for ages admonished younger defense lawyers to reject people of German ancestry because of a stereotype that they are emotionally cold. Germans supposedly punish deviant-looking types who show up in court. Irish and Italians, on the other hand, supposedly favor the defense because they are warm-blooded people, who do not always operate within the boundaries of the law.

Our study shed considerable doubt on these age-old myths. Seventy-four percent of those who indicated that they were Irish voted for "guilty," 50 percent of the Italians voted "guilty," and only 46 percent of those who were German voted "Guilty." Also, jurors who indicated they were from England and Wales had the second highest rate of conviction (62 percent).

Although the totals for each group may not be large enough to make strong recommendations, they contradict what would be predicted from the courtroom stereotypes. The old courtroom stereotypes may produce unexpected results. They were probably more applicable several generations ago, in the time of Darrow, when many of today's old "pros" learned jury selection. By now, strong ethnic tradition is washed out of many Americans, and differences within each group are so widespread that reliance on ethnic traits is simplistic and risky.

Other demographic factors that had virtually no relationship with how jurors felt before deliberating or how they voted were *age, educational level, income, religious preference, religious attendance*, and *political orientation*.[4] Characteristics that mildly predisposed jurors were *sex, race*, and *number of brothers and sisters.*

It has been suggested in other studies that women are more compassionate than men as jurors, and they are more lenient and "acquittal prone."[5,6,7] This study has found just the opposite pattern. Women showed a slight tendency to convict compared with men, but the difference was not statistically significant.

Minorities were mildly inclined to acquit, and people from larger families slightly favored acquittal over those from smaller families.

There were several characteristics that were significant predictors of the final verdict. Jurors who acquitted the defendant were more likely to be married to a liberal or have a less educated spouse. Also, acquittal-bound jurors tended to: (a) prefer reading to watching T.V., (b) have more children, (c) be later-borns, (d) have voted "Not Guilty" on a previous case, (e) disbelieve that criminals were too protected by the courts, and (f) did not agree that jurors too often acquit out of "pure sympathy." The opposite profile is true for those who endorsed conviction. The common thread running through all of these items may be the trait of *broad-minded thinking*. A juror who reads books, comes from a large family and marries a liberal, certainly has a background with a breadth of experiences that might make him tolerant of deviancy. Perhaps the juror who has "seen it all" is somewhat desensitized to the possibility of criminal disobedience.

### The Combined Effect of Juror Characteristics

An analysis of single predictors taken separately does not tell you how they combine to influence jurors' verdicts. For example, let us say that neither a person's age nor educational level will predict appreciably how they will vote on final verdict. In other words, older jurors would convict with about the same frequency as younger jurors, as do degree holders and non-degree holders.

However, when their combined effect is studied, we may learn that one combination convicts significantly more than another and is, therefore, a good predictor of verdict. It might turn out that, while no difference exists between non-degree aged persons and non-degree young people, aged degree holders convict substantially more than young degree holders. This result would not be surprising since older persons with sheepskins would, in all likelihood, have had to battle great adversity back in the time when degrees were rare. Therefore, older people holding degrees might be more "tough-minded" than younger individuals whose degrees were easier to obtain. The result would be that elderly degree-holders convict more than younger college graduates. Two variables may seem unimportant when considered separately, but combined the result may be significant.

Although the combinations in the above illustration could not be tested because of small numbers in each category, other combinations of variables were found to predict initial decision (before deliberation) and final verdict.

Jurors who have fewer children and spouses with higher degrees show a likelihood of conviction. But jurors who have more children and whose mates had lower degrees (e.g., Associate Arts) favored acquittal.

The factors of sex (male or female) and education (does the juror have at least an Associate Arts degree?) combine to produce different rates of conviction.

Females with degrees convicted significantly more (64 percent) than they acquitted (36 percent). Females without degrees were still more likely to convict than they were to acquit, but the difference was not so spectacular.

Males with degrees showed similar patterns as their female counterparts (58 percent = guilty, 42 percent = not guilty). And males without degrees voted for conviction only as often as they favored acquittal. Conviction rates for the four combinations, from highest to lowest were: females with degrees, females without degrees, males with degrees, and males without degrees.

### How the Foreperson Influences the Verdict

The way that jurors perceived the foreperson partially predicted their verdict. Jurors who felt the foreperson was *warmer, more attractive* and not so eloquent were more disposed to acquit. And with *colder,* more *unattractive* forepersons with good word selection, the greater the penchant for conviction. From the data, it would appear that the foreperson had a small, but significant, influence on the verdict. The "acquittal leader" seems to be a social figure and the "conviction leader" a task-oriented, business-like figure.

### Attorney Image and Juror Bias

Jurors who knew victims of violent crime and were affiliated with law-enforcement agencies and who felt a) that the prosecutor was a good attorney; b) that the prosecutor dressed well and c) that jurors in general are too sympathetic to criminals, convicted to an alarming degree. Therefore, attorneys should be acutely aware of any nonverbal reactions veniremen may make toward the prosecutor during voir dire. Attorneys should ask the jurors about their authoritarian attitudes towards criminals.

The *skill* and *likability* of both attorneys interacted with bias toward criminals as a major predictor of jurors' pre-deliberation verdicts. When jurors thought the prosecutor was a good attorney, that the courts protect criminals too much, that the defense attorney was not likable, and that the prosecutor was likable, they consistently felt the defendant was "guilty" before group discussion began. To be sure, the key item in the group dealt with the proficiency of the prosecutor. (The prosecutor seems to play a bigger role in determining verdict than the defense lawyer.)

## Emotional and Intellectual Jurors

An interesting combination of two items that became a strong predictor of initial verdict was whether the juror preferred a good book to television and had ever been a victim of a violent crime (or knew of a close friend, relative, etc. who had). Jurors who had experienced a violent crime and preferred television to reading a book were likely to convict. Those who chose books to television and were inexperienced with violent crimes favored acquittal. It would seem that jurors who often retreat into books and have never fallen victim to criminal violence are more inclined to "intellectualize" crimes rather than react viscerally.

## What Attitudes and Values to Look For in Jurors

A factor analysis of the 74 questionnaire items was completed to determine what items were intercorrelated with each other and were, therefore, measuring the same disposition in jurors. The purpose of this technique is to identify those items that hang together in what is called a factor and then tests its effectiveness in predicting initial and final verdicts. We previously based predictions upon single items of demographic information, such as membership in broad groups like male/female, degree/no degree, and then from various combinations of these classifications. The disadvantage is that being black or white, male or female does not indicate what personality disposition affects jurors' thinking during deliberations. The varimax factor analysis organizes the individual items into a handful of meaningful personality factors. The result of this analysis will reveal what attitudes and values the attorney should look for in individual jurors,—be they old or young, black or white or German or Irish—that will predict the outcome. Hence, instead of relying on whether jurors are male or female or German, Irish, or Jewish to forecast their vote, the attorney will look for traits like "authoritarianism," which will influence any juror in which it is manifested.

    Jurors who perceived their foreperson as weak in verbal ability, intelligence, attractiveness, dominance, warmth and confidence were more likely to acquit than those whose foreperson was stronger in leadership qualities. A possible explanation for this consistent finding might be that juries without a leader compete with each other for leadership rights. In an effort to assert their authority, more people express strong opinions, in opposition to the others, which leads to "reasonable doubt" for the group. With strong leadership there is a greater chance the foreperson will be an authoritarian who will cut discussion short before it can produce reasonable doubt.

Seven items reflected an authoritarian attitude, which was related to more "guilty" verdicts before deliberations and on final vote. Jurors were far more likely to feel the defendant was "guilty" and voted to convict when they thought (a) society is too permissive toward sex, (b) misfortunes are the result of laziness, (c) alcoholics are moral degenerates, (d) jurors often acquit out of pure sympathy, (e) courts protect criminals too much, and (f) the death penalty should be used in some circumstances.[8] According to the analysis, this attitude in jurors will significantly dispose them toward conviction. The more items a juror endorsed in the direction of authoritarianism (versus non-authoritarianism), the more likely he/she would be favorable to the prosecution. The lower the score on this dimension, the greater the likelihood of acquittal.

The factor with the highest correlation with both initial and final verdicts was the "anti-authoritarian malcontent," who had brushes with the law, thought the prosecution was poor and unlikable, didn't like the victim, didn't think jurors were too sympathetic toward criminals, liked the defense attorney, had voted to acquit during a previous trial, and saw the foreperson of the earlier trial as weak. The more a juror possessed these attitudes, the more likely he/she acquitted. This factor had an extremely high correlation with initial verdict and final verdict. In fact, this factor is so strongly related to acquittal, we are naming it the *Defense Factor*.

### Jury Selection Checklist

To sum up the findings of our study, here is a checklist of the 12 key points you should keep in mind during jury selection:

1. The most prominent traits of the foreperson, in order of importance, were *verbal productivity*, *warmth*, and *confidence*. Of lesser importance were word usage, intelligence, and dominance.
2. *Skill* and *likability* of the attorneys were the best single predictors of initial and final verdict. Attorney's dress was insignificant.
3. *Likability of the victim* significantly affected juror decisions. A likeable complaining witness increased the chances for conviction and an unlikeable one made acquittal more likely.

4. The more *attractive* defendents had a better chance for acquittal than less attractive ones. So, clean those defendants up.

5. Secretaries convicted at an alarming rate.

6. High frequency of conviction was also found for jurors in precision occupations, such as engineers, programmers, machinists, bankers, bookkeepers, and accountants.

7. Irish, especially Irish women, were significantly more conviction prone than any other ethnic group studied. Seventy-four percent of the Irish in the study convicted compared with only 46 percent of the Germans. In general, courtroom stereotypes are risky.

8. Women convicted slightly more than men [60% to 53%] and women with degrees were significantly prone to convict more than acquit.

9. Jurors with small families and whose spouses have college degrees tended to convict, while those with larger families and less educated spouses were more likely to acquit.

10. A *leaderless jury* was more likely to acquit than one with a strong and appealing leader.

11. The degree to which jurors have an antiauthoritarian attitude, called the *defense factor*, was far and away the best predictor of acquittal.

12. The authoritarian disposition was an excellent predictor of conviction. We are calling it the *prosecution factor*.

## Notes

1. Stogdill, R., *et al.* Personal factors associated with leadership. *Journal of Psychology*, 1948, *25*, 35-71.

2. Strodtbeck, *et al.* Social status in jury deliberations. *Readings in Social Psychology*, 1958, 379–387.

3. *Supra*, Stogdill, *et al.*

4. An earlier study (c.f., Simon *infra*) agreed with these findings that more educated jurors are likely to convict but a recent study by Mills, C. and Bohanon, W. in the December issue of *The Champion* reported that as age increased so did number of acquittals.

5. Broeder, D. The University of Chicago jury project. 38 Neb. L. Rev. 744 (1959).

6. Simon, R. The jury and the defense of insanity. Boston: Little Brown, 1967.

7. Stephan, C. Sex prejudice in jury simulation. *Journal of Psychology*, 1974, *305*.

8. For a description and discussion of how this personality type influences verdicts, see: Sannito, T. *A Psychologist's Voir Dire*. Dubuque: Forensic Psychologists Press, 1979, p. 11.

# Chapter Three

# *How to Lay the Groundwork for Victory in Your Opening Statement*

The jurors that you have helped select are now sworn in and ready for action. Perhaps more than at any other point in the trial, you have the benefit of their attention and goodwill. If you can only make a strong enough impression on them now in your opening statement, you will have created the necessary momentum to carry your case all the way to a favorable verdict.

You rise to address the jury. You know that this is your best opportunity to get your message across, to lay the foundation for victory, but what do you say and how do you say it? How do you sow the proper words and images that will take root in the jurors' minds and ultimately result in a finding for your client? These are some of the challenges you face in your opening statement, and here to answer them for you are three veteran practitioners who have succeeded time and time again in winning over juries right at the outset of trial—Al Julien, George A. LaMarca and Frederic G. Levin.

Al Julien, known to many as the master of the opening statement, opens this chapter with a personal interview. In it, he discusses the technique behind his opening statements: why a good opening statement should border on summation, the importance of timing in your presentation and how to speak in terms that jurors can understand, and how to handle objections from opposing counsel. "Failure to make use of a proper opening statement to win lawsuits," he warns, "indicates that some lawyers are ignoring one of the most potent weapons in the trial strategist's arsenal."

Trial master George LaMarca follows with some of the most practical and perceptive advice on the opening statement ever to see print. With the help of illustrative examples and checklists, he provides a complete anatomy of an effective opening statement in a civil claim, beginning with your first sentence and continuing step-by-step through the liability, injury, and damage narratives.

"In the opening statement," Mr. LaMarca observes, "counsel must begin to sell himself, his client, and his theory of the case to the jury, all without argument—but hasn't it been said that good salesmanship never was argument in the first place?" Of course, it is *persuasion* which has always been the key to good salesmanship, and in the courtroom setting, persuasion depends upon your seizing the initiative in your opening statement, especially in your all-important opening sentence. Otherwise, your opponent could very well take charge of the trial at your expense.

Mr. LaMarca shows you how to create the kind of opening sentence that captures all the highlights of your entire case in one bold stroke. You will discover exactly what ingredients go into a successful opening sentence, and you get easy-to-follow examples from three different kinds of claims.

Next, Mr. LaMarca provides a sample explanation of the order of trial, giving the jurors in plain everyday terms a brief preview of what to expect (and what is expected of them) during the trial. Then, getting into the meat of your opening statement, Mr. LaMarca reveals the eight essential strands to incorporate into your liability narrative. You will see how to drive home to the jury the full impact of the plaintiff's suffering and how to use your damage narrative to cover each and every category of loss for which your client deserves just compensation.

In addition to helping you build the separate parts of your opening statement, Mr. LaMarca also explains how to put the parts together for maximum persuasive power in court. He ends with a list of pointers for ensuring that *your* opening statement will be the one the jury believes.

A particular opening statement that will long be remembered by attorneys everywhere is featured in the second half of this chapter. It was given by Frederic G. Levin in a wrongful death action where the jury returned verdicts totaling some $18 million, $10 million of which was for punitive damages. Mr. Levin, counsel for the plaintiffs, noted, "The case was, for all practical purposes, over after the opening statements." Now, for the first time, you can see precisely how Mr. Levin constructed and delivered this masterpiece of courtroom strategy. Featured here is the actual case-winning statement together with Mr. Levin's own blow-by-blow commentary.

# The Opening Statement

## Alfred Julien

Alfred Julien is associated with the law firm: Julien, Schlesinger & Finz, New York. He is a past president of ATLA, New York State Trial Lawyers, and Metropolitan Trial Lawyers. He lectures for the Practicing Law Institute, New York State Bar Association as well as other groups on trial techniques and environmental law. He is the author of numerous articles and the book *Opening Statements*; Adjunct Professor of Law, New York Law School and Columnist, *New York Law Journal* on Products and Environmental Law.

### A Good Opening Statement Borders on Summation

EDITOR: You are known as the master of the opening statement. How do you account for the observation made by one of your peers that your opening statement and your summation are almost identical?

AJ: One reason my opening and summation are so similar is because of the emotion that I evoke in each. A good trial lawyer must be able to arouse fervid emotion in himself, and in so doing, will most certainly cause the listener to become emotionally involved. My opening remarks employ all of the techniques that have been taught for years on summation. The key to each is to be persuasive; hold nothing back. During opening, I take advantage of the first opportunity afforded to talk to the jurors apart from jury selection. This is the time to have the jurors feel the capacity of the lawyer; to become attuned to his or her personality and through the proper dialogue, feel the lawyer's deep belief in the case. This is when I touch on all the problems and bring them out into the open. I call this "workshopping."

It is imperative in opening that the plaintiff's counsel present an overview of the entire case so that there is no chance that anything vital will be said for the first time when the defense speaks. The jurors are alert now and their minds are open; they are ready to have you translate to them all of the facts enveloping the case and these facts should be translated by using everyday parlance just as in summation. The jury must understand the context of the parties' legal contentions and know what the law demands, but an astute lawyer conveys this information in a comprehensible manner.

My opening statement in a criminal case also borders on summation in that I give a preview in opening of what will be heard during my summation. I once tried a very important criminal case . . . important because my client was a lawyer who was charged with perjury. I became very emotionally wrapped up in that case because of my closeness to the client, and because I knew that my client was faced with a considerable amount of time to be spent in jail and the loss of his license. The case took a month to try and I gave my usual opening statement representing the defendant; it was very detailed. I told the jury what the case was about explaining how unjustified the charge was against my client. I went into great detail as to why I thought it was unjustified. Not only was this a very long and difficult case, but the judge was leaning heavily against us. Fortunately the jury leaned our way! When the verdict came down in favor of the defendant, a most unusual thing happened, I broke down and cried. I stepped into the hallway and I really broke down. The foreman came up to me and said, "Mr. Julien, why are you crying?" Then he said, "This jury never had any doubt about your case from the time of your first summation a month ago." He had called it summation. Then it clicked with me, of course it's summation. I had been doing that right along during my opening statements, but I had never put a label on it. What smart lawyer wouldn't want to have two full summations? That was the genesis of the idea and I have been teaching that theory throughout the country ever since. I think that I have been able to change the thinking of many lawyers on what was once considered archaic . . . an archaic introductory remark of what's going to happen during the course of the trial.

EDITOR: We are talking about technique; that has to be learned and developed through years of trial experience. You're the expert; but wouldn't your opening statement have to vary with each case?

AJ: I use the same opening summation statement in all types of cases. While I am known for personal injury work, I often try criminal cases, especially white collar crime, anti-trust and security cases. The idea of the opening is always the same whether I am representing the defendant or the plaintiff; it is very detailed. Why is it so detailed on the defendant's side? After all, many experienced trial lawyers have been saying for years that they like to keep things in reserve on the defense so that they can surprise the jury after the case has gone on for some time. That may have been good thinking at one time, but it isn't anymore. In these days of complete discovery, even to some extent in criminal cases, through the use of pre-trial motions, there is little opportunity for complete surprise. A wise lawyer knows what the other side will bring out. That is why it is so important to reach the minds of the jurors early. Perhaps this is even more important for the defense, because the defense comes in early in the case, and a good defense lawyer wants the jury to be aware of some of the things they are going to hear when the plaintiff or prosecutor is putting on his or her case.

A good opening statement in a criminal case *especially* borders on summation. If my opening statement does not draw from the district attorney the complaint that I am "summing up," I am not doing a good job.

The theme of defendant's opening statement in a criminal case must be: "ATTACK!" You must touch the viscera of the jurors by showing how wrong this charge is against the defendant. Stress how important it is to everyone, not only the defendant, that the safeguards of the presumption of innocence, and proof of guilt beyond a reasonable doubt, must be applied rigorously in this case.

I know, in a negligence case, certain things I say are going to evoke a "built-in" response in a jury. If I say, "This case is against a doctor who had a patient who he knew to be critically ill; he was called that night, but he refused to make a house call." Or, perhaps an infant was ill and the doctor would not come to see the infant that night, which later resulted in death or very serious complications, I will get a natural response or reaction of repugnance. Our society still remembers the old "horse and buggy" doctor who did come to the house. There is a very negative response to the doctor who refuses to make a call when somebody is seriously ill. People don't like to think about the "big earner" who refuses to respond to his patient's needs.

A product liability case is really a consumer case and the public is very conscious of the word "consumer." The jury does not have to put itself in the shoes of the litigant in order to identify with a consumer. The patient who is dissatisfied with a hospital for a particular type of wrong treatment is a consumer. I like to say, "this consumer is unhappy or disappointed with a product," or "This is a consumer case involving a defective lawn mower, or vacuum cleaner."

Language is so crucial to your case. You know how lawyers talk? We go through law school and are taught the language of the law. *Res judicata . . . res gestae, executrix, administratrix . . .* why some people don't even know who the plaintiff or the defendant is. We need to use the language of the people. Simply said, "This lady is the mother of a boy who was killed at sea," or "this man is the father of a woman who was recklessly run down by a bus."

A lawyer must forget the language he learned in law school. Return the language of the law to the language of the living. We must use terms and expressions that we live with in our daily lives. The juror hears *res gestae* and he thinks: "What is he saying? I'm a bus driver," or, "I'm a cab driver; I'm a barber." The lawyer who uses difficult phrases once, is going to use them again and again and he does himself a disservice. Jurors wonder why that lawyer is parading that kind of stuff around. While the jurors are thinking about the meaning of some word, they lose the thread of the case. Then, when the other lawyer gets up and speaks in simple terms, the jurors are going to listen. That lawyer will reach the minds of the jurors and that's really what persuasion is all about.

To persuade, we have to tune in not to our wave length, we must tune in on the *listener's* wave length. I find it helpful, when I go out of town to try a case, to arrive a few days early. I read the local paper and I listen to the way the people speak, by visiting bars and restaurants. That's how to pick up expressions and phrases that can later be used in court.

### Don't Make These Mistakes

EDITOR: What are some hyper-taboos you can think of?

AJ: Never, especially during opening or summation, nose-scratch or face-scratch or scratch any other part of the body. It is so distracting, and I've seen it done by both male and female attorneys. There are lawyers who simply cannot stop themselves from doing this. The "picketeer" is most annoying; the picketeer walks up and down the length of the jury rail with his/her head down, rarely looking at the jury. Interminable pacing in front of the jury is a very bad show. Of course there has to be some movement; the trial lawyer cannot remain rooted to one spot, but shifting has to be restrained and not too obvious.

I knew an attorney who used to swing his Phi Beta Kappa key in a most annoying manner. Don't crack your knuckles or use nervous gestures. If you must gesture, make sure they are broad rather than miniscule because no one who expects big money should make less than expansive gestures!

Never focus all your attention on one juror, especially not on a good-looking member of the opposite sex. Other jurors wonder why they aren't as important. You have to eyeball the jury, but use caution and don't show partiality.

### Ways to Handle Opponent's Objections

EDITOR: How do you handle objections?

AJ: As I mentioned before, if I have not been interrupted by my opponent, I am probably not being effective. I want to hear the objection. Of course there are occasions where the judge will side with a particular objection. He may say, "Mr. Julien, I think that is of the nature of summation rather than opening." That ruling is easily handled. I say, "Yes. People of the jury, I mean to prove that." Then I go on with exactly what I was saying before. By adding the magic threshold of words: "I mean to prove that" ... everything becomes admissible.

Ordinarily, I don't recommend saying "I mean to prove," but where it is needed because the court feels more secure in hearing that talismanic phrase, then it must be used. I prefer a good opening ... the telling of a story for instance. I wouldn't say, "We"ll bring a witness here who will tell you ... " I would rather say, "The fact is, this young boy who was killed at sea was doing a job far too much for him. Far too much for any one person. Two or three were needed to do that job." I like that better than, "We will prove to you that it should have been done that way."

Other methods that I have used to handle interruptions from my opponent are, for example, by saying, "I have not interrupted my opponent, although I do disagree with much that he has said to you. I believe we should have the right to speak without interruption as much as possible. Since I did not interrupt him, I am sure that he will not interrupt me." I look at my opponent when I say this. Sometimes that works, other times stronger methods must be used. "Well, I didn't interrupt my opponent, but now he's interrupting me for the fifth time ... for the sixth time and for the seventh!" Once, an opponent said to the court, "I object to Mr. Julien's counting my objections. I want to tell the jury that I have a right to interrupt." The judge said, "Yes. The lawyer does have the right to interrupt. Mr. Julien, please continue." Then I was interrupted again. The judge finally said, "Now that's the eighth time you've been interrupted!"

EDITOR: I imagine you have seen trial lawyers lose cases by *not* using your recommended methods. What about someone taking your advice and using your techniques against you . . . who wins?

AJ: I once had an opponent who "over-played" what I suggest. This was a case involving an alleged stock fraud and the United States government was prosecuting my client. The United States attorney had a copy of my book . . . I knew this before the trial began because they had referred to it in their brief to the court saying: "Mr. Julien usually says more in defense than he's committed to say and I want to stop him before he even starts." The judge looked at the brief and he said, "What else is new?" I knew that they were aware of the book and they were going to use that kind of technique too . . . full disclosure. Now, their case depended upon the testimony of a man (an alleged) co-conspirator who had turned government's evidence in acceptance of a plea bargain. He thought he would receive leniency if he agreed to testify for the government. He had a very bad personal record. He was in the antique business and had stolen, or misused, the proceeds of goods which had been entrusted to him for sale. He had stuck a lot of people; running up bills with everybody. When the people opened, the prosecutor said, "Mr. L. is going to be our principal witness in this case and I want you to know the good as well as the bad." That had a familiar ring to it as I had used phrases like that in my book. He went on, "This man has a bad commercial record." That's where he left it, except he said once his witness had "deep-sixed" some records. When it was my turn, I said to the jury, "I wouldn't have mentioned anything at all about it, but the prosecutor has decided to tell you about his prime witness, Mr. L., but he hasn't told you very much has he? I think you ought to know that this man climbs over partition walls over week-ends to destroy records which his employees are keeping. Also, he stuck hundreds of people by failing to remit monies to them for property that was entrusted to him. The government knows these things, and knows that he's not somebody you can rely on." At this point my opponent stood up and said, "I object to this! Mr. Julien has no right to go into this . . . it isn't material to the case." Whereupon the judge said, "Of course it isn't material, but you opened the door to it, therefore, it is perfectly proper for Mr. Julien to refer to it." I think the prosecution had opened the door and misused the technique which I espouse and he went too far with it. The business of disclosing everything about your case has to be done with a bit of reserve. A good trial lawyer senses what's appropriate and what isn't. When you go too far, you may be bringing in things which your opponent would never have had an opportunity to bring in. Once it is in the open, you'll never have a chance to get it closed.

## The Importance of Timing

Lawyers in the main do not appreciate the importance of timing. Even the cadence, the expression and the tempo employed in language. I speak slowly when I make a speech and even more so during trial. Nobody gets lost. They can keep up with me and comprehend what I'm saying. If you speak too rapidly, you may lose part of the jury. If your voice is constantly on the same level, monotony sets in. You should adjust your voice to that of your opponent. If he or she talks rapidly . . . staccato-like, what a relief it is going to be to the jury when you get up and start speaking in a well-modulated voice; a slower pace, accelerating only when there is a point to be made. The jury that has been bored by your adversary is not likely to be bored by someone who is in contrast.

Timing is so critical throughout the trial: when should you bring in the important witness? What is the best time to introduce the important piece of evidence? If you were to use the time when recess is about to be reached to hit an important point, how wonderful it would be! Just think, to have the jury leave remembering as the last thing that happened in the case, an important piece of evidence that you will capitalize on when it comes time for summation. If it comes, instead, in the middle of the day, surrounded by other things, it gets lost. The jury, already confused, goes home confused. Just before recess is the time to reach the minds of the jurors.

Timing is also vital regarding not only what you say, but how long it takes you to say it. I believe that any opening exceeding forty-five minutes, except in a very unusual case, is probably too long. Likewise, any summation that goes over an hour and a half, and my cases are generally long because they are so complicated and important, is beginning to slide downhill. If there is an occasion where I must take more than the hour and a half to sum up, I ask the Court if we may take a break . . . get some relief, and because of my age, the judge understands what I mean by relief! I'm usually granted that time, and because the jury has been interrupted for a little while, when I get started again, I begin with damages so that I don't lose any climax that I was building previously.

I learned about timing as an actor. I was a terrible actor; in fact, it has been said that I may have had something to do with the killing of vaudeville. Nevertheless, I found this experience to be very valuable later in my life-long profession.

## How Important Are Notes?

EDITOR: Some trial lawyers advocate the use of a notebook for easy reference. Do you keep notes or reference books with you?

AJ: I don't keep notes, but I have notes kept for me. I have an associate with me during trial and he or she takes notes. I do keep memo sheets and references regarding subject matter in advance of trial. I jot down a phrase about something that I want to ask a witness about. I will not be reading anything while I am addressing the Court. I never read notes during opening statement. My mind is fresh at that time. I want to be looking at the jurors. If you have a pad in front of you that you keep looking at, or if you are jotting things down, you detract from the main theme. That's an obstruction. During opening, eye-to-eye contact is the best way to establish a relationship with the jury.

In summation, I sometimes have written-out headings, in other words, one or two sheets before me with subject matter—headings, so that I am sure not to overlook important items. I keep this over to the side, positioned between myself and the jury. Lawyers who do too much writing, harm themselves. You must watch the witness. You must not miss the twist of the mouth, or the tightening of the throat muscles, something vital that is taking place that he or she is reacting to, or you will miss an important chance to use that gesture. It is particularly bad to be wedded to a pad and pencil while jury selection is taking place. You must watch every jury person as he/she moves to the jury box. The way they walk ... the aggressiveness or labile manner of their walk will indicate the difference between possible leaders of the jury and those who just go along with the others.

## How to Lose a Jury

EDITOR: Let's go over your list of losers. You say there are some definite examples of how to lose a jury. What are those?

AJ: The lawyer who begins by saying: "Now, you know neither I nor my opponent was present at the scene ... we didn't see what happened. We don't know all the facts, we only know what we've been told. You will get the testimony from the witnesses. I think they will tell you the following."

It is so much better to be sure of the facts. Better to say, "Now, this is what happened. This is why we are in court." The jury doesn't want to hear that the lawyer doesn't know the facts and is depending on other people to unravel the case. When the lawyer states that there is some doubt, and that this doubt can't be resolved until you hear the witness, the jury loses faith in your ability. That's a sure loser.

The lawyer who uses time-worn expressions, or even up-to-date expressions that are beginning to wear thin like: "the bottom line is" or "you know." The lawyer who has everything written out and insists on reading to the jury. He or she is missing the vital eyeball contact. That's the mirror of the mind; it shows you what that person is thinking. Don't miss that chance!

Remember, there will be many more opening statements than final summations in your career. An opening statement, well delivered, sometimes promotes the very settlement that makes it unnecessary to have summation. That's why we have more of one than the other. Failure to make use of a proper opening statement to win lawsuits indicates that some lawyers are ignoring one of the most potent weapons in the trial strategist's arsenal.

# How to Prepare and Present Effective Opening Statements

## George A. LaMarca

George A. LaMarca is a partner in the West Des Moines, Iowa, law firm of Williams, LaMarca, Maracci & Wiggins, P. C. He received the J.D. Degree from Drake University. He is a member of the Association of Trial Lawyers of America and of the Iowa and Illinois Associations of Trial Lawyers. He is a Fellow of the Iowa Academy of Trial Lawyers and a member of the Board of Governors of the Association of Trial Lawyers of Iowa. Mr. LaMarca is past Trials Editor of *The Iowa Trial Lawyer*.

The opening statement should be an outline of the claim, embellished only by the evidence counsel expects to present as proof of each essential element of that claim. In the opening statement, counsel must begin to sell himself, his client, and his theory of the case to the jury, all without argument—but hasn't it been said that good salesmanship never was argument in the first place?

Your tone of voice and your selection of words should be designed to immediately: (a) capture attention of jury; (b) convey seriousness of case; (c) demonstrate your sincerity; and (d) demonstrate your belief in the case.

Your demeanor, your choice of words, and your method of delivery, of course, are the most important ways you can demonstrate your sincerity and your belief in the case. A short illustration will suffice. For example, consider the persuasive difference in the following introductory phrase:

"*...uhh, I think you will see from the evidence, ladies and gentlemen...*"

as opposed to:

*"Ladies and gentlemen, we will prove to you that . . ."*

The selection of words can make a persuasive difference. For example, if you have a client who has fallen as a result of a defective ladder or scaffolding, never use the phrase, "the plaintiff fell" . . . use the phrase, "the ladder fell", or, "the scaffolding collapsed". The jury will still get the idea of what happened to the plaintiff—the difference is where the suggestion of fault is placed in the minds of the jury as they learn for the first time what happened.

Or consider the differences between these two phrases, when the jury first hears your damage prayer: *"We are asking for $50,000"* or *"We are suing for"* vs. *"We believe the evidence will show we are entitled to $50,000".*

Remember, when organizing your statement and choosing your vocabulary, you must simplify and educate at the same time (and in a brief time). Confusion is deadly to the party with the burden of proof. Therefore, your entire delivery must always be clear and audible, direct, organized, concise, and positive.

### Getting Off to a Good Start

Your opening sentence should be a capsule of the wrong complained (in other words, the entire case in 25 words or less). It should present: (1) what defendant did wrong; (2) what happened to plaintiff; (3) the legal theory of the case; and (4) nature and severity of plaintiff's injuries—all in one stimulating sentence, as the following examples illustrate.

**Product Liability:** Ladies and gentlemen, this case involves John Doe, of Des Moines, Iowa, a 32-year-old press operator who, on April 1, 1976, at the Big Dollar Manufacturing Company, had his right hand amputated at the wrist when the machine at which he was working suddenly and without warning malfunctioned because of a defect in one of its component parts.

**Automobile Rearend:** Ladies and gentlemen, this lawsuit was filed because the defendant's car was following too closely the car being driven by Mrs. Plaintiff, and the defendant was not paying attention to the traffic ahead of him; as a result, Mrs. Plaintiff suffered a ruptured lumbar vertebrae, or what is commonly called a broken back, and she will have this injury the rest of her life.

**Last Clear Chance:** Joseph's case is based on the doctrine of last clear chance—which is, simply, that the railroad personnel operating the train actually saw Joseph in a position of danger and that at that time when the car's movement or dangerous position was obvious, the train personnel had the opportunity and the time to avoid the collision but failed to properly use the emergency braking equipment that this train had. This failure to give Joseph the last clear chance resulted in Joseph's crippling, lifetime injuries that would otherwise never have occurred.

After the opening sentence, counsel should briefly describe the purpose of the opening statement, acknowledging that it is not evidence, but rather a tool for assisting the jury in understanding the order of the trial, legal issues, nature of the proof (evidence), and relative importance of certain evidence to legal issues.

### How to Explain the Order of Trial to the Jury

If permitted, explaining the order of trial to the jury can be vital to their understanding of both the trial process and their duties as jurors, especially in a lengthy or complicated case. For example:

"Before I get into what evidence will be presented in this case, I would like to give each of you an idea on how the case will progress or how the evidence will come before you during this trial. A jury trial in a civil case has four distinct phases.

"Phase One—Once the jury has been selected and sworn in, as each of you has been, the trial starts with the opening statement of each lawyer. These opening statements are not evidence. Lawyers are not witnesses, but representatives. I represent the Plaintiff; Mr. Johnson and Mr. Webster are the lawyers for the defendant. At this time we can only tell you what we think the evidence will be, or what will be demonstrated to you. If, during the trial, you hear or see something different, it is what you determine the facts to be, not what any of the attorneys may say.

"The second phase is the actual presentation of evidence. In a civil case such as this, the evidence is usually from three sources: the first is testimony you will hear from persons called as witnesses; the second is exhibits, or things you can see such as photographs and diagrams; and the third is pre-trial documents, called depositions and interrogatories, that you can both hear and see. These are answers to certain questions asked before trial and answered under oath and reduced to writing. In other words, these are statements of witnesses under oath who will testify, but who may or may not be present here in person in the courtroom.*

---

*This is a good place to advise the jury of deposition testimony and why the deponent is unavailable for trial. Thus, they know in advance that this testimony is equal to all other testimony.

"The third phase is the final argument, which is given by each lawyer after all the evidence for each party has been presented by each party's attorney. Final argument is called an argument, and not a statement, as is this opening statement. It is called an argument because the attorneys are given an opportunity at that time to give our own personal views on what we think the evidence means with respect to the law. In final argument we are allowed to interpret the evidence and give our opinion of what we think certain testimony or certain exhibits prove.

"The fourth, and final, part of the case will be the judge's instructions to each of you on what the law is.

"Lastly, after you have all read the instructions by Judge Fair, you will all go to the jury room where you will decide what the facts are as shown from all the evidence and then apply those facts to the Judge's instructions. This application of the facts that all of you find to the law that you will be given will be called your verdict."

It is also helpful to explain the necessary haphazard order of evidence, and how this opening statement will help them remember how all **parts** of evidence relate to the whole. You might want to use illustrative analogies, comparing the opening statement to the table of contents of a book, the picture on a jigsaw puzzle box, a preview of coming attractions at a theater, or a simple outline.

### Anatomy of a Winning Opening Statement

There are three main parts to an opening statement—liability, injury, and damages.

The first, the liability narrative, is a statement of background and activity which gave rise to injuries. Begin by introducing the players: (1) introduce the parties and their backgrounds; (2) introduce the attorneys; and (3) define the terms 'plaintiff' and 'defendant'.

When carefully prepared and thought out, the liability narrative can be organized to interweave the following:

a) favorable aspects of client's background;
b) background, location, and circumstance of injury-producing occurrence;
c) facts supporting each required element of plaintiff's theory of recovery;
d) definitions of technical terms, a brief explanatory background on technical subjects;

    e) the names of eyewitnesses, their opportunity for observing what happened, and what they heard or observed;

    f) favorable admissions or facts from adverse witnesses obtained from discovery (tell jury how you know this; i.e., depositions, interrogatories, admissions, etc.);

    g) technical experts and their contribution to the facts; and

    h) problems or weaknesses in plaintiff's case, revealed in a way designed to minimize their adverse impact, (be accurate but tactful).

The injury narrative is where you tell the jury what happened to the body of the plaintiff. It should begin with the mechanics of the injury ("this force from the rear caused Mary's head to snap back and then jolt forward into the windshield so hard the safety glass shattered"), and end with the prognosis ("these facial scars are permanent").

    Briefly, describe the anatomy of the injured area or organ, describe the injury using both the doctor's diagnosis and a layman's description, and describe the treatment using both medical and lay terms. For example:

> **Medical** — "Doctor Blair had to perform surgery on this leg; the operation, as you will see from the Mercy Hospital records, is called an open reduction of the tibia and fibula".
>
> **Lay** — "Briefly, what he did, assisted by Doctor Fellows, was to cut open the lower part of the leg so they could see and handle the two lower leg bones that had broken and separated. Then, with their hands, they actually moved the bones back together into their normal position. To hold these broken pieces together while the bones healed, they then drilled holes in the bones with an electric drill so that screws could be screwed into the bones, artificially locking them together".

Other components of the injury narrative are: describing the medication and therapy, stating the prognosis and introducing medical experts or advising of any deposition that will be read due to the necessary absence of any medical expert.

    During the damage narrative, explain that damages are the plaintiff's 'legal losses', and there are separate legal losses from this type of injury to the body. List each separate damage category and tell how the evidence will demonstrate each loss category. The categories are:

    I. Out-of-pocket losses
       a. medical bills
       b. drug bills

    c. property damage
    d. transportation costs
  II. Loss of expected monetary gain
    a. past earnings
    b. future earnings
 III. Human loss—past and future
    a. pain and suffering
    b. mental anguish
    c. inability to enjoy a normal life

**For example:**
    "In our petition that was filed with the court on August 1, 1975, we have stated that we compute Harold Smith's total loss at $40,000. What will the evidence show about how fair is that amount of compensation?
    "The evidence in this case will show you that Harold Smith lost not only $3,212.00 in medical bills and lost not only $1,800 in wages, but that he lost the right to be free from pain, the right to enjoy life as he did before, and the right to be free from worry or mental anguish."

Then briefly outline the expected evidence for each item of damage.

**Inability to Lead a Normal Life:** "There will be testimony from friends that for at least six months after this collision, Harold Smith was unable to enjoy the things he had liked to do before.
    "Each of these witnesses knew and associated with the Smith family before Harold's injuries and also during his recovery. They will tell you the differences in his mood, his recreational activities, and his social activities.
    "These human differences during his recovery period from the time when he was healthy is the measurement or yardstick of a human loss—the law calls it inability to lead a normal life, normal in this case being what Harold Smith was like before he was hurt and laid up."

This combines the legal definition of damage with the facts of damage. This approach lets the jury know that they must start adding up the testimony in dollars and cents, and that a personal injury trial is not a meaningless intrusion into your client's personal and physical activities. You must educate them in advance that there is a purpose for this testimony, and that is to help them with their duty to assess a damage figure for each area of loss.
    Jurors have seen persons injured on TV and recover, they have seen friends hurt and mend; but no one has ever asked them to add all this up in terms of money. And remember, it is money and not sympathy that you

want—sympathy is a mild form of pity; money is a form of compensation for a loss.

Finally, define for the jury the prayer by telling them that it was arrived at by adding up all of the above legal losses, and is what you deem the fair aggregate value or full compensation therefore.

### Courtoom Techniques for Getting Your Message Across

Once the story has been elaborated upon from the capsule sentence, you must explain the importance of certain evidence to the issues and what evidence will resolve those issues favorably to your client. This is done during the liability narrative.

The definition of issues should seem to follow naturally from your narrative; using the rearend case again:

> "I believe you will find that this following too close is in fact what the law calls negligence because we will prove that it is a departure from the ordinary and prudent driving necessary under the circumstances at this busy intersection."

You might want to use a chalkboard or an artist's pad to summarize issues.

Summarize the pleadings. Show how each allegation was answered. Unwarranted or unreasonable denials (in face of abundant evidence) will work to advantage of plaintiff as it will cast doubts on all denials even when there is weak evidence for plaintiff on those allegations.

> "The defendant has denied that he was speeding so in this trial it will be necessary for us to prove that he was going too fast by a greater weight of the evidence. I do not know what evidence defendant will offer to show he was not speeding, but we will let you hear the testimony of Officer Williams, you will see our photographs of the 112 feet of skid marks . . .", and so forth.

You can and you should then refer back to this summary on final argument noting under each issue the witnesses and exhibits supportive on each issue. (The use of an artist's pad for this is again recommended.)

As you present your liability narrative, briefly summarize the essential facts in support of each issue. For example, in a products case state specifically the nature and extent of the defect in manufacture and design that will be proven.

Determine if explanation of technical or medical matters is required in the injury or damage narrative. Remember that the jury may be hearing important words for the first time, it may not know the legal meaning of certain words you are quite familiar with, such as 'mortality table' and its function in helping jury assess damages: or 'prognosis'—tell the jury what it is and why it is important to their deliberations:

> "Prognosis is a medical term for what the future will be like, or, as in Mary's prognosis, how permanently damaged her back will be for the rest of her life".

Use illustrations, photographs, and models as explanatory tools to explain complicated factual statements in liability (enlarged photo of scene or diagram), injury (anatomical model), and damage narrative (list specials).*

### How To Weave The Separate Parts of Your Statement Into a Powerful Whole

The opening statement must be told as a continuous persuasive story with a simple theme—your theory of the case. The organizational ideas I have presented earlier must be correlated into a plan that:

1. tells like a human interest drama;
2. moves with simple logic from the capsule (opening sentence) and shows the inevitable casual connection of:
   a. defendant's conduct (liability narrative),
   b. plaintiff's bodily injury (injury narrative),
   c. plaintiff's legal losses (damage narrative),
   d. jury's duty to award adequate compensation (prayer); and
3. employs transitional language to achieve the objective in points 1 and 2 (above) while persuasively and logically taking the jury from 2a through 2d.

The following examples may be helpful.

> **Transition from Capsule to Defendant's Conduct:** *"Now that we have discussed the purpose of my opening address and we have given you a capsule view of why we are all here, we would like to review with you evidence that you will see and hear that we are certain will prove our case to each one of you".*
> **Transition from Defendant's Conduct and Plaintiff's Bodily Injury to Plaintiff's Legal Losses:** *"We have stated how and why Mary was so seriously*

---

*Be certain these items are not objectionable by prior stipulation, pre-trial order, or faith in both the law and the judge. Also, be certain any illustration (e.g., the scene) is reasonably accurate.

*injured and now it is my duty to tell you what her damages—or legal losses—
have been and will continue to be as a result of this (following too closely or
speeding, etc.), which, in legal terms, is negligence".*

If you have moved in a logical, continuous sequence, all in a persuasive
manner, your pattern of speech will have force—a force that gives off energy known as persuasion, at a time when we know most jurors are susceptible to persuasion—during the opening statement—due to the power
of suggestion.

## What to Say About the Defendant's Case

Briefly anticipate—but do not summarize—defendant's case as learned
from pleadings and discovery. But while doing so, avoid personal attack
on the defendant, counsel for defendant, and the law. As part of the liability narrative you should tell the jury how plaintiff was acting as a reasonable person under the circumstances, and describe evidence that will
prove such conduct. Tell jury that any claim of misconduct must be
proved by greater weight of evidence, and that while you will prove defendant's negligence, defendant must prove their defense of plaintiff's
negligence.

## Checklist of Do's and Don'ts

The above techniques for giving an effective opening statement must be
guided by common sense, tempered by humility, and molded by preparation. And if that isn't enough, remember:

1. Don't overstate your case;
2. Don't apologize for your client or any aspect of case;
3. Don't state as fact something about which there will be no
   evidence;
4. Don't unnecessarily embellish or over-develop any aspect of your
   case;
5. Don't wait for your adversary to be the first one to bring up a weak
   point in your case;
6. Do stress that you are asking jurors for help in reaching a fair result for both sides;
7. Do ask the jury not to reach a decision until it has heard all of the
   evidence and has been instructed on the law by the judge;

8. Do end on a note of fairness, telling jury that you expect to have the opportunity in final argument to comment more fully on the evidence and what you believe to be fair compensation for the plaintiff; and

9. Do convey the idea that you expect to earn the right to receive a substantial award because it is due the plaintiff on the evidence that will be forthcoming.

All the studies on opening statement that I am familiar with confirm that it is well worth the effort to prepare an 'effective' opening statement. Gamblers must always go with the odds, and, after all, if you weren't a gambler you wouldn't have to prepare an opening statement—you would have settled the case when you had a sure thing.

# Strategy for Opening Statement: A Case Study

## Featuring Fredric G. Levin

Fredric G. Levin is a member of the Pensacola, Florida, law firm of Levin, Warfield, Middlebrooks, Mabie & Magie, P.A. His practice is limited to plaintiffs personal injury law. He is a member of the Inner Circle of Advocates and is a Board Certified Civil Advocate by the National Board of Trial Advocacy. Mr. Levin has authored numerous articles on trial tactics and insurance law, and has lectured extensively on the same subjects. He has recently authored a book *"Effective Opening Statements"* published by Executive Reports Corp. Mr. Levin has received many multimillion-dollar verdicts including one for $18,000,000, and another for $13,300,000.

### The Case at a Glance

On November 9, 1977, a Louisville & Nashville Railroad Company train derailed in Pensacola, Florida. Two tank cars carrying anhydrous ammonia ruptured, and the toxic gas leaked onto the nearby property of Dr. Jon Thorshov. As a result of inhaling the gas, Dr. and Mrs. Thorshov died and their two children were permanently injured.

The subsequent wrongful death action, *Thorshov v. Louisville & Nashville Railroad Company*, went to trial in February of 1980. On February 27, 1980, the jury returned verdicts totalling more than $18 million ($10 million of which was for punitive damages) for the deaths of Jon and Lloyda Thorshov. According to Fredric G. Levin, counsel for the plaintiffs, "The case was, for all practical purposes, over after the opening statements."

The plaintiffs' opening statement painted a picture of the defendants wearing black hats, and that was the image the defense labored under for the rest of the trial. To understand how this was accomplished, it is necessary to begin with a brief background of the case.

Pensacola has several major industrial plants which employ thousands, and which are dependent on rail transportation. The Louisville & Nashville (L&N) has served the Pensacola area since the mid-1800's. Starting in 1976, the L&N began having derailments in Escambia County, of which Pensacola is the county seat. The derailments became newsworthy when one caused a major rupture of an anhydrous ammonia tank car in the north Escambia County area and several people were hospitalized as a result. Between the time of the first accident and the deaths of Dr. and Mrs. Thorshov, the news media reported an average of one derailment every month. In one accident, thousands of residents had to be evacuated; another derailment caused an explosion of propane gas and a fire that lasted two days.

In numerous meetings between the City of Pensacola and L&N officials, the L&N maintained that there was no cause for alarm, that the tracks were in excellent condition.

In the summer of 1977, Doctor Jon Thorshov, age 38, his wife Lloyda, age 28, and their two childen (Daisy, age three, and Gamgee, age one) moved to Pensacola. Dr. Thorshov entered into practice as a pathologist, at a salary of $55,000 per year. He was to become a partner after one year, and would have made about $100,000 after taxes in 1979 if he had lived. The Thorshov family was exemplary—the children had been left with a babysitter only once in their lives.

Within a week following the derailment and Dr. Thorshov's death, both the maternal grandparents (Hutchens) and the paternal grandparents (Thorshov), who were the personal representatives for the estate, hired the Pensacola law firm of Levin, Warfield, Middlebrooks, Mabie & Magie, P.A. to file suit against the L&N. The personal injury claims for the two children were severed from the two wrongful death claims.

Plaintiff's attorneys included Fred Levin, D. L. Middlebrooks and Dan Scarritt. Levin was chosen to handle the opening statement.

## Handling the Advantages and Disadvantages of the Case

Levin realized that *Thorshov* was the "ultimate dream case" in many respects: substantial damages, clear liability and deep-pocketed defendants. "But, even the ultimate dream case has disadvantages," Levin heeded. Suprisingly, as the plaintiffs' team developed their theory, they found as many disadvantages in the case as advantages. "The purpose of an effective opening statement," according to Levin, "is to cover the disadvantages in the best light and at the same time present the advantages."

Many of the disadvantages Levin listed were similar to the problems faced in almost any civil case from the plaintiff's viewpoint. For example:

• Pensacola is a railroad town, and the community is extremely conservative. The jurors would not be naturally inclined to award large damages for a handsome, wealthy doctor and his beautiful wife.

• The facts of the accident were complex and technical.

• The jurors would not be sequestered, and the case was to be the most publicized civil case in Pensacola's history. TV cameras would be allowed in the courtroom, and all three networks would carry the trial.

• The defense team was led by Bert Lane, who had an impressive record of defense victories and was well liked by jurors because of his "good old boy," folksy way.

• Plaintiffs did not know prior to trial whether they would be permitted to discuss the facts of specific derailments which had occurred before November of 1977.

• "The Louisville & Nashville Railroad Company had several hundred employees living in the Pensacola area," Levin explained. "Many of these employees were 'old timers' who made excellent defense witnesses, since they would relate well to a local jury." On the other hand, plaintiffs' witnesses were well-educated, bright and quick.

• Seven years prior to the accident, the L&N Railroad had been taken over by the Seaboard Coastline Railroad. Several bright, young, educated executives came over from Seaboard Coastline (SCL) to run the L&N. These new L&N executives also made excellent witnesses.

• Railroad regulations require a railroad to accept every car sent over its line. The tank cars carrying anhydrous ammonia on November 9, 1977, were not owned by L&N, and did not have head shields (extra heavy pieces of metal placed at both ends of the tank cars), even though the federal government had passed a regulation requiring that all tank cars have head shields by January 1, 1980. Although head shields would not have prevented the derailment, they would have prevented the puncture of the two tank cars carrying anhydrous ammonia. It was evident that L&N would argue the common sense position that had it not been for government regulations requiring the L&N to accept these tank cars on its line, the Thorshovs would not have died as a result of the derailment. The owner of the tank cars had not been sued in this case. Although this argument had no real basis in law, it was going to be appealing to the jury.

One of the greatest advantages the plaintiffs had was that "we knew more about the case than defense counsel," Levin told us. "The railroad was unwilling to hire any independent experts to explain how the accident occurred. The railroad relied on its own employees. Defense counsel's opinion as to how the accident actually occurred was limited to the opinion of L&N's own employees. We had hired independent experts, and therefore had a better view of what had actually occurred in the accident. By the time of trial, defense counsel sincerely believed that the railroad had done nothing wrong. This situation created an atmosphere in which we could destroy the defense with an effective opening statement."

Timing was crucial to Levin's opening statement. The defense would be hearing for the first time the plaintiffs' theory of how the accident happened, and Levin did not want to give them a chance to prepare their response. Levin's opening statement ended at 3:30 in the afternoon, and the defense was forced to proceed after only a ten-minute break.

b The following transcript, slightly edited for publication, is accompanied by Levin's comments in italics.

## The Opening Shot

MR. LEVIN: May it please the Court, counsel, Mr. and Mrs. Hutchens, Mr. and Mrs. Thorshov, and you, ladies and gentlemen of this jury. What we lawyers are getting ready to do now is to make our opening statements. And it is here that we tell you what we expect the evidence in the case is going to be, and what we expect the judge is going to tell you the law is at the end of the case. But the opening statement itself is not evidence, and it is not law; it is lawyer talk.

The evidence is going to come to you from the witness stand, and the law is going to come to you from His Honor, the judge.

*How many times has the plaintiffs' lawyer sat down after opening statement and heard the defense counsel say, "What you have just heard is lawyer talk"? The above remarks stole a little of the defendant's thunder. The plaintiffs' attorney should try to diffuse everything that he thinks the defense attorney wants to say in the defendant's opening statement. If counsel for the defendant is a likable individual, an attempt should be made to cover every possible situation that plaintiffs' counsel believes the defendant will attempt to cover in defendant's opening. This will prevent defense counsel from using his likable personality at the start of the case. Of course, the converse is likewise true: If defense counsel has an obnoxious personality, give him the opportunity to show it to the jury.*

## Stressing the Importance of the Case

I would like to congratulate you. You eight people have been selected from what I believe is the largest panel of jurors ever called for a civil case.

And the reason you were selected was because both sides of this case believe that you will be fair and unbiased, in other words, that you will judge this case solely on the evidence and the law.

*Let the jury know just how important the case is. The purpose was to insinuate that the court believes that this must be a very large case or the court would not have called that many, potential jurors.*

I would like to reiterate what the judge has already told you and what he will tell you every evening. And that is if you are watching television or reading a newspaper or listening to a radio, if there is anything that comes on or that you see about this case, about railroads in general, about the L&N, please stop, turn it off, get away from it. If somebody wants to talk to you, whether it is your husband or your wife, parents, children, friends, neighbors, co-workers, tell them you cannot, just cannot talk about this case, because if the judge believes that maybe you will be influenced, he does have the power to sequester the jury. That means he has the power to lock the jury up, and nobody wants that. You don't, the judge doesn't, nor do the lawyers. So if anybody tries to talk to you or if you see anything, please just totally get away from it. Now, this case is going to last, in our opinion, somewhere between three weeks and a month. And it is going to be difficult not to hear things, so again, I urge you to please try to stay away from it.

*We recognized that the jury selected in this case was an excellent plaintiff's jury. The case would last several weeks and the possibility existed that there could be another derailment during the trial. Such an event would be well publicized and could cause a mistrial. In fact, there was a derailment that occurred the day before closing arguments. In addition, we were deeply concerned that the jurors would be influenced by friends, neighbors, family, etc. A general rule to follow is that when asking for tremendous sums of money, outside influence will normally work to the disadvantage of the plaintiff.*

On the defense side of this case for the L&N Railroad are, in my opinion, three of the finest defense railroad lawyers in the country. Mr. Bert Lane is the finest defense lawyer I have ever been up against, and he has been asked to come back out of retirement to try this case. His son Gary is an excellent trial lawyer, and Ms. Dawn Welch, in my opinion, is probably the brightest associate I have seen. But I am not telling you that to gain sympathy for us, because I feel that we are adequate to the task, we are certainly well prepared, and we believe that we are on the right side of the case. And no matter how good you are, you can't change the facts.

*The purpose of the above was to stress the importance of the case and the fact that it was going to be a large case. Complimenting opposing counsel can be a very dangerous tactic if it is insincere. If opposing counsel is not competent, do not compliment him. The worst defeat I ever suffered in a courtroom was when I complimented defense counsel and defense counsel had totally wrecked the defendant's case. In that situation, the jury felt that I was making fun of counsel for the defendant, and the jury sympathized with him.*

### How to Steal the Defendant's Thunder

Now, on November 9, 1977, there was a derailment. Now, as a result of this derailment a young doctor and his lovely wife were killed and two children were very seriously injured. This case involves just the death action, the two cases, one for the death of Jon Thorshov and one for the death of Lloyda Thorshov. The injuries to the children are not being tried at this time. Their condition, though, is going to become important to you in deciding this case.

And you will understand what I mean when I say "condition" by the time I get through with the opening statement.

*Again, I was attempting to steal some of the defendant's thunder. Defense counsel will certainly point out that there are other cases which involve the injuries to the two children. Also, this was an attempt to get the jury ready to understand that the condition of the children will be an issue in the case, whether or not their condition was caused by this accident.*

Now, all of you, all of us have seen criminal cases on television and in the movies, and in those cases you see the criminal defense lawyers and they are exciting and there all kinds of surprises going on, and there is hidden evidence and tactics and delays. Well, that doesn't go on in a civil case. And it's unfortunate, but it's not going to be—we are friends, the lawyers are friends and there are not going to be any fist fights in the courtroom. I saw a movie just recently where the prosecution jumped up and beat the defense lawyer while the judge was trying to call order. That is not going to happen. There is not going to be any cursing in this courtroom. In other words, it is going to be a good, well-tried civil case for damages.

And, I know what must be going through your mind, "Oh, my God, we're going to be here a month listening to this dull civil case." But, if there ever was a civil case, if there ever was a case for damages that was made for television or made for the movies, it is going to be this one be-cause it is going to run the gamut of emotions. When you think of love, and you are going to hear from the witness stand of the love that Jon had for Lloyda and that they had for their children, and it is a true love story. It is the thing that a movie would be made out of. Sympathy, you've got a young doctor and his attractive wife and two beautiful children, well-mannered children, and the doctor and his wife die a horrible death and the children are very seriously injured. And the evidence is going to tear at your heart when you hear the story—well, the psychiatrist will tell you about little Daisy Thorshov, six years old, who sleepwalks at night looking for her mommie and daddy, because she thinks that they were taken from her because she was a bad girl and they will come back if she is a good girl.

*The trial is going to last several weeks and there will be a great deal of technical testimony. The purpose of the above was to tell the jury that the case will be interesting. If you tell someone that the movie they are getting ready to see is a good movie, it is more likely that they will enjoy the movie than if you had told them that it is a horrible movie.*

I think as the evidence comes in you are going to possibly feel disgust toward the railroad. This case—it's not just a simple little accident, it wasn't going too fast or not coming to a complete stop at a stop sign or maybe having a couple of drinks and driving off a road. No, I think you will find in this case that this was the worst stretch of track in the whole L&N system for serious derailments.

*In a deposition of one of the defendant's employees, he mentions (out of context) the fact that Escambia County has been the worst area in the total L&N system for serious derailments. This comment was made in a very lengthy answer to a question propounded by plaintiff's attorney. There were thousands of pages of depositions, and it was hoped that lead counsel for the defendant had no knowledge that the statement had been made. The reader will note that the comment is repeated several times in the opening statement. In the opening statement for the defendant, counsel made the mistake of saying, "The evidence will be that this section of track was one of the best sections of track on the total L&N Railroad system."*

Now, I think you will find in this case that they just didn't care.
You're going to find the case interesting, and being normal people you are going to have normal emotions. But, a month from now when you go into that jury room, you have to leave your emotions behind because a

jury room is no place for emotions. You have got to judge this case on the cold hard facts, the cold hard evidence, and the cold hard law. What I am saying to you is that we don't want any sympathy verdict. Now, again, I think what must be going through your minds, "Here Fred Levin is, he represents the family and he is telling us that they don't want a sympathy verdict. He must be pulling our leg." No, I am sincere when I tell you we don't want a sympathy verdict.

If the railroad was not at fault in this case, you took an oath, and I would hope that you would back up your oath and walk in that jury room and find zero damages for these children. But if the evidence justifies a verdict in the tens of millions of dollars, I hope that you will again abide by your oath and have the backbone to say, "I don't care, I'm going to put it down, because the evidence justifies it."

Now, we don't want a sympathy verdict because as the evidence comes in you will start to see that there are two different philosophies, two different theories. One is the emotional approach. We ought to find enough money to take care of these children to cover their needs for the rest of their lives. But that is not the law, that is a sympathy verdict. That is charity and we don't want charity. And the law says we're not entitled to get that. The other side of the coin is that you should award damages for the fair value of what has been taken, and there is a big difference between what these children need and the fair value of what has been taken from them.

*Plaintiff should always tell the jury that he does not want a sympathy verdict. This is simply stealing defendant's thunder. The most important purpose of the above was to begin to explain to the jury the difference between "taking care of the children" and following the law and awarding "the fair value of what has been taken from the children." The natural tendency of a jury in a death case is to take care of those left behind. Sometimes, this can work to the advantage of the plaintiff. However, in this case, what was taken was substantially more than what the children needed.*

### When to Mention a Dollar Amount

For example, we believe that the evidence in this case will show that Jon Thorshov, the doctor, had he not been killed on November 9th, 1977, and had he lived out his normal life expectancy, which would have been about 33 or 34 years from the date of the accident—approximately 31 years from now—that during that period of time, considering inflation, he would have made over $20,000,000. This will come to you from professors of economics. Well, children don't need that kind of money, and we know they don't need that kind of money. The law says, and you have taken an oath to follow the law, that you should award what you believe has been taken, which is the fair value of what has been taken from them.

The evidence in this case will show that Jon and Lloyda Thorshov were two of the finest parents that you could ever imagine. Those children, the two children were left with a babysitter one time in their life. They were left without at least one parent with them one time in their life. They were devoted to their children. Now, children don't need, they really don't need parents that are that devoted or that wonderful, but that is what has been taken from these children, and that is what you will be asked to replace. Now, at the end of this case we're going to ask you for approximately $12,000,000 for the compensatory damages, that is, the damages for what has been taken. And I am here to tell you that two children don't need $12,000,000, but if you find that that is the value of what has been taken, then you have taken an oath to award that kind of money. So, when I tell you we don't want a sympathy verdict, we don't want charity, I am sincere. I want you, we ask you to follow the law.

*Do you mention a dollar amount in the opening statement when you're going to talk about extremely large sums of money? In this case, we thought so. This case was going to receive tremendous publicity. It would have been impossible for the jurors to totally avoid the publicity. We felt that the media should refer to the case as a multi-million dollar case, and in order to do this, the figures needed to be mentioned in opening statement. In fact, every mention of the case included the adjective "multi-million dollar."*

*It was easy to discuss the amount we were requesting of $12,000,000 when reference could be made to the fact that the deceased would have earned over $20,000,000 during his lifetime. However, this is a dangerous tactic in some cases. For example, assume the case involved the death of a child. In such a case, it would probably be a mistake to mention that plaintiffs were demanding $3,000,000. That evening, when the juror gets home and mentions $3,000,000 to his or her spouse, neighbors, etc., someone is going to start talking about insurance rates, profiteering over the loss of a loved one, etc. As a general rule, mention substantial figures in opening statement only when it can be logically justified with actual economic losses.*

### Explaining the Burden of Proof

Now, the judge is going to tell you that we have the burden of proof in this case, that is, the Thorshov family must prove their case to you by the greater weight of the evidence, and that means exactly what it says, greater weight, 51 precent of the evidence. I like to look at it as the scales of justice. On one side of the scales is our evidence, on the other side is theirs. Which weighs the most in your mind? If you would think about football, if there is a football score 21 to 20, the team that got 21 points wins. We don't have to wipe them out, we don't have to beat them 21 to nothing. In other words, it is simply the greater weight, 51 percent of the evidence. And we don't have to prove anything beyond a reasonable doubt because that is the test for a criminal case, and no matter what you do a month from now nobody is going to go to jail. No matter what you do in this case, no matter how much money you award, nobody is going to go to jail. It is not a criminal case, it is a civil case for damages.

*Always tell the jury that no one is going to go to jail and that no one is going to lose his job because of the case and the verdict. Note that I forgot to mention that no one was going to lose his job. This proved to be a mistake. The case was against the L&N Railroad and the engineer. The engineer was a resident of Florida and was made a party to prevent the removal to Federal Court. When the jury returned a verdict in this case, it found against the railroad but found no negligence on the part of the engineer. As will be seen, a substantial part of the negligence attributed to the railroad was in the actual operation of the train by the engineer. The jury's finding for the engineer on the negligence count could have been critical had the case gone to an appellate court. Therefore, where appropriate, always tell the jury that the defendant is not going to lose his job, and that no one is going to go to jail.*

### Drawing the Jury into Your Case

Now, what is the evidence going to show? I think you are going to have to back up many, many years where the evidence starts in Minneapolis, Minnesota. Mr. and Mrs. Roy Thorshov. Mr. Thorshov was a very successful and *is* a very successful engineer and architect. They are Norwegian and his father before him was an architect-engineer, and it was expected that their son, that the Thorshov's son was going to be an architect-engineer. He was born on February 27th, 1939. His name was Jon, J-o-n. At the start he was going to be an architect-engineer like his father, but by the time he got into the second or third grade he decided he was going to be a doctor. He was an outdoor-type boy, a loving boy, his family was very proud of him. He was extremely bright. You will see some poems that he wrote, and to be perfectly honest with you, half of the words in there I had to go look up in a dictionary. I mean, he was just an extremely bright young man. He graduated from the University of Minnesota High School, and then he went to the University of Minnesota College and graduated there, and then to the University of Minnesota Medical School where he graduated in 1964. He then joined the Air Force and he went into the Air Force and he continued his training, and he became licensed as a pathologist, a medical doctor with the United States Air Force.

*(I am beginning the narrative which paints the plaintiffs with white hats).*

About ten years after Jon was born, in a little town called Rangely, Colorado, in the ranch area, Lloyd and Phillis Hutchens had a little girl. They came from a middle-class background, were not wealthy people, and they had this daughter, and her name was Lloyda, and it's L-l-o-y-d-a, and she was born on October 5, 1949. Now, she graduated from high school and did not go to college. She joined the Air Force and became an x-ray technician. And while they were both in the Air Force, the doctor in the doctor's office, and Lloyda in the x-ray office as a technician, they met each other and started dating and they fell in love. But as usual, what occurred was the doctor, or the officer, leaves town and she was left there at the Air Force base. Jon was shipped off to Germany, and he was in Germany about three weeks and got leave and decided that he loved her, came back to the states and got Lloyda, and said, "Marry me." She did and they took off and went to a judge's office and got married.

*Pensacola is a military town. One of the jurors in this case was a very attractive, single lady in her late 20's. The typical situation in a military community is for the young officer to date the local beauties. Normally, the officer has a good time and then ships out, leaving the young lady behind. The purpose of the above was to show that Dr. Thorshov was not the typical officer, and we hoped that this might have some effect upon the young, attractive female juror.*

As soon as she got out of the Air Force she came to live with him in Germany, and about a little over a year after they got married their first child, Daisy, was born. And she was born November 12, 1973. And then about three years later on May 23, 1976, they had their first and only son Gamgee, which is G-a-m-g-e-e. Jon was then a lieutenant colonel in the Air Force. And then in 1977 an old friend of his, a very good friend of his, Dr. Michael O'Brien, called him, and Dr. O'Brien told him of an excellent opportunity here in Pensacola at the Medical Center Clinic. And Jon and Lloyda Thorshov came to Pensacola with the family, looked it over, and decided to accept the position. Within one year he would have been a partner in the Medical Center Clinic. He was that good. He joined the

Medical Center as an associate on August 1, 1977. This was after he left the Air Force. He remained in the Air Force reserve.

Jon, Lloyda and the two children loved Pensacola. They bought a beautiful home out on Scenic Highway out overlooking Gull Point. It is up on a cliff and it overlooks Escambia Bay, and down below the cliff runs the railroad, and they loved the trains. Jon used to come home early so that they could take the children down to the cliff and look at the train come by. They did everything together; they went shopping together; they went to the movies together; everywhere they went the whole family went together. Jon built pens, he was an outdoor type, for rabbits and chickens for the children there at the home. The family was happy, they were making friends, and everybody who met them were impressed. They were impressed because they were the perfect family.

All but Gamgee were in excellent health. Jon and Lloyda and Daisy were in excellent health. Gamgee had been having some kidney problems with one kidney, and they were hopeful that with medication, possibly surgery, this would be corrected.

On Wednesday, November 9, 1977, Jon was off work, and as usual, he came home and the whole family went early Christmas shopping. The family automobile was a new pickup truck, it wasn't a Mercedes, it wasn't a Cadillac, but a new pickup truck for him and the family. And they went out shopping, and they came home about 5:00. Lloyda began preparing hamburgers for Jon and Daisy and Gamgee, and about 6:05 they heard the train coming north heading up toward the Escambia Bay trestle, coming toward Gull Point. The hamburgers were in the oven, there were vegetables on the stove and she was preparing the hamburger buns. Daisy was eating an apple, and on the radio was WMEZ. Anyhow, they were listening to WMEZ, easy listening music, and at that moment I cannot imagine that they felt that they were ever safer in their lives than they were at that particular moment, nor could they have felt that they could be any happier than they were at that particular moment.

*The above was an attempt to bring the jury into the story that was being told. Note that several unimportant details are mentioned in the same manner that one would do in a normal conversation. Of course, the reference to the pickup truck, not being a Cadillac or a Mercedes, was made for the purpose of trying to show that this was not the typical wealthy doctor.*

### How to Set the Stage for Your Evidence

Now, we're going to have to back up again to pick up the evidence, except this time we have got to go way back, way before any of us were ever born. Many, many years ago the L&N, or whatever it was called then, decided to run their tracks into Pensacola from Alabama. The railroad tracks, and I am not too good of an artist, but I am going to try as best I can, came out of Alabama, came south through Century and Molino and Barth and on into the, what they call the Goulding yards now, which is a little north, this is north up here (indicating), up Fairfield and came down into downtown Pensacola and then—well, they built the passenger station, which I will mark right here (indicating), it turned east. As the tracks continued it crosses Ninth Avenue, then the 14th Avenue crossing, then the 17th Avenue crossing, then that little trestle that goes over the Bayou on down the beach and then it swings back north, and it starts heading north up until it gets to Gull Point, and then it makes a sharp turn left and heads on up.

*As I was giving the above directions, I was drawing a map on the board in order to make it more understandable for the jury. The significant parts of the above remarks were the references to Molino, Barth, and the 17th Avenue crossing. There had been a major derailment in the Barth area some time prior to the accident which injured a number of people. This particular derailment could not be referred to at trial. There had been another major derailment subsequent to the Gull Point derailment in Molino, which likewise could not be mentioned at trial. Also, there had been a major derailment at the 17th Avenue crossing which required the evacuation of thousands of people. Without mentioning the derailments, it was hoped that the jury would recall them by simply mentioning the area and writing the names of those areas on the board.*

Now, it is underneath the Interstate to the Escambia Bay trestle which crosses over the Escambia Bay. And the directions I had given you are correct, the railroad goes south then east then north until it gets to Gull Point and makes a sharp turn to the left and goes up.

Now, when we talk to the railroad people about direction, any time that train leaves Alabama and starts into Florida, no matter what direction it is going, it's heading south. So, when they are on the stand and they say, "Well the train, we were heading south, railroad south at the time," they were actually going north. Now, we will try to keep it straight and we will try to get them to remember that it is geographic north, heading north, even though it's railroad south. A lot of us who drive a lot realize that, for example, I guess the Pensacola Bay Bridge is actually north and south, but it's called 98 East and 98 West. Anyhow, when the train was going up around Gull Point, it was going geographic north, but the railroad people say it was going railroad south. It continues railroad south until it gets to Chattahoochee, Florida, at a place called River Junction, which is the Chattahoochee River. And at that point the railroad tracks belong to the Seaboard Coastline Railroad, it's turned over to them.

*The above was simply to give the background and to explain some rail-road terminology. The opening statement is the place to explain any termi-nology problems.*

For years passenger and freight trains came through Pensacola, and as kids we used to wave at the engineer and he would blow his horn and at the station when the crew would get off, the passenger station, I re-member, you used to look at them the way today in an airport you look at the airline crew, the captain and the co-captain, and the stewardess getting off, there was just this air about them. But times change and in the 1960s it became necessary to stop passenger service through here and we only had freight. And the L&N always made good money, it was always a good railroad. The tracks were well maintained. The old time railroad people wore their railroad caps with pride, and they wore those striped baseball type hats with the big red L&N.

*The above was mentioned for the benefit of any jurors who felt close to the railroads. We knew that none of the jurors had any present connections with railroads or railroad employees. However, it was recognized that some of the jurors, especially the older ones, had to have had some connec-tion with railroads or railroad employees in the past. This was simply an attempt to contrast the wonderful old railroad with what was now becom-ing a corporate giant that was only concerned with making money.*

Now, while all of this was going on in Pensacola, over in Jacksonville, Florida, there were some other things occurring. There was a railroad called Seaboard Airline Railroad, and they had a bunch of bright young good college-educated executives, and they got together with a railroad called the Atlantic Coastline Railroad and merged, forming the Seaboard Coastline Railroad. And the Seaboard Coastline Railroad Company, or holding company, or whatever it is, started buying up other companies. And they called themselves the family company or the family line, and when we speak of the SCL, that is who we are talking about. And during this case you will hear us refer to the Seaboard Coastline Railroad or the SCL, and they started looking over toward the L&N because the L&N was very profitable, very well maintained, and its employees were very happy. And in the 1960s they started buying up stock, the SCL started buying up stock in the L&N and by December 31, 1971, they had 98.2 percent of the stock. And by early 1972 they had bought 100 percent, they had total control of the L&N Railroad.

*1972 was a critical date, as would be shown by the testimony. In an economic analysis of the L&N, maintenance expenses took a tremendous*

*drop in 1972 and continued on through 1977. As a practical matter, the Sea-*
*board Coastline Railroad had control of the L&N since 1967. The purpose of*
*the above was to stress the year 1972 as the year of the takeover. This was a*
*very significant part of the theme of the case. We recognized that defense*
*counsel did not understand the significance of the year 1972. Note that this*
*was being weaved into the general narrative about the background of the*
*railroad. By the time defense counsel realized the significance of the*
*takeover in 1972, it had been mentioned so many times in evidence that it*
*was too late to do anything about it.*

And then the Seaboard Coastline Railroad started sending the bright
young executives over to Louisville to help run the L&N. And they set
down some new policies, and those policies were, "We need to save on
maintenance. For every dollar you can save on maintaining our tracks, it
moves over into profit."

Of course, the old time L&N people said, "What about our safety
rules? They require that we spend a lot of money on maintenance." And
they started talking about this, especially in this day and time when trains
were getting heavier, the chemical cars were getting larger.

MR. LANE: Your Honor, we object to this line of discussion. What the
L&N spent on maintenance has absolutely nothing to do with this case
except on that line of track that went around Gull Point; but what it spent
in Louisville or Oregon or Chicago, or Atlanta, has absolutely nothing to
do with this case.

THE COURT: Objection overruled.

MR. LEVIN: And they began spending less and less money. And they,
of course, like the old L&N people said, "What about our safety rules, and
the old safety rules require that we spend money on maintenance because especially nowadays when the tracks were under heavy trains,
heavy cars, chemicals, things like that." And most of these rules, these
safety rules, are by the L&N and by the AAR—the AAR is the American
Association of Railroads—and this organization consists of all the railroads in the country.

*There were many rules and rulebooks developed by the L&N and the*
*American Association of Railroads. The above is an attempt to distinguish*
*between the old time L&N employees and the new young executives that*
*came over from the Seaboard Coastline. As one can see, the theme of the*
*case is starting to develop. We begin to see the picture of the money-*
*grabbing corporate giant coming in and taking over this wonderful old rail-*
*road back in 1972. The attempt is to make the old time L&N employee an*
*example of what is good about railroads. Note the technique of using an*

*alleged conversation in the above. If the lawyer feels comfortable using this technique, it can be very effective.*

Almost all of these rules concern preventing derailments. Now, a derailment is when a train leaves the track and most derailments occur in a curve. And most derailments are caused by a thing called lateral forces. As you drive a car around a curve there is a force trying to throw you off the curve. Now, when I was in school they called it centrifugal force, but what we are talking about today and we will be talking about for the next month is a thing called lateral forces. Things that will try to derail the train, and that is what most of these rules were for.

*The above is simply definitions. Never assume that a jury understands everything that you understand. The word "derailment" could probably not be defined by 50% of the population.*

*At this point in the opening statement, we had a blackboard in front of the jury. On the board were twelve numbered items. Number one was "heavy train." Number two was "wide gauge." Number three was "bad ties," and so on for twelve specific items. This was a visual display of what we contended were the twelve things that contributed to causing the derailment. In fact, there are over 50 different things that could contribute to a derailment. We decided that the 12 situations would be stressed in opening statement as if there were only 12 possible things that could cause a derailment. We thought that since the L&N employees had convinced defense counsel that nothing was wrong, defense counsel would probably be totally unaware of how many different possibilities existed that could cause derailments.*

*Violations*

1 Heavy train
2 Wide gauge
3 Bad ties
4 Loose spikes
4 Light cars in front
6 Long car-short car in front
7 Super elevation
8 Super elevation runoff
9 131-pound rail
10 Six-axle locomotive
11 Speed limits
12 Braking in a curve

And these rules concern 12 things, the rules that we will be talking about. There are 12 things that can cause a derailment. There are 12 things that can create what we call these lateral forces. And the first one up there is the heavy train, and there are rules against trains that are too heavy. AAR and the L&N have rules. As a locomotive comes into a curve it starts turning. Well, as the locomotive is turning it is not moving as fast forward as the train is behind it, and obviously the more weight you have behind it, the more chance that locomotive has of getting pushed off of the outside rails. And the L&N and the AAR both have rules against that.

The gauge between tracks, it is 56½ inch gauge between the two rails. This is an exact thing and it has been the same for years and years and years. Now, the L&N has a rule, and that is if that gauge gets to 57 inches we've got to correct it, and the reason we've got to correct it is if that train is able to shake back and forth it starts to create more lateral forces. It is the same situation as pushing a car back and forth to get it to move. And the L&N had rules about that.

Bad ties, which is the third thing up there. The L&N has rules, and it has a rule about bad ties. A tie is the timber, the pieces of wood upon which the rail is fastened. And the L&N has a rule that if that tie is bad and rotten we've got to take it out. That is the old time L&N safety rules, and it is still in existence today, and it says we've got to put in new timbers. And then you will hear about the FRA, and Federal Railroad Administration, the Federal Government who governs these railroads. Now, they say they've got minimum, minimum rules. They say, "L&N, you can have a rotton tie and you don't have to do a thing in the world about it, but if you have three totally rotten ties together, you've got to replace one of them." In other words, they can abide by the federal rules by having two rotten ties, one good tie, two rotten, one good, two rotten, one good for the whole line. And so those are the rules in regard to ties.

Now, spikes. The L&N has rules about their spikes. Now, the spikes, you've got a rail, and under the rail is a thing called a tieplate that holds the rail. And these tieplates have these big heavy metal spikes that are driven into the tieplate, into the timber that holds the rails and tries to maintain the gauge. Well, L&N has rules and those rules are, don't let those spikes get too loose. Don't let it be where a train can ride along and the spikes just jump out. And they also have rules that on certain curves, if it's a real sharp curve, you've got to put a certain number of spikes in there to make sure you can hold that rail down.

And then the L&N and the AAR have two rules about train makeup, and that is five and six. The L&N and the AAR say that on a heavy freight train, which we will be involved with in this case, don't ever put light cars up next to the locomotive. Don't put a light car up next to the locomotive with the heavy train behind it because it will again create excessive lateral forces, and the computers tell them this. And then the L&N and the AAR have very strong rules about this long car-short car hookup. They say—and their rules are definite—on a very heavy freight train such as this, don't put a long car-short car hookup next to a locomotive because as they apply the brakes it has a tendency to pop off the track.

As you drive a car around a highway, a major highway, you notice it's banked. Well, railroads have the same thing. When they go around a curve they have a thing called super elevation, and that means the outside rail is higher than the inside rail. They call that super elevation. And the L&N has rules, and they've always had rules that if they design a curve for a super elevation of three and a half inches they must maintain it because the computer says that exact super elevation is necessary for the speed to go around that curve.

And then they have this thing called super elevation runoff. Now, the L&N has a very specific rule that you cannot allow that super elevation in the curve, the high outside rail, to run off into the tangent track. Now, tangent track is straight track. In other words, if you had tracks leading up to the curve this is called tangent, straight track. The L&N rules say under no set of circumstances can you let that run off into the tangent. And the reason for that is, as you can tell if you're riding along on a straight track and it lifts you up and you shift the weight down and you're on this rail as you start around the curve, you've thrown your weight from here to there, the same as rocking a car creating lateral forces and creating a situation that could cause you to overturn a rail.

*I continued to explain each of the twelve numbered items on the board. At this point, I drew freehand a picture of a rail to show the head of the rail and the web of the rail.*

### Driving Your Points Home One by One

Now, the next thing is the 132-pound rail. This is the head of the rail and this is the web, and up until 1947 the standard rail in this country was called 131-pound rail. Now, what that meant was that for every one yard of rail it weighed 131 pounds, and over the '20s and 1930s and 1940s they started realizing in the late 1930s that these rails were breaking, the head was breaking away from the web and they started having troubles. And so the American Railway Engineering Association, and you will hear them talk about the AREA, that is their own engineering association, said back in the 40s, "We have got to do something to stop this." So, they added some weight, one pound per yard at the head and web to increase the strength of it. And it did a good job and it became known as 132-pound rail, and they never again, never again made 131-pound rail since 1947 in this country. But there is a lot of it still in use, and on those tracks where they have 131-pound rail it requires an eye inspection, they walk along with a mirror and they inspect the rail to make sure cracks are not forming.

And then in the late, I guess, the late 1960s, these trains started becoming heavier and these four-axle locomotives, you will hear a lot about four-axle and six-axle locomotives. An axle has two wheels, so if you were looking at the side of a locomotive going past you, a four-axle locomotive would have four wheels facing you. Well, then because the trains were getting bigger and they needed to have bigger locomotives they made a six-axle locomotive; and that is a tremendous thing, it weighs almost 400,000 pounds, and it has six wheels on each side. But, when they started using these six-axle locomotives they began to realize that these six-axle locomotives were causing the outside rails to overturn in some curves, not the four-axle, but the six-axle. And so the industry, the railroad industry, suggested slow the speeds down. If 35 miles an hour was a safe speed around a curve for a four-axle, then we ought to reduce the speed for the six-axle.

Now, there are only two rules about the operation of a train, and that is number 11 and 12.

Speed. Obviously the faster you go around a curve the more lateral forces you're going to create. And the L&N has some very, very specific rules in regard to speeding. They will tell you if they catch an engineer going one mile over the speed limit, some of them say we fire him, others say we discipline him strongly. And there is a reason for that, a strong reason for that, because whereas 55 miles per hour on the interstate highway is the maximum legal speed, it is not the maximum safe speed. You could drive 70 miles an hour, we could five years ago, and it was a safe speed to drive. But on a railroad track they determine what the maximum safe speed is and the engineers are told to drive at that speed, don't go over it. Don't go over it because the computer says it can cause problems. In other words, you're driving at the fastest maximum speed, you've got speed limits and that is what you follow.

And, of course, braking in a curve. That is just good common sense, and all engineers realize that. You don't throw on your brakes in a curve. Now, all of these rules are rules that were created by the old time L&N employees, and even recently the old time L&N employees that remained there kept making these safety rules.

*Some of the L&N rulebooks were written in 1974. This is counter to the theme of the case that the new SCL-L&N employees, after taking over in 1972, were interested only in making money. We had to prevent defense counsel from pointing out that many of the rulebooks were written after the takeover. As will be seen later, we point out a reason for the rulebooks to have been written as late as 1974. This will be discussed under the new bonus plan.*

And these rules are sent down to all L&N employees. But then the SCL executives who had come into the L&N went around to the L&N executives that were making these rules, and they would tell the L&N people it cost money to rearrange a train and take the light cars off of the front and put them in the back. It takes money to take a long car-short car out of a train and put it in the back. It costs money to slow a train down, it costs money to maintain gauge, ties, timbers. It costs money if we don't put enough weight, the more weight we put on a train the more money we make. And we can get more speed if we run off that super elevation onto the tangent track. Of course, the L&N people who had been there for years asked, "What about the safety rules that we have?" Well, the new SCL-L&N executives said, and you will hear it time and time again from that witness stand, "That is not a rule, that is a guideline." So they came in and told them to disregard these safety rules, these are guidelines. Well, some of the L&N people asked, "What is a guideline?" and the new SCL-L&N people came up with an answer for that. They said, "Those guidelines don't apply in Pensacola, Florida, it doesn't apply down here, it only applies to the rest of the L&N system." And so the L&N people here locally, they understood it.

*After the derailment, the L&N employees were called to testify before the National Transportation Safety Board. The L&N recognized that there had been several violations of their own rulebooks. All of the employees began testifying at the NTSB hearings that these "rules" were simply guidelines. When we took the depositions of L&N executives and asked why the guidelines weren't followed, the answer was that the guidelines only applied in the mountainous regions of Kentucky and West Virginia. The above was an attempt to point out to the jury how ridiculous the L&N's position was.*

So, in 1972 the SCL took over the L&N , and the rules were no longer rules and the guidelines just didn't apply down here in Pensacola, Florida. And we began to see the L&N stop spending money in 1972, less and less for maintenance. And you're going to be amazed at how much they saved when you take the inflation out of their dollars and you compare dollars to dollars, oranges to oranges, how much they started saving in 1972, '73, '74, '75, '76, '77, and that is when this case occurred, in '77. And whereas nobody ever heard of derailments before—when you stop spending money on maintenance and safety, eventually it's going to catch up with you. And then about 1975 trains started going off the track. Ammonia started escaping, and then it went into '76 and '77. The City of Pensacola officials became outraged and they turned to the L&N and they said, "Straighten out this mess, at least tell us what it is all about."

*There would be testimony from officials of the City of Pensacola showing that they had warned the L&N. Note that this is being accomplished in dialogue form, rather than by saying, "The evidence will be that the City of Pensacola complained."*

Well, the bright L&N-SCL people came in and they said, "We've got great track, we've got great maintenance, don't interfere with something you don't understand." And the L&N people were convincing. Now, when they were telling the city this story, the L&N knew that this was the worst stretch of track in their whole system for serious derailments, right here. But they convinced the City of Pensacola.

*Again I stressed that this was the worst stretch of track in the total L&N system for serious derailments.*

And the L&N said, "Look out there from the 17th Avenue to the Escambia Bay trestle. In January, 1975, we put in all new 132-pound welded rail." What they didn't tell the City of Pensacola was that when they laid that rail down they didn't put in new timbers, they were rotten. They just laid it right on down, they put down that 132-pound welded rail and they didn't maintain it. There is not one piece of evidence that they did any maintenance on it for two and a half years.

*One of the key points that the defense will argue is that two years before the accident, the L&N changed the rail from 100-pound jointed rail to 132-pound welded rail. We needed to steal their thunder and show that there was no evidence that they put in new ties, nor would there be any evidence of any maintenance on the rail after it had been laid.*

And they also forgot to tell us that when the L&N people put these 132-pound rails together up there in Tennessee or Kentucky, they've got over on one side 132-pound rail and on the other side 131-pound rail. When it came time to put this rail together for Gull Point they sent a guy over to get some of that 131-pound rail, and even though they just put it in one section, but it was a 40-foot section of rail that had been made in 1943, and they decided to put this directly in front of Dr. Jon Thorshov's home. It was a 40-foot strip, and it becomes important as we go along to remember just exactly what they were telling the people of Pensacola. The L&N knew they were telling everybody all of these good things, and at the same time they knew it was the worst area in their whole system for serious derailments.

The L&N knew ammonia was escaping, and they knew ammonia burns, and they knew ammonia causes people to have difficulty breathing. And the train crew will come in here and will testify, and they will tell you if there is an accident where ammonia escapes, that if the L&N would have spent the money to give them air packs, oxygen masks that they would carry—every one of the train crew that comes in here will tell you, "If the L&N would have trained me and they would have given me the air packs, I would have gone up there to Dr. Jon Thorshov's home, and I would have tried to save them." And as the evidence will show, they could have. But the L&N will say, "That costs money, what's the matter with ya'll, it costs money to put *air* packs on a locomotive. We would not only have to put them on the front locomotive, we would have to put them on the caboose, and then we would have to train all five of these people."

*When the crew was questioned on deposition, they could only answer that they would have attempted to save the people if they had had air packs. Again, reference is made to the fact that safety costs money and the new L&N was not going to spend money on safety.*

Well, finally by 1975, somewhere around there, SCL in Jacksonville started getting a little upset at these old-time L&N people that kept making these new safety rules, and they figured, "We've got to do something about these old time people at the L&N in Louisville." So they came up with a little thing called a bonus plan. Now, this bonus plan was for certain key employees, certain L&N executives and key employees, and they went to them and they told them, they said, "If you can produce more profit, we'll give you a bonus of up to 50 percent of what you're making. If you're making $40,000 a year and you can make us more profit, we will give you another $20,000 a year on top of it." Well, they got through, they made their point. And the L&N key employees and executives began to realize what it was all about under the new L&N, the family line: you make money.

*There had to be a reason given to the jury as to why they continued to make new rules up until 1975, even though the takeover was back in 1972.*

*The reason was that the old time L&N employees continued to make the rules until the new executives put in the bonus plan. It is interesting to note that counsel for the defendant had no knowledge of the bonus plan. It was uncovered by plaintiff's counsel in an L&N bond prospectus which was obtained through a stock brokerage house. A decision had to be made whether to use this in opening statement or to hold it for the summation. The reasons for using it in opening were twofold: First, it was necessary to use it to make sense out of the general theme of the takeover by the corporate giant in 1972, and yet safety rules continued to be made up until 1975. Second, it was part of the overall strategy to overwhelm counsel for the defendant in opening statement.*

And there is this thing called per diem, and you will hear a lot about per diem in this courtroom. Per diem is when you go to a crossing and you see an L&N train go by, you start to see cars from the B & O, the Chessie System, The Union Pacific, the Southern Pacific—well, at midnight, every night, whoever has those cars on their system, they pay per diem, they pay rent on those cars.

Now, this doesn't mean the locomotives, there is a different price for that. And the per diem on an average train is $10,000 a day. Now, the L&N people began to realize—on train number 407, we can pick up those cars in New Orleans after midnight, take them all the way through Pensacola, through Santa Rosa County and get them to River Junction and Chattahoochee before midnight and, you know, you can save $10,000. And on number 407 they started doing that. Now, recognize that the L&N does turn the train over to the Seaboard Coastline at Chattahoochee, but the Seaboard Coastline, even though they own the L&N, is a separate company, and the L&N profits would start to look better. And the crew on train number 407 realized very well what per diem was.

*(The per diem was not going to be a surprise to counsel for the defendant. In some situations, it might have been well to have saved this point for summation. However, it was consistent with the strategy of the case to put everything possible in opening statement. At this point in the opening, the total background had been presented to the jury. Everything had been brought up to the point of the day of the accident. The theme of the case had now become evident to everyone in the courtroom. The board with the 12 violations was still in front of the jury and remained there as I began to tell the jury about the accident.)*

### A Dramatic Tale to Capture The Jury

And now for the first time, no matter what you've read or what you've heard, we believe you are going to hear what actually occurred.

On Wednesday, November 9, 1977, the train was scheduled to leave Goulding yard at 4:00 o'clock. As it started to pull out they had brake problems and it had to be delayed an hour and a half. And train number 407 actually left Goulding yard at 5:31, and started heading down through Pensacola.

On the locomotive in the front, the engineer was Walter Brewer; the reserve engineer was Jerry Phillips; the brakeman was Wayne Johnson; and on the caboose at the rear of that train was Warren Kelly, the conductor, and Charles Martin, the flagman.

Now, Mr. Brewer well understood this train was an hour and a half late already. He well understood per diem—I mean to tell you he well understood per diem—since the L&N about five months before then said, "We aren't going to run those four axles anymore, we're going to run those six axles," and that was on May 29, 1977, about five months before this accident. And Mr. Brewer knew what to do because he had been speeding regularly on train number 407. And the railroad knew it and they didn't say a word about it.

*Plaintiffs' counsel had evidence that 80% of the time that train number 407 ran during the five months preceding the accident, it must have been speeding at some point during the run. Also, there was evidence that Mr. Brewer must have been speeding 80% of the time he ran train number 407. These records were obtained from the L&N and analyzed by plaintiffs' computer. The inference could easily be drawn that the L&N had the same knowledge that the plaintiff had.*

So 407 left Goulding with three locomotives, three six-axle locomotives, the train was a mile and a half long and there were nine thousand trailing tons not including the weight of the locomotive.

Now, there was a 10-mile-per-hour speed limit through Pensacola, and as far as Mr. Brewer was concerned that continued until the caboose crossed 17th Avenue. As far as the railroad it was when the caboose crossed Blount Street, and then it went to 15. But as far as Mr. Brewer knew and what Mr. Brewer testified to, that he was to run that train at 10 miles an hour until the caboose crossed the 17th Avenue trestle. And Mr.

Brewer knew the city police, like the city of Pensacola, was looking out for him, and he knew if he went by the Blount Street crossing and the 14th Avenue crossing and the Ninth and the 17th Avenue crossing there could be a police car there, and they've got radar guns, so Mr. Brewer knew to keep that train down to 10 miles an hour.

But he also knew when he got beyond the 17th crossing there weren't any more crossings between there and Santa Rosa County. The only crossing was a little dirt road crossing at Gull Point, and there wasn't going to be any police car on that dirt road just waiting for a train when they didn't know what time it would be there.

After the 17th Avenue, after the caboose crossed 17th Avenue, the rules allow the train to get up to 40 miles an hour until it gets to the Gull Point curve, when it had to get down to 35 miles an hour. Now, as I said, as the train left and got to the point where the caboose crosses 17th Avenue he was doing all right, he was perfectly within the speed limit.

The L&N knew that this train violated the AAR weight limit not just by a few pounds, because that train on just the Gull Point curve that we are concerned with was 50 percent too heavy, 50 percent too much weight for the minimum AAR safety rules. They say 6,000 trailing tons for that curve, and they had 9,000.

The wide gauge, number two up there, the L&N knew that the gauge was too wide, and they had known about it for about a year. The reason they had known it, there is a thing called a geometry car, and that geometry car runs—it's got computers on it and everything, and it has to run under the law twice a year around these tracks. And when this occurred in June of 1977 it showed the gauge was too wide. And they did it back before then in February of 1977 and it showed the gauge was too wide. Well, what did the L&N do? Nothing. Because it was going to cost money to straighten out that gauge.

Bad ties. The L&N knew from 17th Avenue to the Escambia Bay trestle the tie conditions were so bad they violated even those minimum FRA rules, three bad ties in a row. But it is going to cost money to go in there and lift that track and pull and put new timbers in there.

The L&N knew that on the front of the train they had not one, but four light cars on the front of this extra heavy freight train, in violation of the AAR rules and their own rules. But it would have cost money to have taken those cars out and put them behind.

The L&N knew that the first two of those light cars, the first car connected to the three locomotives, and the second car was a long car-short car combination in direction violation of the AAR rules, but again, it would cost money to straighten that out. You know, just to change it around would cost fuel and it takes time, effort and money.

On the super elevation in the Gull Point curve they designed it for three-and-a-half inches, the outside rail. The L&N knew that when that geometry car ran across there five months before that the three-and-a-half inch super elevation had dropped to two inches. They knew that it was in violation and they should have corrected it. But, it cost money to come in and lift up the track and get it straightened out.

They knew when they put that rail on Gull Point in 1975 that they wanted to go a little faster. They knew they let that super elevation run off into the straight track in direct violation of their own rules in order to allow more speed. But it cost money to slow a train down, and they didn't have to slow it down if you give the train that super elevation runoff.

And the L&N knew that that 132-pound welded rail track included one section, at least one section that was made in 1943 of 131-pound welded rail. And you see that was saving them a few dollars by using old 1943 track. That was the track over in that pile, and every once in a while you can slip it in and save a few dollars.

And the L&N knew the only times they had been having any trouble were with these six-axle locomotives, but they didn't slow the speed limit down for them. They just let them run because they had to have them in order to pull that much weight at a good speed.

And we believe you will find from the evidence that on November 9, 1977, everything that they could possibly do wrong in regard to lateral forces and maintenance, they did wrong and they knew it, for the particular stretch of track that we are talking about. In fact, we believe that the evidence will show you that for the stretch of track between 17th Avenue and Escambia Bay trestle, the one they were so proud of, that there were at least 40 FRA violations. These are the minimum standards. If a railroad has 40 in its whole system in one year, that would be a lot. We will show 40 in this stretch of track that they were so proud of.

I say to you that there will be direct evidence of all ten of the first ten things. Now, I know it sounds unbelievable, because I am not giving you evidence, it is strictly lawyers talk, but listen to the evidence.

So, on November 9, 1977, Brewer has got all these things in front of him that he is facing as he comes across 17th Avenue, and he hears from the conductor as the caboose crosses the 17th Avenue crossing. It is about 6:00 o'clock, and the conductor calls to him, "Brewer, you know, we have crossed 17th, now you can go ahead and do what we have to do." And Brewer knows what he has got to do because he has got to beat that per diem, and he goes full throttle. And he gets up to 10, to 15, to 20, to 25, 30, 35, 40. And it's about 6:02, 6:03, and at this time the Thorshov family are in their home. They are cooking, listening to the radio, the children are playing, the food is on, and it's 6:06. There is a crash out in front of the

Thorshov's home. Now, what happened between 6:03 and 6:06, there is some dispute because you see, we weren't on that train, and we don't have anybody on that train willing to testify. So, first I am going to tell you what they say, and then I'm going to tell you what we are going to try to infer from the evidence that we will put in.

The crew says, "We're going 40 miles an hour, we're paying good attention, we're getting into the Gull Point curve and we know there is a 35-mile-speed limit and Brewer slows that thing down to 35." They say, "Brewer blows the whistle for the Gull Point crossing," and they say, "We're in that lead locomotive, all three of us, and we're watching out, everybody is looking as they start into the Gull Point curve." The crew tells you that they were going—all three of them say they were going 35 miles an hour as they came into the curve.

Now, as they go around the curve we do know that the second locomotive overturned the outside rail, and that the third locomotive and 15 or 20 cars thereafter traveled on the overturned rail. As the locomotive overturned the right side rail and continued on around, it kept overturning the rail in front of it. And the right wheels of the second locomotive on back for every one of those cars, the flange, the little thing that sticks down—I am not an artist for sure—anyhow, it is a little thing that sticks down from the wheel. The flange had overturned the track and it was riding in the web. All the right wheels were riding in the overturned web of that track.

The left wheels were over in the dirt. They had already come into the inside of the track and they were just chewing up the dirt and the ties and the timbers. And the crew said, "We were just riding along minding our own business, and the mere fact that we had thrown thousands and thousands of tons behind us, digging up this dirt and everything, we didn't even notice it until our locomotive got beyond the crossing. Eleven or twelve hundred feet we had been riding along derailed, and at that time that doggone 131-pound rail, the head broke off of it and the cars started going every which a way. And at that time the cars broke loose from the coupling, the emergency brakes went on and then, of course, we came to a stop. And that is how the accident happened."

*We had the testimony of the engineer about a simulated run that the engineer made shortly after the accident. If the testimony was to be believed as to his speed from the time he started until the caboose crossed 17th Avenue, then the train had to be going approximately 70 miles per hour at the Gull Point curve in order for the derailment to have occurred at 6:06 p.m. However, counsel recognized that it was impossible for that particular train to be going in excess of 50 miles an hour from the computer studies. Also, there were two witnesses that claimed to have heard the screeching of brakes for 15 to 30 seconds prior to the sound of the derailment. The L&N trial team had no knowledge of the two earwitnesses. How do you handle strong testimony on behalf of the plaintiff when you recognize that it is likely going to be proved to be impossible? How do you handle the surprise of the testimony about braking when the L&N could put on evidence that the screeching actually occurred from the right wheels running in the web of the rail (after the derailment)? In other words, the screeching could have been occurring after the outside rail overturned, and lasted for approximately 15 seconds before the cars began to derail. The following is how we handled these problems.*

### How to Deal with Testimony That Is Hard to Prove

Now, it's not critical to our case what they did on that train, but I think you will find from the evidence that what they did is that when Brewer and the crew in the locomotive got up to 40 miles an hour, he knew he had to make the per diem. It was about 6:02, 6:03, and he let it go up to 45, maybe 50, maybe 55, maybe 60, we don't know, but we know he wasn't paying attention. And at 6:05 we believe the evidence to be that he was going—that he could not have been going over 60 miles an hour, that he was well exceeding the speed limit, and that he was going to Gull Point curve and it was raining. It was drizzling, and maybe he didn't have his wipers on, I don't know what happened, but all of a sudden he realizes as he is about to blow the whistle for the Gull Point crossing, he realized the speed he was traveling, and it was excessive. He knew it, and he knew he couldn't make it and he put on his brakes. Now, again, there is no direct evidence of any of this, but we think that from the evidence there is a good possibility of what I just told you. The first 10 things, there is going to be direct evidence of, but the other two things, we weren't there, so we don't know, but we think the evidence will indicate it. We do know the outside rail did overturn, we do know the second locomotive, the third locomotive, all of these cars behind it were riding along with right hand wheels in the web. And we do know that the left hand wheels were digging up that dirt out there. There wasn't anything in the world they could do at that time because the train was already in emergency.

We believe that there is a good possibility that the 131-pound rail, the only rail that broke in a lengthwise direction, the rail that caused the pile up, we believe it is a good possibility that it was already cracked. Now, I say it is a good possibility, because we have a witness that said when he saw the rail it was rusted. But the L&N took that rail and they sent it up to the AAR laboratory, sent it up to their own lab, and said, "Check and see if this is a new crack in that rail or was it an old one that we should have discovered before." And the AAR came back with this opinion to the L&N that it was a new crack.

So, we said, "Let us see it. Let our experts look at it."

And they said, "We threw away those rails." Knowing that millions of dollars were involved, the AAR just threw the rail away, and they said, "We no longer have this rail." But we do know that the rail did break, and when the rail broke the cars started piling up; wheels started throwing every which a way, and some of the wheels hit into ammonia cars.

*Although it was insignificant in the case, it was important to point out that the rail had been thrown away, contrary to established procedures for any laboratory. This point became extremely important in summation. During the trial of the case, several things were uncovered for the first time that indicated there had been some toying with evidence subsequent to the derailment by the L&N.*

Now, the L&N knew that they were forced to carry these ammonia cars because you've got to carry them. You just can't say, "I'll take this car, I won't take that car." But they knew that these cars didn't have head shields on them. The L&N had to carry them, and they did it for a profit. But they knew they should have slowed the train down because they had cars without head shields. Head shields are extra pieces of metal up on the front.

*Again, the above is simply stealing the defendant's thunder. They would say that they were required to accept every car sent over its line because of federal regulations. I was putting this situation in its best light by saying that the L&N should have reduced their speed when they realized that the tank cars did not have head shields.*

## The Climax of the Story

Jon Thorshov and his family are in the home at this point. The two cars of ammonia are pouring ammonia up over this cliff onto the Thorshov home. They had come home about 5:00, as I have said, in the pickup truck, and Scenic Highway is about this height (indicating) and the home was about on this level, and the cliff, anyhow, the driveway goes downhill to his home. He had pulled the pickup truck facing the water, facing the railroad cars, Jon grabs the little girl and Lloyda grabs the young child.

And obviously they made up their minds that we're going to run through this and we're going to get in the truck and we'll back it up to Scenic Highway and try to get out. And at this time the ammonia is spreading.

They ran out of the house, they get into the truck, he gets it started, he gets it into reverse, and about the time he starts to move it it stops because there is no oxygen. He grabs Daisy, he goes out of the driver's side, he gets about 10 yards and he falls. Lloyda, at the same time, the wife, grabs the little boy, Gamgee, she goes out the passenger side and gets about 15 yards and falls.

Now, before any of this occurs, when the ammonia is spreading out over everywhere, the train has stopped. Now the train stopped just oh, four or five hundred feet beyond the crossing, and the crew gets off and they start walking back to see what's happened. "God knows, everything's done, let's see what we did." And they are walking back and they are looking and they see this cloud of ammonia spreading out over the Thorshov's home. And they knew—I think they testified that they knew there were lights on in the house, that the people were there, and the thought goes through their mind, "Boy, if we had those air packs, if the L&N had paid for those air packs we could go on in there and save those people, because well—no," they said, "no, we'd better go back to the engine."

Well, they start back to the engine and over to their right, to the east of the tracks is Gull Point and there are lots of homes down there and this whole track is blocked, cars are overturned, and everything else. And if that wind changes these people are in trouble. Oh, I am sure the thought must have gone through their mind, "Let's go knock on these people's doors and warn them," or "Let's go run back to the train and blow the whistle and just keep blowing the whistle until they realize what is going on." But, no, they decided not to do that, even though the first L&N safety rule says help people that are in danger. But that was a rule, and the rules were guidelines, and those guidelines didn't apply in Pensacola. So they ran back to the train and they did the smart thing, they unhooked the first locomotive, all three of them jumped in there and they got the hell out of there. No whistles, no calling, no knocking, no nothing. Well, fortunately the fire department didn't feel that way, because they were immediately notified and the fire department crew started in. And they grabbed their air packs, and they are some—you'll probably hear from them tomorrow, and they are some real heroes.

The firemen's oxygen was running out and they went up under train cars, everywhere else, trying to save the people that were trapped in Gull Point. Anyhow, they put on air packs, they go into the Thorshov home and they can't find anybody. And as they were going out they find Daisy, they grab her and get her to an ambulance. The accident happened at 6:06 and at 6:30 Daisy is on an ambulance. They get her on the ambulance and they take her to the hospital.

Well, they know that nobody has left the little girl there alone and they note that there must be other people there, and they go back in again and they find Gamgee, they bring him out. They find Lloyda and Jon and they bring them out and they are put on an ambulance five minutes later.

Jon dies on the way to the hospital and Lloyda and the two children are put into the hospital. Daisy has gotten about 25 minutes of ammonia and she probably has—there is the possibility that she has some lung damage, probably not—

MR. LANE: If Your Honor please, we object to the discussion of these injuries. That is involved in the big case yet to be tried.

MR. LEVIN: Your Honor, I really appreciate the reference to the big case for some injuries while we know that the wrongful death cases are the real substantial cases, but in this case, the condition of these children, whether or not they are going to be dependent to age 22 or for life, is critical.

MR. LANE: We object, Your Honor. That is exactly why he got the cases severed, because he didn't—

THE COURT: Objection overruled.

MR. LEVIN: Daisy got out in 25 minutes and she has very little, if any, lung damage. Gamgee was in there 30 minutes and the doctors will testify that he probably has severe lung damage. He could be a pulmonary cripple.

Jon got out in about 30 minutes, the father, he died on the way to the hospital.

Lloyda got out in 30 minutes, and she lived for 75 days on a respirator and then died.

Daisy had to have a corneal transplant, and you will see some cosmetic difficulties with her eyes when you see her. We are going to bring her in and—

MR. LANE: Your Honor, we renew our objections. It is just not involved in this case.

MR. LEVIN: Your Honor, if the Court please, in the standard jury instructions, under wrongful death, under loss of services and support it is for as long as these children will be dependent—would have been dependent on their parents. Their physical condition is an issue, not whether it is related to the accident or not, but their condition is relevant in this case.

THE COURT: Objection overruled.

MR. LEVIN: Daisy had a corneal transplant and there is the possibility that she will go blind in both eyes.

There is a small possibility of lung damage, and she obviously has psychiatric problems as indicated by the sleepwalking.

Gamgee went ahead and lost the one kidney, probably not related to the accident. But it is important that he only has one kidney, and as the court overruled Mr. Lane when he continued to object, this will be important to you at the end of the case. Gamgee has definite permanent lung damage and he may be a pulmonary cripple. He also has the same possibility of going blind that Daisy does.

Now we filed suit and we basically alleged all of the things that I just told you, and the L&N answered in a magnanimous fashion and said, "we deny everything; and L&N can do no wrong." They even denied that they were in any way at fault.

*When advantage can be taken of the pleadings, take it. The above is simply a method of rubbing in the fact that defendant denied responsibility.*

Now, we also joined Mr. Brewer in this case. We believe Mr. Brewer is at fault, or we would not have filed suit against Mr. Brewer. But, as far as going and collecting the kind of money that we are talking about from Mr. Brewer, there isn't any chance. We are going after the L&N. And the reason Mr. Brewer remains in this case is because we don't want to be in federal court. We want to try this case here in state court.

*The above was an attempt to explain to the jury why the engineer was a party to the case. As explained earlier, the jury found that Mr. Brewer was not negligent because the jury did not want Mr. Brewer to lose his job. This information was obtained from a juror subsequent to trial. We should have explained to the jury that Mr. Brewer was a member of the union and had no chance at all of losing his job.*

Now, the L&N says that neither it nor any of its employees did anything wrong. It just happened. "We don't know what happened. It just happened. The train just went off the track. Why do you blame us?" That is what the L&N says.

And they sent in one of the bright SCL-L&N executives who is now a big vice president over there for us to take his deposition. He had come in and taken over the L&N maintenance in 1972, and he was in charge in '75 when they laid this track and in '77 when they had the derailment. He did such a good job in handling everything after the derailment they made him the vice president. So they sent him to us and they said, "If you want to know what is wrong with our tracks, ask him."

So, we asked Mr. Parker, who is now their vice president up there in

Louisville, who came over from the SCL in Jacksonville. We asked, "Mr. Parker, tell us what is wrong with that track?"

And he said, "You know, I took my own time and came down to Pensacola after that little derailment down there and nobody else wanted to do it. I walked the track from 17th Avenue all the way around—and, of course, in the Gull Point area it was messed up, so I couldn't tell about that, and I walked all the way around to the Escambia Bay trestle." And he said, he told us under oath, that "that track was in perfect condition. There wasn't anything wrong with that track."

*Mr. Parker was the L&N's key witness. The above was simply painting him with the black hat. Throughout the opening statement all of the new SCL-L&N executives had been painted with black hats. The attempt was now being made to make Mr. Parker the perfect example of the new SCL-L&N executive.*

Shortly after the derailment, the L&N had crews working on the track where the derailment happened. They also had crews heading back toward 17th putting those new timbers in, putting those spikes in, making sure it was in good condition. By the time the city got around in December to come and look at all of this track they thought it was beautiful. So Mr. Parker stated, under oath, "The tracks were perfect." The one thing that he doesn't know to this very moment, and I am sure that all of the L&N people will tell him about it because it is going to be here when he takes the stand, we took pictures and he didn't know that.

Between the time of the derailment, after he had looked at it, and before repairs, we went out and took pictures, and he didn't know about it. We were right in front of the L&N crews. They were coming along getting that track straightened out, and we were about a mile in front of them just going right along taking pictures. Not me, personally, but we had people out there, and he didn't know about it until now. But he will know about it tonight for sure.

And so we are going to have pictures, and when they put Mr. Parker on the stand, or if we've got to, we'll put him on the stand, and we'll show him the pictures and we'll ask him to tell you how this was such a perfect track. That is their vice president.

Obviously, anybody who believes what I have told you would be sickened. They would be disgusted. And I am here to tell you when it comes from the witness stand it is going to be worse.

Now, we have the burden of proof. Yes, we've got to prove one of these 12 things by 51 percent of the evidence.

And as I told you, the L&N denies everything. And we had to go out, because this is highly technical stuff when you start talking about lateral forces and super elevations and all of these things like that, we had to go out and find some people who knew something about it. And we have got some former executives, Ed Mann, the executive vice president from Penn Central Railroad, and the vice president from Conrail, and the vice president from Amtrak. These are former railroad people. You know it is rough to get a railroad man to testify against another railroad, but they are coming in and they are going to lay it on you. They are going to let you and the people of Pensacola know how bad it was.

*The above is an attempt to paint the plaintiffs' witnesses with white hats. I was saying that the plaintiffs' witnesses must be honest and good men in order to be willing to testify against their own industry.*

And during this case you will also hear from some employees who actually worked tracks for the railroad, excuse me, former employees. They couldn't be working for them now, believe me. Former employees of other railroads will come in and tell you the same thing.

*At this part of the opening statement, it became necessary to get into the most difficult part of the case, the law of damages. The jury had pads and pencils. The jury was eventually going to be given a special verdict form. All of the testimony as to special damages such as loss of support and services were going to be calculated by economists.*

## The Law of Damages

At the end of this case you are going to be given a special verdict form, and the first question probably is going to ask, "Was the L&N negligent?"

Negligence is the failure to do what is right. Any one of those 12 things. And if the railroad or any of its employees were negligent in any of those ways, then you will be required to fill out the damages.

*At this point, the board facing the jury was replaced with a sample special verdict form.*

And there will be a space for damages to the property, the damage that was done to the Thorshov property. And you will hear testimony as to what damage was done. And then there will be a place on that form that will ask what were Lloyda's medical and funeral expenses, and they were something over $45,000. That is going to be a pretty simple figure to put in, it will be introduced into evidence. And then a space for Jon Thorshov's funeral expense, which was a little over $2,000; and then there will be a place for his accumulations. If Jon Thorshov had lived out his normal life expectancy, how much would he have saved and invested, and how much would have been left for these children? Now, this starts to get a little bit more difficult, and this and most of the other damage questions are going to be more difficult than the $45,000.00. That is the reason you have been given pads and pencils, because there are going to be so many figures to keep track of.

In determining damages, you are going to first have to decide from the evidence, what does the future hold for Daisy and Gamgee Thorshov. In other words, how much longer would they have been dependent if their parents had not been killed and only the children had been involved in the accident.

We do know that healthy children of doctors normally go through four years of college. So we do know that one alternative, that if you believe the children will regain their health, you will determine that they would have been dependent to age 22. That's age 22 for both Daisy and Gamgee. But, of course, the children aren't healthy, and what we believe you will probably find from the evidence is that Daisy, even though she is not healthy would have gone off to college, will go to college, will get out, and she would no longer be dependent. If her parents had lived she would no longer have been dependent on them, and she would have gone off and married and had her own life.

But we believe you will find that Gamgee, because of the possibility of the serious condition that occurred to him, that he may be dependent for the rest of his life, and then of course, the figures vary greatly. They change greatly when you support somebody to age 22 or you support somebody for life.

You will be asked at the end of this case to put in the figures for loss of support for Gamgee, loss of services, net accumulations, loss of Jon Thorshov's parental guidance, his companionship for Gamgee, and for Gamgee's mental pain and suffering. And then you will be asked to do the same thing for Daisy, for each of these elements. They will be combined into one figure, for Daisy for the loss of her father. And then it's going to be necessary to do this for the mother.

Now, three of these things, support, services, and net accumulations, are subject to economic testimony, and we are going to bring in an economist to testify to it because he can give exact figures to you.

Companionship, guidance, mental pain and suffering, no. These are things you're going to have to rely on your common sense and experience. Nobody is going to take the stand and say that the value of the loss of Jon Thorshov's companionship for Gamgee or Daisy was worth two million dollars or six hundred thousand or so much. These are things that we are not going to be able to present evidence about, and that is left to your common sense and experience.

But, on support, services and net accumulations, we intend to bring in some of America's most outstanding professors of economics and they will put figures on the board. They will take Jon Thorshov's salary for the year 1979, what it would have been in '79, and then they know what pathologists have made in the past. They do know what is happening with different economic things, and then they project these figures, the same way they project social security figures, and they know how much money today is going to be worth in the future.

So, they take the salary, and they increase it each year. Then they determine his savings because they know how much the average man in that income category saves. So let's say the doctor after paying income tax would have made $100,000. They know that a man with two children, which is the situation he would be in if he had lived, would have saved a blank percentage, and I think it's 25 percent. So, they put that off to the side for 1980, and then the next year how much would he have made, and then they keep increasing it with inflation until the year he would have died.

This money would then be a tremendous sum of money, 31 years from now. So, then they say, "Well, we are going to replace that money today." How much money will it take today, in dollars invested at a tax-free rate of interest, that 31 years from now will replace exactly what they believe Jon Thorshov would have left for these children had he lived, and that is what they will be talking to you about.

And as to support, they do it the exact same way. They will come in and they will take his income after taxes, and then they will remove the amount that he is going to save. They will then take how much he would have spent on himself, and then they will divide the difference between the two children until each child is no longer dependent. And this is the reason it is important for you to determine whether those children would have been supported beyond age 22, because there is a tremendous difference between supporting Gamgee to 22 and supporting him for the life of his father.

They then take the gross figures for the loss of support and they bring it down to its present value. That is how much money invested today at a tax-free rate of interest will produce the exact amount, in their opinion, of lost support that Daisy and Gamgee would have had.

For the services of the father they do the exact same thing, and for the services of the mother they do the same thing. In other words, a mother who was with these children full time. They are going to have to find somebody to clean and cook and somebody to stay with them. And they go through these figures and they tell you what these things are going to be, and then they bring them back down. The economists will determine how much invested today, when you return your verdict, will it take to pay these amounts for these children as long as they would have been dependent.

Now, I am going to suggest to you that when the professors of economics come in and testify that you take two pages of your pad, one of them for each professor, and put down 22 and 22. Because we'll give you a list of figures for each of these things assuming each child being dependent to age 22. And then on the next page he will then give you figures for Daisy to 22; Gamgee for life.

And at the end of the case you add those figures of loss of the support, services, and net accumulations, and add those figures to the parental guidance and to the companionship, and the mental pain and suffering. It's not going to be all that dull. I am going to have them talk to you about what causes inflation and what prices are going to be like, and it will astound you, 20, 30, 40, 50 years from now. And they will go into the fact that there aren't going to be things called pennies, nickels, quarters, probably, and they will go into astounding things, what wages are going to be some 40 or 50 years from now, and what homes are going to cost and what cars are going to cost and how this all comes into play.

*(The above part of the opening was extremely dull and very difficult to understand. I used the blackboard in explaining some of the complications. Most often, the blackboard was being used to write down certain key words with the hope that the jury would copy those words onto their pads. Also, it was an attempt to get the jurors excited about the testimony of the economists.*

Now, the L&N Railroad has listed three economic witnesses, and if they disagree with what the professors of economics testify to, if they disagree as to what prices are going to be in the future, then I say to the L&N Railroad, don't rely on your lawyer talk in your closing argument here, put your economists on the witness stand. They have got three economists listed. If any one of them is willing to say that Professor Goffman is wrong or President Sliger is wrong, then let him come on. Don't let Mr. Lane come on at the end of this case and say everybody knows plaintiffs' economists are wrong, let L&N come on with their evidence, let them come in and say there is not going to be any inflation.

*The above remarks were extremely important in the eventual out-
come of the case. (The L&N had listed three economists as potential
witnesses. We doubted that the railroad intended to call them as witnesses,
and we believed they had simply listed them in order to require us to prepare for their expected testimony.) We wanted to be able to say in closing
argument, "The L&N economists must have agreed with plaintiffs' economists, because L&N did not put these witnesses on the stand."*


### Concluding Your Statement

Finally, we believe the Judge—and this is the end—will allow you to answer one more question at the end of the case: Did the L&N Railroad,
through its employees, act in a wanton manner or in a manner that was
with reckless indifference to the rights of others? Now, this is different
from simple negligence. I have been telling you about simple negligence,
and that is any one of these 12 things for simple negligence. But, if their
conduct was so bad, so horrible, and you find they did so many bad
things that you determine that they were reckless, they were indifferent,
they didn't care, and if you find that, then the Judge will give you an opportunity at the end of this case to do what the government couldn't do to
them, and that is, control. You have that power. And the Judge will tell
you, and these will be his words, "Look at how much the L&N Railroad is
worth and come up with an amount of money in punitive damages that
would keep them from ever doing this again."

And I believe you will find from the evidence that the L&N Railroad
knew how bad this was, and they knew this stretch of track was the worst
in their system; they knew derailments were happening, and they knew
ammonia was escaping. Now, they didn't want Jon Thorshov and Lloyda
Thorshov to die—but they knew somebody was going to, somebody was
going to get seriously injured out there. But the L&N said, "We are willing
to take that gamble," and I think that is what you will find, and I think you
will find that Jon and Lloyda Thorshov lost that gamble.

Thank you.

*It is important to note that there was one significant bit of damaging
evidence that Levin omitted from the opening statement. As explained,
"One of the major causes of derailments in curves is the application of
brakes. The crew emphatically denied that they applied the train brakes in
the Gull Point curve. We had listed hundreds of potential witnesses who
lived in the area of the derailment. Although most of the witnesses had been
deposed by defense counsel, they had failed to uncover two who had heard*

*the screeching of what appeared to be brakes for 15 to 30 seconds prior to the sound of the actual derailment."*

*Because they were not experts, the two witnesses could not testify that the screeching sound was, in fact, braking. Levin decided not to disclose this evidence in opening statement. "We thought that the better procedure would be to put the train crew on, and follow their testimony with the witnesses of the screeching sound. The summation would be a more effective way to discuss this potentially damaging testimony."*

# Chapter Four

# How to Conduct Direct Examination

Building upon the foundation of your opening statement, direct examination provides the pillars of testimony to support your case. Needless to say, these pillars had better be firmly anchored, or else they will never withstand the onslaught of cross-examination your opponent is waiting to unleash.

In this chapter you will discover how five expert practitioners of direct examination make the most of this powerful, but frequently neglected, phase of trial practice. Michael F. Colley starts us off with a concise roundup of the best ways to increase the interest, the suspense, and the impact of direct testimony—without increasing your preparation time. He explains, for example, that simply by heeding five basic laws of human perception, you can dramatically multiply the persuasive power of your witnesses and their testimony. You will see how something as subtle as your choice of words in a question—and the order of those words—can create the kind of lasting images that stay with the jury all the way through the trial. From the best order to present your witnesses, to the best place to stand when questioning, Mr. Colley capsulizes for you the key principles of verbal and non-verbal persuasion in the courtroom.

One important avenue of persuasion in a criminal case is the introduction of good character evidence in behalf of the defendant. "The testimony not only humanizes the defendant," write Mark Kadish and Rhonda Brofman, "but it may create reasonable doubt in the minds of the jurors." Furthermore, even in cases where the charges are particularly serious, the authors point out, character testimony can be the deciding factor in gaining acquittal for your client.

Kadish and Brofman then tackle the central question of when to use character witnesses and how to select them. Is it better, for instance, to use prestigious people or "just plain folks"? On this matter, you will see how one defense attorney in a bankruptcy fraud trial called the local postman as a character witness. "Although his testimony was brief," the authors note, "the postman (who appeared in uniform) was so likable that the prosecutor asked no questions on cross-examination."

Just as character witnesses can play a big part in a criminal trial, medical experts take center stage in practically every personal injury action. William B. Fitzgerald, Jr. and R. D. Blanchard round out this chapter on direct examination by focusing squarely on the medical expert as witness, both for the plaintiff and the defense.

"The ideal direct examination of the medical expert," Mr. Fitzgerald writes, "leaves opposing counsel with no appropriate questions to ask." To help you anticipate and overcome all possible attacks on your doctor, Mr. Fitzgerald spells out his 17 courtroom techniques for an effective direct examination. Then he demonstrates these techniques in action with a detailed excerpt of testimony of plaintiff's treating surgeon, complete with sample medical reports and exhibits.

Meanwhile, R. D. Blanchard observes that the defense attorney "has some unique problems and opportunities when he undertakes the direct examination of the physician who conducted the adverse (independent) medical examination of the plaintiff in a personal injury action." Mr. Blanchard maps out a no-nonsense defense strategy that minimizes the inherent advantages enjoyed by the plaintiff's medical evidence. You will see how to command the jury's total attention as you disarm their doubts...and how to chip away at the plaintiff's case at every turn.

# Principles of
# Direct Examination

## Michael F. Colley

Michael F. Colley received his J.D. degree from Ohio State University. He served as Assistant City Attorney for the City of Columbus, (1962-64). He also served as Chairman of the Board of Editors for Trial Diplomacy Journal, (1979-1982). Colley previously served as President of the Ohio Academy of Trial Lawyers, the Franklin County Trial Lawyers Association, and the Association of Trial Lawyers of America. He is a member of the National Association of Defense Lawyers in Criminal Cases; the American Society of Law and Medicine and is currently serving as President of the Roscoe Pound - American Trial Lawyers Foundation, (1982-84).

It starts before you interview your first witness when you investigate your case.

For instance, If the hinge issue in your case is the speed of the defendant's car immediately before the collision, your first question to the witness who saw it should be, "How fast was the other car going when it *smashed* into our car", because the way you word a question will influence the witness' answer.

The authority for this proposition is Dr. Elizabeth Loftus of the University of Washington.

### Choosing the Words That Could Win Your Case

Dr. Loftus conducted experiments to determine the effect of the choice of words in a question on the answer. For example, she showed a film of an intersection collision to two groups of students. Both groups were asked to estimate the speed of the same car. Group one was asked, "How fast was the car going when it *smashed* into the other car?" Group two was asked, "How fast was the car going when it *hit* the other car?" The average estimate of group one was 40.8 miles per hour; the average of group two was 33 miles per hour. Why was there a disparity?

The key is the verb *smashed,* which implies greater speed and force at impact than the verb *hit.*

When a witness sees an automobile collision—or any complex, fast-moving event, he forms a "memory representation" of the *actual* event which Dr. Loftus refers to as "*original* information." When you ask the witness, "How fast was the car going when it *smashed* into the other car", your question includes new, external information which enters into the witness' memory, and if believed, will result in an alteration or change in memory.

How about in the courtroom? Will the choice of words affect how a juror, who did not witness the collision, will react?

The answer is unequivocal. Aristotle was the first to observe that our thought process involves imagining what we think in terms of images. He said that you cannot create an image without thinking; and conversely, you cannot think without creating an image.

The choice of words will affect the reconstruction of a past event in the minds of jurors because the meaning we assign to words when we check them against our frames of reference will inevitably incorporate a value judgment.

### How the Order of Your Words Can Sway the Jury

How about the order of words? What effect will the order of words have on the image created in the minds of jurors?

In the 1970 issue of the *Arizona State Law Journal* at page 539, there is an article titled, "Experimental Research on the Organization of Persuasive Arguments and the Application to Courtroom Communication" written by Robert Lawson, who is a law professor at the University of Kentucky.

Dr. Lawson conducted an experiment dividing an audience into two parts, both out of the hearing of the other.

To both groups he described the same person. To the first group he said, "George is intelligent, industrious, impulsive, critical, stubborn and envious." To the second group he said, "George is envious, stubborn, critical, impulsive, industrious and intelligent."

He stated the *same* adjectives to both groups, but in reverse order. Then he asked both groups to state their impressions.

The conclusion of group one was that George was an able person with some minor shortcomings. The conclusion of group two was that George was a problem personality with serious difficulties.

These were intelligent people who heard the *same* words, but in *different* order.

This experiment illustrates that when contradictory information is presented in a single communication by a single communicator, there is a pronounced tendency for those items presented first to dominate the impression received.

The experiments conducted by Dr. Loftus and Dr. Lawson are dramatic proof that the choice of words and the order of words are important because of the impressions or images people assign to words.

The trial of a case in the context of the adversary system is literally a battle between two opposing forces, each contending that its characterization of events and inferences based upon those events is right.

During direct examination, we, as lawyers, cannot persuade *directly*, but we can persuade *indirectly* since we control the order of witnesses presented and the form and content of the questions asked.

What are the principles of verbal and nonverbal communication that apply to the direct examination of witnesses in the courtroom?

Several years ago Professor Ormond Drake, who was at the time Assistant Dean of the College of Liberal Arts at New York University, presented this question to a convention of communication experts from across the country.

He said, "If you could condense into a single, brief statement all that has been written on the art of moving human being to action, what would it be?"

The consensus was, "What the mind attends to, it considers. What the mind does not attend to, it dismisses. What the mind attends to continually, it believes. And what the mind believes, it ultimately does."

If we assume that statement is true, then the key to success in the courtroom is to focus the minds of the jurors on the crux of your case from the start to the conclusion.

That is the objective. How do you achieve it?

First, you must select the motif, thread, or theme of your case. For instance, if you represent a child who suffered severe and permanent brain damage at birth because of negligence on the part of both the obstetrician and the hospital, the theme of your case should be, how will this child and other children injured at birth be cared for in the future. What will be the cost of that care? Who should bear the burden, the child's family, the taxpayer, or the physician and hospital that negligently caused the child's injury?

Second, you should analyze your case in reverse order. In final argument you must argue the legal principles that you expect to be in the court's instructions to the jury. If that is to be your final argument, you must analyze the evidence you will need in order to justify that argument. And that is the evidence you must stress in your opening statement.


### Preparing the Jury to Accept Your Evidence

Your opening statement establishes a "set" which serves as a frame of reference into which jurors will fit later evidence. The set operates to color evidence which is necessarily compared and evaluated when it is presented.

Set phenomena, or synthesia, is a predisposition to respond to evidence in a predictable way. How a juror perceives the evidence presented will depend upon what he is prepared for in opening statement. The central application of set phenomena for the trial lawyer is that a juror will see what he is prepared to see, and he will hear what he is prepared to hear.

At the start of the trial, the plaintiff has the advantage. He speaks first, therefore, he persuades first.

During the University of Chicago jury research studies several years ago, it was found that when a jury was quizzed after opening statement, and again after all the evidence had been presented, 80 percent of the jurors had made up their minds on liability after the opening statement— and never changed their minds. Since the plaintiff addresses the jury first in opening statement and presents evidence first, he has the greatest opportunity for attitude persuasion because of the principle of primacy.

To give a shorthand definition, primacy means that we tend to believe most deeply what we have first heard, and that whichever side of an issue is presented first will have a greater influence on opinion than an equally strong, but later presentation of the opposite view.

The principle of primacy applies to every phase of the trial.

For instance, in a case involving a child who was struck by a delivery truck, assume that the child was taken to the nearest hospital, that he was seen by an intern, was x-rayed, and then was referred to a Board-certified neurosurgeon. Which witness would you present first?

If you presented the witnesses chronologically, you would present the intern, the radiologist, and the neurosurgeon in the order they saw your client. In most cases that probably would be a mistake, because the first witness to testify has to be prepared to withstand the full extent of cross-examination.

The neurosurgeon is probably more knowledgeable, more sophisticated in terms of forensic medicine, and probably best able to blunt the effectiveness of cross-examination. The neurosurgeon should be your first witness. It may not be necessary to call the intern or the radiologist, which will obviate any possible conflict in testimony, since the intern's notes and the x-ray reports will be incorporated in the hospital records.

Another principle you should consider is autistic or idiosyncratic perception, which means that jurors will limit or adjust perception to fit their own needs and values and tend to personalize or even distort testimony to make it correspond to their own frames of reference.

Two factors permit autistic or idiosyncratic perception: (1) vague or ambiguous testimony; and (2) testimony that is of short duration.

Jurors do not retain the details of the testimony of any single witness, and the shorter they are exposed, the more likely they are to forget that testimony.

The antidotes are apparent. Clarity and amplification are essential to every part of the trial. Also note that reception of a message improves with repetition. And persuasion or speed of agreement increases as a function of the number of times a person is exposed to a communication.

Therefore, it is necessary to repeat critical facts during the trial, even though it may be cumulative, to fix them in the jurors' memory. Repetition is especially effective in rebuttal, because we tend to remember best and most vividly what we heard last on a subject. This is the principle of recency.

For instance, if the defense claims your client's ability to drive was impaired because of alcoholic influence, and he denies it, on rebuttal you should call one-fact witnesses. The wrecker operator, the ambulance attendant who took your client to the hospital, or the nurse in the emergency room—in short, any witness who can testify to two questions: (1) Did they see your client after the collision? and (2) Did they smell any odor of alcoholic beverage on his person? Ask nothing else.

There is one caveat. If you call one-fact witnesses, they should be prepared to respond on cross-examination to other issues in dispute. The one-fact witness can be dramatic, but if not adequately prepared, he can be disastrous.

## How to Preempt the Defense

If your case has any potential weaknesses, preempt the defense. For instance, if the plaintiff suffered previous injury to the same part of his body, you should admit in opening statement that he suffered a prior injury that made him more prone to injury; or if the plantiff had preexisting arthritis you should admit it in opening statement but add that he was asymptomatic, without any physical impairment until he suffered a superimposed injury. And, of course, the plaintiff should testify to these facts upon direct examination.

However, when you refer to unfavorable evidence, the order of presentation is important. The conflict theory suggests that favorable evidence should be presented first because it evokes approach tendencies, while unfavorable evidence evokes avoidance tendencies, creating an approach-avoidance conflict.

When jurors hear favorable evidence at the outset, it strengthens the approach tendency to the point where unfavorable evidence can be accepted without causing the loss of the initial approach response. But, if unfavorable evidence is presented first, then an avoidance tendency is established that you may not be able to overcome.

### How to Phrase Your Questions for Maximum Impact

Your questions on direct examination should be short, and should be designed to build your witness' testimony block by block until the word picture you are attempting to create is complete.

To avoid objections which disrupt the flow and continuity of your presentation, your questions necessarily have to be non-leading.

But what do you do if your witness fails to answer your question fully? For instance, if your client testifies she stepped off the curb to cross the street and was struck by a car, what do you do if she fails to state that she was in a crosswalk. The answer is you should key on a word in your client's last answer and form your next question incorporating that word. Your next question should be, "When you stepped off the curb, where were you in relation to the intersection?" Answer, "I was at the intersection." Question, "Was there a crosswalk at the intersection?" Answer, "Yes sir." Question, "Where were you in relation to the crosswalk when you were struck?" Answer, "I was in the crosswalk."

Most lawyers ask questions like lawyers, probably because that is the way lawyers have asked questions since the Magna Carta. However, it is not how we speak in normal conversation, and it is not how we should speak in the courtroom.

Some examples:

—Instead of, "State what, if anything, unusual happened at that time?" You should ask, "What happened then?"

—Instead of, "How long have you been so employed?" You should ask, "How long have you worked for Mr. Jones?"

—Instead of, "Would you relate to the jury what occurred subsequent to your seeing the vehicle in question?" You should ask, "What happened after you saw the yellow car?"

—Instead of, "Would you indicate, sir, at what distance the plaintiff's vehicle was from yours when you first observed it?" You should ask, "How far away was the other car when you first saw it?"

—Instead of, "In your previous statement, you indicated..." You should ask, "You said before..." Or, "A minute ago you said..."

How do we resolve this problem? The answer is to read your transcripts and weed out awkward words and phrases that are stilted, and substitute words that are clear, direct and positive.

## Techniques of Non-Verbal Communication

Where should you stand in the courtroom?

During direct examination you should stand beside the jury, across the room from the witness, in order to: (1) identify with the jury; (2) focus the jury's attention on the witness; (3) force the witness to look at and speak to the jury; and (4) enhance the importance of the witness by expanding his personal territory in the courtroom.

The key to status is personal territory.

For your own witness, you want to non-verbally create importance, and therefore, you expand his personal territory in the courtroom. The reverse is true on cross-examination when you should stand in front of the jury, near the witness. The reason is: (1) to delimit the witness' importance or status; and (2) to control the witness. If you challenge the personal territory of the witness on cross-examination you enhance your own status with the jury, and you exercise control, which can be released or regained once it has been established, by moving toward or away from the witness.

On stage, actors stand in open, closed, and profile positions with respect to their audiences depending upon the emphasis required. If the actor is in the open position, he is facing his audience and commands its full attention; in the closed position, his back is to the audience and attention is diverted; and finally, in the profile position, he is at a right or left side position to the audience, sharing the attention of the audience with other characters in the drama.

In the courtroom on direct examination when you and your witness are sharing the emphasis, you should both be at profile to the jury with the witness in a more open position, turned slightly toward the jury.

On cross-examination, when you want the emphasis directed toward you, stand in an open position in front of the jury.

The objective on direct examination is to create interest, suspense and impact, which is achieved by staging the order of witnesses with imagination.

The great British barrister, Sir Edward Marshall Hall, said this:

> A lawyer and an actor are akin. It is true I have no mask, I have no set lines, I have no black cloth and I have no floodlights to help bring illusion; but out of the miseries and the joys and the strivings and the experience of men, I must create an atmosphere of living reality so that it may be felt and understood by others, for that is advocacy.

What we as lawyers attempt to do in direct examination is to recreate the past before the jury, to produce images that instill the miseries, and the joys and the strivings and the experience of our clients.

# Direct Examination of Character Witnesses in a Criminal Case

## Mark J. Kadish and Rhonda A. Brofman

Mark J. Kadish received his law degree from the New York University Law School. He is a senior member of the law firm of Kadish and Kadish, P.C. of Atlanta, Georgia. Kadish is a member of the American Bar Association, New York State Bar Association, Georgia Trial Lawyers Association, Georgia Association of Criminal Defense Lawyers, member and secretary of the American Trial Lawyers Association (Criminal Law Section), and member of the National Association of Criminal Defense Lawyers. He is the co-author of *Criminal Law Advocacy, Trial Investigation and Preparation* as well as the author of numerous articles in the criminal law area. Kadish is an Adjunct Professor at Woodrow Wilson College of Law in Atlanta, Georgia and has lectured widely throughout the United States.

Rhonda A. Brofman, a member of the Atlanta law firm Davis & Brofman, graduated from Emory University School of Law in 1978. Ms. Brofman has co-authored the full-length book *Trial Investigation and Preparation*, as well as, several articles and chapters in the criminal law area, including: "Drug Courier Characteristics—A Defense Profile"; "Trial Strategy and Tactics"; "Polygraph, Hypnosis, Truth Drugs, and the Psychological Stress Evaluation"; "Direct Examination Techniques for the Criminal Defense Attorney"; "Racketeering Influenced and Corrupt Organizations: and "Defense of Servicemen". She is Vice President of the Georgia Association of Criminal Lawyers, Editor of the *Georgia Defender* (a quarterly newsletter of the Georgia Criminal Defense Lawyers) and a faculty member of The National Center for Paralegal Training. When Ms. Brofman had been practicing law for less than one year, she was appointed by the State to assist in the defense of a highly publicized rape case. Since then, she has defended numerous criminal cases of all kinds.

Very rarely does the trial of a criminal case turn on a brilliant cross-examination. Cases are more often won by diligent preparation and presentation of direct testimony, including that of character witnesses.

The general rules governing proof of character in a criminal case, in both federal and state jurisdictions, are complex; and counsel must closely follow the applicable state and federal statutes or rules of practice in presenting the defendant's case.

### Federal and State Rules

Federal Rules of Evidence, Rule 405, sets out the methods of proving character:

(a) Reputation or opinion. In all cases in which evidence of character or a trait of character of a person is admissible, proof may be made by testimony as to reputation or by testimony in the form of an opinion. On cross-examination, inquiry is allowable into relevant specific instances of conduct.

(b) Specific instances of conduct. In cases in which character or a trait of character of a person is an essential element of a charge, claim or defense, proof may also be made of specific instances to this conduct.[1]

Pursuant to F.R.E. 405(a), counsel should note that there is a fine distinction between (1) character testimony based on reputation and (2) character testimony in the form of an opinion. "Reputation" testimony is based on the community's opinion of the defendant's character while "opinion" testimony is based on the witnesses' *personal* opinion of the defendant's character. Reputation testimony is based on personal knowledge. Permitting witnesses to state personal opinions may simplify the process of testifying since, with reputation evidence, witnesses often fail to grasp that they are permitted to give *only* the "opinion" of the *community* and not their own opinions.

Federal Rules of Evidence, Rule 405(a) does not necessarily limit character testimony to lay opinions; the Advisory Committee's Note, F.R.E. 405, states:

> "If character is defined as the kind of person one is, then account must be taken of varying ways of arriving at the estimate. These may range from the opinion of the employer who has found the man honest to the opinion of the psychiatrist based upon examination and testing."

A few courts have held that expert witnesses may give opinions on a person's character.[2] In *U.S. v. Staggs*,[3] the defendant was found guilty of assaulting a federal officer with a deadly weapon. The defendant, who was being sought for desertion from the Marine Corps, testified that when his wife let federal agents into his apartment, he picked up a gun because he intended to injure himself so that he would not be taken back to the Marine Corps. The trial court excluded the testimony of a psychologist who examined the defendant, and whose proferred testimony was that the defendant was more likely to hurt himself than to direct his aggressions toward others. On appeal the Seventh Circuit reversed, stating that the psychologist's testimony was evidence of a character trait of the defendant, offered to prove that he acted in conformity with that trait in his encounter with federal agents.

## When to Use Character Witnesses

It is important to introduce good character evidence on behalf of the defendant when available. Many attorneys feel that the severe limitations on character testimony render it ineffective. In certain cases, however, the importance of introducing good character evidence cannot be overstated. The testimony not only humanizes the defendant, but it may create reasonable doubt in the minds of the jurors. For example, in the military courtmartial of Captain Ernest Medina,[4] charged with deliberately killing civilians in My Lai during the Viet Nam war, many character witnesses were called on Captain Medina's behalf. This character testimony, when considered along with the other evidence, seemed to have played a significant role in Captain Medina's acquittal. Defense counsel F. Lee Bailey was able to stress the defendant's good character during closing argument:

> "The uncontradicted evidence would surely lead you to believe that this was a rigid, although not unfeeling, disciplined commander, who had been

viewed by all of those who had been his superiors . . . as an outstanding person, certainly far above average. One of great dedication, sincerity. One who honored and loved the uniform that he wore and the country he represented. One who took to assigned tasks with a good deal of vigor and tried very hard to discharge the duties given him. We went to some length, as my opponent pointed out, to demonstrate the character of Ernest Medina . . . would you have wanted to judge this man without knowing all you could about him? I doubt it. I surely would not. If you were about to get him in your outfit wouldn't you like to know what his former commanders had said . . . if we have taken too much of your time on this kind of evidence, you have my apology."

More recently, character evidence was presented in the trial of Bert Lance, former Director of the Office of Management and Budget. Of the 22 counts in which Lance was named a defendant, he was acquitted of 19 counts and the jury could not reach a verdict on the remaining three counts. Character testimony seemed to have had a major impact in this case, and similar testimony may be equally effective in a case where the defendant is a popular politician charged with a first offense.

Look at your client and your client's case objectively to determine whether character evidence would benefit him.

### How To Select The Character Witness

In presenting this evidence, use the opportunity to its best advantage. The character witness you select should know the defendant well and should be familiar with the defendant's reputation in the community in which he lives or works. The witness should be one with whom the jury will feel some kind of affinity. It is paramount that the jury be persuaded that the character witness is, himself, a well-respected person who really believes in the defendant.

In a recent trial in which the defendant was charged with bankruptcy fraud, the trial judge on his own motion moved the place of trial from one division to another in the same district due to pre-trial publicity. However, the importance of character evidence in this case was such that, after weighing the issue of substantial pre-trial publicity against the advantages of a trial by a jury who knew and could relate to the defendant and the character witnesses, defense counsel vehemently objected to the transfer from the division where the defendant was well-known. The court ultimately moved the trial back to the original division in the defendant's home town. Thus, counsel must weigh a motion for a change of venue (or object to the court, *sua sponte*, moving the place of trial) because of pre-trial publicity, against the impact on readily available good character testimony.

In this same bankruptcy fraud trial, the local postman was called as a character witness on behalf of the defendant. The postman was a well-known, well-respected member of the community. He testified that he had known the defendant for thirty-five years and that the defendant's reputation for truth and veracity in the community was exemplary. Although his testimony was brief, the postman (who appeared in uniform) was so likable that the prosecutor asked no questions on cross-examination.

In another trial, a grocery store clerk was charged with the theft of forty dollars ($40.00) from a customer. At trial the store manager was called as a character witness on the defendant's behalf. The manager's willingness to testify as a character witness for the defendant was even more important than his testimony. His presence effectively expressed the confidence and trust which he felt for his employee.

Prestigious individuals are often sought as character witnesses. One issue which has arisen is whether or not it is proper for a judge who has been subpoenaed by the defense to testify at trial as a character witness. In a recent federal tax evasion case,[5] defense counsel called a superior court judge as a character witness on the defendant's behalf. The trial court called a bench conference and questioned the propriety of a judge testifying in a trial as a character witness. On appeal, the Fifth Circuit held that the trial court had no power to bar the judge from testifying *under subpoena* and that since the subpoena was valid on its face, it insulated the judge from any violation of the judicial Canons. The court stated that the trial court's concern about the possibility of an impropriety by the witness-judge should have been handled by appropriate action before local bar authorities. Counsel should study the Canons carefully before submitting character evidence from a sitting judge.

The question arises as to whether prestigious people or "just plain folks" are better character witnesses. Much of this depends on the locale where the case is being tried and the attitude of jurors to religion, politicians and judges. Counsel may have to line up a variety of character witnesses for trial and decide which witnesses to call *after* jury selection when something more is known about each juror. After learning about the jurors, counsel can determine which character witnesses will relate best to jury members.

Thus, character witnesses must be selected carefully. Whether prestigious or "just plain folks," their sincerity and credibility are essential.

## Laying the Proper Foundation

The proper foundation must first be laid before character evidence is admissible at trial. Counsel must address its character evidence to the specific traits called in question by the charge against the defendant. Thus, counsel may prove the trait of "peacefulness" where the defendant is charged with assault and battery, but not perjury. On the other hand, counsel may prove the trait of "honesty" where the defendant is charged with perjury, but not assault and battery.

## How to Present Reputation Testimony

When defense counsel is presenting "reputation" testimony in either federal or state court the proper foundation is established by showing that the witness knows the defendant is familiar with the community in which the defendant lives or works; and that the witness knows the defendant's reputation in the community for a particular character trait. The following character testimony was effectively used in a recent conspiracy trial:

Q: What is your name, please?

A: Stuart DeMar.

Q: And where do you live, Mr. DeMar?

A: In Decatur, Georgia, DeKalb County. 418 Virginia Drive.

Q: How long have you lived in Decatur, DeKalb County, Georgia?

A: 56 years.

Q: How old are you, Mr. DeMar?

A: 62, sir.

Q: Then you have lived in DeKalb County practically all of your life?

A: Yes sir.

Q: And what is your occupation, Mr. DeMar?

A: I am Sheriff of DeKalb County.

Q: What has your adult life been devoted to?

A: Law enforcement.

Q: In what capacity?

A: First as a city police officer and then as a deputy sheriff and then as sheriff.

Q: Mr. DeMar, do you know the defendant in this case, Kenneth Lane?

A: I do, sir.

Q: How long have you known him?

A: All his life.

Q: Have you had occasion to work closely with Mr. Lane on many occasions?

A: I have, sir.

Q: Do you know other people in Decatur who know him?

A: I know many who know Mr. Lane.

Q: Have you had occasion to discuss with these people Mr. Lane's reputation in the community in which he resides?

A: I have sir.

Q: What is his reputation, Sheriff?

A: It is very good.

Q: And what is his reputation in the community for truth and veracity?

A: It is excellent.

Q: Is Mr. Lane a friend of yours?

A: Yes sir.

## How to Present "Opinion" Testimony

Before the witness can express an opinion as to character, counsel must again lay the proper foundation. The witness must show that he has sufficient personal knowledge on which to base an opinion and cannot rely on the defendant's reputation to support his opinion. While the opinion may be based on specific instances of conduct, the witness may not relate on direct examination any of the incidents which he thinks support his opinion.[6]

Remember that the distinction between reputation and opinion testimony is that the former is actually based on hearsay (what the community says) while the latter is based on personal knowledge. The following is an example of the latter:

Q: Will you state your name, please?

A: Samuel Hart.

Q: Are you better known as Judge Hart?

A: Well, I was judge of the probate court for 25 years.

Q: And when did you leave public office?

A: Last June.

Q: What is your occupation at this time?

A: I'm Executive Director of the Housing Authority of Pittsburgh, Pennsylvania.

Q: And how long have you been Executive Director?

A: Nearly 38 years.

Q: Do you know the defendant John Thomas?

A: Yes sir.

Q: And how long have you known him?

A: 25 or 30 years.

Q: In what capacity have you known him?

A: Well, I knew him first as a member of our Sunday school class and then he was elected President of the Sunday school class a few years later.

Q: Does your organization do business with him?

A: Yes we do.

Q: What kind of business is that?

A: We have bought large quantities of metal from him.

Q: Do you have an opinion as to Mr. Thomas' honesty?

A: Yes, it is excellent. I would entrust him with any of my financial and business affairs.

Q: Would you believe him under oath?

A: Yes sir.

## Dangers of Introducing Character Testimony

In many cases, the defendant does not have a good character and may have prior convictions which will be admissible if he makes an issue of his character. It may be important for the defense to insure that the defendant's character does not get into evidence.

The defendant's character cannot be put in evidence unless he chooses to put it in issue. In federal court and some state courts, if a defendant testifies he may be impeached like any other witness by showing his bad character.[7] In other state courts, however, the fact that the defendant testifies is not a sufficient condition for introducing his bad character, and the state may only ask questions related to the defendant's direct testimony and then attempt to impeach him.

Calling a character witness on the defendant's behalf also puts his character in issue. Once "reputation" or "opinion" testimony is inquired into on direct, your opponent may cross-examine the character witness.[8] On cross-examination, the prosecution may ask whether the witness has heard about or knows about specific acts of misconduct committed by the defendant, in order to test his testimony that defendant has a good reputation. Prepare your witness for the prosecutor's "attack" prior to trial, by taking him through a thorough and sifting cross-examination. An effective direct examination can be destroyed on cross if the witness is not told what to anticipate and how to handle the "tough questions." For example, the prosecution may ask a defense character witness whether he has heard that the defendant was arrested or convicted or did a specified evil deed on a certain date. This is allowable, although evidence of this sort is excluded for all other purposes in the law.[9] Witnesses should be chosen who can answer these questions in an effective manner. Also make sure the witness understands the present charges against the defendant; and it is often effective for the witness to be able to state, if the prosecutor opens the door, that the defendant has discussed the charges with him, that he has denied the allegations and that the witness believes the defendant.[10]

## Notes

1. F.R.E. 405(b) permits proof by specific instances of conduct where character is an "essential element of a charge, claim or defense." The cases in which character is an ultimate issue in a criminal case are rare. One example is where a prosecution under federal statute requires that the defendant be shown to be engaged in the business of gambling.

2. U.S. v. Staggs, 553 F.2d 1073 (7th Cir. 1977). King v. State, 248 N.W. 2d 458, 75 Wis. 2d 26 (1976).

3. 553 F.2d 1073 (7th Cir. 1977).

4. Represented by F. Lee Bailey and Mark J. Kadish.

5. United States v. Callahan, 588 F.2d 1078 (5th Cir. 1979).

6. Advisory Committee's Note, F.R.E. 405.

7. United States v. Walker, 313 F.2d 236, 238 (6th Cir. 1963).

8. Fed. R. E. 405(a).

9. Michelson v. United States, 335 U.S. 469, 93 L.Ed 168 (1948).

10. Amsterdam, Trial Manual 3 for the Defense of Criminal Cases.

# Direct Examination of the Medical Expert

## William B. Fitzgerald, Jr.

William B. Fitzgerald, Jr. is a partner in the Waterbury, Connecticut, law firm of Carmody & Torrance. He graduated from Harvard Law School in 1961, and practices in civil litigation, including plaintiff personal injury, medical and legal malpractice, and commercial litigation. Fitzgerald is a Fellow of the American College of Trial Lawyers.

The ideal direct examination of the medical expert leaves opposing counsel with no appropriate questions to ask. It anticipates all attacks on the doctor including, where applicable, his compensation for testifying for the defense, the fact that he has only examined the plaintiff one time in behalf of the defense, the fact that he customarily testifies for the plaintiff or the defendant, and the fact that he has some bias, expressed through his published materials or past testimony, for one side or the other of the subject issue. If, for instance, your expert is an orthopedic surgeon who has a bias against motorcycles, you should acknowledge it and inform the trier of the fact of the reasons, grounded in personal experience, for the doctor's bias.

### 17 Courtroom Techniques for an Effective Examination

1. You should control the examination and not permit the doctor to deliver a lecture or to give a long narrative answer based on his notes without the guidance of questions. The questions should be short whenever possible and designed to elicit one fact at a time. Usually, you will want to follow the patient's course chronologically. The jury is hearing the doc-

tor's testimony for the first and only time, and you do not want the doctor to give the testimony so fast that the jury cannot absorb it.

2. When an objection is made, before arguing it on the merits consider whether you can meet it by rephrasing the question, minimizing the interruption of your presentation and maintaining your control of the testimony. Also, to avoid distracting interruptions, seek advance agreement from opposing counsel for the admission of exhibits which you plan to offer during the examination.

3. You must have the doctor translate every technical term he uses into plain language for the jury. It is also helpful to personalize the doctor's testimony by relating it to your client by name. The doctor may tend to testify about "the patient" rather than use his or her name, but you can inject the name in the questions.

4. Lead the witness. You may properly lead until you get beyond preliminary matters. This is particularly useful for the less experienced trial lawyer as it will provide a comfortable beginning to the examination and get it started well.

5. Prior to the testimony itself, you will have invited the expert to suggest to you visual aids and demonstrative evidence to illustrate his testimony. They may range from an x-ray film to a video tape documentary of the type of surgery involved. Be sure that the expert knows that such evidence is admissible and ask for his suggestions. If a particular x-ray film is critical to the case, you can obtain a positive print of the film to go to the jury like any other photograph. Simple anatomy charts displaying only the particular matter in issue, such as the tibia and fibula in the sample testimony cited below, are preferable to complicated charts showing much more detail than you need. Examples of useful demonstrative evidence include a sample of the hip implant, photographs of the physical therapy unit showing the equipment which the patient had to use as part of the therapy, photographs of the patient in various stages of recovery, and, in cases of severe permanent disability such as quadraplegia, films showing the daily life of the patient.

Most plastic surgeons make before-and-after photographs of the patient, and the photographs taken in advance of the surgery should be of interest to you.

6. You should always consider whether your proposed demonstrative evidence will offend the jury. Also, any such evidence that relates to treatment of the patient rendered when the patient was under general anesthesia is of questionable use to you. But you might use such a film in an exceptional case, for instance, to justify the plaintiff's protracted convalescence by illustrating in detail the seriousness of the procedure.

It is important not to overdo the demonstrative evidence. As Professor Irving Younger has stated, to prove that the patient died it is not necessary to exhibit his heart to the jury.

7. Prior to presenting the testimony, you will have discovered the doctor's attitude toward pain in general and toward pain in this particular case, and you will not ask questions about pain unless you are satisfied in advance with his answers. Physicians' attitudes toward pain, both physical and mental, vary widely. You may want to have the doctor characterize the pain in terms of mild, moderate, moderate to severe, or severe. If the doctor minimizes the pain too much, you may elect not to ask him about it at all, and then prove it through the patient without, of course, permitting the patient to exaggerate it. On direct examination do not ask the doctor any questions to which you have not already learned the answers from preparation.

8. Take all the time you need to explain in detail the qualifications of your expert. Do not assume that the jury understands, without precise explanation, the specialty in which your expert is qualified.

Do not accept opposing counsel's offer to stipulate that your physician is an expert, but rather establish his qualifications by his testimony. You have an absolute right to qualify the witness even where the concession is offered. *Murphy v. National Railroad Passenger Corp.*, 547 F2d 516 (4th Cir. 1977). It is reversible error to exclude testimony of his qualifications.

9. Alternate questions that call for short answers with those that call for long answers. Do not bore the jury.

10. Do not repeat either the question or the answer. Nothing is more unappealing than the following sequence:

Q: Are you a doctor, doctor?

A: Yes I am a doctor.

Q: What kind of doctor are you, doctor?

A: I am a medical doctor.

Q: Oh, are you a medical doctor?

A: Yes.

11. Some parts of your expert's testimony will be so important that you will want to have a transcript for your summation or for various motions during trial. You can arrange some system of signals with the court re-

porter to let the reporter know that you need a partial transcript. Such a system can save you valuable time later by eliminating the necessity of reviewing all of the reporter's notes for the particular witness.

12. If you plan to use a hypothetical question in the examination, it should be written out in advance with copies typed to be given to all other counsel and to the court. It should also be cleared in advance with the witness. The hypothetical question will often draw objections, require rereading from the court reporter, and generally cause an interruption of the presentation of the testimony. If you have it typed, and the court rules that it must be changed, you can make the changes readily on your typed copy.

13. It is advisable that you have memorized in advance or, if absolutely necessary, written out, the last question for your expert witness. This will permit you to finish the direct examination in a positive and confident manner.

14. If your physician's diagnosis will be attacked, you should take pains to show the foundation of the diagnosis. For instance, if your defense doctor concludes that plaintiff does not have a low back strain at all or that it is of minimal significance, you should fully detail each and every test that he did prior to making the diagnosis. It is of little use to have the doctor say, "all neurological tests were negative" or "I did all the standard tests for low back strain and they were all negative."

15. Take the doctor through each test. Have him illustrate, for example, the straight leg raising test and ask him why he did it. Have him explain normal range of motion and detail what the test might have shown were it positive and what that could have meant in connection with his diagnosis. Explain, through him, that "negative" means normal. Explain the difference between "symptoms" (subjective) and "signs" or "findings" (objective).

16. If your doctor's diagnosis is not in accord with the majority view as expressed in the relevant literature and as held by the physician for the opposition, you should particularly emphasize your doctor's qualifications and experience with this type of case. If he is the treating physician, emphasize that this is his diagnosis made to treat this patient and not a diagnosis made as part of a defense examination. Emphasize that in treating this patient, he was not treating the "majority" of patients who present similar symptoms, and he does not make his diagnoses simply by "going by the book." Emphasize the role of this physician's own judgment in making the diagnosis. Emphasize the obvious fact that where there is a majority view applicable to most cases, no one claims that it is applicable to every single case, and you are only dealing with one case here. In so doing, you are protecting the doctor's diagnosis and anticipating the

cross-examination. This witness, of course, can readily agree with a treatise presented on cross-examination to attack his diagnosis. He can agree that the treatise correctly deals with the average case and he can repeat that this is not the average case.

17. Conversely, while treatises are generally used on cross-examination, you can use them on direct examination if they are recognized as authoritative [Federal Rules of Evidence, Rule 803 (18)], in which case they can be offered to prove the truth of the matter asserted. If the authority is overwhelmingly on your side on a disputed issue, you may want to introduce a treatise excerpt on direct examination as cumulative evidence.

## The Order of Testimony

Generally speaking the doctor's testimony should follow the following order:

(a) First contact with patient—when and where and under what circumstances did he first see the patient.
(b) The patient's history.
(c) The first examination.
(d) The initial findings.
(e) The initial diagnosis.
(f) The treatment.
(g) Present condition and prognosis.

## Sample Direct Examination of a Medical Expert

The following is an excerpt of testimony of plaintiff's treating orthopedic surgeon. It illustrates the use of short questions, chronological sequence, short answers where possible, the use of exhibits and the anticipation of cross-examination.

The reports are presented herein. Note that the examination goes well beyond the literal content of the reports. It is rarely, if ever, sufficient to merely have the doctor "read the reports."

Q: State your name and address please.

A: Kristaps J. Keggi, M.D. My professional address is 1211 West Main Street, Waterbury, Connecticut.

Q: And you are a licensed medical doctor?

A: Yes, I am licensed in the State of Connecticut, New York, New Hampshire, Arizona.

Q: Without going through all four states, when were you first licensed anywhere?

A: I was first licensed in 1960 in New York.

Q: Tell the jury please where you went to medical school and something about your internship and residency.

A: I graduated from the Yale Medical School in 1959. I did general surgery in New York for two years; then I came back to Yale and did three years of orthopedic surgery; then went in the Army. I spent a year in Vietnam where I was chief of orthopedic surgery in a MASH-type hospital, came back to Yale, was on the full-time faculty for three years in orthopedic surgery and in 1969 I went up to Waterbury in the private practice of orthopedic surgery.

Q: In Vietnam were you in orthopedics?

A: In orthopedic surgery, yes.

Q: And what is orthopedics?

A: Orthopedic surgery is a specialty; surgery that deals with the so-called musculoskeletal system, bones, joints, muscles, ligaments, nerves of the human body.

Q: Are you affiliated with any hospitals?

A: Yes, I am on the staff of the Waterbury Hospital and the staff of St. Mary's Hospital in Waterbury. I am also on the staff of the Newington's Children's Hospital in Newington.

Q: Do you have any affiliation with any medical schools?

A: The Yale University School of Medicine.

Q: And what is the nature of your affiliation?

A: I am an assistant clinical professor of orthopedic surgery.

Q: I assume you belong to a number of medical associations and academies.

A: Approximately 12.

Q: Are you board-certified?

A: Board-certified in orthopedic surgery.

Q: What does that mean? What do you have to do to be board-certified?

A: You have to be fully trained, which means five years after medical school, and you have to be in practice for two years and then you have to pass national level-type examinations.

Q: And have you published any professional articles in your field or given any lectures?

A: Yes, I have.

Q: Approximately how many articles have you published?

A: I would say 20.
   *[If the witness had published anything concerning injuries of the type in question, the publication should be mentioned, but you should make sure that the doctor is ready to explain, on cross-examination, any apparent inconsistencies between his articles and his diagnosis in this case.]*

Q: Now, doctor, did you have occasion to treat the plaintiff, Sheila Murphy?

A: Yes, I first saw Sheila in the emergency room on January 2, 1976.

Q: And was a history of why she was there made available to you?

A: Yes, she was brought in by ambulance, having been in an automobile accident.

Q: And did you examine her?

A: Yes, she was examined and from an orthopedic point of view I found her to have a fracture of the tibia and fibula, which is her lower leg, fracture of the radius, which is her forearm, and shortly after admission she was also complaining of low back pain.

Q: Now, I call your attention to this chart here, and ask you what does it show? (*Chart is shown.*)

A: Well, that's a picture of a forearm and wrist.

Q: Will this picture help you explain to the jury and help them understand something about this wrist fracture?

A: Yes, I think if you had to show where the fracture was you would probably say it was in this area here, this being the radius.
   (*Mark as exhibit. It is admissible because it helps him explain and helps the jury understand.*)

Q: How did you treat that fracture of the wrist, doctor?

A: That fracture was set and placed in a cast, in a plaster cast.

Q: And did that particular fracture cause any pain to the plaintiff?

A: Yes it did.

Q: I show you another chart and ask you what is shown on that one. (*Chart is shown.*)

A: This picture is basically one of the leg, this being the thigh and the femur and this being the lower leg, the tibia being the larger of the two bones, and the fibula being the smaller one.

Q: Now, do I understand that this patient had fractures in both the tibia and the fibula?

A: Yes, this patient had fractures in both the tibia and fibula.

Q: And, is the tibia the bone in the front of the leg?

A: Yes, that's basically the shin bone, if you touch your own leg you'll find that you are touching the tibia.

Q: Where would you touch your leg to touch the fibula?

A: The fibula would be to the side. (Demonstrating)

Q: And how did you treat those fractures, doctor?

A: Those fractures were also reduced; in other words, aligned properly and then immobilized, placed in a cast extending from the thigh down to the toes.

Q: Did those tibia and fibula fractures resolve eventually?

A: Yes, these fractures all healed without any major sequelae, and she went through the usual period of casting followed by the usual period of stiffness of the joints above and below the fracture site, but eventually she recovered quite well.

Q: And again, did those fractures cause pain to the plaintiff?

A: Yes, they caused her pain for several months.

Q: Now, you mentioned at the time of this admission she had some low back complaints. Did you follow her after discharge?

A: Yes, she was followed after discharge and was also placed on physiotherapy for all of her injuries, her arm, leg and also back because she continued to have back pain, and for this she was given physiotherapy.

Q: And did the physiotherapy cure the back pain?

A: No, as a matter of fact as she became somewhat more active as her fractures were healing, she started having more back pain and more leg pain, specifically left leg pain.

Q: And so what course ensued with this back pain?

A: She was treated in a so-called conservative non-operative manner until the summer of 1976 when it was obvious that she had to be treated in ways other than just bed rest, massage, heat and that sort of thing.

Q: In what respect was it obvious that you had to do a different treatment?

A: She wasn't getting better on so-called conservative treatment.

Q: Was she in pain, doctor?

A: Yes, she continued to complain of back and leg pain.

Q: Are you familiar with the manual for orthopedic surgeons of the American Academy of Orthopedic Surgeons?

A: Yes.

Q: For evaluating disability? Do you have a copy with you?

A: Yes I do.

Q: There is a part in there, doctor, where pain is divided into four categories or grades, grades one through four. Are you familiar with that?

A: No, I usually concentrate on the back part of the book rather than the front. Which page are you referring to?

Q: Page 7 at the bottom characterizes pain as mild, moderate, severe and very severe. What I want to know is this, there came a time with Sheila Murphy when you decided that you had to take other steps. How would you characterize the pain that her back was giving her at the time when you decided to put her back in the hospital?

A: I would characterize it as being moderate to severe.

Q: And before we get to the second hospitalization, did you inform yourself of any prior history of this patient with back trouble?

A: Yes, as part of the history it was established that in 1971, the patient had had another accident which had eventually led to a back operation in 1972, that operation being the excision of a lumbar disc.

Q: And would you locate the lumbar for the jury.

A: The lumbar area is—when you talk about a lumbar spine, it is that portion of your spine which corresponds approximately to your belt line. You are talking about this portion of the back, approximately the level of a belt.

Q: And what was that operation in 1972?

A: What she had is she had a laminectomy with the excision of the L4 - L5 disc. The spine is made up of blocks of bone that are called vertebrae that sit on top of each other.

Q: Do you see any on this chart, doctor, vertebrae? (*Chart is shown.*)

A: Well, this is an example except it doesn't show the entire vertebral body, this is just sort of cut off; anyway that's about the way they are, and in between these bones are discs which are rubbery material which are supposed to act as shock absorbers. Occasionally, as a result of an injury, you can have a piece of this rubbery material pop out of place, which is then called a ruptured or herniated or slipped disc, and as this happens that piece of disc which has slipped out of place, not the whole thing but a piece of this material that slips out of place, pushes on a nerve and as a result of this causes back pain, back spasms, and also leg pain if the nerve involved is one that goes down to the leg.

Q: Now this next chart, doctor, does that show such a nerve as you are talking about? (*Chart is shown.*)

A: Yes, these are the nerves that we are talking about. This is a disc here.

Q: It is a top view, isn't it?

A: Well, if you want to call it that. It's like a slice of bologna, if you want to call it that. And there is a disc and here are the nerves which are in back of these bones, and the disc as it slips out of place would be pressing on one of these nerves, thus causing pain.

Q: So, in 1972 Sheila Murphy had a disc out at—at what level was that?

A: L4 - L5, between the fourth and the fifth lumbar vertebrae, L referring to lumbar 4, lumbar 5.

Q: And, what do you call that operation?

A: That is called a disc excision, obviously, but also very frequently people will refer to this operation as a simple laminectomy. A laminectomy being to laminize. Another structure that enters into the picture is this portion of the spine. In the back of these blocks of bone, the vertebrae, are these knuckles of bone that are all interconnected and they are called spinous processes and lamina, and the lamina is a sort of a shield of bone along the back of the spinal cord and spinal nerves, and in order to get into the spinal canal and to get at the disc and to get at the nerves you have to make a hole in this bone in the back of the disc and that is called a laminectomy. In other words, you go in and you make a hole, and very often when people talk of disc excisions they also say laminectomy, using that term synonymously.

Q: Now, you did not do that surgery in 1972?

A: No, that was done at Yale.

Q: But did you inform yourself from records about how she went after that surgery?

A: Yes, she did rather well. She was only followed for a couple of months and then discharged, having had a rather successful result.

Q: Would being followed for a few months, would that be a relatively short period for this operation?

A: Yes, I think that's very good.

Q: What do you know, doctor, about Sheila's history after she was discharged a few months after the operation? That's with respect to her back.

A: This is in 1972?

Q: That's right. During the four years leading up to the day of the accident.

A: She was described as being symptom free, apart from occasional backaches. As far as I could determine, she was participating in sports and went on and had a child. There is no history of any major problems with pregnancy and delivery and obviously neo-natal care of the child, housework, diapers.

Q: She had occasional backaches as the only symptom of trouble with her back during this period that we are talking about?

A: Yes.

Q: How would you describe her functional disability, if any, during that period of four years with respect to her back?

A: Minimal or mild, to use the word, I believe, in the manual.

Q: Now, does the science of orthopedics automatically assign some amount of disability to a patient who has had this operation?

A: Yes, I think there are several ways of doing it. One is, you know, you can go through all kinds of elaborate measurements of back motion and you can measure millimeter by millimeter the hole that you made in the back to get into the disc and then you can just sort of use basic guidelines in terms of again, mild, moderate, severe, and the net result is approximately the same. I have been following this broader approach using the manual of the American Academy of Orthopedic Surgeons.

Q: All right now, recognizing that she had very little in the way of symptoms, do you nevertheless recognize some degree of disability from the simple fact that she had the operation in 1972?

A: Yes, there is no question about the fact that somebody who has had a slipped disc or a herniated disc and who has had surgery has a back that is weaker than the normal back in the similar patient, same sex, same age and so on. I think that for that reason alone, even if the patient is symptom free, we assign partial/permanent disability of the back because there is scar tissue, there is a hole in the lamina, the disc has been removed, there is scarring around nerves.

Q: Can you, doctor, on the basis of this history, tell us your opinion as to what her disability was before the accident?

A: If I had seen her at a time, well after she was discharged or at about the time she was discharged by the surgeons in New Haven, I would have probably pinned a 10% disability of the back on her condition if somebody had questioned me about that.

Q: And you would assign that notwithstanding the fact that she had only occasional backaches in terms of symptoms.

A: Yes, I would definitely rate her as having some permanent disability, damage to her back.

Q: Even though as you say the functional impairment to her at that time you characterize as mild?

A: Yes, I think even though she was functioning perfectly well I think she would definitely have a disability.

Q: Now, you told us that you had her admitted again after this conservative treatment was not curing her. What **did** you do when you put her in the hospital?

A: She underwent a myelogram.

Q: What's a myelogram?

A: A myelogram is a test designed to show the inside of the spine, if you will. It's a test designed to show ruptured or herniated discs. It's a test where we put a needle into the canal, this canal here, where the nerves are, and we instill some dye that shows up in x-rays. The nerves and discs themselves do not show up on x-ray. The only thing that shows up on ordinary x-rays is bone, so in order to visualize the nerves in contrast, we put in this dye and then we can tell by little notches in the column of the dye whether or not there is a disc out of place.

Q: What do you put the needle in, doctor?

A: The needle is put into the upper lumbar area, I would say two or three inches above the belt line.

Q: And do you fill the entire spinal column with this dye?

A: No, you instill just enough to fill the lower portion of the spinal canal, the area of pain in her case.

Q: And the dye, if there is any problem with a disc or nerve, the dye will illustrate this for the doctor?

A: Well, I think myelograms show discs in approximately 85% to 90% of cases, and in 10% to 15% of the cases the disc does not show up even with this particular test. But usually it is a fairly reliable examination.

Q: And so you did this procedure on Sheila Murphy?

A: Yes we did.

Q: And with what result?

A: This showed that she now had a disc injury one level below her injury of 1972. In other words, her previous disc injury had been at L4 - L5, which is this level, and now she had a disc that was out of place in this area here, L5, which is the lumbar, 5th vertebral body, and S1 referring to the sacrum, which is sort of a solid piece of bone connecting the spine to the pelvis.

Q: Now, having done the myelogram with those results, what did you do next?

A: Well, having seen the myelogram and having diagnosed the disc problem, it was decided that she had had enough symptoms, disability and pain in the preceding six months to warrant surgery and the risks thereof. Also, it was felt that because of her previous operation and six months worth of back pain, that she should not only have the excision of the disc, in other words an operation similar to what she had in 1972, but she should also have a fusion to prevent any further problems with these discs. A fusion is an operation where you take some bone graft from the pelvic bone and you lay it around these bones in this area here and then eventually the bone graft turns into a solid chunk of bone that prevents all motion of these lower bones of the back.

Q: You did this one from the back?

A: From the back.

Q: And how long did that operation take?

A: That operation took approximately three hours.

Q: And how was Mrs. Murphy's condition subsequent to the operation?

A: Her condition was good. She improved, her fusion took and she had a fairly satisfactory course even though she was still left with some back pain and leg pain and some disability obviously.

Q: And incidentally, could you describe for us the type of scarring this fusion operation causes to the patient?

A: Well, in order to do a fusion, you have to not only get into the back, which is, you go right in the middle of the back, but you also have to get the bone graft. Very often the bone graft part of the operation remains painful longer than the fusion part itself. Because what you have to do to get the bone graft is you have to go out to the side of the pelvis, to the hip area, to approximately the area where your back pocket is, you have to strip off the gluteus maximus muscle from the bone in this area and then, with gouges and chisels, you have to sort of gouge out these chunks of bone, then transplant into the mid portion of the back and that sometimes hurts.

Q: How does that leave any scarring, or can you do that without scarring?

A: There are two ways of doing it. One way is to do a mid-line incision and sort of undermine your way to the side and get it sort of obliquely; and then there is another way of getting it where you make a second incision and you go straight down on the bone and the patient is left with two incisions. We usually do it through one incision, especially in women. It's cosmetically more pleasing.

Q: Is that what you did for Mrs. Murphy?

A: Yes we did.

Q: One incision?

A: One incision.

Q: So the incision at the site of the fusion, what kind of a scar does that leave?

A: Well, it leaves a scar approximately 6 inches long.

Q: And width to that scar?

A: Oh, sometimes they spread, not too bad, half a centimeter, one-quarter of an inch, that sort of thing.

Q: That's a permanent scar, of course?

A: Right.

Q: Now, I would like to know, doctor, about Mrs. Murphy's condition when you stopped treating her in terms of any limitations on her activities.

A: She still had some difficulty, she still had some back pain and some pain going down her left leg, and she also had difficulty with some of the basic activities that one must engage in such as housework. Apparently her husband now has to help her with the chores.

Q: She testified earlier before you came, doctor, that she had to give up her sports activities. Is that testimony consistent with this type of operation and her condition as you know it?

A: Yes, I think there are many people after major back operations and injury such as she's had and then subsequent fusion and so on, that have significant limitation of activity.

Q: Now you mentioned, doctor, that both before and after the operation she had some pain radiating. Now would you tell the ladies and gentlemen of the jury what that means?

A: That means that the pain starts out in the back and then in a ray-like fashion it goes down the leg, is radiating pain.

Q: Does the chart on the board, doctor, show anything in that connection?

A: Well, I think it just shows that the reason for this radiation is the fact that the nerves are irritated in this area, the patient feels a pain down in the leg where these nerves end up.

Q: Now, you can answer the next question yes or no. Do you have an opinion, doctor, based on a reasonable medical probability as to whether or not Mrs. Murphy has any more disability after this accident than she did prior to it?

A: Absolutely. She has quite a bit more difficulty and disability as a result of the accident, surgery and so on.

Q: Okay, you characterized before that her preaccident disability in terms of functional impairment was mild, I think. If you used the same terms, how would you characterize her disability today, functionally?

A: Oh, moderate to moderately severe.

Q: And in terms of percentage, you said earlier that she probably had a 10% disability on her back before the accident. Do you have an opinion as to a percentage disability of her back now?

A: Yes, her disability was assessed at 20% of the spine or back.

Q: And is that permanent in your opinion?

A: That's a permanent disability.

Q: Is this 20% disability of the back, is this a condition that Sheila will have for the rest of her life?

A: Yes she will.

Q: And doctor, do you have an opinion as to whether or not this increase in her disability, which you just described, whether or not it has any casual connection to this accident?

A: Yes, I think it is directly related to the accident.

The foregoing case presents a fairly neat medical picture and leaves little room for effective cross-examination. In more complicated cases, you should determine whether particular elements of your medical position are worth presenting at all, in view of the anticipated destructive effects of cross-examination. Such cross-examination will not only attack such questionable medical propositions directly, but it may well affect the credibility of the more solid parts of your position. It is often advisable to limit your medical claims to avoid involving the doctor in controversy of marginal benefit.

# Direct Examination of an Adverse Examining Physician

## R. D. Blanchard

R. D. Blanchard is a partner in the Minneapolis law firm of Meagher, Geer, Markham, Anderson, Adamson, Flaskamp & Brennan. He is an active member of the Defense Research Institute, and has been primarily involved in civil litigation for the past 22 years. He is the author of "Cross Examination of a Treating Physician" (DRI) and the book, *Litigation and Trial Practice for the Legal Paraprofessional*.

A lawyer has some unique problems and opportunities when he undertakes the direct examination of the physician who conducted the adverse (independent) medical examination of the plaintiff in a personal injury action. The problems stem from the facts that the adverse medical examination is usually conducted many months after the alleged injuries were sustained, and that the adverse examiner is not involved in the plaintiff's medical treatment. Whereas the treating physician sees the plaintiff on numerous occasions, beginning soon after the accident, the adverse examiner sees the plaintiff only one time. The treating physician's testimony certainly has a "head start" for persuasiveness. If the treating physician and the adverse examining physician have reached conflicting medical opinions about the plaintiff's condition and the evidence seems evenly balanced, the treating physician's testimony will probably prevail.

The problem is compounded because the defendant's entire theory of defense on the damages issue centers upon the persuasiveness of the adverse examiner. The jury usually knows that he was selected by the defense. They may even come to believe that he was "hired" solely for the purpose of providing favorable medical evidence. If he lacks authority, the jury will resolve doubts in favor of the treating physician's testimony. If he lacks necessary facts and information to be knowledgeable about the case, his expert opinions may appear contrived. If his credibility is shaken, the entire defense will be contaminated.

## Mapping Out Your Defense Strategy

Recognizing plaintiff's advantages in the medical aspects of the case is the second step toward preparing an adequate strategy for the defense. The first step, of course, is to determine which, if any, of plaintiff's claims are in error or subject to question. Only those claims should be controverted. It is a mistake to spend time on matters that should not be disputed or cannot be refuted. Like all other facets of litigation, the evidence concerning injuries and a medical evaluation must be based upon a theory which ties everything together. A theory points the direction for discovering evidence and establishing the truth. Having a theory enables a lawyer, and hopefully the jury, to understand and explain the interrelationship of all the relevant evidence. If the evidence is consistent with a valid theory of the facts, corroboration occurs automatically. A theory on the facts tends to become self-validating if it is correct. If a case is successfully defended without having a theory on the facts, the favorable result is sheer luck. You didn't win; the other side merely lost.

The defense lawyer's challenge, which is considerable, is to minimize plaintiff's obvious advantages in dealing with the medical evidence and effectively utilize the several opportunities permitted by the Rules of Civil Procedure applicable in most courts of record.

The defense lawyer has a responsibility to convince the jury that the physician was selected because of his professional competence—not because he harbors a bias against plaintiffs or is dependent upon the defendant or insurance industry for his livelihood. It is absolutely imperative that the witness appear to be honest and sincere. He must be fully prepared on the case before he takes the stand. In addition to fully understanding the medical aspects of the case, he should have a general understanding of the case as a whole. There is no reason for the adverse medical examiner to see himself as an advocate for the defense. But he should see himself as an advocate to support the medical information he has assembled and the medical opinions he has rendered to the parties through his medical report. More physicians would be willing to conduct adverse medical examinations if they realized that all the defendant's counsel needs is a competent medical examination and opinion that he can rely upon.

A format for the direct examination of the adverse examining physician should take into consideration the inherent weaknesses of such testimony and utilize fully the available opportunities. The basic source of the witness's testimony is his written report. The substance of his testimony will come straight from the report and, possibly, some office notes. The lawyer's task is to establish a smooth dialogue by asking relevant questions based upon the matters read from the report. With adequate planning and some consultation with the witness about the format, the witness's testimony can appear to be almost extemporaneous. His use of the report should appear to be like a reference to an important record.

Presumably, the examiner was selected because he is highly competent in his field and because the plaintiff's medical claims are within his area of expertise. Therefore, it is particularly important to inform·the jury about his education, specialty training, board certification, government appointments, writings, and teaching positions. A lawyer should never stipulate to his witness's qualification to give medical opinions. The jury should be led to feel that the plaintiff would have done well to have placed himself in the care of this highly qualified physician. Though the adverse examiner has not treated the plaintiff, the jury must be made to appreciate that he does treat many patients. For that reason it is important to bring out the fact that he is on the staff of one or more hospitals. His profession is that of healing.

Almost as important as competency is the examiner's professional standing—his acceptance by his peers. Professional acceptance can be shown by having him identify and describe the professional associations to which he belongs, and the offices he holds or has held in those associations. Whenever a physician is asked by other physicians to act as a consultant, he has professional acceptance and his role as a consultant should be brought out. What could be more delightful than showing that the treating physician consults the adverse examiner or his group on occasion! Some "city specialists" routinely travel to rural communities to provide medical consultation services. Certainly they enjoy peer acceptance. Any special appointments that the adverse examiner has should be mentioned. For example, a physician may be designated by the Federal Aviation Agency to conduct bi-annual physical examinations for commercial pilots. Even though such experience has nothing to do with the case at hand, the federal appointment speaks well for the examiner's credibility. If he is associated with other physicians in the practice of medicine, their identity should be made known.

## How to Present the Witness in Court

When the witness is being introduced to the jury, the lawyer's mode of questioning should *elicit* from the witness his achievements. A lawyer should not force the witness to give a narrative expounding his own greatness. Rare is the person who can eulogize himself without irritating or boring his listeners. It is the lawyer's function to create the framework for his witness's testimony and to establish a dialogue within that framework. In other words, if the direct testimony turns out to be unintelligible or dull or unpersuasive, it is usually not the witness's fault. The witness may be pretty much on his own during cross-examination, but not on direct.

Through a proper introduction of the witness, the defense counsel can mitigate the problem that the witness was not involved in the plaintiff's actual treatment. Though the adverse examiner did not see the plaintiff immediately after the accident and has seen him only once before trial, he usually has ample information from which to make his diagnosis. After all, before the examination he had the opportunity to review and *consider* all the tests, records and reports prepared by the treating physicians and consultants. Furthermore, the adverse medical examination is usually conducted after the plaintiff's deposition was taken, so it is possible for defense counsel to provide the adverse examiner with relevant, detailed information about the accident and plaintiff's history which the treating physicians probably never had.

The jury should be told about the adverse examiner's many sources of information before the witness discusses his own examination of the plaintiff. But it must be made clear that he has only *considered* this collateral information and has not *relied* upon it for his diagnosis. The importance of this point will be discussed below. Obviously, the adverse examiner is able to direct his medical examination to the controversial matters relatively quickly. Though the actual examination may have taken only an hour or less, the time was fully adequate, considering the wealth of information available to him to prepare for it. He should tell the jury, in response to questions, that he didn't need any more time for the examination in order to make an accurate diagnosis. If he needed more tests, he would have ordered them.

If the adverse examiner does choose to *rely* upon any portion of plaintiff's medical records, those portions should be specified and expressly adopted. For example, if a myelogram was performed and reported as negative, there should be no need to repeat it. The radiologist's report should be referred to and adopted, perhaps even quoted, in the adverse medical report and testimony.

Too often defense lawyers see cases where the plaintiff gives the adverse examiner an erroneous or incomplete medical accident history in which the matters omitted may be important to the defendant's theory of the case. As a general rule, it is best to pursue the significance of these important omissions only after the adverse examiner has given his opinion based upon the information actually supplied by the plaintiff. But the plaintiff's failure to mention the important facts—whether or not intentional—should be clearly indicated while the history is being related from the adverse medical report.

Whether or not the adverse examiner alludes to plaintiff's medical records during the direct examination, there is a possibility that plaintiff's counsel may take the tack of asking the witness if he "considered" various statements contained in the reports which are particularly favorable to plaintiff. In this manner, plaintiff's counsel has seized upon the opportunity to merely repeat facts which were important to his case-in-chief. Ordinarily, he would not ask the witness how he explains or reconciles those facts to the witness's own conclusions. Consequently, the defense counsel and adverse examiner should be prepared to develop the appropriate explanations on re-direct. If handled correctly by the defense, plaintiff's counsel will wish he had never tried to embellish his case by asking such questions. The counter attack can succeed only if there has been good anticipation of the problem and adequate preparation.

The defense lawyer must meet with the physician at least once before trial so that they can prepare *each other* for the court appearance. The lawyer should be able, at that point, to explain where the significiant controversies are. They should be able to agree on the medical theory and what explanations should be given to the jury. Both should review the records before the meeting. It's best to schedule the meeting for the end of the day so that the physician doesn't have patients waiting to see him.

### Highlighting the Medical Report

The adverse examiner's testimony is necessarily predicated upon his own report which usually runs several pages in length. I don't think there is anything wrong in having the witness read from his report. In fact, it may be best if he reads it verbatim, but a dialogue must be established and maintained in order to keep the jury's attention. An adequate dialogue can be effectively established by politely interrupting and asking appropriate questions as the report is being read. The questions should elicit additional relevant information concerning the history, complaints, examination, etc.

After the physician's introduction, the testimony usually proceeds as follows:

Q: Doctor, did you conduct an *independent* medical (neurological) (orthopedic) examination of Mr. (plaintiff) at my request?

A: Yes.

Q: When did you conduct the examination?

A: Date.

Q: Where was the examination conducted?

A: My office in the Medical Arts Building.

Q: Did you obtain a history from Mr. (plaintiff)?

A: Yes.

Q: Did you have any other information available about Mr. (plaintiff)'s medical history and condition?

A: Yes. (Describing records, reports).

Q: What did Mr. (plaintiff) tell you?

A: He told me that . . . .

As the medical history is related by the witness from his office notes or the report, ask him questions for clarification and emphasis to make the evidence more vivid. Ask the physician why he inquired about certain aspects of the history such as prior accidents or medical conditions when it is relevant to your theory. Of course the adverse examiner is not required to reiterate plaintiff's version of the disputed facts about how the accident occurred. For example, plaintiff's claim of the green light or plaintiff's claim of an unlawful speed on the part of the defendant. The statements are self-serving hearsay. If such statements are in the report, the physician should be advised to omit them or rephrase them. If plaintiff's history states that defendant was driving 35 miles per hour in a 30-mph zone at the moment of impact, it's enough for the physician to state that plaintiff described a forceful impact on the side of his vehicle. Where the witness quotes the plaintiff, the lawyer may want to emphasize that it is a quote. The emphasis can be accomplished by asking the pertinent questions.

After the plaintiff's history is covered per the report, it is desirable to bring out the patient's failure to volunteer information about certain important facets of his history, such as a prior history of similar symptoms or other accidents. Perhaps the deposition or investigation revealed that the patient has engaged in strenuous activities since the accident in question, such as skiing, tennis, football, or moving his household furniture into a new home. He may have made a previous claim of permanent disability. Again, there is no need at this point to follow up the questions about the significance of the omissions. Do that later. Sometimes experienced physicians break down the plaintiff's history into categories such as *Personal History, Occupational History, Prior Medical History* and the *Accident History*. The breakdown aids the lawyer to establish a dialogue.

The next section of the report should list the plaintiff's complaints and symptoms, preferably in the order of their importance to him at the time of the examination. Past symptoms that have resolved should be mentioned last. Of course it's important to know just how long the symptoms persisted. Though at first blush it may seem counterproductive, I think the symptoms should be as detailed as possible. If subjective symptoms are diffuse or recur only at certain times of the day or recur with normal activity, they are suspect. Counsel's questions concerning the recorded complaints and symptoms should be aimed at clarifying their character and lifting the specific areas of the anatomy involved.

Usually the next section of the adverse medical report details the examination, medical tests and findings. A physician should use the language of his profession when describing the examination because it's comfortable for him, he can be more precise with his descriptions and he tends to sound authoritative. However, whenever medical jargon is used by the witness concerning a significant part of the examination, the lawyer should ask him to explain the technical words "for us." This approach, I think, is preferable to allowing or requiring the physician to repeatedly volunteer a layman's definition each time. He will probably do it too often. This recommended procedure aids in maintaining a dialogue and helps the witness to avoid the appearance of "talking down" to the jurors.

The witness should identify each medical test by its technical name. The lawyer should ask for a description of each *relevant* test, i.e., how it is conducted. He needs to show the jury why it was conducted. Then he should have the physician explain the significance of the findings or test results. The same format should be employed in describing the more elaborate diagnostic procedures such as electroencephalograms, electromyograms, myelograms, and psychometric tests.

## How To Make The Most of Negative Findings

Too many defense lawyers fail to take full advantage of the opportunity to ask about the significance of negative findings. They erroneously assume that the jurors understand all of the ramifications of a negative finding, but they don't. For example, the adverse examiner may report that the straight leg raising test was negative. The direct examination should provide a full description of the test—the patient's positions on the examining table, the active movement of the patient's legs and the passive motions. After the jury is shown what was done they must be educated to understand why the test was done, viz. to test for impingement of nerves emanating from the lower spine. Though a negative finding may not be conclusive against the existence of an herniated intervertebral disc, it strongly mitigates against a disc problem. But it does more. It may demonstrate a full range of motion of the hip and thigh muscles. The absence of true muscle spasms is manifest.

The medical report may state that the patient has a full range of motion of the neck. The finding is too important to leave it at that. Through additional questioning the lawyer should obtain a clear description of each of the several motions tested: flexion, extension, rotation and tilting from side to side. The range of motion test usually demonstrates that the muscles have good strength, the ligaments are not impaired, there is no swelling, no muscle spasm was present or produced by the movements. There probably was no atrophy of the musculature. And the joints were functioning normally.

If cross-checking tests show inconsistent responses, the adverse examiner should not be burdened with having to characterize plaintiff as dishonest. For example, if plaintiff complains of radiation of pain into his leg and foot when the straight leg raising test is performed, but has no such symptoms when he sits on the examining table with his legs dangling, there is a physiological inconsistency. After the adverse examiner points out the inconsistency it is sufficient for the lawyer to ask the physician if there is any "medical or physiological explanation" for the inconsistency. He can comfortably respond that there is none. He should not be asked to directly attack plaintiff's honesty. He should not be asked if plaintiff is telling the truth or whether he believes plaintiff's subjective complaints. If the examination shows there is no muscle atrophy of an extremity, where there are subjective symptoms, pursue the significance of it. Ask him what that indicated about the condition of the muscles, nerve supply and the current use to which the extremity is being put. If there is a past history of "disuse use" atrophy, it is particularly important to demonstrate that the present full circumference manifests normal use of the extremity during the recent past and present.

Obviously, the lawyer must know the reason for each medical test to appreciate its value and limitations. Again, by way of example, the straight leg raising test is employed primarily to detect any impingement on nerves emanating from the lumbar spine. So a ten-degree limitation in the range of motion, or more, due to hamstring tightness does not make the test positive. Nevertheless, I have been treating physicians' reports describing the test as *positive* on that basis alone, though no radiculopathy was produced. The adverse examiner must educate the jury about the test when it's been erroneously used or described by the treating physician.

## Clarifying Medical Terms for the Jury

A lawyer must be sure that he understands what his witness means by the words he uses. It is not enough to have and use a good medical dictionary, though that is a good beginning. For example, some physicians use the words "strain" and "sprain" interchangeably. Other physicians may use "strain" to mean that muscles and ligaments were merely overstretched without any significant tearing. No permanency could result from a "strain". Whereas, a "sprain" involves a tearing of muscles and/or ligaments with internal bleeding, scarring, etc. Permanent disability might result. The term "muscle spasm" is used by physicians to describe an involuntary contraction of muscles where the muscles are, apparently, trying to splint themselves. An athlete's common "Charlie horse" is a good example of an acute muscle spasm. It hurts! Muscle spasm is strong objective evidence of injury and pain. However, I have found that some physicians refer to voluntary muscle guarding and tightness as spasm. Voluntary guarding or tightness is a subjective symptom. Its value as evidence is significantly less and is often subject to challenge. If relevant, the adverse examiner should be prepared to explain the physiology involved.

Permanent disability is a term which members of the medical and legal professions use frequently, but there is not always agreement on just what is meant by it. We have become so used to reducing any injury and its consequences to percentage figures as used in worker's compensation cases that we have fallen into the habit of using percentage figures in court cases. The medical profession, especially orthopedic surgeons, has fallen into the vice of converting even symptoms into a percentage disability rating. For example, a patient who has recurring subjective pain in his back for over a year is *automatically* evaluated, by some physicians, as permanently disabled by about 5%–10%, regardless of the physician's expectation that the symptoms will eventually resolve and regardless of the fact that the patient is able to engage in all of his pre-accident activities and has full motion and strength. If the plaintiff has pain on movement or develops soreness and stiffness after strenuous use, he should be compensated for his "pain and suffering", but there is no measurable disability. Or, said another way, there is no real basis for awarding damages for disability which is different and in addition to the elements of pain and suffering. Disability should be related to function such as strength, range of motion, function of senses, or inability to perform work or other ordinary activites.

An expert opinion must be based upon reasonable medical certainty. I have found that some physicians assume that an opinion on permanency should be given if the symptoms or disability are going to last "indefinitely"; that "indefinitely" is tantamount to "permanently" for purposes of court. It is not. A condition is permanent only if, based upon reasonable medical certainty, the problem will last the rest of the patient's life. The fact that it will last into the indefinite future is not sufficient to make the condition permanent.

## How to Reinforce the Credibility of Your Case

After the adverse examiner has given his medical diagnoses and other expert opinions predicated upon the history given by plaintiff and his own examination of plaintiff, the defense lawyer has the opportunity to utilize some of the other evidence in the case to obtain helpful clarification about medical matters, explanations and even additional opinions. An example will help illustrate the point. In *Molin v. Tyson Truck Line, Inc.*, 307 Minn. 510, 239 N.W.2d 461 (1976) plaintiff claimed numerous injuries, including an injury to her spine caused by a truck striking the rear of her automobile. The adverse medical examiner, a highly qualified orthopedic surgeon, was given a history by the patient that her automobile was stopped at a traffic light when struck in the rear by defendant's truck; she soon developed pain in her neck and back. The symptoms continued to worsen to the point that she could no longer do her housework, etc. She obtained a lot of medical attention over the next couple of years. The independent medical examination was completely negative. The examiner's initial diagnosis was that she had suffered a musculoligamentous strain of the neck and back, and there was no satisfactory medical explanation why she should continue to have symptoms persisting for over two years. Obviously, his testimony was helpful to the defense because his testimony mitigated against any significant injury to the spine or nerve. However, his testimony tended to confirm *an injury*. Other evidence already in the case showed that the contact made by the truck was so minor that no damage was done to the truck. Only a very small dent was put in plaintiff's bumper. According to the defendant truck driver, plaintiff's deposition testimony was that she could not remember if her vehicle was moved by the contact. At trial she described a forceful jolt and movement. The jury correctly refused to award Mrs. Molin any damages, though she had incurred thousands of dollars in medical expenses for treatment of her *alleged* injuries. Her problems were psychosomatic and pre-dated the accident.

The teaching point to be gleaned from the *Molin* case is that the defense lawyer can develop the additional facts after the adverse examiner has rendered his opinion based upon his own examination. Though the jury should be aware early in the witness's testimony that he had additional information records and reports available, his initial opinion should be based upon the history he secured from the plaintiff and upon his own examination. By delaying use of the additional facts, the examiner's credibility becomes stronger. Perhaps the defense lawyer can show the jury that the treating physician and examining physician reached the same conclusions when they relied upon only plaintiff's history and subjective complaints. But with the additional reliable evidence, the diagnosis may be significantly modified, hopefully for the better. The same approach, of course, may be used where causation is the primary issue.

As a general rule, the adverse examiner should testify even though liability is the primary issue. He can add credibility to the defendant's case as a whole. Almost never can the defendant elect to present his medical testimony by deposition or even video, because he needs the adverse examiner to cope with and explain the medical evidence presented by plaintiff at trial.

Like most people, physicians do not like to be put into the position of having to pass judgment on the patient's credibility. The responsibility for determining credibility of the plaintiff should belong to the jury only. Some judges allow lawyers to ask physicians if they believe the plaintiff's complaints. If the new rules of evidence do permit counsel to ask medical experts whether or not they *believe* the patient's subjective symptoms, complaints or history, the rules of evidence do the physicians and juries a disservice. Lawyers ask such questions hoping to force the defense to object or to obtain testimony that their client is believed and, therefore, believable. The adverse examiner should be prepared to respond to such questions by answering merely that he has taken the subjective complaints into consideration—unless he is willing and *prepared* to joust with plaintiff's counsel about plaintiff's veracity. It is a course of action fraught with danger and possible disaster. In most cases it is best for both parties to let the jury reach their own conclusion about which witnesses are to be believed and to what extent.

The new rules of evidence permit a lot of testimony that would have been excluded under the common law rules. Some lawyers are tempted by these new rules to abbreviate foundation questions, omit use of the hypothetical question and to rely upon hearsay testimony, such as treatises, though better evidence is available. There is a tendency to expand the role of the expert witnesses to the point where they invade the province of the jury. See *F.R.E.* 704. Full use of the new rules of evidence can lead to less effective advocacy. A lawyer should lay a good foundation for his expert's opinions even though it is possible to get by without it. Avoid asking leading questions on direct even if they are permissible. Let the witness testify. A lawyer detracts from the witness's credibility by leading him on the direct examination.

# Chapter Five

# *The Art of Cross-Examination*

Cross-examination has been called a mental duel between counsel and witness—and nothing is more important at trial than winning this duel in a dramatic and convincing way. Properly handled, cross-examination can be the finest of all courtroom tools for demolishing your opponent's case. By robbing the other side's witnesses of their credibility in the eyes of the jury, you make your own case all the more compelling.

To begin this chapter on the art of cross-examination, Trial Master John A. Burgess approaches the subject purely as a means of "achieving a result through persuasion." He sets out six active principles of cross-examination to guide you every step of the way, from deciding whether or not to question a particular witness to recognizing the biological signals that tell you when a witness is most vulnerable to attack. Mr. Burgess shows you how to pin your witness down as you block off every avenue of escape. Then you will see how to move in for the kill, and most important, how to grab the attention of every person in the courtroom just before you finish the witness off.

Nothing wrecks the composure and credibility of a witness more than tripping him up with a prior inconsistent statement. Courtroom wizard Leroy J. Tornquist demonstrates how to use this weapon with the most devastating results for your opponent's case. Mr. Tornquist covers everything you need to know, including how to find the prior inconsistent statement in the mass of material in your case file . . . when during the course of your questioning to spring your trap on the witness . . . and how to underscore the impeachment, spotlighting the fatal contradiction with every means at your disposal.

Cross-examining the expert witness presents special problems for the attorney, and here to provide the solutions is noted trial lawyer Ted M.Warshafsky. Because this is an area where the pre-trial preparation goes a long way in court, Mr. Warshafsky shows you where to dig up material you can use to discredit the expert even before the first depositions are taken. You will also see how to commit the witnesses in their depositions to specific positions they will have to live with—and live down—at trial, where the real action begins. Here Mr. Warshafsky gives you practical pointers to help you take apart the expert on cross, exposing the biases and subjective values that distort the testimony of even the most accomplished witness.

Next, noted attorney **Bruce Walkup** provides a case in point. His penetrating cross-examination of the opposition's expert witness was the deciding factor that led to a jury award of $2.6 million for Walkup's client. Portions of this piercing attack are excerpted here, showing how Walkup skillfully discredited the expert by establishing a prejudicial motive for his testimony.

Trial Master **Fred Peters** takes another approach, demonstrating that laughter can be a potent ally in winning substantial verdicts. Faced with a self-important expert who threatened to destroy his case, Peters was able to puncture his self-esteem with a ridiculing cross-examination until his credibility washed away in the waves of laughter that came from the jurors. "The jury was in hysterics," says Peters. "They were laughing out loud, tears streaming down some of their faces. They were having the time of their lives."

Faced with the perplexing problem of proving proximate cause in a million-dollar personal injury action, attorney **Lou Ashe** had to maneuver his way through a whole array of medical experts in a process that he calls "accentuating the negative." By skillfully negating each and every proposed cause that might avoid liability, Mr. Ashe demonstrated at trial— and here recounts for his fellow practitioners—the cross examination techniques he used to break down the opposition piece by piece.

In this fascinating case study, you will watch as Mr. Ashe methodically zeros in on causation, eliminating a number of possibilities one after another until he wins the crucial point—a definitive diagnosis of the tragic and needless suffering that befell the plaintiff during hospital treatment for injuries arising from a motorcycle accident.

"As matters previously resolved by the courts continue to pass to administrative forums," Lawrence G. Malone writes, "the legal profession is being forced to pay increased attention to the fine points of administrative trial tactics." Mr. Malone closes out this chapter with a succinct review of the special cross examination methods that work best at administrative hearings, where the rules of evidence do not necessarily apply and where the mental duel between counsel and witness is particularly keen.

# Principles and Techniques of Cross-Examination

## John A. Burgess

John A. Burgess is founding partner in the law firm of Burgess Associates in Berkeley, CA. Mr. Burgess is former State's Attorney of Bennington County, Vermont; past President of the Vermont Trial Lawyers Association; Governor of the Association of Trial Lawyers of America; State Chairman of the American Bar Association Prison Reform Committee; and President of the Roscoe Pound Foundation, American Trial Lawyers Association. He has lectured widely on trial practice and substantive law.

The name of the game is persuading the jury that the verdict you advocate is justified by the facts and essential to their sense of justice. We will not concern ourselves here with cross-examination as an instrument in the search for truth. We are concerned here with achieving a result through persuasion.

### The Six Principles of Cross-Examination

**1. The first principle of cross-examination is to have a purpose when you cross-examine.** Don't do it merely because it is your turn. Don't do it because you want to demonstrate your brilliance as a cross-examiner. Don't do it because your client passes you a note that says, "Ask him this or that question." The justification for cross-examination is not because somebody else wants it, or because emotionally you need it, or because it's your turn. It is because you have a purpose. Know what that purpose

.is. Be able to say in your own mind, before you rise to speak, "I will accomplish the following purpose with this witness."*

If you cannot articulate that purpose in your own mind, exercise the highest degree of legal education—do the most courageous thing a lawyer can do: don't get up.

**2. Cross-examination is not something that is ad-libbed in the courtroom. It is something that is prepared in the office.** When do you start preparing your cross-examination? The honest answer is, you start the day you take the case. You prepare your cross-examination while you're driving to and from work. You prepare your cross-examination in the shower. You prepare your cross-examination on that little receptacle which in most houses is next to the shower.

The eminent Polish pianist and statesman, Paderewski, played a concert at Carnegie Hall. Shortly after the concert, after encores and standing ovations, a little girl from the Juilliard School ran up, eyes aglow, and asked, "Dr. Paderewski, what made you such a genius?"

"My darling," he replied, "before I was a genius, I was a drudge."

**3. Don't cross-examine a witness unless you can say to yourself, from the heart and not from the ego, "I know I have to."** Cross-examine not to be a great performer, but to be a good lawyer. Do it not because this witness has just said something you don't like, or because he has just said something that offends your client; but because he has undermined the persuasive impact of what you want this jury to believe.

Think of cross-examination as elective surgery, and you are both the surgeon and the patient. If you don't wield the scalpel carefully, you might perform a pre-frontal lobotomy on yourself.

---

*Following are some of the purposes for cross-examination:
    To show that the witness is lying;
    To show that he is prejudiced;
    To show that his testimony is unlikely;
    To force him to admit certain facts;
    To explain his testimony;
    To destroy his testimony by showing his inablity to see or hear the facts;
    To prove his contrary statement/s;
    To show conviction of a crime (credibility);
    To destroy expert witness's testimony by showing lack of qualifications;
    To obtain evidence by examination of an adverse witness.

(Alan E. Morrill, Trial Diplomacy, 2nd Edition, Court Practice Institute, Chicago, 1972 §4.5)

**4. Don't give the witness a chance to explain why he did something implausible or incriminating.** Dramatize the implausible or incriminating act in such a way that the jury cannot forget it, and simply leave the matter in the minds of the jury. But don't ask the extra question. When you come to the summation, recreate the drama of that cross-examination, and then you make the point.

A great cross-examination does not end with the witness standing before the jury, clasping his head and saying, "I confess." That only happens when Earl Stanley Gardner writes the script. Rather, a great cross-examination sets up a great summation.

Edward Bennett Williams tells the story of a lesson he learned as a young lawyer. He was representing a Washington, D.C. streetcar company. This most preeminent of trial lawyers was then still learning the fine art of wielding the scalpel of cross-examination. The decedent, whose estate was suing for the negligence of the streetcar company in having run over and killed him, was a man of known alcoholic tendency. As a matter of fact, he had been known to have one or two or five or six on almost any occasion, and the setting of the sun was a sufficient occasion to trigger this celebration in his mind.

Late one evening he and his young son were walking down the street in Washington, the evidence demonstrated. He had walked an uncertain path in front of an oncoming streetcar. The streetcar, as streetcars are wont to do, had severed him. His young son, Williams established on cross-examination, had run into the street after his father. The young son had knelt down next to his dying father.

Q: And what did you do then?

A: I put my face down next to my father's face.

Q: And isn't it a fact that witnesses close by could hear you inhaling?

A: Yes, that's true.

Later in summation it could have been argued that this young man ran out to sniff his father's breath to see if the investigators could tell that there was the aroma of the devil's brew upon him. But the cross-examiner had not yet learned this principle, and asked the next question.

Q: Why did you put your face down close to your father, and emit the sound of inhalation?

A: Because he was the only daddy I was ever going to have, and I was kissing him goodbye.

**5. Remember Charles Darwin.** Charles Darwin taught that there are some lesser orders from whom our ancestors descended. So what do we know about them? We know that when their ancestors were feeding and were attacked by sabre-toothed tigers, and they were backed up against a wall, their hearts instinctively began to beat faster; they instinctively prepared either to run away or to grapple; their muscles instinctively tensed; instinctively the hair on the back of their heads rose, so that if the tiger bit, he would go away not with a cervical cord, but with a mouthful of hair. We know that instinctively they perspired so that in grappling, the palms of their hands would be liquid and flexible. We know these things because we have read Desmond Morris's book, *The Naked Ape.* We know, much as we don't like it, that engineers and doctors still have the traits of their primeval ancestors.

What does this have to do with cross-examination? Have you ever seen a "treed" witness? Have you ever had the experience of watching a witness's posterior involuntarily twitch? Have you ever seen them wiggle in their chairs? Have you ever seen their mouths go dry? Have you seen the beads of perspiration form on their foreheads? Have you ever been close enough to watch their ancestral eyes dilating the pupil so that they would have adequate tunnel vision of the target that was attacking?

If you haven't observed that and thought about that, then you're cross-examining by listening only, and not by watching. A good cross-examiner examines with all his senses, and assaults the witness in his total being.

You, as a cross-examiner, must remember that Clarence Darrow was right in the Scopes trial when he said that evolution has validity. You must read the witness's agitation, nervousness, and frustration by the beads of perspiration, by the involuntary twitching of the muscles, and by the absence of saliva in the mouth. The absolute biological signal that the witness is in a danger zone, or believes he is, is the time for you the cross-examiner to uncoil and strike—as truly as the rattlesnake would have stricken that witness's ancestor the ape.

**6. The final principle I will discuss here is, "Remember the Greeks."** The Greeks, as you know, had gods, and they framed certain beliefs about how the gods dealt with mortals. One of those was "He whom the gods will destroy they shall first make mad."

Anger is not consistent with rational thought. Anger arises from frustration. A frustrated witness is the predicate to an angry witness. A twice-frustrated witness is ready to become an angry witness. A thrice-frustrated witness will immediately become an angered witness; and an angered witness, manifesting the Darwinian symptoms of the need to run away or grapple with you, is now, and only now, prepared for the collision that is inevitable for cross-examination to be successful.

## Where To Begin Your Cross-Examination

Where you begin your cross-examination is crucial because it may open many doors for you if chosen well.

Many a cross-examiner is tempted to begin where his predecessor, the direct examiner, left off. He feels he must undermine the points scored by the direct examiner. That is the wrong place to begin. At that place the witness has that subject fresh in his mind. Unless your opponent is a moron, he has made the high point of his case, and ended on a strong note. A good direct examination has left the witness with a feeling of confidence. Don't begin by attacking an impregnable fortress.

Begin your cross-examination where the witness isn't ready for you, at a place where he has less confidence, at a place where you can begin to score points. Most important, begin at the place from which you can proceed to accomplish your purpose—the purpose you articulated in your mind before you got out of your chair.

On occasion it may be necessary, in order to accomplish your purpose, to at once "strike a swift and damaging blow" to the witness even if the point is not a vital one.

> "The impression thus to be made on the [jury] will be helpful to counsel's case; and what is even more important is the effect on the witness. An initial reverse may make him much easier to handle than he would otherwise have been."*

In some cases, it may even be necessary to begin with questions whose sole purpose is to give you the measure of the witness—questions about

---

*Gary Bellow and Bea Moulton, *The Lawyering Process*, The Foundation Press, Mineola, NY, 1978. Page 780

the witness himself, which may have little bearing upon the case, but which will teach you something about the witness.

### How to Block Off Every Avenue of Escape

If there was a rat running around in the courtroom, and the judge ordered the bailiff to catch the rat, what is the first thing the bailiff should do? What would you do if you were trying to catch the rat? First, you would close the doors so it couldn't get out of the room. You've got to corner the rat before you can catch him, you've got to close the space he can move in; you've got to close the doors.

Similarly, you've got to walk around that witness. Think, prepare, and plan for every conceivable way that he can wiggle off the hook, every way that he might get away from your grasp, every way that he can move out of the area where he's a target; and pre-close every avenue of escape. Pin him down, so there is only one way out, and that's the way you want to take him.

When you are closing off the avenues of escape, develop a pattern in your questioning where on the third or fourth question on a certain subject you create a slight distortion. While he is waiting for the opportunity to resolve this distortion, you change the subject. Do this a few times and he will begin to get frustrated. You are twisting and he can't get at you. Remember the Greeks: frustration is the predicate to anger. He whom the gods will destroy they shall first make mad.

When you change from one subject to another, do so in complete disregard of chronological order. This can throw the witness's train of thought out of whack, and will frustrate him further.

Now you have blocked all exits. The witness is frustrated, getting angry. You have finally come to that point in your cross-examination where you are going to drop the bomb and eviscerate the witness. You are about to ask that crucial question, the zinger, the one that will fulfill your purpose and help win your case. You've been looking forward to this moment for days, maybe weeks. You glance at the jury and see that the retired fireman in the second row is dreaming about the blond in the back row of the gallery, and at this moment doesn't really care who is on trial. You must get the attention of every member of the jury for the zinger.

There are several ways to do this. You could move over near the jury, raise your voice, and say, "Now, Mr. Witness, listen very carefully because this is the zinger." This will get their attention—but it will also warn the witness that it is coming, and he had better prepare for it.

I have found that the most effective way to gain the attention of everyone in the courtroom is to do just the opposite. Invoke the only thing that Americans never indulge in: the enjoyment of quiet.

We live in a switched-on society. We turn on the TV and don't know what is on it, just to have something on. In our car we play the stereo, or, if we haven't been successful in our practice of law, we play the radio. Whatever it is, we keep the buzzing going all the time. We're used to noise. The most shocking thing to the American ear is the grating, overpowering sound of absolute silence.

So before you spring the zinger, before you snap the trap, stop. The jurors, will bring their minds back to the trial, because the humdrum of the noise has been interrupted.

### Closing In on the Witness

In some jurisdictions where trial practice is about to become obsolete, the judge forbids not only voir dire in the jury selection process, but also addressing the witness close up. So this technique is only good in about 40 of the 50 states—but we hope for the salvation of the other ten. If your state is one of those ten, by the way, you can move for permission to approach the witness.

Approaching the witness accomplishes two things. First, you invade his territory and that makes him uptight. If you don't believe that, next time you get into an elevator and there is another person on it, walk right up close to that person and watch his reaction. If it's true in an elevator, where people are relaxed, anticipating the delights that await them in the suite on the 14th floor, think of how it will affect a witness in a courtroom when he is already nervous. Gradually approach him, and unnerve him, as you get closer to unleashing the zinger on him.

Second, approaching the witness gives you a chance to observe him closely. Remember Darwin?

# The Art of Using the Prior Inconsistent Statement

Leroy J. Tornquist

Leroy J. Tornquist received his law degree from Northwestern University Law School in Chicago, where he practiced law until 1971, when he began his teaching career. Currently, he is Dean of the Willamette University Law School at Salem, Oregon.

The credibility of a witness is for the jury to determine. In doing so they may consider his manner and demeanor on the stand. Therefore, commit the witness to the inconsistent testimony before confrontation with the prior statement. Wellman, in his classic, "The Art of Cross-Examination", stated this as follows:

> "You should never hazard the important question until you have laid the foundation for it in such a way that, when confronted with the fact, the witness can neither deny nor explain it. The correct method of using such a letter is to lead the witness quietly into repeating the statement he has made in his direct testimony, and which his letter contradicts ... Then let your whole manner toward him suddenly change and spring the letter upon him."

### How to Underscore the Impeachment

Use questions that underscore the importance of the impeachment. For example, assume the witness testified on direct that the defendant did not stop at the stop sign, and had made a contrary statement in his discovery deposition. The following line of questioning may be helpful in emphasizing the contradiction:

Q: Were you in my office on January 1, 1978 for the purpose of giving a deposition? (The date indicates the deposition was closer to the event or occurrence than the testimony at trial.)

A: Yes.

Q: Was a court reporter present?

A: Yes.

Q: Was your attorney present? (Or—was the attorney for the plaintiff present? This indicates that an attorney was present to protect the witness from improper questioning.)

A: Yes.

Q: Did I ask you certain questions and did you give certain answers?

A: Yes.

Q: Were you under oath to tell the truth? (Indicates that prior testimony was also under oath.)

A: Yes.

Q: Did you tell the truth?

A: (Any answer to this question will be favorable to your impeachment.)

Q: Did I ask you this question and did you give this answer:

"Q: Did the defendant stop at the stop sign?

A: Yes."

One method of emphasizing the important part of the impeachment is through voice inflections or a pause at the important part of the impeaching question. In speaking, unlike writing, we cannot underline or italicize the important words within a sentence or series of sentences. To make sure that the jury, however, understands the important part of the question, the attorney may use nonverbal methods of communication. For example, he can raise or lower his voice, use movement, or pause to bring the jury's attention to the important part of the question.

## When to Strike and When to Stop

Exactly when the prior inconsistent statement should be used has been argued for years, and the two most popular theories seem to be: (1) right at the start, and (2) after obtaining favorable admissions from the witness.

Because the jury is keyed for the first question on cross-examination, the first few questions may be the best time to confront the witness with the inconsistency. If you make an important point concerning credibility immediately, this is not likely to be lost on the jury. In addition, the witness may fear that you can impeach all of his answers, and he may be truthful on subjects upon which you are not prepared to contradict.

On the other hand, it is arguable that you should first obtain admissions from a witness before impeachment. The primary purpose of cross-examination is to obtain admissions favorable to your side of the case. And if enough favorable admissions are obtained there may be no need to use a prior inconsistent statement. Obviously, this approach depends entirely on the circumstances of the particular case.

Once the witness admits the prior inconsistent statement, it is an easy temptation to ask additional questions to highlight the impeachment. Questions such as: "Were you lying then or are you lying now?" ... "Which of the two statements is true?" ... "Isn't it likely that what you said before trial is true since it was made at a time closer to the event and was not influenced by the pressure of trial?"

There are several valid reasons for not asking additional questions after the actual impeachment has been obtained. First, jurors identify with the witness, not with the examining lawyer. They resent an unjust and overly aggressive attack on the credibility of the witness, and may react by sympathizing with the witness and searching for arguments reconciling the two statements. In other words, the jurors should come to the realization by themselves that the witness is not worthy of belief.

McCormick's cardinal rule of impeachment should not be overlooked:

> "Never launch an attack which implies that a witness has lied deliberately, unless you are convinced that the attack is justifiable and essential to your case. An assault which fails often produces in the jury's mind an indignant sympathy for the intended victim."

Second, the significance of inconsistent statements can be explained in detail during closing argument, and at that time it is too late for the witness to seek an explanation for the inconsistency, whereas if additional highlight questions are asked during cross, your opponent may be forced to seek an explanation of the inconsistency during redirect examination.

Third, the question itself may be objectionable on the grounds that it is argumentative, and the court may protect the witness from undue harassment or embarrassment; as the California Supreme Court indicated in People v. Southlack:

> "Control of cross examination of a witness as to which of his conflicting statements is true should be in the sound discretion of the trial judge. The purpose of such cross examination is ascertainment of the truth, and if, as here, that purpose can be furthered by direct questioning as to the truth or falsity of prior statements, such questioning may be permitted; the trial court, however, must be ever alert to protect the witness against being badgered or tricked into statements unintended by the witness".

## How to Succeed at Extrinsic Impeachment

Assume that the witness, after being confronted, is evasive or denies making the prior inconsistent statement, and that the examiner has a transcript of a deposition to the contrary. What procedure should you use to complete the impeachment?

It is obvious that the prior inconsistent statement must be proved by another witness or documentary evidence. This is called extrinsic evidence.

Before introducing extrinsic evidence, however, the accuracy of the deposition containing the prior statement should be highlighted. For example, if the witness to be impeached signed the deposition or waived signature, that fact should be brought out during cross examination, through questions such as:

Q: You reviewed the deposition before you signed it, didn't you? *or*

Q: You knew you had the right to make any changes in it, didn't you? *or*

Q: You didn't make any changes, did you? *or*

Q: You reviewed it recently before testifying, didn't you? (It would be unusual if the witness didn't read it before testifying.)

If the witness had the opportunity to review the deposition but waived the right, that fact should be elicited. In most cases waiver of the right to sign the deposition will be expressly waived by the witness during the deposition. Therefore, the witness could be impeached if he stated that he did not knowingly waive signature.

Once the accuracy of the deposition has been established, the court reporter should be called and requested to bring his or her original short-hand notes. After properly qualifying the reporter/witness as an expert court reporter, the shorthand or machine notes should be marked for identification and the reporter/witness should be referred to the contra-dictory testimony. After establishing that the witness whom you are at-tempting to impeach was under oath at the deposition, the reporter/witness should be asked whether the deponent was asked the following question (in line with our earlier stop sign illustration) and gave the fol-lowing answer:

"Q: Did the defendant stop at the stop sign?

A: Yes."

If the court reporter/witness is not available, the prior inconsistent state-ment may be proved by any person who heard it at the deposition. While this type of impeachment is less satisfactory, it should be kept in mind in case of an emergency.

Obviously, the testimony of an impartial witness such as a court re-porter is effective in showing that the witness is not worthy of belief—not only did the witness make inconsistent statements, but he denied under oath that he made the prior statement. An independent witness, the court reporter, testified to the contrary.

## Principles of Impeachment

Principles applicable to cross-examination in general are also applicable to impeachment by contradiction. For example, leading questions are permissible. Indeed, every question should be leading. During an effective prior inconsistent statement impeachment every answer by the witness should be a simple 'yes.' Surprisingly, many inexperienced lawyers fail to lead during inconsistent statement impeachment. Obviously, this reduces its effectiveness, as the following examples illustrate:

*Non-leading Question:*

Q: What question, if any, did I ask you about the color of the traffic light?

A: I don't remember.

*Leading Question:*

Q: Did I ask you this question, and did you give this answer:

"Q: What color was the light?

A: Red."

A: Yes.

A non-leading question can often result in confusing both the witness and the jury, whereas the leading question can direct the witness to the specific source of impeachment and maintain control by the cross-examiner.

Another general principle of cross-examination that should not be ignored is—listen to the answer. Many lawyers are so wrapped up in their next question that they do not listen to the answer. The cross-examiner must analyze each answer and if it is evasive, the witness must be required to take a definite position. An evasive answer usually occurs where the material is favorable to the cross-examiner. A definite answer produces such testimony and reveals the witness's attempt to conceal relevant facts. This principle is particularly crucial where the question is important such as the last question in impeachment by prior inconsistent statement:

Q: Did I ask this question and did you give this answer:

"Q: What color was the light?

A: Red."

A: I may have. *or*

A: I forget. *or*

A: If that's what it says there, I must have.

Such answers are evasive and cry out for further questioning and/or extrinsic evidence to complete the impeachment. Yet many lawyers do not followup, because they were not listening to the answer.

Another principle is—do not permit the witness to explain the inconsistency. If the witness attempts to explain the inconsistency an objection should be made:

"Your honor, I move to strike the last answer as not being responsive to the question and request the court to instruct the jury to disregard the answer."

The court should grant the request if the question was leading and called for a limited answer.

To avoid the appearance of being unduly harsh, the cross-examiner should state that this is his time to conduct examination and he would like his questions answered—the witness's counsel will be able to ask further questions during redirect. In my opinion, it is a mistake to ask a non-leading question which allows the witness to explain. For example:

Q: Why did you make two different statements on the same subject?

Such a question violates the rule against asking a 'why' question during cross-examination and can only hurt your cause. If the witness is able to dream up a satisfactory answer, the impeachment is destroyed. If the witness does not answer, you have gained little because the impeachment had already implied that there is no satisfactory answer.

An adverse witness may give an undesirable answer. If he does, you must be able to impeach or the question should not have been asked. Without the use of statements made before trial, this would be an extremely difficult principle to follow.

For example, in civil litigation it is commonplace to take the deposition of every important witness for your opponent and then order a transcript of the depositions. Before trial and in preparation for cross-examination, every statement made by the witness is examined for possible use at trial. Every fact favorable to the examiner's case can then be elicited from the witness during cross-examination. If the witness changes his testimony, he should be impeached by the prior statements.

### How to Pinpoint Prior Inconsistent Statements

How do you find the prior inconsistent statement in the mass of material in your case file? For effective use of the prior inconsistent statement, you must be able to find it or at least remember where to find it. To do that, the file must be organized so that the location of all prior statements made by the witness is known. Unless effort is spent in the organization of the documents prior to trial, it will be difficult to find the impeaching statement when it is needed.

The jury and trial judge are not going to be impressed by the lawyer who wastes time fumbling through his file looking for a particular comment. Furthermore, while he is shuffling through the papers, the witness has time to think about his answer, and to anticipate the crucial impeaching questions.

Discovery in modern civil litigation has mushroomed the quantity of documents in either lawyer's files at the time of trial. The sheer number of documents in the file at the time of trial—statements made in pleadings, interrogatories, affidavits attached to motions for summary judgment, oral and written statements of witnesses, prior testimony, transcripts of discovery depositions, admissions of fact, letters, memoranda, expert opinions, etc.—can be enormous.

It takes extensive pre-trial preparation in reading and cataloging every document to be able to recall and use every inconsistent statement made by a particular witness, and if there is more than one witness, as is usual, the problem is even greater. Yet this penchant for thorough preparation, in my opinion, is what separates the competent trial lawyer from the average lawyer.

There are many systems used by experienced trial lawyers to organize the file. The important thing is to develop a system of organization that is compatible to you.

One method that I have used is to make notations on the inside of the deposition indicating the pages where testimony on a particular subject can be found. In really 'big' cases, there are commercial firms that can perform this task, but as we all know, such cases are the exception. However, it is not too great a task to prepare an index relating to key words in the case—such as 'stop sign'—and then list the witnesses and documents in which 'stop sign' is mentioned.

# Cross-Examination of Technical Experts

## Ted M. Warshafsky

Ted M. Warshafsky received his law degree from the University of Wisconsin. He served as Wisconsin Court Commissioner for Milwaukee County in 1965 and served as Tort & Educational Chairman for the National Association of Claimant's Counsel, 1964-65. Warshafsky is a member of the State Bar of Wisconsin (Director, Litigation Section, 1972-73; Director, Individual Rights & Responsibilities Section, 1977 - present); member of Wisconsin Academy of Trial Lawyers of America (National Secretary, 1965-66); member of the American Board of Professional Liability Attorneys (Director, 1976 - present); member of the Inner Circle of Advocates; member of the International Society of Barristers; and member of the American Board of Trial Advocates. He has lectured for the University of Wisconsin Law School and is the author of numerous articles.

No other part of the evidentiary phase of a civil jury trial presents as much opportunity for deep involvement and the partisan taking of sides by jurors as the cross-examination of expert witnesses. It is the time in the trial when borderline cases are won and indignation that finds its final reflection in the verdict is created.

All trial lawyers know that a brilliant, incisive, and destructive cross-examination of a lay person can easily backfire, if the jury identifies with and becomes protective of the witness. With a technical expert, that problem falls away. A well-prepared advocate can enlist strong jury support as he meticulously exposes and discredits the direct testimony of one who has been offered as having special knowledge and experience, which is, in fact, either lacking or is being used to obscure the truth.

The arguments that can be made for occasionally not cross-examining do not apply to experts. The failure to challenge authoritative opinions will be noted by jurors at the time, and provides the basis for a devastating closing argument by one's opponent.

## Five Good Reasons to Cross-Examine the Expert

There are a number of distinct and usually interrelated objectives that will vary with a particular witness and the relative importance of his or her testimony. While a flexible trial lawyer will seize opportunities that arise during the course of the trial, the goals of a particular cross-examination should be fairly well defined before it is started.

Five general categories of purposes may be stated as follows:

**1. Neutralizing the Impact** of a credible and persuasive witness who is not subject to impeachment by eliciting admissions and concessions.

Such a witness can be asked to agree to a sequence of general principles. This can be followed by short questions that relate directly to the examiner's theory of the case. Phrasing the questions in the language of a previous expert of the examining lawyer or of the opening statement is a persuasive technique for lending weight to one's interpretation of the facts.

Oftentimes the examiner, by eliciting agreement through narrowly structured questions, may obtain concessions that are more apparent than real. At least room is left for doubt about the validity of the otherwise omniscient witness's conclusions.

If the questions are skillfully put, the witness must agree or appear biased and, ergo, less credible. Sometimes this is the only method for neutralizing an otherwise devastating witness. It can leave the impression that the sum total of the testimony was not of great importance, thereby directly affecting the weight if not the credibility.

**2. Direct Attack** upon the foundation or conclusions of the witness.

Demonstrating that one lacks sufficient qualifications and adequate knowledge whereby to hold the conclusions given is an effective way of neutralizing testimony without becoming involved in a personal attack. An examination of this type considers such concepts as acquaintance with the specific facts of the case, educational background, experience, personal biases of which the witness is unaware, and faults and weaknesses in investigation, research, and methodology. It in a sense asks the question of whether or not this witness is entitled to hold the opinions that have been given.

**3. Eliciting Damaging Information** that is important to the entire case and valuable for impeaching or diminishing the weight to be given to testimony of other expert witnesses.

An expert witness may offer little on direct that is of probative value. Frequently, employee-experts are called to testify to only one limited aspect of the case.

However, such a witness may be the key to impeaching others who have already testified. They may be used to demonstrate a general lack of ability on the part of the individual defendant or company.

For example, in products liability and engineering cases, apparently believable and credible witnesses may be called from within the defendant company to testify to particulars of manufacture and design. This may present an opportunity to: (a) test probabilities in relation to testimony about how manufacturing is carried on; (b) introduce evidence of the statistical nature of quality control and inspection (i.e., a certain number of defective products are permitted to get through); and (c) demonstrate that on-the-job personnel who are actually in charge of procedures have an abysmal lack of knowledge about quality control and inspection in general.

It is also an excellent point at which to introduce the concept that foreseeability of ordinary use was never a real consideration in design.

From a plaintiff's standpoint, the more expert witnesses of the defendant that can be deposed and examined the better. The defendant is usually better served by relying upon a small number of sophisticated experts than by exposing a multitude of individuals to examination, the development of discrepancies, and the demonstration of weaknesses.

**4. Impeachment** by the use of prior testimony, depositions, statements, or writings; interrogatories and admissions; learned treatises; and the testimony of other experts within the organization named for purposes of trial.

Impeachment should not always be thought of as directly insinuating a lie. It may also demonstrate a lack of knowledge or credibility on the part of another witness; a lack of believability on the part of the witness being examined; or a general lack of believability of the whole case of the party being impeached.

**5. Collateral Cross-Examination.** On occasion, the only cross available is collateral, in that it does not really touch the main issues or ultimate facts of the case. It ranges from a subtle discrediting of the witnesses' ability, all the way through to a demonstration of bias, interest, and cupidity.

A collateral examination is always dangerous. There is a temptation to nitpick, perhaps best illustrated by overemphasizing the fact that an expert is paid for the time spent in court. However, when appropriate, it can be the most devastating of all examinations, because it puts into question the integrity of opposing counsel for having called such a witness.

This examination makes the point that the witness was called because your opponent believed that his qualifications and conclusions would be persuasive, not because of any search for the truth. When successful, the jury can draw the legitimate inference that the testimony was aimed at confusing or fooling.

## Where to Find Ammunition to Use Against the Expert

Before the first depositions of technical experts are taken, counsel must be thoroughly conversant with relevant areas of a witness's expertise. This process has to continue up until trial and should be broad enough to permit counsel to immediately seize upon errors or misstatements.

The witness's background, job history, writings, areas of specialization, and limitations should all be known. The societies, references, and texts upon which he ordinarily relies should be checked. Previous testimony and reports rendered in other cases should be obtained. The more thoroughly one delves into this area, the more likely one is to obtain valuable, impeaching material. For example, a person who has written a doctoral thesis should have not only his writings, but those of the professors under whom he studied, analyzed; and a medical witness in a malpractice case should have the writings of professors under whom he did his residency checked.

Comprehensive depositions of *all* expert witnesses should be taken well in advance of trial and as close together as possible. Inevitably, when there are large numbers of witnesses, particularly if they have not had time to study depositions of others, there will be major discrepencies in the testimony. In taking depositions, it is absolutely important that witnesses be pinned down to specific positions that they will have to live with at the time of trial.

All of the discovery and investigation must be correlated and cross-indexed. There should be easily usable summaries of every material fact to which the witness has previously testified and these should be cross-referenced to other witnesses for discrepancies.

What kind of a person is the witness, and what type of cultural biases and prejudices does he or she have? Truth invariably has a subjective component. Witnesses who testify that a product is or is not defective are always including their own risk philosophy. Academics who come from departments in universities that are heavily subsidized by particular industries may well have been subtly corrupted without being aware of it.

Literature in the area of the expert's field should be carefully studied to find points on which the testimony is inconsistent with generally recognized principles. Learned treatises, not written for purposes of litigation, are always an extremely useful tool in cross-examination.

## How to Conduct a Successful Cross-Examination

In commencing the examination, one should realize that no fact finder, no matter how sophisticated, is going to assimilate large numbers of highly technical points elicited during the course of an oral examination. For that reason, demonstrative aids, models, lists, maps, graphs, and charts, particularly those that can go to jury room, should be used.

If counsel wants the jury to remember specific glaring discrepancies, they should be sufficiently limited so that they can be recalled.

As important as any fact or specific point is a general impression of the witness. A squirming witness, trying to cover not only his tracks but those of another expert who has already testified, may not be remembered for any specific, but the general demeanor will stick, create indignation, and usually be of much more value than an admission of a specific error.

The more technical and remote from common knowledge the area of examination, the more necessary that it be presented to the jury in terms and analogies that they can understand and incorporate into their usual frame of reference. This can only be done if, as in all cross-examinations, the examiner, whatever his personality style, controls the examination, uses short concise questions, appropriate word choice, controls the witness, and demands a specific answer.

Details should be obtained early. The witness must be committed to those facts upon which he bases his conclusion, so that he cannot later color his testimony to meet a developing logic of cross-examination when and if it becomes apparent.

The rules and value of using learned treatises and prior writings and testimony are patently obvious and need no repetition here. However, what is sometimes forgotten, is that the statements and testimony of each person designated by one's opponent as an expert witness then may be used in the same way that one would use a learned treatise.

Specifically, despite the general rule that one witness may not be called upon to pass judgment upon the testimony of another, for the reason that this invades the province of the trier of fact, one expert witness of a party may be asked about the statements of another.

It is not unusual, late in a trial, to find an expert called by the defendant who attempts to explain away previously received damaging testimony. It is quite proper to read a portion of the deposition testimony of another expert for the defendant, or of an in-house engineering expert who was offered for deposition, and pointedly ask whether or not the witness agrees. If so, there is a change of testimony. If the witness disagrees, he is at a minimum attesting to the incompetency of the in-house technician.

The fact that a witness has testified before and the amount that he is being paid for his testimony, if it is large, can be valuable points to develop. However, if the charge is reasonable it should not be pressed, the amount of income received from testimony being only meaningful if such sums would indicate bias and a financial interest in providing a certain kind of testimony.

Most of the large manufacturers that are sued repetitively develop a traveling stable of experts. While they may use someone new, or one or two locals, they usually call upon the same people.

Those who work for the corporation are obviously biased; their jobs are on the line; and they will inevitably never concede *any* possible defect of any kind in any product or procedure utilized by their employer. Those who come from without the company may have a high financial stake, directly or indirectly, in the company. It is not unusual to find an "independent research laboratory" or a university providing testimony for a manufacturer that provides grants or gives business to the institution.

Questioning about previous testimony for the same company, or in similar kinds of cases, is also a good method of placing before the jury a history of injuries, defects, and damages caused by the same products or manufacturer.

## Probing for Weak Spots in the Expert's Testimony

Most of the testimony of all technical experts does not fall within the usual definitions of exact sciences. Think of the non-medical areas in which expert witnesses are most frequently utilized: design, material selection, quality control, reconstruction, warnings, ballistics. All of these evaluations contain subjective considerations, social values, and cost factors. Also, consider the degree to which experts, even when they are dealing with exact sciences, are highly specialized within our modern industrial society, and the limited extent to which any technical expert is a Renaissance person who has a handle on the whole problem.

It is perfectly proper and important to expose the subjective and societal values that enter into conclusions that are presented under the banner of "reasonable certainty." It is equally valid to demonstrate the two-dimensional brilliance of the witness.

Think of the effect upon a jury of learning that most material selections in large industries are done by people of demonstrably little personal expertise, who are trained in the use of technical jargon, and who make their selections from catalogs that list properties of the materials.

The larger the company or institution, the more likely that the "Peter Principle" applies. The first to be deposed, and probably the least knowledgeable person in any company, may be the chief engineer or the person in charge of the particular product. Knowing this permits the examiner to create a conflict between the deposition testimony of that witness, and the expert called at trial. Once the fact is developed that the head of the project lacks real knowledge and must rely completely upon underlings, one raises the proper inference that no one has an overview of the entire job.

Witnesses should be questioned closely about their knowledge of prior occurrences or product failures of a similar nature. In-house experts should be made to explain why they did not modify procedures, designs, and techniques in the light of past experiences. If they have no knowledge of demonstrable product failures, they should be questioned about what they would have done had such information been relayed to them by sales or complaint divisions of their company. The responses may demonstrate a wide range of objectionable conditions, ranging from callousness through to a lack of procedure for assimilating customer information.

Experts hired from without a company should be asked to explain how similar failures occurred. The very fact that they were not supplied with this information by opposing counsel is valuable in reducing the impact of their testimony.

Risk philosophy should be explored with expert witnesses. Although the law demands reasonable certainty or probability as a predicate for liability, a competent expert is negligent if he or she did not foresee a reasonable possibility. The examination should be rich in analogies that relate to the members of the jury. For example, in a malpractice case failure to consider foreseeable possibilities would be negligence. In a products liability case, not anticipating the broad spectrum of human limitations that users bring to a product is equally negligent.

Another aspect of the risk philosophy of the witness that should be investigated is the degree of danger of injury, failure, or harm that the expert considers acceptable. The best illustration of this is in quality control and inspection where cost is always inversely related to the degree of inspection, but seldom correlates to the potential for serious harm. Demonstrating that the decision not to exercise more control was conscious and a function of cost should be followed up by a correlation and comparison with the potential for serious harm. Even a slight risk is unacceptable if it carries with it a potential for infliction of massive damages that are ultimately more expensive than eliminating the risk.

# Impeaching the Expert:

## Featuring Bruce Walkup

Bruce Walkup is the senior partner in the San Francisco law firm Walkup, Downing, Shelby, Bastian, Melodia, Kelly & O'Reilly. He is a member of the American Bar Association and the Association of Trial Lawyers of America. He was president of the Inner Circle of Advocates (1977-78) and is a fellow with the American College of Trial Lawyers, and the International Society of Barristers.

The last sound Jim Peebles heard before his Kawasaki 500 motorcycle veered out of control was a strange noise that seemed to come from the rear wheel.

Seconds later, he lay in a gravel ditch alongside the highway, his body badly broken. As he recalled, he had fallen from the bike when it suddenly and unexpectedly veered off the road and crashed into a roadside culvert. The motorcycle traveled another 94 feet without its passenger before settling alongside the two-lane highway Peebles had been traveling just outside of Eugene, Oregon.

The accident rendered Peebles a quadriplegic. In the ensuing lawsuit, his lawyer, Bruce Walkup (Walkup, Downing, Shelby, Bastian, Melodia, Kelly & O'Reilly of San Francisco), argued that the accident should not have happened because the bike was relatively new with little more than 1,000 miles on it. The strange noise Peebles heard indicated that the bike was defective and that the distributor and dealer had not properly serviced it as promised, Walkup argued.

A jury eventually awarded Peebles $2.657 million although the case seemed evenly matched, if not in Kawasaki's favor. Walkup's decisive success was his cross-examination of the defense's star witness, an engineer whose direct testimony had shifted responsibility for the accident from defendant to plaintiff.

Walkup's performance exemplifies a prime objective of expert cross-examination: to discredit the witness by establishing the prejudicial motive for his testimony. As Walkup explains, he was able to demonstrate for the jury and argue in his closing argument that the witness was a "Kawasaki expert in the truest sense of the word."

## Kawasaki's Expert v. Plaintiff's Past

Before Kawasaki's expert took the stand, Walkup's stiffest challenge was establishing his client's credibility. Motorcyclists are often stereotyped as speedy and reckless drivers. The defense played on this bias, gathering eyewitnesses to testify that Peebles was racing faster than 60 MPH when his bike crashed. And in a bedside interview soon after the crash, Peebles blamed himself for the accident, saying he had been speeding.

The plaintiff's background did nothing to dismiss the biker stereotype. He had a history of drug use going back to his service days in Vietnam. His best witness and close friend was an ex-con.

The defense's leading witness was William Otto, an engineer. If the plaintiff fitted the stereotype of a calloused biker, Otto easily played his role as the respected, honest conveyor of truth. He was a "very distinguished looking, white-haired gentleman . . . a physicist (with) a beautiful bedside manner, if he were a doctor, you would just listen to him (for) he is so poised and calm," Walkup would say in his closing argument.

Otto's purpose, of course, was to offer the jury a believable explanation for the accident that would exonerate Kawasaki and eliminate any question of its liability.

## The Expert's Theory for the Accident

Walkup's experts had testified that the bike jerked out of control when a loose rear-wheel chain popped off of its sprockets (accounting for the noise Peebles heard before veering off the road). The bike was either defective when it was transported from Japan, or the loose chain had not been detected during a routine checkup by the Kawasaki dealer five days before the accident, Walkup argued.

For the defense came Otto. He testified that the bike was not defective and that any marks on the motorcycle were a result and not a cause of the accident.

As the trial continued, Otto developed a theory for the accident that was supported by an impressive display of demonstrative evidence. The accident occurred, Otto said, because the motorcycle's kickstand came down as Peebles rounded a slight curve in the road—a result perhaps of the rider's negligence. The plaintiff had probably forgotten to kick the kickstand back into place, Otto testified. It was this kickstand, scraping against the road, that caused the bike to slip out of control. Otto even displayed scrape marks on the bottom of the kickstand to illustrate his point.

### Showing the Jury the Expert's Bias

Otto also showed movies that demonstrated how difficult it is to shake loose the chain of a Kawasaki motorcycle. As Walkup recalls: "Mr. Otto's testimony was impressive. He was very good at explaining excessive speed on the part of our motorcycle and his kickstand theory sounded interesting. He also created a direct conflict with our experts on whether the defect was before or after the accident.

"It is my belief that if an expert goes out of his way to try to hurt your case, you must let the jury know his bias and prejudices and why he is working for this particular defense. Later in my final argument I could say of Otto that 'he is really a combination lawyer and investigator and tester (testifying for) $60 an hour.'

"But when the cross began, I had very little information about Mr. Otto because I was not allowed to take his pretrial deposition. Much of what I learned developed during the cross-examination as I pried into his relationship with Kawasaki.

"The cross-examination of Mr. Otto was conducted in a very polite, gentlemanly way with no obvious bitterness. But without it, I believe the jury was willing to accept his testimony," Walkup says.

The cross-examination follows.

Q: (BY MR. WALKUP): First of all, going back to your background and experience, I believe you indicated that you do some work for some motorcycle industry group.

A: (BY MR. OTTO): Yes, I do some work for the Motorcycle Industry Council.

Q: What is the Motorcycle Industry Council?

A: It's an association of manufacturers, both OEM's and after-market manufacturers. OEM's is original equipment manufacturers; people that manufacture whole motorcycles. And the after-market people manufacture accessories.

Q: Now, as I understand from your previous testimony that it has been about the last seven years that you have developed an interest in motorcycles?

A: Well—

Q: As opposed to the type of work you were doing before, marine engineering and aircraft and so forth.

A: On a technical basis, yes. I have ridden motorcycles since 19—well, since 1950.

Q: About how many miles have you ridden, would you say?

A: In excess of 90,000 miles.

Q: And now your general background and experience up until about seven years ago when you started getting more into the technical end of motorcycles was in other fields of your profession as a physicist, right?

A: That is correct.

Q: And then after you got into the last seven-year period, where you did work for the Motorcycle Industry Council, did you do work for some of the manufacturers of original equipment motorcycles?

A: Yes, I have done work for—well, specifically Harley Davidson, Yamaha, Kawasaki, BMW, Suzuki, practically all of them.

### Helping Kawasaki

Q: And with reference to Kawasaki, particularly, what type of work did you do for them—for Kawasaki, for the company?

A: I have done two types of work: One is accident reconstruction work and the other is engineering work, dealing with stability, high-speed stability.

Q: Let's take the work that you did for the company first that didn't have to do with accident reconstruction. And now I'm just talking about Kawasaki. When did you first start doing work for Kawasaki having to do with the stability of the Kawasaki motorcycle?

A: I think that was in 1975.

Q: And who employed you to do that work?

A: A gentleman named Jim Corp.

Q: And what is his position with Kawasaki?

A: He is in the technical group. I don't know exactly what the title is, but he is in their technical group in Santa Ana.

Q: And in connection with the work that you did with Kawasaki as to stability of their motorcycle back in 1975, what did that project involve? How long? Where did you go? And what did you do? What was the general nature of your Kawasaki assignment?

A: The general nature of the work consisted of taking the S-1, which is their 900 cc motorcycle, mounting it on a torsional pendulum, which I have in my laboratory, and measuring moments of inertia of the motorcycle about the various axis of interest. I disassembled the front end from the motorcycle and measured (it) independently.

   (I measured) all of the geometric properties of the motorcycle: the cg location, center of gravity location. Locations, I should say, of both the motorcycle as a whole and the front assembly. And then (I plugged) that data together with the tire data of various kinds, camber coefficient, slip-angle coefficient, lateral compliance, vertical compliance, spring rates, etc., into a computer for simulation of a motorcycle and determining the inherent stability of the machine and the effects of various modifications to the motorcycle on the inherent stability characteristics of the machine. Specifically: changing tires; lengthening the swing arm; shortening the swing arm; shifting the cg into various positions; changing the rake angle, changing the geometry to the front end—(A) very wide variety of modifications that might be done to the motorcycle by people outside. And possibly by the factory as well.

### Other Projects

Q: That sounds like a project that consumed quite a bit of time for Kawasaki.

A: No, it took approximately, oh, I would say two-three weeks.

Q: And during that—

A: Certainly not more than that length of time.

Q: During that time were you working with the Kawasaki engineers and personnel?

A: No, I was working by myself.

Q: Under the project which they gave you?

A: Yes. They asked me to do a stability analysis of the S-1 and various modifications to it.

Q: Was this all done here in this country?

A: Yes, it was.

Q: Now, have you done any other projects for Kawasaki other than accident reconstruction, I will get to that next, besides that project that you did in 1975?

A: Yes.

Q: Tell us about some of them.

A: I did a similar analysis of the S-1 Police motorcycle. And that was done recently.

Q: When was that done?

A: Oh, that was within the last couple of months. We did that—we measured the mass properties over one weekend and then I ran the computer simulations over the next weekend. I think, roughly, a month and a half, two months ago.

Q: Shortly before the start of this trial?

A: Yes, it was.

Q: And who, from Kawasaki, did you work with on that project?

A: That was a gentleman named Bob Chote that I was doing the work for. He is head of the police program.

Q: And where is he in Kawasaki, (the) Santa Ana office?

A: No, he's in Lincoln, Nebraska.

Q: Had you done—I think you did indicate there were some more projects you had done for Kawasaki besides those two.

A: No, I don't think so. I think—well, I did some road tests of police motorcycles.

Q: For Kawasaki?

A: Yes. Right. That was part of the latter—that was the last project. I should say a follow-on to the last project. I actually took some bikes out.

Q: How long did the last project consume?

A: The road test was done in one day at Riverside Raceway and the moment measurements and computer runs consumed two weekends.

Q: Now, have you also—before we get to the accident reconstruction, have you also, for Kawasaki, written some papers about their bikes?

A: Not that I can recall, no.

Q: Any technical reports to them that you have ever rendered about their bikes.

A: Well, the first stability analysis resulted in a technical report, yes.

Q: To Kawasaki?

A: To Kawasaki.

Q: Which was not published?

A: No, not published.

Q: It was an in-house type of thing where you would just give it to them?

A: Right. That's correct.

Q: And was there a similar type of in-house report that you made about your findings in the police special Kawasaki?

A: Not really. The net results of that was the production of a set of curves showing the dampening characteristics as a function of speed and a discussion of those curves with Bob Chote and a group of police officers at Riverside Raceway.

Q: Did you go back to the Kawasaki facility at Lincoln or was this all done out here?

A: No, this was all done out here.

Q: They came out to see you?

A: Well, Mr. Chote did. I won't say, "they."

Q: Well, their representatives?

A: Yes. That's correct.

## Keeping Track of Time

Q: And then has Kawasaki indicated to you that they have any more programs coming up where they're going to give you special projects to do for them?

A: Well, that police bike program was done on the 900 cc version of the police bike. And I anticipate that there will be another stability analysis run on the 1000 cc version of the police bike.

Q: Would that—do you know approximately when you're going to do that for Kawasaki?

A: I really don't know. As soon as I can find time, I think. But really, you know, there's no definite schedule or date for that.

Q: All right.

A: We have talked about it.

Q: With reference to finding time, I haven't looked through your sheets there yet, but you have kept time records of how much time you spent on this case against Kawasaki?

A: I have a time record. But I don't have it with me and honestly don't know how many hours I have put in on it.

Q: Well, let me just ask you a couple of questions about that, because we live out in the same Valley River Inn.

A: Right.

Q: Have you been here substantially everyday during the trial of this action in Eugene, Oregon?

A: Substantially. Excluding weekends, yes. I have been here, I think, starting on the 12th and substantially every trial day, excluding weekends.

Q: And you weren't in court testifying during all the days, of course.

A: No, no.

Q: And you weren't expecting to be testifying all those days?

A: No.

Q: What were you doing spending your time up here all those days?

A: In part working with—or on this particular case, reading transcripts of the proceedings, the witnesses' statements in particular, and, in part, doing other work, dictation, examining photographs that I have taken of other accident cases, things that I could bring along with me. Writing a paper on motorcycle cruise controls. Doing part of a paper on stability analysis, or on stability of motorcycles. For *Road River* magazine.

Q: And I'll come back to that in a moment. But you indicated that in addition to these projects that you have done for Kawasaki, and anticipate doing in the future, that you have done accident reconstruction work for Kawasaki. Could you tell us about that? When that started and how much of that you have done for Kawasaki?

A: Yes. I believe that started in 1975 and in terms of quantity of work, I really don't—don't know exactly what you want, number of hours?

Q: No, I'd like to know how many different times Kawasaki has come to you and asked you to be a consultant or expert for them where there has been a case involving a Kawasaki product.

A: I honestly don't know. I don't keep a record of numbers of times. I have made up records of this nature on—at various times. The last time I made such a record was in January, 1976, I think. Or December of 1975.

Q: What was the purpose of making that?

A: An attorney asked me to.

Q: In other words, was that in another case for Kawasaki (where) some other attorney asked you to tell him what I'm asking you to tell me and you went to the records and dug it out?

A: Yes, that's correct.

## Where the Expert Testified

Q: Do you remember as of 1976, when you made that compilation for that attorney, how many Kawasaki assignments you had in the field of accident reconstruction?

A: I believe I had about eight or 10 at that time.

Q: That was up until what date?

A: That was the end of 1975. Essentially—well, first of January of 1976.

Q: And where was that case tried that that attorney asked you to do that?

A: That was in New Jersey.

Q: New Jersey?

A: Yes.

Q: And what—have you testified out of state for Kawasaki other than in New Jersey?

A: Yes, I have.

Q: Tell us the states where you have gone up until 1975, when you made up the list for the attorney in New Jersey.

A: States that I testified in have been New Jersey, Oklahoma, California, Oregon, obviously.

Q: Well, we're not up to Oregon yet.

A: No.

Q: We're working up to Oregon.

A: Georgia. Those are the ones I can recall right offhand. As I say, I don't keep that kind of record.

Q: Those are states, but in some of the states it was more than one trial, was it not?

A: No, I don't think so. Not that I recall. Well, California, perhaps.

Q: Yes. Wasn't there one case in California where the case was tried twice?

A: No, not that I am aware of.

Q: But anyway, between all the states up until the end of 1975, was it, or 1976?

A: Well, now, the states that I have given you are definitely to 1976—well, through today.

Q: Now then, after the New Jersey attorney asked you to prepare the list, which you did, which showed about eight or 10 times up to then (that) you testified for Kawasaki (on) accident reconstruction, how many cases has Kawasaki consulted you about since that time to do accident reconstruction, whether you have testified or not?

A: I would say a grand total of perhaps, oh, 20 or 25 cases.

Q: Since the New Jersey?

A: No, no. Grand total. That's everything.

Q: OK. Now, have you also done similar types of work for other motorcycle manufacturers in addition to Kawasaki?

A: Yes, I have.

Q: Will you tell us what other companies that manufacture motorcycles you have testified as a reconstruction expert?

A: Let's see. One that I have actually testified for is BMW. Moto Guzzi. I don't think I have actually testified for Honda. I have testified against Honda, but not for them.

 I take that back. I'm sorry. I think there is one Honda case in which I have given a deposition.

Q: For Honda?

A: Yes. For Honda. Suzuki, Yamaha, Harley Davidson. I take that back. Harley Davidson I have not testified for. I have testified against Harley Davidson.

### The Expert's Fee: $60 per hour

Q: Well now, for instance, in the case of the Yamaha and Suzuki and some of those other names that you mentioned, has it been on more than one occasion that they have retained you to examine and reconstruct an accident involving their motorcycle?

A: Yes. See, the ones that I have given you are ones that I have testified for.

And there is a distinction, obviously, between testifying and being retained to examine a motorcycle accident. And I have been retained by practically all of them on one occasion or another and—but I have testified for, you know, just the ones I told you about.

Q: And the examinations, though, probably outnumber the times you actually get to court and testify, do they not?

A: Oh, yes. Many, many times.

Q: Then I take it that in the past seven years this has been a fairly substantial part of your business, has it not?

A: Yes, it has.

Q: And has it been a fairly substantial part of your income?

A: Yes, it has.

Q: Tell me, and I'm not saying that critically, because we know that people charge for their time, but what do you charge, like Kawasaki, per hour or per day for this time of work for them? I'm talking now about accident reconstruction court testimony.

A: Well, I charge anybody, Kawasaki included, $60 an hour.

Q: The $60 an hour, is that whether you are testifying in Court or sitting reading transcripts in a motel room or whatever you are doing for them?

A: That's for the time that I'm working.

### Physicist and Counselor

Q: And now getting back to your trip to Eugene—well, let's go back further than that. When were you first consulted about this case?

A: I really don't have specific recollection of that. It would be sometime prior to the March 9th examination of the motorcycle.

Q: Would your file that I have had marked but haven't looked at yet assist you in telling me who, when and where you were first consulted about this case?

A: No, I don't think so.

Q: Do you have any independent recollection as to who first contacted and told you that they wanted to use your services in connection with this case?

A: I really can't say positively. It would have been one of two people.

Q: Who?

A: Either Mr. Arrowood or Mr. Gearin.

Q: Two gentlemen, distinguished gentlemen, sitting here at counsel table?

A: Right.

Q: And Mr. Arrowood is located where?

A: In Santa Ana.

Q: And his position is what?

A: He is with Kawasaki.

Q: And had Mr. Arrowood been known to you before this time?

A: I believe I met Mr. Arrowood for the first time in 1975.

Q: And was that in connection with you being retained to do some accident reconstruction work for Kawasaki on some other cases?

A: No, no. That was a result of a discussion that we had regarding the stability analysis that I was doing.

Q: And then subsequently, when you have worked on cases for Kawasaki, where it's taken you out of state or out of town, have— has Mr. Arrowood been involved in those in any way?

A: Yes.

Q: What way?

A: He has traveled with me. As Kawasaki's representative.

Q: And have you sort of, in this work you have done for them, acted, in addition to being a physicist, sort of as a counselor, you might say, as to how to present the case, what lines of approach to follow in deciding their cases?

A: Well, I have advised them on, you know, whatever cases I have been retained on regarding the facts of the accident. And, you know, how they present them is their business. But as far as presenting the facts of the accident are concerned, yes, I have advised them on that because that's my job. That's what I consider a part of my job.

## A Pleasant Lodge

Q: And have you, on previous cases for Kawasaki, when there is a trial out of town, gone and lived in the town with the attorney (who's) trying it (in) the same motel or hotel and stayed there during the trial?

A: Yes, I have.

Q: And have you, when you did that, gotten these qualified, shorthand reporter daily transcripts and read it over everyday to see what was happening in court by way of evidence?

A: No. I, frankly, think this is the first trial that I have ever done that on.

Q: All right.

A: For the most part, if I do go to listen to the evidence in the trial, I go and listen to the evidence in the courtroom.

Q: I see. Well, in this case I asked for an order excluding witnesses and the court excluded witnesses so in this case you weren't able to sit through the trial and be of assistance to counsel in the courtroom, correct?

A: That's correct.

Q: So, in this case there was a daily transcript with two reporters alternating to get the transcript. Did you get it daily, every evening? Or early the next morning?

A: No, I would say that there were occasions when I didn't get it for a couple—get the transcripts for, you know, a day or so.

Q: But as soon as you got it you would spend your time reading over the transcript, analyzing it, looking for things that you could advise Mr. Arrowood and Mr. Gearin about your opinion about what was going on, right?

A: I would say that in general I tried to read the transcript before court was out, or before I would have my next meeting with them as the case may be, yes.

Q: And with relation to meeting (them), you have enjoyed socializing with them, meeting together with them at the Valley River Inn and enjoying meals and social activities with them?

A: Valley River Inn and company are very pleasant, yes.

Q: All right.

## Closing with the Cross

Walkup's cross-examination of Otto set the stage for his closing argument to the jury, edited portions of which follow:

...How do you determine the credibility and how much weight do you give to the testimony of various witnesses?

What is their interest? What is their motive? What is their bias? What is their interest in the outcome of the litigation?

I will tell you right now, if William Otto, one witness, is going to decide the outcome of this case, then I'm going to pick up that briefcase and go home right now. We are not here to have a trial by a man who works almost full time for Kawasaki; who is a member of their team; who goes all over the United States defending their cases and sitting in court or in a motel, telling Kawasaki how to handle a case—is that an independent and unbiased witness?

...I will admit, when Mr. Otto walked up on that stand and he sat there—he (was) very dignified-looking: white-haired gentleman, a physicist and he has a beautiful bedside manner. If he were a doctor, you would listen to him, for he is so poised and calm.

But then I got a crack at him. And, frankly, I didn't know that much about him. But lo and behold, it develops that he is a combination lawyer and investigator and tester during trial at $60 an hour. You know, he has a cushy job and you (indicating the jurors) didn't leave your common sense at home when you came to court.

He said that he was busy doing projects for Kawasaki testing their bikes and that he is waiting to do another project when he has time.

Well, he didn't have time, if he was living up here in Eugene, Oregon, coaching Kawasaki and looking for hypotheses to exonerate them.

# Cross-Examination of an Adverse Medical Witness: "Keep the Jury Laughing"

### Fred Peters

The late Fred Peters was a senior partner in the Brooklyn law firm of Peters, Berger & Koshel. He lectured on law and trial technique at Brooklyn Law School, St. Johns Law School, Hofstra Law School and the Practicing Law Institute. He was past president of the Inner Circle of Advocates; member of the American Board of Trial Advocacy; and member of the Association of Trial Lawyers of America.

Dr. Johnson, the bespectacled gentleman on the witness stand, was the embodiment of a professorial physician.

He was a leading cardiologist at a major New York City hospital—the chief of his department and an expert with impeccable credentials. His terse but steady testimony under direct examination threatened to rip the guts out of Fred Peters's case.

It was left to Peters (Peters, Berger & Koshel, P.C., Brooklyn, N.Y.) to revive his case by discrediting Johnson on cross. To do so, Peters sized up the doctor—"steely grey-colored hair, very professional in appearance, obviously filled with his own self-importance"—and then the jury: "a normal cross-section of Brooklyn residents, working-class and middle-class people."

And he decided to pierce Johnson's self-esteem with a ridiculing cross-examination until his credibility washed away in the waves of laughter that came from the appreciative jurors. The transcript of the cross-examination and Peters's italicized comments on strategy follow.

## The Background Behind the Case

Peters's client claimed that he had developed a serious heart problem of undetermined diagnosis after his eighth-grade teacher assigned him to carry a heavy package of art supplies up several flights of stairs.

The boy had collapsed while carrying the packages and complained of severe chest pains, dizziness and nausea. An electrocardiogram, read by the family doctor, was abnormal and the boy was referred to Dr. Johnson.

Johnson examined the youth, placed him on strict bed rest for one month and limited activity for another month and then discharged him from care.

Subsequently, several other cardiologists concluded that the boy had a heart problem of undetermined diagnosis. On the basis of several cardiograms, including the original, the plaintiff charged the New York Public School System with negligence and claimed that his problem was traumatic myocardial infarction, induced by the stress of the sustained effort of carrying heavy weights up the steps.

Seven years after the incident occurred, the case came to trial.

## A Resurrected Witness

*Early in the litigation, I was not the attorney. I inherited the case after it had been lying in another attorney's office for a long time.*

*When I got the file and looked it over, I saw a note that said Dr. Johnson had been interviewed several years before and had expressed absolute disdain in giving the lawyers any help whatsoever. He said that he didn't want to appear in court—that he was too busy. So I assumed that it would be a waste of time to approach him, and I promptly forgot all about him. The defense resurrected him.*

*My theory of the case was that this boy had sustained a traumatic myocardial infarction, the trauma having been precipitated by the negligence of the defendant. But Dr. Johnson came in as a surprise witness during the defense and testified that he was the actual cardiologist who treated the boy many years before—at the time of the occurrence. He testified that it was his opinion that no trauma played a role in the disability. In fact, he said that the boy had made a full and complete recovery after several months of treatment and bed rest.*

*If you were to believe the witness, my client was perfectly normal after three months of the occurrence. This, of course, was devastating testimony.*

## The Purpose of the Cross

*The purpose of the cross-examination was to destroy him as completely as possible. Before beginning the cross-examination, I sought and got permission to review the doctor's file notes.*

*I quickly realized that his notes were sparse and contained almost no details or history. Realizing that so many years had elapsed, I sought to establish that the doctor's recollection of events would be hazy and that he wouldn't be able to say he remembered something that wasn't in his notes.*

*From the outset of the cross, he was very professional; obviously, he was filled with his own sense of self-importance. He took the stand and testified in a very arrogant manner. He answered questions as if he looked down on his audience. I felt that he would be amenable to being made to look ludicrous or ridiculous.*

## The Cross-Examination of Dr. Johnson

Q (BY PETERS): Dr. Johnson, I wonder if you would be good enough to tell me whether or not you have an independent recollection of the physical examination which you made of this boy— independent from any notes you might have.

A (BY DR. JOHNSON): I have no extra material stored in my brain concerning this particular case other than what I have been speaking about. The passage of time, years in fact, make such retention of facts impossible.

Q: Your answer then is no?

A: Yes, my answer is no.

Q: And that is because, of course, you see so many patients during the course of each year, is that correct?

A: That's right.

Q: And without such notes you would have no recollection whatsoever after so many years of any of the events of that examination, is that correct?

A: Well, there are some generalizations that one can or may remember with a fair degree of accuracy, but certainly in certain areas, this may become somewhat limited, the degree of which cannot be stated consistently.

Q: Is that a yes answer to my question, Sir?

A: Yes.

## Is That a Yes Answer, Doctor?

*His answers are perfectly typical of his attitude. The language he chooses to use is very pedantic. I ask a simple question and he comes back with a complex answer.*

*The jurors sympathized with me. They didn't understand the answer. It seemed round about and when I emphasized the evasiveness and pomposity of his responses by simply stating "Is that a yes, sir?" the jury giggled. They giggled right then and there and that prompted me to attack him in the fashion that I did.*

## Questions of His Age

Q: Doctor, keeping in mind what you have testified to, you said that the plaintiff had myocarditis and that you base that upon the fact that he had some sort of an infection; an underlying or causative infection—is that correct?

A: Yes.

Q: If in fact the plaintiff did not have such infection, either bacterial or a virus infection, then of course your diagnosis of myocarditis would not have ensued—is that correct?

A: No, that is not true.

Q: Well, did you say that you made your diagnosis of myocarditis based upon the fact that he had had some sort of bacteria infection which invaded the heart?

A: That's correct.

Q: Please assume, Doctor, that no such bacteria had been contracted by my client. Would you still have decided that he had a myocarditis?

A: Yes.

Q: What besides this infection, which you seemed to stress in your direct testimony, caused myocarditis in this case?

A: I am only talking about this case, and I refer to either a virus or a streptococcus, both of which may be implicated in various types of upper respiratory infection.

Q: Is it your testimony that before the myocarditis could follow, there would have had to be either a virus or a streptococcus or some other microbe or virus infection?

A: Yes

Q: Assume, doctor, that there had been no such infection prior to your first examination when you made your diagnosis. Would that diagnosis of myocarditis have been changed?

A: Not necessarily.

Q: You say, sir, if I understand you correctly, that in order to have a diagnosis of myocarditis, there must have been some pre-existing infection—is that so?

A: Yes.

Q: I am asking you now then to assume there was no pre-existing infection; would that alter your diagnosis of myocarditis?

A: Not necessarily.

Q: Did you consider it extremely significant in making your diagnosis that he had a history of a virus infection?

A: Yes.

Q: It was so significant that you based your diagnosis upon it—is that not so?

A: No.


### You're Making Me Sound Like an Idiot

Q: Well, what other factors did you take into consideration, in addition to an antecedent virus in arriving at your diagnosis? Please enumerate them one by one.

A: Well, his age simplified this problem to a great extent.

Q: Let's stop at each one if you don't mind, sir. You say because he was 14 years old he had a myocarditis?

A: I didn't say that at all; you said it.

Q: Did you just testify that his age simplified the problem of diagnosis?

A: Yes.

Q: Did you mean that if he had not been 14 years old the diagnosis would have been more difficult?

A: That has nothing to do with it.

Q: What has nothing to do with it?

A: His age.

Q: Well, haven't you enumerated that as one of the factors?

A: Do you want the reasons?

Q: Did you not list age as one of the factors that simplified the problem in making the diagnosis?

A: I didn't say he was 14 years old.

Q: When you refer to his age, you were referring to his being 14 years old were you not?

A: Yes. But obviously, you are drawing a false conclusion.

Q: Doctor, suppose we leave the conclusions to be drawn to the court and jury. I am asking you merely to enumerate, one by one, the factors which you used to form your conclusion that this boy had a myocarditis.

A: Well, I have given you some of them.

Q: You have told us that he had a history of virus infection and that he was 14 years of age; what else?

A: Well, the age level was most important for the following reasons...

Q: I don't ask you for your reasons yet, sir, just the facts that you considered, that is my question.

A: I am trying to give you all of the factors.

Q: Well, tell us the rest of the factors.

A: The age level and also this was a diagnosis that was made with great infrequency at that time.

Q: Are you saying that one of the reasons you decided that this boy had a myocarditis was because that diagnosis was so rare?

A: You said it was rare, not me.

Q: When you said the diagnosis was made with great infrequency did you mean that it was commonplace?

A: No, just the opposite, it was relatively rare.

Q: Well now, does your use of the word rare mean we can accept that such a diagnosis was hardly ever made?

A: Yes.

Q: All right. Are you now saying that since the diagnosis was hardly ever made at that time, that was one of your reasons for making it?

A: That is obviously a very absurd statement.

Q: Did you consider the absurdity of it when you used it in your testimony as a factor in arriving at your diagnosis?

A: It was not absurd at the time.

Q: Has it become absurd since?

A: Of course not.

Q: Well, what other factors, if any, did you take into consideration when you decided he had a myocarditis, besides the precedent infection, his age, and the rarity of such a diagnosis?

A: I meant I was aware of it because I was writing on the subject in a text book I had published.

Q: Are you telling us that because you happened to be doing some writing on the subject of myocarditis at the time you made the examination that that was one of the reasons you made such a diagnosis?

A: That is another absurd statement.

Q: Didn't you just tell us about your book in response to my asking you to list the reasons for making your diagnosis?

A: This is becoming ridiculous.

Q: What is becoming ridiculous, my questions or your answers?

A: You are making me sound like an idiot.

THE COURT: Doctor, please don't make comments; just answer the questions that are put to you.

## The Jurors Had a Good Time

*The jury was in hysterics. They were laughing out loud, tears streaming down some of their faces. They were having the time of their lives. And the more they laughed, the more discomforted the doctor became. The more ridiculous were his answers. The judge was barely able to stifle a laugh.*

*In point of fact, there was nothing about the cross-examination that was improper. There is only one point where the judge interfered and that was when the doctor started arguing with me.*

*You have to appreciate the scene. If I had agreed with him or said something to the effect of, "Well, you are an idiot," I might easily have turned the jury around in his favor.*

*I let him stew in it. He had never been treated in that fashion in all of his professional life. He was not accustomed to having his word questioned.*

## Athlete's Foot

Q: Are you telling us that one of the factors you relied upon in arriving at your diagnosis was that you happened to be writing a book on that subject?

A: Yes, and I can explain that.

Q: Do you mean that if you had been writing a book on, let us say, athlete's foot, you would have diagnosed his problem as athlete's foot?

A: I don't write on foot infections.

Q: Do you write on gunshot wounds of the heart?

A: I do.

Q: Then I will substitute gunshot wound in my last question for athlete's foot.

A: What has that to do with my diagnosis?

Q: Doctor, what has your writing a book on myocarditis have to do with your diagnosis in this case?

A: It was one of the things I considered.

Q: Going back to the virus, if there were no such virus, would that have had some significance in making your diagnosis?

A: It may have been an evanescent virus.

Q: Doctor, I haven't asked you about anything evanescent. I asked you to assume that there were none, n-o-n-e, no infection whatsoever.

A: That is an important factor.

Q: The fact is, doctor, is it not, that it is so important that if you knew that there had been no infection, you would not have arrived at a diagnosis of myocarditis due to a virus.

A: Not at all. There are some negative factors.

Q: You mean there were both positive and negative factors which you considered?

A: Yes.

Q: Tell us what some of the other negative factors were?

A: I will conclude with one negative factor.

Q: And what was that, sir?

A: The boy had no murmurs.

Q: Do you mind if I jot that down?

A: Please do.

Q: Since there were no murmurs, did you consider that significant in arriving at your conclusion that the boy had myocarditis?

A: Absolutely right.

Q: Do I take it, doctor, that if he in fact had had a murmur you would have decided it was not myocarditis?

A: Of course not. Again, you are making me sound idiotic.

Q: Doctor, is the lack of a murmur significant in making a diagnosis of myocarditis?

A: Well, as I told you, it was a negative factor.

Q: Were there any other negative factors which you considered?

A: I will conclude with one negative factor because there were so many positive factors involved here.

### Please Take Your Time, Doctor

Q: Doctor, have you listed all the positive factors already?

A: Well, I haven't told you about the rest yet.

Q: Well, tell us now—what were the rest of the factors?

A: He had a history of virus infection.

Q: You already told us about that, sir, I'm asking for any additional factors.

A: Well, he had a temperature elevation.

Q: Doctor, I assume that when you stated that he had a temperature elevation, you refreshed your recollection from a note in your records?

A: Yes.

Q: Can you show me where in your records there is any reference to a temperature elevation?

A: I am looking.

Q: Please take your time.

A: I cannot seem to find that note.

Q: Is that because no such note exists on your records?

A: I simply can't find it. Yes.

Q: Will you agree with me now, Doctor, that if he did not have an antecedent virus, and in fact he did not have a history of temperature elevation, nor did he have a temperature elevation at the time of your examination, you would not have come to the same conclusion of myocarditis?

A: Not the same conclusion, no.

Q: And that means, doctor, that assuming no virus had existed then no myocarditis existed, is that correct?

A: Yes.

### Let the Admission Sit In

*Having firmly established the fact that if no virus existed then no myocarditis existed, I could move on to other points. I didn't hammer home this point because more often than not that leads to witness backtracking. You can lose the admission, or it gets watered down.*

*Once I get an admission, I let it sit. I may pause a bit to look at the jurors, without asking a question, so I know that they are aware of the answer and that it has percolated in. But I won't ask any more about it because the witness might back off.*

*My next question really nails down my point. I say, "Let us inquire whether in fact he had a virus." The previous question was let us assume he had none.*

### Was His Mother There?

Q: Well, then, let us inquire into whether or not he in fact had a virus infection. What investigation did you make with respect to determining exactly whether or not he had it, what this so-called virus infection was?

A: History.

Q: Did this 14-year-old boy say he had a virus when you examined him—were those his words?

A: His mother was along with him.

Q: You told us you had no independent memory of this examination, is that correct?

A: Right.

Q: Show us on your notes, doctor, where it states the identity of the person who accompanied the boy to your office, if anyone.

A: It doesn't say.

Q: Do you have any record that his mother was with him at all?

A: I did not expect this to be a legal matter.

Q: Whether or not you expected it to be a legal matter, is it not a fact that nowhere on your records is there any indication that a mother gave you a history?

A: I didn't expect to take copious notes about the appearances of various collateral family members or other people.

Q: Since you say that this virus infection was extremely significant in the making of the diagnosis, I simply want you to tell this court and jury what investigation you made into its character, what kind of an infection it was, and any of the other details about it

A: Since I don't possess an electronic microscope and other complicated instruments and since these were not readily available,
anyhow, and since they weren't performed anyway except during research study on this type of problem, one simply relies on
the history as obtained and if there are any objective evidences of
such primary infection which may persist, they may be easily recognized by the examiner.

## A Layman's Advice

Q: Since you have told us that you relied on history, may I take it
that there was no objective evidence of such infection
whatsoever?

A: Yes.

Q: And you simply related that reliance that there was a virus to a
myocarditis, is that correct?

A: I was concerned with all the facts in the case in arriving at a
proper diagnosis.

Q: Since the presence of an antecedent virus played such an important part in your diagnosis, I would like you to tell me what your
investigation revealed to you about the character of the virus—
what did you discover about it, what kind of virus did he have?

A: I think that even you as a layman know as well as any physician
does what I am saying.

Q: I do not understand what you just said, sir. Do you mean that we
should all know what you have said without your explaining it?

A: What I mean is, I believe it is common knowledge as to what the
ordinary or common cold means, whether you're a layman or a
physician. In fact, most of these diagnoses are made by laymen
themselves, and seldom do they go to a physician.

Q: Are you now saying that the boy had an ordinary common cold
and based upon that history you decided that he was suffering
from myocarditis when you examined him?

A: I am saying that either he or his mother told me he had a virus.

Q: What was it that you claim he had, a common cold or a virus?

A: There is no difference to me.

Q: Are you saying, sir, that you relied on a diagnosis by a layman of virus in order to formulate that as a cornerstone for your own diagnosis?

A: It was important.

Q: Is your answer to that then yes?

A: Yes.

## Spur of the Moment

*Everything that happened was done on the spur of the moment. I started the cross and took it on the wing—so to speak. Once he started down the road he did, the questions simply suggested themselves. And his answers very properly led to the next question.*

*My main point at all times was that there was no basis for the doctor's diagnosis because antecedent infection didn't exist. Everytime he raised the question of antecedent infection, I had to somehow slap it down. Suddenly he was saying that the antecedent infection was not, in fact, his observation, but something someone had told him. My obvious reply to that is what kind of big shot doctor would base his whole diagnosis on what some layman said.*

## Impugned Integrity

Q: As a matter of fact, doctor, on your examination, the boy had no elevated temperature whatsoever, did he?

A: That's correct.

Q: And further, doctor, as a matter of fact when somebody is suffering from myocarditis, an elevated temperature is one of the signs one customarily sees—isn't that true?

A: Not necessarily.

Q: But it is one of the signs one customarily sees—is it not?

A: It may be low grade or it may not be present on a specific occasion; it may be elevated for the rest of the day or during the night or at various other times.

Q: Doctor, I merely ask you whether one would expect to find an elevated temperature in a patient suffering from myocarditis?

A: That's correct.

Q: In any event, on this particular occasion, there was no elevated temperature, true?

A: I don't know. I didn't take the temperature; I was told that he had an elevated temperature.

Q: Do you now say that you had some conversation with somebody during which you were told that the boy had an elevated temperature—is that your testimony?

A: Yes.

Q: When you make an examination of a child for the first time in which you suspect myocarditis you don't even bother to take the temperature yourself?

A: Are you impugning my integrity as a physician?

THE COURT: Doctor, do not argue with counsel.

Q: Would you answer my last question, please?

A: I did not take the temperature, no.

Q: Well, in this conversation that you recall, do you recall it distinctly.

A: I have a note here that he had sometime a temperature elevation.

Q: I want to know when you spoke to whoever it was who told you that, what were the circumstances, when and where?

A: I don't recall any other facts other than what I have stated here. There may have been a temperature elevation.

Q: Your notes do not say anything about conversations, do they?

A: You brought that up.

Q: Doctor, didn't you state a few moments ago that you may have obtained that information in a conversation?

A: I got it from the doctor who sent him to me along with his electrocardiogram.

Q: You told me you got the virus-information from the mother or from the child—that you relied on a layman, did you not?

A: The doctor may have told me.

Q: Did you now say a doctor may have told you about it, meaning you do not absolutely recollect?

A: I have no record. This much I do know. The mother was there. I am not going to make up any stories. That is all I know about it. There is no more I can answer, regardless of what you ask me about it.

Q: I am not asking you to make up any stories, am I?

A: No, but you are trying to deliberately weight some of these matters, as far as I can tell from the line of questioning.

Q: It was your own testimony, was it not, that you relied on a layman's expression of virus?

A: I have no distinct recollection as to who gave me that information.

## He Dug His Own Hole

*Hopelessly entangled in his own answers, he is being whipped back and forth by the absurdity of his replies. He finally says, "There is no more that I can answer."*

*He says that he is not going to make up any stories. Obviously, he feels his testimony looks like it is made up. It is a defensive statement. So I said, "I'm not asking you to make up stories, am I?"*

*He goes right back into it deeper by saying, "You are deliberately trying to weight some of these matters." I reply with his own testimony: "It was your testimony, was it not, that you relied on a layman's expression of virus."*

*I am whipping him, but I am also very careful. I am amused. I simply put questions to him and his answers are the ones which give me and the jury enjoyment. Occasionally, my questions fan the flames a little.*

## Rheumatic Fever

Q: Did any physican, to your knowledge, make a diagnosis of a virus infection, either a bacterial or any other type, prior to the examination?

A: I have no record of it down in black and white.

Q: The question is, was any made to your knowledge—yes or no?

A: I have no record of it in black and white.

Q: Doctor, whether or not you have it down in back or white, to your knowledge was any such diagnosis ever made?

A: No.

Q: Now, doctor, rheumatic fever may be a common cause of myocarditis; isn't that so?

A: That's true.

Q: It is also true, is it not, that this boy never in his life had rheumatic fever?

A: He may have had.

Q: Doctor, as far as you know, I don't care what may have been.

A: Well, you don't recall what I said, because I said the myocarditis could have been either post-viral or rheumatic.

Q: Did you ever obtain a history or did anybody ever tell you that this boy had rheumatic fever?

A: I just answered that question.

Q: Would you please answer it once more?

A: Nobody ever told me he had rheumatic fever.

Q: Isn't it a fact that you are arrived at a diagnosis of myocarditis for some reason, and now you are saying that, if you were correct, it might have come from rheumatic fever?

A: The most likely etiologic factor here was post-viral, but rheumatic basis for it may be a possibility.

Q: Now we have already agreed that the viral infection may not have been there at all, so let us go on. If a 14-year-old boy is asked in a school to lift 70 to 80 pounds at the time, and while doing so experiences severe chest pain, dizziness, nausea and collapses, and that he had never had such an experience before and that he had never been called upon to lift that type of weight before, and thereafter a cardiogram is taken which was interpreted to reveal myocardial damage, would you not say that an explanation for the symptoms and the myocardial damage was the activity he was asked to perform and the strain it put on his heart?

A: It could have contributed, yes.

Q: Doctor, are the electrocardiographic changes which take place with myocarditis, transitory in nature?

A: They usually are, yes.

Q: In view of the fact that you have testified that you successfully treated this myocarditis and it had entirely cleared up in three months' time, would you expect, in view of that, for him to have had an abnormal electrocardiogram four years later?

A: The electrocardiographic fndings had not only cleared up four years later, they were cleared up by the time of my second examination three months later.

Q: So that if he had myocarditis, as you say there should have been no abnormality in the subsequent electrocardiograms, is that correct?

A: That's correct.

Q: Have you ever heard of Dr. Pete Jones?

A: Yes.

Q: Do you recognize him as an eminent and prominent cardiologist?

A: Yes.

Q: Is he a cardiologist in this city?

A: I believe he is.

Q: Have you ever heard of Dr. Sam Smith?

A: Yes.

Q: Is he an eminently qualified cardiologist in your opinion?

A: Yes.

Q: Are both of those gentlemen capable of interpreting and reading electrocardiograms, in your opinion?

A: Certainly.

Q: I want you to assume that both of these gentlemen have testified in this case and have interpreted the subsequent cardiograms as being abnormal.

A: Yes.

Q: Let me show you Plaintiff's Exhibit Three and call your attention specifically to lead V6 on that cardiogram.

A: Yes.

Q: And would you please note, Doctor, that this is a cardiogram taken subsequent to the time you say his myocarditis had cleared up.

A: Yes.

Q: Looking at the V6 lead Doctor, do you consider that an abnormal reading?

A: Yes.

Q: Does it indicate that the patient has myocardial damage?

A: Yes.

MR. PETERS. Thank You, Doctor. I have nothing further.

## Testimony from Left Field

*The truth of the matter is that he came to court and testified to a diagnosis that I thought was out in left field. While he may have, in fact, made such a diagnosis, there was no basis for it, I felt. I believed the diagnosis was wrong when he made it seven years ago and it was certainly wrong in court.*

*My client won a substantial verdict. I cannot absolutely claim that the cross-examination won the case, but had I not destroyed the doctor's credibility, it could have gone the other way.*

# Proving Proximate Cause:
# A Million-Dollar Case Study

## Lou Ashe

The late Lou Ashe practiced law in Los Angeles. He received his JD degree, cum laude, from Boston University Law School; he also received the LLM degree from Boston University. He was a Fellow of the International Academy of Trial Lawyers and of the Internatonal Academy of Law and Science. He was a national president of the Association of Trial Lawyers of America. He received honorary degrees of Doctor of Laws and of Doctor of Humanities; was a member of the World Policy Committee's Commission for chairman of the American Bar Association's Committee of Trial Techniques.

DRAMATIS PERSONAE*
  Druffy v. Coastview County General Hospital, et al

THE HOSPITALS: South Marina Community Hospital
      Emergency Room
    Coastview County General Hospital
    and its Coastview County Medical
    Center

PHYSICIANS: First surgery:
    Chief plastic surgeon: Dr. Everett Anson
    Assistant resident: Dr. Jan Mason
    Second surgery:
    Chief resident surgeon-otolaryn-
     gologist: Dr. Harry Kilvair
    Professor and staff surgeon:
      Dr. Franklin M. Turnside
    Neurological consultants:
      Chief of Staff: Dr. Jason Franks
      Resident: Dr. Byron Brock

NURSES: Recovery room: Carlotta Ryan, RN

---

*All names of persons and places are fictitious

## The Initial Accident and Its Aftermath

Until approximately 10:00 pm, on September 10, 1969, Sandor (Sandy) Druffy II was an energetic, good-looking, fun-loving, athletic young student, in excellent health, preparing to begin a new college semester as a business administration major. He was an accomplished, well-trained motorcycle operator.

On that evening—September 10, 1969—Sandy was operating a Jamasaki motorcycle owned by his friends Christine and James Shaw, and was observed by them, at the intersection of Pacific Coast Highway and McArthur Street in Coastview, California, to accelerate the bike from a dead stop to about 25 mph. In a bizarre action, the bike went out of control, striking the tailgate of a parked station wagon. The major force of the impact was exerted against Sandy's neck and chin.

Within 48 hours, by approximately 4:00 p.m. on September 12, Sandy had undergone two surgeries, had suffered brain damage and the eventual loss of his voice, among other despairing disabilities, flowing from his affliction as an essential quadriplegic. We shall relate these sequentially as the facts unfold.

In the pages that follow, we hope to delineate the techniques employed to establish—from testimony adduced from the defendants themselves—the sequence of events under their control that either directly or indirectly caused, influenced, or aggravated the pathologies that imposed upon Sandy a laryngeal stenosis which robbed him of his voice, and the litany of dramatic disabilities and suffering consequent upon a brain injury that was sustained, as we contended, because of a negligent failure to keep this young man's airway free from the accumulation of biological fluids, thus denying oxygen to the brain—leaving Sandy an essential quadriplegic.

## The Missed Diagnosis

At approximately 10:20 p.m., Sandy, despite the traumatic episode, remained conscious, alert, and oriented. Driven to the South Marina Community Hospital by his friends, the Shaws, Sandy walked into the emergency room under his own power, but with these steps began the compounding of errors that would lead to his victimization as a quadriplegic.

Emergency room personnel failed to verify any injury other than an obvious avulsion wound of the chin. They administered a tetanus toxoid injection, but they failed negligently to investigate and/or observe:

1) the cause of blood in the throat;
2) a fracture of the larynx;
3) emphysema in the neck tissues;
4) bilateral rib fractures; and
5) a probable pneumothorax.

Having determined that he could not pay for services, the hospital discharged Sandy, who had to travel by car to the Coastview County General Hospital, almost an hour away, with his lacerated chin in a gauze fold and a container to catch his blood production. (*This activity by the hospital was in violation of the California Health and Safety Code, Section 1407.5, as amended.*)

When Sandy arrived at the Coastview County General Hospital Medical Center at aproximately midnight he was suffering from multiple injuries to the internal structures and soft tissues of the neck, which should have been recognized by the trained eye. In fact, these were recognized finally, and preoperatively diagnosed (in addition to the obvious extensive avulsion defect of the lower lip and chin) as: (1) progressive interstitial emphysema of the neck; (2) abrasions of the left side of the face; (3) patient complaint of difficulty in breathing; (4) patient spoke in a high, squeaky voice, and (5) marked fullness of the neck threatening obstruction to respiration.

### Eliciting the Facts Surrounding the First Surgery

The first surgery was planned solely for repair of the avulsion wounds of the lower lip and chin, despite a preoperative diagnosis of progressive interstitial emphysema of the neck. When the patient arrived in surgery, he was in great respiratory distress and required an emergency tracheotomy.[1] With improvement of respiration, the surgery of repair at the hands of Dr. Anson continued. After surgery, with a finger over the trache tube, Sandy could speak, but again only in a high, squeaky voice. Despite this now recognized symptomatology, no further procedures were undertaken or immediately planned.

Dr. Anson, the plastic surgeon, was deposed, to establish, among other things, the standards and responsibility of the admitting doctors, as well as his own, and to establish (a) the significance of the preoperative presenting signs and symptoms, and (b) the life or death necessity of maintaining the patient's airway.[2] It was pursued in this manner:

MR. ASHE: Doctor, when you are called to treat a patient with an avulsion defect of the chin requiring plastic repair, and you find that he has developed a progressive interstitial emphysema of the neck, abrasions of the left side of the face, and if you should further find from the history that a man struck a fixed object with his head and neck, fell off his bike, and sustained that much injury to his chin, would that not raise a suspicion in your trained mind that there might be some possible threat to his airway?[3]

DR. ANSON: Yes, it would.

Q: You will agree, won't you, that an intern or resident receiving a patient in a great hospital such as this, would, following good standards of practice, take a history covering all essential data he or she thought necessary as a basis, in part, for developing a diagnosis?

A: He should.

Q: Is not the training of a doctor who is received for further training as an intern or resident required to be sufficient so that should he or she observe signs of interstitial emphysema, bruises, and abrasions about the face, ecchymatic areas anterior to the throat itself—and the patient being conscious and, when spoken to, responds in a high, squeaky voice, that there is enough here to raise a strong suspicion that there was something wrong with the pharynx or larynx?

A: *Yes, that should be.* (Emphasis added.)

We inquired further to establish that the swelling sufficient to cause interstitial emphysema would induce a doctor knowledgeable as to the ENT (ear, nose, and throat) phases of this injury to conclude that such swelling might in and of itself "*restrict the passageway and deny a proper airway to the patient*". There was objection that this query was outside the witness' expertise. However, he answered:

DR. ANSON: If it were to become progressive, yes.

MR. ASHE: As a well-trained doctor, whether you are an ENT specialist or not, you will agree, the answer solicited is not outside your field of knowledge?

A: No, I wouldn't say that it is. No.

Q: You know from the range of your studies, don't you doctor, that a pharynx that swells may so shut off the airway that within a relatively short period of time the patient is dead, right, sir?

A: *This could happen.* (Emphasis added.)

It was firmly established that any threat to the airway would have contra-
indicated undertaking of the second surgery. This was affirmed in the following fashion:

MR. ASHE: Dr. Turnside, with your obvious expertise at hand, certainly
neither you or your chief resident would ever have gone ahead
with this surgery as a matter of good medical practice if, during
such a procedure, in some fashion, there was a threat to this man's
life because of any inadequacy of his airway—right, sir?

DR. TURNSIDE: That is correct.

Q: So, I may assume, sir, that throughout this surgery, there was no
threat to this man's life or to the integrity of his brain all through
entire surgery?

A: There was no indication of that at all.

Nor would the patient have been transferred postoperatively were there
any threat then to the airway.

MR. ASHE: Sir, at the hands of a highly trained specialist such as yourself, you will assure us that this patient never would have been
turned over to the intensive care unit if, within your judgment,
there was any possible—and even more so any probable—threat
to continuity of the airway?

DR. TURNSIDE: That is correct.

Q: That would be consistent with good medical standards of care?

A: Yes—to make sure that the bleeding is controlled and that the
airway is adequate before going to intensive care.

Q: Then, we are in agreement that anything less than that would be
below the standards of care?

A: I would agree with that.

Q: Thank you, sir. Thus we have it that both you and Dr. Kilvair were
satisfied fully in this regard before you were willing to release this
patient to the intensive care unit, right?

A: That is correct.

## The Transit to Tragedy

The obvious trauma to Sandy's neck now led to a consultation of five doctors from the Otolaryngologic Services (ENT). The decision was: a second surgery for Sandy. The preoperative diagnosis this time was: "Probable laryngeal and tracheal fracture". A four-hour procedure was performed by Dr. Harry Kilvair, chief resident surgeon, with Dr. Franklin M. Turnside, a senior surgeon, attending.[4]

Throughout the surgery, there were no untoward incidents indicating any threat to the patient's airway. Vital signs remained stable and the patient left the surgical suite in good condition, and was delivered to the recovery room nearby, arriving at 2:55 pm, September 12, 1969—approximately 41 hours after the initial accident had occurred.

Examination of all attending nurses and doctors established firmly that vital signs remained intact and that there was no evidence of any brain damage.[5]

At 3:50 pm—less than an hour after leaving surgery—Sandy, with an indwelling tracheotomy tube in place and determined to be stable with no respiratory problem contra-indicating his transfer, was ordered moved from the recovery room to the intensive care unit.

Whatever other misfortune had befallen Sandor Druffy II, he had not yet sustained brain damage.

But tragedy was only moments away.

Even now, years after the events I am relating, it tears at me to concede that in multiple depositions we could not elicit a flat admission from any defendant, or establish by any record, the identification of any staff doctor, resident, intern, nurse, nurses' aide, or orderly who could or would testify as to precisely how, in what manner, and by whom Sandy was transported from the recovery room to the ICU.

However, there were peripheral concessions that helped to light the way, irresistibly, to convincing conclusions.

Testimony regarding the reasonable elapsed time for the movement of a patient under those conditions from the recovery room to the ICU varied from four to six minutes or more.[6]

When the transit was completed, the well-trained nurse who received Sandy in the intensive care unit observed and reported classical signs of brain damage: (1) the patient's pupils were fixed, dilated, and nonreactive to light, (2) there was a substantial increase in his respiratory rate, and (3) his blood pressure was advanced.

Within an hour, by 5:00 pm of the same day, there were more pronounced signs of brain damage: (1) decerebrate movements, and (2) twitching and convulsions. Sandor Druffy II was at the threshold to disaster!

## Zeroing in on Causation

Dr. Kilvair, the otolaryngologist, had seen the patient in the recovery room at 3:05 pm; when advised of the brain damage discovered at approximately 3:55 pm by the nurse receiving Sandy in the ICU, he responded emotionally when asked for his reaction. We report verbatim:

> MR. ASHE: At this point, had you any discussion with other doctors on the staff as to what conceivably went wrong with this patient, what caused the brain damage?

> DR. KILVAIR: Yes . . . I can't recall exactly what time or with whom, but we discussed it at length. *I was quite upset by it and I discussed it with a lot of people.* (Emphasis the witness.)

> Q: How about Dr. Turnside, did he have an opinion?

> A: Well, he was as flabbergasted as I was, and neither of us could make a judgment as to what went wrong, or when . . . as far as it was humanly possible to tell, the surgery, (pause), went well. *It was just like someone dropping a bombshell on you when they told us this had happened.* (Emphasis his.)

When we pressed the doctor as to whether, at that time, he had formed a medical impression that 'somewhere along the line there had been a denial of oxygen to the brain', he answered:

*I had not made a judgment as to that . . . I couldn't pinpoint what went wrong, but that is one of the possible causes, definitely . . . as to when, where, how, I have not made a judgment.* (This more than two years after the fact.) However, he is in agreement that:

> MR ASHE: . . . at 3:05, or thereabouts, the same patient you had seen less than an hour before and had determined to be in no respiratory distress now was noted as "suctioned with bloody return with a few clots. Pupils dilated and nonreactive to light. . . .

> DR. KILVAIR: Yes.

> Q: And that would indicate that something happened to this man which had caused a neurological deficit. Do you agree to that?

A: Yes.

Q: A deficit which you did not find at 3:05 when you saw him?

A: Right.

Despite his total reluctance to indict the transport period as the crucial moments of hypoxia and/or anoxia because, "*There were other variables that can cause this type of problem*", when pressed further his reply was significant:

> MR. ASHE: Doctor, as you consider all the variables and what you see to have been the final result in this case—that we have here a man with severe brain injury, is it not true that if we should put all the variables into the hopper, the most likely cause of the brain injury would be a denial of oxygen to the brain, hypoxia and/or anoxia?
>
> DR. KILVAIR: It could.

Dr. Turnside, the staff otolaryngologic surgeon and professor, somewhat guardedly, was, nevertheless, in agreement.

> MR. ASHE: Although I appreciate your field is ENT—you are first a finely trained doctor and you will agree, won't you, that anoxia was the cause of this man's brain damage? (Colloquy and objection.)
>
> DR. TURNSIDE: Let's say that he has had brain damage and anoxia in one possibility. (Colloquy.)
>
> Q: Have you ever voiced a personal opinion as to the probable cause of the brain damage to Mr. Druffy?
>
> A: Yes, the possibilities were discussed on my teaching rounds.
>
> Q: May I respectfully suggest to you, sir, that one of the possibilities you discussed . . . was the fact that there might have been a denial of oxygen to the brain for some reason?
>
> A: That is correct.
>
> Q: In light of the fact that this young man was intubated at the time he went into this condition of cerebral anoxia, would that not point to the cause being most probably—the lack of oxygen? (Objection—beyond his expertise.)
>
> A: I think so—more or less.

Earlier in our examination of Dr. Anson, the plastic surgeon, we had ventured this question:

> MR. ASHE: If, in fact, a failure to maintain the airway of Mr. Druffy, in this case, resulted in an accumulation of biologic fluids sufficient to obstruct the airway, and if this condition were permitted to exist long enough to create brain damage—if this were the fact, would you agree with me, sir, that would be below the standard of care observed by reputable physicians and surgeons in this community?

> DR. ANSON: Yes—it would.

## A Technique for Breaking Down the Opposition

It has long been this contributor's belief that no case is ready for the plaintiff until the defenses and the techniques which may be employed to assert them are explored, exposed, analyzed, and methods are contrived to dissipate or dissolve their impact on the desired result.

Our persistent inquiries continued through dispositions, interrogatories, requests for admissions, and medical-legal consultations at various periods of the developing file. Having anticipated an array of defenses calculated to dissipate the basic etiologic causation of the quadriplegia, we were faced with the necessity of negating each and every proposed cause that might avoid liability. I refer to this as accentuating the negative and punctuating the positive.

Dr. Byron Brock, the neurological resident, conceded a post-paralysis conference with his chief, Dr. Jason Franks. Pursuing this, we inquired in part:

> MR. ASHE: Surely, doctor, there is no question in your mind that Sander Druffy suffered brain damage while a patient in this hospital?

> DR. BROCK: No.

As the dialogue continued, Dr. Brock revealed that Dr. Franks and members of the staff were 'sifting the possibilities' in their attempt to determine the etiology of the brain injury.

> MR. ASHE: Doctor, though you may speak of 'sifting the possibilities', eventually it is axiomatic in medicine that one must have a diagnosis in order to treat?

DR. BROCK: Correct.

Q: Do you equate 'possibility' with what is commonly referred to as seeking a 'differential diagnosis'?

A: Yes, that is correct.

With that preamble, we can examine, in brief, the confection of possible causes of the brain injury by the defendants.

First, with Dr. Franklin M. Turnside, who had earlier conceded that anoxia was a 'good possibility', and who volunteered other possibilities, including: (a) trauma, (b) hemorrhage, (c) vascular accident.

We queried:

MR. ASHE: Was it ever determined by anyone in ruling in or out the causes or the cause of this young man's brain damage as to whether he had suffered any insult to his brain at the time of the motorcycle accident?

DR. TURNSIDE: To my knowledge that was not proved, and it was only discussed as a possibility.

Q: Brain damage by trauma would be the least likely etiologic factor, wouldn't it?

A: I feel that's a fair statement.

Q: Have we ended the possibilities?

A: I would say he could have suffered a cerebral vascular accident, too.

Q: Do you know one vascular surgeon who was asked to see this young man on the theory that he had had a vascular accident in the brain which caused this damage?

A: This would be in the domain of the neurosurgeon.

Q: Do you know any place in the patient's record that any neurosurgeon has postulated the possibility of a vascular cerebral accident here?

A: I have not read the notes that the neurosurgeons have made.

Q: Absent any postulation here by neurosurgeons on the record of this hospital that one of the etiologic factors of this man's brain damage was a cerebral vascular accident, could we, based upon that absence alone, say that in a teaching hospital like this that we could eliminate that as a probable cause.

A: I would say as a probable cause.

Next, the neurosurgeons, Drs. Franks and Brock. Dr. Brock circumvented trauma as a cause by reference to subdural or epidural hematoma.

> MR. ASHE: Now the next one—Dr. Franks questioned this in his own mind in the record: 'doubt subdural or epidural hematoma' . . . didn't he question, in his own mind, that there had been a traumatic incident strong enough, forceful enough, to have created a subdural hematoma?
>
> DR. BROCK: There was no evidence of any skull fracture or any trauma directly to the head . . . I mean by head the cranial vault excluding the fact.
>
> . . .
>
> DR. BROCK: (volunteering): Another way of trying to rule in the presence of a subarachnoid hemorrhage[7] is a lumbar puncture—a puncture of the subarachnoid space to determine if there is any blood in it.
>
> MR. ASHE: Was it done?
>
> A: Yes.
>
> Q: Was there any blood?
>
> A: It was relatively clear . . . indicating there was no significant subarachnoid hemorrhage.

Another possible cause of Sandy's brain injury, which had to be ruled out, was bilateral cerebral ischemia. This, it was speculated, would have resulted from a thrombosis of the carotid arteries bilaterally, which in turn could have led to the subarachnoid hemorrhage discussed above.[8]

The carotids, adequately tested, were determined to be 'full and equal bilaterally'. Dr. Brock explained their importance:

> DR. BROCK: . . . The arteries in the neck that are the prime vehicles of transport of oxygenated blood to the brain were full and equal and so were the temporal arteries, which are branches of these.

MR. ASHE: Then, presumably, there was no occlusion?

A: No.

Next, we considered fracture. The lack of evidence of trauma to the head and the absence of the "Battle Sign", encouraged the belief that this type of pathology did not exist. It was brought out that an examination of the ear canals indicated no bleeding had occurred. Also, the possibility of a cervical fracture as a contributing cause of the brain injury was medically discarded. There was no rigidity or other evidence of pathology.

### Winning the Crucial Point

Ultimately, after all was said and done, a type of definitive diagnosis was arrived at.

How? Dr. Brock advised:

. . .

DR. BROCK: A diagnosis of exclusion was arrived at.

MR. ASHE: A diagnosis of exclusion, by definition, is what, doctor?

A: A diagnosis that cannot be definitively proved, but that can only be assumed from the ruling out of other diagnoses that can be proved.

Q: What was the diagnosis arrived at by the exclusion process as you understand it, doctor?

A: Cerebral hypoxia and/or anoxia.

Dr. Franks, the chief of neurosurgery, having earlier raised issues challenging the etiology of the brain damage, was then asked to confirm the medical cause of Sandy's brain damage. He did so swiftly.

MR. ASHE: This diagnosis arrived at by exclusion, cerebral hypoxia or anoxia—was it one determined by you?

DR. FRANKS: I agree with this diagnosis.

Q: Would not this indicate that somewhere along the line there was a denial of sufficient oxygen to the brain?

A: That is correct.

Q: And the most probable reason for the brain damage?

A: Yes.

## A Million-Dollar Recovery

Sandor Druffy II suffered through various stages and degrees of coma for approximately four months following his second surgery of September 12. Upon achieving a state of consciousness, he was paralyzed in all four extremities, incontinent of bowel and bladder, unable to talk, and unable to visualize a single object.

In the period that followed, he underwent the following procedures and endured these illnesses: (1) direct laryngoscopy, on three occasions; (2) laryngoplasty; (3) laryngectomy (removal of larynx); (4) left thalamolectomy (surgery of the brain); (5) bilateral burr holes; (6) release of muscle contractures, right arm; and (7) removal of kidney stones.

Agonizingly, his mentality was preserved. With an IQ of 125, Sandy's only real method of communicating was by employing an alphabet board, somewhat in the style of the old ouija board, which he used to express himself by moving the pointer, laboriously, one letter at a time, to form words. One day, never to be forgotten, he formed the perplexing question, uppermost perhaps in his mind—the answer to which took some three years, long hours of research, and determined effort to achieve.

Sandy asked:

```
A        P
 H         T
D      N      W
E
```

WHAT HAPPENED?

We pray that the question has been answered adequately for this young man, whose endurance amazed us at every turn; and that his revovery beyond the million-dollar mark may afford him a semblance of human dignity and the will to persevere despite the personal devastation he has suffered.

### Notes

1. The emergency tracheotomy was performed under a local anesthetic, and at the wrong level. One of the reasons asserted for performing the tracheotomy at the wrong level was the "sudden emergency" faced by the plastic surgeon. He agreed he had prior experience in the performance of tracheotomies, and . . .

MR. ASHE: Normally, doctor, a tracheotomy is placed lower than the first ring of the trachea?

DR. ANSON: Yes, sir.

Q: There is a definite reason for that?

A: Yes, sir.

Q: The reason is what, sir?

A: In this area, there is the possibility of postoperative stenosis ... My goal was to save the patient's life ... It was difficult to be certain what area I was in.

(We note, sadly, that there was, in fact, postoperative laryngeal stenosis, and that the patient did undergo a laryngectomy and lost his ability to communicate verbally.)

2. The entire report of the first surgery was never located. The surgeon stated: "This is redictation—first dictated on 9/12/69, but I am informed that there is no record of this dictation ..."

3. Dr. Anson's appreciation was further emphasized in the following dialogue:

MR. ASHE: What other outside signs were there of trauma to the structures of the neck as distinguished from trauma to the chin itself?

DR. ANSON: There appeared to be some edema of the neck, or should I say some degree of fullness of the neck.

Q: Having observed this about the patient, prior to taking him into surgery, did you get into any discussion with this conscious patient as to how he felt inside his throat, sir; whether or not, for example, he could swallow without a problem? Did you ask him that?

A: I am not certain whether I did or not.

Q: Did you attempt to palpate the pharynx or the larynx in any way, doctor?

A: Not until I examined the patient in the surgical suite.

Q: Then did you attempt to palpate the pharynx or the larynx, doctor?

A: Yes, sir.

Q: Were the pharynx or larynx palpable at that time?

A: Not distinctly.

Q: Which would indicate what to your trained mind, doctor?

A: That there was a problem with the pharynx or larynx, that it was involved in the trauma.

4. The surgeons performed: (1) a direct laryngoscopy, (2) a repair of the avulsion of the thyroid membrane, (3) a repair of the laryngeal laceration and fracture. A new incision was made at the fourth tracheal ring and a new tracheotomy tube with a cuff was inserted. The improperly placed tube at the first tracheal ring was removed and the wound closed.

5. The nurses in training and practice were oriented fully to the dangers of hypoxia and anoxia when dealing with this type of patient intubated with a tracheotomy tube with cuff and carrying an inflatable balloon at its distal end to keep it in place and prevent passage of fluids into the trachea. One sample excerpt from the testimony reflects the appreciation:

> MR. ASHE: It was axiomatic as part of your training that you understand that should the airway become occluded and the patient denied sufficient oxygen that the potential for brain damage is there?

> NURSE RYAN: Yes, sir.

> Q: And no matter what order had been written as to the intervals of time for suctioning of the airway that in the face of any symptom or signs reflecting occlusion, the nurse is to act immediately to relieve the situation?

> A: Yes, sir.

> Q: And you were taught and instructed that this was the normal expected course of conduct and the standard of care for such nurses at this hospital?

> A: Yes, sir.

6. The intensive care unit at Coastview County General Hospital was four floors removed from the recovery room. The patient would have to be transported by bed or guerney in an elevator and then down a long hall. Dr. Kilvair, asked whether this could take five minutes, stated: "*It could, definitely*".

7. Conceivably a vascular accident secondary to previously asymptomatic berry aneurysm . . . a congenital defect of the arteries serving the brain which occurs at the junctions of the arteries where they branch.

8. Further inquiry revealed that if in fact someone had a head injury, and underwent two surgical procedures in two days, if an anesthetic gas was used, an ischemia might result, because the brain tissues had been altered. With normal concentrations of anesthesia a normal person can withstand it well, but with an abnormal brain some will not awake from the anesthesia. However, as was conceded, there was no direct trauma to the calvarium in Sandy's case.

# Cross-Examination Before Administrative Law Judges

## Lawrence G. Malone

Lawrence G. Malone is Assistant Counsel for the New York State Department of Public Service. He has represented the consumer in formal proceedings involving utility rate requests, as well as generic energy questions. Mr. Malone has also represented the Department of Public Service before a wide variety of state and federal courts. He has published several articles on administrative trial tactics in *Litigation* and *Public Utilities Fortnightly*, as well as *Trial Diplomacy Journal*.

As matters previously resolved by the courts continue to pass to administrative forums, the legal profession is being forced to pay increased attention to the fine points of administrative trial tactics. Attorneys involved in "hearing work" recognize it as an art unto itself which, like judicial practice, is acquired only with years of experience.

Because administrative hearings are not bound by the rules of evidence, the attorney has a certain degree of additional freedom (vis-a-vis the courtroom) in questioning the witnesses. Many Administrative Law Judges (ALJs) tend to allow witnesses wide latitude in their responses. In the hands of an expert witness this freedom can become most troublesome to the questioner.

### How to Plan Your Attack Ahead of Time

The complex nature of most administrative hearings, and the growing preponderance of expert testimony, are forcing administrative agencies to require pre-filed direct testimony. Irrespective of whether you receive written testimony before the hearings, it is essential that you understand *all* aspects of your opponent's case before preparing cross-examination. That is, one must fully understand all assumptions, calculations and studies which are inherent, but generally not explained, in the expert's testimony. These underpinnings usually represent the controversial portion of the witness's presentation. In order to attack them in cross-examination, the attorney must discover and critique them long before the hearing. If you discover them for the first time while conducting cross, you will not be in a position to test them.

How does one quickly get to the crux of the opponent's case? As soon as an attorney is hired, he or she should ask the opposition to accompany all direct testimony with a copy of underlying workpapers. If necessary, seek an order from the ALJ directing parties to provide *all* workpapers. Because your request obviously is intended to avoid fact-finding cross-examination, it will be welcomed by most ALJs. Also, see to it that your expert, or preferably team of experts, is prepared to work extensively on the preparation of interrogatories. These written questions are a valuable tool in identifying the crux of your opponent's case. For example, a financial expert in a utility rate case often presents a particular model forecasting required profits for the company based upon a variety of inflation, interest and monetary assumptions. Before contesting the accuracy of the model, one may wish to change the underlying assumptions to reflect reasonable future expectations, and ask the witness (in an interrogatory) to rerun it. If the results support your own case, you may not desire to impeach the witness. The important point to remember in filing interrogatory requests is to submit them early in the proceeding because the answers are essential to the preparation of cross, and you must give your opponent a reasonable period of time to answer. Responses provided on the day of cross-examination are of little value.

Once all underlying assumptions are clearly understood, the attorney and his experts should establish definite goals for cross-examination. Most testimony is sponsored by individuals who are expert not only in their academic pursuits but also in the art of testifying. In establishing goals for cross-examination, one must evaluate the relative competence of each witness. What can be fruitful questioning of one expert may be disastrous with another. If you have never cross-examined a particular witness, call a lawyer who has, or obtain a transcript of prior testimony to measure his or her abilities.

Most testimony rests upon theoretical analyses or empirical studies. What you can accomplish on cross-examination turns mainly on the worth of the analysis or study. Objective, well-done studies, when sponsored by a solid witness, do not make for ambitious cross-examination. However, irrespective of its excellence, if testimony rests on judgment it is worthwhile, at least, to identify its subjective nature. From the witness's description of the suppositions in his presentation, you can weave a web of agreement between his study (forecast, opinion, theory) and the testimony which your own witness will sponsor.

If testimony rests upon a questionable theory or is sponsored by a weak witness, cross-examination can be more engaging. However, the attorney should consider whether he or she can *best* document the opposition's weaknesses by questioning or rebuttal testimony, or both.

For example, if there are two legitimate sides to the issue and you plan to sponsor rebuttal testimony, you can rest assured that the opposition will confront your witness with *its* side of the story. Will your witness be able to answer effectively the opposition's argument? If so, you may not need to broach the subject with your initial cross-examination. On the other hand, if your witness is inexperienced you may wish to establish the point fully on cross-examination and argue it in your brief. However, remember that most jurisdictions allow *reply* briefs to the ALJ; and if your position is such that it belongs in your *initial* brief, the opposition will enjoy the last word in reply (Briefing strategy is yet another topic worthy of future discussion).

The point is: anticipate the entire argument of each potential question, in terms of the strengths and weaknesses of your position as well as your witness, *before* beginning to prepare cross-examination.


### Seven Rules for Questioning the Experts

When testimony is either highly subjective or simply flawed, the question becomes, How should one prepare for cross-examination? Obviously, the general rules of courtroom cross-examination apply (lead the witness, know the answers to your questions, avoid the why question, etc.) However, additional rules may be helpful.

**1. Place all relevant discovery material into the record.** Most often cross-examination addresses material obtained during discovery (as opposed to the expert's prefiled direct testimony). Of course, discovered material must be placed into the record prior to questioning. After the witness has adopted his own sworn testimony and is offered for cross-examination, the cross-examiner should lay a foundation for the admission of the discovered materials into the record:

> Q: Were the responses to these interrogatories prepared by you or under your direct supervision?

A: Yes.

In placing materials obtained through discovery into the record, the cross-examiner should be selective. Occasionally, opposing counsel may attempt to offer all responses; but most ALJs will require a showing of relevancy before granting such a motion.

**2. Use your own expert.** Experienced experts are invaluable in assisting in the preparation of cross-examination. Not only can they supply the attorney with useful ideas for impeaching the opposition's testimony, but they can also serve a useful role in mock cross-examination. If they are able to evade the thrust of your questions, the opposition will likely do so.

It is a serious mistake for any attorney to rely on his expert to assist him once cross-examination has begun. Lawyers who allow experts to whisper in their ears while they conduct cross-examination rarely obtain a useful product. If an attorney is not confident that he will be able to understand a witness's responses and follow up accordingly, he should not cross-examine on that issue.

**3. Never repeat a point for emphasis.** Most ALJs are highly schooled in the matter at issue. Their main concerns are to develop a thorough record and complete the case expeditiously. As a result, repetitious questioning, which might be effective in emphasizing an issue to the jury, will be poorly received by the ALJ. Not only will repetition annoy the judge but it inevitably will allow the witness an opportunity to diminish the effectiveness of your point.

**4. Establish a rhythm to your questioning.** Experienced witnesses will pause before *each* response. In doing so, they not only prepare their answers and make necessary pauses inconspicuous, but they think ahead to where the attorney is going. As a result, many lawyers find their line of reasoning frustrated before its completion. There are several ways to avoid this. One device is to ask questions fairly quickly to disrupt the witness's rhythm. Another method is to ask one or several very simple questions at the onset and then look at the judge or opposing counsel (or both) each time the witness pauses. Some experts will feel compelled to answer quickly under these circumstances.

**5. Control the witness.** Irrespective of the intelligence and experience of the Administrative Law Judge, it is rare that the judge will understand fully every technical point raised in the proceeding—even after reading the parties' briefs. In these instances, the judge is forced inevitably to rule on intuition. That is, the judge will resolve questions in favor of the party which seemed most reliable. As a result, experienced parties vie for the judge's reliance by exhibiting candor and competence during the hearings.

Many expert witnesses take pride in an ability to buttress their cases during the opponent's cross-examination. If you know the judge is receptive, obtain a ruling at the outset precluding the witness from volunteering information. Because some ALJs (especially non-lawyers) resent obvious attempts by an attorney to control the witness, know your judge before requesting such a ruling. If you make the request and it is denied, the witness will feel free to ramble. If you know the judge does not keep a rein on witnesses, be *extremely* specific in your questions. If the witness still deviates (and most will), gently interject that his comments are interesting and you may discuss them later, but they are not responsive to your particular question.

Often a tug-of-war between the attorney and expert will ensue with both apparently vying for control of the record. In some instances, it is better to allow an obstinate witness to ramble and destroy his credibility. However, it is crucial not to allow the witness to ramble unless he first appears obstinate. That is, the attorney must take all reasonable measures available to control matters. For example, if you are in a highly technical area and are attempting to educate the judge by defining certain terms, don't ask the witness for definitions. Such questions merely allow the expert to demonstrate his knowledge. They place the lawyer in a pupil-teacher relationship with the expert. Instead, supply the definition yourself, as part of your question, and simply ask the witness whether he agrees. The lawyer should do the educating, with the witness's affirmance.

Another way to control the experienced witness is to move quickly from one topic to the next. A good witness will bring a pad to the stand and take notes for redirect. However, if the attorney takes control and moves along briskly, the witness often will forget he or she has the pad.

**6. Keep the judge interested.** Most lawyers properly save the linchpin to their questioning for rebuttal testimony or brief. However, the attorney should take pains to make the questioning coherent and interesting to the Administrative Law Judge. This goal can be accomplished by simplifying complex points, with the use of plain language, and periodically turning to the judge and establishing eye contact during questions. Not only will you keep the judge interested but your manner will reassure him or her that you are trying the case for his benefit as well as the agency or board which reviews his recommendation.

**7. Beware of Making Your Case on Cross.** Evidence generally belongs in one's own direct case. However, if your witness will not withstand cross-examination well, you may be tempted to make your point through cross-examination of the other side's witness. Avoid this dilemma if at all possible. An experienced witness, asked to accept an exhibit or calculation on cross-examination, will respond that he does not consider himself in a position either to accept or reject it without time for review. Moreover, his attorney will object that the evidence should be sponsored by your own witness. Of course, if you provide the witness with a copy of a work sheet explaining the calculation well before the hearing, you will be able to answer this objection. Also, the witness is free to answer the question "subject to check." That is, most jurisdictions allow questions to be asked subject to the witness's veryifying the accuracy of the calculation later (assuming he is unable to verify on the stand). If the witness subsequently checks the calculation and wishes to challenge it, he can do so through a letter from his attorney to the ALJ.

Making one's case on cross is dangerous. If overdone, it creates the impression that the witness is being treated unfairly.

## How to Work Smoothly with the ALJ

Administrative trials often involve millions of dollars and far-reaching policy questions. When one considers their innate complexity, along with the significance of the remedies at issue, one can appreciate the strain under which ALJs labor. It is essential that the attorney cooperate with the judge in scheduling and conducting the case. Cross-examination which clarifies issues is welcome. Emotional questions and obvious attempts to confuse a witness are seen as obfuscatory and an insult to the judge's intelligence.

Avoid taking unreasonable positions. If the opposition is clearly correct on an issue, concede it. Even if you are successful in attacking your opponent on minor points with cross-examination, the illogic of your argument would be revealed eventually, with the net effect being a loss of credibility.

Cross-examination is probably the most exciting aspect of litigation because it is the least predictable. For the ill-prepared, it can be devastating. But for the studious and realistic advocate, cross-examination before Administrative Law Judges can be most rewarding.

# Chapter Six

# How to Make the Most of Final Argument

Final argument represents your last chance to influence the verdict, to give the jurors the extra push they may need to decide the facts in your favor. As Melvin Belli, the King of Torts, puts it, "The final argument is just that. It argues finally, before the jury goes into the jury room where you won't be able to follow them. You might even say to them, 'My voice is stilled; I can't follow you into the jury room. If you feel that there has been an injustice here, then you must become champions and carry through in the jury room to a just verdict.' "

Mr. Belli's remark is part of an informative interview that begins this chapter on final argument. Explaining the key elements of his highly effective summation techniques, Mr. Belli tells us how to make a strong, convincing argument even when the factual background supporting your case is weak or ambiguous. He reveals a strategy that lets you hit the high points of your case as you take the jury on a carefully mapped-out guided tour of your best evidence. You will also see how to get maximum advantage from your demonstrative aids by developing the same evidence no less than three different ways during the course of the trial, culminating in "one of the great moments of the trial," your final argument.

Mr. Belli cautions against certain all-too-common mistakes that attorneys make in summation and explains a simple technique to help you overcome what is perhaps the worst of them—failing to analyze your case totally from the point of view of your client. And to wrap up this wide-ranging dialogue, Mr. Belli shares his tools of the trade for making a successful final argument, covering both what to say *and* how to say it.

For Trial Master Robert E. Cartwright, final argument in a personal injury case is the time when you must get the jury to identify strongly with the plight of your client. "You have got to make the jury believe," he writes, "that 'There, but for the grace of God, go I.' If you can implant . . . that seed in their minds, you are going to win."

To help bolster your winning effort, Mr. Cartwright spells out seven psychological principles to unlock the hearts and minds of the people in the jury box. Based on Mr. Cartwright's quarter-century of experience in trying cases before juries, these seven principles, properly applied, can make your next final argument a truly memorable one.

You will see, for instance, how to give the jury an easy-to-grasp story or analogy guaranteed to hit home harder than any ordinary statement could do. Mr. Cartwright provides several examples to get you started and suggests how to accumulate a whole storehouse of these case-winning gems. You will also discover how to captivate the jury during final argument by striking again and again at your opponent's jugular...how to take the sting out of your opponent's argument before he even has a chance to deliver it...and how to hook the jurors with subtle understatement, getting them to complete your final argument for you by leaving just the right gaps for their imagination and sympathy to fill in.

Criminal defense attorney David Cohen rounds out this chapter with a penetrating look at reasonable doubt in summation. A former prosecutor and magistrate, Mr. Cohen knows from experience exactly what defense counsel is up against at trial. With the aid of several sample arguments provided by Mr. Cohen, you will see not only how to combat the prosecutor's definition of reasonable doubt, but also how to give the jurors a choice of *many* reasonable doubts from which they can pick the one they will use as the basis of their acquittal.

# Final Argument

## An interview with Melvin M. Belli

Melvin M. Belli is the senior partner of his law firm, with principal offices in San Francisco, California, and with offices in Beverly Hills (Los Angeles), Pacific Grove, San Diego, Stockton and Sacramento, California. Mr. Belli is Director, Dean Emeritus, Fellow and Co-Founder of the International Academy of Trial Lawyers; past President of the Association of Trial Lawyers of America; past President of the American Trial Lawyers Association Western States; Provost of the Belli Society and founder and moderator of the annual Belli Society seminars; and author of over 60 books including *Modern Trials* (six volumes), *The Belli Files*, *The Wayward Law*, and his 1976 autobiography, *My Life on Trial*. He is a member of the Board of Editors of *Trial Diplomacy Journal*.

### How to Set Up a Strong Summation

EDITOR: What should you have accomplished with respect to persuading the jury before you begin your summation? In other words, what advantages would you like to have as you go into your summation?

BELLI: You would like to have a thorough, logically structured factual background. That is the prosaic background for any final argument, where your case is a good one. Of course, if you don't have a good case, you can't have a very good background. But with a good final argument you could still win your case with a bad factual background.

The final argument is just that. It argues finally, before the jury goes into the jury room where you won't be able to follow them. You might even say to them, "My voice is stilled; I can't follow you into the jury room.

If you feel that there has been an injustice here, then you must become champions and carry through in the jury room to a just verdict."

Summation is adding together everything that went on during the trial. But a *good* summation is a lot more than that. You can pick a lot of flowers and put together a bouquet—that will be a bouquet, but it won't be a work of art. To make it a work of art you've got to place the flowers carefully, you've got to arrange them by color, you've got to emphasize, you've got to make people appreciate what is before them.

To do a good final argument you've got to have made a good opening statement. For example, if you try a case on *res ipsa loquitur,* use the term *res ipsa loquitur* in the voir dire: ask the jury if they would follow the doctrine of *res ipsa loquitur* if the judge instructs on it. If the judge cuts you off and says you can't talk law, regardless, you can still say, "I just want to use the words *res ipsa loquitur,* your honor." And to the jurors, "If his honor instructs on the law, will you, ladies and gentlemen of the jury, follow the law that his honor instructs on?"

Then you tell them in your opening statement that you can try a case on *res ipsa loquitur,* but you tell them very little of what the doctrine is all about—you lead them up to that door, but don't open it for them. You tell the jury that there is a lot of illumination behind that door, and encourage them to look on the other side of it. The final argument is that which causes jurors to become champions in the jury room and go beyond the door and look themselves for what is there. A good final argument brings jurors to champion your side, and lets them find out what is good for your side; and you are then much better off than if *you* told the jury what was behind the door. A beautiful final argument is one that opens the door just so wide and no wider; wide enough so that they will see the whole thing; and not so narrow that they will miss it.

Coming back to *res ipsa loquitur*: you've mentioned it in your voir dire, you've mentioned it in the opening statement, and you've come to argument. You tell the jurors, "Ladies and gentlemen of the jury, I remember trying a case in Sacramento the other day, and I told the jury there that I was going to try my case by *res ipsa loquitur,* and the jury came back against me. It was almost as clear a case as this one that I am trying before you today: I went up to the jury afterwards and asked them, 'Why didn't you go for the plaintiff?' And the foreman said, 'Mr. Belli, you said we were going to try a case by *res ipsa loquitur,* and you never even called that Mexican as a witness.'

"Now ladies and gentlemen of the jury, *res ipsa loquitur*—whether he is Mexican or of another ethnic group—means that you don't have to call a witness. If a case is supported without proof, that is the most important thing. You don't have to call Manuel Resipsaloquitur as a witness, the case speaks for itself. *Res ipsa loquitur* means the case proves itself. And I have asked you from the beginning, I talked about it in the opening statement, and you told me that you would follow the doctrine if his honor instructs on it—he *will* instruct on it. Now you see if this thing doesn't speak for itself." There you have carried a case from voir dire through opening statement to final argument.

In your notes, set a page aside called "arguments," and make notes for arguments from voir dire, opening, direct, cross, through final argument, so that you can just pick it up at any time of the case when the judge says, "Do you want to argue?" and you have your notes and you can go right into your argument. And you better say yes, because you've got the burden of proof if you are a plaintiff. Your argument should be the ornaments that go on the Christmas tree, the infrastructure of the Christmas tree being the opening statement and the voir dire.

EDITOR: How would you structure your final argument if you feel you haven't accomplished what you wanted to with respect to the factual background of the case, and you are at a disadvantage going into final argument?

BELLI: If your evidence in some particulars is so bad that you can't do anything with it, for heavens sake don't try to do anything with it; just completely ignore it. The jury will give you more points for having completely ignored it than for making a bad argument with it.

If you've got some evidence that is half bad, half good, then by all means, explain it. And if you've got evidence that is good, get that first. Get your good evidence in right off the bat when you stand up in front of the jury, and then go along with your argument.

I think a closing argument probably hits four or five points at the most, and you should structure those four or five points so that they carry the flesh of the whole closing argument. In my closing argument I put four or five of the exhibits in strategic places around the courtroom, so that I walk over to one which in my mind's eye may be on the clerk's desk—maybe an exhibit or a deposition. I finish with that piece of evidence on one subject, and finish that conclusively—don't come back to it—then I move to the next piece of evidence which I have placed over on the counsel table or put on a chair someplace. Finish with that conclusively, and then go to the third piece, in a different area of the room. Have them physically separated around the courtroom, and go to the different areas as you physically and forensically complete the different areas of summation.

## How to Get Maximum Use from Demonstrative Aids

EDITOR: Do you use a lot of demonstrative aids in your final argument, as well as during witness examination?

BELLI: Yes, you use them not only then, but you use them in opening, and you go into the judge's chamber *in limine,* and have it understood with the judge that you are going to be allowed to use certain demonstrative evidence: charts, illustrations, serial photos, diagrams, mark-ups, models. You are going to use those for the purpose of illustration in your opening statement, and you assure his honor that these are all going to be offered into evidence and that they are all admissible, and if you use them in opening and during the trial you will also use them in the final argument.

Sometimes you are going to have an exhibit that you won't use during the trial, such as a hospital record. You may and you should refer to it just briefly in opening statement. You might have a nurse identify the hospital record—be sure and get it into evidence. Then when you come to the final argument, you pick up that hospital record and you read extensively from it. In other words, just get some of the most important pieces of evidence into evidence, and don't dwell on them during the trial, but hit them hard in final argument, because the jury will be curious by then. Also, invite the jurors to bring these exhibits into the jury room with them. Now, that is just a matter of procedure.

On the other hand, in some cases you will want to do just the opposite: you will want to exploit the evidence during the trial, such as a hospital record, and put a nurse on for two days and have her read the number of times that drugs, morphine sulfate, things that are given for pain, are administered. Let her go through and read those, read those, read those, ad nauseam, until the jury is just utterly and completely convinced by the repetition of "morphine" that this patient had terrific pain during that period of time. Let her read the doctor's orders, let her read the patient's complaint; and let her read the nurse's description of how the patient was at that time. Now, you might want to do that during the trial, and just refer to it then in argument. Or you could do it the other way around, whichever fits beautifully into the case.

EDITOR: During argument, if the jury has seen a certain piece of demonstrative evidence twice already, how do you decide whether you should show it to them a third time?

BELLI: There is no law against repetition and showing it to them a third time, any more than there is during public speaking or in ordinary conversation. The test is whether the jury has absorbed it. Frequently, you will refer to something in final argument that has been gone through thoroughly during the trial and you might even get a juror's nod. If you get that, don't hit him over the head with it.

Develop it in different ways. One way to develop the evidence is by showing it on exhibits, such as blowups. Another way to develop it is by having a nurse read it, and then another way to develop it, the third way around, is to paraphrase it during final argument, so that you get three ways. Sometimes you don't need it that much, sometimes it is sufficient by itself.

Be careful of big words. Exsanguinate. I remember a case that I had once, a child that died from loss of blood in the recovery room, and the hospital records said that the child was exsanguinated. Knowing what it meant myself, I asked the doctor to define exsanguination. He said, "If you hold a chicken up by its feet with its head down, you cut its throat and all its blood spurts out and the blood is all gone, that chicken is exsanguinated."

When you come to final argument you might not even say the word. You just go to the board and write "exsanguinated" without even saying the word—or maybe just whisper the word—because the impact has been made.

### Criminal Cases vs. Civil Cases

EDITOR: What different techniques would you use in criminal cases that you might not use in a civil case?

BELLI: I think it is the same. There is a technique of interesting the jury, making the jury curious, creating suspense and bringing the jury up to the door—not pushing them through it, or not taking them in, but letting them be curious enough to open it and want to know further.

Of course, in a criminal case you don't have the last argument, so you've got to shoot all your works in one argument, which isn't too different because I always shoot everything that I have in the opening argument. I think you make a serious mistake if you make a weak opening and then you let the defense answer and then split up by making a final argument trying to catch him. You can't.

### Common Mistakes in Final Argument and How to Avoid Them

EDITOR: What are some of the common mistakes that you've seen lawyers make in final argument?

BELLI: Droning on and on; not analyzing; not paying attention to what the jury is doing; reading or quoting from passages without seeing whether the jury is listening to you, or whether they are interested. You can read, but practice reading, and look up at your jury to see that they are following you, and be sure that they are interested in what you are reading.

EDITOR: When you say analyzing, what do you mean by that?

BELLI: Just exactly what the word analyze means. What the hell is your case all about? Sit down by yourself without a notebook and pencil, and see what you've got.

For example, if you've got a child darting out case, you want to get rid of the words "dart out," you want to use any other word or expression than that. You put stress on the point of view from which you look; you want to look at the case from the child's point, not from the motorist's point. From the child's point, the child is entitled to sanctuary on the street; under five in most states he can't be held responsible in contributory negligence, and nothing that he can do will make him responsible or guilty. The motorist has to be aware of the proclivities, the idiosyncrasies, the tendency of children to run out into the street, to act like children. What you would find abnormal in an adult is ordinary conduct that should be expected from a child. This is what the motorist should expect, and you shouldn't lose, although I just lost one and I was offered five hundred thousand dollars in a so-called dart out case. I call it a non-attention by the motorist case.

### The Key Elements of a Great Summation

EDITOR: How can a lawyer who is not a great orator make a great final argument?

BELLI: I think that when you stand up to begin your final argument it is one of the great moments of the trial, and one of the great moments of your week. Just stand up there until you are relaxed, and then just start talking leisurely. Don't orate, don't bellow, don't yell at the jury.

Now, I don't mean that you shouldn't bellow and yell sometimes during the trial; but bring your voice up to a crescendo, and then when you get to a point where you are insulted at what the ******* defendant did to you, then let him have it by a good yell and a good bellowing. But stand back from the jury rail, because the offense that most of the lawyers make is that they bellow or yell or emphasize too close to the jury rail. I think that you should be completely at ease, you should take your time, you should have a glass of water, and you should have your exhibits placed around the room.

The night before, when you go to bed, think in your mind's eye about what you are going to discuss. For example, the cop. His testimony and everything pertaining to him is over at counsel table; when you go over there, you're going to take all of the stuff pertaining to him and exhaust it. Then you are going to leave the cop and go to the doctor. You discuss the doctor, with all the stuff pertaining to the doctor, his hospital records, charts, and so forth, over at the other end of the counsel table.

You separate the parts of the trial. This allows you in your own mind to think, before you leave one part of the evidence, that you have exhausted that completely. Then you go to the next part and you exhaust that. Then put some other papers or exhibits or depositions on the clerk's bench, and go over and pick that up. It makes nice packing, it separates your argument into the parts, it makes you cover everything that you should cover, and it is a nice way to get rid of the stereotypical putting of notes on a lectern and following that. If it is a deposition, you can have some notes written down; maybe a hospital record in which you can have notes written on your copy.

When you review the case the night before, as you are thinking about it, you know which of the four parts of the case you are going to hit as you go from one place to another. And when you add something to one, then just put your paper over there, or just add it in your mind's eye to what is over there.

Be sure that you summarize your exhibits when you do your final argument; and indeed your exhibits can be the pieces of paper that you put in one area of the courtroom to develop. Take five or ten minutes on each piece of paper and everything that relates to it, and then invite the jury to take that paper into the jury room with them. Invite them to take the nurse's notes into the jury room with them and discuss those. Be sure that they are familiar with all of the exhibits. Tell them to come back and ask the judge to send the exhibits in if they don't have them in the jury room.

What you must do during the trial, I'd say even in the opening statement, is to blow up the most important pieces of testimony: the officer's testimony, the doctor's orders, the prescription, and so forth. Blow them up so that they are on boards of about four by five feet. You can show that in the opening, you can cross-examine the doctor on that during the trial, and then you can argue from it during the closing: "Now, this is the important thing. Witness Jones said to Officer Smith before any lawyer got to the scene, before *anyone* arrived, that the defendant was going twenty-five miles an hour in a fifteen-mile zone. How do we know that? Here are the notes blown up for you, and if you want to see the original, get the original; these are the notes of what this man said to the officer at the scene of the accident before any lawyer, before any lawsuit; this is a completely objective fact, and this is important." That is one of those four or five things, as I say, that you place around the courtroom.

Blow up some instructions, and show the instructions of the law to the jury. You might do that in opening, then you will do it in final argument and you will say, "This is the law, his honor will instruct you on this and the law means exactly this. Now let's dissect that." Take five or ten minutes going through that important instruction. For example, in a child case, it is very important to realize that a child is under five and there can be no contributory negligence, and no comparative negligence. The defendant is absolutely responsible.

In the final argument say, "Now you remember in my opening statement I told you I was going to make a bond with you; I was going to prove these things to you and then I will come back to you at the end of this case and I will ask you in my argument to return a verdict for the plaintiff in the sum of x dollars. All right, here is what I told you I was going to prove." And you have a chart of these things written on the blackboard. "I proved these things by Officer Jones, Officer Smith, Dr. Wiles, and so forth. We are now at the point of damages." Then you put the damages on the blackboard in the final argument of the costs, the hospital costs, the doctor and so forth, and your general damages, and use a formula which we developed in *Modern Trials* for that.

When you get to the last two minutes of the argument, be pointing to it when you come to it, say those last two minutes, and sit down. For example, in a case where there was radiation, your last two minutes should be as follows:

"In a radiation case, ladies and gentlemen of the jury, there is hazard and there is novelty. The greater the hazard and the greater the novelty, the more care that should be used; and what you do here today is going to set a standard for a new industry of atomic power. We've heard about Ten Mile Island and everything else. There are no standards, really, and there won't be any standards until you, ladies and gentlemen of the jury, decide what is a standard of due care—which in a case where there is too much hazard and too much novelty, must be the *utmost* care.

"Hazard and novelty. If this were an ordinary case, to install an interlock would be superfluous. Superfluous, to look it up in the dictionary, means unnecessary, or it might mean redundant. But redundant is the word that is used in the atomic power industry. You've got to have redundant safety devices; superfluous; more than we have in any other industry; because there is great hazard and there is great novelty, and you've got to have duplication of safety devices."

Have that argument memorized, and when you say that—period—sit down.

# Winning Psychological Principles In Summation

## Robert E. Cartwright

Robert E. Cartwright, a senior partner in the San Francisco firm of Cartwright, Sucherman, Slobodin & Fowler, Inc., received his law degree from the Boalt Hall Law School, University of California. His professional memberships include: a Fellow of the International Academy of Trial Lawyers, a Fellow of the Dean Roscoe Pound-ATLA Foundation, a Fellow of the American College of Trial Lawyers and a Fellow of the International Society of Barristers. Cartwright is the author of numerous articles on legal subjects, and co-author of *California Products Liability Actions*. As a member of the ATLA Faculty of the Nation, he has lectured for many years in over three-quarters of the states in the United States on all phases of trial practice and procedure, and on various substantive law matters such as medical malpractice, products liability and outrage suits.

I think the most important thing in final argument is to project candor, honesty, sincerity, and utter belief in your client and the merits of his or her case. It should come out of your pores that you believe in your case, that you believe in your client, and that you sincerely believe that he or she is entitled to recover. Above all else, you must try to get the jury to identify, because if you cannot get them to identify, you are going to lose the case. You have got to make that jury believe that "There, but for the grace of God, go I". If you can implant or convey that idea, that seed, in their minds, you are going to win.

It is my opinion that many lawyers do not take sufficient advantage of fundamental, basic, elementary psychological principles that exist with reference to the thinking of people. I want to discuss some of the more important of these principles, because they apply to virtually all cases.

## 1. Making Your Point with a Story

Everybody loves a story, and if you can give your listener a story or an illustration, an anecdote or an analogy that will sink in, rather than simply baldly stating to the jury that this is the law or that is the law and therefore they have to do this or that, you will have a much better chance of winning your case. As you go along in your careers you should have a book or a notepad in which you set aside a storehouse of stories and analogies, and give them a name which will make them easy to recall—as for example, "the ball story," "the vase story," "the ladder story," "the tire story," etc. You should have 50 to 100 stories with a key word, so you can immediately call into play one of these stories or analogies to answer points raised by the other side, as for example contributory negligence, pre-existing injury or condition, or whatever else foreseeably might be thrown at you. Let me illustrate.

Suppose, as in so many of our cases such as the routine neck or back case, the plaintiff has a pre-existing condition of congenital anomaly, has had a prior accident, is a fragile person, or any one of the numerous other situations we find so often; this should not be an impediment to your case. This should be an advantage, and in fact should explain why your client not only suffered for three months, which maybe would be the most that would have been suffered by a very strong person, but it demonstrates why your client had problems for a year, or two years, or three years, or longer. You should have analogies and illustrations that make this point clear to the jury, drive it home to them, and show them why the client, in spite of these things, is entitled to recover for all of the detriment suffered.

You can tell the jury that under the law, the judge is going to tell them that the negligent defendant has to take his victim as he finds him, that he is responsible for all harm caused or additional harm caused, and that it is no defense for the defendant to say that the plaintiff was more susceptible to being injured or more likely to be injured than someone else. You can tell them that this is no defense and that His Honor is going to so instruct them. But in spite of this, the jury may or may not understand or agree or follow you or the law. It is much more effective if you drive your point home by giving them a story or an analogy that will make the point clear. There are at least ten different ones that I know of, and a number that I have used. I am going to use one in this article that I have personally never used before, and that is "the doll analogy." You tell the jury:

"To illustrate what we mean by this doctrine, imagine that we have three dolls, all dressed in the same clothing. They look just alike from the outside, but one is made of lead, one of wood, and the other of glass. Someone comes along and negligently knocks all three dolls to the floor. The glass doll shatters into a thousand pieces. Now, ladies and gentlemen of the jury, can you imagine this defendant saying, that although he was negligent, that the plaintiff should not have had a glass doll, that it too should have been made out of lead or steel, that it should not have been so brittle? Ladies and gentlemen, this is no defense. As I have told you before, in substance, the defendant has to take the brittle plaintiff, the strong plaintiff, the old plaintiff, the young plaintiff, the weak plaintiff, or whatever plaintiff he has injured, as he finds him, and as I told you before, he is responsible for all the consequences that follow. This is a good law if you think about it. It protects the old, the young, each of us and all of us as we get older and start to deteriorate. In fact, we all start to die a little bit from the time we are born. We have degenerative changes in our backs and our necks. These changes may never bother us and we might even go through life with these conditions and never have any problem. They may be asymptomatic, and yet a negligent tortfeasor, a wrongdoer, as in this case the truck driver, comes along and runs into this person and it lights up or flares up his condition and he is in misery. Under such circumstances that negligent person is responsible under the law.

"Let me give you another story or analogy, ladies and gentlemen, to illustrate the point. Suppose a farmer is taking his wares, a truckload of eggs, to the market. And a negligent person runs into his truck, turns the truck over and all the eggs are broken. Can you imagine the person who did that trying to escape responsibility for paying for those eggs by telling the farmer that he should not have been carrying eggs, that he should have been carrying golf balls? This is no defense, ladies and gentlemen."

Now, you should not only use techniques such as this as defensive mechanisms, but you should use them as an offensive mechanism. For example, in a case which I tried fairly recently in Orange County, California we had precisely one of the problems that I have mentioned, namely, a congenital anomaly, a condition called spondylolisthesis, commonly called a "spondid." The plaintiff had a low back sprain, a soft tissue situation with no objective findings. We were able to turn this case from what was perhaps a $4,000 whiplash case into a case worth many times that sum by recognizing the psychological principle that I have been talking about. The doctor testified that this plaintiff had a *mechanical* defect in his back from birth. He stated, "Now, the ordinary person, from my experience, will ordinarily get over a soft tissue injury such as this man sustained in perhaps three to six months. But this man had the trauma superimposed upon this mechanical defect and it caused it to light up, to flare up, and it is well recognized in the medical literature that a dormant or asymptomatic condition such as that can be triggered by trauma, and this explains why this man has suffered so much during the last two years."

The jury was able to appreciate and understand this fact, and it explains why we were able to obtain a proper award. It explained why the disability was two years instead of three to six months in this low back injury, soft tissue case.

Now let us take another rather typical type of situation where you have to have an analogy, where you have to have a story, or you are not going to sell your case. I have had at least two of these types of cases, and I can tell you that the analogy which I am going to tell you about works. The jury can understand it. I am talking about the typical case that most of us have at one time or another where the person has a low back sprain or neck sprain, and the person goes along for three months or six months or, as I had in one case, eighteen months, and the disc blows. This person finds that he cannot straighten up and he is in terrible pain. I recall one case where this happened to my client six months after the accident while she was opening an oven, and in another case where it happened to my client some eighteen months after the accident when he was bending forward to pull on a hand brake. Now, how are you going to explain this to the jury? I asked my doctor, an orthopaedic specialist, to explain to the jury why, six months after the accident when the lady is opening the oven, her disc blows out. He stated, "It's very simple, it is like when you park your car and hit the curb too hard. This may weaken the tire, it may cause an imperceptible weakness, crack, or fissure, and then with normal everyday wear and tear thereafter and the use of the vehicle, six months later the tire blows out.

Well, this is what happened to this lady. This accident, this trauma, weakened her back and injured her back, she suffered some pain, she had a strain or sprain, we know that, and then, with her routine work—hanging laundry, opening the oven, and so forth, and in this particular case when she bent down on the morning in question to open her oven—her back went out." The jury could understand that. Suppose we hadn't used some sort of analogy that made sense and was understandable to the jury, and had just tried to explain in technical terms what had happened to the plaintiff? I am not at all sure we would have won the case if we had done only that.

## 2. Leaving Something for the Imagination

I think understatement rather than overstatement, particularly with respect to damages, or at least not exaggeration, is very important. You shouldn't try to overkill or overlitigate every case—leave something for the imagination. We have all heard the statement that a smart woman remains partially draped because it leaves something for the imagination. Do the same thing with your jury. Lead them to the water but don't try to force them to drink. They may balk or rebel.

As the legendary Mo Levine said in a case where he obtained a very substantial verdict, "Ladies and gentlemen, I am not going to torture you by going through the torment of my client's experience, by going through each and every item of suffering that he has endured in the past or that he will face in the future. This man lost both of his arms and I have been trying to think of how to best tell you what it is like to live without two arms. Let me tell you what it is like. I had lunch with my client. I ate with my knife and fork. Do you know how he ate? *He ate like a dog."* His argument on damages consumed less than five minutes but he got a very large verdict.

### 3. Using the Rhetorical Question

The rhetorical question, in my judgment, is one of the most effective techniques there is, yet you don't see lawyers using it very often. I gave you an example of how to do it with the golfball story when I posed the question to the jury, "Do you mean to say that the plaintiff should have been carrying golfballs?"

In a products liability case, to use another example, one of the questions that you might ask the jury—and you can think of dozens—is this: "Ladies and gentlemen, with reference to the dangerous propensities of this product, its tremendous potential for harm, and its capacity to either injure or kill in the absence of an inexpensive safety device, do you believe that this manufacturer should have put profits first as it did? Or should it have given some thought to safety? Should it have used some of the known safety devices such as guards and shields that are available to protect working people from this type of injury?"

In a slip-and-fall case you might ask the jury: "Ladies and gentlemen, this defendant did everything possible with its Madison Avenue advertising campaign to distract this plaintiff, to cause this plaintiff to take his eyes off the floor, and to look at the displays, the fancy ribbons, the beautiful packaging, and all of the other things on which they spent hundreds and perhaps thousands of dollars for display purposes and advertising purposes. Now, I ask you, do you think it is fair for this defendant to now say, having purposely and deliberately taken the plaintiff's eyes off the floor, 'Mr. Plaintiff, you should have been walking along looking at the floor rather than at the things that we wanted you to look at.' I submit that such an argument by this defendant is both poor taste and bad manners. Four-legged animals walk along with their heads down, but human beings walk erect and upright."

## 4. Striking for the Jugular Vein

Do you build up to the climax in a slow deliberate manner, or do you give them the climax and then have the anti-climax? Do you strike for the jugular vein, or do you toy with them and then build up to your key point? Every psychological study that I have seen shows that you strike for that jugular vein, because if you don't, by the time you get to it the jury may be asleep. They may no longer be interested, you may have lost them and it may be too late. They may be completely turned off with reference to your case.

Winston Churchill once said, "The approach to winning an argument is to strike for that jugular vein and to hit it once, hit it twice, and then really hit it for the third time—this is the way to win an argument".

Let me give you an illustration. As chairman of the California Trial Lawyers Association Amicus Curiae Committee for many years, I have had the privilege of participating in scores of landmark cases. About once a year I will argue one of these cases in the Supreme Court of California. The rest of the time I will assign the responsibility to other members of our committee, as I don't want to be seen there too often. I decided as chairman to personally argue the case of *Brown* v. *Merlo,* which is the first case in the United States in which a court by judicial fiat declared an automobile guest act unconstitutional. I never argue for more than five minutes during these presentations. The plaintiff attorney has to relinquish part of his 30 minutes to our Amicus Curiae Committee. The court knows this and it knows that I or the other people I assign to argue are going to strike for the jugular vein, they know that we are going to hit hard with reference to what the really important point is in that case.

In *Brown* v. *Merlo* the plaintiff's lawyer—and he is an outstanding lawyer and is now a Superior Court judge in California—talked for approximately 25 minutes and did an outstanding job, a lawyer-like job. What he said was right, but it was difficult to perceive whether the court was agreeing with him one way or the other. When it came time for my five-minute argument, I used the Winston Churchill approach, the "1-2-3, bang" type of argument. I will paraphrase some of the comments I made, as follows:

"May it please the court, California's automobile guest act is an impermissible discrimination under the equal protection clauses of both the

United States and California constitutions. For such a law to stand there has to be some rational reason for this discrimination among different users or classes of people who ride in automobiles. With reference to this law, there is no such rational reason. I can think of none and I challenge defense counsel to give a rational reason for this rank discrimination. Very frankly, these laws—which were passed in about half the states, not all of them—were passed in the 1920s to help the insurance companies out, to help them make more money. That is the only reason they were passed, and in my judgment this is not a legitimate or permissible reason under the equal protection clause for this discrimination. These laws are nothing more nor less than anachronisms of the 1920s and they should be eliminated. Let me show you how ridiculous and absurd this discrimination is." (I then proceeded to use the reductio ad absurdum argument, which I think is a marvelous approach in any argument.)

"Number one, suppose, your Honors, that my client, who is driving his car and who is insured with friendly Allstate, has a passenger who is his best friend in the right front seat. The driver goes through a red light or a stop sign negligently, he hits a stranger, and injures both the stranger and his friend. Under the present law, the stranger can recover but his friend cannot. Now who do you think this man would rather see collect from his insurance company, the stranger or his friend, for the harm, for the injury that he caused?

"Suppose he is traveling to the state of Arizona, which has no guest act, and he is ten feet from the border. If he had been eleven feet further— yes, eleven feet further—his friend would have been able to recover from the insurance company for the grievous harm that was done. To put it even more clearly, suppose that he has two friends in the car, one in the front seat and one in the back seat, and he has straddled the border, his friend in the front seat could recover and the one in the back seat could not. Does this make any sense?"

This is when the court started to smile. This is what I would call striking for the jugular vein.


### 5. Taking the Sting Out of Your Opponent's Argument

I believe that it is very important to take the sting out of your opponent's argument by anticipating it and discussing it in advance. Rob him of his potency by putting the point in the light most favorable to your client before opposing counsel has an opportunity to discuss it with the jury.

For example, in a slip-and-fall case, if your plaintiff was distracted because of the displays, you should tell the jury that the reason the plaintiff did not see the banana on the floor, or the water, or whatever else it was, was because he was distracted. "It was because he was looking at the displays or signs which the evidence has shown the defendant put there for him to look at as he was walking along. His Honor will tell you in his instructions that the business proprietor must anticipate and foresee that the business patrons may oftentimes be absorbed in their own thoughts or that they will be distracted for one reason or another, or that even if they knew about the danger in question, that it is common to have momentary forgetfulness. All of these matters are traits of human character and nature which a business proprietor who invites the public into his premises for the purpose of making a profit must anticipate and foresee and guard against."

If it is the type of slip-and-fall where the plaintiff simply didn't see because of the lighting or the blending of colors, you should explain this fact to the jury so they will understand why your plaintiff didn't see and why probably the ordinary average plaintiff probably wouldn't have seen either under the same or similar circumstances. You should talk about these matters, and explain them rationally and logically in your own way, rather than attempting to talk about them in a defensive manner in rebuttal. It is sometimes too late to explain in rebuttal what you should have explained to begin with. It sounds as if you are making excuses.

### 6. Using the Promissory Note Technique

In your voir dire of the jury, you should get the jury to sign a promissory note, or to put it another way, to make a pledge, and then in final argument you should call in that pledge and get them to sign on the dotted line. In your voir dire you should condition the jury, you should ask questions of the jury as to whether or not they have the ability and whether or not they would be willing, if the evidence justified it, to return a verdict for substantial damages in favor of your client if in fact the evidence shows that those are substantial damages justifying such an award. You should get a pledge from each one of them to this effect. You should get a pledge from them that they would be willing to follow the law which holds that an injured victim, an injured plaintiff, is entitled to receive general damages for his injuries, and by that we mean compensation for all of his injuries, pain and suffering, and for all of the mental and emotional suffering which he has sustained and which he will sustain in the future. You should tell them that under the law the plaintiff is entitled to be compensated for each and every item of general damages he has sustained or will sustain in the future; and once again, you should obtain their agreement and pledge that they will be willing to allow damages for all of these items. You should obtain their commitment in summary that they will take the law from his honor, who is going to tell them what it is, and that they will follow it, and that this will include following the law with reference to the law of damages. You should make sure that they will have no hesitation in awarding damages for any element of damages that is proper under the law and which is proven by the evidence.

Then in your final summation you should remind them of their commitments, the pledges they have made, and you should perhaps explain to them why you have made such a point of their pledges, their commitments. You might tell them, "The reason is that we know from experience that every once in a while some juror will go into the jury room and, when it comes time to discuss the general damages, the juror will say, 'I do not believe in awarding money damages for pain and suffering and all of the other human losses as distinguished from out-of-pocket losses that the victim has sustained.' Or in the alternative, the juror may say, 'Well, even though it is proper I don't know how to translate these matters into dollars and cents, and therefore I won't try and I won't award anything.' Any juror who did this would, of course, be violating his or her oath as a juror to decide the case based on the law and the evidence; the juror would be breaching the pledge and agreement made at the start of the trial. I know that in this case none of you will do that and that we can count on you to provide full, just, reasonable, and proper compensation to the plaintiff."

## 7. Selling Your Case with Demonstrative Aids

It is a well-known principle of psychology that after two or three days most people remember only a small percentage of what they hear, and that if you not only tell and/or explain the point in question to them but also demonstrate it to them visually, the chances of their both understanding and remembering the point are dramatically increased. You have got to recognize that many people are bad listeners. Lots of peoples' minds go fast and they tend to drift into their own thought processes and problems rather than listen to you, even though they might be nodding at you and pretending to listen. They may have things on their minds that cause their minds to wander, and they may only hear half of what you say. Or, they may be just plain lazy, and in some cases may not be too bright. Accordingly, on your critical points, the crucial points in your case, it isn't sufficient to just tell them about them. You must make them see, you must force them to see the point if necessary, and then it may sink in and you may win your point. If you don't use both approaches you are running a terrific gamble on the critical points of your case that either they are not going to hear you because they are thinking about something else, or, in the alternative, that perhaps they really don't understand. This is human nature. I would like to give you just a few suggestions as to how to handle this problem.

1. People like to be taught. From grammar school, high school, and in some cases college days, they are used to the professional type of approach where the teacher uses the blackboard. This is something they understand and can relate to. You can be the teacher, you can be the professor, and in many cases you can go to the blackboard and write the critical points on the blackboard for them so that they can both see and hear. Sometimes it is good, in order to keep their attention, to make a slight mistake, perhaps in addition, and then to catch it and correct it.

2. We have a service in San Francisco, where I practice, that will blow up almost any document into a large chart for the sum of five dollars. For example, a medication record from the hospital records, or certain critical entries in the nurse's notes, or a typewritten sheet you have prepared setting forth the computation of your damages. These can be blown up and you can then show the jury, as for example in the case of a medication record, the tremendous amount of pain medication your client had to take, which in turn helps to substantiate the degree of pain and suffering your client has testified to.

3. A very inexpensive and simple technique I have often used is to use butcher paper or a large artist's pad. You can prepare many of the points you are attempting to explain to the jury in advance on the pad, and you can then point to them as you explain them to the jury and flip the pages as you proceed with your presentation.

4. One of my favorite techniques is to use the 3-M overhead projector, not only in summation but all during the trial from time of opening statement. I like the 3-M particularly because you do not have to turn the lights off in the courtroom in order to use it. You can have it all set up, and as you come to a point you want to explain visually you simply press a button, having prepared your transparency in advance, and there it is on the screen in large letters for the jury to see. You can even then underline in front of the jury in color on the transparency certain particular points you want to stress. This is a wonderful procedure to use, for example, where you have had testimony from the trial transcribed and you want to show a particular admission or inconsistency or other pertinent point, or where you want to show an admission or an item of impeachment from a deposition. It can, of course, be used to illustrate almost any type of documentary proof that exists in the trial. You can have transparencies made of

excerpts from hospital records or any other documents that have been introduced during the trial. When they actually see the nurse's notes on the large screen showing that the patient was screaming for pain medication, it has a much more impressive effect on them than if you have simply read those notes to them. You might want to make transparencies of five or six entries, or even more sometimes, from the hospital records or the doctor's records to show the terrible suffering, pain, etc., that your client sustained.

In short, with reference to points that are critical and crucial to your case, in my judgment you must demonstrate them to the jury either by way of the overhead projector or through some other visual aid technique, in order to make sure that the jury both appreciates and understands the point.

Let me give you an example. Several years ago I tried a case involving a boiler that exploded in the Hearst Building at Third and Market Streets in San Francisco, California. When the plaintiff maintenance man pressed the button to light up the boiler in question, it exploded and blew him backwards. He sustained industrial blindness in one eye and painful injuries to his leg and hip. He was laid off work for some six months. He was a man approximately 60 years old who prior to this accident was able to do his work without pain or difficulty, although he did have a heart condition he had incurred some years before but that, after treatment, was in a state of compensation and was not causing him any difficulties. In other words, he was functioning well at the time of this explosion. After he went back to work following the six-month layoff after the explosion, his heart condition flared up and he had to start taking nitroglycerine tablets once again. He thereafter continued to work with this problem for approximately a year and a half, at which time he had an acute heart attack and died. Our contention in the wrongful death case was that the additional stress, strain, tensions, and anxiety this man had after he went back to work because of the constant and continual pain he had in his leg and hip, and the difficulty that he had in doing his work, climbing stairs, ladders, etc., is what caused the heart condition to flare up, to worsen, and to ultimately result in the heart attack. There was one key entry in the Workmen's Compensation doctor's records in which the doctor who was treating him said, at the time that the heart condition first flared up, that it appeared that all of the additional strain and tension that the man was under, because of the pain that he was in from his injuries, had contributed to the flareup of his heart condition. At the time of trial we of course had testimony that this had continued to contribute to his problem and that, in the doctor's judgment, was a proximate cause of the heart attack. We argued vigorously all during the trial and in final summation that the injuries he received in the accident caused stress to him, strain and anxiety, and that he worked under difficulty—that this activated, precipitated, and flared up his heart, and ultimately contributed to his death, or at least was a substantial contributing factor thereto. We told them that it was true that his cigarettes and his drinking may also have been contributing factors, but under the law of doctrine of concurrent causes as it will have been explained by the court, this does not make any difference; that it makes no difference even if there were a hundred other causes as long as the cause in question was a substantial contributing cause. At this point in time in what many would think was a rather difficult case, we flipped the button that caused the transparency of the Workman's Compensation doctor's notes to go on the screen, and there the jury was able to see, in large print, the entries of that doctor which were made long *before* the man died and long before there was any thought of a wrongful death lawsuit. I then underlined these notes in color for emphasis. I sincerely believe that if I had just read this telling entry to the jury, it would not have had the same effect. I have always believed that the use of the transparency projection materially helped us to win that case.

During summation, and in fact throughout the trial, you are trying to sell the jury on the sizzle of your case, you are trying to persuade, so use every tool that is available to you. If you have a critical instruction of law or point of law, you should have that blown up in one of the fashions I have mentioned, and then go through it carefully with the jury so that they can see it, hear it, and perhaps better understand it. Explain it to them in your own way, and then when the judge reads it to them they will hear it again and perhaps now they will understand it because they have already seen it and heard it. This can be an extremely effective technique.

# Reasonable Doubt in Summation

## David Cohen

David Cohen has practiced for the past fifteen years as a criminal
defense attorney in Liberty, New York. Before that he was a
Sullivan County, New York, prosecutor; and a magistrate in Liberty. He is the author of *How to Win Criminal Cases by Establishing a Reasonable Doubt* and *Admit the Act and Win the Criminal Case* (Prentice-Hall).

Weaving your theory of reasonable doubt into the evidence should be the
highlight, the crucial moment, of your summation. You must logically and
reasonably explain how the facts that you have been presenting create
reasonable doubts which necessarily must acquit your client.

Do not parrot testimony or review it chronologically. The jury will be
easily bored and stray in their thinking. Bring out certain highlights of testimony from which you can logically deduct, infer or point up reasonable
doubt.

### 3 Ways to Highlight Reasonable Doubt

In discussing reasonable doubt, unless you have caught a police officer in
a blatant lie, never pit his testimony against the defendant's. That is, don't
make it a credibility contest. You must pit the police officer's testimony
against what is probable, what is reasonable, what is logical, and what is
rational.

Refer to many reasonable doubts. It is wise to refer to many reasonable doubts and not limit your expression to a single reasonable doubt.
Give the jury a choice of several reasonable doubts that exist in the case,

and allow them to take their choice as to which of them they will use as the basis of their acquittal. To effectively do this, you must probe the testimony given to find the inconsistencies, the clouded memories, the discrepancies, and the lack of evidence, all of which foster doubt.

Give the jury your definition of reasonable doubt. In discussing the definition of reasonable doubt, don't usurp the judge's function by attempting to define in detail the meaning of reasonable doubt. You may mention that it is any doubt, based upon reason, that the jury may have from the evidence or lack of evidence. You may also tell the jury that the words "reasonable doubt" are usually coupled with the words "to a moral certainty," and that you suspect the judge will charge the jury with that before they can convict anyone of a crime. The jury must be convinced of the defendant's guilt "beyond a reasonable doubt and to a moral certainty." The word "certainty" may have a more permanent effect on some jurors than the word "doubt."

### How to Combat the Prosecutor's Definition of Reasonable Doubt

Undoubtedly, the prosecutor will discuss reasonable doubt in his summation. In some jurisdictions, the prosecutor delivers his *summary* first. As a prosecuting attorney, I often used the following language to warn the jury to be leery of the phrase "reasonable doubt":

Now, ladies and gentlemen, reasonable doubt will be defined to you by the judge. However, I would like to make some comments to you concerning its application in this trial. Now, we all know that the world is round; that is a scientifically proven fact. If someone should come along tomorrow and say that the world is flat because he once walked to the point where it ended, you couldn't possibly entertain a doubt about the world being round. Similarly in this case, if the prosecution has satisfactorily proven to you by competent, believable, established evidence that the defendant is guilty, then merely because the defendant denies being guilty does not mean that the doubt is a reasonable one.

You, ladies and gentlemen, do not have to be satisfied beyond every and *all* doubt; you don't have to be satisfied beyond a *shadow* of a doubt; you must be satisfied by those *reasonable* standards that reasonable people adhere to. If at this stage you say to yourself that based upon the evidence, "I am reasonably satisfied that the defendant committed this crime," then you do *not* have that reasonable doubt that is referred to—and under those circumstances, you must find the defendant guilty of the charge. Remember, you do not have to be absolutely certain; you need only to be reasonably satisfied.

To combat this type of approach, as a defense lawyer you must be realistic, logical and believable. If you are not, the the word "reasonable" will have no significance in your appeal to the jurors. You cannot be overly speculative or leave too much open to conjecture, or the jurors will soon realize that you are not being fair with them. I suggest that you employ the following:

> You cannot convict my client on speculation, belief or conjecture. To do so would be to violate every concept of decency and fairness. The theory of reasonable doubt does not contemplate possibilities or probabilities, as the district attorney would have you believe. Think of what a world we would live in if people were jailed because a jury of their peers thought they were *probably* guilty. That is the kind of reasoning that gives rise to fascism and the doctrines that Hitler built his dictatorship on. The sound principles upon which our laws were established would not tolerate guilt by belief or suspicion. A man must be proven guilty beyond a reasonable doubt—to a moral certainty.
>
> The prosecution charges my client with the commission of a serious crime. The law, which you are sworn to uphold, says, "Mr. District Attorney, you must establish the defendant's guilt by credible evidence. It is not sufficient that you produce evidence which indicates that the defendant is probably guilty. You must produce evidence which clearly establishes beyond doubt founded in reason that no one else might have committed this act. You must, Mr. District Attorney, overcome every possible obstacle, every possible logical doubt. If you do not do this, you have not met your burden of proof."
>
> Nothing can be left to surmise or guess work. How tragic it would be if a man's life could be taken from him because twelve people thought that they were satisfied that he was guilty—but were not sure. That is why the law says that every man accused of a crime must be proven guilty beyond every reasonable doubt. If there is any doubt whatsoever that sounds reasonable to you, then my client, under our great system of justice, is entitled to the benefit of that doubt, and should be acquitted. Ask yourself, "Am I morally certain of his guilt?" If you are then I say that you must find him guilty. However, if you are not morally certain, then he must be acquitted.
>
> You see, this is not like an accident case or a suit involving real estate, where only property rights are determined. In such a case, the side which brings the suit need only produce evidence that outweighs his opponents to be successful. In those cases, if the jury makes a mistake, all that is lost is money. But in this case, if the jury makes a mistake and sends an innocent man to jail, no money in the world could ever compensate him for that injustice. Therefore, the law places upon the state a heavy burden of proving guilt, not merely by the weight of the evidence, but *beyond doubt*. You, as intelligent, civic-minded people, can appreciate the difference in the amount of proof required, and can now see what reasonable doubt really is.

If you are not sure—if you have reservations—if you feel that the prosecution has left out a missing link; if you believe that this incident could have
happened in any other way than the prosecution suggests—then you must
give to my client the benefit of your uncertainty and find him not guilty.
That's what reasonable doubt is all about.

The prosecutor might try another tactic and try to reduce reasonable
doubt to the simple argument, "Whom do you believe?" He will try to convey reasonable doubt as a contest between the witnesses and their respective credibility. He will likely say that if the jury believes the prosecution witnesses, there can be no reasonable doubt. You must dispel this
notion and create in the jurors' minds an image of reasonable doubt that
will destroy the elementary "Whom do you believe?" argument. You might
say:

> Reasonable doubt, ladies and gentlemen, is not a question of whom you be-
> lieve, as the prosecutor has attempted to indicate. You may listen to the
> people's witnesses and having heard them say to yourself, "Why, they
> sound believable and logical." Then you may hear the defendant's version
> and say to yourself, "Why, his version sounds believable and logical . . . I
> don't know whom to believe." Ladies and gentlemen, if this be the case, you
> have a reasonable doubt and you must acquit. You cannot send a man to jail
> because of conjecture or speculation. So, you see, reasonable doubt is not
> necessarily whom you believe. You may believe both sides and have a rea-
> sonable doubt. Even if you only believe the prosecution witnesses, you may
> *still* have a reasonable doubt if what they have told you is insufficient to
> prove their case. You may find reasonable doubt from the lack of evidence,
> as well as from conflicting evidence. So I implore you not to be deceived into
> the thought that reasonable doubt may be reduced to a credibility contest,
> for as you see, it cannot.

Even if the prosecutor does not attempt to reduce his argument to the
"Whom do you believe?" method, it is nevertheless suggested that you
employ language similar to the above statement. However, in most jurisdictions you have the opportunity of summing up first, and you must
therefore anticipate the prosecutor's arguments and negate them
beforehand.

### A Successful Technique for Applying Reasonable Doubt to the Testimony

The task of weaving the testimony into your discussion on reasonable
doubt is not an easy one. Each case has its own unique features, themes

and propositions. Do not take each witness, one by one, and review his testimony in an endeavor to demonstrate reasonable doubt. The following is a technique that you may employ:

Ladies and gentlemen, you have heard the term "reasonable doubt" mentioned many times during the course of this trial. The judge will charge you on reasonable doubt; however, at this juncture I am sure you all appreciate and agree that one, single, solitary, reasonable doubt must result in an acquittal of my client. I will now, in my closing remarks to you, show you not one, not three, not five, but ten—yes, ten—reasonable doubts that are in this case. Ten areas, ladies and gentlemen, which, if you will reflect, consider, and analyze, must result in your saying to each other and yourselves, "yes, they are all areas where there is a reasonable doubt." For example:

Reasonable doubt #1: Where is the gun? Did the prosecution ever offer or attempt to offer a gun into evidence? No, they showed you a dead body and a bullet hole in the form of physical evidence and nothing else. Don't you, as reasonable people, say to yourselves, where is the gun? Are there any fingerprints? How do they tie the defendant with this case without a weapon? Doesn't that in itself create in your mind a reasonable doubt—the failure of the prosecution to produce the murder weapon? You heard eight police officers say that they could find no weapon. You heard eight police officers testify that when he was arrested and searched, my client had no weapon. You heard eight police officers testify that my client told them that he has never handled a gun in his life. I say to you, ladies and gentlemen, that this in and of itself is sufficient to create a reasonable doubt and to acquit my client; but there are more—many more—there are ten.

Reasonable doubt #2: Where is an eyewitness? The prosecution could not bring into this courtroom one person who saw the alleged crime committed. Certainly, there was not one shred of evidence by anyone who saw or heard the crime being committed. Doesn't this fact logically create in your mind a reasonable doubt? How are you going to know who committed a crime, if a crime was in fact committed, when no one has seen it? Remember the words "moral certainty." Are you convinced to a *moral certainty* where there is no eyewitness? Isn't this a reasonable doubt? Of course it is. I don't think that twelve people, sitting in judgment, under the oath you took as jurors, are going to send a man to jail for a long, long time on evidence such as this—or should I say, "lack of evidence."

So, you have had Reasonable Doubt #1, no gun—and now you have Reasonable Doubt #2, no eyewitness. Each one, sufficient on its own to acquit; but we have eight more to go. Eight more reasonable doubts for you to consider in analyzing the evidence in this case.

You should continue until you have demonstrated all areas to the jury where they can resolve reasonable doubt. You must capitalize on any doubtful aspect of the prosecutor's case, as well as any doubt that you may have introduced in presenting your own case.

### How to Discuss Circumstanial Evidence in Your Summation

When the prosecution relies principally on circumstantial evidence, each piece of circumstantial evidence lays a foundation for your ultimate argument on reasonable doubt. The evidence, being circumstantial, lends itself to more than one interpretation. It is imperative that you give the jury as many interpretations as possible, consistent with the innocence of your client. By your employing this method, the jury will be given a choice of many explanations and will undoubtedly say, "Well, it could have happened that way."

For example: In an arson case, the prosecution has proved that the defendant purchased two gallons of gasoline the day of the fire. They have proved that the very same cans were found at the site of the fire, and that the defendant was seen in the area an hour before its occurrence. They have presented a strong case of circumstantial evidence, using the facts to create an inference of guilt. It is now your duty to use the same facts and render an interpretation consistent with the innocence of your client. You may say:

> The district attorney asks you to convict my client based upon certain circumstances from which he asks that you infer guilt. I will now show you how these same circumstances imply innocence.
>
> My client purchased two gallons of gasoline the day of the fire. Any one of you may have purchased two gallons of gasoline that very same day. The fact is that my client owned a power mower and his grass needed to be cut. How many times have you and I picked up gasoline in gallon cans at a gas station and used the fuel for a power mower? The prosecution takes an innocent act of mowing a lawn and the preparation done by my client and they ask you to convict him of arson because a fire occurred the same day. Is that logical?
>
> They have brought to this courtroom the garage man who sold these gallons of gas, and the man told you that the cans that were found at the scene of the fire were the same cans that my client purchased from him. He said that the cans looked like the same cans.
>
> Ladies and gentlemen, gallon cans are gallon cans; most of them look alike. I defy anyone to make a statement that these cans were the same cans—and this gentleman, in all honesty, could not say they were the same. But, this man did tell you that he knew my client and that he had on several occasions in the past sold him similar gallons of gasoline. Are you going to

call my client a felon because two gallon cans were found at the scene of the fire which resembled cans that he purchased? Isn't this coincidence remote, speculative, conjectural? Any one of you folks could have made a similar purchase that day, involving gallon cans similar to the ones that were found at the premises; but does that make you guilty of this horrible crime?

They tell you he was seen in the area an hour before the occurrence. I tell you it's only a natural coincidence; he lives only two miles down the road. This is his neighborhood. He has a right to live and travel in his very own neighborhood. Is this criminal? Does this make him guilty, or is it more logical, more sensible and more understandable that he was on his way home to his wife and children when he was seen in the area. We are all seen in the neighborhood in which we live—and yet we are not condemned every time a fire occurs in that area merely because we bought fuel for our lawn mowers that day.

Now, they introduce a bracelet bearing the letters F.P., and since my client's name is Frank Parker, they tell you that this locks up the case for them. There is not one iota of proof to establish that this bracelet is my client's. They want you to infer guilt because of these initials. Well, I have checked the records to see how many firemen were on the scene of this fire and how many spectators were there, and curiously enough, I found that fireman Fred Poley, fireman Frank Pettis, and fireman Fess Porter all participated in helping to subdue this fire. Why couldn't that bracelet belong to any one of those gentlemen, or to any of the spectators whose initials were F.P.? Is there any testimony in this case to show that this particular bracelet was not owned by the three men whose names I have given you? Why didn't the district attorney eliminate these men as being the owners of this bracelet, merely by calling them to the witness stand and having them deny ownership? Ladies and gentlemen, he didn't because he couldn't. This could have been anyone's bracelet. It's a coincidence that my client has those initials.

Please do not confuse circumstantial evidence with pure coincidence. Don't you see how unjust, how unfair, how illogical it would be to send a man behind bars based upon coincidences which strangely enough could have happened to any one of us? The fact remains that the prosecution has not proven anything which directly ties my client into this fire. To the contrary, everything they have established is more consistent with the client's innocence than with his guilt. Don't convict because of coincidence, and that is all that you have in this case.

*Chapter Seven*

# How to Win Substantial Damages for Your Client

Recovering a substantial verdict for the plaintiff in a personal injury action might be considered the supreme test of an attorney's courtroom savvy. It's not enough simply to establish liability. You have got to go beyond liability and give the jury clear-cut, compelling reasons to award your client a sum fully commensurate with the loss or injury caused by the defendant.

No matter what sort of claim you are handling, "each case has its winning point," according to renowned advocate John G. Phillips. In the frank and revealing interview that opens this chapter on damages, Mr. Phillips discusses specific strategies for recovering large verdicts in such cases as serious injury, non-permanent injury, child death, and breadwinner death. Beginning with voir dire, Mr. Phillips explains how to set the stage for a large award right at the outset of trial. You will see why Mr. Phillips seldom uses the word "damages" in front of the jury ... when and how he broaches the subject of actual dollar amounts ... and what phrases he uses to impress upon the jury the importance—and the necessity—of a substantial verdict for his client.

Mr. Phillips also shows you how to enlist your client's aid in collecting the kind of hard-hitting damage evidence you need in order to win big at trial. In addition, you will see how to present the *effect of injuries* in a way that no jury will ever forget. And even if the plaintiff did not suffer permanent injury, Mr. Phillips explains how to stress the other elements in your case that can also justify a large award.

"An attorney can usually make a good estimate of his chances of proving liability," writes Gerald D. Martin, "and he can easily determine the range of awards made in his jurisdiction. His most difficult task is in guessing the size of the loss an expert would arrive at in a formal evaluation." Why attempt such a guess in the first place? Dr. Martin, a financial expert who is frequently called on to give evidence in damage suits, explains several reasons why it pays you to make a preliminary estimate before you hire an expert. As you will discover, just a few minutes' effort on your part can strengthen your case dramatically along basic, bottom-line issues—and save you time and money, too. Using nothing more than a hand-held calculator, anyone with a knowledge of simple math can turn Dr. Martin's easy-to-follow directions into surprisingly accurate loss estimates in less than five minutes. You will find formulas to cover five typical situations, plus a fully worked-out example illustrating the entire process step-by-step.

Armed with your preliminary estimate of loss, you are now in an ideal position to discuss your case with an economist. In fact, you have already assembled much of the information he will need. Picking up from here, noted economist **Charles M. Linke** will give you a valuable inside look at exactly what an economist can do to help you win damages in a disability or death action. You will see how the expert weighs all the relevant factors and assigns precise dollar amounts to every kind of pecuniary loss, including money earnings, fringe benefits and non-paid services. The end result is a proven figure you can present to the jury without apology as the definitive compensation to which your client is justly entitled.

But is it wise to stop at compensatory damages? Should you seek punitive damages, as well, if they are allowable? Careful—this question is tougher than it first appears. The way you answer it could very well determine the outcome of the lawsuit, as Trial Master **Tom Riley** points out in his thoughtful analysis at the end of this chapter. Mr. Riley spells out five good reasons for asserting punitive damages, but he also reveals when it is best to confine your prayer to compensatory damages alone.

# Arguing Damages

## An Interview with John G. Phillips

John G. Phillips of Chicago, Illinois, received his law degree from De Paul University. He has served as President of the Illinois Trial Lawyers Association, and as Governor of the Association of Trial Lawyers of America. He has authored numerous articles on trial technique and trial advocacy in the *Trial Lawyer's Guide* and in *American Jurors Trials*.

### Setting the Stage for a Large Recovery

EDITOR: How should a plaintiff's lawyer address the jurors during voir dire, when he intends to request a substantial verdict in the case?

PHILLIPS: In jurisdictions where a liberal judge permits voir-diring the jury, lawyers may inquire into matters that relate to prejudice against awarding sums for the intangible or specific pecuniary losses and even on the issues involved or law applicable. In death cases, one may ask whether in following the law the juror can accept and implement presumptions of substantial pecuniary loss and conversion of services into money. Whenever possible, to set the stage for a large recovery, one may request the juror to act as a judge of the facts and not evaluate the case on either his own earnings or personal evaluation of his own business affairs.

If the case involves an aggravated liability situation or a clear-cut defendant responsibility, such as drunkenness, a plaintiff's lawyer may seek to commit jurors on whether they could return a sum certain. In cases involving serious injuries, multiple parties and third-party actions, it is advisable to phrase questions in a vein indicating that the real issue involves *who is going to pay, rather than whether the plaintiff is entitled to recover*. Where defendants furnish an opening or an individual judge permits, you might give some examples as to how the jury should consider this case, such as Uncle Sam suing Boeing for a $52,000,000 defective B-52 bomber, or Mohammed Ali suing for $8,000,000 because he spent 45 minutes pummeling an opponent, etc.

Finally, if you have liability weaknesses, expose them in the beginning. Conviction of a crime, admissions in depositions and other adverse bits of information should be elicited by plaintiff himself if such evidence may have a shocking impact when injected by the defendant during his presentation of evidence. You should phrase your questions in a courteous, straightforward and non-offensive tone, giving the jury the message you intend to carry throughout and, like any other good movie producer, laying the groundwork or the scenario for your production.

EDITOR: Do you think the word *damages* has a tendency to turn off jurors?

PHILLIPS: The words *damages, recover, awards,* or similar terms suggest unrestricted compensation which should be avoided if they can be negatively interpreted by a skillful opponent. I personally rarely use the word *damages*. I like to use *compensation* or *reimbursement*. Sometimes I use alternative phrases such as "That which will make my client whole," or "That which will put him in the position that the law says he ought to be," or "That which will make it possible for my client to attain the right kind of justice." The effect of just payment is more acceptable to the average juror's mind.

## How to Talk About Actual Dollar Amounts

EDITOR: In cases where the liability is clear, do you talk actual figures?

PHILLIPS: Yes, but only where the liability is crystal-clear. However, if you have doubts or there is a significant question of liability, it is poor policy to commit yourself (or the jury) to specific sums of money, especially where jurors may compromise a verdict in proportion to your liability weakness. You can, nonetheless, preface your prayer in general terms: "If we are entitled to a substantial amount of money," or "A large sum of money," or "If it becomes necessary for you to decide on a recovery in six figures," is an acceptable technique which does not totally commit. It is strategically better to wait until summation before deciding what to ask.

Of course, if I were a defendant, I'd counteract this tactic by telling the jurors: "Mr. Phillips asked you if you could return a verdict for

$3,000,000. As you know, anybody can ask for absurd amounts of money by simply mentioning big figures. One can add zeroes by a single stroke of a lead pencil. But the law requires you to look at the crux of this case, not hand out money indiscriminately as though it's coming off a money tree. Can you follow the law that limits a plaintiff to recovery only to simple compensation? That is to say, if he is entitled to $100, that's all you'll give him, not a penny more?"

Often defense lawyers will say, "Well, you know they can simply file suit papers in the clerk's office and we have to come here and defend even if they don't have a case; will you insist that they prove what they say in these papers?" Or, "Counsel asked you for $900,000, I don't know where he got that figure, but you understand that anyone can throw figures around just because they sound big. Every time that they ask you for money, will you look at the evidence·to see whether or not they are entitled to anything at all? It doesn't cost any more to file a lawsuit for a million dollars than one for a thousand dollars. If we're not obligated to pay money, you're not going to oblige us to pay simply because somebody is asking for it."

As you can see, the plaintiff talks big, and the defendant talks it down to actual damages, if at all.

EDITOR: If both arguments are convincing, how does the jury decide?

PHILLIPS: That's where skill and salesmanship enter into the picture. A likable lawyer can accomplish more through eye-to-eye contact and a smile than one who has an abrasive personality. Some plaintiff's attorneys feel that if the juror is a friendly, warm, South European, he is more inclined to be plaintiff-oriented. Some defendant's attorneys, on the other hand, are more prone to accept the cool, Nordic, conservative, strictly logical mind. Whether plaintiff or defendant, however, it is always advisable to impress upon the juror the importance of his role and the effect of his decision on society. Logic, honest argument, sufficient evidence and clarity usually decide cases for the jury.

Of course, the use of such phrases as "Human life is sacred"; "I wouldn't take a million dollars to have that happen to me"; "Society is dedicated to protecting the public"; or "We spend millions to protect, we should do likewise to compensate," is important. The extent to which you can use catch phrases like these depends on the particular judge before whom the case is being tried.

## Finding the Winning Point in Each Case

EDITOR: What suggestions do you have in specific cases such as child death, breadwinner death, serious injury, and not-so-serious injury?

PHILLIPS: As you know, each case has its Achilles heel or its winning point. In child death cases, for example, recovery is limited to pecuniary loss; there is no recovery for bereavement, sorrow or even filial relationship. In most jurisdictions there is a presumption of substantial pecuniary loss. This phrase should be magnified and equated with substantial amounts of money, and examples should convey to the jury its real significance to that family. In conveying this message, Webster's definitions are very handy, as are newspaper and magazine accounts of precedents where substantial amounts of money were awarded.

In breadwinner death cases, more than income is actually lost because most jurisdictional instructions permit recovery for services furnished by the decedent, such as loss of education, religious instruction, other services, goods, etc. The lawyer should ask the jury to evaluate each such service provided by the decedent. For example, parents drive children to Sunday School. You now need a chauffeur to do that. How much is a good chauffeur worth? How are you going to pay for a chauffeur? If the parent was washing walls, painting, cleaning and fixing the plumbing, you are now required to hire skilled workmen. Such costs are phenomenal. If you start to add those services by present hourly costs, large money recovery flows naturally.

Relate the losses to present day prices. One has merely to mention the spiral of gasoline prices to understand the effect of inflation.

## Dramatic Ways to Present the Effect of Injuries

EDITOR: How do you convince the jury that your client deserves a substantial verdict when the injury has not resulted in death and may not be serious?

PHILLIPS: If you have a not-so-serious injury it is wise to admit in the first place that the injury isn't serious. Honesty pays. But even if you don't have permanency, you should stress the one element in the case which has intrinsic value—"Who would take x dollars for this particular experience?" If a man falls two floors and gets up, walks, and concedes, "I've just got a wrenched knee," you concede on the issue of permanency; but when he says that he relives again and again the experience of falling two flights, the jury believes him and should award him compensation for the experience alone. In short, while you may not have proof of permanency elements, you've got other elements which have great value.

EDITOR: Do you ever use videotapes of a person who is seriously injured?

PHILLIPS: Yes, if you've got a serious injury. To reenact the life of a handicapped person requires visual as well as auditory impression. The jury should be permitted to see in order to appreciate how handicaps affect people. One can talk incessantly about difficulties in arising from bed; but jurors are haunted by the visual image of hardships, impediments and difficulties. Of significant effect are videotapes of a person who suffers brain damage with resulting epilepsy. Unless an epileptic episode manifests itself in the courtroom, jurors cannot understand what an unforgettable visual experience it is to witness a person frothing at the mouth, shaking and quivering with the prospect of a tongue which may be bitten off. A videotape of that experience is an unforgettable one.

But videotape is not the only way to relive or present the effect of injuries. Evidence of an objective nature is available, even in cases where routine medical media such as x-rays or EKG's are negative. The testimonial approach that sets the stage for damages is extremely effective since a neighbor, co-employee, minister, scoutmaster, grocer, nurse or newspaper boy are highly believable when they testify that they witnessed different facets of impediments or difficulties experienced by a plaintiff. The technique of attestation bombarded by the advertising media works for industry, and ought to work in the judicial system.

## How to Work with the Plaintiff in Collecting Strong Evidence of Damages

EDITOR: What questions can you suggest for presenting evidence of damages through the plaintiff, in order to have material for effective arguments?

PHILLIPS: Make a list of damage elements as experienced by the plaintiff. I usually tell the plaintiff not to tell me what he can't do, because I believe they've tried to do everything. I want to know what he experiences, and tell what he has tried to do. Inevitably, I will fill three to six pages of such things as: "When I kneel, I notice that it feels like my knee locks; when I try to lift packages, I favor the injured leg; in the morning it takes me ten minutes before I am able to ambulate with my sore back; I have to twist to one side and sort of throw my feet onto the floor."

Various lawyers have innovatively used systems and techniques that break down and itemize handicaps accurately or chronologically reflecting the plaintiff's problems, through diaries, calendars and tabulations. I personally insist that clients keep a calendar tabulation of handicapping experiences. In addition, shortly before trial or discovery depositions, it is advisable to ask a client to list all of his individual handicapping experiences or problems so that he can relate them when asked.

The lawyer can assist by asking the client such questions as: "What do you notice about yourself when you get up in the morning? What do you experience when you try to get up? What do you feel when you have to swing out from the bathtub? What experience do you have in putting your body into the bathtub? How do you climb over? What do you feel when you are bending to reach for a towel and it happens to be several feet away? What difficulties do you notice when you try to put on trousers? Or attempt to tie your shoes? Are you able to do that? How long does it take? If you use a razor, are you able to hold it? Are you as steady as you were before? What kind of clothes do you wear now as compared to those you wore before?"

The list of these difficulties is endless, and will vary only with the ingenuity of the lawyer and the memory of the client. And, when all is said and done, the more accurate and convincing permanent injuries can be displayed, the greater the damages.

# How to Estimate the Present Value of Lost Earnings

### Gerald D. Martin, D.B.A.

Gerald D. Martin is Professor of Finance at California State University, Fresno. He holds the Doctor of Business Administration degree from Arizona State University, and is the author of numerous articles in professional journals. He is called on frequently to give evidence for both plaintiffs and defendants in damage suits, minority stockholder suits, and class actions, some reaching all the way to the U.S. Supreme Court. Martin is the co-author (with William C. Clay, Jr., Esq.) of "How to Win Maximum Awards for Lost Earnings: A Guide to Estimating Damages and Proving Them in Court," *Executive Reports Corp.*, 1980.

An attorney can usually make a good estimate of his chances of proving liability, and he can easily determine the range of awards made in his jurisdiction. His most difficult task is in guessing the size of the loss an expert would arrive at in a formal evaluation. This latter task is the focus of our following comments, where we offer specific techniques for making an accurate guesstimate of the present value of the loss.

### Why You Should Make an Estimate

There are several reasons why you should make a preliminary estimate. First, it forces you to consider and gather evidence relating to the major elements of an appraisal. Should you decide to use an economist, you will already have much of the information he will need. Second, you have a better idea of what the case is worth when you begin your pre-trial negotiations. Third, should you hire an economist you will have a knowledge of what he is doing and will be able to question either him or your opponent's expert intelligently if your figure differs significantly from the expert's. Fourth, by having a rough idea of what the expert's appraisal will show as the value of the loss, you are in a better position to make the decision of whether to commit your firm and your client to paying the expert's fee.

## The Time Value of Money

A dollar in hand today is more valuable than a dollar to be received in a year. One reason for this is that, with inflation, an item that can be bought for a dollar now will cost more than a dollar in a year. Another reason is that a dollar in hand now may be lent out or placed on deposit—at compound interest—so that a year from now you can reclaim the dollar plus the interest it has earned. Thus, because the dollar you have now can generate additional money over the coming year, it has more potential value than a dollar to be received a year from now. Or, to put it another way, the present-day equivalent of a future dollar is somewhat *less* than a dollar.

This last fact is now recognized by virtually all courts. In essence, when you determine the lost earnings of the deceased ten years hence but demand payment now, you cannot expect to receive an *equal* amount now, but rather, an *equivalent* amount that will be smaller. The award must be reduced, to be stated as the present value of an amount that would not normally be received until some future date. The reason is that whatever is received today would presumably grow until a later time, when it will be used to replace earnings. Failure to adjust earnings to their present value, then, gives a figure that overcompensates the plaintiff, unfairly penalizes the defendant—and jeopardizes your chances of winning the maximum award for your client.

## Present Value at a Glance

In any present value problem there are only four variables that must be dealt with: the time span in years or periods, the interest rates, the value in the future, and the value in the present. When the values for any three variables are known, the fourth can easily be found. Future value is the estimate of earnings over the worklife expectancy. The interest rate is your best estimate of the long-term return that could likely be earned by the plaintiff if he invested the award now. The present value is what that stream of future income is worth if paid in a lump sum at the time of the trial.

Regarding terminology, two sets of terms must be understood.

When a future payment, or amount, is known for the end of a period, the equivalent amount at the beginning of the period is found by *discounting the future value to the present value*. On the other hand, given a known payment at the beginning of the period, the equivalent value at the end of the period is found by *compounding the present value to the future value*. Only two dollar amounts are involved: the present value, and the future value. The time period may be days, months, or years, but it is a specified period. The interest rate is also a specified amount, and is called either the discount rate or the compound rate, depending upon whether you are converting backward or forward through time, respectively.

In terms of a lost earnings appraisal, the $10,000 may be an estimate of what the deceased would have been earning in ten years, and the $5,084 is the equivalent value today. To find this equivalent amount, one need only consult a table of present value factors. Unfortunately, a lifetime loss estimate is not this simple but, in essence, the economist is making the above calculation over and over again.

To further complicate the process, the expert must work not with annual income, but with weekly or monthly paychecks. Further, interest is rarely compounded (discounted) annually. It may be daily, monthly, quarterly, or even semi-annually as is the case with corporate bonds. When the deceased was young at the time of the accident, literally thousands of calculations are required and, for this reason, most experts today use rather complicated computer programs to handle the sheer volume of mathematics. Few law firms have the time, the staff, or the equipment needed for such an appraisal.

### The Key Factors in Your Estimate

Several factors exert a strong influence on any appraisal of lost earnings. The first is obviously whether the accident resulted in death or in disability. In a death case, all future earnings are lost; but this is not always true when the victim survives. It is necessary to determine the extent to which earnings are impaired. This is often directly related to evidence provided by medical and rehabilitation experts describing the degree of disability and the type and amount of work that can be done after recovery.

Personal consumption is another variable that must be considered.

All persons who earn an income spend some portion on their personal needs, such as food, clothes, dental care, and so forth. When the accident victim dies, the amount normally spent for personal use is not an amount lost to his survivors or his estate. Consequently, this would not be considered as part of the loss. State laws, however, are not uniform on this subject. While some states require a deduction in death cases for personal consumption, others permit recovery of gross earnings. The attorney must know the law in his state and advise his expert.

There is no disagreement when the victim survives. He, rather than his survivors, is seeking recovery for his loss, and his personal consumption or use of income survived with him. In many instances his personal consumption actually increases as a result of continuing medical bills and the diminished ability to purchase life and health insurance.

Fringe benefits are often overlooked but are a major element in the total pay package for many employees, particularly union members. As a percent of pay, these benefits range from five to twenty-five percent for many persons. At the very least, the employer's portion of a worker's social security tax should be added to the loss.

Work life expectancy is yet another variable to consider. The economist can determine this down to two decimal places, but such accuracy is not required for your rough estimate. Without a lengthy digression into work life calculations, you will be reasonably accurate if you assume that employment would have continued to age 62 for both men and women. Given the victim's age when injured, you can determine the number of years earnings would be received.

Annual income at the time of the accident can be obtained from tax returns or from the employer. The assumption can then be made that earnings will increase over time at some rather constant rate. Several guidelines are available. For example, the legal minimum wage has increased annually at about six percent for the last 41 years. At this writing, the wage guideline set by the Administration is eight percent and union contracts recently negotiated call for 10-12 percent increases. For your estimate, select a rate on the conservative side that seems appropriate in the case you are handling.

One other variable needed is an appropriate interest (discount) rate to be used to convert future earnings to their present value.

One last item must be mentioned because it is so frequently misunderstood. It is true that most income is subject to federal and state tax and it is common to hear the defense attorney argue that an award must be reduced by an amount equal to the tax that would have been paid. As Dr. Linke correctly pointed out, the expert's appraisal will be the same regardless of whether he is retained by the plaintiff or the defendant. But while it is advantageous for the defense to argue for a tax reduction, most experts working for the defense would prefer it not come up because it too often proves to be a trap. It is true that future income will be taxed, and it is true that an award is exempt from tax. What is overlooked, however, is the fact that the award will be invested and will earn interest, that the award and accumulated interest together replace future income, and that all of the interest earned will be taxed.

Consider a simple example. Assume the jury awards $400,000 for lost earnings to the survivors of a young decedent. Further assume that in the first year following death, the decedent would have earned $20,000. With usual deductions, the tax on his income may have been, say, $3,500. On the other hand, a $400,000 award deposited or invested at seven percent would earn $28,000 in that same first year. Not only is this greater than the lost income for that year, but the family, because of the death, has lost one of its personal exemptions. As a result the tax is likely to be $7-8,000. The plaintiff's attorney can now argue that, because of tax, the award should be increased! In reality, something close to an offset is occurring. Had the decedent lived a normal life, his income tax liability would increase each year. The taxes on earnings from an award, however, are high in the early years and then decline as the award is depleted. When both types of taxes are discounted to a present value, they tend to cancel out each other. For this reason, taxes need not be included in your rough estimate.

### How to Use Simple Formulas to Estimate the Loss

With an understanding of the elements discussed above, specific techniques for making an informal estimate can be introduced. While this may appear on the surface to be rather complicated, it is really quite simple. With the use of a hand-held calculator, the problem can be solved in less than five minutes. Five situations are covered, but in no case are more than two steps required.

The economist will use dozens of documents to pinpoint the proper value to be assigned to each variable, but a reasonably close approximation can be made by an attorney with a minimum amount of research in a small number of sources. First, the level of earnings and the growth rate in earnings can be established by examining the annual "Handbook of Labor Statistics" published by the Department of Labor. Earnings in nearly all occupations increase annually and historical evidence shows that increases tend to be at some constant percentage rather than a constant dollar amount. For most jobs, a proper rate of growth can be found in the "Handbook." Fringe benefits for most jobs also can be found in this document.

Worklife expectancy is easily found. About once every ten years the Department of Labor publishes tables showing the number of years a person is expected to work, given the age that person has already attained. The current document is Special Labor Force Report 187, "Length of Working Life for Men and Women."

The discount rate to be used is the interest rate one can earn on relatively risk-free investments. The monthly "Federal Reserve Bulletin" is one source of information about rates available through banks, savings and loan associations, and U.S. Government Securities. A good single source for data on personal consumption is in the Department of Labor Report 455-4, "Consumer Expenditure Survey Series."

Five formulas are given here to cover the five most commonly encountered situations. If you find a need to use them, be sure you select the correct one. Before moving to the formulas, however, let's set up a standard set of symbols.

| Symbol | Definition |
|--------|------------|
| g | Constant growth rate of earnings |
| d | Discount rate |
| i | Function of g and d |
| E | Annual earnings |
| n | Number of worklife-expectancy years earnings will be received |
| P | Present value of future earnings |
| C | Personal consumption as a percent of pay |
| D | Degree of disability or earnings impairment |
| F | Fringe benefits as a percent of pay |

The values for g, d, i, E, and n are assumed, in the basic formulas, to be annual values; but each can be adjusted for shorter periods. For instance, if the annual values are known but calculations are desired on a monthly basis, proceed as follows: Because there are 12 months in a year, the adjusted value for g is g ÷ 12. The adjusted value for d is d ÷ 12. Since i is a function of g and d, it is automatically adjusted. The adjusted value for E is E ÷ 12, and the adjustment for n is n × 12. If a quarterly basis is desired, then just change the 12 to a 4 to represent the number of quarters in a year.

All percentages are used in their decimal equivalents. For example, a discount rate, d, of 7 percent is entered into the formula as .07. This applies to d, g, i, F, D, and C. E and P are dollar amounts and n is a time period. When there is to be no deduction for personal consumption, C, nor any addition for fringe benefits, F, these values automatically assume a value of 1.0 and have no effect on the calculations. In the case of a death, the degree of disability, D, is 100 percent, or 1.0, and also has no effect.

The formula to be used depends on the answers to two questions that you already know or can reasonably assume. First, is the growth rate, g, less than, equal to, or greater than the discount rate, d? Second, are base earnings, E, the amount earned during the year prior to the accident or the amount estimated for the first year following the accident?

The choice of whether to use earnings prior to or following the accident depends on the information available to you. Assuming the victim worked, the earnings for the last full year prior to the accident will always be known. For persons working under contract, such as union members, earnings for a year or two following the accident are usually already set. Whenever possible, use post-accident earnings because it reduces by one year the amount of speculation in the estimate. Given this information, one of the five following formulas will give a good approximation of the loss.

**Formula I.** Use this when base earnings, E, are for the year *prior* to the accident and when the discount rate, d, is greater than the earnings growth rate, g. Two steps are required. First, find the value of (i) as follows:

$$i = \frac{(1 + d)}{(1 + g)} - 1$$

Then, with the following formula, calculate the present value of the loss, P.

$$P = E \left[ \frac{1 - (1 + i)^{-n+1}}{i} + 1 \right] D(1 + F - C)$$

**Formula II.** Use this when base earnings, E, are for the year *after* the accident and the discount rate, d, is greater than the earnings growth rate, g. Again, two steps are required. First, find i where:

$$i = \frac{(1 + d)}{(1 + g)} - 1$$

Next, find the present value with:

$$P = E \left[ \frac{1 - (1 + i)^{-n}}{i} \right] D(1 + F - C)$$

**Formula III.** This is used when base earnings, E, are for the year *prior* to the accident and the earnings growth rate, g, is greater than the discount rate, d. The two steps are:

First, find the value of $(1 + i)$ as:

$$i = \frac{(1 + g)}{(1 + d)} - 1$$

Then, find P where:

$$P = E \left[ \frac{(1 + i)^{n+1} - 1}{i} - 1 \right] D(1 + F - C)$$

**Formula IV.** Use this when base earnings, E, are for the year *after* the accident and the earnings growth rate, g, is greater than the discount rate, d. The two steps are:
**Step one:**

$$i = \frac{(1 + g)}{(1 + d)} - 1$$

**Step two:**

$$P = E \left[ \frac{(1 + i)^n - 1}{i} \right] D(1 + F - C)$$

**Formula V.** This is a one-step formula to be used when the discount rate, d, is equal to the earnings growth rate, g. It is immaterial whether base earnings, E, are for the year prior to or after the accident because g and d, being equal, cancel each other out. The result is that estimated future annual earnings are the same as current base earnings, E, for each year of worklife expectancy.

The present value of the loss is:

$$P = E \times n \times D \times (1 + F - C)$$

## Solving a Typical Case

Now let's set up a situation showing how to determine and use the correct formula. Suppose that, for simplicity, the accident occurred on January 1, that the deceased had signed a contract calling for a base salary of $12,000 for the coming year, and that fringe benefits were valued at $1,800, or 15 percent of the base salary. Earnings have been increasing annually at a rate of 6 percent, and are expected to continue at this rate. The deceased personally consumed, on the average, about 25 percent of his income. At the time of death, his worklife expectancy was 30 years. A conservative and realistic discount rate is estimated to be 7 percent.

Converting this information to a usable format, we find that:

$$
\begin{aligned}
g &= 6\% = .06 \\
d &= 7\% = .07 \\
E &= \$12{,}000 \\
n &= 30 \text{ years} \\
C &= 25\% = .25 \\
D &= 100\% = 1.0 \\
F &= 15\% = .15
\end{aligned}
$$

Because the discount rate, d, is greater than the earnings growth rate, g, and base earnings, E, are for the year after death, formula II must be used.
Step 1:

$$
i = \frac{(d + d)}{d + g} - 1 = \frac{(1 + .07)}{(1 + .06)} - 1 = (1.0094) - 1 = .0094
$$

Step 2:

$$
P = E \left[ \frac{1 - (1 + i)^{-n}}{i} \right] D(1 + F - C)
$$

$$
P = 12{,}000 \left[ \frac{1 - (1.0094)^{-30}}{.0094} \right] 1.0(1 + .15 - .25)
$$

$$
P = 12{,}000 \left[ \frac{1 - .75527}{.0094} \right] 1.0(.90)
$$

$$
P = 12{,}000[26.0353]\ 1.0(.90)
$$

$$
P = \$281{,}181
$$

In this case, the present value of the loss is approximately $281,181. But remember, there are several reasons why this is less accurate than a computer-generated estimate. In the example it is implicitly assumed that the deceased would be paid only one time a year, at the end of the year. Also, the accident date and the present-value date are treated as being the same date. Another consideration is that the single formula method does not permit the value of any variable to change over the period of worklife expectancy. For example, personal consumption changes as children enter and leave a family, but only one rate is allowed in the formula. Consequently, all these factors combined cause a slight understatement of the present value of the loss.

## A Word of Caution

We would be remiss not to insert a caution. Whenever you must choose within a reasonable range of values, always lean toward the conservative end. Specifically, use care in selecting g, the growth rate in earnings and d, the interest rate used to discount those earnings to the present. The *higher* the earnings growth rate, the higher will be the loss estimate. Conversely, the *lower* the interest rate, the higher will be the loss estimate. Obviously, a high growth rate and a low interest rate will best serve the plaintiff, while a low growth rate and a high interest rate will best serve the defendant. Your expert, if he is truly unbiased, will not attempt to serve either but will choose the rates that best reflect the general socio-economic conditions to which the victim was subject.

# Measuring the Pecuniary Value of Human Capital

## Charles M. Linke, Ph.D.

Dr. Charles Linke is Professor of Finance and Chairman of the Department of Finance at the University of Illinois (Urbana-Champaign). Prior to joining the faculty of the University of Illinois in 1966, he taught at Miami University and Indiana University. Professor Linke has published numerous articles and books, and he consults with industrial firms, financial institutions, utility companies, and lawyers on a variety of economic and financial issues.

## Valuing Human Life As a Capital Asset

The attempt to place a monetary value on human life in law can be traced back over four centuries, but it has only been in the last two decades that the expert economic witness has emerged as an appraiser of pecuniary damage in death and disability actions.

The conceptual and practical problems of estimating human capital value revolve around the meaning of the term "value." "Value" of a person in what sense? "Value" to whom?

Economists have used a variety of alternative definitions of "value" in their studies in human capital theory. The issue being analyzed ultimately dictates the appropriateness of the "value" definition employed. Generalizing, economists have viewed the "value of man" in terms of his worth as a productive asset, having some gross productivity per period and a consumption requirement per period. A man's period of productivity and consumption functions typically have been operationally defined as his expected future earnings stream and his expected personal consumption expenditure pattern. Thus, the economist chooses to view the value of human capital in much the same fashion that he views the value of any capital asset.

To an economist, the gross present money worth of a productive or capital asset is the present value of the future income the asset will produce over the expected life time of the asset. Algebraically, the gross present value of an asset may be represented as follows:

$$PVo = \frac{E1}{(1+i)^1} + \frac{E2}{(1+i)^2} + \frac{E3}{(1+i)^3} + \ldots + \frac{En}{(1+i)^n}$$

where

$PVo$ = *present value of the asset's future earnings in time zero or today dollars*
$E1$ = *income of asset in year 1*
$En$ = *income of asset in year n*
$(I+i)^t$ = *discount factor in year t*
$i$ = *discount rate of interest or investment yield*
$n$ = *life expectancy of the asset's income earning ability.*

PVo, the price or present value of an asset, is that amount of money which, when invested at the discount rate (i), would exactly generate from both principal and interest the time configuration of expected annual income. An estimate of the asset's net present value would be obtained by reducing the annual income estimated (the $E_t$) to account for any costs, such as consumption or maintenance expense, incurred in generating the income in years 1, 2, 3, . . . , n.

## Human Life Value in Law

In law as in economics, the conceptual and practical problems of estimating the capital asset value of man revolve around the meaning of the term "value." Without stopping to explore damage instructions for particular jursidictions, it is sufficient to state that the law attempts to provide practical answers in death actions, at least, to the two value questions, "Value of a person in what sense?" and "Value to whom?"

Generalizing, the law indicates the assessment of the "pecuniary value of a decedent" should be consistent with the present pecuniary value of the money, goods, and non-paid work services (net of terminated personal consumption expenditures) the deceased might reasonably have been expected to contribute to the maintenance of his family had he not encountered a premature ending of his life or income-generating ability. As such, the legal concept of human life is consistent with the economic view of man as a capital asset.

## What to Expect from the Economist

The apparent simplicity of the economist's capital asset valuation model which was presented above is deceptive. Superficially, at least, the appraisal of a decedent's capital value appears straightforward. For example, given the age and the lost earnings rate of the injured person, present value tables exist which permit the reduction of the expected future income flows to their present value at an assumed future "prudent man" investment rate of interest or discount. And this is essentially what the plaintiff's attorney has done over the years to provide damage information for the jury.

Unfortunately, appraisal of the economic loss that can properly be associated with the premature ending of an individual's working life tends to be a complex problem requiring sophisticated economic analysis of a number of economic relationships in the economy. That appraisal of the economic value of man is complicated is not surprising. After all, valuing non-human capital such as business machinery and land as capital assets has not made the appraisal activity a simple and straightforward calculation devoid of expert knowledge and judgment. It follows that valuing man as a capital asset does not provide the appraiser of human capital with a task less difficult than that encountered by the appraiser of physical assets. Indeed, the task of human life valuation is likely to be more complex.

The principles of capital asset appraisal are well established in economic theory. In practice, opinions may vary regarding the appropriate values for variables in the capital asset valuation framework, such as estimated income in one or more years. But there is no argument among economists that this is the approach to take to determine the present value of a productive asset, regardless of whether the asset is physical or human capital.

The general approach to appraising pecuniary loss in a death action involves estimating the death-terminated flow of money earnings, fringe benefits, non-paid work services to the household, and the terminated personal consumption of the decedent. Econometric estimation of these flows requires specific socioeconomic information about the decedent, general socioeconomic data relating to the decedent's "statistical cohort," and regional and national general economic data.

Below is a summary table that suggests the end result of an economic appraisal of the pecuniary damages to be associated with premature death.

| Pecuniary Losses To Be Associated With the Premature Ending of the Decedent's Working Life | Present Value In Trial Date Dollars | |
|---|---|---|
| | Pre-Trial Loss | Post-Trial Loss |
| Money Earnings | $ | $ |
| Fringe Benefits | $_____ | $_____ |
| | $ | $ |
| Plus Value of Non-Paid Work Services to Household | $_____ | $_____ |
| | $ | $ |
| Less Terminated Personal Consumption Expenditures | $_____ | $_____ |
| Loss in Trial Date Dollars | $_____ | $_____ |

Money earnings, fringe benefits, and non-paid work services represent lost economic value the decedent would have generated for the benefit of himself and his household had he not encountered a premature end of his working life. Usually the largest loss element is the annual money earnings to be associated with the decedent under the assumption he would have completed his expected working life (as distinguished from life expectancy).

Fringe benefits, or supplementary payments, are benefits that increase the real earnings of a worker but not his current money earnings. Included in fringe benefits loss are such items as employer-financed retirement plans and family health care insurance. Accordingly, the monetary value of these fringe benefits must be evaluated if a realistic picture of the economic loss associated with the decedent's premature death is to emerge from the analysis.

Another economic value arises from the non-paid work services the deceased would have provided his household had he lived. The value of services performed by the decedent prior to premature death which will now have to be purchased by his household in order to maintain the same standard of living is the value in question.

The above losses must be reduced to reflect any reduced expenditure outflow or death-related inflow that occurs as the result of the decedent's premature death. The main deduction is the termination of the decedent's own personal consumption expenditure. Another source of possible deductions are those flows of value that occur due to the decedent's death. For the economist, the "collateral source" rule and/or the attorney's instructions supersede economic logic in specifying whether such offsetting "collateral source" flows are incorporated in the analysis.

The final step in the valuation process is to convert all estimated dollar quantities to present value. This requires separating the flows into two time periods: (1) a pre-trial period extending from the date of death to the trial date; and (2) a post-trial period extending from the trial date to the end of decedent's work life and/or life expectancy. The flows in the pre-trial period are compounded forward to permit pre-trial flows to be expressed in trial date dollars or present value. Post-trial flows are discounted back to present value as of the trial date.

Inasmuch as the valuation logic is similar for impaired earnings capacity and death actions, the following discussion will revolve primarily around wrongful death actions. The discussion is structured around activities and considerations common to all appraisals. This permits the various types of appraisals (i.e., appraisals of employees as distinguished from the self-employed, professional practitioner, mother-housewife, or child with no prior demonstrated earnings) to be discussed jointly.

## What Kind of Information the Economist Will Need

An economist will require a substantial amount of specific information about the decedent. The retaining attorney (defense or plaintiff) typically can provide or obtain the needed information which would include the following:

1. Race
2. Sex
3. Date of birth
4. Date of death
5. Marital status (parent data if decedent was a child)
   birthdate of spouse
   number and birthdates of children
6. Education

7. Geographic location
8. Occupation or profession
  earnings rate at time of death
  money earnings
  fringe benefits
  anticipated earnings/promotional potential
  demonstrated earnings capacity
9. Expected trial date.

An economist's interest in specific socioeconomic data about the decedent should not be interpreted to mean he is prepared to forecast what would have happened to a particular individual who encountered a premature end to his working life. Economic analysis cannot generate answers to questions about the future of a specific individual. However, an economist can forecast with a reasonable economic certainty the most likely economic future of the average or representative person in the subset or statistical cohort of individuals having socioeconomic characteristics similar to the decedent.

Of course, the economist is prepared to "individualize" the data as much as possible. But in the final analysis, an economist's appraisal is for the average individual in the decedent's statistical cohort. Stated differently, an economist cannot know what any specific truckdriver, for example, would have earned had he lived to complete his expected work life but he can estimate what the average truckdriver with the deceased's socioeconomic characteristics can be expected to earn. The use of the statistical cohort concept is an accepted econometric approach to projecting the uncertain future, and a technique federal agencies such as the Social Security Administration, insurance companies, and other organizations forced to forecast the future utilize when making projections.

The economist will use the decedent's socioeconomic data in conjunction with published source documents and studies of general socioeconomic data to determine the decedent's life expectancy, expected work life, non-paid work services value to his household, and expected personal consumption expenditures had he lived to his life expectancy. Much of the general socioeconomic data needed by the economist is gathered and published by departments and agencies of the United States Government. The Department of Labor and its Bureau of Labor Statistics, and the Department of Commerce and its Bureau of the Census compile and publish data and studies on age-education-occupation earnings patterns, "fringe benefits" patterns, monetary value of non-paid work services to the household, family consumption expenditures, employment-wages-prices-interest rates-productivity patterns, and other similar types of relevant data.

Methodology as well as data sources useful in integrating a decedent's socioeconomic data with occupation, industrial, national, or peer group averages to generate an appraisal of economic loss are examined below.

## Life Expectancy or Expected Working Life?

General socioeconomic data from published federal government sources are used to estimate the decedent's expected working life and life expectancy. General population life and mortality rates by age, race, and sex are published by the United States Center for Health Statistics in an annual publication, *Vital Statistics of the United States.* Life expectancy data may enter into the analysis of economic loss in several ways. Years of life expectancy as of the trial date will indicate the length of time to be used in calculating the value of decedent's terminated personal consumption expenditures and the value of non-paid work services rendered to the household. Also comparative life expectancy data on the decedent and the statutory beneficiaries, usually the spouse and minor children, are required to reflect the longevity of loss to justify the argument for replacement of decedent's lost future earnings for living dependents.

Working life rather than life expectancy is the appropriate time period for which lost earnings should be estimated. Expected working life is an actuarial estimate of the average number of years remaining in an age cohort's work life after separation from the labor force due to death and due to both temporary and permanent withdrawals for other reasons have been considered. The difference between expected work life and life expectancy provides an estimate of the probable period of retirement and the social security and/or other pension eligibility period of the decedent.

The Bureau of Labor Statistics has for some time gathered data and published estimates on the expected working life of men. Unfortunately, the tables of work life expectancy are not as extensive or as current as life expectancy tables.

Work life data are particularly limited for women. However, the Department of Labor provides a set of work life expectancies for females at various ages, classified by marital status, and presence of husband and/or children. While helpful, the data reflect the social and economic climate of the 1960s. The economic climate for women has changed dramatically in the past two decades in ways that have caused more attractive and rewarding employment opportunities to be available to women.

Expected working life data are suggestive, at best, of a decedent's lost productive earning period. For men, the statistical cohort for work life expectancy is defined only on one characteristic, age. The data for women, as noted above, has similar shortcomings. Thus, an economist will consider the decedent's occupation and other factors, such as the existence or absence of a mandatory retirement age, in addition to expected working life data in selecting the earnings loss period.

### How the Economist Estimates Lost Earning Capacity

The calculation of lost income during the pre-trial period or from the date of death to the assumed trial date is comparatively simple relative to the post-trial calculation. Consider, for example, the case of a decedent with a demonstrated earnings record in a particular occupation. The decedent's annual money earnings rate as of the date of death provides an initial estimate of lost pre-trial earnings capacity when adjusted for contractual and/or general wage changes which may have occurred during the pre-trial period. Corroborating evidence on the money earnings capacity of the average worker in the occupation in question with decedent's age-education-location characteristics can be developed from data available in publications of the Bureau of the Census and the Bureau of Labor Statistics.

Projection of lost future earnings after the date of trial or during decedent's post-trial expected working life requires an economist to draw upon his professional knowledge and make earnings estimates for the median worker in the decedent's statistical age-education-occupation group according to trends which are economically logical and consistent with the characteristics of a particular case. These earnings estimates will typically be generated by applying an average annual money wage rate(s) of growth the economist analytically deduces to be appropriate for the particular case to the decedent's trial date annual earning capacity. In selecting the money wage growth rate, an economist will select a rate based upon an evaluation of wage-price-productivity trends in the economy and in the industry and/or occupation of the decedent.

Selection of an appropriate money wage growth rate to generate money earning estimates for several decades into the future is not "too speculative" an activity as some critics argue. Failure to consider future wage increases would be indefensible in that the realities of theoretical and empirical economic analysis would be ignored. There is no debate among economists about whether an individual's income will grow. In a growing economy, every individual may expect an upward trend in his own earnings. This economic view differs importantly from the methodology used by the actuary which establishes the income during a base year, extrapolates the same income level for the remaining working life of the worker, adjusts for the probability of living by actuarial tables and discounts the amount to obtain a present value.

Some judges and lawyers question whether economic projections beyond a few years are so subject to uncertainties as to be "speculative in nature". The choice is not between quantifying and not quantifying expectations about the future for purposes of decision making—but rather between quantification that is explicit and reasoned or quantification that is implicit and unexamined. It is noteworthy that both public agencies and private business firms engage in such long run economic projection activity. For example, the Social Security Administration's *Annual Report of the Board of Trustees of the Federal Old Age and Survivors' Insurance and Disability Insurance Trust Funds* contains projections of workers' future income levels over a 75 year period, or to past the year 2050. Life insurance companies, pension management firms, and similar organizations make projections extending fifty or more years into the future with respect to the average worker's income in a particular occupation. One court expressed a reasoned attitude toward expert economic testimony as follows:

> This court agrees that the testimony and exhibits . . . were speculative in nature, but no more so than any other evidence that has for its purpose the proof of future action or events. The issue before the trial judge . . . was whether the testimony . . . should be allowed, in order to give the jury some basis upon which to reach a conclusion in regard to the possible future earnings of the decedent, or whether to leave the jury unguided and hope that by their common knowledge and sense of justice they might arrive at a more accurate estimation of damages. It appears . . . that in this particular case the element of conjecture is reduced significantly as to the possible future earnings of the decedent. *Krohmer V. Dahl*, 145 Mont. 491, 402 P.2d 979, 981 (1965).

## How Much Would the Decedent Have Earned?

At what rate might the average worker's income be expected to grow? One rate that could be used to estimate growth of income would be the long term annual rate of increase in output per man hour in the American economy which averages about 2.75 to 2.95 percent per year. This 2.75 to 2.95 percent rate reflects growth in real earnings and is an average annual adjustment for the increase in real productivity in the economy, not for the inflation of prices. A somewhat higher rate of growth would have to be used to take into account expected gains in money income due to both productivity and price levvel change. When the longer term rate of increase in the general price level of roughly 2.5 to 3.0 percent per annum is superimposed upon the real growth of approximately 2.85 percent, a 5.25 to 6.00 percent estimate of the annual growth of workers' money earnings cmerges.

Without stopping to present the data, it is sufficient to state that analyses of the historic growth in money earnings of a wide range of occupations, using decennial and annual United States Department of Commerce/Bureau of the Census post-World War II income data, and the Bureau of Labor Statistics wage data extending back to the turn of the century, reveal most occupations experience a longer term average rate of growth in money earnings of 4.5 to 6.0 percent per annum, which is consistent with growth in the general economy and with the annual labor productivity plus price level change total. Economists would expect money wages to grow in real terms in line with real productivity increases and thus with the economy. Stated differently, if productivity grows about 2.85 percent per year, and if average wage settlements exceed that figure, prices will rise enough in the longer run to hold real wage gains—money wage gains adjusted for inflation rate—to the productivity increase.

Specification of an appropriate average annual rate of growth in money earnings will emerge from an analysis of the growth of workers' earnings in general, of the growth of workers earnings in the decedent's occupation in particular, and of the consensus outlook for the economy in the post-trial period. Although an economist will examine carefully the historical average annual rate of money earning growth experienced by the decedent's occupation, an extrapolation of past rising wage rates several decades into the future would hardly be a defensible assumption without a supporting explanation. Similarly, the choice of a different rate than the historical average would also require a reasoned economic explanation. An economist might select the historic growth rate in money earnings of the median worker with the decedent's characteristics because his analysis revealed the economic forces causing the historical pattern of increase could, with reasonable economic certainty, be expected to continue to operate into the near future. He might also increase or decrease the expected growth rate away from the historical average because of economic forces and trends which he judges will persist during the post-trial period.

Annual money earnings losses during the pre-trial and post-trial periods are estimated to be the money earnings during these same time periods of the average worker with the decedent's socioeconomic characteristics. Pre-trial money earnings estimates may be based upon the decedent's demonstrated earning capacity at death when adjusted for earnings growth and/or the money earning capacity of the average worker in the decedent's occupation. Post-trial annual money earnings are estimated by applying the "appropriate average annual growth rate" to the trial date earning capacity of the average worker with the decedent's occupation. These annual money earnings estimates for the average worker in the decedent's occupation must then be adjusted to give effect to the decedent's educational level, to the age-education life cycle of income pattern observable for the occupation in question, and to the probability of periods of unemployment and other work stoppages. An adjustment for the probability of not living through each successive income period is implicit in the use of a post-death work life expectancy loss period.

Projection of the post-trial earnings losses for a decedent with an earnings record in an identifiable occupation is more straightforward than projecting the loss for the professional practitioner, business executive, entrepreneur, mother-housewife, or child. However different the technique, the economic logic underlying the analysis is the same. In the case of an individual with no demonstrated earning capacity, statistical cohort averages must be used. For example, if an eighteen-year-old boy is killed the day after graduating from high school, the economist will estimate the decedent's future income as the lifetime income expected for the statistical cohort composed of male high school graduates. No attempt is made to use industry and/or occupational information since there is no basis for determining likely occupation with reasonable economic certainty.

In cases involving professional practitioners, business executives, or self-employed individuals, more reliance is placed on the past earnings record of the individual. The reason for this is simply that not as much useful data on the average worker may exist as with other more common occupations. In these types of cases, an economist is forced to make reasonable professional judgments as to the values that should be associated with such items as the division of income between capital and labor in a small business, stock options, etc. Nonetheless, an economist will want to integrate whatever occupational or professional peer group data are available into his analysis.

The economic loss to be associated with the wrongful death of an individual without a paid position, such as a housewife and/or mother, is perhaps the most difficult type of case to assess. To an economist, the value of non-paid work services to a household is the price the household would have to pay a worker in the labor market to perform the work. This approach to valuing a mother and/or housewife is objective and does not have the economist concerned with the immeasurable aspects of the wife-mother role such as love, moral guidance, inspiration, etc.

## The Importance of Fringe Benefits

An appraisal of a decedent's lost earnings would be incomplete if the value of fringe benefits were ignored. Fringe benefits refer to payments employers make to, or on the behalf of, employees. Some fringe benefit values are already reflected in the decedent's basic money earnings. Such benefits would include paid vacation, holiday, sick leave, and overtime or shift premium payments. Other fringe benefits values, such as family coverage health insurance, pension and retirement plans, and savings and stock option plans are not reflected in the decedent's earnings record, nor are these benefits considered in occupational earnings data.

These fringe benefits values cause the cost of labor hour to an employer to exceed the money wage payment to the worker. Recognition must be given to the economic value of employer contributions to pay for a worker's insurance and retirement plans if a realistic evaluation of the worker's real income is to emerge from the analysis. Thus, an economist is not concerned with the total cost of fringe benefits to the employer, but rather with the value of these benefits to the employee or his beneficiaries.

Valuation of the two major types of fringe benefits, health insurance and retirement pension, requires an economist to examine both occupational fringe benefit data which value these benefits as a proportion of wage earnings, and the specific plans of the decedent's employer. From an economic vantage point, the value of a worker's benefits can be estimated on the basis of employer cost, replacement cost if the worker were to buy the same benefits privately, or on the basis of benefits received over a period of time. A good valuation guideline is to value insurance and retirement plans at employer cost (as a percent of employee money earnings) for younger workers since fringe benefits display a reasonably stable percentage relationship to wages and may be expected to rise in line with wages in the future. In the case of older workers, the discounted value of the cost of providing comparable insurance coverages for dependents of the decedent, and the discounted value of the expected retirement payments had the decedent lived, provide useful estimates of lost fringe benefits.

## Valuing Non-Paid Work Services

Another value to be considered in a death action arises from non-paid work services rendered by the decedent to statutory beneficiaries. The value of services performed by the decedent prior to premature death and which have to be purchased by the household in the post-trial period requires that the beneficiaries have a higher income to sustain their former (pre-death) consumption level. Thus, the economic loss will be understated unless the value of decedent's non-paid work services are added to the estimated lost money and fringe benefits.

Cash benefits cannot be expected to replace the loss of the decedent to his survivors. But consideration can be given to indemnifying the family unit for the loss of decedent's non-paid work services, which must now be purchased. The value to be imputed to these non-paid work services is the present value of the dollar cost of these services in the marketplace or the present value of the additional income the remaining family unit will require to sustain its former consumption level.

Until recently, little authoritative data existed on the dollar value of work services in the household. For an excellent review of the value of non-paid work literature, see Bordy, *Economic Value of a Housewife* (U.S. Dept. of Health, Education, and Welfare/Office of Research and Statistics of the Social Security Administration, 1975).

## Deducting the Decedent's Terminated Consumption

How much of the lost earnings would have been consumed by the decedent had he lived? From the projected flow of lost earnings, fringe benefits, and non-paid work services, the personal consumption of the decedent must be estimated and deducted since this amount would not have been available to his statutory beneficiaries had he lived.

The average consumption per family member is not a useful measure of lost income which has been been consumed by the decedent. Two cannot live as cheaply as one, but neither can one live for half (the average) the cost of two people. Stated differently, there are economies of scale in living units. What is needed is a measure of changes in family consumption related to ages of family members and changes in family size.

Although several comprehensive studies have sought to measure the needs of families of various sizes and ages, none of the methods evolved have gained general recognition. However, the Bureau of Labor Statistics analyzes family budget data and publishes useful general guidelines for estimating the proportion of a family's consumption allocable to specific family members.

## Special Situations Where Legal Precedent Guides the Economist

In appraising the economic loss to be associated with a death action, an economist attempts to generate a present value estimate that causes the statutory beneficiaries to be in the same pecuniary position in which they would have been but for the decedent's premature death. However, no mention was made of how pecuniary benefits such as life insurance proceeds and social security and pension benefits, which were caused by decedent's death and which otherwise would not have occurred, should be handled in the analysis.

This issue poses no conceptual problem to the economist who has a valuation model to guide his decisions regarding how the various inflows should be treated. However, and more to the point, the treatment of these "collateral source benefits" is dictated by legal precedent. The economist looks to the attorney for instructions regarding those issues such as taxes or collateral source benefits where legal requirements supersede economic logic.

## Present Value and Discount Rates in Action

The pre-trial and post-trial estimates of decedent's annual lost money earnings, fringe benefits, non-paid work services, and terminated consumption expenditures must be stated in terms of present value or trial date dollars. Determination of the present value of the pre-trial loss involves nothing more than asking what sum of money would decedent's beneficiaries have at trial date had they received the projected pre-trial economic losses as earned and invested this flow of value at the selected investment rate. The estimated economic loss plus the interest earned would add to the present value of the pre-trial loss as of trial date.

Calculating the present value of the post-trial economic loss in trial date dollars can be thought of as comparable to determining what sum of money, invested at the selected investment or discount rate, should be awarded so that periodic payments of principal and interest equal to the estimated earning capacity destroyed will be received throughout the life or work life expectancy of the decedent, with nothing remaining as either interest or principal at the end of that period.

Consider, for example, the calculation of the present value of a decedent's post-trial money earnings under the following hypothetical assumptions:

(1) trial date money earnings rate is $10,000 after age-education life cycle adjustment and work interruption adjustment;

(2) 5.5 percent is the appropriate average annual growth rate of money earnings, or earnings of $10,550 in one year, $11,130.25 in year two, etc.;

(3) post-trial loss period is 5 years;

(4) end of year cash flows; and

(5) 6.0 percent is an appropriate time value of money rate.

The present value of the decedent's post-trial money earnings when discounted at 6.0 percent is $49,296.89. Table One demonstrates that the principal amount and the earned interest are consumed in providing the decedent's expected future earnings in the time configuration that would have occurred had the decedent not encountered a premature ending of his working life.

Perhaps the logic of present value can be better explained by considering the following question: How much money must be placed today in savings accounts—an account for each year of lost earnings—in order for the decedent's beneficiaries to receive what the decedent would have earned but for a premature ending of his working life? Table Two shows that the previously determined present value amount of $49,296.89 can be distributed between the five savings accounts so that the decedent's estimated earnings are exactly replaced in the time configuration that would have occurred if not for the decedent's premature death. "The Logic of Present Value" table makes clear the present value amount or principal along with the interest earned are entirely consumed in replacing the decedent's anticipated earnings.

### Table One

| Year | Principle Beg. of Year | + | Interest Earned at 6.0% | = | Principal Before Withdrawal | less | Earnings Withdrawal | = | Principle End of Year |
|------|------|---|------|---|------|------|------|---|------|
| 1 | $49296.89 | | $2957.81 | | $52254.70 | | $10550.00 | | $41704.70 |
| 2 | 41704.70 | | 2502.28 | | 44206.99 | | 11130.25 | | 33076.74 |
| 3 | 33076.74 | | 1984.60 | | 35061.34 | | 11742.41 | | 23318.93 |
| 4 | 23318.93 | | 1399.14 | | 24718.07 | | 12388.25 | | 12329.82 |
| 5 | 12329.82 | | 739.79 | | 13069.61 | | 13069.61 | | 0 |
| | | | $9583.62 | | | | $58880.50 | | |

## Table Two

| | SAVINGS ACCOUNTS | | | | | |
| | #1 | #2 | #3 | #4 | #5 | Total |
|---|---|---|---|---|---|---|
| Principal: Year | $9952.83 | $9905.88 | $9859.15 | $9812.66 | $9766.37 | $49296.89 |
| Year 1 interest | 597.17 | 594.35 | 591.55 | 588.76 | 585.98 | 2957.81 |
| Year 2 interest | | | | | | |
| on Principal | | 594.35 | 591.55 | 588.76 | 585.98 | 2502.28 |
| on Year 1 Interest | | 35.67 | 35.49 | 35.32 | 35.16 | |
| Year 3 interest | | | | | | |
| on Principal | | | 591.55 | 588.76 | 585.98 | 1984.60 |
| on Year 1 interest | | | 35.49 | 35.32 | 35.16 | |
| on Year 2 interest | | | 35.49 | 35.32 | 35.16 | |
| on Year 1 interest | | | | | | |
| from Year 2 | | | 2.14 | 2.12 | 2.11 | |
| Year 4 interest | | | | | | |
| total | | | | 701.21 | 697.92 | 1399.13 |
| Year 5 interest | | | | | | |
| total | | | | | 739.79 | 739.79 |
| Amount Available | $10550.00 | 11130.25 | 11742.41 | 12388.23 | 13069.61 | 58880.50 |
| Earnings Withdrawal | 10550.00 | 11130.25 | 11742.41 | 12388.23 | 13069.61 | 58880.50 |
| Balance | 0 | 0 | 0 | 0 | 0 | 0 |

Present value amounts vary inversely with the discount rate or interest rate available upon appropriate investments. The interest rate to be applied to the pre-trial losses normally will not be the same as the discount rate applied to post-trial losses, the former being a short-term interest rate and the latter a longer-term rate. As such, determination of the pre-trial period present values poses no difficulties since the needed rate data is observable.

Specifications of an appropriate average annual rate of discount to be used to express post-trial losses in trial date dollars or present value is an important decision in pecuniary damage determination. Fortunately, the development of capital market theory or capital asset pricing theory during the past two decades has given a precision to the meaning of terms like "prudent investments" that was not previously possible. Also capital market theory clearly reveals one can generalize about only two prices in the capital markets, the price of time and the price of risk. Since an economist has no expertise in choosing the risk-return level or tradeoff the court and the decedent's beneficiaries deem acceptable, the default-free rate of return or the pure time value of money rate is used to convert past and future dollar estimates to present value. A useful discounting approach employs the observable default-free current yield on United States Government securities with maturities matching the issues being analyzed, along with an appropriate reinvestment rate at which interest in excess of withdrawals in early years could be reinvested.

Inflation could confound the estimation of the present value of expected future earnings were inflation not also a variable influencing the appropriate rate of discount. The discount rate and the money wage growth rate must be economically consistent. Conceptually, the discount rate can be thought of as representing the productivity of capital, while the real earnings growth rate is appropriately viewed as the productivity of labor. The theoretical relationship between the productivity of labor and capital would suggest that the real rate of interest and the growth in productivity and real wages should be comparable. Econometric evidence suggests that the real rate of interest exceeds somewhat the output per man-hour growth rate proxy of labor productivity which averages nearly 2.85 percent. Just as the nominal money wage growth rate was equal to the real productivity increase plus allowance for price level change, the relevant rate of discount is the current or nominal market rate which approximates the real rate of interest plus the inflation rate. Generalizing, economists visualize the appropriate money earnings growth rate and the appropriate discount rate to be approximately equal whether expressed on a real or nominal basis.

Without stopping to explore the underlying logic for the economic relationship between the interest rate level, change in prices, and the rate of growth of workers' money earnings, it is sufficient to state both theoretical and empirical research support that these three variables generally tend to move together in the same direction. The correlation is not perfect, but the relation between money wage growth rates and interest rates is important. For if wage growth rates and interest rates tend to move together in the same direction, then the differential rate will not vary much even during such periods of economic change as the past decade.

## Should You Hire an Economist or Not?

Expert economic testimony contributes to the presentation of wrongful death damages by providing the jury with an analytical persuasive scenario regarding the pecuniary implications of the decedent's premature death to the surviving household. Non-economists, and these jurors, experience difficulty when attempting to visualize the pecuniary potential or value of a worker, child, or housewife in the dynamic American economy. An expert economic witness can assist a court and jury in determining the economic loss sustained by a decedent's survivors by offering his objectives, mathematically correct, economically logical, and consistent appraisal for consideration.

Not all cases, or economists for that matter, are amenable to this trial technique. The preceding discussion regarding what an economist is prepared to do and how he does it suggests that the decision to utilize the expert testimony of an economist should be carefully considered.

An economist would suggest attorneys make this decision on the basis of a cost-benefit analysis. While the question is complex, the general answer can be stated simply. If the use of an economist's services increases (decreases) the expected value of the negotiated settlement or jury award substantially more than the cost of the economist's services, then the plaintiff (defense) attorney should consider using an economist. Clearly the size of economic loss in a case and the probability of a favorable judgment on liability issues are two important variables for a lawyer to consider before reaching a decision on the use of an economist.

In passing, it should be noted that the burden of establishing liability and the present value of pecuniary damages has caused plaintiff attorneys to utilize professional economists more frequently than their defense counterparts. The most effective and perhaps most economical way for a defense attorney to prepare for cross-examination of the plaintiff's economic expert is to retain the services of another experienced economist. This observation does not propose a "battle of experts". The defense economist can critically review the plaintiff economist's written report, deposition, and/or testimony and can identify possible biases in the data used, alternative sources of data on which projections could be based, unjustified omissions or inclusions of benefits and/or costs, etc. A defense attorney well versed in the subtleties and complexities of determining pecuniary damages will be able to cross-examine an economist effectively.

It should also be mentioned that the economic expert should be indifferent as to whether he is retained by the plaintiff or defense. The data needs, information requirements, and statistical methodologies employed, and thus the present value of pecuniary losses that may be associated with the decedent's premature death, are identical in either instance.

# When and When Not to Claim Punitive Damages

## Tom Riley

Tom Riley, a graduate of the University of Iowa College of Law, is a Fellow of the Iowa Academy of Trial Lawyers. He has lectured at CLE courses conducted by Association of Trial Lawyers of Iowa and Association of Trial Lawyers of America. He is the author of the book *Proving Punitive Damages: The Complete Handbook*, published in 1981 by Prentice-Hall. On April 20, 1982 he obtained the first judgment against Procter & Gamble for Toxic Shock Syndrome involving the use of Rely tampons.

*"For all manner of trespass, whether it be for ox, for ass, for sheep, for raiment or for any other manner of lost things, which another challengeth to be his, the cause of both parties shall come before the judges; and whom the judges shall condemn, he shall pay double unto his neighbor."*

*Exodus 22:9*

After Mr. Grimshaw obtained his $125 million punitive damage judgment against Ford Motor Company recently, the suggestion that there are times to forgo punitive damages may sound like legal heresy. Most assuredly, in cases involving target defendants, of which Grimshaw is the epitome, punitive damages should be sought where the evidence supports their award. But there are occasions when punitive damages are allowable and it may not be good tactics to seek them.

393

## Five Reasons For Seeking Punitive Damages

As a general rule, whenever you have a defendant who is wealthy or has a liability insurance policy with high limits (in a jurisdiction where punitive damages are collectible from the insurer),[1] the plaintiff should ordinarily seek punitive damages. Assuming conduct which allows punitive damages, the plaintiff's aggregate award of compensatory and punitive damages should be higher for several reasons:

1. The punitive damage claim is unique in that the objective does not concern itself with recompense for an injured party. The objective is the noble one of improving our society by discouraging reprehensible conduct. A substantial jury award is the means of achieving this objective and, unlike penal fines imposed by society for objectionable conduct, your client's bank account, and not the public coffers, is the happy winner.

2. Asserting a claim for punitive damages prevents the defendant's admitting liability and trying the case solely on the issue of compensatory damages in order to keep the jury from becoming incensed by the defendant's outrageous conduct. Putting it another way, the claim for punitive damages guarantees that the jury will hear of the defendant's conduct and become incensed which should have its effect on the actual damages award as well as the punitive damages award.

3. The evidence of a defendant's wealth or ability to pay is ordinarily not relevant in a damage action but is admissible where the right to punitive damages is established. Such evidence of the defendant's wealth should add to the size of what the actual damages would otherwise be, in addition to resulting in a separate award for punitive damages. This last factor applies even in the case of the obviously wealthy defendant, such as a Ford Motor Company. Chances are that the jury, while generally aware of the wealth of a large corporate defendant, may be surprised upon learning the daily (weekly, monthly, etc.) profit of such a defendant, which can only be learned in the presence of a punitive damage claim.

The plaintiff can make a very effective argument in terms of tying the punitive damage award to a day's, a week's, or a month's profit in the case of a giant corporation. For example:

"Ladies and Gentlemen, we are not asking that you destroy the defendant, or even take one brick from its billions of dollars of net worth. We are only asking that you apply the law of punitive damages to 'smart' the defendant by denying it the profits of one day (one week or one month, as the case may be), which is $10,000,000 (etc.). Leave the other 259 work days (51 weeks, 11 months) profits of X million dollars for the defendant. I submit it will take at least that much to deter and, even then, I'm not certain that only one day (week, month) will 'smart' sufficiently to ensure deterrence from similar misconduct in the future. If an ordinary citizen were guilty of this type of misconduct, wouldn't he be happy to get off with a loss of income of only one day (week or month, as the case may be)."

4. Another reason for asserting punitive damages lies with the leverage it may bring in settlement, especially in states that do not allow liability coverage for punitive damages, or in the situation where the policy does not cover them. The claim for punitive damages would then amount to an "excess judgment" exposure problem for the insurance company should the plaintiff offer to settle his compensatory damage claim within the policy limits and offer to dismiss his punitive damage claim. Should the plaintiff recover within the policy limits on his compensatory damage claim and, in addition, obtain a punitive damage award which the assured is obligated to pay, the insured may have a claim against his own insurance carrier for either negligence or bad faith in not settling within the compensatory damage limits. A pre-trial demand to settle the claim within the policy limits may provide the extra leverage to plaintiff to obtain a reasonable settlement.

5. An additional reason for seeking punitive damages is the nondischargeability of such damages in bankruptcy. Technically speaking, a judgment that is based on malicious or willful injury to persons and property is nondischargeable in bankruptcy, whether in the form of compensatory or punitive damages.[2] As a practical matter, however, the proof in bankruptcy proceedings that the judgment represents one for malicious and willful injury to personal property is made easier if the award is for punitive damages. If the plaintiff seeks only compensatory damages, the absence of a specific finding that the acts were malicious may require an examination of the whole record of the Court entering judgment to determine if the judgment is one which is nondischargeable. Where the action complained of may include elements of negligence, breach of contract or a constructive rather than actual type of fraud, the record may be muddied as to the basis for the verdict. A claim for punitive damages which is reduced to judgment in that instance should satisfy the inquiry. A year or so ago, the author obtained an $80,000 judgment for false arrest of which $45,000 represented punitive damages. The defendant promptly petitioned for bankruptcy but was chagrined to find that the punitive damage award wasn't dischargeable. Recently, the defendant compromised the judgment for punitive damages for a substantial sum after having earlier received his discharge in bankruptcy for his other debts.

## When to Confine Your Prayer to Compensatory Damages

One might conclude that punitive damages should always be sought wherever and whenever the facts render them allowable. Unfortunately, however, for the victims of malicious acts and other outrageous conduct, their perpetrators are often not wealthy and, in fact, many are downright poor and the only virtue that redeems them is their foresight to be insured. This is especially true for the victims of drunk drivers.

Where the defendant is impecunious, plaintiff's counsel should avoid the knee-jerk reaction of a punitive damage request and, instead, analyze the advisability of seeking only compensatory damages. If he determines that the defendant has insurance covering punitive damages and the jurisdiction permits insurers to pay punitive damage claims, he may decide to seek punitive damages. If the defendant's policy excludes punitive damages or the jurisdiction prohibits insurers from paying punitive damage claims, the plaintiff should think twice about seeking punitive damages. The reason in this situation is that he may win a large verdict but find most of it awarded in the form of uncollectible punitive damages. The jury may temper the award for compensatory damages, which would be totally or partially collectible in insurance, while allowing the plaintiff a great Pyrrhic victory in punitive damages. One commentator has written:

> "The theory of punitive damages (without the name) is built into the average juror's value system; the latitude permitted in calculating personal injury award is so wide that proof of defendant's outrage will enhance some verdicts without express instruction allowing punitive damages ... He may find that the insurer is not liable for punitive damages and lose part of an award that he would have gotten as compensatory damages had he not formally asked for punitive damages."[3]

Secondly, the rule that a defendant's wealth is admissible in punitive damages cases works in reverse in many jurisdictions. Proof of the defendant's poverty, thus, may be admissible.[4] Therefore, the defendant might not only succeed in holding down the noncollectible punitive damages awarded but the fact of the defendant's poverty might also diminish the collectible compensatory damage award.

Another reason for confining one's prayer to compensatory damages exists where the claim for punitive damages is borderline and there is risk of reversal if the court submits punitive damages. Counsel may decide not to risk having to retry a good compensatory damage claim because an appellate court finds that punitive damages should not have been submitted. The facts that tend to justify punitive damages will undoubtedly enhance the compensatory damage claim as Professor Morris contends. The author obtained a $498,000 verdict against Volkswagen of America for the loss of a client's leg when a four-day-old Porsche sports car overturned allegedly due to loose retaining bolts on the rack and pinion steering. What made the result interesting is that the plaintiff was a paraplegic before the accident, having had his spinal cord severed by a bullet five years earlier. What made this verdict possibly the highest ever for the loss of a numb leg was the activity of the representatives of the defendant in tightening one or both bolts while the driver and the plaintiff-passenger were lying in hospital beds. The defendant contended it was merely carrying out a recall campaign to test the tightness of the bolts. However, the unusual fact that this was done at the residence of an investigator hired by the owner's attorney to protect the car and allegedly without the claimed consent to the tightening of the bolts by either the attorney or the private investigator, undoubtedly incensed the jury and resulted in the unusually high damage award. The verdict has since been sustained by the Iowa Court of Appeals and the judgment paid. When this case had been pled by other attorneys, no punitive damages had been sought. Had they and the trial court submitted punitive damages to the jury, a punitive damage award would probably have been rendered based upon the alleged "tampering" with the evidence. However, the conduct of the defendant in tightening the bolts did not cause the accident and, since there was a legitimate recall campaign in progress, rather than one that was contrived, the question of submission of punitive damages was not clear-cut and could have engendered error. As suggested earlier in this article, the plaintiff in the Volkswagen case undoubtedly obtained some punitive damages in the form of compensatory damages without the risk of error by their inclusion.

## Beware of the Reasonable Relationship Rule

Another problem that can be created when a punitive damage award is extremely high is the rule in most jurisdictions that the amount of punitive damages bear a reasonable relationship to the actual damages. This rule has been rightfully criticized because it is in conflict with the objective of punitive damages which is to deter. Limiting the amount of punitive damages to a reasonable ratio to actual damages may result in the punitive damage award falling far short of what it is necessary to "smart" and, therefore, to deter. Nevertheless, the reasonable relationship rule has survived. A better rule would be to relate the punitive damage award both to the outrageous nature of the misconduct and the wealth of the defendant. A $125 million punitive damage verdict against Ford Motor Company in the Pinto case would have no trouble standing judicial scrutiny under such a proposed rule. However, until such an enlightened view replaces the "reasonable relationship" rule, the addition of punitive damages adds an extra risk of reversible error—one that many attorneys may be willing to take, especially where the risk is only of *remittitur* versus a new trial. The author's state, Iowa, is unique in refusing to remit an excessive punitive damage award. It adopts an all or nothing stance. Other states will remit an excessive verdict and only set it aside in its entirety if it appears to be the result of passion and prejudice.

### Special Factors to Consider

From a tax standpoint, the IRS exempts punitive damages for personal injuries from the federal income tax.[5] Damages for fraud are not exempt. A suit with elements of both personal injuries and property damage where fraud is one of several theories submitted to the jury might incur income tax liability on a punitive damage judgment. In that situation, plaintiff's counsel might decide to let the jury vent its outrage on non-taxable compensatory damages.

Respecting multiple disaster cases, where one act has damaged many persons and there have been previous awards to these other persons based on the identical act of misconduct, the question arises whether the defendant will be permitted in your action to show these other punitive damage verdicts in order to establish that it has been sufficiently "smarted". Of course, the defendant may not wish to do so and, instead, deny liability.

Presently, the rule would seem to exclude evidence introduced by the defendant of punitive damage awards against it in other litigation based on the identical act of misconduct, the rationale being that the punitive damage claim belongs to the individual plaintiff and should not be lost or diminished by awards in cases involving other plaintiffs. However, considering each case in a vacuum flies in the face of the logic behind the imposition of punitive damages, which is to deter a defendant and others from similar misconduct. The purpose is not to reward the plaintiff or create a windfall, rather that it is a consequence of the imposition of the "smart" damages. Therefore, the author predicts that the courts will ultimately permit evidence of punitive damage awards in multiple disaster cases if offered by the defendant (but not if offered by the plaintiff since its only effect in that situation would be to create an inference of liability).

The justification will be to aid the jury in determining whether an additional punitive damage award is indicated and, if so, the extent thereof. If and when the courts permit the introduction of such evidence, plaintiff's counsel will have to decide whether to omit a claim for punitive damages and trust that the evidence of the defendant's misconduct will enhance the compensatory damage award or, on the other hand, maintain a prayer for punitive damages in the case and hope the jury believes that the defendant needs additional "smarting."

Assume counsel has concluded that a punitive damage award is uncollectible because of lack of financial responsibilty, either in the form of the defendant's personal wealth or insurance. He decides to omit punitive damages with the expectation that the jury will award a more substantial compensatory damage judgment. But, if he does so, the defendant may admit liability in order to keep out the inflammatory evidence of misconduct that would incense a jury. In that case, plaintiff should consider seeking a nominal award for punitive damages or withdraw the punitive damage claim at the close of all the evidence. Keeping a small punitive damage claim in the case can permit plaintiff to argue that his client doesn't want a windfall but only damages to compensate him for his loss. Presumably, such a posture to the jury should result in additional damages being awarded for compensatory damages that would otherwise go in the form of punitive damages.

## Notes

1. See Anno. 20 ALR 3d 343 and 25 Fed. Ins. Counsel 309 (1975) for partial list of cases involving insurability for punitive damages.

2. U.S.C. §35(a)(8) (1970)

3. Morris *Punitive Damages in Personal Injury Cases,* 21 Ohio S.L.J. 216, 226–227 (1960).

4. *Hall v. Montgomery Ward & Co.,* 252 N.W. 2d 421 (Iowa 1977).

5. Revenue Ruling 75-45-1975-1, C.B. 47.

# Chapter Eight

# How to Use Demonstrative Evidence in the Courtroom

Research studies show that we tend to believe and to remember best what we can actually see with our eyes. That's why a picture is worth a thousand words, and why one good piece of demonstrative evidence is worth hours of ordinary oral testimony.

In this chapter, four leading practitioners share with you their favorite strategies for developing and presenting demonstrative evidence in court. For starters, George A. LaMarca explains 12 simple yet effective ways to enhance the impact of your demonstrative evidence and its acceptance by the jury. Here in a nutshell is your complete guide to the courtroom use of physical evidence, covering everything from how to handle the exhibits in the presence of the jurors, to specific pointers on displaying pictures, charts, free-standing objects, and more.

"Keep in mind," attorney Susan E. Loggans writes, "that demonstrative evidence can be used at all stages of trial." For your opening statement, the testimony-taking stage, and your final argument, Ms. Loggans describes a variety of techniques to get your message across to the jurors by *showing* them, not simply telling them, the facts. She provides a hypothetical personal injury case, illustrating how liability can be proven conclusively—and quite vividly—with the aid of accident wreckage, photographs, recordings, and other physical items.

You will see how to handle the foundation testimony necessary to get your exhibits admitted into evidence ... why models and diagrams are sometimes more effective in court than the original objects they represent ... and how to avoid the potentially disastrous pitfall of conducting an in-court experiment that fails just at the crucial moment.

Not only is demonstrative evidence essential in proving liability, it is also your key to proving damages, according to William P. Wimberley. Indeed, what better way to convince the jurors that your client is entitled to a substantial award than to show them the physical evidence that speaks so poignantly of injury and suffering? Mr. Wimberley explains how to make the most advantageous use of X-rays, models, and medical appliances in court. He also includes tips for turning certain everyday items such as blackboards, cardboard sheets, and even butcher paper into impressive demonstrative aids. And when the time comes to talk damage sums, you will see how to hold the jurors' attention as you visually engrave your dollar figures in their minds.

One visual tool that is becoming increasingly important in the trial of personal injury cases is motion pictures. "It is your best and most compelling witness," writes Solomon L. Margolis, who concludes this chapter with a step-by-step approach to making a quality film, getting it admitted into evidence, and presenting it at trial in a way that hits the jury dead center.

To demonstrate how these ideas work in actual practice, Mr. Margolis reveals the complete outline of the brief day-in-the-life film that helped him recover a $6.5 million award for his client in a spinal cord injury case. "The jury was visibly moved and was in tears when the lights went on at the conclusion of the film," observes Mr. Margolis. "The picture had been worth its weight in gold."

# Courtroom Use of Demonstrative Evidence

## George A. LaMarca

George A. LaMarca is a partner in the West Des Moines, Iowa, law firm of Williams, LaMarca, Maracci & Wiggins, P.C. He received the J.D. Degree from Drake University. He is a member of the Association of Trial Lawyers of America and of the Iowa and Illinois Associations of Trial Lawyers. He is a Fellow of the Iowa Academy of Trial Lawyers and a member of the Board of Governors of the Association of Trial Lawyers of Iowa. Mr. LaMarca is past Trials Editor of *The Iowa Trial Lawyer*.

Demonstrative evidence (real evidence) is evidence that is addressed directly to the senses of the court or the jury without interposing the testimony of witnesses (except for its foundation). Essentially, demonstrative evidence is a tangible object or thing which in itself is a nonverbal demonstration or illustration of a relevant fact. In other words, it speaks for itself.

Demonstrative evidence includes objects or articles produced at trial and exhibited to the court and the jury, such as: photographs, x-rays, motion pictures, diagrams, drawings, models, comparisons of writings, fingerprints, palmprints and footprints, the exhibition of one's person or body, and experiments, demonstrations, or tests conducted either in court or out of court with their results or conclusions present in court.

### Why and When to Use Demonstrative Evidence

There are three reasons for using demonstrative evidence as a part of your case. First, demonstrative evidence may be used to describe or explain ideas that are difficult or virtually impossible to verbalize. A picture, you have heard, is worth a thousand words. Second, jurors tend to remember what they see longer than what they hear. Of course, visual testimony and verbal testimony on the same point of fact can mutually reinforce each other so as to produce the evidence best remembered. Third, demonstrative evidence tends to make the trial less boring for the jury.

Generally, when a fact in issue is sought to be established by demonstrative evidence, it is proper to educate the jury by producing either the object or a different but representative object. However, rules governing the admissibility of actual samples or pieces of the disputed whole are more restrictive.

Foundation testimony for the admissibility of a sample must establish (to the court's satisfaction) all of the following: (1) proper identification as to source; (2) similitude to the condition of the entire substance at time involved; and (3) that it is a fair representation of the whole.

Alteration of the sample does not necessarily prevent its admissibility when the alteration does not obliterate or change the condition sought to be shown. For example, in an action against a silo contractor, a sample that a farmer testified to be representative of soiled silage was admissible even though there had been a change in color, which was explained to the jury.

Demonstrative evidence must be of self-explanatory value to a relevant issue. Its explanatory value must be of such instructive importance that its use outweights any prejudicial value of such evidence. The explanatory value of demonstrative evidence is within the discretion of the trial court, as the soiled silage example illustrates.

When a fact in issue may be explained by the production of an article or object to which the testimony relates, it is always proper to bring that article or object into court and exhibit it to the jury. This also applies when the condition (not the existence) of the object or article is in controversy. Additionally, in a suit for personal injury, it is admissible to exhibit to the jury the actual injury or physical impairment to show the condition or limitation thereof, and such a demonstration will not be considered as creating passion and prejudice.

## How to Select Demonstrative Evidence

Selection of an object to aid, illustrate, explain, or itself testify requires planning and imagination. The trial lawyer's choice of demonstrative evidence must be both practical (for courtroom use) and persuasive.

Whereas demonstrative evidence "speaks for itself," most items need the explanation of a witness to tell the jury the role that the item (whether model or actual) played in the factual pattern of the issues sought to be resolved. Thus, the selection of the best and proper witness must be taken into account when deciding to use such evidence.

Ordinarily, the witness whose testimony is non-verbally demonstrated (aided, clarified, or assisted) is the same witness (or the best witness) who will provide the necessary foundation for the admissibility of the particular exhibit. However, the persuasive trial lawyer will not stop there. Expert testimony to the technical accuracy (dimension, color, texture, size, structural composition, etc.) of a particular thing is often necessary to add further probative quality and dimension to lay witnesses' identification and confirmation of the particular object. A combination of lay and expert testimony is advisable (and sometimes necessary) to provide the foundation for some exhibits, such as: accident scene, property boundaries, irregularities in terrain, samples, and finger-, palm-, and footprints.

Whenever it is necessary to show the condition or quality of a certain object or substance, the object or substance itself is the most persuasive evidence that can be produced. This type of evidence should be introduced together with supplemental testimony of witnesses (lay or expert).

Whenever demonstrative evidence may clarify a fact sought to be proved, it should be used.

### 12 Ways to Enhance the Impact of Your Evidence in the Courtroom

The trial lawyer gives persuasive impact, evidential quality, and relative importance to demonstrative evidence by the way he treats these items in the courtroom. The jury will give no greater significance or gravity to physical evidence than is warranted by the lawyer's own treatment or presentation of these objects in their presence.

I have discovered that observance of the following courtroom techniques will enhance both the importance and juror acceptance of physical evidence.

1. Have the evidence readily accessible but well concealed before its actual use.
2. It should be clean, and in an unmarked and undamaged condition.
3. A physical exhibit should be complete for all that it is intended to depict.
4. Single-item paper exhibits or photographs should be enclosed in clear plastic binders and blocked or framed for rigidity and ease of handling.

5. If paper exhibits (such as medical records or a series of invoices) are voluminous they should be bound in notebook form, properly indexed, numbered, and sequentially placed with reference or locater tabs to facilitate witness or juror examination.
6. The exhibit should be well packaged in an appropriate enclosure (e.g., objects are more impressive when they come out of a carrying case or a zippered cover rather than a grocer bag).
7. Handle the exhibit with dignity and utmost care in the presence of jurors.
8. Place or locate free-standing objects at a prearranged place where all jurors can have easy and complete visual access.
9. Plan in advance to have available necessary stands or supports.
10. If an object is not to be used in evidence, it should not be permitted to remain in the view of the jury. If you suspect your opponent may exhibit objects or articles not to be received in evidence, a motion *in limine* should be obtained. Such a motion is also the best way to decide any disputed matters of admissibility; that is, proper foundation, relevance, explanatory value, or probative vs. prejudicial value.
11. The contents of voluminous writings, recordings, or photographs that cannot conveniently be examined in court should always be presented in the form of a chart, summary, or calculation. (See Federal Rules of Evidence, Rule 1006.)
12. Have a pre-trial run in the same courtroom to someone seated in the jury box in order to detect problems in seeing, hearing, or understanding the demonstrative article or object.

In summary, the use of demonstrative evidence requires careful pre-trial planning if it is to be of persuasive probative value. Failure to carefully plan the pre-trial selection, courtroom handling, and juror presentation can turn demonstrative evidence into a hindrance to the attorney who indiscriminately presents such evidence.

# How to Use Demonstrative Evidence to Prove Liability

## Susan E. Loggans

Susan E. Loggans, of Chicago, Illinois, graduated from DePaul University College of Law in 1974; is Chairman of the Aviation Law Section of the Association of Trial Lawyers of America, and former Chairman of the Aviation Law Section of the Chicago Bar Association.

The term, "demonstrative evidence," has sometimes been used as a generic label for all tangible items used at trial. This label is misleading; often an item is used to illustrate, summarize, or explain testimony or other evidence, but is *not admitted as evidence itself.* In fact, some jurisdictions severely limit the admissibility of all demonstrative evidence to illustrative purposes[1] or refuse to recognize such evidence as having any independent evidentiary value.[2]

Although the effectiveness of the demonstrative item in presenting one's case may be no greater when admitted into evidence than when not, formal admission may be preferred when counsel wishes the exhibit to go to the jury room,[3] or when the exhibit is crucial to a reviewing court because its evidentiary value is substantially important to the case and is not present in other evidence.

Trial counsel should be aware of the distinctions between evidence that is formally admitted and that which is not. Frequently, a piece of demonstrative evidence that has been denied admission can be used for illustrative purposes only, and thereby serves its purpose under another guise.

A juror will remember the facts better if they are presented both visually and verbally. Keep in mind that demonstrative evidence can be used at all stages of trial.

### How to Use Demonstrative Evidence During the Opening Statement

The first opportunity to use demonstrative evidence is the opening statement. Before deciding whether to give the jury its first view of such evidence now, weigh the advantages versus the disadvantages. Since most lawyers feel that the liability portion of a case may be won or lost during opening statement, it is here that technical aspects of the case are first discussed; demonstrative evidence may be essential for the jury's understanding of these aspects. The balancing disadvantages of using demonstrative evidence at this stage are loss of the evidence's dramatic effect at a later point in the trial, and the opportunity provided opposing counsel to prepare a later objection to such evidence.

The procedure for introducing demonstrative evidence during opening statement is simple. Nothing need be said to the court or opposing counsel; nor do you have to lay any type of foundation. If an objection is made, a promise to provide foundation testimony later should suffice.

If the demonstrative object is very large, it may be better to bring it into the courtroom before opening statement begins. This avoids having to stop the statement in order to bring the evidence in. But the evidence can be very distracting unless it is kept covered or pushed out of sight. A photograph or diagram of the original may be used at this point to avoid these strategic problems, with the original brought in later. If the demonstrative evidence is small enough to be handled easily during opening statement, it should be kept from the jury's view until the appropriate time, then placed or held before the jury by counsel.

### Demonstrative Evidence in Action

The following hypothetical case will help explain how various items of demonstrative evidence, both real and illustrative, can and should be used during the testimony-taking phase of a trial:

**Facts:** *Icharus v. Albatros Aircraft and the Stick-E Corporation*

On a summer day, plaintiff, enroute from Sundance to Sun City aboard his Sunbird aircraft, suddenly fell from the sky and crashed into the desert below. Plaintiff, Icharus, sustained serious injuries.

The National Transportation Safety Board (NTSB) report revealed that just prior to the accident the pilot, Icharus, radioed the control tower that a liquid substance was dripping from a point beneath the wing assembly's connection with the fuselage. Shortly afterward, the pilot reported that the wing had torn loose and the aircraft was plummeting out of control. A recording of these statements was recovered from the cockpit voice recorder.

Further investigation showed that the wing had been connected to the fuselage by a revolutionary new wax-based adhesive substance. Our theory, as plaintiff's attorney, is that the wax used to secure the wing to the fuselage was defective because it melted under the increased ultraviolet radiation from the sun at high altitudes.

Defendants in the case are the manufacturer of the aircraft, Albatros Aircraft, and the manufacturer of the wax adhesive, the Stick-E Corporation.

At trial, the following items of a demonstrative nature will be used:

a. the wreckage of the accident aircraft wing assembly;
b. a duplicate or model of the wing assembly;
c. a diagram of the wing assembly;
d. photographs taken after the accident;
e. ultraviolet lamp (sun lamp) and model or duplicate of wing assembly for in-court experiment;
f. the cockpit voice recording of pilot's statements prior to the crash.

## How to Handle the Foundation Testimony

Any item that was itself involved in the incident, such as the wreckage of the accident aircraft, is potentially useful as real or original demonstrative evidence. Such tangible objects that have played an active role in the controversy are in contrast to ordinary demonstrative evidence such as diagrams, models, or photographs, which have themselves played no part in the history of the case, but are tendered instead for the purpose of illustration or clarification.

To be used in court for any purpose, the wreckage must, of course, be relevant or probative of some fact in issue. In this case, the fact that a crash occurred is uncontroverted. Opposing counsel could attempt to block its usage by asserting that the only thing shown by the mangled mess is that an accident occurred, which is undisputed. However, the damaged wing assembly may be used for *several other purposes*. For instance, as evidence of causation, i.e., to show that the wing snapped from the fuselage because the wax adhesive did not hold, a fact likely to be in issue; to show the wing had separated in-flight and not on impact (through the damage pattern); or that the aircraft was incapable of sustaining flight once the wing detached.

To be admitted in evidence on this issue, counsel must initially prove that the wreckage is, in fact, that of the accident aircraft; and secondly, that its condition is substantially unchanged from that at the time of the accident.[4]

Since the parts of the aircraft impacted with the ground after separation, it may be difficult to prove that the wing assembly is in the same condition as it was at the time it separated. However, a reconstruction expert can testify that the crash did not affect those parts of the wing assembly relevant to the issue of causation,[5] nor did any effect destroy its ability to supply some information on the point.

The foundation testimony necessary to use anything as demonstrative evidence is simple and logical. The question to be put to a witness whose testimony you seek to support with demonstrative evidence is, "Would the use of this object assist you in clearly and accurately supplying your testimony to the jury?" An affirmative answer places the use of the proposed demonstrative evidence within the discretion of the trial judge. Some judges require it be shown that the thing is reasonably accurate and not misleading. This question can also be asked of the witness.

## Using Duplicates or Models

If the original wing assembly is not available or cannot be used, it is possible that a duplicate or model may be substituted. In a design defect case, as opposed to a manufacturing defect case, the generic characteristics common to all such assemblies are at issue, and often the original product is less desirable because it distracts the jury.

By way of foundation, it must be shown that the duplicate is substantially similar in all material respects to the original. This is usually proven by the model maker. It need not be identical.[6]

Alternately, if a duplicate is unavailable, or its use in the courtroom is awkward or impractical, a model of the wing assembly could be used in its place. As is true of all demonstrative evidence, the admissibility of a model is predicated upon competent testimony that it is a substantially accurate representation of the original.[7] If there are inaccuracies or significant variations in scale which render the model misleading, the court may reject it.[8] Any inaccuracies should be pointed out and explained during direct examination so as not to alienate the jury and also to present a fair, and therefore a more favorable, position for its admission to the judge.[9]

The advantage of a model over a duplicate or the actual wing assembly for illustrative purposes is that the relevant parts can be made so that they are easily removed, thus facilitating their exhibition to the jury. In addition, the model can be made small or "cutouts" can be made so that it can be handled more easily by the witnesses or jury. The jury should also be provided with an opportunity to see it without distraction.

### Why Diagrams are Often Preferable to the Real Thing

A diagram of the wing assembly can be an effective visual aid during opening and closing argument or in providing a graphic representation of an expert witness's testimony. Often diagrams are preferable to the real thing simply because they are much easier to handle. Diagrams can be prepared outside of court. It is unimportant who creates them. If opposing counsel has produced the diagram, it is likely he will stipulate as to its accuracy. If not, the witness aided by the diagram can testify as to its accuracy. He need not have prepared it. A witness may also be asked to draw a diagram while on the stand.

Obvious advantages of diagrams are reduced expense and physical ease of use. Another consideration is the negative effect a model can have on the jury. In a smaller case, for example, the impression that the plaintiff or his lawyer can afford expensive models should be avoided.

If several witnesses are to testify about similar facts or issues, it must be decided whether the same diagram should be used. If the testimony of several witnesses is likely to be consistent, the same diagram can be used for all witnesses, and each witness "adds" any additional information to it. However, by way of example, if each witness is marking the scene of the crash with an "x" and the witnesses do not agree, any inconsistency will be made obvious by the use of only one diagram. By use of separate diagrams, contradictions or variances are avoided.

What is true of models is also true of diagrams or sketches: they need not be perfectly accurate representations as long as a witness vouches for their substantial fidelity and explains major discrepancies to the jury.[10] It should be noted that one advantage of a diagram produced on paper is that it may, if admitted in evidence, be preserved as part of the record at the discretion of the court, or it may be taken to the jury room for inspection. A chalk drawing on a blackboard, however, will simply be erased.[11] Wreckage and other similar physically large items of evidence are very difficult to handle during the trial and appeal process. Some courts made the distinction that if the diagram (particularly a map) is to scale, it is admissible and therefore goes to the jury room.

## Telling Your Story With Photographs

The foundation question for admission of a photograph into evidence is similar: "Does this photo clearly and accurately depict the _____ as it existed on the day of the occurrence?" A photograph is extremely helpful to the testimony of a reconstructive expert and allows the jury to see exactly what facts about the airplane post-crash position led the expert to his conclusion.

A recent development in photographs is computer-created photographs. A computer can be given all of the variables in an accident sequence; for instance aircraft speed, altitude, and distance from a certain object. By analyzing an existing photograph with all those variables known, a computer can create a second photograph with one or more of the variables changed to show what the pilot would have seen had his airspeed or altitude been different.

## How to Conduct In-Court and Out-of-Court Experiments

A strong caveat must be given with reference to all experiments, more strongly to in-court experiments than out-of-court experiments. If the experiment fails or does not duplicate the result expected, the impact can be devastating. Since most states allow broad pre-trial discovery, the results of a failed out-of-court experiment may some day be disclosed to the opponent, creating a powerful weapon for cross-examination of that expert at trial.

One method of circumventing the danger of out-of-court experiments is to have them initially performed by an expert who is merely a consultant and who will never testify at trial. The chances are good that the opposition will never discover the experiments. When the experiment is perfected, the testifying expert can then repeat it. An in-court experiment should never be done unless it is certain that it will succeed.

In the case here, in order to prove the contention that the wing fell off as a result of the melting of the wax adhesive upon exposure to increased levels of ultraviolet radiation at high altitudes, an out-of-court experiment could be performed. A video tape of the experiment could also be made and shown in court. These experiments need not be attended by opposing counsel or meet any other "bipartisan" requirements, as long as the necessary foundation of similarity is laid at trial.

Black and white film may be preferable since it is the most dramtic and makes detail more distinguishable. A variety of angles of the experiment should be filmed so that the trier of fact can see the progressive effect of the heat on the wing assembly as the wax begins to drip. The film should be slowed and the camera should zoom in on the source of the dripping. A narrator can explain each stage of the experiment and what is occurring.

The greatest hurdle in the path of in-court experiments is the requirement that the conditions under which the experiment is performed be similar in all material respects to the conditions existing at the time of the incident.[12] The key word is "material" and as long as the "material" conditions are similar, the experiment should be allowed.

In the particular experiment proposed here, the expert will testify that either a duplicate or scale model of the wing assembly and fuselage was made with materials identical to those of which the subject aircraft was made, that the wing assembly is attached to the fuselage with the same adhesive and in the same fashion as the original aircraft, and that the same level of ultraviolet radiation is produced as existed during the ill-fated flight of "Sunbird."

Such similarity of conditions would appear sufficient to allay objection. However, the experiment will take approximately 2½ hours before any result can be expected, and for this reason the experiment may well be excluded as excessively time-consuming.[13] This problem can be solved by time-lapse photography of the experiment out of court, having an expert testify as to reported results only; or still photographs of key points.

## Tape Recordings or Transcripts?

The recording of the pilot's statements would provide direct evidence of events immediately preceding the accident. If this recording is attested to by an expert as an accurate reproduction of the conversation or the recording methods, or if otherwise verified, it should be admitted. A "chain of custody" witness can establish that the tape has not been altered since originally secured.

Like the wreckage of the aircraft, this tape recording is "real" demonstrative evidence in that it was itself involved in the accident. If admitted, it may be played to the jury. In an aircraft case, for example, the pilot might call the control tower to report, "My left engine is running rough, I'm gonna shut it down," and later an investigation reveals that it was, in fact, the right engine with problems so that when the pilot mistakenly shut down the left, he shut down his only good engine.

As an alternative to playing the recording in court, a "read-out" or typed transcript of the recorded statements can be made. This avoids any objection to the recording's admissibility on the grounds that parts of the tape are too garbled to be understood in open court. Since any drama of voice intonations is lost by the use of a transcript, the recording itself is perferable *if* the drama is desired.

### Demonstrative Evidence During Closing Argument

All of the demonstrative evidence used during the trial will have been marked with an exhibit number. When the evidence is only demonstrative, its number will be followed with the notation, "for I.D. (identification)," such as "plaintiff's exhibit #2 for I.D." If the item is accepted into evidence, the I.D. notation is stricken and it remains "plaintiff's exhibit #2." In this way, there is a record of every tangible item when used at trial. In some jurisdictions, the custom is to permit items in evidence to go with the jury to the jury room when they retire to deliberate. In those jurisdictions, demonstrative evidence not formally introduced is usually excluded from the jury room.

The end of witness testimony, however, should not be the end of use of demonstrative evidence. If it was important during witness testimony, then it may be even more important during closing argument, where such testimony is reviewed. In most jurisdictions, all demonstrative evidence used earlier in the trial can be used during closing argument. More importantly, you may be able to use *new* demonstrative evidence during closing argument.

Just as many trial lawyers believe liability is either won or lost during opening statement, they also believe that damages are either won or lost in closing argument. The damages portion of the close in all but the lightest cases will occupy most of the time. This is the time when summarizing, conceptualizing and simplifying occur, and therefore, the use of charts that utilize and organize is beneficial. Computation and listing of each element of damage, such as medical expenses, pain and suffering, etc., can be made on a large poster in front of the jury. These charts should also be marked and are preserved as part of the record.

Special interrogatories to the jury, i.e., special verdicts or findings often confusing and difficult to explain during close, can be handled in a novel but exciting way. The position can be written on a large white poster board, exactly as it will be given to the jury, including a space for a yes or no vote. A large "x" at the appropriate answer is a visual reminder which should insure against a possible mistake.

When the jury retires to deliberate, the court in many jurisdictions will inquire which items of demonstrative evidence counsel wants taken to the jury room. The ruling is discretionary and many courts frown upon purely demonstrative evidence going to the jury room. Only those items which are really favorable should be submitted. Foisting unnecessary or confusing evidence upon the jury in the form of superfluous demonstrative evidence should be avoided.

## Notes

1. McCormick, id., at S212 n.33

2. 9 A.L.R.2d 1044; McCormick, Evidence, S213 n.39

3. Id. at S217

4. 95 A.L.R.2d 681

5. E.g., in an action brought against a soft drink retailer and bottler for injuries sustained when plaintiff consumed part of the contents of a soft drink bottle containing a cigarette, the admission of the same was proper even though two years had elapsed between the incident and the trial, in view of testimony explaining to the jury the changes that had taken place in the contents of the bottle. *Pulley v. Pacific Coca-Cola Bottling Co.*, 415 P.2d 636 (1966).

6. E.g., where expert testified that an oxygen tent, offered in evidence by defendant hospital in a personal injury action for burns sustained from flash fire, was "substantially like" the tent he observed at the scene shortly after the fire, admission of the tent was proper. *Watson v. Elbertson-Elbert City Hosp. Auth.* 186 S.E.2d 459 (1971).

7. 7 Proof of Facts 611, Proof No. 2

8. E.g., in a products liability action, scale models of wire container load lifted by plaintiff forklift driver at time of accident were properly excluded in that the models were less than true representations of the interlocked wire baskets which comprised the actual load and evidence was cumulative. *Christopherson v. Hyster Co.* 374 N.E.2d 858 (1978).

9. 69 A.L.R.2d 424, 429.

10. E.g., map of intersection in automobile collision case, although inaccurate in certain details, was properly admitted since the inaccuracies were fully explained to the jury, plaintiff admitted that the map was illustrative only, and plaintiff was subject to cross examination thereon. *Miss. Road Supply Co. v. Baker* 199 So. 2d (1967).

11. One technique of preserving the chalk drawing is to take photographs. 3 Am. Jur. Trials 288.

12. E.g., where courtroom conditions were unlike those at home of plaintiff who was allegedly burned as a result of flash fire caused by flammable fumes from fingernail polish, court did not err in refusing to permit plaintiff's expert to conduct test of same in courtroom. *Whitehurst v. Revlon, Inc.* 307 F Supp 918 (1969). In another case, the court did not abuse its discretion by refusing to allow a courtroom demonstration of the operation of a slot machine where, in an action for injuries allegedly caused when employee of casino opened slot machine which struck plaintiff's hand, the spacing between the two machines in court did not simulate the actual positions of the machines at the time of the accident. *Way v. Hayes,* 513 P.2d 1222 (1973).

13. 3 Am. Jr. Trials 431; 8 Proof of Facts 173, Proof No. 2.

# How to Use Demonstrative Evidence to Prove Damages

## William P. Wimberley and Chris N. Brumfield

William P. Wimberley is a partner in the Spokane, Washington, law firm of Richter, Wimberley & Ericson, P.S. He is past President of the Washington State Trial Lawyers Association, and a Fellow of the Inner Circle of Advocates and the International Academy of Trial Lawyers.

Chris N. Brumfield graduated with honors from Gonzaga University School of Law in 1982. He is an associated with the law firm of Clausen & Brown in Spokane, Washington. He is a member of the Washington State Bar, American Bar Association, Washington State Trial Lawyers Association and the Association of Trial Lawyers of America.

Demonstrative evidence is a powerful tool available to the trial attorney in proving damages sustained by his client. Unfortunately, many trial attorneys still fail to see the immense value of demonstrative evidence and use it rather sparingly.

### X-rays: Negative and Positive

X-rays should be used by the doctor during his oral testimony to assist him in his explanation of the nature and extent of the traumatic injuries sustained by the plaintiff, especially a serious injury which has little or no superficial evidence. The X-ray can also be used in illustrating a diseased condition of the body to the jury.

Attorneys too often do not take advantage of the use of a positive X-ray. A negative X-ray can be made into a positive X-ray for approximately $10.00. A positive X-ray is beneficial because it is actually a photograph. A positive X-ray will show whatever type of injury appeared on the negative X-ray, but the positive one will be a better illustration of it. The positive X-ray can be used without the "shadow" box required to view a negative X-ray.

### Making the Best Use of Models During Trial

When models are used during trial it is essential that the attorney establish the qualifications of the person who prepared the model and the method used to prepare the model.

The most valuable models for the attorney in proving damages are the medical models. Medical supply houses can provide skeletal, organ, nervous system or vascular models. Most college science departments also have many anatomy models available for use by the attorney. Since the majority of people making up a jury will be uninformed about the basic human anatomy, the attorney should make use of medical models whenever possible. For a medical model to serve its maximum purpose it should, like the x-ray, be introduced by a doctor during his oral testimony to assist him in explaining the plaintiff's medical problems to the jury.

One source of medical information often forgotten by the attorney is medical textbooks. These textbooks contain illustrations, cross-section views and diagrams which often prove valuable if used during the oral testimony of a doctor. The pages from the medical textbooks can be either photographically reproduced or shown via an overhead projector. This type of medical demonstrative evidence can be beneficial to the attorney who does not have a medical model available for use during a trial.

### Demonstrations, Experiments and Exhibitions

Demonstrations before the jury of the use of traction devices, head halters, cervical collars, back braces or artifical limbs can be invaluable in illustrating to the jury the awkwardness and discomfort involved in their use. The demonstration of these devices by a witness is usually permitted, and is usually the most effective method.

Experiments are another useful demonstrative evidence tool for proving damages which is often ignored by the attorney. For example, if the plaintiff has sustained brain damage, the attorney can have the testifying doctor talk with the plaintiff to illustrate to the jury the extent of the brain damage. Another method would be to have the testifying doctor conduct an experiment with the plaintiff to show what the plaintiff can or cannot do. Having the injured plaintiff attempt to perform actions or submit to manipulations of a testifying doctor is frequently allowed and can be invaluable in illustrating the extent of the plaintiff's injury to the jury. The caveat in this area is that the experiment must contribute to the knowledge of the jury regarding the subject matter in dispute.

Every attorney is aware of the value that the displaying of the plaintiff's wound or physical injury has towards proving damages. A simple viewing of the plaintiff's injury will often have a greater impact on the jury than all the oral testimony regarding the seriousness of his condition. Remember, a trial court is rarely reversed for permitting the exhibition of the plaintiff's wound or physical injury.

### Grabbing the Jury's Attention with Photographs and Movies

All types of photographs are used during trial. Their value in proving damages is undeniable. Photographs are excellent to preserve the severity of an injury. This is especially helpful when the plaintiff has sustained an injury in which the superficial evidence of the injury tends to dissipate in a relatively short time (i.e., black eyes, burns, etc.). Photographs can be used to portray the horror of injuries such as deformed or amputated limbs or the pain and suffering which accompanies a skin graft. The attorney can also use photographs to replace the necessity of the jury's viewing the plaintiff if the plaintiff is unable to be in the courtroom.

Remember that photos can be enlarged. A photo can be englarged to three feet by four feet for approximately $15.00. A photo this large can be kept in view of the jury during an entire trial. The attorney will be able to continually refer to it and, if appropriate, can make the photograph the theme of his case.

Movies are another demonstrative evidence tool which few lawyers take advantage of to assist them in proving damages. An excellent use of a movie in trial is the so-called "day in the life of" type. This type of movie can be used to show the jury the limitations on every day activities the plaintiff has suffered as a result of the injuries sustained. A movie of this type is especially valuable when the attorney is working with a paraplegic case. For obvious economical reasons this type of movie should only be used in a case with a potentially large jury verdict. Another valuable use of movies is to illustrate to the jury the severity of the surgical procedure the plaintiff had or will have to go through. Movies of surgical procedures are available through local hospitals, medical schools or some prosthetic device sales companies. If the attorney is able to get the Court to admit a movie of a surgery, it can help immensely in proving the severity of the plaintiff's injury which mere oral testimony would be unable to adequately describe.

## How to Spotlight Hospital and Medical Records

Records from the plaintiff's hospital are excellent tools in front of a jury. They are not costly to use and are capable of keeping the jury interested while the attorney makes a point regarding the plaintiff's damages. One note of caution about the use of the plaintiff's hospital records, often the records will contain damaging entries in them pertaining to the plaintiff; therefore, the attorney should carefully read the entire hospital record before trial to ascertain if there are any damaging comments which should be omitted.

Another part of the plaintiff's medical records which should not be overlooked are the nurse's notes and the doctor's prescriptions. Both of these records are excellent for proving the pain and suffering of the plaintiff. The nurse's notes will contain entries regarding the plaintiff's condition and complaints of pain during each day. The doctor's prescriptions can be used to show the type and strength of the drug the plaintiff is having to use to obtain relief from the pain resulting from his injury.

## Easy and Economical Demonstrative Aids

There are many devices which can be used in conjunction with demonstrative evidence. Discussed below are a few of the easiest and most economical to use.

The overhead projector is a helpful device to the attorney. The overhead projector allows the attorney to enlarge a photo or drawing onto a screen. It is useful in increasing the jury's understanding of the subject matter and in persuading the jury. Another positive aspect of the overhead projector is that it can be used with the courtroom lights left on. In this same area the attorney should not forget about possibly using an opaque projector.

The attorney should take advantage of any opportunity during trial to make use of a blackboard in describing something to the jury, especially when defining terms or performing arithmetic calculations.

Butcher paper is another type of demonstrative evidence which is inexpensive to use. A positive aspect that the use of butcher paper has over a blackboard is that the defense attorney cannot erase it. If possible, the attorney should have the butcher paper marked as an exhibit so the jury can take it into the deliberation room with them. An example of the use of butcher paper is when a doctor is testifying to the elements of a certain type of infection. The attorney can place the butcher paper on the wall and have the doctor write down each element of a diagnosis for this infection. Entries from the plaintiff's medical record can then be written on the other half of the butcher paper showing that the plaintiff suffers from each of the necessary elements. There are a myriad of possible uses for butcher paper to assist the imaginative attorney in proving the plaintiff's damages.

Another demonstrative evidence device which can be useful is cardboard sheets. The attorney can take large pieces of white cardboard and outline on them each aspect of the damages the plaintiff is seeking. For example, the attorney could title one sheet medical damages and then list the plaintiff's medical damages with the appropriate dollar figures after each entry. A card like this could be made up for each area of damages that the plaintiff is seeking. The attorney then has a visual aid that he can refer the jury to when he is discussing the plaintiff's damages. This not only keeps the jury's attention, but will assist the attorney in implanting his damage figures in the jurors' minds.

# Motion Pictures—An Effective Tool in the Presentation of the Personal Injury Claim

## Solomon L. Margolis

**Solomon L. Margolis is a senior partner in the law firm of Margolis & Sakayan, with offices in Washington, DC, and Rockville, Maryland. He graduated from American University Law School in 1960, and is a member of the Maryland Trial Lawyers Association. His use of the "day-in-the-life" film recently helped him win a seven-figure verdict in a personal injury case.**

Obviously not every personal injury case lends itself to the use of film. It is equally obvious that the economics of the case are important. The cost of a good film, properly edited, will probably start at around $2,000. A good rule of thumb is not to consider film for anything which can readily be done in the courtroom. A broken leg or a limping plaintiff can be demonstrated in person before a jury. Another good rule to follow is to use film when the particular injury is of such a nature as to be embarrassing to the client and to the jury if displayed or demonstrated in person.

### Two Rules for Making A Quality Film

There are two important rules when it comes to the actual mechanics of film making. First, hire a professional. Admit that there is an art to film making and that as an attorney you must not assume that you can do everything. Take the professional with you to interview the client, to see how the client lives, how the client spends the day, what appliances the client uses and the emotional setting in which the client operates. The second rule is to use a professional cameraman to actually shoot the material, properly edit it, and blend it so that the final product is a smooth, flowing visual story.

### How to Get Your Film Admitted into Evidence

Admission of films is ultimately discretionary with the trial judge. Experienced trial lawyers know that one must expect no gifts from the defense. The film will be objected to by defense counsel claiming that it is inflammatory, deceptive, or has the effect of giving undue weight to phases of the injury. Hang in there. If the film is fairly made, it should make it into evidence. It is, however, extremely important, if not imperative, to insist that the trial court view the film well in advance of trial. In this way, should the court feel that certain portions are objectionable, they can be edited out before trial. If you wait until trial you may end up with the entire film being excluded because of the objectionable portions.

### When to Use the Film for Maximum Impact at Trial

So you've made a film and it's been approved by the trial judge in advance of trial. Now you've got to decide where to place it at the trial in order to maximize its impact on the jury, and you've also got to determine who will narrate the film, describing what the jury is seeing. If you've done a good job with the film there is only one place to use it in your presentation of the plaintiff's case—last. It is your best and most compelling witness and will send the jury off to deliberate with the reality of the plaintiff's plight engraved in their minds. With respect to the narration, a member of the family or the treating doctor are good choices to describe what is being seen.

### Case History of the Making of a Film

Let's talk about a specific case which will demonstrate much of what we've been discussing. I recently tried a case involving a woman who sustained a spinal cord injury when her new car left the road and crashed because of a defect in its drive train. The woman was a quadraplegic after the accident, with no voluntary motion below her neck other than an awkward, gross movement of her right shoulder. We decided early in our trial preparations that we would not subject the client to long hours in the courtroom, both because she couldn't sit for more than several hours at a stretch, and because we felt that we did not want the jury to get used to being around her. To hear lengthy descriptions of the plaintiff's disaster heightens the jury's curiosity, so that one can achieve maximum psychological impact by bringing the plaintiff into the courtroom for a very short appearance and then ultimately concluding the trial with a motion picture.

In the course of a visit to the client's apartment, I took note of the equipment which she utilized in everyday life and asked that it be demonstrated for me. She used a hospital bed, a special wheel chair, a mechanical lift, a special feeding device and a special telephone apparatus. In addition the client required an indwelling catheter for drainage of the bladder. Clearly, it would be impossible to bring all of this equipment into court. It was also clear that the jury would not appreciate having to view firsthand the use of these many devices. Our feeling was that the jury would be embarrassed and perhaps even indignant if we put the client through her paces like some kind of freak. We concluded that psychologically there was something about the use of film that tended to insulate the jury and the client from embarrassment and would enable us to educate the jury to the client's daily life in a relatively short motion picture.

So where does one go once one decides to make a film? In my case I called my still photographer and asked if he also made movies. He was honest and told me that he really didn't have the equipment that would be adequate to provide what I wanted. I asked him to check around and see if he couldn't find me someone who knew how to create motion pictures. As always, he didn't let me down. He located someone who had been making pictures on the care of paraplegics, and we were off.

The professional and I again visited the client in her home. We checked the appliances, scouted the stairways, the parking lot, and just watched the interaction between the client and her family in their natural setting. After this meeting I met again with the professional and we discussed those items which we felt would be visually most significant and which had to be included in the film. I then left the preparation of the film outline to the pro. We ultimately shot about 70 minutes of film, which was edited down to 18 minutes depicting a day in the client's life.

### Outline of a Case-Winning Day-in-the-Life Film

The following is arranged to suggest that we are following Client's activities chronologically through a "typical" day. Clearly, it is difficult to give a full sense of the boredom and pain involved. The events chosen, however, are typical of the severe limitations and inconveniences she suffers. Although not scripted, occasional reaction shots of Client's face may help serve as useful reminders of the human element in the middle of what are sometimes very mechanical preparations.

1) *Exterior Day.* Establishing shot of where Client lives, to set the stage for later shots of transportation difficulties in leaving home. Open on *close-up* of sign, "Handicapped Resident." Camera *zooms out* to show apartment building and then *zooms in* to bedroom window of her upper story apartment.

2) *Interior.* Low angle *medium shot* of Client in bed, framed by bed rails in foreground. Bedside drainage bag will be visible here (although other more detailed shots of toilet activities should probably be omitted in the interests of good taste). Bed rails lowered by Client's husband.

3) *Medium shot* as Client's husband begins to sponge-bathe her in bed. (We need not show this entire process.)

4) *Wide shot* as Client's husband begins to dress his wife in her bed. Some *closer* shots here will also be useful in showing need for assistance in getting hands into sleeves, handling buttons and other simple elements of getting dressed that we tend to take for granted.

5) *Wide shot* as Husband moves wheel chair and Hoya lift to bedside.

6) *Series of medium close-ups* shows the nature of the net that will hold and lift her, and show Husband's activities as he attaches hooks, makes adjustments, sees to her comfort and begins to operate the lift.

7) *Wide shot.* Client being moved from bed to wheel chair, as Husband operates lift. When transfer is complete, he sees to her comfort, disconnects lift (*close-ups*) and removes it. At this point, if her wheel chair has been made operational, she will move herself to her accustomed location in front of the television set. Otherwise, Husband returns and moves chair to that position.

8) *Another series of close-ups* as he sees to her comfort. These shots will particularly emphasize the hand wrappings that keep her wrists stiff, the difficulty she has in sliding her hands to positions of comfort, and the adjustments that must be made to the chin brace holding her head upright.

9) *Medium shot. Low angle.* Husband turns on television set, as an indication of the only kind of passive entertainment and activity she has available to her.

10) *Wide shot* as Husband moves feeder-device into place behind wheel chair.

11) *Series of medium close-ups* as he makes necessary attachments.

12) Husband or other family member brings in breakfast meal.

13) *Low angle medium shot* as she works at feeding herself. This may also include *close-ups* of hands as she tries to grip utensils and of Husband's hands as he assists her. We need only show the beginning of this eating process, keeping with it long enough to indicate the types of difficulties she has. In the interest of time, it will probably not be necessary to show the dismantling of the feeding device, unless we decide to emphasize particularly the time-consuming repetition her life is composed of. If we omit or condense this, the passage of time can be indicated by a camera *fade-out* to black and then *fade* back in on the next scene.

14) *Fade in on wide shot* as visiting therapist enters.

15) *Series of medium close-ups* indicate some of the activities and exercises she goes through with the therapist. Sequence ends with *fade to black*, after therapist places telephone remote control on wheel chair.

16) *Fade in on close-up* of telephone on Client's bureau.

17) *Medium shot* of Client in wheel chair, with telephone visible beyond. Phone remote control is visible on wheel chair table. She looks—as best she can—in direction of phone, to indicate its ringing. She then tries to reach for remote control. *Zoom in to medium close-up* as her hand works at manipulating device.

18) *Medium close-up* of her face—phone visible beyond—as she attempts to conduct brief conversation. *Fade out* to black.

19) *Fade in on medium shot* of family member applying minimal makeup, to help emphasize Client's own natural desire for neatness in contrast to her own inability to effect it.

20) *Wide shot* as Husband and fire department representative enter and prepare to carry her for trip to hospital.

21) *Close-ups* of preparation, including readying of two-man carry and movement of Client from wheel chair.

22) *Wide shot* from hallway outside apartment, as they maneuver her through apartment and doorway.

23) *Low angle wide shot* looking up stairs from bottom as they carry her down.

24) *Exterior wide shot* as she is brought out of building, positioned on stretcher, and manuevered into ambulance. Doors are closed, and vehicle drives away. *Fade out* to black.

The film was shown on the last day of the trial after the client had made a brief appearance and after many doctors and nurses had described the injuries in great detail. We used a very large screen, and the client's husband described what was being shown in a soft voice which was compelling. It added a great deal to the impact of the film. The jury was visibly moved and was in tears when the lights went on at the conclusion of the film. It was at this point that I could move right into final argument. The jury now understood to a certainty what the full dimension of quadriplegia was. They had been educated to the injury and were ready and receptive to be educated to the financial aspects of damage. The verdict for this 52 year old plaintiff and her husband was $6.5 million dollars. The picture had been worth its weight in gold.

*Chapter Nine*

# *Secrets of Courtroom Psychology*

In an interview you will find in this chapter on courtroom psychology, Trial Master **Harry H. Lipsig** remarks, "The lawyer who tries his case concentrating only on adducing the evidence, without continually being sensitive to what's happening in the jury box, is making a grave mistake." In other words, to shortchange the psychological angles in court is to risk handing over control of the trial to your opponent, because, as every experienced trial attorney knows, the outcome of many cases, whether civil or criminal, hinges as much on the laws of human nature as on the rules of law.

Here, to illustrate the psychological strategies that can help you win at trial, are five of the best legal minds working today. Forensic psychologist **Thomas Sannito** leads off the chapter by explaining the practical courtroom applications of some basic laws governing human perception. You will see, for example, how the proper timing and sequencing of your evidence can help fix it securely in the minds of the jurors. Dr. Sannito reveals where to place your emotional evidence as opposed to your factual evidence. He tells how to blunt the edge of your opponent's damaging evidence, and how to make sure your own best evidence hits home every single day of the trial.

In addition, you will see what steps you can take to mold the right sort of image for yourself and your client, plus five simple techniques to intensify your persuasiveness as a speaker *without* any of the high-pressure tactics that can turn a jury off.

Just as a sports team enjoys a psychological advantage on its home field, a trial lawyer gains that same winning edge when he feels throughly at home in a particular courtroom. **Francis Elwood Barkman** shows you how to scout the courtroom ahead of time for certain features that may seem insignificant on first glance, but could prove decisive at trial.

You will see, for example, how to protect yourself against awkward seating positions, blocked views of witness or jury, blind spots, and other obstacles to a smoothly presented case. Mr. Barkman also explains how to familiarize your key witnesses with the courtroom setup so that they will remain psychologically cool even in the most heated moments of the trial.

Harry H. Lipsig's phenomenally successful career can be attributed largely to the keen psychological insights he brings to the courtroom. In the candid interview with Mr. Lipsig featured in this chapter, you will discover this legendary advocate's secrets for getting the jury on his side and even for getting the jury to *try his case for him*. In a similar vein, **Judge Randall Evans, Jr.** will show you how to sway the jurors by transferring to them your own absolute conviction that right and justice are on your side. Judge Evans illustrates his key points with a gripping and psychologically astute closing argument that speaks to the minds as well as to the hearts of the jurors.

For defense counsel in a criminal case, psychology can be a potent weapon in overcoming cultural bias in jurors. "In my opinion," states **Susan B. Jordan** in the informative interview that concludes this chapter, "the defense attorney's job is to explain to the jury what psychological and social factors put this person in the defendant's chair."

From voir dire to closing argument, Ms. Jordan shows how to break down the myths, the stereotypes, the psychological and social barriers that often stand between the defendant and a just verdict. She explains her techniques for "humanizing" the defendant for a jury that may be unfamiliar with his social background and his way of life. You will see how to choose jurors with an ability to maintain an open mind and how to sensitize the judge on the cultural and psychological issues essential to your defense theory.

# Psychological Courtroom Strategies

## Thomas Sannito, Ph.D

Thomas Sannito is professor of Psychology at Loras College, Dubuque, Iowa. He specializes in Forensic Psychology. He is a lecturer and consultant to trial attorneys on the applications of psychology to the courtroom. Dr. Sannito is on the Board of Editors of *Trial Diplomacy Journal*. He is also coDirector of *TDJ's* jury study.

No one can listen to two people at the same time. So, in the interest of fairness, trial advocates take turns presenting their evidence so that each has a chance to command the jury's undivided attention. Except by raising objections, counsel is powerless to prevent jurors from hearing the opposition's arguments or evidence.

So it was in an earlier era, when Clarence Darrow could do little else but smoke his cigar as the prosecution developed its case. Watching him in his mummified state, one could only judge the passage of time by the length of his cigar ash. It grew longer and longer, as many eyes in the packed courtroom watched it. Jurors and spectators alike seemed to be anxiously waiting for the dangling ash to drop from its stub, but it wouldn't. Now, with curiosity piqued, no one dared to turn away until the tension broke with the ash's descent. The tantalizing ash wouldn't fall because Darrow had put a wire through the center of the cigar.

Regardless of the veracity of this folklore vignette, it was not beyond Darrow's inventiveness to use such a psychological tool to dull prosecution testimony. He, like many of the legendary courtroom craftsmen, relied on psychological instincts rather than on a formal understanding of the psychological principles involved. This sly old fox may not have fully understood the gestalt principle of *figure and ground* in perception, or the *Von Restorff* effect of novelty on attention and memory; but he knew the human mind could only concentrate on one thing at a time.

### Using the Laws of Human Nature to Enhance Your Case

A psychological strategy, in contrast to the intuitive stratagems of Darrow, is a carefully calculated plan to enhance the effectiveness of your case by using the laws of human nature to your fullest advantage. Would you plan various aspects of your case differently if you knew the following psychological principles?

A. Sequencing and Timing of Evidence
  - We are better visual than auditory learners.
  - The first and last things in a series are learned better than those in the middle.
  - The attention span narrows under stress, fatigue, and boredom.
  - Unique events are "burned" into our memories.
  - Metaphors, similes, and stories are forgotten last.

B. Impression Formation
  - Sympathy appeals leave us cold.
  - Certain people appear better than they really are when we experience them after someone unlikable.
  - Sincerity is the trait of greatest appeal.
  - First impression counts the most.
  - If a person is described as "warm," a whole cluster of positive traits will be ascribed to him.

C. Persuasion
  - Bright people are insulted by a "one-sided" message, but ignorant people are influenced by it.
  - Superlatives weaken your speech, while descriptive words make it more powerful.
  - Crisp answers and long narratives increase credibility.
  - People resist changing their stories unless you first join them and then "walk them away."
  - When our freedom seems threatened by high-pressure messages, we rebel with the opposite decisions.

D. Theory or Theme
- Jurors have a need to resolve conflict, and it gets greater as the trial wears on.
- We remember a general theme, theory or principle better than individual details.
- Jurors look for the explanation that reconciles the greatest number of discrepancies.

From these laws of human nature, strategies can be fashioned to (a) give your evidence greater impact, (b) help you create favorable impressions for you and your client, (c) make you a more persuasive communicator, and (d) make your case more meaningful to jurors.

## Timing and Sequencing of Evidence

In music, two different melodies can be created from the same set of notes: one a harmonious masterpiece that caresses our eardrums, and another one a melodious disaster that makes us grimace with displeasure. The difference between a work of noise and a work of art is the *order* in which the notes occur and the *timing* of certain sounds. The genius comes in knowing how to create the overall effect by the right combination.

So it is with the presentation of evidence at trial; the proper timing and sequencing of the various segments can produce a courtroom *chef-d'oeuvre.*

**1. Serial Position Effect.** Once you have determined the evidence you intend to introduce, the question becomes: "How can I arrange the segments of my case to achieve the greatest impact on the jurors?" Unlike music, in which each note is theoretically equal in value to every other note, certain pieces of evidence are more important than others. The quandary, then, is where in the trial order should you present those parts of evidence that will make or break your case.

Our memory of items presented in a sequence is not equal at each point in the series. Anyone who has ever ridden a train through a big city knows that you learn the stations in the beginning and end better than those in the middle. This phenomenon, in which the first and last things in a series are learned more quickly than those in the middle, is called the *serial position effect.* Generally speaking, then, your best witnesses should go on first and last, since jurors will forget much of what occurs in between.

**2. The Primacy-Recency Law.** The next question that arises is, "Should I position the evidence that I want to give the greatest significance to first or last?" One of the beginning efforts to determine the comparative power of the two positions is attributed to Lund, who in 1925 formulated his Law of Primacy in Persuasion.[1] He found that the argument of a controversy presented first would have the greatest impact on the audience. Other studies have supported the "primacy effect." Asch asked one group of subjects to consider a person who was INTELLIGENT, INDUSTRIOUS, IMPULSIVE, CRITICAL, STUBBORN and ENVIOUS. To a second group he described a person as ENVIOUS, STUBBORN, CRITICAL, IMPULSIVE, INDUSTRIOUS and INTELLIGENT.[2] Note that the two lists with the same words are in reversed order; so that the first one opens with positive traits and finishes with negative traits, while the other list is negative to positive. The impressions formed from the two lists were quite different. The person depicted from the first list was seen as "an able person who possesses certain shortcomings which are not serious enough to overshadow his merits." The person portrayed after exposure to the second list, by a different group of subjects, was "a problem person whose abilities are hampered by serious difficulties."

Similarly, Luchins found a strong primacy effect using a two-paragraph description of a person named "Jim," in which the first paragraph described Jim as an extrovert while the second paragraph described Jim as an introvert.[3] The group that heard this description (extrovert-introvert) perceived Jim as extroverted. When the order of the paragraphs was reversed (intro-extro) and read to a different group, the second group perceived Jim as introverted.

In all of these studies, what came first determined the impression. Thus, the correct strategy for establishing a lasting impression of your client or the opposition's client is to advance your description early. Prosecutors and plaintiff's attorneys have a decided advantage built right into the system. Since they go first, they can create the strongest impression. First impressions do count most, and once formed they resist change, even in the face of evidence to the contrary. The first impression becomes the reference point, and all subsequent information must be reconciled with it. Information that is different will seem to be "discrepant" and less reliable. As time goes on, the discrepant information will be distorted to make it consistent with the initial impression.

Fortunately for defense attorneys there are exceptions to the primacy over recency rule. The primacy effect is weakened as the length of time between contrary messages increases.[4] The longer the trial, the more the memory of first impression fades, making the last impression the strongest one. In a one-day to two-day trial, attorneys for the people and plaintiff will have a "primacy" advantage, but in trials of three days or more, counsels for the defense will savor a "recency effect." Two tactics for neutralizing the primacy power of adverse first impressions are: (a) lengthen the trial, so that memory of the first impression is stale and weak, while recall of the last impression is fresh and strong, and (b) have a parade of character witnesses that by their sheer numbers will cause a breakdown of the first impression.

Another reversal of the primacy-recency law happens when you're dealing with objective information of experts rather than emotional impressions from lay witnesses or opposing competition. What gives first impression descriptions their lasting effect is the strong emotional tone of the describer. Feelings are remembered more easily than facts. With the lack of emotion in the testimony of experts, it takes more mental energy of jurors to remember it. The more factual the communication, the more quickly it withers over time. Therefore, put your strongest experts on last so the fact-finders can deliberate on things they have just heard.

From this discussion of primacy and recency effects, several strategies for sequencing evidence emerge.

A. Put emotional evidence first to get the primacy effect of first impressions. Once an emotional decision has been made, we construct a logic to justify it.
B. Put factual evidence on last to gain the recency effect of memory.
C. If a damagingly negative first impression is created by the opposition, lengthen the trial to allow the impression to fade, and add more witnesses with opposite portrayals.
D. Put your best evidence first on each separate day of the trial for a souped-up primacy effect. The attention span of jurors is greatest in the morning, when they're fresh and alert in contrast to a narrowed interest later in the day, when fatigue and boredom set in.

**3. The Von Restorff Effect.** The *Von Restorff* principle in learning states that unique or novel events that stand out are virtually unforgettable. How many parties can you remember? After a while, they all seem alike, but you can't forget the one in which the jealous lady "accidently" shoved the plate of spaghetti on the coquette's lap. Research by Sears and Friedman reveals that if subjects are merely told that a particular message they are about to hear is novel, they are substantially more influenced by that message than the same message without the belief of novelty.[5] Legendary attorneys who electrify courtrooms always have this effect going for them. However, every attorney can make use of the *Von Restorff Effect* during the course of a trial. First, have a novel theory or theme in your case, one they haven't heard before. Second, save "hair raising" evidence for the boring part of a trial to ensure that it will be remembered during deliberations. In this way, you can make the middle part of the trial, which is usually dull, work for you. Also, create your own *Von Restorff Effect* anytime you wish by talking in a low voice and a slow tempo for a while and then suddenly accent your point in a loud, quick voice.

Finally, if you are a judge, be conservative with the order to "strike it from the record" and the admonition to the jury to forget what they heard. By making it stand out, you are burning it into their memories.

### How to Mold the Jury's Impression of You and Your Client

An irresistible human tendency is to form impressions of others, even when very limited information is available. There is no way to prevent jurors from forming impressions about the plaintiff, defendant, attorneys, and judge, because it is human nature. What is even more disconcerting is that their "emotional impressions" in about 20% of personal injury and criminal cases may be affecting their verdicts.[6] Humans are not necessarily "rational" creatures as the philosophers tell us. Just to satisfy your curiosity on this point, the next time you go to your banker for a loan, ask him where he hides the batteries to light up his pants. Now, being a completely objective, rational person, he will explain that money is "tight" right now. We make emotional decisions about others, then seek rational evidence to justify them. When confronted with contrary information, we are even willing to delete, distort, or rearrange it or demean its source to make it consistent with our impression. Once formed, the enduring whole impression jurors have of you and your client will affect their interpretation of the event in question.

Attorney Image.  In forming their impressions of you as an attorney, jurors will want to know four things about you:

1. They will ask themselves "Do I like him?" *Liking* is the first decision we make about another person, and it has a subtle, but powerful, influence on our thinking. If they like you, they unconsciously want you to win and will find it difficult to vote against you.

2. Jurors watch you and wonder, "Can I *trust* him to tell me the truth?" Avoid casting the image of a "slick" who is sly and cunning. Jurors are impressed with an honest and sincere lawyer. Psychological research has shown that sincerity and honesty are two of the most admired traits in others.[7] If they judge you to be sincere and straightforward in your ap-

proach and not trying to trick them, you satisfy their intellectual quest for the truth.

3. Are you *efficient and competent*, or are you a stammering bumbling lawyer in their eyes who robbed his client of effective representation? It is hard to go against efficiency and quality.

4. Your own *confidence* will color their judgment in the case. If you appear shaky and tentative, they conclude the case for your client is worth very little. On the other hand, if you seem confident and certain of your case, your arguments are more believable. The image that has universal appeal to most jurors is an attorney who is likable, sincere, efficient, and confident.

You may wish to adjust your courtroom image slightly as you change from a predominantly male to a largely female jury. According to Lind and O'Barr[3], men believe the job of the attorney is to win; whereas, women expect him to be sensitive and considerate. Hence your ideal image for a male jury would be *CONFIDENT*, EFFICIENT, SINCERE, and LIKABLE; and for women it would be altered to *LIKABLE*, SINCERE, EFFICIENT, and CONFIDENT. The two images differ only by the trait of greatest importance, with men favoring the competitive spirit and women underscoring warmth. A more aggressive approach can be taken in front of a male-majority jury, since they will key on the "confidence-efficiency" part of the image and the female accent on "likable-sincere" will dictate a softer tone. Men will expect you to be a little rougher on cross-examination, while women will give you points for finesse.

There are many things you can do to improve your attorney image in the courtroom. Concerning liking, it is true that zealous efforts to get jurors to like you will be interpreted as shallow "ingratiation" or begging for a verdict, but actions which naturally promote liking may be quite successful. For one thing, try to bring out similarities between you and the jurors during voir dire. For example, if the juror served in Vietnam and you did too, ask him about a few of the places and events with which you are familiar, to establish a common bond. We feel best in the company of those who are similar to us in their past experiences, attitudes, values, and interests, and we are uneasy about aliens who are dissimilar. There is hardly a better feeling than discovering someone went to the same school, got knocked around by the same teachers, belongs to the same church, or likes activities that we like. That's why people are driven to attend class reunions in which they can reminisce on common experiences. Remember, "birds of a feather flock together," so tease out those similarities whenever possible. Also speaking to them in their language instead of lawyer lingo will tell them that you came from their ranks. A feeling of comradery naturally accrues when the vernacular is spoken (if you feel comfortable with it).

For the efficiency part of your image, prepare your case thoroughly so that you manifest an economy of words and actions. And avoid shuffling·frantically through papers in the courtroom, which spells disorganization to jurors, by being well organized. Lastly, be yourself as much as possible to convey authenticity.

**Defendant Image.** In criminal cases, the defendant image becomes a particular concern, because as a group they have a dubious reputation. Most jurors have an initially bad impression of anyone who has to defend himself in court. They wonder, "What's he doing here in a fix like this, the police don't go out and pick up innocent people." According to the research of Schulman, *et al.*, about 80% of prospective jurors begin with a belief that there is something to a case when someone is on trial.[9] In the impression formation of a defendant, he may well be "Guilty" until proven "Innocent."

The only way the attorney can control the image of his client is to keep him off the stand. In most criminal matters, there is no choice but to swear him in, since he may be the *only* evidence in his own defense. When a defendant tells his story to the jury, the "defendant impression" will be formed mostly from the emotional reactions jurors have to him. They will trust their own instincts in sizing him up, in spite of your efforts to present a "clean" character. In forming their impressions, they will use the cues most often relied upon in short-term person perception, "social attractiveness" and "demeanor while speaking."

Since time won't allow you to send your client to acting school to learn desirable affectations, concentrate on his dress and grooming with the idea that beautiful is good and ugly is bad. Our emotions tell us that attractive people don't have to resort to crime to get what they want, while homely people may go bad out of desperation. Psychological research is replete with studies showing that "unattractive" people are judged guilty more often and receive harsher sentences than "attractive" persons.[10] [11] If your client looks as if he crawled out of a swamp or fell off a flatcar, it won't matter much what he says. Who knows, maybe in their tendencies to want to acquit those who are attractive and convict those who are unappealing, they may be reasoning, "She's too good looking to be behind bars" or "He's too ugly to be out on the street." You can bleach the tainted image of the defendant by making him more esthetic in appearance. Keep in mind, though, that juries will detect phoniness. Don't dress a factory worker like a banker, and don't try to make a prostitute seem like a Girl Scout.

In insanity or diminished capacity defenses, in which a special image is required, the best strategy is to leave the defendant off the stand. In trying to prove "He was temporarily insane" or "He didn't mean to do it," he can only hurt his own defense by taking the stand. If he appears lucid and clear-headed, they can't visualize him going berserk; and if he acts crazy enough to convince them, they may want the mad dog securely in prison rather than in a mental hospital where some do-gooder may let him go. If he never takes the stand, the attorney and a good expert can project an image of a normally rational person who "cracked" while under unusual strain or while in a rare mental and emotional state. With the defendant on the sidelines, all eyes will be on the defense attorney to reassure them that he's safe. If the manner in which he defends his client conveys security, confidence, and calm, their fears will abate. If, on the other hand, he acts uneasy about defending his client, jurors may get an uncertain feeling about the defendant. With this strategy, the defense counsel becomes an extension of his client's personality, presenting a rational, calm figure.

At the same time the attorney soothes them emotionally by representing the now-rational side of his client, the expert witness gives the defendant an identity and explains his ephemeral insanity. Keeping the defendant mute while the attorney and expert characterize him allows defense counsel to control the impression the jury forms of his client.

**Plaintiff Image.** Probably the best image a plaintiff can have in a personal injury case is *understated.* Jurors know you're there to ask for money, but they want to see if you're going to beg or not. The evidence may determine which way the verdict goes, but their impression of the plaintiff will influence the amount. Don't let your injured client whine on the stand, it will turn jurors off. Sympathy appeals usually backfire and result in lower verdicts. We feel most compassionate toward those who are trying to cope with their miseries. Which paper boy would you tip the most when you inquire how cold they are, the one who says "Boy it's cold our here" or the one who replies "No, I'm ok" as he shivers uncontrollably? The effect works best when the injury is visible, experts give strong testimony about the abjection of the plaintiff, and there is no doubt of the victim's suffering. Playing down a big injury is seen as courage, which should always be rewarded, while begging is to be discouraged. The impression jurors have of the plaintiff as a "resolute soul" making the best of it, or a "beggar" exaggerating his ills, may determine whether they will be generous or chintzy in their award.

To add to the impression of understatement in a personal injury case, bring the plaintiff in sparingly. Understatement will work only if the jurors are emotionally moved by the injury; overexposure will attenuate their emotional reaction. The longer the victim is in court, the greater chance there is the jury will get used to the injury and become "desensitized" to the misery it has caused. Then the plaintiff's understatement may lead to the jury's underevaluation of the case. The best way to heighten the effect of plaintiff understatement is to build the suspense by withholding the plaintiff; then, near the end, expose the jury to the plaintiff's condition at the same time she or he takes the stand.[12] In this way, the understatement will come at a time when the jury's emotional reaction to the injury will be the greatest, and the whole effect will remain fresh for jury deliberations.

## 5 Techniques of Persuasive Speaking

All of us have been captivated at one time or another by an accomplished orator like John F. Kennedy, Hubert Humphrey, or the great Clarence Darrow, any of whom could hold audiences spellbound for long periods of time. Besides the unique charm of each individual, all three had "powerful" speech patterns. What makes speech in the courtroom powerful and persuasive? Recently, sociolinguists have identified several variables of courtroom speech that differentiate a "powerful" style from a "powerless" style.[13]

1. Persuasive lawyers avoid the use of intensifiers (e.g. "very, very much"), hedges (e.g. "kinda," or "sort of") and questioning intonation (i.e. finishing an answer with a rising pitch, as if asking a question). We are much more convinced by detailed descriptions than by these meaningless expressions of speech. When we hear Harry described as "super great," we are left with a hollow ring to the words, but if he is depicted as "warm, friendly, kind, and soft-hearted," we form a vivid picture of his greatness.

2. On the handling of witnesses, the most "powerful" style was judged to be when attorneys encouraged their witnesses to speak in a narrative form rather than the shorter staccato style controlled by the attorney. With the long narratives, the attorney is signaling the jury that he is giving up his control and prompting, which makes the whole examination more credible.

3. Attorneys who get into verbal clashes with their witnesses, in which both speak at the same time, are perceived to be "powerless." Jurors watching this simultaneous speech see the attorney as losing control and being less fair. It is much more skillful if the attorney acquiesces.

4. Increase your courtroom power by teaching your witnesses to answer in a crisp tone instead of a tentative manner. I have seen many witnesses of dubious reputation look believable by a firmness in their answers. Over the long haul, altering your speech patterns to fit these findings can give you stature as a powerful, compelling persuader.

5. Refrain from using expressions like "... you will be compelled to find the defendant," or "...you must then turn in a big award." Also, never sum up by saying "Ladies and gentlemen of the jury, you must come in with an acquittal," because you may thereby make it difficult for them to find him innocent. If you do anything, tell them, "My opponent will tell you that you have no choice...." Also, if you stand in about the middle of the courtroom, you take the pressure off them; and if they feel less pressure from you they are more malleable. If you stand too close, they feel pressured, and you are risking the "boomerang effect."

The "boomerang effect" is the rebellion jurors feel for high-pressure attorneys, which results in their reduced compliance. It was first described by Brehm in 1966 who contended that if a person's freedom is restricted or threatened with restriction, he will rebel against the mandate or order by doing the opposite to insure his freedom.[14] In one of Brehm's studies, he reported 70% compliance from subjects subjected to low-pressure messages and only 40% compliance from those who received high-pressure tactics. This same desire to act contrary to the force that is constricting one is called the "paradoxical effect" by psychotherapists. Therapists have observed that ministers who preach at their kids often have hellions. The courtroom moral to the story is avoid overselling your cases with a dominant, aggressive style; use the soft sell to reassure jurors that you are not making the decision for them.

Notwithstanding the success of two or three prominent attorneys who use dynamic force, the best results will be achieved by a smooth, low-key effort.

### How to Develop a Powerful Theme

A theme or theory is an explanation of how and why things occurred. Some attorneys present fragments of evidence and others develop themes. A theme is the common meaning running through all of the evidence in a case. Each piece of evidence should say the same thing in a different way. Adding "filler" witnesses detracts from the theory and weakens its effect. The theory is stronger when it is tight and tidy, with no distractions. When every segment of evidence adds to the theory, the explanation becomes compelling. Jurors will forget most of the details unless they are bound together by a common thread. A good theory or theme is one that is (a) simple, (b) unique, and (c) tidy, making it easier for them to remember. Jurors will buy the theory that makes sense out of the greatest number of facts and reconciles most of the inconsistencies. Therefore, try to work the other side's evidence into your theory, and delete any evidence that doesn't fit in with your theory.

## Notes

1. Lund, F. H. "The psychology of belief. IV The law of primacy in persuasion." *Journal of Abnormal and Social Psychology*, 1925, *20*, 183–91.

2. Asch, S. E. "Forming impressions of personality." *Journal of Abnormal and Social Psychology*, 1946, *41*, 258–90.

3. Luchins, A. S. "Primacy-recency in impression formation." In C. I. Hovland (Ed.), *The order of presentation in persuasion*. New Haven: Yale University Press, 1957. Pp. 33–61. (a)

4. Luchins, A. S. "Experimental attempts to minimize the impact of first impressions." In C. I. Hovland (Ed.), *The order of presentation in persuasion*. New Haven: Yale University Press, 1957. Pp. 62–75. (b)

5. Sears, D. O. and Freedman, J. L. "Effects of expected familiarity of arguments upon opinion change and selective exposure." *Journal of Personality and Social Psychology*, 1965, *2*, 420–25.

6. Kalvin, H., Jr. and Zeisel, H. *The American Jury*. Boston: Little Brown, 1966.

7. Anderson, H. Ratings of likableness, meaningfulness, and likableness variances for 555 common personality traits arranged in order of decreasing likableness. *Journal of Personality and Social Psychology*, 1968, *9*, 272–279.

8. Lind, E. A. and O'Barr, W. M. "The social significance of speech in the courtroom." In H. Giles and R. St. Clair (Eds.), *Language and social psychology*. Oxford: Basil Blackwell, 1979. Pp. 66–87.

9. Schulman, J. "A systematic approach to successful jury selection." *Guild Notes*, 1973, *2*, 13–20.

10. Landy, D. and Aronson, E. "The influence of the character of the criminal and his victim on the decisions of simulated jurors." *Journal of Experimenntal Social Psychology*, 1969, *5*, 141–152.

11. Efran, M. G. The effect of physical appearance on the judgment of guilt, interpersonal attraction, and severity of recommended punishment in a simulated jury task. *Journal of Research in Personality*, 1974, *8*, 45–54.

12. See Stanley Karon, "Developing Evidence of Damages in Personal Injury Actions," *Trial Diplomacy Journal*, Fall 1980 (Vol. 3, No. 3), pp. 14–19.

13. Erickson, B., Lind, A., Johnson, B., & O'Barr, W., "Speech style and impression formation in a court setting: The effects of 'powerful' and 'powerless' speech." *Journal of Experimental Social Psychology*, 1978, *14*, 266–279.

14. Brehm, J. W., *A Theory of Psychological Reactance*. New York: Academic, 1966.

# How to Make the Courtroom Your Home Ground

## Francis Elwood Barkman

Francis Elwood Barkman is Professor Emeritus of Law at the University of Toledo College of Law in Toledo, Ohio. He taught primarily trial practice, evidence, remedies, torts, criminal law, law and medicine, and insurance. Barkman was associated for a decade with Sullivan & Cromwell of New York, N.Y., in the practice of law as a member of that firm's litigation department. His practice included the fields of commercial, corporate, antitrust, banking and investment banking law.

The trial advocate competes with his* adversary in the role of producer-director of the courtroom drama. Just as a theater director must first know the dimensions, boundaries and limitations of the stage, and just as a World Series or Super Bowl team will arrive early to practice on the grounds of the home team, so should the advocate visit the courtroom before a trial. He should visit the courtroom when it is empty, and should be accompanied by a few assistants who will aid in the inspection.

Counsel should be looking expressly for defects, handicaps, and disadvantages, to either side or to the other participants. I do not purport to have examined all of the courtrooms in the United States; however, I have found some feature in every courtroom that I have ever visited which, by keen observation and consummate showmanship, might be converted into an advantage against an adversary.

---

*"His" henceforth designates both sexes in this piece.

## How to Stake Out Your Territory

First, counsel should ascertain from the clerk of the court the local practice as to the seating and stationing of the advocates. As a general proposition, it seems that counsel to the party having the burden of proof takes the seat or table closest to the jury, if there be one. I have found no statute or rule of law which so prescribes, although such may exist. In some jurisdictions it seems to be a matter of first arrival, first choice.

After learning the applicable custom, counsel should also ascertain the extent to which any rearrangement of the furniture in the room is possible. Counsel should then sit at the place to which he will be assigned and have the assistants sit at various places in the room: the witness box, opposing counsel, parties, the reporter's table, the judge's bench, the jurors' seats, seats for counsel inside the bar not involved in the present case, the bailiff, spectators, the press, the television camera, etc. In each instance, the advocate should determine whether the view is unobstructed, whether there are problems with acoustics, problems with mobility of counsel or others in the handling of exhibits, or problems with verbal or non-verbal communication.

Next, the advocate should sit in the seat of his adversary and engage in the same observations. Does the adversary have any advantages or disadvantages by virtue of the location? After comparing these seats, the advocate should return to his assigned position to determine its advantages or disadvantages.

Sitting in the seats assigned to him and adversary counsel, the advocate should consider the possible ploys which he may encounter, or possibly desire to use, in connection with that court's custom governing the location and posture of counsel. In my opinion these ploys detract from the ideal trial and, if intent to disrupt were easily established, might warrant discipline for contempt. However, they often are so smoothly executed that a judge is reluctant to find intent and instead allows some leeway for frailities of the human condition. Their aim is to upset opposing counsel.

Suppose that custom, or judicial direction, requires counsel to be seated when questioning witnesses, but to stand at a rostrum when addressing either jury or court. Shifting the rostrum or the table a foot in any direction may block the adversary's view of jury, witness or judge.

If counsel are free to stand and move about at will, movement of one counsel may be a studied insult to opposing counsel but so well performed, with a display of disarming innocence, that the possibility of con-

tempt does not even occur to the judge. For example, in one case plaintiff's lawyer (PL) was doing poorly in cross-examining an executive of
defendant corporation:

> Q (by PL, handing document to witness): Look at this and tell me
> what it is.

> Defense Counsel: Your Honor, I object. I don't know what he has just
> handed the witness and I am entitled to know.

> PL (quickly): Your Honor, I'm sorry, may I have permission to hand
> the document to defense counsel?

> The Court: Certainly.

Plaintiff's lawyer, apparently engrossed in studying the document, walked
the long way around the tables to Defense Counsel's seat, obviously intending there to hand him the exhibit; Defense Counsel, meanwhile, had
been pursuing PL around both tables in the same direction.

> PL (after looking all around and finally seeing Defense Counsel, apol-
> ogetically): Counsel, I hand you Defense Exhibit No. 1.

> Defense Counsel (with some irritation): No objection, Your Honor.

PL appeared confused, returned to his table, shuffled documents again,
and proceeded as above, except that this time he reversed his direction in
apparently pursuing Defense Counsel, while actually forcing the latter to
track him. A few repetitions of this scenario and Defense Counsel's blood
pressure reached volcanic proportions and he exploded to the court.

> Defense Counsel: Your Honor, I object to PL's rudeness.

> PL: Your Honor, if I offended Defense Counsel, I apologize to the
> Court and to him.

> The Court: Let's get on with the trial, counsel.

Plantiff's Counsel, following the same script, handed the witness a different document, Defense Counsel's view of which was obstructed.

PL: That's your signature on this document, isn't it?

A: Yes.

Defense Counsel was so angered that he didn't realize until several questions and answers too late that PL had obtained testimony as to an otherwise inadmissible document damaging to defendant's case, to which no objection was made until PL offered it to be marked and received into evidence.

## The Importance of Position

Another ploy, blocking adversary's view of witness or jury, may be successful under either the fixed or mobile customs. For instance, in one case the Government was engaged in rebuttal closing in criminal prosecution of a labor racketeer, D, whose career of criminal violence was met by proof of good character, D's numerous worthy charitable endeavors, as testified by a parade of high ranking prelates, which the Government had not been able to rebut. The prosecutor was immediately in front of the jury. Defense and court saw only his back. Counsel, a Protestant, knowing that a majority of the jury were of Roman Catholic faith:

> You heard a parade of priests come here and tell you what a fine person this defendant is. We proved him to be a thug. Ladies and gentlemen, you know it's awfully hard (counsel now fumbles around his tie and produces a crucifix, fingers it a moment, and then pushes it back inside his shirt) for a member of the faith to disagree with the hierarchy, but we all know that priests are priests.

Defendant, counsel and judge were unaware that the credibility of the character testimony had been demolished.

Where the advocate persists in blocking his adversary's view, the latter should calmly request the court either for permission to move or to direct the advocate to change position. I once observed a trial where defense counsel, tired of requesting the court's aid, simply leaned back in his chair, contemplated the ceiling and became completely unaware of improper questions for about 15 minutes. He was dumbfounded when he asked the judge how his case was lost and the judge replied that he couldn't understand defense counsel's failure to object. Only a reading of the record for appeal persuaded defense counsel that, in his anger, he had tuned the trial completely out and had made no objection to prejudicial testimony of doubtful admissibility. He had even twice replied, "No," when the judge asked whether he desired to object.

In another case a young prosecutor was determined not to let defense counsel block his view of witness and jury; he simply changed his location in the courtroom every time defense counsel blocked his view. When he interviewed the members of the hung jury about what proof they found persuasive, he was stunned to learn that a majority of the jurors thought he had been intentionally discourteous in an effort to disrupt the defendant's testimony, which they then accepted as credible.

Thus, the advocate should consider the extent to which the custom or seating and location of counsel may permit his opponent to engage in such games and impair an otherwise impressive case.

Counsel should then sit in the seats of several of the jurors, survey the room and consider carefully the construction and arrangement of the jury box.

Do the jurors seated in front block the views of the jurors in back? Does each juror have an unobstructed view of the witness? Of either counsel? Of the parties? Of the judge? Of the reporter?

Are the jurors going to be reasonably comfortable? Are their chairs similar? Do all jurors have sufficient leg room? Are the rows of chairs far enough apart that there will be little disruption as the jurors are brought to or from the jury room?

I have never seen a trial in which the jurors always filed in and out in the proper order. If the space between rows of jurors is narrow, the tardy juror will be both inconvenienced himself and annoying to the other jurors. The alternative is for the jurors to line up in the jury room in the sequence in which they would enter the courtroom. Having been a juror, I know that the panel on which I served resented lining up in a pseudo-military formation. Do the jurors' seats lift up, or are the seats fixed so that the tardy juror must crawl over seated colleagues? The disruption can increase anxiety or anger, perhaps directed toward the lawyer who made the jury's retreat and return necessary.

Counsel should give special attention to problems of security. Is the table so close to the railing that during a recess a member of the public could reach across and relieve counsel of his briefcase and its contents? Many a lawyer has suffered theft of evidence, equipment or clothing perpetrated in the courtroom. Can exhibits or other papers be removed from counsel's table by anyone, including the adversary? Can jurors in leaving or returning to the box look over and read notes or documents which counsel has not yet presented? There have been reports of contraband disappearing in the courtroom before it was admitted in evidence.

Counsel should then sit in the witness box. Can the witness see all of the jurors, and vice versa?

Have both a tall, well-built associate and one of more slight physical dimensions try the various positions of participants, the different locations in the jury box, and elsewhere. A juror who has difficulty seeing the witness may tire of the endeavor and withdraw substantially from active attention to the evidence or, in later deliberations, simply vote against that witness's side.

The reporter should not be ignored in this examination of the premises. Too often trial lawyers do not recognize that, so far as the appeal is concerned, the ability of the reporter to hear may be the most crucial factor in the ultimate outcome. The reporter cannot record that which is not heard. What kind of problems will the trial present to the particular reporter?

It is my belief that most trial advocates take reporters for granted and do little or nothing to help them with their important task. Give the reporter an alphabetical list of names and addresses of witnesses and parties. The reporter can then get them correctly without having witnesses or counsel spell out the names. See that the reporter's facilities permit the efficient discharge of that responsibility.

Counsel should sit at the judge's bench. Under what limitations does the judge operate? Does he lack office supplies at the bench or are these automatically available there? Do the furnishings indicate that the judge will be only casually attending to the case being tried, while he is writing letters or drafting an opinion on some motion argued before him in another case a month before? Will the judge assiduously be taking notes? Will the judge be writing messages to friends in the courtroom in the fashion of the late Justice Felix Frankfurter? Will the judge have any difficulty in seeing any of the participants? A number of courtrooms have so architecturally exaggerated the status of judge as to handicap his view of witness, reporter, or bailiff. Only one who has sat in the judge's seat would learn this limitation.

## How to Size Up the Battlefield

Having considered the problems which the relative seating arrangements may present, the advocate should examine other things about the room. A tape measure would help counsel to know distances which could then be used as estimates in framing questions to witnesses, especially in personal injury cases. It may be helpful to know the exact distances among clearly defined objects, corners, doors, or railings.

Is the lighting adequate for all participants? Does the lighting create a particular problem for some? Sunlight reflected from an office window across the street may blind a witness, juror, or counsel.

If diagrams or blowups of exhibits are used in the trial, which participants will thereby be handicapped? An exhibit may block the view of, or not be visible to, opposing counsel, the witness, or the judge. In one libel case, a blowup of the offending newspaper column was 4' × 8' instead of 3" × 6" as it appeared in the newspaper. For the advantage of the jury, this blowup was located behind the libeling defendant during his testimony. Plaintiff's counsel constantly used a pointer to refer to selected phrases in the offending piece. The jury easily read, but the witness was thoroughly confused as he turned around and could simply not decipher the offending phrases because they were too blurred to him. It was 20 minutes before his counsel realized that the witness's inability to respond was caused by inability to perceive. To a casual observer the jury had already assessed credibility unfavorably; the subsequent effort to rehabilitate the witness by asking the same questions while he had a normal copy of the document to look at was unsuccessful. Only the appellate courts saved the defendant from a staggering award of both compensatory and punitive damages.

I have seen courtrooms where counsel shared a table. The position, spacing, and location of seats around the table may carry advantages and disadvantages in viewing either a jury or the judge. If plaintiff's counsel faces the judge and defendant's counsel has his back to the judge, defendant's counsel is seriously inconvenienced in gaining information from the judge's body language, which the plaintiff may find so helpful in timing objections. If both counsel face the judge by a simple turning of the head, then there is a corresponding advantage and disadvantage between counsel with respect to eye contact with the jury.

In one multi-party case, a lawyer, representing a nominal defendant and the real power behind the throne, found his view of the judge blocked by plaintiff's counsel while the latter was standing and delivering his opening statement. Whenever defense counsel wanted to object to improprieties in plaintiff's opening, he was forced to stand up. He never learned that other counsel had rigged the seating and the location of plaintiff's counsel in opening so as to force him to stand, and that his standing conveyed to the judge that he represented the real party in interest when he was trying to play the role of a shrunken violet.

Some consideration needs to be given, especially in multiple-party cases, to a simple thing like chairs. Will there be enough? If not enough chairs for counsel, where will additional chairs come from? Will it be necessary for some counsel to stand? In the early stages of proceedings in multiple-party cases, it may be that many defendants have not retained counsel, and, in order to save money, are seeking to ride the coattails of some other defendant's lawyer; some counsel may be seeking to be retained by additional defendants. Such a situation may even degenerate into an absurd game of musical chairs. Assume a preliminary proceeding, say, of an antitrust or administrative nature, with perhaps 50-200 defendants and in which prestigious firms A and B are competing to be selected as lead counsel for the bulk of the defendants. Firm A may simply preempt the available seats with a number of its most recent associates and thereby demonstrate to the many defendants present that Firm A has the manpower to do the job. Firm B and its star advocate of national fame may arrive moments later and have to scrounge for a chair for its star. For a few minutes, which may seem like a century to the star advocate, there will be no room for him, just as was the case of the parents of the Saviour at the Inn. Those few moments may result in Firm A becoming lead counsel for most of the defendants. Such calculated rudeness of Firm A may make the star advocate of Firm B seem like an unimportant fool and minimize Firm B's role in the case to insignificance.

Acoustics should be carefully considered and tested. Are there dead spots? Are there sound centers where a whisper between client and counsel will reverberate throughout the room? Scrutinize the floor for loose tiles or boards, slick spots, etc.

All in all, every aspect of the courtroom must be examined for flaws which may impair counsel's effectiveness or present unique opportunities which he can turn to his advantage.

### Make Your Witnesses Feel at Home

Having determined comparable things from firsthand inspection, the advocate should then familiarize his more important witnesses with the empty courtroom during a second visit. The goal is to enable them to feel comfortable while on the witness stand. A juvenile court referee of some years experience recently was summoned to testify as a witness in the Court of Common Pleas. When his name was called, he moved forward and for the first time saw the railing which keeps spectators from intruding. The referee's hearing room had no such railing. He became rattled and halted. After some delay, the judge said, "Up here." He accordingly moved toward the bench. The bailiff then said, "Over here." The referee turned and headed to the side. The bailiff said, "Wait until we are ready." The referee-witness now felt like a fool. The oath was finally administered and he was told to take his seat. He was by now thoroughly confused and did not see the witness box at the other end of the judge's bench. When he finally sat down in the chair to which everyone pointed, he didn't remember his own name. He later said that he survived the ordeal only because the judge leaned over and said, "Well Tom, I guess you find it a little bit different up here in the big league," and the resulting laughter dispelled his anxiety. Isn't that a terrible emotional price to have to pay for fulfilling the basic duty of telling the truth as one knows it?

Having the witness sit in the judge's chair reduces the terror which otherwise strikes the heart of the average person first confronting the black-robed angel from on high. Have your witnesses sit in the witness chair and look all around the room. Let them know where to find friend and foe. Especially try to get your witnesses to look at the jury. Of course, in many courts where counsel are permitted to be mobile, questioning counsel can manipulate the witness by taking a position at the end of the jury box and insist on repetition when he cannot hear the witness.

The last decade has witnessed enormous expenditures on new courthouses and new and remodeled courtrooms. Judges have taken the lead in the creation and design of these facilities. Distinctive features of new courtrooms may answer problems of security, efficiency and economy, but create new problems and perhaps even manifest some personal idiosyncracies. I have not had the opportunity to view more than a few of these.

I have read descriptions of the marvelous facility at McGeorge School of Law, University of the Pacific, in Sacramento, California. "The Courtroom of the Future." This $460,000 complex seems ideally suited to overcome past deficiencies, as Dean, former Judge, Gordon B. Schaber has justifiably asserted:

> They [pre-1955 courtrooms] are poorly lighted, subject to numerous distractions; and offer few improved means of presenting or preserving evidence. Security for the judges, jurors, witnesses and the public has not been a great concern in the past. Nor has a procedure to eliminate undue pressure on the jurors, witnesses and others been a part of the design.

But even the most experienced trial advocate in the nation would be well advised to orient himself thoroughly in such an outstanding facility before conducting his first trial there. While he may not have to guard against some of the problems outlined earlier, it would certainly require adjustments to pace a trial presentation to allow jurors to take notes at their desks, to avoid running afoul of the security system, to observe whether jurors were being attentive to exhibits being televised to their individual TV monitors from the evidence pedestal (which is housed below floor level when not in use), and to cope with all of the other technological advances incorporated.

In short, the advocate, like his counterparts in other endeavors, must know his terrain. Every military man wants to distinguish grass, cliffs, mountains, plains, water, ice, and sand. Every horse trainer wants to know whether the track is fast, dusty, or muddy. Every football coach wants to know whether the field is astro-turf or grass. Every tennis player has a preference for either grass or clay. Every outfielder wants to know whether he crosses a cinder track before crashing into the wall in pursuit of a fly ball. Similarly, any lawyer trying a case in an unfamiliar courtroom should thoroughly explore the arena beforehand for its advantages and disadvantages and to familiarize himself with technological advances. With this preliminary scouting and orientation, he is better equipped to excel in his capacity as a co-producer/director of the trial and concentrate more effectively on the substantive basis for a just outcome.

# Having the Jury Try Your Case for You

## An Interview with Harry H. Lipsig

Harry H. Lipsig was graduated from Brooklyn Law School in 1926, and is now senior partner in the New York law firm Lipsig, Sullivan and Liapakis, P.C. He is a Fellow of the International Academy of Trial Lawyers, President of the Public Awarness Society, and taught trial advocacy at New York Law School. He became the first male member of four New York women's bar associations.

Harry Lipsig was selected by the New York Criminal & Civil Courts Bar Association as "The Outstanding Lawyer of the Year" and then presented with its Rober Daru Award.

### What It Takes to Be a Successful Trial Lawyer

EDITOR: What makes a successful trial lawyer?

LIPSIG: A charming personality. A tactful man who affronts nobody. A man of sincerity. This is the day of the soft sell. The days of oratory are in great measure gone. The only place, possibly, for oratory is when the lawyer in summation can give of his whole soul, his whole heart, his whole being on behalf of his client; but of necessity preface it with the hard facts of the case, and the clear, cool, intelligent logic that the more sophisticated jurors of today have a right to expect.

### Courtroom Techniques for Getting the Jury On Your Side

EDITOR: In your interview with *US* magazine, you were asked what you look for in jurors, and you said "open hearts, understanding and compassion." Do you not look for a reasonable, rational, and logical juror?

LIPSIG: Oh, I like people of intelligence. My feeling is that the jury and I are working *together*. I try to give them that viewpoint right from the start. At the beginning, in the course of selecting a jury, I say, "A trial is a search for the truth. And you, ladies and gentlemen of the jury, are here, and I am here with you, in that search for the truth, as to who *really* is responsible in this case. And I shall be most happy to work with you and do what I can to bring that truth out."

At every step that I try in the case, as I bring out evidence, to the extent to which I am permitted, my approach is that I'm producing it and laying it in the lap of the jury. And as I bring out a piece of evidence I accentuate, within reasonable limits, the import of it by the type of questions I ask. I look to the jury as if to say, "Look—this is it! And do you see what we're bringing out?!" When I get a witness who is insincere, and I am able by some question to bring that lack of sincerity out, as he gives the answer that makes it clear, I immediately look to the jury and I let my face and my stance and my whole mood express the significance of what that witness is saying.

Any lawyer who just proceeds with cold logic in the handling of his questions and answers is doing a job; but how much more effective is it when he gives it the proper setting, when he stages every phase of the case with life, with meaning, and not just with the cold facts—because you're dealing with human beings on the jury? And if you use your attitude, your tone of voice, your mood, and your facial expression to *illuminate* the cold facts that are coming out, or hot facts that are coming out, to give them more meaning by what you do, you're giving life to the feelings and reactions of the jury in that regard.

However, on occasion there is a different approach, especially for young lawyers. I once delivered an address before one of the conventions, and the theme of the address was to have the *jury* try the case for you. Sounds ridiculous? Well, early in my career, I tried a case in a city far distant from where I was accustomed to practice—the wonderful city of New York was my usual place of activity. This was at the height of the Hitler propaganda against the Jews, penetrating then even the United States. And in that particular city, out of my twelve jurors I think ten of them were of German background. And here was I, a Jew from New York, trying that case. And the only Jew who was part of the panel excused himself from the case. When I bumped into him in the washroom afterwards and asked him why he excused himself, he said to me, "In the present antisemitic atmosphere in this community, heightened by the Hitler propaganda, if I'd have stayed on that jury and ever dared to utter one remark on the evidence in favor of your client, with you as a Jew, they'd have rent me limb from limb."

Well, being sensitive to that atmosphere, I tried that case as if I was somebody who didn't understand the meaning of the answers. I called the witnesses on the defendant's side first, as I so often do. As I got them in an inconsistency, I didn't say aggressively, "Now what is the fact, what you said ten minutes ago, that your speed was 40 miles an hour, or what you say now, that your speed was only 25 miles an hour?" On the contrary, my approach was one of unbrilliant puzzlement: "Well," hesitantly, and almost stutteringly, "Well, uh, I er, I don't understand," apologetically, "a little while ago you said 40 miles an hour, and now you say . . . you were going . . . 25 miles an hour, well, I-I-I-I'm puzzled . . . as to what . . ." See, I'm highlighting the inconsistency, but I'm too dumb to understand it. And I did that enough times for the jury to think, "What the blazes is the matter with this dumb cluck from New York? Doesn't he realize that they're not telling the truth, doesn't he see that?"

So within themselves they begin to see what I'm too unbrilliant to see for myself, and they begin to feel that they wanted to force it down my throat, to make clear to me what's going on, and so they were trying the case for me. They were condemning the witness for me, because I was too obtuse and too simple-minded a soul in my inoffensiveness, to realize that the witnesses were being inconsistent and so terribly insincere.

Well, additionally, I had learned the wisdom that when you are in a foreign jurisdiction you should get well-known local counsel to sit in with you. Whereupon, instead of doing that, I selected a young man who had just moved into the community who had a good Jewish name, when I should have picked a German-American. I couldn't stay for the verdict, since the jury was locked out at the end of the time of the trial, and I left him to take the verdict. Fortunately for me, my technique had worked with the jury beautifully—they were so indignant at my lack of understanding that they saw it very strongly on my behalf. When the verdict came in, the very eminent attorney for the defense, the second most outstanding lawyer in that particular community, said to the judge, "If juries are going to render verdicts like this there is no sense my trying cases," and he stormed out of the courtroom. That was the story as related to me.

So there's a psychology for you. And I say to any experienced lawyer: if he has an adversary that he's burying, he'd better be careful, because he may be burying himself. That was part of my experience in this case that I spoke of before, where I wanted the jury to try the case for me. My adversary made me the laughing stock of the courtroom the first number of days of the trial, humor at the expense of this little Jewish lawyer from New York. In the long run it did him no good.

I had said to my clients, who were Italians from Brooklyn, "The only way I can hope to win this case is to let the other lawyer walk all over me.

And you've got to understand now, that when I try this case you're going to see your lawyer as a most ineffectual individual." At the end of four days, one of my clients came to me and said, "Do you *have* to let him get away with so much?" He was *horribly* perturbed over the way the other lawyer was just romping all over me in the courthouse, and I doing *nothing* to stop him in any direction.

I said to him, "Look, I warned you in advance, you've got to sit tight. Don't think that I enjoy being made a laughing stock. But let's see who smiles at the finish of the lawsuit."

I have strongly advised, in some of my lectures to young practitioners, that they shouldn't hesitate to try a case just because they were inexperienced. They should prepare their case to the hilt, make sure they have every aspect of it at their fingertips, and then go into court and make clear to the jury by their hesitant conduct, such as I delineated in the psychology of this other case, that they were just beginners. As a matter of fact, say to the jury apologetically, "Would you hold against my client the fact that his lawyer is now trying his first case of this kind?" or "Would you hold against the client that this is the first case that I have tried in the Supreme Court?" And thereafter be inoffensive and diffident, and if he is of as slight build as I am, on occasion, as he apologizes to the jury, to sort of look up at his overtowering adversary.

So for the young practitioner I say, parade your youth! Parade your inexperience! Because there is one thing I find beautiful about our American juries. For me it is one of the most beautiful things in the world. The American people, who are our American jurors, take care of the underdog. They all but take some helpless creature to their bosoms, be they male or be they female, and take care of them against the all-too-powerful forces against them.

### The Perfect Way to Start a Case

EDITOR: You have said that in a negligence case you normally call first the defendant as an adverse witness, or someone related to the defendant's side of the case.

LIPSIG: Well, I do especially where we subpoena records and there are records strangely missing. When you start off the trial highlighting the strangeness of the missing records, a jury is immediately put in suspicion of the defendants. Why should they be missing? Either they have been destroyed with time, up to the time the case has come to trial, or have been deliberately destroyed, or have been screened out of what is produced, which happens all too often.

Where the defendant is insincere, I'll call him first, on the theory that any lawyer with a reasonable amount of experience should be able to bring out that lack of frankness and parade it before the jury—and that this will poison the minds of the jury against the defendant's side of the case.

Of course, if you have defendants with conflicting interests, it is a grave mistake not to call those defendants in the early part of your case, at the very beginning, and ask barely enough questions to provoke the attorney for the *other* defendants, to take over the questioning of the particular defendant produced. You are then in a position where the defendants will be fighting among themselves, and whatever conduct is sparked by the conflict is all to your advantage, even where the defendants in such situations make deals among themselves not to fight, not to quarrel. The underlying worry with each one of them is always that his particular client may be the one held liable. So despite all agreements, subconsciously there is a drift to a conflict. You can sit back while the conflict goes on, and be as inoffensive as possible, while they on occasion quarrel among themselves.

The perfect way to start a case is with the jury aroused, either because of suspicion or because of their reaction to the battle being waged among the defendants.

### Staging Your Case for a Dramatic Climax

EDITOR: At what point of trial do you call the plaintiff?

LIPSIG: Every case should be staged just like a play. Every lawyer should be aware of the fact that you have to stage your drama to a high point of conclusion—you save your most important witness for last. And your most important witness, if you are representing somebody seriously injured, is that person who is there to portray the tragedy that has been visited upon him, the agony that has followed therefrom, and the terrible loss sustained by it. Of course, if you have a doctor or other witness who is what we call a "clincher," you leave that clincher for last.

There is great wisdom in starting with a good point in your behalf, and that is why I try to use a defendant who is insincere as my first witness—that's a good beginning. And you finish at a high point, or make that point as close to the finish as you can. Once you've hit your high point, you should bring that case to a close as quickly as possible.

Only the most experienced lawyer should conduct a lengthy cross-examination. No matter who is conducting a cross, if a witness has once made a seriously damaging statement, where it is a high-point admission or inconsistency, one should immediately and abruptly bring it to a close at that point, leaving it with the jury.

In your examination of a witness, always try to leave an important point before a recess, so the last thing in the minds of the jurors is the high point that you've achieved that moment. You should stagger your questions in such a fashion that you leave that important point for when the recess is likely to take place. When in doubt, it is perfectly proper to ask the court how long the court intends to sit before the next recess, or when the next recess will be. Or having achieved a high point in the trial, at that point appeal to the court for the seventh-inning stretch. Bear in mind that the jurors are confined within a space—they're in prison—so when they are given a chance to relieve the burden of sitting there in that fashion, they like the man who applies for it.

One must in the course of the trial be *ever* aware of the jury, and of their mood. The lawyer who tries his case concentrating only on adducing the evidence, without continually being sensitive to what's happening in the jury box, is making a grave mistake.

The most important attribute for a lawyer in the trying of a case is for him to have the jury feel that he is sincere. And no lawyer must ever say anything that he is not prepared to prove. And if he attempts to prove that which is unbelievable, he better not do it, because he may be proving himself out of the consideration of the jury. Everything has to be reasonable, no matter what your jury is composed of. I have the *highest* respect for the composite underlying of twelve people on the jury, even when it is reduced to six. Even when you have doubts about the intelligence of some of the folks on the jury, you would be surprised how much common sense they have in the aggregate. I pay high tribute to them, these good people of ours in this U.S.A., their concern for the underdog. You see that played up in the movies that are so popular, the westerns, where there is one poor soul fighting the combined villainy of the gang that controls a western community; and how the audience is waiting hopefully for the time when he'll be free of their overpowering influence. Try a case where you can have that atmosphere working for you, and you're going to have the underlying sense of concern and fairness on the part of our American juries working for you. Study how you get that powerful force working for you, and you'll win almost all of your cases.

# Reaching the Hearts and Minds of Jurors

## Randall Evans, Jr.

Randall Evans, Jr. began practicing law at the age of 18. He served as Mayor of the City of Thomson, as Georgia State Senator, and as Speaker of the Georgia House of Representatives. He was appointed to the Court of Appeals of Georgia in 1969, and selected Outstanding Appellate Court Judge in the United States by the Association of Trial Lawyers of America in 1975. Now retired, he is the author of *Opening and Closing Arguments: The Law in Georgia* (1978).

To make a creditable argument on behalf of your client, you first must be able to step into his shoes and be convinced of the righteousness of his cause. Unless you can do that, let some other lawyer try that particular case. But being convinced that justice is on the side of your client, you must attempt to transfer your own conviction into the hearts and minds of the jurors; you must undertake to establish rapport with them—to feel your own heart beating in time and in turn with the hearts of twelve jurors. Often, your conviction that RIGHT and JUSTICE are on your side will inspire you with the earnestness, the zeal and the fervor to make the RIGHT come true—to cause the jury's verdict to be rendered on the side of *Righteousness*. Your conviction will enable you to impress the jury with your honesty and sincerity in the fierce battle you are waging for your client and will oftentimes be reflected in the jury's verdict.

### Establishing a Strong Foundation for the Verdict Your Client Deserves

Of course, a lawyer must reach the *mind* before he has any basis whatever for reaching the *heart*. That, stated another way, means you must have *evidence of negligence* against the defendant before you have standing to reach the *hearts* of your jury.

Many lawyers frequently punctuate their opening remarks with the statements, "We expect to prove," and "The evidence will show." While such remarks undoubtedly are formally correct, and in most cases are probably used unconsciously while the speaker thinks of what he is about to say, they should be avoided. They are distracting to the jury and tend to erode the impact of a well-told story. An opening caveat that the words of the lawyers are not evidence is sufficient, and thereafter the scenario may be painted in effective terms, without constantly reminding the jury of their lack of probative value.

Of prime and utmost importance is that a verdict for *something* be awarded the plaintiff. In that respect, "if I had my druthers," I would prefer two reliable witnesses who could testify that the left front wheels of the truck were two feet to the left of its center-line of the highway, rather than a concluding argument by Demosthenes playing on the heart-strings of the jury as to the *amount* of the verdict.

But let us assume there is sufficient evidence, though contradicted in places, to authorize verdict for the plaintiff. Now we come to that high place in the drama—a real-live, honest-to-goodness chapter in the lives of people of flesh and blood, where the fortunes and future of many people will be directly affected by the verdict and the *amount of the verdict*.

### Final Argument: What to say And How to Say It

The skilled and dedicated lawyer has studied his case so well that he knows it forward and backward; knows the law and the evidence; knows the high points in his client's case and the pitfalls; knows the strength and weakness of his opponent's case. Nothing—but nothing—can take the place of work and study, which includes attention to minute details. "There is no royal road to geometry. " That was the advice given to Ptolemy more than 2,000 years ago; and it is just as true today in any discipline, including law.

You should ever bear in mind the fact that the jurors are strange to the case you have studied so well for weeks or months; the evidence is presented to them in its totality, and they are expected to separate the wheat from the chaff, the important from the unimportant, and none of them is an expert in that field. They will not remember all of the evidence; they will not remember all of the charge of the court. They would be supermen if they did.

Your task in argument, among others, is to select the strongest points of your own case and the weakest points in the case of your adversary, and emphasize them. Explain to the jury that it is not expected that they shall remember every word of testimony or every sentence in the court's charge, but for their aid and benefit in coming to a correct and proper conclusion, you are going to outline some of the more important areas in the evidence, and some of the very important principles of law you expect the court to give them in the charge.

Spare no legal effort to obtain the closing argument. It is far and away the most desirable spot in the entire trial. It is doubly important. First, your having it denies a skilled and brilliant lawyer on the opposing side the right to be heard last—the right to advance arguments and make points that you will not be allowed to answer; though perhaps you might have a ready and plausible answer. But more important, it gives you the right to be last heard, to advance arguments and to make points your adversary will not be allowed to answer. There you can marshal and array the strong evidence which supports your case, and point to the faults, the weaknesses, and the large cracks in the armor of the case of your adversary.

The manner of the delivery by counsel of his closing remarks often may outweigh in effect the substance of his sentences. Artificial phrases or speech patterns are the earmarks of insincerity to even the least sophisticated juror. The use of emotionally directed argument can be treacherous if handled clumsily, and should be undertaken with care until it is spontaneous and unaffected to the listeners. This is not to condemn the practice; for when utilized properly, the stirring of the right emotional chord of the jury can yield the most extraordinary results, provided it is done with taste and feeling.

Although reading verbatim from a prepared argument is to be avoided, and rote memorization of a lengthy summation rarely can be handled by most practitioners, an outline of the closing argument, either mental or written, supplemented by notes on the evidence or the lack thereof is a must.

The final summary or conclusion should end as forcefully as possible; and, where a point of strong impact has been made, but some further summary is needed, it should be as brief as possible and should not detract from the high point thus established.

Remember those twelve jurors facing you were sons and daughters, brothers and sisters, now mothers and fathers, before they were jurors, and to each of them that former role is far and away more important than the role of juror. Speak to them, then, as human beings, who know much more about life and its values than they do about rules of law.

## Sample Closing Argument

"The little six-year-old boy in this case was on the school grounds at recess. He and his schoolmates were playing ball. Automobiles were parked all around the school on the streets. The wild throw carried the ball into the street and the little boy darted after it. Ladies and gentlemen of the jury, he was of that tender age when a little boy thinks the all-important thing in this world is to recover the ball as quickly as he can—he thinks the whole world will wait for him—be careful not to hurt him or kill him. Later, he will have more judgment, but let us thank Almighty God for that period in a child's life when he has not yet come face-to-face with the real facts of life; when he has a child's trust in the goodness of the universe. Do you remember when you were not yet selected as jurors, on voir dire examination, I asked you, in a body, if any one of you had ever experienced a little child suddenly running in front of your automobile? Many, many hands went up. But then that next all-important question: "Did any one of you run over the child?" NOT A HAND WENT UP! You knew to watch out for children; you were alert; your speed was such and your control of the car was such that you could and did stop your car before running into and over the child! Not so with this defendant. He did not show the same circumspection, alertness, and diligence that you showed; and when he stopped his car and went back, a little boy was lying in the street with the light of life gone from his eyes—gone forever!

"This child had not reached that place where he had selected a vocation. We do not know what he might have become in our society. He might have become a truck driver; a common laborer—both honorable means of earning a livelihood. He might have become a president of a bank; or he might have become an attorney who could earn fees commensurate with these great lawyers who represent this defendant (and how we wish they had been on our side—what a difference there would have been in the way he portrayed the case to you!). He might have become a doctor, and on some fateful day he might have stood at the bedside of one of your loved ones in extremities and might have been able to act as an agent of Almighty God in keeping health, strength and life in the body of that loved one.

"But oh, ladies and gentlemen of the jury, we need not speak of what might have been—it never will be. His little life has been cut down and ended at the very threshold, as the broad panorama of this wonderful world was unfolding before him.

'Of all the words of tongue or pen
the saddest are—it might have been!

"The law allows me to speak of certain matters though not introduced in evidence, matters of common knowledge, such as history; that the mighty Titanic sank in 1912 with a tremendous loss of lives; that Jesse James was an outlaw in the era of 1865-1880; etc., etc. So, I am well within the mark when I tell you that in 1955 there was a picture of that great race horse, Nashua, in the New York daily papers, with a price tag of $1,255,000 upon him. Think of that for a moment! A racehorse, whose body at death goes back to the dust; and here we have a little boy—a human being with a soul that goes back to God. In Biblical days the psalmist looked up and asked of the Creator:

> 'What is man, that Thou art mindful of him
> Or the son of man, that Thou visiteth him?'

And the answer came—was written down by the Prophets—and comes ringing down the corridors of time until this good day:

> 'Thou has made him
>   a little lower than
>   the Angels,
> And crowned him
>   with honor and
>   glory.'

"This humble little boy, whose mother was of very moderate means, was MADE IN THE IMAGE OF GOD, AND CROWNED WITH HONOR AND GLORY! I tell you with all of the fervor and earnestness of my soul that the most humble little black or white child in this state is more valuable than the best-blooded race horse that ever ran!

"Go with me now to the little boy's home. He used to be a little negligent in the care of his clothes and his room—about average. Often his mother came into his room after he had gone to school, and picked up his pajamas from the floor; straightened out the bed covers; smoothed the little pillow that was rumpled and sometimes on the floor.

"But now—what a change! The mother goes into that little room, and everything is neat and in order; the clothes are neatly hanging in his little closet; the bed is neatly made; the pillows are smoothed. No little head slept on that pillow last night. But wait! I said *everything* is neat and in order. Everything but one thing: a mother's heart has been broken into one thousand pieces. And all the king's horses and all the king's men can never put that heart back together again.

"That mother would give a king's ransom, if she had it, to be able to walk into the room just one more time, and find the bed-covers and the pajamas on the floor, the pillows rumpled from having been slept on, to be able to straighten up a room that had been slept in by a little boy.

"But the little boy that lived there has gone away to Heaven, never to kiss his mother goodbye again, or to greet her again.

"Ladies and gentlemen of the jury, I almost tremble in thinking of the awesome task that is yours: of equating and translating the value of a little boy's life into mere money. It seems profane and vulgar, but we have followed the law of the land, and prayed for the only thing that we ask of you. May you somehow be enlightened by a higher power when you come to grips with the amount you will write in your verdict as to the worth of a little boy.

"If the evidence in this case warrants a verdict for the Plaintiff, I believe it will be your duty to write a verdict for the Plaintiff—in the amount you think proper.

> 'Right is right—since
> God is God
> And Right this day must win!
> To doubt would be disloyalty—
> To falter would be sin
>
> So near is grandeur to our dust—
> so near is God to man—
> When DUTY whispers "Lo, thou must!"
> The answer is "I can." '

"Ladies and gentlemen, whatever verdict you may render, I earnestly pray that it will be a verdict that will console your future steps by day, and bring comfort to your pillow at night.

"Thank you, Ladies and Gentlemen of the Jury."

# Overcoming Cultural Bias in Jurors

## An Interview with Susan B. Jordan

Susan B. Jordan is a sole practitioner in Ukiah, California and San Francisco, California. She has taught trial advocacy and other subjects at the New College of California Law School, and the National College of Criminal Defense Lawyers and Public Defenders. In addition, she has lectured on criminal law and trial advocacy at numerous seminars throughout the United States.

*A brief background of People v. Garcia\* will be helpful to the reader of this interview. Inez Garcia was raped in Soledad, California in 1973 by a man with an accomplice. About 30 minutes after being raped, she shot and killed the accomplice, Miguel Jiminez. In her first trial, Inez Garcia was convicted of murder, when the jury apparently rejected a plea of impaired mental state.*

*Susan B. Jordan represented Inez Garcia in her appeal and retrial, and in 1977 Miss Garcia was acquitted on the basis of a self-defense plea.*

### How to "Humanize" the Defendant for the Jury

EDITOR: When you are representing a woman charged with a violent crime against a man, I assume you wouldn't want an all-male jury.

JORDAN: Surprisingly, I don't think it makes any difference. What generally happens in a criminal trial is that the District Attorney puts on trial one

---

\*Cr. No. 4259 (Super. Ct. Monterey County, Cal. 1977).

instant in time: did the defendant pull the trigger? From the DA's point of view, that is basically all he or she has to prove, unless he is trying to prove a case of premeditation, in which case he must show some planning in that. But he doesn't go much further back in time to explain how the defendant came to be in this spot.

But when someone comes to pull a trigger, there are significant social and psychological reality events which preceded that. No matter who the person is, something, often a very complex set of things, preceded the pulling of that trigger. In my opinion, the defense attorney's job is to explain to the jury what psychological and social factors put this person in the defendant's chair, in a case called *People v. John or Jane Smith.*

Voir dire is the beginning of this explanation. I think that one can never underestimate how unfamiliar jurors are with the criminal process and criminals; and as a result of that, how often they come to court believing that they are open-minded, intending to do a good job, when in fact their heads are filled with stereotypical images of crime and criminal defendants, derived from the media and not from personal experience. The defendant in a criminal case—your client—may or may not fit the jurors' image of a stereotypical criminal, and in fact may appear very scary, strange and foreign to them. Voir dire is the time when one begins to humanize this defendant for the jury.

Most judges do not feel that one can go to elaborate lengths to give a social, political, or psychological explanation to the jury in voir dire. Some judges allow more latitude than others. But any judge will permit exploration into questions of bias.

Consider, for example, the case of Inez Garcia. Initially, before she was a defendant in a criminal case, she was a rape victim. At first glance it wouldn't appear that society in general had any bias against rape victims. One would expect that the initial reaction might be to feel sorry for her. But on closer examination, it turns out that just about everybody harbors some attitudes, which I call stereotypical notions, about rape victims. For example some believe that a woman who is raped probably asked for it, or in some way wanted it to happen; was dressed so provocatively that it had to happen; was out alone in a bar at night, therefore she could expect to be raped. If one believed any of those things even without thinking about it, then one was biased against the rape victim. If you believe that Inez Garcia asked for the rape, then you would never believe that she acted in self-defense.

After her first trial, when she was convicted, one of the jurors was interviewed as to why he convicted her, and he said, "Well, you can't shoot somebody just because he tried to give you a good time." That indicates an initial bias against rape victims. No matter what kind of a case the defense puts on, no matter who the lawyer was, no matter what was going on, the jury could never believe she acted in self-defense if they believed she shot a man who was trying to give her a good time.

That is what I call a threshold myth, that rape victims always ask for it. It is a myth that if you get raped you wanted to get raped. Women do not like violence of their bodies. And each rape has its own set of facts— far more complex than "she asked for it," or "she was out alone, so naturally . . . ."

In Inez Garcia's case we were permitted to ask a series of questions on voir dire which went something like: "Do you believe that rape victims ask for it?" And many people didn't know the answer to that question. I mean, jurors often in voir dire do know how they are expected to answer—they are supposed to say they are not prejudiced against blacks, they are supposed to say that everyone deserves a fair trial. But for rape they didn't know the answers. So people would think about it and say, "Well, maybe, maybe they ask for it."

Then we would ask, "Do you think that when a woman is raped she enjoys it?" And some people would honestly answer yes.

And then we would ask, "Well, don't you think that rape is a violent assault?" And they would say, "Yes, absolutely."

The next question would be, "Well, what if *you* were violently assaulted?" They'd say, "I wouldn't like that."

And then we would go back and say, "What about *her?* If she were violently assaulted, and you agree it's a violent assault, do you think she liked it? Do you think she had a *good time?*" And you know, they'd start thinking about it.

Once a juror starts thinking, that pleases me. That is why in response to your question, do I want all women or all men on a jury, I don't care. The jury in Inez Garcia's second trial, where she was acquitted, was ten men and two women. The DA bounced off the jury all of what he called the sympathetic women; he thought anyone under the age of forty would be "women's lib," and should go off the jury. But for our choices we went more on who responded to our questions in a way which demonstrated that they were willing to have an open mind.

### Choosing the Openminded Juror

EDITOR: So you might accept a juror who is biased, if he is honest and open about his bias?

JORDAN: If it came to a point where somebody would say, "I can *never* get rid of the notion that a woman who gets raped asks for it"—and there were one or two people who said, "I'm sorry, that's what I believe"—then they would be rejected for cause, because the judge agreed that that would be a bias against her defense. But by and large, a juror who demonstrates that he or she can be open-minded, someone who will listen to the evidence and determine if it was justifiable to shoot in a homicide case, is a wonderful citizen and a wonderful juror. And the people that we chose on the Garcia case came from all walks of life. They were not pro women's liberation, they were not from any special sector of the community, they really came from all walks of life; and they demonstrated a particular ability to respond honestly and openly to our questions and to maintain an open mind, which I think is the best jury that you can have.

EDITOR: So your experience in the Garcia retrial indicates . . .

JORDAN: And many other trials following, also.

EDITOR: . . . that men can be sensitive to women's issues in a criminal trial, if these issues are presented correctly. Does that apply as well to race— can whites be sensitive to blacks' issues in a criminal trial?

JORDAN: Yes, if the issues are sensitively explored. Does a white person from the north side of Chicago understand what it is like to live in the south-side black ghetto? All the north-sider knows about it comes from television, newspapers, and possibly whatever stereotypes they grew up with. It would be only guessing for a white person from the north side to imagine what it is like to be a seventeen-year-old kid at 63rd and Halsted on a particular day and time.*

So in order to explain how it is that Johnny Jones, for example, from 63rd and Halsted, came to shoot Alvin Smith, and it was not a violent gang-related assault but it was in self-defense, one would have to understand a little bit of what it was like to live out there, how he grew up and what it was in his head, and why he perceived danger such that he would shoot.

EDITOR: I've heard of cases, such as "The Trial of Big Man," where the jury was taken to visit the scene of the crime, to see how this danger might have been perceived.

JORDAN: Okay, but in that case there are twelve jurors, let's say that five of them are white, and you go accompanied by marshalls or sheriffs, and

---

*63rd and Halsted is a rough ghetto neighborhood on the south side of Chicago.—Ed.

you go accompanied by the judge, and you are all in a group and you are all protected—it doesn't tell you what it is like to be a seventeen-year-old living in a gang neighborhood. It does give you some more indication than if you had stayed in the courtroom, and it is only the *beginning* of the process we have been talking about. My feeling is that you still have to look beyond that. Jurors are well-meaning people. I don't think they are really out to *get* anybody at the start. But if you don't offer them the information, then they'll have no basis for understanding another culture or another environment.

One time when I worked in Chicago I represented a member of a gang who had shot somebody in a rival gang. It was a murder case, and I was given a guided tour by the sympathetic gang into the unsympathetic gang's territory. And I want to tell you that it was terrifying. The level of tension and the emotional and psychological feeling of being in a wrong gang's territory were something. We were under minimal protection, you know, there were no police, there was no big group; I never had an experience like that before. It was a war zone, and we were taken there to see the scene of the crime so that we could better understand, and it was an experience that I have never forgotten. And you know, even after that experience, along with my previous experience working with black people in all kinds of situations, unless my client had explained the culture and the environment to me, I wouldn't have understood well enough to handle the case effectively. Nobody could understand, unless it is explained.

Defendants in the criminal justice system come from very different walks of life. Inez Garcia was a Latin. Now, in California, we have a lot of Chicanos. To Inez Garcia, the difference between a Chicano and a Latino is very large. I didn't know before she explained to me, that a Latino is someone who comes from Latin America—she was Puerto Rican and Cuban. A Chicano is a Mexican American. Culturally, there is a big difference. Language-wise, there is a whole different slang, pronunciation is different, some of the cultures' mores are different.

And while it may not seem the most crucial thing going on, there was one small aspect in Inez Garcia's case which helped to explain how she came to be in a situation where she would get raped. She was a foreigner in the town she lived in. To the jury she looked like one of those other Chicanos down there. But the Chicanos looked at her as a complete outsider; they had never seen anything like her before. She grew up in Spanish Harlem in New York City. Soledad is a small town, and she was much flashier than anyone else there, not because she was a "sexy broad" looking to get raped, but because when you grow up in Spanish Harlem you look a lot flashier than when you grow up in the tomato fields of Soledad, California. She looked flashy, she wore a lot of make-up and tight clothes and high heels, because that is how they dressed where she grew up. And she was seen as a foreigner, an outsider there. If we didn't explain that, the jury would look at her picture, or look at her in the courtroom, and say, "The Chicanos around here don't look like that, she must have been asking for it that night." But if you understand her background and the difference between her and the Chicanos, then you come to understand how she would be looked at in that town as a foreigner, which she was.

You can't make the whole trial out of psychological and social differences, but I think a small amount of that kind of explanation will help the jury to understand the case. I think that jurors do like learning. Coming to court is a learning experience for them. They all leave saying, "My goodness, I didn't know any of this." If you treat them with respect in the selection process and believe that most of them want to learn, and choose your jurors for open-mindedness and a willingness to learn, you will have a very good chance of finding people like that.

### When and How to Emphasize Social Background

EDITOR: At what point in the trial do you make these cultural distinctions clear? How much of this can you do in voir dire, and how much do you do in opening statement?

JORDAN: Okay, two questions arise: how much do you *want* to do, and how much *can* you do? I think that the answer to the first question, how much do you want to do, depends on the particular case, facts of the case, and the client. Again, you cannot explain every crime on somebody's social or psychological background, you just can't. And you don't want to belabor it forever. So it is a question of sensitivity, what do you think needs explaining?

The first thing I do is sit down and analyze; what are the significant factors that need explaining in order for the jury to understand the defense? Now, let's take a simple example, which is a case I actually worked on in Chicago. A black young man was accused of shooting a white neighbor during a racial incident. He was in fact innocent of the shooting, the killing. We knew who had done it, because the actual committor of the offense had basically confessed to us, even though he wasn't charged.

The wrong kid was charged. It was a case of mistaken identification. The accusing witnesses were all white, and they were all accusing this one black kid. Now, to many jurors, it sounds simplistic, but all blacks look alike, especially teenagers of the same size, with the same clothes, with the same, you know, body motions. They look alike. Not because jurors are inherently racist, but because they don't have experience. They haven't lived in and around the blacks enough to begin to distinguish racial characteristics. The same with Asians, Chicanos, Latinos; you don't develop a sensitivity to different characteristics as you do in your own race.

That is one of the things I would begin to understand in order to defend that case. What would I do about it? In the pictures, in the identification process, I would call attention to details; noses, eyes, mouths, hair and ears, very specifically. In voir dire I would talk about people's experience. How many blacks do they know? Without confronting them I would find out whether they are prejudiced or biased. I don't urge confronting each juror, accusing them of being prejudiced or biased, because I don't believe people are inherently that way if they can help it. If someone has had no experience with blacks whatsoever, is terrified of black teenagers, then probably he or she is not going to be perceptive of the black culture and its characteristics.

There are expert witnesses, I don't know if I would use them in every case, but there are people who specialize in eyewitness identification and who can testify that culturally white people often misidentify black people. There are experts that testify that eyewitness identification is inherently untrustworthy because people so often make mistakes; and you add to that the cultural factor. That kind of testimony is not allowed in every court. Some judges will reject it, saying this is common knowledge, thus you can't present expert testimony on it. But you can argue that. You can argue that without confronting the juror and without saying, "You are a terrible racist." You can say, "Think of your experience. How many times have you walked up to somebody on the street and started to say, "Hi—"; you think it is John and it is really Sam, or it is really nobody that you know. You think it is your friend and all of a sudden it turns out to be somebody else.

EDITOR: Someone of the same culture as yourself.

JORDAN: Even the same culture or the same color, yes. Apply that to someone who is very different from you, and it compounds the problem. So I begin by identifying what I think are the main problems in the case. You can't address every one, society is too complex. But in the women's cases we have worked on, we started to identify what we thought were impediments to understanding the defense, and we noticed that jurors, courts, and even district attorneys were ready to be sympathetic.

Let me give you an example. You can help jurors understand the state of mind of Inez Garcia, for example, after she had been raped by comparison to a different situation. John comes home and finds his wife in bed with Sam. Sam runs out of the house, John picks up the gun and goes out after Sam. Let's say John kills Sam. Everybody would say, "Oh, John, you shouldn't have done it. You were over-reacting, you should have gone to the police. But we understand. We can see how this could happen and we don't blame you for getting mad and losing your head." At most a manslaughter in the heat of passion. At *most* a manslaughter.

Nobody said that John is responsible for Sam sleeping with John's wife. Nobody blames John for that. But here they were *blaming* Inez Garcia for accusing this teenager of raping her. And then, when she *herself* had been violently attacked, *she* was blamed for getting mad and losing her head. That is a real inequality of treatment, not merely because there is sex discrimination in this society, but because of the stereotypical notions of a woman who gets raped: she must have asked for it.

The same with battered wives. There have been a lot of cases lately of women who shoot, *finally*, after years and years of being battered. They finally are driven to the point where they believe that they are going to be killed, and they respond with force. Now, a very difficult thing to present to someone who is unfamiliar with the situation of battered women is the fact that a battered woman would stay at home and not leave. Let's say that the defense is self-defense, or some kind of impaired mental state. If you are presenting a long history of abuse, which you have to do to show provocation—years and years of getting beat up—the first thing that everybody asks is, "Well, if she was so beat up, why did she stay? Why didn't she just leave; that's what I would have done," people often say.

If you read the literature, and there is starting to be a substantial amount of literature around, a psychological syndrome develops by which the woman leaves two, three, four times—I mean actually leaves— and she always ends up going back. The courts urge her to go back, the social system urges her to go back, her mother urges her to go back to try again, her husband finds her, and she comes to believe that she cannot escape. It becomes a psychological belief that she can't escape. In addition, there is a cycle which women in this situation fall into, which we present by expert testimony all the time, and the juries understand completely.

### Defeating the Myths That Could Damage Your Case

EDITOR· Who is the expert, a social worker?

JORDAN. There are many people who study this. There is a psychologist named Lenore Walker, who has written a very good book on the subject and done many studies, in which she says that the first thing that happens is a build-up phase. The tension builds, and finally the man hits the woman. Stage one is the build-up phase; stage two is the hitting of the woman by the husband; stage three is a kind of winding down. What follows is stage four, which is like the honeymoon all over again. He brings flowers, he brings presents, he apologizes. It is like the day they were married, they want to get everything back together. It is a high following a terrible event. And the cycle begins to perpetuate itself. Men feel guilty for hitting women. I don't think it feels very good to them either. They send flowers, gifts. The men feel bad. The woman feels, well, maybe next time it will be different. This time he sent more roses than last. This time he really has come to understand his behavior, he will never do it again.

In order for a jury to believe the woman's assertion of self-defense, they have to believe that what went on before that was two years of ferocious beatings. If they believe that any woman who is beaten will automatically leave, they will never believe that she had been beaten before. Therefore, not only do you have to prove that she was beaten, which is hard—these men don't come in and cop to it, you know, they don't like to get up in public and say that they battered their wife; it is embarrassing. You have to factually try and prove it. Maybe the neighbors heard screams. But even beyond that, there has to be some explanation of why a woman would stay in that situation, or return. You have to defeat the threshold myth that any woman who is beaten will leave.

EDITOR: That psychology could apply as well to a child in a bad family environment, or a person living in the ghetto.

JORDAN: We live in such an incredibly culturally varied society, and most defendants do not come from the same culture as the jury. Statistically, defendants are largely third-world and largely poor—it is not across the board, but I would say overwhelmingly so. Jurors come from a great cross section, which doesn't often match the cross section of the defendants. Therefore, there is a lot of explaining to be done; and to the extent the rules of evidence permit, it should be done. I don't want to say it should be overdone—one still has to try the facts of the case, one still has to address the ballistics, the time, the sequence, the measurements, the factual issues—but I think to the extent that it is relevant, and a misunderstanding would be an impediment to the defense, it should be explained, yes.

Another threshold myth is that any woman who shoots her husband or a rapist has got to be crazy. Lawyers for years and years urged these women, if they were going to trial, which was rare, to go on some kind of an insanity or lesser impaired mental state defense, or plead guilty immediately. And what we found, and we find now, is that the prisons and jails are filled with women who pled guilty in factual situations that are very similar to the Garcia case, because there was no understanding.

In Inez Garcia's first trial the defense was a combination of impaired mental state—which in California is called diminished capacity—and self-defense. The self-defense was played down, the impaired mental state was really emphasized. Well, now, Inez Garcia was not crazy in any way, shape, or form, and in her first trial she came across as being completely sane. I mean very sane, and the jury looked at her and said, "There is nothing wrong with this lady, what is she trying to put over on us?"

Again, it is a bias, which came from this whole series of myths about women, this one being that any woman who shoots some guy has got to be crazy. So women are urged to plead guilty, or do these insanity defenses or impaired mental state defenses. But they didn't work. The jury would look at these women and say, "They are not crazy, I don't buy that." Indeed, we presented Inez Garcia as a reasonable woman. She acted reasonably in shooting Miguel Jimenez. She was in fear for her life, he already had raped her, he had a knife, it was all very reasonable and made complete sense.

That is not to say that the impaired mental state defenses are unusable. In many situations that is the only explanation; something has gone wrong, for example, from years of being beat up. She may not be acting reasonably, her mental state may have been affected by this. I think that anybody who gets beat up every night when a man gets home from work, or gets drunk, may not have been well; so there are situations where impaired mental state makes absolute, complete sense. The impaired mental state defenses have their place. But in the situation where it is really a self-defense case, we should be able to see through the stereotypical attitudes and say, "No, this is a self-defense case."


## The Crucial Jury Instructions

EDITOR: What instructions are crucial?

JORDAN: The instructions that are crucial are, of course, reasonable doubt, the standard instructions regarding self-defense, and whatever you know is basic to your case. In addition to that, you are still thinking, what are the impediments in the jury's mind?

The jury is given instructions—the judge reads them the law, and they must apply the law. No matter how much sympathy and understanding and explanation they may have acquired from you, if the law is not on your side, or if the judge reads them some law that has nothing to do with what you said, then you are not going to win anyway. So, in fact, I think of instructions first, even before I do my opening argument. Let me give you a very simple example. In Inez Garcia's case the prosecution—in fact everyone that I ever talked to, defense lawyers included—said to me, "Well, didn't she go out and hunt that guy down? Inez Garcia was raped in her apartment, and a half-hour later she left the apartment, and went out to hunt this guy down. That's not self-defense." I saw that one as a big impediment, even if they *did* believe she was raped, even if they believed that she had a terribly hard time.

But here were the circumstances: Inez shared an apartment with a young man named Freddy, who was a friend of the man who raped Inez. The rapist had a key to Inez's apartment. In fact, Inez lived in apartment number one, and the rapist lived in number three. She also received a phone call in the interval saying, "We are going to do worse to you next time." It didn't say when it was going to be. These guys were drunk when it happened, they could come back any hour and start all over again on her. The fact that the rapist had a key was crucial to understanding Inez's state of mind.

Now would *you* stay home under those circumstances? I wouldn't, I would be afraid to. I would leave, now that I think about it, if I were Inez Garcia.

EDITOR: And you would not go out unarmed.

JORDAN: She would not go out unarmed, she is certainly not going to stay home and wait for this rapist to come back. You would have to be crazy to stay home. So I thought about the instructions. In the California penal code, there is a provision which says a person is entitled to carry a loaded weapon in public if he is in fear for his life. All you do is translate that into an instruction, and say, "The law permits one who is in fear of her life to carry a loaded weapon in public."

In closing argument, the simpler the theory, not simplistic, but the simpler, the clearer, the more straightforward the theory is, the easier it is for the jury to understand. Again, for the jury, the whole procedure is very foreign, coming into court, getting sworn in, listening to these objections, jumping up and down, papers, motions, I mean it is all another world. It is all this other world to them, and the clearer your message can be the much better chance you will have, if you have a defensible case.

There are some special instructions that you could suggest. If you represent a woman, you certainly have to insist that the feminine gender be used. *She* has the right to act in self-defense if *she* finds *herself* in a life threatening situation. Judges are certainly willing to say that the use of the masculine pronoun applies to the feminine. But that is not enough; because what the jurors have to do is imagine themselves in that person's situation. What they are asked to do is apply the "reasonable person" standard: What would a reasonable *person* do in this situation? Not a reasonable man. I think it is a "reasonable woman" if you are talking about a woman, but some judges have argued with me about that. But a reasonable person I guess combines the characteristics of both. What would a reasonable person do in *her* situation, not *his* situation.

The mere semantics of it are not the essence of the defense, but they do remind the jury that they are dealing not with two men in a bar who were fighting because they were drunk; they are dealing with a woman who found herself in a life-threatening situation.

Inez Garcia was maybe five feet tall and weighed about 98 pounds. The individual that she shot weighed three hundred pounds, had just been the accomplice in her rape, and was carrying a six-inch knife. You can direct the jury's attention to those facts in the case which will help them interpret the law as it's written. The law says you have to be in reasonable fear of great bodily injury or death. What is reasonable for a five-foot, 98-pound woman may be different from what is reasonable for a 300-pound man.

## Sensitizing the Judge on Cultural Issues

EDITOR: In addition to educating the jury, is it advisable—or possible—to educate the judge on cultural issues? Perhaps *in limine*?

JORDAN: I think we should use the word "sensitize" the judge. I feel that good judges, like good people, are anxious to learn. Judges, more than any of us, deal with people day after day, in all walks of life, in all situations; and one of the things about staying a good jurist is the ability, I think, to keep learning.

In a situation where I realize that I am presenting what is a novel defense, or a novel application of the law, something that hasn't been done before, I know that I have had a lot more time to read about the subject than the judge has. It would be arrogant of me to assume that he should have as much knowledge in specific areas as I do. For example, if there was some reading that I had done, or studies or some information that I had, which I felt would help the judge understand the presentation of expert testimony, or help him understand a particular instruction that I wanted that was based in law and not merely in theory, I would make every effort to share that material with the judge. There are a lot of ways to do this. Sometimes I have just gone into chambers and said, "This case is going to involve battered women or rape victims or blacks, and there are some new studies or some law review articles that I think really elucidate the area, I will be referring to them in argument, they are cited in my pleadings, let me give you the originals." And give them to the DA, too. Most judges don't have time to read volumes on any given subject, but if you can excerpt for them or give them a short study, I find most judges are very anxious to know what you are talking about. They may reject it, they may say this has nothing to do with anything, but they will read it. And it makes life easier for the defense attorney when the judge knows what you are talking about. It is very unfair to spring on a judge, for example, as we were talking about before, the cycles with the battered wives, during argument.

The judge in the original Inez Garcia trial might have felt, "Well, what else is there to know about rape? We all know about rape. What else is there to know?"

But there are some very well-respected and well-documented studies that show, for example, that something like 87% of all women who are raped fear for their lives, even if the perpetrator is not carrying a weapon. They believe that during or after the rape they are going to be killed. Nothing will convince them that is not the case, whether the guy has a weapon or not, because that is the kind of life threatening psychological and physical experience it is.

In the Garcia case I gave the judge all those studies, and he read them all. He was really interested. I don't know that it changed the outcome of the trial; but I think it broadened his understanding of the issues that he was dealing with, and therefore helped us present our case.

EDITOR: Did you get any rulings that you otherwise might not have gotten?

JORDAN: Yes, in the first trial they substantially limited the expert testimony on rape. On the retrial we got it admitted. In the retrial we presented one psychologist, herself an expert in the rape field, on the reactions of rape victims in general. Fear for their lives, humiliation, how long the fear lasts. That was a real important question in Inez Garcia's case, because she shot him twenty to forty minutes later. Now, if you were unknowledgeable, you might think, "Well, the rape is over, what else are you worried about?" But women are haunted by this for years. They have nightmares years later; they go around nervous on the street. Once you get raped, that is it for a long time. You become much less trusting, the fear stays with you. So forty minutes was *nothing* for her. I mean the fear was just as alive as if it was one second ago.

So we were permitted to present expert testimony from the psychologist on rape victims. Then we presented a second expert, also a psychologist, who was just wonderful. She was a Latin herself. She addressed herself specifically to the question of rape within the Latin American cultures. She added a whole other factor in which—now the jury didn't love this testimony, I will tell you what the foreman said later—but she added the factor that a Latino woman who is raped is practically expelled from her family; she is considered dirty, and she doesn't get any sympathy—so that was going through Inez Garcia's mind on top of everything else. She was very tight with her family, so that added another factor to why she would be in such an angry state.

The jury foreman who was white told me, when I asked him about this, that he didn't find that testimony appropriate. He felt that *his* wife would have been just as outraged, and that we tried to say that Latino girls were better than his wife. But it was interesting. I never looked at it that way, and I learned something from talking with him about it.

Again, the question of experts and what they say and what you put on is really a question of sensitivity. What do you want the jury to hear? What message are you putting across? Are you insulting anybody? Are you educating anybody? You can't try your case simply on education of the judge or the jury, because that is a sociology class and not a jury trial. But where it is relevant and where it is helpful, I think it should be done.

# Chapter Ten

# *A Treasury of Courtroom Tactics*

In this concluding chapter of *The Trial Masters,* eleven eminent practitioners will join you as co-counsel in solving some very special courtroom challenges.

Suppose, for example, you are suddenly called on to represent a witness before a grand jury investigation. What are the witness's rights and liabilities? Should your client invoke any privileges, or should he elect to waive them and testify? One wrong turn could mean "the forfeiture of the witness's Fifth Amendment privilege, and perhaps other rights, which may never be redeemed," says Herald Price Fahringer, who is on hand to guide you step-by-step through this mine field of procedural dangers. You will see exactly what to do, from the moment the subpoena arrives to the all-important debriefing session immediately after the grand jury appearance is over.

Next, the Honorable Jerome Lerner shows you how to take full advantage of an extremely useful trial tool in both civil and criminal cases—the motion *in limine.* This move to bar your opponent from introducing irrelevant, prejudicial or inflammatory evidence is often the best possible way to protect your client against an unfair verdict. Furthermore, as Judge Lerner points out, "there is no limit to the scope of matters that may indicate an appropriate invocation of this motion." You will see how other attorneys have used the motion *in limine* in cases ranging from personal liability to murder...the risks and benefits for the movant...and how the adverse party can preserve error for review.

For plaintiff's counsel Harry M. Philo, "you only get product reliability out of liability." In the no-holds-barred interview with Mr. Philo featured in this chapter, you will discover how to try your next tort case not simply to gain compensation for the victim of an accidental injury, but to *prevent* future injuries and deaths by making it too expensive for the culpable wrongdoer to proceed in an unsafe way.

In a tort claim, and in virtually every other kind of case, your success depends to a large degree on how you structure the presentation of proof.

Here to address this strategic problem are **Trial Masters Philip H. Corboy and Peter Perlman.** First, Mr. Corboy reveals a variety of courtroom tactics he uses to present a swift and pointed case that creates no difficulties for the jury while creating insurmountable difficulties for the defense. Then, Mr. Perlman, concentrating on medical proof, shows you how to put your case across with the help of such sure-fire visual evidence as medical hardware, surgeon's tools, and blow-ups of hospital records, those "living entries of pain and suffering."

Mr. Perlman reminds us that the sense of sight has a far greater impact on learning and retention than any of the other senses. There are many ways to exploit this fact at trial, but perhaps the most unusual and effective is described by **James Krueger,** who shows you how to use medical videotapes to establish proof of informed consent in a medical negligence case. Widely used by health care providers in educating patients scheduled for surgery or other treatment, these medical videotapes, as you will soon discover, are an ideal means to demonstrate at trial whether appropriate standards of disclosure were met in the case of the plaintiff.

"The trip-and-fall case or the slip-and-fall case are often maligned areas of personal injury practice," observes **Neil G. Galatz.** Yet these cases can be rewarding ones when the plaintiff's attorney adopts the special tactics which have worked so well for Mr. Galatz and which he now reveals for his fellow practitioners. Taking another kind of case and cutting it down to size, **Samuel Langerman** discusses the ins and outs of third-party bad-faith actions, where the interests of an insurance company and its insured come into conflict. You will see how to recognize and evaluate a potential bad faith case . . . how to line up the witnesses and pick the kind of jurors you need . . . and how to prove bad faith even in the most conservative of jurisdictions.

Representing the family in an action for the wrongful death of a child is "one of the more difficult and wrenching experiences faced by the modern trial lawyer," according to **Allan R. Earl.** To make your job easier and to assure a just recovery, Mr. Earl spells out a complete plan for trying your case, including a sample argument you will want to make when you have little or no concrete proof to establish actual pecuniary loss. You will also find three sample final arguments to help you demolish the defendant's chief contentions as you inspire the jury to return a substantial verdict.

Surely one of the landmark cases of our time is the $10.5 million verdict against Kerr-McGee Corporation that **Gerry Spence** won on behalf of the Karen Silkwood estate. In the following pages, you will find a riveting interview in which Mr. Spence recounts the highlights of the trial and the techniques he used to prove an injury that not only can't be seen, but can't even be shown empirically.

Whether you are a trial veteran, like Mr. Spence, or a novice, every case does not work out as planned, which is why effective appellate advocacy should be among your arsenal of courtroom weapons. To conclude *The Trial Masters,* Alfred C. Scanlon will lend you his formidable expertise in writing a strong, persuasive brief and in delivering an oral argument that is at once flexible, incisive, and above all, successful.

# Representing a Witness
# Before a Grand Jury

## Herald Price Fahringer

Herald Price Fahringer gradúated from the University of Buffalo Law School and is a partner in the law firm of Lipsitz, Green, Fahringer, Roll, Schuller and James, with offices in New York City and Buffalo. He is a Fellow of the American College of Trial Lawyers; a Fellow of the International Society of Barristers; General Counsel to the First Amendment Lawyers Association; and author of numerous articles on various legal subjects. He lectures frequently on trial advocacy at Continuing Legal Education seminars throughout the country. He is a member of the Board of Editors of *Trial Diplomacy Journal*.

Any lawyer runs the risk of receiving a call from a friend, a neighbor, or a former client, explaining that he or she has just received a subpoena to appear before a grand jury tomorrow morning at 10 a.m. The probability of a general practitioner receiving this call for help is enhanced by the fact that the witness, unlike a person accused of a crime, is unaware of his jeopardy. Therefore, the client sees no need to hire a lawyer experienced in the defense of criminal cases. The attorney's dilemma is compounded by the need to make certain decisions quickly, which may commit the client unalterably to a course of action which could end in calamity. The most prominent of those choices is whether or not the witness will invoke any privileges before the grand jury, or will elect to waive them and testify. A single response to one question may mean the forfeiture of the witness's Fifth Amendment privilege, and perhaps other rights, which may never be redeemed. On the other hand, his failure to answer a proper question accurately, assuming he has received a grant of immunity, may result in a contempt or perjury indictment. Thus, it is imperative that the lawyer, advising a client called before a grand jury, be fully aware of the witness' rights and liabilities. Our modern-day grand jury system is heavily mined with deadly procedural faults and dangers. Consequently, no phase of our work places heavier demands upon a lawyer's skills and knowledge.

### What to do When the Subpoena Arrives

After a client receives a subpoena, it is absolutely essential that the lawyer secure sufficient time to fully investigate all of the circumstances surrounding his client's connection with the grand jury's inquiry. Therefore, the witness's appearance before the grand jury, if on short notice, must be adjourned. If the prosecutor will not consent to a reasonable postponement, the witness may wish to go before the grand jury and simply read a card that states:

> "I have not had an opportunity to secure counsel and therefore request that my appearance before this body be adjourned for a reasonable period of time (a week or ten days) so that I might obtain a lawyer's advice."

A witness who has merely been invited to appear before a grand jury should arrange to receive a subpoena. The Fifth Amendment only protects a person against *compelled* disclosures. A voluntary appearance may result in the relinquishment of certain rights that may never be recovered. Furthermore, some subpoenas are instructive. It normally lists the sections of the law claimed to have been violated and, therefore, may provide some idea of the direction of the grand jury's investigation.

A prosecutor has no authority to subpoena a witness to his office. And yet, some district attorneys persist in exploiting this unfair tactic. A witness is not obliged to appear any place other than before the grand jury. On the other hand, counsel may wish to visit the prosecutor to discuss with him his client's appearance before the grand jury. A conference of this kind can be, under certain circumstances, helpful.

The scope of the subpoena should be carefully examined to determine whether or not it is too expansive or burdensome, and therefore, vulnerable to a motion to quash. Although the chance of succeeding in such an application is roughly zero, give or take a percentage point, it is an avenue which must be pursued in order to protect fully the client's rights. A full-scale discussion of motions to quash would support a separate article of this size.

## Getting a Head Start in Your Investigation

The area in which failure among lawyers representing witnesses before the grand jury is most evident, concerns the initial conference with the client. An enormous amount of time must be devoted to investigating all the circumstances relevant to the witness's appearance before the grand jury. Many lawyers loiter through this area of representation. You must completely understand the witness's role in the investigation before you can properly advise him of what rights he should invoke. You must search out other areas of peril, such as potential tax problems, or other areas of misconduct, unknown to the grand jury, which may surface during that inquiry. It is important that you learn whether or not he is a target of the grand jury's investigation, or merely a witness. The official manual issued to all United States Attorneys provides that a witness before a grand jury must be informed of his status before that body.

One method of gaining this form of vital intelligence is to call the prosecutor and ask him what the investigation is about. If he is seeking your client's cooperation, he may be willing to discuss the grand jury's interest in the person you represent. If the prosecutor is uncooperative, you may be able to contact lawyers for other witnesses, who have appeared before the grand jury, and find out what they said.

Under Rule 6(e), of the Federal Rules of Criminal Procedure, the government and the grand jurors are foreclosed from disclosing what transpired in the grand jury room. However, this restriction does not apply to a witness. Therefore, a witness is at liberty to disclose to the press or any other interested persons what he said or did before the grand jury. Courts have held that it is inappropriate for a prosecutor to direct a witness not to discuss his grand jury testimony with any other person. *In re Grand Jury*, 321 F. Supp. 238 (N.D. Ohio W.D. 1970), and *King v. Jones*, 319 F. Supp. 653 (N.D. Ohio E.D. 1970).

If, after a complete exploration of the facts surrounding your client's role in the investigation, there is the slightest chance he may endanger himself by testifying, the privilege against self-incrimination should be invoked. There is an exasperating reluctance on the part of most clients to avail themselves of this safeguard because it is so often misinterpreted by lay people as a confession of guilt. Nevertheless, such slight embarrassment must take precedence over a possible five-year prison term.

## How to Prepare Your Client for the Ordeal

A witness is entitled to invoke his privilege against self-incrimination where his words might furnish a single link in a chain of evidence connecting him with the commission of a crime. *Maloy v. Hogan*, 78 U.S. 1 (1964). Furthermore, the Supreme Court has concluded that no person may be penalized for asserting his privilege against self-incrimination. Thus, the court has nullified the ouster of a public school teacher, *Slochower v. Board of Education*, 350 U.S. 351 (1956); has repudiated the disbarrment of an attorney, *Spevack v. Klein*, 385 U.S. 511 (1967); has revoked the suspension of a police officer, *Garrity v. New Jersey*, 385 U.S. 493 (1967); has overruled the removal from office of a public official, *Perla v. New York*, 392 U.S. 296 (1968); *Lefkowitz v. Cunningham*, 431 U.S. 801 (1977); has rescinded the discharge of public employees where the individuals were disciplined merely because they invoked their privilege against self-incrimination, *Uniformed Sanitation Mens Association, Inc. v. Commissioner of Sanitation*, 392 U.S. 280 (1968); has forbidden the elimination of a contractor's right to do business with the state, *Turley v. Lefkowitz*, 414 U.S. 70 (1974).

Although the privilege against self-incrimination is the one most often relied upon before a grand jury by witnesses, it is by no means the only right available to the client. Out of an abundance of caution, you may wish to have the witness invoke the provisions of the First, Fourth, Sixth and Ninth amendments to the United States Constitution.

The First Amendment covers a witness's right to remain silent if the investigation is overly broad, unauthorized, or intrudes into other areas insulated by the First Amendment, such as political or religious beliefs.

The Fourth Amendment includes unlawful searches and seizures of either a witness's words or his records, and today embodies a complaint that the questions asked of the witness were derived from the illegal use of electronic surveillance.

The Sixth Amendment guarantees to the witness the assistance of counsel throughout the grand jury proceedings, and the Ninth Amendment generally includes any other rights which must be asserted in an extraordinary case, such as one involving a right of privacy. Accordingly, the witness may wish to read a card before the grand jury which says:

> "On advice of counsel, I respectfully decline to answer that question on the grounds that my answer may tend to incriminate me. And, furthermore, to answer that question would violate my rights under the First, Fourth, Sixth, and Ninth amendments to the United States Constitution."

Most witnesses are ill-equipped to manage the claims which must be made before a grand jury without having them written out in large type on three-by-five cards. Counsel should try to accommodate every situation that may possibly arise in the grand jury room with written directions to the witness. Counsel must make certain that the witness's testimony is not protected by any other privileges, such as attorney/client; husband/wife; physician/patient; clergyman/penitent.

If the witness is granted immunity or decides that he or she would like to appear and testify before the grand jury, it is important that the client be adequately prepared. The witness must understand that he will be subjected to an open throttle cross-examination that may lurch back and forth between as many as two or three prosecutors. The client will enter a state of siege, bordered on the east with perjury; on the west with contempt; and on the south with indictment. Therefore, counsel may want to put the client through several sweaty scrimmages of cross-examination to prepare him for what he is about to face.

Explain the grand jury setting to the witness. You may wish to take the witness to an empty grand jury room and familiarize him with those surroundings. Explain to the witness that the prosecution's attempt to squeeze him dry by a grinding cross-examination cannot be avoided with answers such as, "I can't recall". Explain to him that any mistakes made before the grand jury can be corrected if promptly brought to the grand jury's attention through a letter. Keeping his answers short and to the point will help him realize his yearning to go home.

Alert him to those special questions which are normally followed by trouble, such as:

"Are you absolutely certain that Dracula wasn't present at that meeting?"
"Are you absolutely certain you never met a Mr. Barracuda?"

These telltale questions normally forebode that the prosecution has information that contradicts what the witness has said. A witness faced with these danger signals may wish to review his testimony and protect himself by saying, "I believe that's the fact, but I cannot be sure," or, "I may well have been mistaken."

Sometimes, the more aggressive prosecutor will frisk a witness in the grand jury room by asking the indiscreet question, "How did you get Mr. Jones as your lawyer? Who is paying your lawyer? How much is he being paid?" The client may wish to stand up against such unseemly questions by asking, "How is that question relevant to this grand jury's investigation?" If the witness is dissatisfied with the prosecutor's explanation, he may ask to be taken before a judge for a ruling on the propriety of that inquiry. Warn the witness that he may be asked when was the last time he talked with or saw the target of the grand jury's investigation. He should be prepared to answer these questions frankly and forthrightly.

Many witnesses who appear before a grand jury are quite nervous and will often take tranquilizers as a form of chemical comfort. If that is the fact, the client should advise the jury of his reliance on any pharmaceuticals.

If the witness is elderly and has a bad memory, the grand jury should be told about it. At the conclusion of the grand jury session, your client may wish to ask of the grand jurors:

> "Are there any other questions that the grand jurors would like to ask me? I would be glad to try to answer them."

If the prosecution has in mind a contempt indictment, this unsolicited inquiry may prove to be useful in a subsequent trial.

### The Right of Consultation and How to Handle It Properly

In most states, a witness before a grand jury has no right to have counsel present with him inside the grand jury room. However, the grand jury witness has a constitutional right to confer with his attorney outside the grand jury room. *In re Tierney,* 465 F.2d 805 (5th Cir. 1972); *United States* v. *Duncan,* 456 F.2d 1401 (9th Cir. 1972); *People* v. *Ianniello,* 21 N.Y.2d 418, 288 N.Y.S.2d 462 (1968).

However, the witness and counsel should be careful not to abuse this right of consultation. If it becomes apparent that their conferences are being conducted for "strategic purposes," rather than to secure "legal advice," further discussion may be foreclosed. "Strategic purposes" involves the lawyer's instructing the witness how to answer the question; whereas, a conference on "legal rights" concerns the witness' obligation to answer the question. Consequently, when it is necessary for a witness to consult with his lawyer, he should be sure to advise the grand jury that the purpose of the conference is to obtain advice covering his "legal rights". He should ask:

> "I request that I be allowed to confer with my attorney so that I might be advised of what my legal rights are concerning this question."

The next most important question that the witness should ask the grand jury is:

"Are any of the questions that will be asked of me based in any way upon evidence acquired through any form of electronic surveillance?"

If the prosecutor admits that the inquiry will be based on evidence acquired through electronic surveillance, the witness is entitled to go before a judge to ascertain whether the electronic surveillance was conducted by court order. He is not entitled to a hearing on that issue. Once it is established that eavesdropping forms the basis for much of the inquiry before the grand jury, the witness may well then wish to ask to hear the tape, or see a transcript of the electronic surveillance. To date, a witness has no absolute right to that relief.

### What You Must Do As Soon As the Grand Jury Appearance Is Over

When the witness's appearance before the grand jury is terminated—run, do not walk, to the nearest exit. It is imperative that your client be fully debriefed. Using a tape recorder, you should try to get as much from the witness as is possible concerning his recollections of what he said to the grand jury. This is usually a tedious, unglamorous ordeal, but it is a task that must be borne if your representation of the witness is to be successful. The record of what he said should then be typed up and preserved. If it turns out that the witness before the grand jury was unfriendly to the government's position, he may never have a chance to see his grand jury testimony. Your memorandum will be the only record available to him when he is called to testify at the trial, some six months to a year later. It will be invaluable to him at that time.

If your client is not indicted, you've done your job well. If he is, hopefully your representation of him was skillful enough to lead to a successful defense of those charges. And should that not be true, then—appeal immediately!

# The Motion *in limine*: A Useful Trial Tool

## The Honorable Jerome Lerner

Judge Lerner is a Judge of the Circuit Court of Cook County, assigned to the Law Jury Division. He has served on the bench since 1976 and has presided over numerous major civil jury trials. Judge Lerner is presently chairman of the Illinois Judicial Conference Study Committee on Dispute Resolution. Prior to serving on the bench, he was engaged in the general practice of law and as an instructor of law. Judge Lerner is a frequent lecturer to the bar on the subject of jury trials.

The term *in limine* is defined as "on or at the threshold; at the very beginning; preliminarily."[1] A motion *in limine* is a trial procedure "usually used to prohibit mention of some specific matter such as an inflammatory piece of evidence, until the admissibility of that matter has been shown out of the hearing of the jury."[2] It has also been described as a pre-trial motion which seeks an order excluding certain evidence on the ground that its admission would violate some ordinary rule of evidence.[3] Although it is ordinarily made prior to the commencement of the trial, it may be invoked during the course of trial, as occurred in *Bruske v. Arnold*.[4] The ruling granting the motion, until it can be addressed during the testimonial phase of the trial, is a "preliminary-prohibitive" order. The ruling prior to trial that precludes any further reference to the subject matter of the motion is an "absolute-prohibitive" order.

Although this procedure, as a trial tool, has been extensively and effectively utilized by experienced jury trial practitioners, its function may be unfamiliar to the general bar whose members have infrequent occasion to try cases to a jury. The lack of notoriety of this procedure may be due to its comparatively recent recognition. One of the earliest decisions to recognize its use in a civil trial is reported to be a case decided by the Alabama Supreme Court in 1933.[5] The earliest reported decision of the recognition, with approval, of such an exclusionary motion in a criminal case emanates from the Supreme Court of Washington in 1937.[6] In the latter decision, the trial court was upheld in its ruling barring the prosecuting attorney from inquiry into discreditable circumstances of the defendant's termination from military service. It has been held to be within the inherent power of the court to entertain such motion.[7]

## What the Motion *in limine* Can Do for You

The motion may request the court to bar the opposing party from introducing, or attempting to introduce, certain evidence which the movant contends is irrelevant and the effect of the question and/or answer, although ordered stricken, would produce a prejudicial effect. This motion may also address evidence which, although relevant, would have a prejudicial effect that would far outweigh its probative value. The Federal Rules of Evidence specifically provide for the exclusion of such evidence.[8]

One might argue that the admonitions to the jury contained in the very first of the standard jury instructions invariably given to the jury both in civil and criminal cases[9] should suffice to erase any prejudicial effect of evidence attempted to be introduced at trial, and statements of counsel to which objections were sustained. It was held in *Department of Public Works v. Sun Oil Co.*[10] that the State's violation of an order granting a motion *in limine* in favor of the defendant "was not cured and the prejudice removed by the trial court's ruling, and admonition to the jury to disregard the question and response made by the witness . . . . It is most difficult to determine what effect such conduct and error had on the minds of the jurors."

In *State v. Church of Nazarene*[11] the following language from an earlier decision was quoted with approval by the Indiana Supreme Court:

> Motions *in limine* are a part of the Indiana practice. The trial court's authority to entertain 'motions *in limine*' emanates from its inherent power to admit and exclude evidence. This inherent power to exclude extends to prejudicial questions and statements that could be made in the presence of a jury, and thereby interfere with fair and impartial administration of justice.
>
> If prejudicial matters are brought before the jury, no amount of objection or instruction can remove the harmful effect, and the plaintiff is powerless unless he wants to forgo his chance of trial and ask for a mistrial. Once the question is asked, the harm is done. Under the harmless error rule many

of these matters would probably not be reversible error even though they have a subtle but devastating effect on the plaintiff's case.


## How Other Attorneys Have Used the Motion *in limine*

There is virtually no limit to the scope of matters that may indicate an appropriate invocation of this motion. The following cases are cited merely for illustration of some of the matters that have been the subject of an *in limine* motion.[12]

In *Benuska v. Dahl*,[13] a personal injury action, defendant moved *in limine*, prior to trial, to preclude plaintiff from introducing any evidence of drinking on the part of this defendant. It was contended that unless it could be shown that the drinking caused this defendant to be intoxicated at the time of the occurrence, it would be irrelevant and prejudicial.

In an action to recover from lower back injuries allegedly sustained in an auto accident, plaintiff moved *in limine* to exclude evidence by defendant of plaintiff's prior accident and unrelated injuries.[14]

The holding in *Burger v. Van Severen*[15] indicates that a motion *in limine* would be appropriate to exclude evidence of a settlement with another party. Similarly such motion would exclude evidence of prior negotiation and settlement offers previously made in condemnation proceedings.[16]

In *Hulsebus v. Russian*,[17] a color photograph taken in an operating room which disclosed plaintiff in a gory and hideous condition was excluded from evidence as being likely to influence and prejudice the jury. It should be noted that there was detailed medical testimony describing the injury. The *Hulsebus* case provided an example of the procedure undertaken by plaintiff to obtain a "permissive" ruling in advance of trial to allow the introduction of color photographs.[18] Only one of the four photographs for which permission was sought, relative to subsequent use in evidence, was objected to, and excluded by the trial court.

In *People v. Ross*[19] defendant moved *in limine* to exclude from evidence two color photographs showing the victim's dismembered body. Defendant contended that the exhibits were so gruesome as to be highly prejudicial and to be unnecessary to establish a cause of death because a complete description of the injuries had been stated by a pathologist. The Appellate Court held, following the precedent of *People v. Foster*[20] and *People v. Lindgren*[21] that trial judges have discretion "to admit, if they choose, photographs of the victim at the scene of the crime which are probative of any fact in issue."

Numerous additional illustrations of the general use of motions *in limine*, and similar exclusionary rulings, in civil and criminal cases in other jurisdictions may be found in 20 Am. Jur. Trials 441, the Annotations at 84 ALR2d 1087 and 63ALR3d 311, and 15 Cleveland Marshall Law Review 255, Motions *In Limine*.

## Risks and Benefits for the Movant

When and whether one should employ the motion *in limine* requires careful analysis. Unless there has been an adequate investigation of the facts and a complete discovery process, it could be that the movant would be educating the opposing party to facts and circumstances which might be detrimental and prejudicial to the movant. It would appear unwise by the motion to advise one's opponent that his party had been drinking sometime prior to the occurrence or had a prior criminal conviction involving dishonesty, if such information had not been previously disclosed during investigation or as a result of discovery.

On the other hand, a motion *in limine* seeking a ruling in advance of trial on the admissibility of certain testimony may save the expense of calling a particular witness, as well as avoid the impact on the jury of the failure, as a result of a sustained objection, to present the testimony for which the witness had obviously been called. Illustrative of this circumstance is what occurred in *Mareci v. General Motors*.[22] In *Mareci*, in the midst of his testimony, a consulting engineer was barred, as a result of a sustained objection, from rendering an opinion on a critical evidentiary issue. If the proponent of this testimony had reason to expect a challenge to the foundation for the witness's opinion, an advance ruling by motion would have settled the question. This result must be measured against the risk one takes of inspiring an objection to admissibility and of an adverse ruling if the motion suggests the movant has a tentative or doubtful position on admissibility.

## The View of the Courts

The Court, in *Bradley v. Caterpillar Tractor Co.*,[23] confirmed the usefulness of the motion as a trial tool but cautioned against an indiscriminate application lest parties be prevented from even trying to prove their contentions. "Nor should a party ordinarily be required to try a case or defense twice—once outside the jury's presence to satisfy the trial court of its sufficiency and then again before the jury .... The motion is a drastic one, preventing a party as it does from presenting his evidence in the usual way. Its use should be exceptional rather than general."[24]

In *People v. Garfield*[25] the trial court had granted the state's motion *in limine* preventing the defense from any mention during the trial of defendant's intoxicated state or drugged condition. By this order the reviewing court held that the trial court had deprived defendant of raising a valid defense to the charge. The motion should be used with caution particularly in a criminal case where the granting of a motion *in limine* would have the effect of preventing an accused from raising a defense."[26]

The Appellate Court in *Department of Public Works v. Roehrig*[27] expressed a far more receptive view toward the "correct" use of a motion *in limine*: "Because the correct use of these motions promotes jury trials that are devoid of prejudice, this court believes such motion should be explicitly recognized as part of the civil procedure of this State [citations]. Even in the absence of authorization by statute or Illinois Supreme Court rule, the inherent power of a circuit court to admit or exclude evidence is sufficient to enable it to entertain a motion *in limine*."[28]

Addressing a serious evidentiary question immediately prior to trial via this motion provides a more relaxed and in-depth analysis of the issue both for the litigants and the court. As was noted in *People v. Shrader*,[29] counsel should be encouraged to bring such motions in advance of trial "to enable the trial court to exercise its discretion to grant or deny such motions under less hectic and more thoughtful circumstances" than is normally available during the testimonial aspect of the trial.

Assuming counsel have researched and are well prepared with legal authority in support of their position on the motion, it is more probable that a correct ruling will follow. As the Supreme Court of Indiana noted in *State v. Church of Nazarene*,[30] "Another advantage in the use of these motions is to allow the trial judge an opportunity to study the question and the authorities involved. If presented in advance of trial with a brief and with the time to study it, the court will be more inclined to grant the motion."[31]

## Key Factors Affecting the Court's Ruling

The trial court's ruling at the outset of the trial also provides an early opportunity for counsel to know whether or not they will need to address this evidentiary issue during trial. Certainly the ruling must affect trial strategy and the marshalling of evidence. Whether or not one must face the issue of the non-use of a seat belt or the nature and extent of prior injuries presents a problem that entails considerable expense, as well as preparation. It has been suggested by trial counsel that an early ruling may result in the settlement of a case "since a key evidentiary issue may have been decided."[32]

Counsel may be so far-sighted as to seek a ruling on a motion *in limine* during the discovery stage of the case to determine a particular issue well in advance of trial. In Cook County, Illinois, the Motion Section could be the forum for such a ruling. However, an earlier ruling by a judge in the Motion Section could, on motion, be reconsidered by the trial judge, and since the initial order would be interlocutory, there could be a change in the ruling.[33] Additionally, later discovery could cast an entirely different perspective on the admissibility of the evidence at issue. The trial court itself, as a result of evidence developed at the trial, may reverse its own former ruling. This occurred in *Benuska v. Dahl,* where because of the late stage of the trial at which this change of its ruling occurred and its detrimental effect on one of the defendants, the reviewing court held the trial court had committed reversible error.[34]

The trial court must be provided with enough factual information to make an informed ruling. It is incumbent on counsel to provide such an adequate factual basis. When the court, in the exercise of its discretion, is of the opinion that an insufficient basis for its ruling is present, or is of the opinion that the development of evidence in the normal course of trial will provide greater clarification, the court may reserve its ruling until that point in the trial is reached.

When the court, at the pretrial hearing, reserves its ruling for later determination, it must then consider whether or not it will allow any reference to the subject matter during voir dire and opening statement. This decision requires weighing the potential for prejudice should the motion later be granted.[35]

It is in the interest of the movant that an exclusionary order be sufficiently broad so as to prevent any statement or other reference to the prejudicial matter not only during the testimonial aspect of the trial but also during voir dire and opening statement. It is in the interest of the respondent that the order be as free from ambiguity as possible to avoid an interpretation, not previously contemplated, with potentially dire consequence. In *Bradley,*[36] counsel for the defendant was held in contempt of court for violating the court's *in limine* orders.

The Illinois Supreme Court, in *People v. Graves,*[37] upheld a conviction of counsel for contempt: "When certain matters are withdrawn from the consideration of the jury, counsel may not, through question or comment, expose the jury to the very matters withdrawn from its consideration, and a summary conviction of contempt based on such conduct is not a denial of due process."

The hazard of an *in limine* order that may be overbroad, or lacking in clarity and specificity, is clearly illustrated in *Bradley*,[38] and the consequent confusion that may follow is vividly observed in the opinion of *Reidelberger v. Highland Body Shop.*[39]

Customarily, motions *in limine* made prior to trial are, and should be, in writing. The order granting the motion should also be in writing even though it may not be necessary for the record. There is less likelihood for misinterpretation if the motion and order are in writing.

### How the Adverse Party Can Preserve Error for Review

When the ruling granting the motion excludes evidence, the adverse party, to preserve error for review, should make an offer of proof on the record. It has been held that "In order to preserve error alleged to have resulted from the exclusion of evidence, an offer of proof is usually necessary, and if not properly made, any alleged error will be waived."[40]

If required, the offer "must show what the offered proof is or what the expected testimony will be, by whom, or how it was made and what its purpose is." *Scaggs v. Horton.*[41] In *Scaggs*, it was contended that the trial court erred in excluding evidence of prior collisions at the intersection where plaintiff's injury occurred. The reviewing court held that defendant had failed to make a sufficient offer of proof to preserve error.

The failure to make a formal offer of proof does not waive the right to urge error, where the record disclosed, on the hearing on the motion, the judge was fully apprised of the nature and content of the testimony the witness would have given.[42]

There do not appear specific guidelines for the manner in which the court should conduct its hearing on the motion *in limine*. It generally consists of representations by counsel, reference to sworn answers to interrogatories, statements of witnesses, deposition testimony or formal offers through witnesses. In *People v. Eddington*[43] the Illinois Surpeme Court approved a thorough and lengthy hearing in which the trial court itself questioned the witness and the prosecutor.

McCormick on Evidence poses the following hypothesis.

"Suppose . . . there are several witnesses who are available, but not in court, to prove a line of facts, and the judge's rulings on the law have indicated that he will probably exclude this line of testimony, or the judge rules in advance that the line of testimony is inadmissible. Must the party produce each of these witnesses, question them, and on exclusion, state the purport of each expected answer?"[44]

Some cases hold that a witness must ordinarily be placed on the stand and questioned in connection with the making of an offer of proof.[45] The Illinois Supreme Court, in *Garvey v. Chicago Rys. Co.,* appears to countenance an offer without the production of witnesses.[46] The line of cases which hold that an offer is not necessary when the trial judge understands the character of the evidence and the nature of the objection, and rules on that basis, would support the view that the production of witnesses for the purpose of the offer is not necessary.[47] *Hession v. Liberty Asphalt Products, Inc.*[48] supports the rule that where it is obvious that the witness is competent to testify to the fact, and it is obvious what his testimony will be, if permitted to testify, a brief statement by counsel may suffice.

When the motion to exclude is denied, moving counsel must determine whether to rely solely on the order of denial itself to preserve error on the ruling, or to proceed to make objection during trial when the evidence is proffered. There is authority the latter course must be taken.[49] There is also authority that to preserve error, objection need not be renewed at the time the evidence is offered.[50] Prudence would dictate the former procedure as the safest course to follow.

## Notes

1. *Black's Law Dictionary Fifth Edition,* 1979, West Publishing Co., St. Paul, Minn.

2. *Bradley* v. *Caterpillar,* 75 Ill.App.3d 890, 394 N.E.2d 825 (1979) quoting the opinion in *Lewis* v. *Buena Vista Mutual,* (Iowa 1971) 183 N.W.2d 198. *Gendron* v. *Pawtucket Mutual Insurance Co.,* 409 A.2d 656 (Me. 1979); *Burrus* v. *Silhavy,* 293 N.E.2d 794 (Ind. 1973). See also: *State* v. *Tate,* 261 S.E.2d 506 (N.C.App. 1980), *State* v. *Quick,* 597 P.2d 1108 (Dan.1979).

3. *Dept. of Pub. Wks.* v. *Sun Oil Co.,* 66 Ill.App.3d 64, 383 N.E.2d 631 (1978). *Wilkins* v. *Royal Indemnity Co.,* 592 S.W.2d 64 (Tex.Civ. App. 1979).

4. *Bruske* v. *Arnold,* 100 Ill.App.2d 428, 241 N.E.2d 191 (1968). *City of Corpus Christi* v. *Nemec,* 404 S.W.2d 834 (Tex.Civ.App.1966); cf *State* v. *Johnson,* 183 N.W.2d 194 (Iowa, 1971) (Motion in limine should not be used to reject evidence until trial); but see *Berger* v. *Superior Court,* 499 P.2d 153 (Ariz.1972).

5. *Bradford* v. *Birmingham Electric Co.,* (Ala. 1933) 149 So. 729.

6. Rothblatt and Leroy, Motion In Limine Practice, 20 Am.Jur. Trials 441, citing *State* v. *Smith,* (Wash. 1937) 65 P.2d 1075.

7. *State* v. *Church of Nazarene,* (Ind. 1978) 377 N.E.2d 607; *Dept. of Pub. Wks.* v. *Roehrig,* 45 Ill.App.3d 189,359 N.E.2d 752 (1976). See *Burrus,* note 2; *People* v. *Jackson,* 95 Cal. Rptr.919 (1971).

8. FED. R. EVID. 403

9. IPI 2d Edition (Civil) 1.01; IPI (Criminal) 1.02 and 1.03.

10. See note 3, supra. *Sacramento & San Joaquin Drainage District* v. *Reed,* 29 Cal.Rptr.847 (1963); *State* v. *Jensen,* 216 N.W.2d 369 (Iowa, 1974); but see *Montgomery* v. *Vinzant,* 297 S.W.2d 350 (Tex.Civ.App. 1957).

11. *State* v. *Church of Nazarene* (Ind. 1978) 377 N.E.2d 607. *Lapasinskas* v. *Quick,* 170 N.W.2d 318 (Mich. 1969).

12. The criminal cases cited herein involve evidentiary questions and principles common to the civil cases.

13. *Benuska* v. *Dahl,* 87 Ill.App.3d 911, 410 N.E.2d 249 (1980). *Jordan* v. *Berkey,* 611 P.2d 1382 (Wash.App.1980).

14. *Khatib* v. *McDonald,* 87 Ill.App.3d 1087, 410 N.E.2d 266 (1980). *Calvanese* v. *A.S.W. Taxi Corp.,* 405 N.E.2d 1001 (Mass.App.1980).

15. *Burger* v. *Van Severen,* 39 Ill.App.2d 205, 188 N.E.2d 373 (1963). *Hartford Accident and Indemnity Co.* v. *McCardell,* 369 S.W.2d 331 (Tex.1963); *Bruckman* v. *Pena,* 487 P.2d 566 (Colo.-App. 1971).

16. *Dept. of Pub. Wks.* v. *Sun Oil Co.,* see note 3, supra.

17. *Hulsebus* v. *Russian,* 118 Ill.App.2d 174, 254 N.E.2d 184 (1969). But see *Holmes* v. *Black River Electric Cooperative, Inc.,* 262 S.E.2d 875 (S.C. 1980).

18. This motion requests a "permissive" order as distinguished from the "prohibitive" forms.

19. *People* v. *Ross,* 89 Ill.App.3d 128, 411 N.E.2d 1187 (1980). *State* v. *Oughton,* 612 P.2d 812 (Wash.App.1980); *State* v. *Vernon,* 385 So.2d 200 (La.1980).

20. *People* v. *Foster,* 76 Ill.2d 365, 392 N.E.2d 6 (1979).

21. *People* v. *Lindgren,* 79 Ill.2d 129, 402 N.E.2d 238 (1980).

22. *Mareci* v. *General Motors* _____ Ill.App.3d _____ filed Nov. 5, 1980. Docket No. 78-1538 (1st Dist.).

23. See note 2, supra.

24. Id. at 900. See *State* v. *Johnson,* note 4, supra; cf *State* v. *Flett,* 380 P.2d 634 (Or. 1963) (trial court need not conduct "dress rehearsal" in which defendant may explore the State's case).

25. *People* v. *Garfield,* 72 Ill.App.3d 107, 390 N.E.2d 612 (1979).

26. Id. at 113. See *State* v. *Bradley,* 576 P.2d 647 (Kan. 1978). Perhaps it was due to the problems encountered by trial counsel and the trial court in the interpretation of the *in limine* orders that gave rise to the view expressed by the Illinois Supreme Court in *Reidelberger* v *Highland Body shop* that the *in limine* motion is

a "powerful weapon" and "a potentially dangerous one." This particular Supreme Court Opinion is so recent that we don't have a reporter number for it. It has the Supreme Court of Illinois docket number 53051, and it was an opinion filed in the January term of 1981. (See footnote 39—the Supreme Court opinion affirms the Appellate Court.)

27. *Dept. of Pub. Wks.* v. *Roehrig*, 45 Ill.App.3d 189, 359 N.E.2d 752 (1976).

28. Id. at 195. See *Burrus*, note 2 supra.

29. *People* v. *Shrader*, (Mich. 1979) 279 N.W.2d 47.

30. *State* v. *Church of Nazarene*, (Ind. 1978) 377 N.E.2d 607.

31. Id. at p. 611-12.

32. Skolrood, Medical Evidence, ch. 4. Ill. Institute for Continuing Legal Education (1976). *Russell* v. *Lake Sherwood Acres, Inc.*, 388 So.2d 822 (La. 1980); cf *Gendron* v. *Pawtucket Mutual Insurance Co.*, 409 A.2d 656 (Me. 1979) (motion in limine may be used to narrow issues, shorten trial and save costs for litigants).

33. See *Towns* v. *Yellow Cab Co.*, 73 Ill.2d 113, 382 N.E.2d 1217 (1978). Cf *People* v. *Lopex*, 356 N.Y.S. 2d 481 (1974) (inappropriate for judge at Motion Term to bind trial judge by ruling on particular items of evidence); see also *Jordan*, note 13, supra.

34. See note 13, supra. Cf *Lapasinskas* v. *Quick*, 170 N.W.2d 318 (Mich. 1969) (reversible error for trial judge to permit violation of ruling excluding prejudicial remarks); see also *Burdick* v. *York Oil Co.*, 364 S.W. 2d 766 (Tex.Civ.App. 1963).

35. In Benuska, see note 13, supra, the appellate court noted the significance of the early ruling's effect on voir dire and the content of the opening statement.

36. See note 2, supra. The contempt conviction was subsequently reversed in *People* v. *Bernard*, 75 Ill.App.3d 786, 394 N.E.2d 819(1979).

37. *People* v. *Graves*, 74 Ill.2d 279, 384 N.E.2d 1311 (1979). See *Burdick*, note 34, supra.

38. See note 2, supra. See *Lawrence* v. *Lawrence*, 384 So.2d 279 (Fla.App. 1980) (one cannot be held in contempt for violation of order which is not clear and definite); see also *Wilkins*, note 3, supra.

39. *Reidelberger* v. *Highland Body Shop*, 79 Ill.App.3d 1138, 399 N.E.2d 247 (1979).

40. *Scaggs* v. *Horton*, 85 Ill.App.3d 541, 411 N.E.2d 870, (1980); *Simon* v. *Plotkin*, 50 Ill.App.3d 603, 365 N.E. 2d 1022 (1977); cf *Pioneer Hi Bred Corn* v. *Northern Ill. Gas*, 61 Ill.2d 6, 329 N.E.2d 228 (1975). See also *International Harvester Credit Corp.* v. *Formento*, 593 S.W.2d 576 (Mo.App. 1979).

41. See *Scaggs*, note 40, supra at p. 546.

**42.** *Lindley* v. *St. Mary's Hospital*, 85 Ill.App.3d 559, 406 N.E.2d 952 (1980); *Schusler* v. *Fletcher*, 74 Ill.App.2d 249, 219 N.E.2d 588 (1966). *Mixis* v. *Wisconsin Public Service*, 132 N.W.2d 769 (Wis. 1965).

**43.** *People* v. *Eddington*, 77 Ill.2d 41, 394 N.E.2d 1185 (1979). See *Flett*, note 24, supra.

**44.** McCormick on Evidence, 1972 West Publishing Co., St. Paul Minn.

**45.** Id. at 112 footnote 17, citing the annotation in 89 ALR2d 279, 283-286.

**46.** *Garvey* v. *Chicago Rys. Co.*, 339 Ill. 276, 171 N.E. 271 (1930); but see *Austin Liquor Mart* v. *Dept. of Revenue*, 18 Ill.App.3d 894, 310 N.E.2d 719 (1974). See also *State* v. *Dodge*, 397 A.2d 588 (Tex.Civ.App., 1966).

**47.** See note 43, supra.

**48.** *Hession* v. *Liberty Asphalt Products*, 93 Ill.App.2d 65, 235 N.E.2d 17 (1968) but see *Nielson* v. *Brown*, 374 P.2d 896 (Or. 1962) (suppressing testimony of witness in advance is "not commended").

**49.** *State* v. *Church of Nazarene* (Ind. 1978) 377 N.E.2d 607. See *Wilkins*, note 3, supra; but see *Biard Oil Co.* v. *St. Louis Railway Co.*, 522 S.W.2d 588 (Tex.Civ.App. 1975).

**50.** *State* v. *O'Connell* (Iowa 1979) 275 N.W.2d 197; *State* v. *Miller* (Iowa 1975) 229 N.W.2d 762. See *Mixis*, note 42, supra; *State* v. *Miller*, 229 N.W.2d 762 (Iowa, 1975) (if decision on motion in limine indicates that it is beyond question whether or not challenged evidence will be admitted during trial, decision on motion has effect of ruling and objection need not be raised at trial).

# Torts, Common Sense
## and the
## Empathetic Juror

### An Interview with Harry M. Philo

Harry M. Philo, of Detroit, Michigan, is a past President of the Association of Trial Lawyers of America. He is past President of the Michigan Trial Lawyers Association, a member of the faculty of the National College of Advocacy (ATLA), a member of the Editorial Board of the Journal of Products Liability, and author of *Lawyers Desk Reference: Technical Sources for Conducting a Personal Injury Action* (six editions).

EDITOR: Your prescription for preventing or reducing injuries, as you put it in one of your articles, is by making it too expensive to proceed in an unsafe way.

PHILO: Right, You only get safety in our society out of liability. You only get product reliability out of liability. You don't get it any other way in our society. You have to make it more expensive to do it in the unsafe way. As soon as it's made too expensive to do it in the unsafe way, they will do it in a safe way.

The taxpayers have paid the whole shot in the past for the culpability of business. Now in the last twenty years plaintiff's tort lawyers have started to shift the burden of accidental injuries and death and their cost from the taxpayer to the culpable wrongdoers. Instead of the taxpayer having to pay all the welfare cost—all the welfare, extra hospitals, extra doctors, extra nursing, extra drugs, extra transportation for medical, extra prosthetic devices—now some of that's being shifted to culpable wrongdoers. But we have to expand liability far beyond where we've expanded it, because there's still all sorts of unreasonable privilege in the law to business.

EDITOR: You wrote about the inability of some attorneys to understand applicable standards of care.

PHILO: I think the biggest task in educating the plaintiff's bar is to get the less experienced lawyers to understand that safety is not common sense, that safety is very sophisticated business, and that all accidental injuries and deaths can be prevented. And they are not prevented primarily by safe practices: drive safely, operate your machine safely, be careful. They are prevented by industrial hygiene, safety systems engineering, failure mode and effect analysis, good quality control, adequate instructions for reasonably safe use, and adequate warnings against reasonably foreseeable misuse as part of basic design of every product. We kill and maim just too many people in this society, and the cost of accidental injuries and deaths that can be prevented in a year exceeds the whole defense budget. It's one of the great aspects of immorality within this society.

The essential purpose of tort law is accident prevention. It's the job of the tort lawyer to know it. It's the job of the tort lawyer to be the expert in safety and know as least as much as their own expert about it, even prior to consulting the expert, because they have to make a critical evaluation of the competence of their own expert. Most of the complicated tort cases for plaintiffs have been lost in the last twenty years because the plaintiff's attorney relied on either an expert to reject liability, or a token expert that didn't know a damn thing about safety.

EDITOR: While we're on the subject of the expert, you wrote that "the expert must be a social architect charged with formulating social rules of behavior to minimize the harm associated with our advanced technology."

PHILO: We seek the expert who understands the social architecture and who is part and parcel of the group of experts that are trying to make a safer society. So the expert, when he presents that kind of testimony for the jury, for the trial judge and for the appellate court, is making a major contribution to the social architecture as far as the prevention of accidental injury and death. You not only save the tragedy, but you save tremendous cost within society if you do it. So, the expert that the plaintiff seeks to employ has to be somebody who is interested in a safer society. Unless they're philosophically interested in a better society, they don't undertake the hard task of equipping themselves with what is reasonable prudence in design, manufacture, sale, construction, or what have you; or they don't undertake the hard task of understanding mechanics of injury, etiology of disease, etiology of chemical insult, mechanics of ignition, the foreseeability of intervening conduct, or human factors engineering that will allow them to understand the injured person or the decedent in relationship to their environment. So, the expert that the plaintiff employs has to be a very capable individual.

### The Two Key Points on Which to Build a Winning Case

EDITOR: Let's go to trial techniques.

PHILO: The first point is that every good plaintiff's lawyer wants an intelligent, down-the-middle, hard-working jurist who allows the lawyers to try the case, but has some discipline. But even before going to court we always prepare a safety brief, in addition to legal and medical briefs, that would give the jurist who tries the case some understanding of the safety engineering that's going to be involved in the case—the safety standards that are available, the technical literature that's available, the patients, the statistics, the case histories, competitor's data, and so on. So the judge who is oriented to the proposition that safety is common sense gets a little greater sophistication before any evidence is received.

The second thing that I believe philosophically in the trial of a case for a plaintiff is in the selection of a jury. I think that the prime consideration in selecting a jury is to understand something about intelligence. The first quality of intelligence is empathy. It is not how many years in college or graduate school, or whether one is an executive, or so on. The first quality of intelligence is empathy. That's a reasoned concern for the rest of humanity. So I want jurors who have empathy; not sympathy from the heart, but empathy from the mind, a reasoned concern for the rest of society. The degree to which a juror has been oppressed in life, to that extent are they potentially good jurors. To the extent that one has been a selfish person in life and has no empathy and has no concern, but just worries about their own family and their own self, to that extent are they bad plaintiff's jurors. And I don't select a juror depending on the color of their tie or their body language or anything else. I pick it by seeking that first quality of intelligence: empathy.

### Reaching the Empathetic Juror

EDITOR: How do you distinguish between the empathetic juror and the selfish juror?

PHILO: Status in life. I think the working class on the whole, and the working class jurors on a whole, are brighter than middle-class jurors or wealthy jurors. I think that the average person on an assembly line in an industrial plant is brighter and is more capable of understanding the issues and being a fair jury than the engineer or the architect or the corporate executive or the insurance company vice-president. And I think you distinguish it basically by station in life or status in life. To that extent, going into the trial I have a little different philosophy than some other plantiff's lawyers.

The next thing that I think is important is the use of demonstrative aids in the opening statement. I always have a large blowup of our theories of liability, which I think allows the jury to understand better the theories of liability in the case. And I usually have charts of the relationships of the parties and what I intend to prove. And most often I use an artist's sketch of the accident scene in the opening statement, because that can be much better understood by the jury than just a verbal picture.

I construct the opening statement to include an introduction to the opening statement, the theories of liability, the evidence to support the theories, and the witnesses to bring the evidence; but next, the defenses of the defendant and the evidence to meet those defenses and the witnesses to bring that evidence; and then the theory of damages, the evidence to support the damages and the witnesses to bring that evidence. The opening statement is very important and I think every plaintiff's lawyer believes that.

EDITOR: Specifically what would you say about the defendant's case?

PHILO: "There is another aspect of liability that I must tell you about. The defendant in this case claims that my client assumed the risk. The defendant in this case claims my client was guilty of contributory negligence. The defendant in this case claims that my client misused. I want to tell you what my evidence will be to meet those defenses and my witnesses to bring that evidence to you." Because you're entitled to tell what the nature of your case is. Well, the nature of your case is not just your affirmative thrust, but involves your ability to defend. And I think that is overlooked by 99.9% of the plaintiff's lawyers. They don't seek to tell that aspect of their proofs. I think it's very important.

### How to Win the Liability Aspect of Your Case

EDITOR: Do you agree with some plaintiff's lawyers that you should try to win the liability aspect of the case in opening statement?

PHILO: In the cases that I try or the cases that many major plaintiff's tort lawyers try, you should win liability before you ever go to court. I think with the propaganda, the associations of business today and the Chamber of Commerce or the insurance industry, where they have a thirteenth juror in every jury room because of their massive advertising and the unfair nature of their advertising, then if a plaintiff does not have an 80% case when he goes in, he shouldn't even wait for the jury verdict. You get the 80% case before you go in by your recognition of liability and your development of liability, and your preparation. And I think it's a mistake to suggest that you win it on opening statement. I think that, to the extent that you can without arguing, paint culpability in opening statement by telling your theories of liability, by having a correct theory of liability, by having the correct evidence, and having the correct witnesses, and having the correct material to meet defenses, to *that* extent do you start to shift to damages. But the cases that are tried with good plaintiff's lawyers tend to have some difficult factual problems that prevented you from settling the case. So, you can desire all you want to paint a picture of liabiity in the opening statement, and that's your duty; but these cases are, for the most part, contested on the liability. You're not quarreling as much about the damages as you are quarreling about liability.

I want to paint as good a picture of liability without arguing as I can in opening statement. You can start to teach a jury safety engineering in opening statement. I think every last juror in the United States can be taught safety engineering, and will know more about safety engineering if it's presented correctly during the trial than the defendant did. And I don't care who the defendant was, it can be General Motors or DuPont or Monsanto or Ford or anybody. The jurors will know more about that aspect of safety engineering than the defendant knew at the time they put out a product or undertook an activity.

But if you think that you can teach a jury safety engineering with just an opening statement or an expert witness, you're mistaken. I think one of the ways that you qualify liability most is in cross-examination of defense experts. I think at that moment the jury begins to get substantial clarity. But it also takes a final argument to tie it together. Remember that jurors tend to make up their mind early on which side they're on. And then they rationalize after that a great deal. That's part and parcel of the picture, too.

Now, the next thing that I think we do differently than most plaintiff's lawyers is we tend to put on the safety expert as the very first witness in the trial. Historically all of the plaintiff's tort cases have been developed by proving the *violation* of the standard care, and then later bringing on an expert to give them the standard of care. I believe you must give the jury the standard of care first, and then show the violation of that standard of care. Why? Because if you put on the factual situation first, the injury occurred because your client was using common sense. Common sense doesn't prevent the injury; common sense *causes* the injury. But the jurors only bring common sense to the jury box. So if you put on the facts first and the jury applies common sense, they're blaming your client. But if you put on safety engineering first, a standard of care or reasonable prudence first, then before they hear the facts they're waiting for the accident to happen and understand the culpability of the defendant in having caused the injury to the plaintiff. So I think that's a major difference between my approach to the trial strategy and tactics and some of my colleagues! But those colleagues of mine that have heard this and tried it, I think, basically agree.

### Courtroom Techniques for Examining Expert Witnesses

EDITOR: Do you establish your own rules for examining experts?

PHILO: Well, one of the tools of anyone who directs a visual art form of any kind is economy. There must be an economical presentation of the proof.

Secondly, the examination must fit within your liability theme or your damage theme. I think that it's necessary to be ultimately fair to anybody that you're examining or cross-examining. Anybody who testifies for me as an expert witness is told to lean against me in every answer and never go outside their area of expertise. So that's part of the rules of examination of the expert.

EDITOR: Lean against you so as not to appear biased?

PHILO: If the expert leans toward me, it becomes obvious to most of the jurors. If the expert is right in the middle, the two most conservative jurors think that my expert is leaning my way; whereas if the expert constantly leans against me in any close answer, it even becomes obvious to the two most conservative jurors that this expert is fair and reasonable with them. And I want the jury to think at the end of the trial that my individual conduct has been fair and reasonable with them, and that all of my witnesses, including my experts, have been fair and reasonable people.

I think the jurors tend to identify with anybody in the witness box, unless that person is totally incompetent or totally obnoxious or totally dishonest; then the jurors tend to identify against that witness. But they would prefer that the lawyer examining a witness be courteous to the witness, even on cross-examination. And I try to be courteous with a witness. I try to be reasonable with a witness.

There are only three kinds of experts that I know that can come in opposition in liability. If the expert is very sophisticated and very competent, he has to agree with my case completely because he knows safety engineering and knows how to have prevented the injury. So that witness has to agree with me completely, and I'm happy to take that witness that way. If the expert for the defendant is totally incompetent and stupid, then that expert can be exposed rather quickly as incompetent and stupid. If the expert is half and half, half-competent and half-incompetent, then you take him both ways. You have him try the case for you with their competence, and you expose his incompetence.

I think it's only a small percentage of experts that you totally seek to destroy. If you seek to destroy an expert, you'd better be sure you *can* destroy that expert. And if you intend to destroy an expert, I think it's well to announce to the jury as you get up to examine the witness that you are going to make the witness crawl out of the courtroom.

EDITOR: How do you do that?

PHILO: I had one major verdict a few years ago in which I started my examination by saying to the expert, "You graduated from grammar school, didn't you?" And the expert said yes. And I said, "But you didn't graduate from high school, did you?" Because the nature of the evidence being offered was rather sophisticated evidence, I was announcing to the jury by those two insulting questions that I'm going to make this witness crawl. Here is another example:

A: You've been offered as an expert in industrial safety?

A: Yes.

Q. And you consider yourself an expert in industrial safety?

A: Yes.

Q: When I took your deposition two weeks ago you knew so little about industrial safety that you thought the National Safety Council was in Washington DC, isn't that right?

I'm announcing to the jury by a very insulting approach, "sit up and take notice because this witness at the end of this examination is going to crawl out of the courtroom." And some people can only be handled in that way. They *should* have to crawl out.

EDITOR: How do you expose the incompetent, stupid expert?

PHILO: Well, the stupid expert in the field of accident prevention has never been on a safety standards committee, is not a member of the National Safety Council, has never been to the National Safety Congress, is unfamiliar with the patent literature, is unfamiliar with how to even get into the technical literature, has not done the right testing, has not made a critical examination of the test procedures, doesn't know the composition of material, or has not preserved the evidence.

### Developing a Persuasive Liability Theme

PHILO: I think it is extremely important to have a liability theme and possibly have a liability sub-theme, to have a damage theme and a damage subtheme; to use every tool that you can to get identification for you or your client, for your theory, for your damages; and to get every aspect of identification against the defendant's attorney, the defendant, the defendant's theory of defense and the conduct of the defense during the trial.

EDITOR: What is a sub-theme?

PHILO: A sub-theme is a lesser theme, not an alternative theme. For example: Safety is not common sense, safety is sophisticated business.

Your theme might be the defendant didn't know about safety, didn't care about safety, didn't do anything about safety—as your basic theme to show the culpability of the defendant. But then maybe have as a sub-theme the lack of risk recognition on the part of your client.

I think it is important to present some evidence in terms of reaction rather than action. And I think that it's also important to use the tools that any good director uses of pulling power—to prove things *not* in the easiest way at times, but to use every legitimate means in the trial to have the jury start pulling for a point to be proven rather than just to prove it easily. You need the cooperation of the defense counsel in that respect, but generally you get it: Objection. Objection. Sustained. Sustained. And then you put in the evidence. And you not only have achieved pulling power, but you may have achieved impact. And they understand that there has been tremendous impact by the one that did it, where they wouldn't have gotten the impact without the tool of pulling power.

EDITOR: What do you mean by reaction versus action?

PHILO: Young lawyers tend to present all evidence in terms of action, rather than some of the testimony coming in by the witness testifying as to the reaction, testify in terms of the reaction to the scene as opposed to the particular action. The best example I can give you is something that every lawyer has seen many times in the presentation, say, of a movie or television production: a kiss. There's the action in the kiss. Now if you just see the action, you're not told the full story. But if you see reaction, you're always told the full picture. So you always get the full story in the reaction, but you might not get the full story in the action.

## Demonstrative Aids and How to Use Them at Trial

PHILO: I try to use a lot of demonstrative aids during the trial, and particularly the artist's sketch is important. I seek to put in much more evidence of either actual or constructive knowledge of the defendant than I think most other plaintiff's lawyers do. And either seek to have it introduced in evidence as part of my case, or have it identified as part of my case so it's available for a cross-examination of the defendant. I think that part of the privilege that has been given to business historically still exists in the form of too many limitations in evidentiary and technical literature.

In closing argument I go to the sketch pad a great deal and list on the sketch pad all the major areas of jury instruction; and review the witnesses for their ability to know, their competence, their truthfulness, their reasonableness. That's how you review every witness. Then I list and review every undisputed fact on one sheet, and every disputed fact on another sheet. Then list the damges that have been proven, and so on. But I make extensive use of a sketch pad in the closing argument.

EDITOR: You mean a big pad—bigger than 8″ × 10″?

PHILO: Oh, yes, it would be 2½ by 3½ feet, on an easel.

EDITOR: Would you make it available for the jury to take back to the jury room with them?

PHILO: Well, during a trial you use a sketch pad rather extensively. And if it is the kind of potential evidence that might very well be received, then you mark it as an exhibit and have it admitted. And then the jury can take that back. Once in a while a jury asks for my final argument sketch pad, but it's not in evidence and not admissible, and defense counsel hasn't agreed to let the jury have it. So, I don't get the chance of making it available to the jury unless it's in evidence.

# Structuring the Presentation
# of Proof or Evidence

## Philip H. Corboy

Philip H. Corboy received his J. D. degree, cum laude, from Loyola University Law School. He is a Fellow of the American College of Trial Lawyers and the International Academy of Trial Lawyers; a member of the International Society of Barristers and of the Inner Circle of Advocates; past president of the Illinois Trial Lawyers Association and member and past president of the Chicago Bar Association. He has written more than 40 articles on the preparation and trial of civil litigation, and has been a lecturer and panelist in many cities. He is a member of the Board of Editors of *Trial Diplomacy Journal*.

I believe that the ultimate ambition of every plaintiff's lawyer in the delineation of proof should be "restrained speed." In other words, do it fast.

Jurors are pretty smart people who know what they are doing, and who cannot be fooled in an important case because an important case takes a long time, generally, and the longer you are in front of a jury, the easier it is for them to see through any false sophistication or flimsy technique. Furthermore, I believe that the plaintiff has to present a case in which something is left for the jury to do. Consequently, not everything has to be—or should be—put into proof. The jury should not go into the jury room with no decisions to make. If you totally usurp their responsibility with too much evidence, in any type of a lawsuit, that "too much" may be what tips the scale in favor of the defendant.

I think the best explanation of restrained speed was given by Melvin Belli some 25 years ago, when he said that a trial is a race for the truth; it is nothing more than supplying, as fast as you can, the truth so that the jury can absorb it and go on to their own business. One of the first persons I met who won a million-dollar verdict was J. D. Lee from Tennessee. J. D. won a million and a half-dollar verdict in a case that lasted a day and a half—his final argument was 20 minutes.

## How to Save Time by Marking Exhibits in Advance

I am not aware of any rule of court, nor am I aware of any case decision, that says the court reporter has to mark an exhibit. So we don't do it any more; we call it Plaintiff's Exhibit No. 1—not Plaintiff's Exhibit No. 1 For Identification. We so mark every exhibit ahead of time, supply copies to the other lawyer, and present a list to the judge. We also keep a list with space for checking each item as it is introduced and marking the date it is introduced. In our experience, judges appreciate this. They know what type of evidence will be offered, and they know in advance; they won't have to mark down in their notebook what is being offered and what is not being offered. The other lawyer seems to appreciate this—at least we've noticed that most of them respond by doing the same thing.

Everybody hates bills, whether receiving them as individuals or, as jurors, having to wade through a stack of them. We have not put a bill into evidence in the last ten years. Of course, each bill has to be marked "paid" or testimony presented that they should have been paid, but we collect, the first time we meet with the client, all such specials, mark and photostat them, and send them to the other lawyer together with a sheet of paper on which the total has been entered. Why do we do this? In addition to making it easier and not wasting the time of the court and the jury, it is also an excellent method of informing the jury that these specials are actually the smallest part of the lawsuit. It is a relatively simple step, therefore, to throw in $25,000 worth of specials in less than a minute if they have been totaled and are on a single piece of paper. We've seldom had an argument from the other lawyer concerning this, and certainly it makes it easier on the jury for them to consider one piece of paper rather than a pile of individual bills.

The real advantage, of course, is in your being able to refer to this in your opening statement:

> "Plaintiff's Exhibit Number so-and-so, ladies and gentlemen, is going to show what is probably the smallest part of this lawsuit. There is only 18 or 19 thousand dollars in medical expenses involved in this suit."

Usually this will go in quite easily, and you can refer to it later if necessary. In the meantime, the jury is not waiting while you waste time with the court reporter while he marks Plaintiff's Exhibit No. X ID, and marks off the ID, and puts each individual bill into evidence. This does not apply in most federal courts, because most of them will not allow you to do it.

## What to Do During Jury Selection

Determining what your evidence is going to be should start with jury selection. I sincerely believe that a lawyer is guilty of malpractice if he does not get into the courtroom before the jury does; he is guilty of gross negligence if he does not watch the jurors as they walk toward and enter the jury box. I like to see whether the juror is carrying anything; if a male, if he is wearing black socks, white socks, or argyle socks; if there seems to be an alliance already formed between any two jurors. On this last point, the alliance, I want to know when I knock one off, do I have to knock the other off.

As you well know, these are the people who are going to find the facts and I think, as a lawyer, you have the duty to try and determine what type of facts they want. Observing them before they become jurors can only help you determine this.

During jury selection, I strongly recommend that your client never be present in the courtroom while the jury is being selected. I am fully aware of the practice of many lawyers, both plaintiff and defense, who go through the charade of talking to their clients before excusing or accepting the juror. I think this is bunk. I don't believe that jurors think that a client has the first thing to say about who is going to be on the jury; and if they do, you shouldn't be in the courtroom. I don't think any lawyer worth his weight in salt is ever going to allow a client help him select a jury.

There is another, equally valid reason for not having your client in the courtroom during the selection of a jury, particularly in seriously injured cases or in representing the spouse of a deceased-person: familiarity, if it does not breed contempt, at least breeds acceptance. Once the jurors accept a person with a crippling or otherwise serious injury, or once they accept a widow or a widower, they are less apt to regard that person as needing their help. So while I have not made it an ironclad rule, I have at least made it a rule of thumb not to have the client, or the clients, present during the picking of jurors.

I can recall, too vividly, one of my first cases when my client happened to be in the courtroom, by my choice, sitting behind me. It was a railroad case, involving injury to the right side of the brain, and I proved, through use of expert medical testimony, that my client would have difficulty with his left hand. We won, a sizable verdict for those days, but nothing approaching what I had expected it to be. I talked to one of the jurors afterward who told me: "Well, you had a good case, Mr. Corboy, but almost all of the jurors remembered, back when you were picking the jury and your client was there, you dropped a pencil. You didn't see it, but he picked up that pencil with his left hand, and he had no difficulty bringing it from the floor to the table". Of course, I had no idea he had done that.

So, if you must have a client present during jury selection, keep him or her as virginal as possible. Remind him or her not to talk in the elevator. I haven't gone so far as ever telling a client not to move—or even breathe—in the courtroom, but I've been tempted. So remember, the less chance you give the jury to become familiar with your client, the better off you and your client will be.

## A Revolutionary Technique for Opening Statement

We all know the classical method of delivering an opening statement: stand up and tell the jury that this is a personal injury lawsuit in which your client is seeking reimbursement or damages, or this is a death case in which a widow is seeking damages, then recite as much as we can about the evidence on liability. Many plaintiff's lawyers believe it is a truism that opening statements are designed to acquire liability and that final arguments are designed to acquire damages. I heard this the minute I stepped out of law school—and I have no idea where it came from. However, I accepted it for years and only recently began to question it.

I dropped it during a recent, eight-week case in Kentucky; actually, I turned it around. I had learned beforehand that the judge didn't give a damn how long the lawyer took for opening statement, but he restricted final argument. So I decided to give my final argument before the proof went in. In anticipating and structuring our proof, we decided to give our opening statement by giving damages first. I talked for about 45 minutes on the subject of damages, starting out by telling the jury that this lawsuit had its genesis in an operating room at a certain hospital at such and such a time on such and such a date, and that as a result of that operation our client, a 14-year old girl, suffered terrible injuries.

So we talked about damages first and then liability. Afterwards, we talked to jurors and to lawyers in the courtroom. Both said they had never seen it done before, they were laudatory, and they said it worked. The jurors told us they were more aware of what the liability aspect should be than they would have otherwise been. Although the outcome of that particular suit was not entirely to my liking, I did come away with the feeling that the technique had promise. So I tried it again in another case, this one involving a railroad. This time it worked much better to my satisfaction.

There is another aspect of talking about proof in opening statements, something that I think most lawyers neglect or at least have a reluctance against doing. I'm talking about using evidence, such as a blackboard, during opening statement.

If you recall my earlier suggestion about setting out your exhibits and giving a copy of your exhibit list to your adversary, you can find out early in the game which exhibits are going to be agreed upon and which aren't. So you can talk about them during opening statement. In a motorcycle case I brought the motorcycle in during opening statement and talked about the lack of safety guards and was careful to introduce the term, "unreasonably dangerous" . . . and reintroduce it. If the jury did not know by the end of opening statement what the issues were, I think both the defense lawyers and ourselves failed miserably.

## How to Arrange the Order of Witnesses

Your first witness, in a personal injury case, should be the doctor. I have done this dozens of times, and I have been told just as many times that this is taking your doctor out of order. I don't know what "out of order" means. I try, and usually succeed, in bringing the medical witness on first so that the jurors are aware of the significance of the injury, and the importance of the injury, which we hope is going to be tantamount to restitution by way of damages.

By the same token, I like to put my client on last, whether it be a widow or somebody injured. Why? Well, if you play it right, you can build up to a beautiful crescendo and have the jury sit there just waiting to hear the final movement—or see the play end.

As with virtually everything else, there is an exception to this: if you know your client is going to get impeached, then put him or her on second, rather than last. Then hope that somehow or another that while he is being impeached, the jury is still thinking about the medical testimony. So in these instances, get the client on, get him off fast, and go on to something else.

We also try to prove as many damages as possible using witnesses other than the plaintiff. For example, we have had good results using the surviving spouse's mother-in-law or father-in-law. If, as most often happens, it is the husband who had been killed, and if the jury hears an in-law tell what a great marriage it was, the jury might well believe that this widow really does miss her husband. Whereas I think it's a waste of your breath to ask a widow if she misses her husband. The jury might very well believe she misses her husband—but what her motive for missing her husband might be is anybody's guess. So we have done our best to prove these non-tangible, or non-dollar, damages in death cases with someone other than the widow.

### The Role of Demonstrative Evidence in Proving Damages

I think it is extremely discourteous to any jury to "show-and-tell" the actual injury to the jury. Even if it didn't conflict with my major premise of restrained speed, I think it is an abominable way to prove damages. Any time you have to declothe a man or a woman inside a courtroom you give some of the jurors the idea that, "Boy that g.d. lawyer will do anything to get money". So I don't believe it is in your best interest to show the jury the stump, or the scar, or anything if it means the taking off of clothes to do it.

Showing a photograph of the injury, however, is something else. In fact, on the motorcycle case, we obtained the photographs from the doctor. When we asked him why he took them, he said, "You know darn well why I took them: so I wouldn't have people like you suing me later". As it turned out, as I was laying the proof of the photographs, I asked the doctor who, actually, took the photographs, and he said, Sister Mary so and so. The jury knew, then, that we were not in the emergency room when this young person's leg was amputated, but rather that the photographs were taken by a nun.

Another point concerning photographs. We introduced five different photographs we obtained from the doctor, knowing that we probably wouldn't get them all in. We didn't, but we wanted two and we got three—50 percent more than we had planned on. So if you are going to introduce photographs taken prior to trial, take more than you need, offer all of them—ahead of time so you won't waste time in front of jury—and eventually you'll probably get the two or three or four that you really need.

What about movies? Specifically, movies or videotaped presentations showing a day in the life of a seriously injured patient? There has been a lot of talk about these—a lot of lawyers, including myself, have done them; are they that good?

We've talked to jurors about this, and they tell us that they are not impressed with "A day in the life of . . ." presentations. With the omnipresence of television showing things practically as they happen—planes exploding, people being shot here and abroad, accidents—presentations of this sort just don't seem to have the punch they did a decade or so ago.

There is another argument against using them: in a long trial, it may be two or three weeks between the time the jurors see the movie and the time they begin their deliberations. So we tried something different. We hired a photographer to go into the room where the patient lived and take pictures starting when the patient woke up in the morning and continuing every half hour during the day. These were not posed photographs, although, human nature being what it is, some of them ended up looking posed. We then sent all the photographs to the other lawyer, who objected to some—mostly because they did look posed. Eventually we got knocked down to 45 photographs. We learned later, after talking to the jurors, that they liked this idea, they appreciated having tangible evidence with them in the jury room.

## How and When to Use the Hypothetical Question

For many years, I thought that the hypothetical question was an excellent device to get all of my proof and all of my arguments before the jury. I thought it was just a personification of my ability to get up and talk for ten or more minutes without looking at a note, and that it showed the jury how smart I was and how well prepared I was, to be able to talk that long, or longer, before I popped the hypothetical question. Well, again, we asked jurors about this technique—they told us they don't like it, and that they think hypothetical questions are a pain in the neck.

Under federal rules, and under the rules of some states, you do not need a hypothetical question to elicit an opinion from a witness. Frankly, I like that. I think hypothetical questions are dangerous. During a recent case, the other lawyer gave a hypothetical question. In fact, he gave the same hypothetical question I had previously. His witness started talking about things that were not in the hypothetical: he started talking about what the policeman said, and telling what the policeman did. None of this was in the hypothetical. What he had done is mix up what he had read in the file and what he had read in depositions with the question. So he became extremely vulnerable on cross-examination, not because I am such a great cross-examiner, but simply because he made a mistake. Although the longer the hypothetical, the smarter the lawyer may look—also the more vulnerable the witness becomes on cross-examination.

Obviously, nothing so crude as, "Now, Mr. Engineer, would you repeat that question", although some judges might allow that, exposes the witness during cross-examination, but why take the chance.

If you must use the hypothetical question, never call it by that name. Use the word "assume" and use it once. I've heard lawyers say, "Assume this, doctor, then assume that, and then assume something else . . . ", until they've used the word assume a dozen or more times. And the jury ends up thinking maybe these are just assumptions, maybe they are not facts, maybe the lawyer is asking us to assume too much. Also, if you slant your hypothetical in such a way that it becomes argument prior to final argument, you've tipped your mitt and revealed a weakness.

# Preparation and Presentation of Medical Proof

## Peter Perlman

Peter Perlman received his J.D. Degree from the University of Kentucky. He is a Fellow of the International Academy of Trial Lawyers; former President of the Kentucky Association of Trial Attorneys; Member of the American Board of Trial Advocates; Trustee of the Melvin M. Belli Society; Served on the Trial Techniques Committee of the American Bar Association; Former Negligence Section and Law Day Chairman of the Kentucky Bar Association; Lifetime Fellow of the Roscoe Pound Foundation and former Member of the National Board of Trial Lawyers of America for more than a decade and during 1983-84 he served as Vice-President. Perlman is Professor at the University of Kentucky, College of Law; he serves on the Advisory Board of the American Journal of Trial Advocacy and on the Board of Editors for Trial Diplomacy Journal.

Each personal injury case is probably the only one that an individual claimant will ever have. With this thought in mind, a maximum effort is required of the personal injury lawyer to achieve a maximum result. The method and manner by which the medical proof is presented to the jury are the heart and soul of the case.

The trial counsel has available to him various techniques which, in some instances, at a minimum of expense, can make the presentation of medical evidence more understandable to a jury, and hopefully lead to a more equitable result for the client in his only day in court.

## Getting Your Case Across to the Jury with Visual Evidence

We have come a long way since the days when demonstrative evidence was thought of as a theatrical device available only to bring skeletons and gruesome objects into court to inflame the mind and passion of the jury. Demonstrative evidence is now recognized as a sophisticated and necessary part of courtroom proceedings. All trial counsel, no matter whom they represent, should fully recognize the astounding impact that visual evidence plays in the trial setting. Psychological studies show that the senses play the following roles in connection with learning and retention:

$$
\begin{array}{ll}
\text{Sight} & \text{—85\%} \\
\text{Hearing} & \text{—10\%} \\
\text{Touch} & \text{— 2\%} \\
\text{Taste} & \text{— 1½\%} \\
\text{Smell} & \text{— 1½\%}
\end{array}
$$

How many times do we hear counsel state that his case was not sufficiently large to justify the introduction of visual or demonstrative evidence. Every case should be developed to its fullest potential.

The type of visual or demonstrative evidence presented in a case is limited only by the imagination and resourcefulness of counsel. The attached citations represent a sampling of cases illustrating the development of damages through visual evidence.[1] The criterion for admissibility is simply whether it would aid the jury in understanding the witness's verbal testimony and supplement it.[2]

A seldom-used but highly effective technique is the presentation to the jury of the surgical hardware required to treat the injuries. In a hip injury case, for example, counsel may be expected to produce x-rays showing the fracture before and after a prosthesis has been inserted. In addition, medical drawings and anatomical charts are available to illustrate the anatomy and nature of the operative procedure. It is submitted that the impact and severity of the injury can be driven home to the jury much more effectively by showing the various tools used by the surgeon. This would include a replica of the metal plate, the surgical screws, hammer and screwdriver. These materials are readily available from surgical appliance houses or can often be borrowed from the surgeon involved.[3]

Explanation of technical language should be done in advance of any medical testimony in the form of a large chart or tablet containing the major medical terms involved in the case and their definitions. This may be approved as being accurate and of assistance to the jury through testimony of the expert medical witness, blown up for purposes of demonstration, and used throughout the trial.

### How to Prepare and Present Your Medical Witnesses

Counsel must thoroughly organize the hospital and medical records and discuss these with the medical witness in depth before he is expected to give his testimony. A medical brief informing the attorney of the nature of the injuries, and some respected authorities concerning treatment and prognosis are essential. In many instances, this can also be used to enlighten or refresh the recollection of the medical witness.

The medical witness should also be alerted as to possible areas of cross-examination. This not only prepares him, but gives him a feeling of self-confidence, as he in many instances is a stranger to the courtroom atmosphere and needs assurance like any other witness. One classic area of cross-examination to be discussed with your witness concerns the question of whether his treatment achieved a satisfactory or excellent result. He should be prepared to testify that the result was satisfactory considering the nature and severity of the injuries.

The Federal Rules of Evidence add a new dimension to the cross-examination of expert witnesses through the adoption of the "Federal Treatise Rule," 803 §§ 18.[4]

One application of this rule is to have the treatise or publication established as reliable or authoritative through the testimony of your expert, and thereby become substantive evidence for any and all purposes, including cross-examination of the opponent's expert witness.[5]

With regard to the qualifications of your medical witness, never allow these to be stipulated. In fact, the exclusion of the witness's qualifications is improper, as the jury has a right to know about his background, skill and veracity.[6]

In addition to the testimony of the treating physician, various other non-physician medical personnel are also available. In many cases the testimony of a physical therapist is invaluable, as he has a great quantity of meticulously detailed medical records available. These are admissible on the same basis as hospital records, or under the Uniform Business Records Act. In addition, he usually sees and physically examines the patient more often and more thoroughly than the orthopedist or other treating physician. Since therapists are not limited in the time they can spend with a patient, patients are freer in discussing their ailments and limitations than with a physician or nurse. As a result you are able to develop a better picture of the pain, limitation of motions, flare-ups, exacerbations and remissions than you would with the testimony of a physician.[7]

The use of a nurse is particularly effective in conjunction with a medical chart or hospital record. Even though she may not be the nurse that was on duty, she can help explain the make-up of the hospital chart, various medical terms and definitions and read pertinent entries once the hospital record has been admitted.

In any case involving permanent injuries, the testimony of a psychiatrist or psychologist is imperative, because it's impossible to have a permanent physical injury without having some mental effects.

Many attorneys reject the testimony of a chiropractor as not being sufficiently authoritative. However, it's a fact that many jurors have had some contact with chiropractors, either personally, or by some member of their family, and believe in them. In addition, chiropractors have received a considerable amount of education and are very qualified at detailing and describing anatomy.

### How to Bolster the Impact of Your Case by Videotaping the Medical Proof

The jury should have the benefit of all the evidence presented in such a manner that they may utilize all of their senses in arriving at a just and proper determination of the issues, including the nature and extent of Plaintiff's injuries. The customary practice of reading written depositions is a totally lifeless and unimaginative method of presenting the medical proof, and the use of the videotape recording device should be greeted as a welcome relief from this boring and archaic practice.

This obviously was the intended result of Federal Rule 30.02(b)(4) which authorizes the taking of depositions by "other than stenographic means." Many recent decisions have recognized the fact that the use of written depositions is at best a poor substitute for the live testimony of a witness.[8]

Other factors to consider are the opportunity for a jury to watch the witness testify, and the instant replay capabilities of videotape devices. In addition, in many instances, the Court has no subpoena power over a physician. The rule allowing the videotaping of depositions provides that they will be subject to a Court Order regarding the method of recording and preserving the testimony. The testimony will be greatly improved as the witness may use x-rays and visual aids to explain his findings and opinions to the jury.

From a strategic standpoint, the opposing lawyer appears much more accommodating and less likely to make frequent objections; and the physicians like it as it gives them an opportunity to express themselves and their knowledge to a jury.

Many modern courtrooms now feature equipment for the taking of videotape medical depositions.

In any case, it adds life to a lawsuit, requires preparation on the part of the attorney, keeps up the jury's interest, and generally expedites the trial of the case.

### Strategies for Using Hospital Records at Trial

The introduction of the hospital record into evidence expedites the trial of the case by eliminating the necessity of calling all persons who made entries in the record. In many instances due to the unavailability or forget-fulness of witnesses, the hospital records may be the only evidence of a fact or condition, and it would be unduly disruptive to bother the hospital and the court to require all entrants to appear personally. There are many authorities which allow the use of the hospital record as substantive evidence where a proper foundation has been established.[9]

Once admitted, many strategic uses can be made of the hospital record.

(1) *Demonstration of pain and suffering.* The doctor's order sheet listing medications, narcotics, etc., are living entries of pain and suffering. This is also true of nurses' notes showing fulfillment of the orders, patient complaints, special calls, etc. The nurses' progress notes are a daily record of the patients' ordeals which can be catalogued. Use of this portion of the hospital record thereby presents to the jury graphic, verified entries of the victim's pain and suffering recorded by persons in the ordinary course of their business without any interest in the lawsuit, and without any intent to exaggerate. Emergency room records are in many instances invaluable, showing the manner and condition of the person upon admission, loss of blood, and initial treatment.

(2) *Specific use of isolated portions.* Once the hospital record has been organized in a chronological manner with an index, tabs and cross-references, isolated portions of the record may also be blown up and used for any purpose throughout the trial. In many cases a graph may be used, showing the patient's course with entries detailing specific events, and may be very helpful in supplementing the hospital record. Blowups,

charts, graphs and other similar documents are particularly effective during closing argument. Trial attorneys who are anxious to demonstrate their eloquence often forget that the sense of sight has a much greater impact than all other senses combined with regard to learning and retention.

(3)*Use "a silent witness" during closing argument.* The hospital record is a valuable aid to counsel during his summation to the jury, as he can point out to the jury that it has testified in the case in a silent way through uncontradicted entries, made by persons with no interest in the lawsuit, and clearly demonstrates the patient's pain and discomfort during his hospitalization.

## Notes

1. *Visual or Demonstrative Evidence—*
   Admissibility of Electroencephalograms and Electrocardiograms
   > *Malford v. Gauss and Brown Const. Co.,* 17, Ill. App.(2d) 497, **151 N.E. (2) 128** (1958)

   Admissibility of Medical Charts
   > Illustrative drawings and medical charts may be used to explain testimony:
   > *First Federal S & L Assn. of Miami v. Wylie,* Fla., 1950. 46 S.2d 396
   > *Lackey v. State,* 1952, 215 Miss. 57, 60 S.2d 503
   > *Segee v. Cowan,* 1941, 66 RI 445 20 A.2d 270
   > Medical Chart (or Illustration): 58 A.L.R.2d 689, 690
   > *First Fed. S & L v. Wylie,* 46 S.2d 396 (Fla. 1950)

   Admissibility of Casts, Braces, Collars, etc.
   > 1. Leg brace—*Glowacki v. Holste,* 295 S.W.2d 135 (Mo. 1956)
   > 2. Thomas Collar—back brace
   > *Hampton v. Hauteustrauch,* 338 S.W.2d 105 (1960)
   > *Hulke v. International Mfg. Co.,* 14 Ill. App. 2d(5) 142 N.E.2d 717.
   > 3. Plaster Casts—
   > *Dinwiddie v. Siefken,* 299 Ill. App. 316, 20 N.E.2d 130
   > 4. Surgical pins—
   > *Norman v. Norman,* 103 Ga. App. 626 (1961), 120 S.E. 242
   > 5. Glass eye—
   > Exhibit of eye socket to jury
   > *Bowermann v. Columbia Gorge Motor Coach System,* 1930, 132 or 106, 284 P. 579

   Exhibition of Plaintiff's Injuries
   > 1. Proper to permit plaintiff to exhibit injured arm to jury
   > *Mulhado v. Brooklyn City Railroad,* 30 N.Y. 370, 372 (1864)
   > 2. Exhibition of plaintiff's injuries generally allowed Richardson on *Evidence,* § 134 at p. 107, 66 A.L.R.2d 1334

With Trial Court's discretion:
  *Stegall v. Carlson,* 6 Ill. App.2d 388 (1955)
Demonstration of Effect of Injury
  1. Sticking plaintiff with needle to show no sensation permissible in most
     cases:
  *Osborne v. Detroit,* 32 F. 36 (Mich. 1886)
  *Stephens v. Elliott,* 36 Mont. 92 P. 45 (1907)
  *Anthony v. Public Transit,* 130 A. 895 (N.J.)
  *Wilson v. Campbell,* 157 P.2d 465 (Okla. 1945)
  2 Show jury difficulty with walking
  *Missouri Co. v. Lynch,* 46 Tex. Civ. App. 543, 90 S.W. 511 (1905)
  *Villegas v. Kercher,* 11 Ill. App.2d 282, 137 N.E.2d 92
  *Barnstable v. Calandro,* 270 Ill. App. 57 (1933)
  *Tindall v. Chicago & Northwestern Railroad Co.* 200 Ill. App. 556 (1916)
Skeleton or Model of Human Body
  58 A.L.R.2d 689
  *Smith v. Ohio Oil Co.,* 13 N.E.2d 526
X-rays
  10 A.L.R.2d 918
  5 A.L.R.3d 303 (Proof re: authentication)
  53 Am Jur. *Trials* § 924.
Use of Colored Slides or Drawings
  *Slow Development Co. v. Colter* 353 P.2d 890 (Ariz. 1960)
Admissibility of Motion Pictures
  8 Am. Jur. *Proof of Facts* 167 (1970)

2. *Criterion for Admissibility—*
  66 A.L.R.2d 1334; *Darling v. Charleston Community Memorial Hospital,* 211
    N.E.2d 253 (Ill. 1962); also *Smith v. Ohio Oil Co.,* 13 N.E.2d 526 (Ill. 1956)

3. Demonstration of Surgical Hardware—Procedure discussed approved in
*McMann v. Reliable Furniture Co.,* 140 A.2d 736 (Me. 1958)
  Admissibility of Braces, Crutches, or other Prosthetic or Orthopedic Devices
    (also surgical appliances) 83 A.L.R.2d 1271

4. Federal Rules of Evidence, Rule 803 §§ 18, eff. July 1 1975 as an exception to the
hearsay rule:
  (18) Learned treatises. To the extent called to the attention of an expert
       witness upon cross-examination, statements contained in published
       treatises, periodicals, or pamphlets on a subject of history, medicine, or
       other science or art, established as a reliable authority by the testimony
       or admission of the witness or by other expert testimony or by judicial
       notice. If admitted, the statements may be read into evidence but may
       not be received as exhibits.

5. An example of this application is *Heilman v. Snyder,* 520 S.W.2d 321 (Ky. 1975)

6. *Dotson v. Allied Chemicals*, 178 S.E.2d 27 (N.C.1970)

7. *Testimony of Physical Therapist*
   See Wolfstone, 1974 *Personal Injury Annual*, p. 156
   Robb, "Use of Lay Witnesses," 1962 *P.I. Annual*, p. 489

8. *Admissibility of Videotape Depositions*
   Federal Rule of Civil Procedure Rule 30(b)(4)
   "Videotape: The Coming Courtroom Tool." 7 *Trial* 55 (1971)
   *State v. Moss*, 498 S.W.2d 289 (Mo. 1973) (Rep. in 17 *ATL Newsletter*, **108 April,** 1974)
   *Rubino v. G. C. Searle & Co.*, 340 N.Y.S.2d 574 (S.Ct. 1973)
   "The Practical Uses of Trialvision and Depovision," John J. Kennelly *Tr. Law Guide*, Vol. 16 p. 183 (Summer 1973)
   "Televised Medical Testimony" *Current Medicine for Attorneys*, Vol. **20** No. **79** (Feb. 1973)
   "Expanding Videotape Techniques in Pretrial and Trial Advocacy" John W. Thornton, *The Forum*, Vol. 9 No. 1 p. 105 (Fall 1973)
   "Implementing the Videotape Deposition in New York," William P. McCool, *New York Law Forum*, Vol. 19 p. 851 (Spring 1974)
   "Videotape Trials: Legal and Practical Implications," *Columbia Journal of Law and Social Problems*, Vol 9 p. 363 (Spring 1973)
   "Videotape: Use in Demonstrative Evidence" James J. Stewart, *Defense Law Journal*. Vol. 21 p. 252 (1972)
   "Videotape: A New Horizon in Evidence," Bruce E. Krell, *John Marshall Journal of Practice and Procedure* Vol. 4 p. 339 (1971)
   *Use of Videotape in the preparation and trial of lawsuits* Thomas J. Murray, Jr., XI *Forum* No. 4 Summer, 1976, p. 1152

9. *Use of Hospital Records*
   McCormick on *Evidence*, 2nd Edition, p. 604
   A. It must be in the ordinary course of business
   B. The entrants are unavailable, or it would cause undue inconvenience to make them available.
   C. The entries are either original or contemporaneous with the events referred to
   D. The entry represents first-hand knowledge of one whose job it is to know the facts
   E. They are regular entries made as a continuing part of the job of the person making the entries.
   *Federal Shopbook Rule* (Model Act for Proof of Business Transactions), 28 U.S.C. 1732; 6 *Proof of Facts* p. 135; Cotchett and Elkind, *Federal Courtroom Evidence*, 1976 Chapter 22, p. 146-150.
   *Federal Rules of Evidence*, eff. July 1, 1975 Rule 803, §§ 6 "Exceptions to Hearsay Rule."

Am. Jur. *Proof of Facts*, Vol. 6, p. 135 50 A.L.R.2d 378

*Darling v. Charleston Community Hospital* 211 N.E.2d 253 (Ill. 1962) 44 A.L.R.2d 553

Vol. 37 No. 3 *Albany L. Rev.* p. 579 (1973) 44 A.L.R.2d 553

Foundation for Admission

7 Am. Jur. *Proof of Facts*, Proof 3

# Informed Consent by Videotape

## James Krueger

James Krueger of Maui, Hawaii is a trial lawyer specializing in civil litigation on behalf of plaintiffs. He is past president of the Western Trial Lawyers Association, a member of the Board of Governors of the Association of Trial Lawyers of America, National Vice-Chairman of the Committee on Medicine and Law of the American Bar Association, and past president of the Maui County Bar Association. Krueger is a Fellow of the International Society of Barristers, Fellow of the International Academy of Trial Lawyers, a Trustee of the Melvin Belli Society, member of the American College of Legal Medicine and member of the American Society of Hospital Attorneys. He is an instructor at the ATLA National College of Advocacy and has served as speaker at the following conventions: ATLA, WTLA, CTLA, Haw. TLA, and Wash. TLA.

My aim here is to describe a new method of establishing proof of informed consent in a medical negligence case. Use of medical videotape gives the trial lawyer a novel approach to establishing whether appropriate standards of informed consent disclosure have been met in a given instance.

### The Doctor's Obligation to the Patient

Since Cardozo[1] trumpeted the right of the patient to determine what should be done with his body, the doctrine of informed consent is predicated upon negligence concepts.[2]

The duty of disclosure is a major component of the informed consent doctrine. Those matters which must be discussed and disclosed by a doctor to a patient are:

(1) the nature of disease or condition;[3]
(2) those known and/or reasonably foreseeable risks of care to be rendered including frequency of risk occurrence;[4]
(3) those known and/or reasonably foreseeable side effects occurring subsequent to treatment;[5] and
(4) the patient's probable course if treatment is not performed or is rejected.[6]

Writing recently in the New England Journal of Medicine, Dr. Drummond Rennie notes the difficulty which "arises because of the inevitable and gross inequality between the two parties interested in consent to a medical procedure. One is fit and medically knowledgeable, the other sick and medically ignorant."[7] Dr. Rennie notes that the "paternalistic role," maintained by doctors, must give way to counseling and advocacy by

attempting to give patients equality in the covenant by educating them to make informed decisions.[8]

Thus, it is the doctor's ultimate responsibility to ensure that the patient has given an "informed consent."[9] Whether the doctor's obligation to disclose is based upon the "professional standard,"[10] (referring to the practice engaged in by reasonable physicians similarly involved) or upon the "material risk standard"[11] (under which a more extensive duty exists to disclose all material and significant risks and alternatives known), *disclosure must occur.*

No longer may the medical profession arrogate upon itself the right to determine what patient needs which information. To the contrary, The American Hospital Association Board of Trustees, in 1972, promulgated a statement entitled "A Patient's Bill of Rights." Paragraphs 2 - 4 of the AHA statement declare:

2. The patient has the right to obtain from his physician complete current information concerning this diagnosis, treatment, and prognosis in terms the patient can be reasonably expected to understand. When it is not medically advisable to give such information to the patient, the information should be made available to an appropriate person in his behalf. He has the right to know by name the physician responsible for coordinating his care.

3. The patient has the right to receive from his physician information necessary to give informed consent prior to the start of any procedure and/or treatment. Except in emergencies, such information for informed consent should include but not necessarily be limited to the specific procedure and/or treatment, medically significant risks involved, and the probable duration of incapacitation. Where medically significant alternatives for care or treatment exist, or when the patient requests information concerning medical alternatives, the patient has the right to such information. The patient also has the right to know the name of the person responsible for the procedures and/or treatment.

4. The patient has the right to refuse treatment to the extent permitted by law, and to be informed of the medical consequences of his action.

Similarly, the Joint Commission on Accreditation of Hospitals, in promulgating the 1979 version of the "Accreditation Manual for Hospitals" (AMH), imposed upon JCAH accredited hospitals firm and stiff obligations relating to the nature of information which must be disclosed to a patient and the data upon which the patient's consent to such procedures must be grounded.[12]

Comprehension of the disclosed data is requisite. Patient lack of comprehension of disclosed data is rampant. In the area of surgical consent forms, for instance, most patients believed that such were meant to protect the physician's rights.[13] Lack of comprehension of surgical forms results, primarily, by reason of the fact that the forms are written by committees composed of lawyers and physicians, and the data contained in the forms are written for the intellect of the upper-division college undergraduate or graduate student.[14]

Recognizing that there are significant problems with respect to comprehension, the states of Florida, Hawaii, Kentucky, North Carolina, Ohio, and Vermont have promulgated statutes specifically mentioning that the informed consent must be one comprehensible and comprehended to and by the patient.[15]

Ludlam notes the doctor's "primary duty to communicate with the patient"[16] but goes on to say that the

law does not say how he must communicate. In other words, he has considerable leeway in the methodology he may use . . . The critical point is that the method used must be comprehensible to the patient.[17]

Ludlam notes the important role of the hospital in patient education and states that such things as seminars and visual aids are appropriate to back up the physician's personal explanation to the patients.[18]

## Videotapes as Demonstrative Evidence

Barristers have long used photographs and, since their advent, motion pictures as demonstrative evidence at trial. With respect to videotape,

> [logically], the standards for admitting this type of videotape evidence should be substantially identical to the admissibility standards for similar evidence recorded on motion picture film. As a means of presenting demonstrative evidence videotape should be readily interchangeable with more traditional media. As noted previously, videotape has substantial advantage over still photographs and motion picture films, and apparently raises no new evidentiary difficulties. The utility and desirability of encouraging proper use of this flexible tool should therefore be manifest.[19]

Nationally known medical facilities and private educational media firms, such as the UCLA School of Medicine and Audio-Visual Partner, Inc., among others, now develop videotape presentations for use by doctors and hospitals as an adjunct to explaining various procedures as are anticipated to be used upon a given patient.

In recent years doctors have made the requisite disclosures imposed upon them by the doctrine of informed consent and, having done so, presented their patients an in-office or in-hospital viewing of a videotape depicting the disclosures which the doctor has orally presented. The patient is thereby benefitted by receiving similar information twice but, more compellingly, in the latter occasion, visually.

## Trial Techniques Using Videotape

Take, for example, the circumstance where a patient is required to undergo arteriography. At the UCLA School of Medicine/Hospital, a very well-done videotape will be presented to the arteriographic patient. If the videotape made by this outstanding medical institution is good enough to educate patients undergoing such procedures at that facility, surely the same videotape could be utilized to demonstrate during the course of trial what disclosure should have been made in a case wherein a claim is made that a patient, undergoing arteriography, was not given adequate disclosure of those matters inherent in such invasive procedure.

The trial lawyer having access to such videotape at trial should, during the direct examination of plaintiff's medical expert, obtain testimony from the expert as to what matters necessarily should have been disclosed to the patient. Therefore, having obtained testimonial proof that the videotape describes the minimum disclosures as should have been made in the particular case, the lawyer should ask for and obtain court approval to show the videotape to the jury.

The practitioner may logically argue to the trial judge that the videotape presentation represents disclosure of the minimum data as should have been presented to the patient, according to the standards of a nationally renowned medical institution. The videotape may then be contrasted with evidence of what the defendant-physician incompletely or inaccurately disclosed to the plaintiff-patient. Accordingly, under Rule 401 of the *Federal Rules of Evidence* (FRE), the videotape becomes relevant.

Under the above approach, in essence, the medical institution becomes the expert and the videotape contents become its testimony. This evidentiary submission may seem Orwellian when viewed in the above context, but, thereunder, the videotape may rise to the level of a learned treatise and be admissible under FRE 803 (18). See also FRE 702.

Another method which may be employed in presenting the videotape to the jury as demonstrative evidence can be via testimony by plaintiff's medical expert that the content of the videotape constitutes data or a basis upon which the medical expert's opinion is established. If the medical expert testifies that the matters depicted in the videotape were used by him in order to arrive at whether adequate disclosure was made, the videotape may be offered as independent evidence supporting the expert's opinion, or alternatively as illustrative of the expert's testimony.

Use of videotape in any of the above fashions presents a thorny problem to defense counsel because of the difficulty in cross-examining an inanimate object. If defense counsel wishes to have a defense expert criticize the videotape, the courtroom would again be darkened, the videotape re-run, all the while the defense expert critiques the same and the jury, doubly influenced thereby, again reviews plaintiff's visual evidence.

## Notes

1. *Schloendorff v. Society of New York Hospitals*, 211 N.Y. 125, 105 N.E. 92 (1914).

2. *Natanson v. Kline*, 186 Kan. 393, 350 P.2d 1093 (1960) clarified 354 P.2d 670 (1960).

3. Rosoff, Informed Consent (1981), ch.2, p. 41.

4. *Canterbury v. Spence*, 150 App.D.C. 263, 464 F.2d 772, 786 (1972).

5. *Id.*

6. *Id.*

7. 302 New England Journal of Medicine 917 (1980) Rennie, "Informed Consent by 'Well-nigh Abject' Adults."

8. *Ibid.* p. 918.

9. Ludlam, Informed Consent, American Hospital Association (1978), p. 13.

10. *Natanson,* supra, 350 P.2d 1106.

11. *Canterbury v. Spence, supra,* 464 F.2d 785-787; *Cobbs v. Grant,* 8 Cal.3d 229, 104 Cal. Rptr. 505, 502 P.2d 1, 11 (1972).

12. Pengalis and Wachsman, 1 American Law of Medical Malpractice, §3:5, pp. 124, 125.

13. New England Journal of Medicine 896 (1980) Cassileth, *et al.,* "Informed Consent—Why Are Its Goals Imperfectly Realized?"

14. 302 New England Journal of Medicine 90 (1980) Grundner, "On the Readability of Surgical Consent Forms".

15. Fla. Stat., §768.132(b) (1975); 1976 Sess. Laws Haw., §3(c); Ky. Rev. St. §304.40-320(2) (Supp. 1976); Ohio Rev. Code Am. §2317.54 (as amended 1977); N.C. Gen. Stat., §90-21.13(a) (2) (Supp. 1976); Vt. Stat. Ann. Tit. 12, §1909(a) (Supp. 1977).

16. Note 9, *supra.*

17. Ludlam, *supra,* p. 12.

18. Ludlam, *supra,* p. 16.

19. 23 *Am. Jur. Trials,* Videotape in Civil Trials, §102 p. 184.

# Staying on Your Feet in the Trip- or Slip-and-Fall Case

## Neil G. Galatz

Neil G. Galatz, senior partner in the Las Vegas firm of Galatz, Earl
& Catalano, received his law degree from Columbia University
Law School. His professional membership includes: American
Bar Association; The Association of Trial Lawyers of America
where he has been actively involved for over 20 years; Nevada
State Bar Association; Arizona State Bar Association; New York
State Bar Association; New York State Association of Trial Law-
yers; California Trial Lawyers Association. He is a Fellow of the
International Academy of Trial Lawyers and a member of its
Board of Directors; and he is a Fellow of the International Society
of Barristers. Galatz has held various offices in the Western Trial
Lawyers Association; Nevada Trial Lawyers Association; and the
Southern Chapter of Nevada Trial Lawyers Association. He has
lectured widely and published numerous articles.

The trip-and-fall case or the slip-and-fall case are often maligned areas of
personal injury practice. Repeatedly, we hear the comment that these are
terrible cases. I disagree. I believe they can be good cases, often excellent
cases, IF . . . first, an injury is involved, preferably an objective injury, and,
second, the attorney taking on such a case is willing to put forth thought
and effort to develop the case properly.

### Conditioning the Jury During Voir Dire

When first approaching the trip-and-fall or slip-and-fall case, the plaintiff's attorney should have an awareness that the jury has two contradictory reactions: the first is that if the plaintiff slips or falls in a hotel or store

or similar establishment, then the establishment is responsible because it happened on their premises—this attitude is, obviously, quite beneficial to the plaintiff; the second reaction follows this line of reasoning: "Well, I fell once and I didn't sue anybody, people fall all the time and I don't know why they should sue when they do—it's just one of those things."

Which of these two attitudes will prevail in the minds of the jury will be determined, I believe, to a good degree by the nature and extent of the injury. I believe that the degree of injury is a very significant aspect in this type of case. Where the injury is minor, or subjective, usually the "you don't sue" attitude will prevail; with a severe, readily demonstrated type of injury, the "establishment is responsible" attitude will usually prevail.

Therefore, in the voir dire of the jury, conditioning is absolutely essential. It is vitally important that you point out that "certainly, people fall all the time and don't sue," but go beyond that and point out that this particular fall is not due to the fault of your client, but to the fault of the defendant, and be certain to point out that there is a real and a significant injury.

Regarding the jury's viewing of the typical slip-and-fall or trip-and-fall case, the plaintiff has at least one advantage; he almost always has the benefit of a target defendant.

If there is a single area that creates difficulty in this type of case, it is not anything inherent in the case itself, but in the lawyer's attitude toward the case; or, in other words, his falling down in the job.

### How to Help Your Client Outwit Defense Counsel's Tactics

Preparation of your client is an important step, but watch out you don't overdo it. Your client, having all the basic human tendencies, wants to do all he can to help. After you have explained to him that negligence on the part of the defendant must be established by a preponderance of the evidence, watch out for overreaction and exaggeration by your client. To illustrate:

The most effective defense technique I have come up against in these cases involves the situation where, during cross-examination, defense counsel asks himself, "what is the plaintiff's major contention?" Once he has come to a conclusion, he might say, "well, fine, he is going to claim that it was too dark—let's work on that darkness." He then has the plaintiff, who is aware that he must establish the condition of inadequate lighting, try to describe how dark it was. The defense counsel will then proceed to draw the plaintiff on and on until he has him describing an area blacker than the Black Hole of Calcutta, and the jury becomes aware of the obvious exaggeration. Defense counsel finds it much easier then, to build on the defense of contributory negligence.

Or perhaps the cause was a defect in the sidewalk or in concrete, which may have been a few inches in depth or diameter to begin with (large enough, of course to be significant) which suddenly becomes—during cross-examination—a manhole. Obviously, then, the plaintiff should have been able to see this manhole-sized defect and should have avoided it.

There are other ways that the defense counsel can build on the defect, to make it grow and grow or whatever, to establish contributory negligence, simply because of the plaintiff's very human desire to stress the elements of his own case. This is something the plaintiff's attorney should constantly guard against.

A related area that has caused otherwise solid cases to turn soft is the failure by plaintiff's lawyer to caution and prevent his client from attempting to describe something that simply cannot be described in a meaningful or understandable way. For example, defense counsel may ask the plaintiff to describe how he or she was walking. The plaintiff, unless he has been forewarned, may attempt to go into a detailed, anatomical and physiological description of how he or she was walking. The number of muscles and bones that are involved in the coordination of walking in an ordinary manner is extremely difficult to describe without sounding quite silly. Far better if your client simply answers, "I was walking in a normal manner, if you want something more than that, I'll get up and demonstrate". Or, "I was walking in an ordinary manner, I can show you, but I cannot verbalize it". If, however, a verbal description is attempted, what may come out is a description that has the plaintiff walking poised and balanced in such an inane way that he, or she, didn't fall because of any defect—he fell because his limbs became hopelessly entangled.

Another area wherein inadequate preparation of the client by the plaintiff's attorney has repeatedly lost cases is the causation link. Generally, the plaintiff didn't see the defect upon which he tripped or the object upon which he slipped. If he had, he would have avoided it. Sometimes you become fortunate and have another witness who can establish the fact that your client actually tripped over something, or he saw him slip. More frequently, however, there will be no other witness, and the attorney will have to establish causation by circumstantial proof. For example, the plaintiff cannot say, "I saw the object and tripped upon it," but he can say, "I had a catching sensation of the toe or the heel and was catapulted forward" . . . or "there was a definite sliding sensation." Then, of course, the nature of the defect or the object—which was observed after the fall in detail—can be described. If you're fortunate, there will be a skid mark or a squashed object to tie in. If this was the only defect or object present of adequate size to cause the trip or slip, and if the tripping or slipping sensation is described as presented above, this is generally adequate to link up the causation.

An area that is important in combating contributory negligence in the trip-and-fall case has to do with where a person looks when he walks. A clever defense lawyer would have us believe that people walk around like penguins . . . eyes glued to the floor exactly three feet ahead, so that we can carefully scrutinize each little area upon which we are about to step. In truth, nobody walks that way—the jury doesn't walk that way, you don't walk that way, therefore it is ridiculous to expect your client to walk that way.

The plaintiff needs only to conduct himself as a reasonable and prudent person would, and the reasonable and prudent person walks with his eyes taking in an area well ahead of him. He doesn't keep his eyes fixed and focused directly ahead of him . . . his gaze wanders to the right, to the left, in all directions. This is the way we all walk. Generally, we are able to avoid getting hurt because we see an area somewhere between seven, ten, 15, 20, or even 30 feet ahead of us, and it is from this distance that we gauge what the condition of the area will be. This can be the key to establishing liability, because from 15 or 20 feet away, defects or objects usually can't be seen. They can only be seen when the person is almost right on top of them—three or four feet away. But if the plaintiff was walking the way most people walk, he or she was looking some 15 or 20 feet ahead, and he was not looking with a fixed gaze . . . his eyes were wandering, his head was turning.

Distraction is another area that the defense loves to dwell on in building up the trip- or slip-and-fall case. Your opponent will emphatically state that your client wasn't looking where he or she was walking, but instead was looking at a display, or looking for a particular product, if in the supermarket. The built-in answer to that is obvious, and has more than enough case law to substantiate: the defendant created the distraction. There are distracting circumstances, and the law recognizes the fact that people do become distracted and will excuse this, and will hold that this leaves a question for the jury as to the reasonableness of the case where there is a distracting circumstance. And of course you are in the position to argue that "how can the defendant complain–how dare he talk about your client being guilty of contributory negligence when the client himself has spent thousands of dollars bringing in experts to create eye-catching displays of pop-up soap or some other marvelous new product? These dollars were spent for the single purpose of causing your client to do exactly as he was doing—to make him look away from the area where he was walking, to look at the fancy display, and, hopefully, to go over and buy whatever it was that was being displayed."

Momentary forgetfulness is, again, a case where the law is clear. The fact that a person knew there was a defect or a danger, then crossed the area and was injured because he forgot for a moment that the danger was there is not an automatic winner, but again the law is reasonable and recognizes that people do forget.

If the forgetfulness argument isn't strong enough, another way of handling the problem—and here again there is case authority to support your contention—is that there was no other reasonable alternative available.

## How to Combat the "No-Other-Accident" Argument

The astute defense counsel may attempt to show that there have been no other accidents as a result of the condition you are claiming was negligent. The only aspect of this defense that surprises me is that it is used relatively rarely—I am amazed it's not used more frequently.

But when you are up against the contention and the proof that thousands of people have walked across the same area and nobody else was hurt therefore it's perfectly safe, you'd better be on your guard. First, make sure that defense counsel lays a proper foundation to get that proof in. They must show a substantial identity of circumstances, and often that can be difficult, if not impossible, to show. To illustrate, in one case in which I was involved, defense counsel attempted to offer proof that literally thousands of people had walked across a specific area at the exit of a hotel where some concrete had broken loose and which caused our client to fall. However, the proof of identity of circumstances was a stumbling block for them, because our client was injured when she was coming out of the hotel right after a nightclub show had broken. Many people were present at the same time, and this added a different factor in. Because of the press of the crowd, our client was no longer able to do what most people do, that is glance ahead as she walks—she couldn't see the ground ahead of her because of all the people. This was sufficient, in the opinion of the court that heard this case, to prevent the proof of no other people falling because the defense counsel had not established the fact that this crowding condition had occurred during the other time periods.

A separate factor to be considered in the "no-other-accident" type of argument or proof, even if the defendant is able to put this in, is that "no other accidents" does not necessarily mean there were no other falls or slips. At best, all it does mean is that the defendant does not know of another fall or slip occurring there. When most people fall, they are not hurt but they are embarrassed. If you've ever watched a person fall, the universal reaction—unless of course they are seriously injured—is to get up and get away from there as quickly as possible. So accidents may very well have happened at that specific location, they just weren't reported and therefore they were not brought to the attention of the defendant. This argument is always available and can be very helpful in persuading a jury.

The defendant might have yet another argument to bring out, particularly in the slip-and-fall case involved in wet or waxed floors: dwelling on the shoes your client was wearing. They're new shoes, and that's no good because new shoes are slippery; or if the shoes are worn that's no good because worn shoes are slippery; or the shoe has a little nail sticking out; or the shoes have soles made of leather, or heels made of leather; or something similar. What the defendant is attempting here is to create a diversion and swing the issue to something that is unreasonable. First of all, there is nothing wrong with a person wearing new shoes or old shoes, or shoes with holes in the soles for that matter. The temptation for the plaintiff's lawyer is almost to argue that what the defendant is asking here is to have your client wear nothing but sneakers or suction-cup shoes. This whole line of argument by the defense attorney strikes me as so silly that I have been tempted at times to bring in the little old shoe repairman and have him point out how often and in what condition shoes are brought into him for repair—or even have the new shoe salesman testify how many pairs of brand new shoes are sold in his store each day. I have never done either of those, but I have been tempted on occasion, especially if the defense tries to claim that it is unreasonable for people to wear shoes of the type or kind my client was wearing.

### How to Take Advantage of the Plaintiff's Evidentary Advantages

A major area to work on is the fact that the defect had caused other falls or slips. The proof of prior falls is proper to go to in these cases—not to the issue of negligence per se, but to the issue: did the defendant have notice of the dangerous condition? This, of course, relates to an equally important issue—the existence of the defect. Is there in fact a defect?

A second evidentary advantage to the plaintiff is in the area of subsequent precaution or subsequent repairs. Very often, someone from the defendant's business, or his expert, will stand up and tell the jury how perfectly safe the condition was. There is considerable authority supporting the proposition that when a claim is made, that the condition was not defective, that it was safe. It is perfectly proper to impeach that claim by showing proof of subsequent changes or repairs made in the condition or premises. Subsequent precautions can go in under the issue of control; which of several defendants has actual control of the premises? It is reasonable for a jury to infer that the party who did the repair is responsible for the maintenance.

Another area where you can put in proof of subsequent precautions is in establishing the reasonableness and feasibility of making the condition safe. To illustrate:

For approximately two years after a new terminal was opened at a busy airfield, there was asbestos tile on the public walkways. Discovery established that during the first year of operation of the new terminal, over 100 slip-and-fall injuries had occurred. And there were 100 injuries that were actually reported—no one knows how many occurred that were not reported. Additional proof was brought up through some of the personnel employed there to establish that they saw lots of persons fall and just get up and move. But there was on file the 100 reported slips and falls.

Evidence was allowed in to establish (1) that the condition was, in fact, defective, and (2) that the defendants had notice of it. After the second year of operation, the entire terminal was carpeted. Proof of that carpeting was properly admitted to establish the reasonableness and feasibility of making the repair to show that there was an alternative way of doing it that was financially sound, reasonable, and proper. In fact, in that specific case, in addition to establishing reasonableness, we were able to put in actual correspondence from county officials regarding the cost feasibility of the carpeting as opposed to the tile.

In addition to this, proof went in to establish control. The county had said, "No, it's not our fault; it's the janitorial service and the contractors. They should have kept the floor from being so slippery, that was their job." The janitorial contractor said, "No, it's not our job. We only were doing what the county told us to do." The carpeting, put in and paid for by the county, was proper to establish the control by the county over the area.

Another area of proof you might do well to explore to help establish that the defendant created an unreasonable risk is to show, for example, that the defendant department store did $4 million in business in a certain period, but would not spend $50. for a rubber mat for its entryway; or the supermarket did $2 million in business, but didn't think $40. was a valid expenditure for something to soak up spilled water in front of its produce counter.

## Using Building Codes As an Ally

There are four model building codes, each popular in a different geographical subdivision of the country, that a city or county may adopt. Or it may decide to draft its own. So whatever code is in use in the jurisdiction in which the trip-and-fall occurred, that code should be explored and perhaps put into evidence.

If a provision, or provisions, of the code can be put into evidence, here is a good case for bringing in experts. They can not only identify the code, but they can point out how the code was put together and—equally important—why the considerations that are set forth in the code as safety practices are there. An expert can also often explain the custom in a given situation. For example, one case involved a meeting held at a public hall where an arrangement was set up involving a microphone being placed at a podium, with the cord draped across the floor. As an expert, a chief of maintenance was put on the stand and testified that the customary procedure when a cord had to be draped across a carpet or floor was to take a couple of towels and wrap the cord in the towels, because the towels, which are big and obvious, serve as a flag. Whereas the flat cord, laid across, in this case a red and black checkered carpeting, was effectively camouflaged and caused the plaintiff to trip over it and fall.

To the uninitiated, a building code can be, at first glance, frightening and full of strange words. But everything in there is there for a purpose. Let me illustrate, with a review of several specific types of slip-and-fall situations, and how the building code* can become an ally.

**1. Stairways:** the code requires handrails when there are more than three risers. Why? Because experience has shown that people need the assurance and safety of something to hang onto, both to assist them and to grab onto in the event that, for any reason, they lose their balance.

If the handrails have verticle rails within them, a maximum gap of nine inches is allowed. Is this an arbitrary figure? No, it isn't. Engineers have learned that younger children love to clamber through the railings and have discovered that nine inches is close enough to prevent children who are capable of trying this from squeezing through.

If the stairway is more than 88 inches wide a railing is required in the center in public premises, not only at the sides. Why? Because obviously to do any good, the railing must be in a location where it can be utilized. If

---

*Code requirements used as illustrations are taken from the most recent edition of the Uniform Building Code, used primarily in the western states, published by the International Conference of Building Officials.*

the stairway is too wide, having rails only at the ends will leave the people using the center of the stairway without protection. The code recognizes this and require an additional rail in the middle.

At least six feet, six inches of clear head space above the steps is required by one code: other codes require even more. Silly? Certainly not. The code drafters are aware that even though most people are shorter than this, as they come down the steps they often bounce or step lively and end up several inches higher than their own height. The code, therefore, requires some clearance to allow for this common occurrence.

There are requirements as to how wide the stairwell has to be, which vary according to type of occupancy. Landings on the staircase are covered—because the engineers again recognize that when a person comes off the steps, he or she is walking with momentum and needs an adequate space to slow up to negotiate the next turn. Speaking of landings, the engineers also realize something else; that people get tired and as they tire their balance becomes affected, so the code requires that not more than 12 steps be put in without a landing.

2. Lighting: the codes, regarding exitways, steps, and corridors, talk about lighting. A light meter can measure this and tell you whether the light is sufficient. Also, look for alternating bright spots and dark spots, because the eye takes time to adjust adequately from light to dark and vice versa.

I suggest that every attorney might do well to purchase a copy of whichever code is most popular in his area of practice. If you're not sure, call your local building department.


### How to Zero In on Hidden Dangers

The simple failure to warn people concerning an ordinary, common situation, which normally we would not consider dangerous, is yet another area to explore. Ordinarily, we would not consider the simple act of washing floors to be dangerous. Unless we don't know about it. To illustrate: a person goes into a restaurant, sits at a table, drinks his 45-cent cup of coffee, then gets ready to leave. Meanwhile, in back of him, someone's busy washing and/or waxing the floor. The washer never bothers to tap the customer on the shoulder, and say, "When you get up, don't step back, because I've just washed the floor." He, or she, never puts up a rope barrier, or even a barrier of chairs. Instead, our customer—soon to be a client—finishes the meal, pushes the chair back, gets up and takes a step, and promptly slips on the wet surface and sustains a herniated disc.

While we're on the subject of floors, let's not forget waxing. Generally, the mere waxing of a floor is not sufficient to show that the defendant was negligent. You must show that in some way, this simple task was done so as to become dangerous. The defendant will no doubt argue that everybody, and every place of business, washes and waxes floors. It is your task to determine if the proper procedures were utilized in the application of that wax. For example, look for different waxes being used at different times. Sometimes, when different waxes are used, they don't meld properly and leave a floating surface where the top layer of wax floats on the lower layer. Water, when applied to certain types of self-polishing waxes, can cause the wax to become soft and when wax is soft, it's often slippery. Likewise, some types of asphalt tile coverings become soluble with certain types of wax. Variation in the application of wax in adjacent areas is another thing to look for, as changes in the coefficient of friction of a floor are difficult to pick out—and dangerous to walk on.

The entire pattern of maintenance should be explored. Often, believe it or not, the defendant will not have had an adequate cleanup schedule or program. To establish this, our experience has been that it's not good to wait until formal discovery, because when interrogatories are sent, or when depositions are taken, we have invariably received replies about what "a wonderful maintenance program is employed. Why, there even is one person who does nothing but walk around looking for things on the floor and cleaning them up . . . oh, yes indeed, we do have a rigid schedule of cleanup."

But what we found, however, when we sent an investigator in to talk to some of the people who work there is that: "Well, yes, Jones is supposed to do the cleanup, but they also have Jones unloading trucks, carting out garbage, taking care of empty pop bottles, stacking shelves, retrieving shopping carts from the parking lot . . . gee, he's supposed to check floors, but he never really gets around very often." Or, "Oh, you know: Jones was sick the day that lady fell, and when he's sick they don't bother to have anyone else do that."

(Incidentally, we found that, where the case involves a supermarket, box- or bag-boys are very good people to talk to, because there's a high turnover among them, they are not career employees, and don't have that same feeling of loyalty to prevent them from talking frankly.)

Also, while we're still in the supermarket, observe how things are stacked. Often, someone will pile boxes or bags so poorly that they were bound to fall—spilling their contents on the floor.

In terms of discovery, then, the chief areas to look for in preparation are: *(1)* establishing prior complaints and falls, and *(2)* establishing exactly what the conditions were at the time your client was hurt so that you can duplicate them and prepare them for testing and use as demonstrative evidence in the courtroom. A coefficient of friction board is a handy device. With this, you can show properly and improperly waxed surfaces side by side.

## Jury Instructions That Will Help Your Case

In terms of jury instruction, spend a little time on research; you'll find some good instructions. For example . . . when one has a choice of two ways of performing an act, one of which is known to be safe and the other, in the exercise of reasonable care, is subject to danger, the choice of the dangerous way ordinarily constitutes negligence. This is true in the absence of the showing of the existence of an emergency, sudden peril, or other circumstances justifying such choice.

The fact that the less dangerous method might take more time, be inconvenient, or be otherwise attended with difficulties furnishes no excuse for knowingly choosing the more dangerous of the two methods.

A second important instruction to the jury: while the measure of duty of both the plaintiff and the defendant is said to be that of ordinary care, there is a greater duty resting upon the defendant who is engaged in the business of inviting people onto its premises to discover whether there exist any dangerous condition(s) upon the premises that devolve upon an invitee who has the right to assume that the premises are reasonably safe for his use.

Even if the court will not give the specific instructions set forth above, the plaintiff's attorney can apply the points in his final argument.

# Third Party
# Bad Faith Actions

## An Interview with Samuel Langerman

Samuel Langerman is senior partner in the Phoenix, Arizona, law firm of Langerman, Begam, Lewis and Marks. He is past President of the Association of Trial Lawyers of America: Founder and past President of the Arizona Trial Lawyers Association; past President of the Western Trial Lawyers Association; and past Chairman of the Board of Editors of *Trial Magazine*. Langerman is a past member of the Board of Editors of *Trial Diplomacy Journal*.

## When the Interests of the Insurance Company
## and the Insured May Conflict

EDITOR: Please give us a little bit of background on the third party bad faith action.

LANGERMAN: The typical liability insurance policy such as the one that each of us has on our automobiles contains a provision that an insurance company agrees that it will defend any actions brought against its insured and arising out of his use or his operation of the automobile; and also it provides that if it loses that suit the company will pay on behalf of its insured the amount of the loss, up to the limits of the insurance company's policy.

This is what we mean by a typical third party claim. There are three parties involved: the insurance company, the insured and the ultimate injured victim who brings the claim against the insured person.

Ordinarily, the insurance company's interests and that of its insured are the same. But where the claim has a potential value larger than the limits of the insurance policy, the interests of the insurance company and its insured may conflict.

For example: the insured has a $25,000 policy and he has allegedly injured somebody who appears to have sustained about a $100,000 injury. Under the circumstances the insured's interest may be served best by settling that claim and removing the risk of a verdict of approximately $100,000. Should such a verdict be entered against him, ordinarily his insurance company would only owe the $25,000 policy limit, and the insured would owe the balance. If the injured person is willing to settle that claim for $25,000 or less, the insured would almost certainly benefit from a decision by the insurance company to go ahead with that settlement.

If I represented the injured victim in that situation, I would probably obtain his permission to say to the insurance company, "I'm going to give you a chance to settle this case and thus avoid the possibility that your insured will end up with an excess verdict."

Before the development of the law of "bad faith," the typical reactions of an insurance company in that situation would be, "Why should I give you my full $25,000 policy if that's the most that I can ever lose anyway?"

And you would be likely to respond by saying, "That may be the most you can lose, but if the verdict is larger than the policy limits, your insured will be responsible for the entire verdict, so he can lose a lot more."

That kind of discussion between the victim's lawyer and the lawyer or adjuster for the insurance company twenty-five or thirty years ago would frequently end up with the insurance company still maintaining that it did not want to settle the case unless it received a discount on its policy limits. If the discount was not offered, the company would go on trial; and if a verdict was entered in excess of the policy limits the company would tell its insured that he owed the rest. The insured would probably find there was little law in his jurisdiction that would obligate the insurance company to pay the balance of that "excess" verdict.

Today, essentially all over America there is law creating a duty on the part of the insurance company in that kind of situation to exercise good faith toward its insured. A frequently used test of good faith is to require the company to settle the case if the company would have paid the demanded amount of money had the policy limits been higher. Under this test, if the injured party's demand is for a $25,000 settlement, the insurance company is required to evaluate that demand as though the company had an unlimited policy. If under those circumstances the insurance company would have decided that $25,000 was a fair settlement, then it would have the obligation to settle at $25,000 even though the insured only had a $25,000 policy. If in fact the demand is rejected, and a verdict of $50,000 or $100,000 is entered, a jury in a subsequent "bad faith" trial will be instructed to find against the insurance company if the jury finds, from the evidence, that the company would have accepted the $25,000 demand if its insurance policy had been unlimited.

In California it may be hard to distinguish bad faith from ordinary negligence because bad faith can consist of such things as failure to do what a reasonable company would have done under the circumstances if its coverage had been larger. Bad faith can consist of failure to defend the case properly, failure to investigate it properly, or not keeping your insured advised of what was going on. Many other things can be bad faith in a liberal jurisdiction like California.

In other jurisdictions, a litigant who is claiming that an insurance company was guilty of bad faith may actually have to prove that the insurance company had almost an *intention* to injure its insured. Each lawyer needs to know how the courts of his state have defined "bad faith."

In my jurisdiction, one rule that applies is a rule that requires the insurance company to give equal consideration to its rights and to the rights of its insured. So when a settlement demand is received by a company, it must ask not only what risk will the company face if it rejects the demand, but also what risks will its *insured* face. I believe that under that test an insurance company has the duty to do what it would have done if its coverage had been unlimited. If the company can persuade the jury in a subsequent "bad faith" trial that it would have rejected the demand even if it had had an unlimited policy, then the failure of the insurance company to accept the demand was not bad faith. If, however, the insurance company, in the opinion of the jury, would in all probability have accepted that demand if the coverage had been unlimited, then the failure to accept it with the more limited coverage constituted bad faith on the part of the insurance company.

Plaintiff's lawyers should use discretion in selecting cases for policy limit demands. The lawyer who indiscriminately makes a policy limit demand every time he has a claim will create a situation where the insurance company can establish that it had no reason to pay much attention to his policy limit demands, because he makes them in essentially every case.

When a lawyer makes a policy limit demand, he should give the insurance company a great deal of information—essentially everything that he has. He should tell the insurance company his expected testimony on liability, to establish that it is a case of probable liability or at least a case where the insurance company has considerable exposure. He should give the insurance company all of the available information pertaining to injuries and damages.

An insurance company's duty is not limited only to those cases of good liability. Consider, for example, this situation. An insurance company is defending a claim that it could reasonably expect to win nine times out of ten, but the damages are large and would reasonably support a verdict of $200,000. The company should not conclude that because it expects to win nine out of ten times it has no duty to accept the policy limit demand if the policy is a small one. Thus if the policy limits are $15,000, then the company might very well find that it was guilty of bad faith for turning down a $15,000 policy limits demand.

Just figure it out for yourself; what would this company probably have done in that same case if it had had a million-dollar policy and it received a demand of $15,000? Would it say to itself, "We're going to win nine times out of ten, and therefore we don't want to settle," or would it say, "Let's figure it out mathematically and economically; if we had ten of these cases and tried all ten we would win nine out of the ten, but in the tenth one we would lose $200,000. Thus each of the ten cases would average a loss of $20,000 plus the cost of processing the case"? The company's logical conclusion would probably be that a $15,000 settlement demand was realistic and should be accepted. If the same company rejects a $15,000 demand in such as case when it has only a $15,000 policy, a jury will probably conclude the company recognized that one out of ten of such insureds would end up on the losing side of a $200,000 verdict, but decided to take the risk in the hope that its insured and not the company would be saddled with the large verdict.

Frequently, a company will turn down the demand originally because it believes and hopes that the lawyer doesn't mean it when he says in his letter, "If you don't give me the policy limits and give it to me within a fixed, reasonable time limit, I'll never again settle for such a small amount." The companies have learned that some lawyers who write such letters don't mean it; they will later settle for the policy limits or even for something less than the policy limits. A lawyer who has that reputation will have difficulty in persuading a jury that the company acted unreasonably in ignoring the deadline in his demand letter. A better policy is to tell the company, "This will be your only chance to settle this case within the policy limits," only in those cases where no second chance will be given to the company.

Lawyers should keep in mind that the bad faith claim belongs to the insured and not to the victim who has been injured by that insured. But the insured can usually be persuaded to assign his bad faith claim to the victim who obtained the large verdict against him; and the injured victim then processes the bad faith claim against the insurance company. If a jury in that second trial decides that the insurance company acted in bad faith in failing to settle the case, and by so doing subjected its insured to a verdict that was larger than his policy limits, the insurance company will owe the entire judgment.

A plaintiff's lawyer in a bad faith suit will be able to "discover" the contents of the insurance company's file concerning its processing of the original claim against the insured. The plaintiff in the bad faith suit stands in the position of the insured, and that file is not privileged insofar as the insured is concerned. Thus the plaintiff's lawyer can obtain the memorandums that relate to settlement negotiations. He can obtain the evaluation that the insurance company lawyer made and the letters that the insurance company lawyer sent to the insurance company evaluating the case. Sometimes those letters will disclose that the lawyer told the company that this was a case which the company had a significant chance of losing and that if the insured lost, his lawyer anticipated a large plaintiff's verdict.

The insurance company may offer the testimony of the lawyers and adjusters who were processing the case for the company originally, to the effect that they didn't think the case was worth the amount of money being demanded. And the plaintiff will offer testimony of experienced lawyers in the field, and perhaps experienced adjusters, saying they would have evaluated the case at more than the demand, and had the coverage been there they would have thought the case was worth more than the amount that was being demanded.

### A New Area of Bad Faith Claims

EDITOR: There is a new area of bad faith that I know you have been lecturing on recently. Could you tell us about that?

LANGERMAN: The type of case that I've been lecturing on recently is different because it's a case in which the insurance company is not denying that the case is worth the full policy. Instead, the company insists that there was an exclusion in its insurance policy which makes the policy not applicable to the particular accident.

I'll give you an example of an airplane case where the company's policy provides that the coverage will not apply if the plane involved in the crash did not have a regular airworthiness certificate. The company, having denied coverage, obviously is reluctant to get involved in settlement negotiations. So it may never make a decision as to whether the case is or isn't worth the full policy limits.

Take another example, in the automobile field; the company has a policy exclusion that says that it does not provide coverage if the claimant is a relative resident in the same household as the insured. The insurance company claims the exclusion applied to the claim your client is making. You, as the plaintiff's attorney, disagree—you define the word "residing" to mean long-time or permanent resident, and you claim your client was only a temporary occupant of the insured's household.

I could give other examples, but the significant thing is not for me to name as many exclusions as I can, but to tell you that any time the insurance company thinks it has an exclusion, the insurance company has several choices available to it. One choice is to surrender when the plaintiff's attorney insists that the exclusion really doesn't apply and to agree with him that they will not rely on that exclusion. Most companies aren't willing to do that. If the company thinks it has an exclusion, it usually isn't willing to surrender on that exclusion unless and until a court has ruled that the exclusion is not valid or is not applicable.

A second thing for the company to do is offer to defend the case under what is called a "reservation of rights." The company will tell the insured that it will defend him under this reservation. Frequently, if not always, the company won't even ask him to agree, but will send a letter to the insured saying, "We believe we have an exclusion and that we don't have any coverage, but in order to be fair to you we will go ahead and defend your claim just as though we did have coverage, but without surrendering our position that we really do not have coverage. Similarly, we don't ask you to surrender your position that there is coverage." On its face, that looks like a fair position for the company to adopt, because it looks like it is saying to its insured, "We're not asking you to give up your rights and we don't want to give up ours, and what could be fairer than that?"

The problem is that when a company does that, it is unlikely to consider settling the case; and one of the rights that the insured had if he had coverage was the right to have that company act in good faith when a settlement demand is made. If the company believes there is no coverage, however, the company may be unwilling even to *consider* the question of what the case is worth. In a case where the plaintiff's injuries are worth a lot more than the policy limit, if the company then rejects a policy limit demand it is subjecting its insured to a great risk. Without the policy exclusion, a different result would probably have occurred. Unless the liability situation was tremendously one-sided in favor of the insured defendant, the insurance company probably would have responded to a policy limit demand by deciding that it was too dangerous to reject the demand, and the case would have been settled.

Thus, notwithstanding the assurances in the "reservation of rights" letter, the insured will not receive from this company all of the rights he would have received if coverage had been conceded. If you are the insured in that case, it isn't very satisfactory to you to have your insurance company tell you that they won't even discuss settlement with the claimant until the company has litigated the coverage issue in a separate declaratory judgment action. That action might not be concluded for one to five years, depending on the jurisdiction.

Even though an insured's rights are not being fully protected by a conditional defense, most insureds, because they aren't experts on insurance law, are very likely to conclude that the company's offer is fair, so they accept the conditional offers to defend. If you are faced with such a situation, I advise you to give a lot of consideration to urging the insured (or his personal lawyer) to reject the conditional offer.

Let me give you an example. The insured, when he gets the conditional offer from the insurance company, may discuss it with his personal attorney. You should find some way to advise the insured that you have made or intend to make a policy limit demand. Many companies will send a copy of your demand to the insured, because the company is afraid that failure to advise the insured that there was a policy limit demand may constitute bad faith. In the demand you should point out that the insured is not being treated fairly by his insurance company because the company, having adopted the position that there is no coverage, is not really considering settlement, and the insured is being harmed or has the potential of being harmed very substantially by that position. Your letter will tell the insurance company that in your opinion it should advise the insured to get himself another lawyer to advise him independently as to what his rights are. Most companies will be very reluctant not to pass that on to the insured, and they'll be very reluctant to tell him anything other than the fact that maybe that's good advice: maybe he *should* have another lawyer.

If he already has another lawyer, there's nothing unethical about talking to the lawyer. You're not limited to a discussion with the insurance company lawyer, if there are two lawyers representing the same person. You should tell the private lawyer this important rule: a denial of coverage by an insurance company, which turns out to be wrong, creates an obligation on the company's part to satisfy the entire judgment which is ultimately entered against its insured, even if the denial of coverage was made in good faith.

In short, this is one area where the company not only has to have a logical reason for thinking that it had an exclusion, but the company has to be right! If it had a logical reason for thinking it had an exclusion but a court ultimately holds that the exclusion did not apply and that there was coverage, then the company has acted in bad faith and it owes the entire amount of the verdict.

Now, this is very important because frequently, if not always, the company's position that there is an exclusion is not an outrageous position. There are indeed facts from which the company could logically believe that its exclusion may apply. The problem is that if the company turns out to have been wrong, it will then be a company which has been unwilling to enter into any settlement negotiations even though it had coverage. And a company which has coverage has a duty to act in good faith when a settlement demand is made.

The California courts have explained this rule of law as follows: If a company has coverage it has a duty, when a policy limit demand is made, to evaluate that in good faith and to accept it if good faith would have required it to accept. If the company refuses to consider the demand because it thinks it has no coverage, it has denied the insured a right which the policy gave him—the right to have this claim against him settled. And if the company's reason for rejecting the demand, for failing to analyze it as all other demands are analyzed, was the *mistaken* belief that there was no coverage, the company has breached its contract. If in fact it turns out that there was coverage, then the company must explain why two years or three years earlier it had refused to settle the case for the policy limits when it was clearly worth the policy limits. If its explanation is that "We thought we didn't have coverage, but we turned out to be wrong," the court's position is, "We don't give you any benefits for being wrong. We won't punish you for being wrong if you had a reasonable basis for thinking you were right, but we won't put you in a *better* position than you would have been in if you hadn't made the mistake. And if you hadn't made the mistake, good faith would have required you to accept that reasonable policy limits demand."

It's extremely important for plaintiff's lawyers to understand this rule. Because this is the one rule that I know of where making a logical mistake does not avoid the finding of bad faith. In all other circumstances, if the company had a logical, sound reason for thinking its position was correct, it probably will not be held to have been in bad faith.

Thus, for example, if the company evaluates liability and decides that liability is strongly in favor of its insured, and if a jury subsequently finds that that was a logical and reasonable evaluation, the company will be judged by the fact that it has a logical reason for thinking there was *probably* no liability. And the fact that a jury subsequently found for the plaintiff may very well not cause the insurance company to have been in bad faith.

Similarly, if the insurance company thought that the plaintiff's injuries were really the result of some factor other than the accident—they thought his arthritis was acting up rather than the injury had produced his symptoms—and if the jury finds that logically that's what almost any reasonable insurance company would have thought at that time based on the available information, then the company very likely will not be found to have acted in bad faith, because they relied on their logical evaluation of the medical evidence.

EDITOR: In effect, when the insurance company loses the declaratory judgment action, then it is strictly liable in the bad faith action.

LANGERMAN: That's right. If it is conceded that the only reason it rejected the policy limit demand earlier was its erroneous belief that it did not have any coverage, that belief no longer counts, and the company, in effect, is strictly liable in that situation.

### How to Recognize and Evaluate a Potential Bad Faith Case

EDITOR: How do you recognize a potential bad faith case when it walks into your office?

LANGERMAN: Obviously, when a case first walks into the office you start processing it without reference to the question of bad faith, because at that moment you're merely trying to decide how good or bad your case is and how large it is. However, the moment you begin to have the reaction that this is potentially a fair-size case, one that may be larger in value than small or modest policy limits, at that point you should begin thinking of bad faith. At that point you will find out what the policy limits are, if in your jurisdiction that is permited. In the federal courts it is now permitted, of course, by filing an interrogatory that requests that information. In many of the state courts the same rule has been adopted. In those courts, the moment you file suit you can find out what the policy limits are.

If you're in a jurisdiction which permits you to find the limits by filing suit, the insurance companies may give you the policy limits without suit because they know you can get them anyway.

If you can't find the policy limits, that will not stop you from considering the question of a potential bad faith suit, because you can send a demand letter to the insurance company that in many respects will be like your usual demand letter. You will tell the company that you're representing the plaintiff and here's why he's entitled to win, and here's what his injuries are, and here's our demand—what you think the case is worth. You will then point out that you don't know how much insurance the defendant has. Assuming that his insurance is smaller than the demand, your letter will state that you have obtained your client's permission to settle for your policy limits if the company corroborates in writing all coverages available to the defendant in this case.

I usually set a time limit, too, because I tell the lawyer or the adjuster that if we're going to settle for a lot less than the case is worth, we're going to be doing it only because there is not adequate coverage. One of the considerations for this small demand is that the company settle quickly. I make it very clear this is the one case in which I'm not making a "negotiating" or "opening" demand. Similarly, I tell the company that I'm giving a relatively small amount of time—and I mean to adhere to this unless the company seeks a reasonable, small extension. I make it clear that I expect prompt action, and I expect the full amount of money. I don't expect to be bargaining when we're already agreeing to settle for a lot less than this man's injuries are worth. Again I remind your readers, don't send those letters in cases where you intend to bargain.

### Picking the Witnesses Your Case Demands

EDITOR: *What kind of witnesses will you then line up in the second lawsuit, the bad faith lawsuit?*

LANGERMAN: You should understand that at the time the bad faith suit is being processed, the first lawsuit, which was the personal injury lawsuit, has gone to a verdict in an amount that is meaningfully higher than the policy limits. Otherwise, you won't be processing the second suit—the "bad faith" case.

So you start with the second jury knowing that another jury thought that this case was worth, say $36,000 but the insurance company rejected a $15,000 demand. The insurance company must persuade the jury that when the $15,000 demand was made, it had a valid reason to believe the case wasn't really worth $15,000. The company is unlikely to try to persuade the jury that the injury wasn't worth $15,000 from a damage standpoint, if in fact a jury has given a $36,000 verdict. Obviously, the larger the discrepancy between the policy limit and the size of the verdict, the more difficult it becomes for the insurance company to argue the damage issue. Usually what the company will be arguing, then, is that this looked like a case of no liability or very poor liability from the plaintiff's standpoint, and thus the company had a reason for believing that it would win the case. And even though it knew that if it lost it could lose more money than its policy limits, it thought the odds were good or overwhelming, that it would win the case.

When you have that kind of a case, who are you going to look to as witnesses? You're going to get lawyers and adjusters who are experts in this field, who evaluate cases of this sort all the time. And you're going to have them testify that you made available to them all of the information that was known at the time the settlement demand was being made. You give your experts the same information you gave the insurance company. Hopefully, your witness will get on the witness stand and say, "I don't disagree there was a chance for the insurance company to win the case; but I strongly disagree with their position that they were going to win it 80 or 90 times out of 100. It looks like the kind of case that they probably would win 40% to 50% of the time. That's how I would have evaluated it as of the date when the insurance company made the decision to turn down the demand. And if I had evaluated it as a fifty-fifty case, I sure as blazes would not have turned down a $100,000 demand if I were the insurance company. I would have said to myself, "If the company loses this case it's going to lose several times $100,000 and perhaps as much as $1,000,000. And the fact that the company may win this kind of case about half the time doesn't mean it isn't worth $100,000."

That same witness would probably tell the jury that in his opinion, based on his experience, even though the insurance company is denying it, and even though their witnesses are denying it, he believes that if the insurance company had had a $50 million policy it would quickly have accepted this $100,000 demand; and as a matter of fact it probably would have paid more than that to settle, because even though it hoped to win, its exposure was sufficiently great that it would have paid this larger amount.

He would testify that in his opinion the only reason the company rejected the demand is because it had a limited policy, and it hoped that if it lost the case a subsequent jury at a bad faith trial, this jury that is now hearing this case, would believe the company when it brought a witness who said, "Oh, we wouldn't have settled this if we had a $40 million policy. We wouldn't have paid $100,000."

The wonderful thing about this area is you're not limited as to who can be your witness. When you have an eyewitness to an accident, he's the only eyewitness, and he's the one you have to call. You can't call a substitute if it turns out that the eyewitness is inarticulate, or unattractive, or if he has a bad record. He's the only eyewitness, and you either call him or get along without an eyewitness. However, when you're in *this* field and you're talking about experts, any lawyer in town—or for that matter, any lawyer in the country who's an expert in handling cases of this sort—is a potential witness on your behalf.

If you're lucky, and if you have good relationships with the defense bar, you may also persuade one or two or three defense lawyers to testify for you, if they do not represent this particular insurance company and don't have any feelings that some day they hope they'll get this account. Such an attorney may look at your case and say to you, "It's so flagrant that even though I'm usually on the other side, I am still willing to get on the stand and say this is a flagrant case." This witness will subsequently tell the jury that ordinarily his work is *defending* these cases and representing insurance companies, and that he frequently is called upon to evaluate cases of this sort for insurance companies—companies who face the same problems the defendant in this case faced. He then places a value on this case, taking into consideration the facts known at the time the company rejected the plaintiff's demand. He'll discuss liability and damages, and tell the jury his evaluation. Presumably it'll be a lot larger than the policy limits. You then ask him if he has an opinion as to whether the company should have accepted the policy limits demand. "Were they acting the way a normal, reasonable insurance company does when they rejected the demand?" And he says, "My companies wouldn't have turned this down." And of course, that's very persuasive.

You can also pick an insurance adjuster who says, "I've been a claims man for many years, and here's my background and experience, and here's how I would have evaluated the case."

You should understand that one of your witnesses is almost certainly going to be the plaintiff's lawyer who was negotiating the case and who made the policy limits demand.

## How to Handle Your Opponent's Witnesses

EDITOR: *How would you handle the other side's witnesses?*

LANGERMAN: The other side will bring the defense lawyer who defended the personal injury case, if they can. Sometimes the company is in the sad position where he has recommended that the case be settled. You will be reading to the jury his letter; it will be an exhibit in evidence. But if he hasn't recommended settlement, the company may bring him in. Your cross-examination of him will try to establish that there are many cases that he's settled, or in which he recommended settlement, in which he thought there was disputed liability; and that he has not adopted the position that if liability is disputed, then it doesn't matter how bad the damages are, the case shouldn't be settled.

If you happen to know of a specific case that is similar to this one, in which he has been involved in a settlement, than you may be able to cross-examine him on that specific case and have him try to distinguish the case. The jury will understand that you're showing that the only real distinguishing point is that there was more coverage in the other case or, alternatively, the company in the other case acted in good faith and didn't subject its insured to the gamble involved in rejecting the demand.

I don't know of any tricks in terms of how you cross-examine the defense lawyer. You're just trying to establish the methods one uses in evaluating these cases, and that in this case the insurance company appears to have deviated from those methods.

### How to Prove Bad Faith Even in Conservative Jurisdictions

EDITOR: How would you handle one of these cases in a conservative jurisdiction where the court will instruct the jury that bad faith requires a finding of almost an evil intention, wickedness, on the part of the insurance company?

LANGERMAN: The one thing that is quite clear, even in those jurisdictions, is that you don't have to prove your case by showing an admission by the insurance company that it intended to act in bad faith. You prove your case by showing that its conduct was so different from the conduct in cases where it had larger insurance policies, that the jury can reasonably conclude from this that the company's motives were bad.

Sometimes, if you're lucky, you can find something in the file that will show the bad motives. There's a rather famous California case, the Critz case, in which the insurance company file disclosed letters from the local adjuster to his boss pointing out that the case was worth more than the policy limit of $10,000, but that he believed he could save something because everyone understood that in order to get this $10,000 the litigant or claimant would have to file a suit, and take a long period of time, and pay a lawyer a fee; and thus the claims man thought he could persuade the plaintiff and her attorney to settle for less because in the long run they would end up not getting the whole $10,000 anyway, because of these costs and expenses.

That was a relatively early case when the law of bad faith wasn't that well established in California. I doubt that any California insurance company would now engage in such communications. But there may still be companies around the country that are doing it. The correspondence in that case also showed that eventually the claims manager gave the adjuster the $10,000 worth of authority, with both of them agreeing the case was worth that amount, but advising him that he wanted him to save something if he could and the adjuster then made an offer of $8,250. That kind of correspondence obviously proves a course of conduct on the part of the insurance company that even in the more conservative jurisdictions would almost certainly be held to be bad faith. And occasionally you will find something in the file that will help you on that.

For the most part, though, you'll try to persuade the jury that this was such a *clear* case in which the evaluation should have been above the policy limits, and such a *clear* case in which the policy limits should have been offered, that the jury can presume from this failure to settle in this clear-cut case that there was this bad conduct on the part of the insurance company.

Insurance companies have learned that the letters they write may go to the jury ultimately, and frequently now you'll find the defense lawyer giving you a jury argument answer to your demand letter. Instead of answering by just saying no, or this is a case in which we want to do some more discovery, you'll get a letter that will express outrage that you should have put a three-week time limit on your letter when no depositions have been taken yet, and the company doesn't know all of the evidence yet, and you expect the company to jump every time you say jump, and this is outrageous and one-sided, and it demonstrates the fact that you're not a fair guy, and so forth. What they're doing is writing a letter that they hope to read to a jury later on.

### The Kind of Jurors You Want in a Bad Faith Case

EDITOR: What kind of jurors do you want in these cases? Do you want intelligent jurors who can understand the complexities of the insurance business?

LANGERMAN: I don't really think so. You start out with a named insurance company, and my guess is that you're likely to find that business and professional people who have worked with insurance companies empathize with them. People whose only contact with insurance companies has been that they've made claims against them, or they've complained about premiums, are less likely to have empathy for the insurance company. I'm not suggesting that they may not nevertheless be very intelligent people; but I am suggesting that you might very well stay away from the head of the local bank, or the president of the largest corporation in town, because they've been working with the insurance companies and they've been on their side so often that they tend to identify with them.

Secondly, I think the issues aren't nearly as complex as they may sound. Basically, the jury understands that this insurance company had a chance to settle this case and avoid the very large verdict that was entered against the insured. Jurors are told they're not supposed to judge by hindsight, but they do know now that the insurance company lost the case and that the verdict was much larger than the policy limits. I'm sure that the jurors try not to judge by hindsight, but it's hard to ignore that large verdict.

Thus when they hear some good expert witnesses telling them that without hindsight, they would have evaluated this case as being worth more than the policy limit demand, the jurors tend to find these witnesses more believable than the adverse witnesses. If you've selected those cases which warranted the policy limits demand, and follow up with good experts at the bad faith trial, your success ratio in those cases should be good.

# The Wrongful Death
# of a Child

## Allan R. Earl

Allan R. Earl is a partner in the Las Vegas, Nevada law firm of
Galatz, Earl & Catalano. He is a past president of the Nevada Trial
Lawyers Association; a past president of the Western Trial Lawyers Association, and a former State Committeeman from Nevada
to the A.T.L.A.

One of the more difficult and wrenching experiences faced by the modern
trial lawyer is representing the family, usually the parents, in an action for
the wrongful death of a child. It is a sensitive task, demanding an appreciation of deep-seated feelings and values that most personal injury cases
never reach. The task is made more complex because presenting the
death case of a 17-month-old infant differs dramatically from the presentation of the death case of a 17-year-old high school student. We will focus
primarily on the accidental death of children below the age of 14, although mention will be made of certain circumstances which deal with
the death of older teenagers.

### Handling the Threshhold Question of Liability

In child death cases, as in all areas of personal injury practice, the
threshhold question is liability. Usually when a child is accidentally killed,
the fact issues that are raised concern the possible comparative or contributory negligence of the child and of the parents in supervising the
child. Each state, by case law, has determined the extent to which deceased children and their parents can be contributorily negligent. I will
not attempt to analyze the case law of each state. As a general rule, chil-

dren are held to that standard of care which would be expected from an ordinary child of the same age, experience, knowledge and discretion. In those instances, however, where a child is engaged in an adult activity (such as driving a car), he can be held to an adult standard of care.[1] In some jurisdictions, minors below a certain age are considered incapable of contributory negligence. Some states use age seven as the cut-off date, and one state has extended the cut-off date to nine years of age.[2] Most states, however, do not define the age when children are incapable of contributory negligence, but handle it on a case-by-case basis.

A far more difficult question involves the contributory negligence on the part of the parents, who are generally the plaintiffs. The cases in this area hold that it is a question of fact for the jury to determine whether the parents of the minor child were negligent in failing to supervise the activities of the child under all the circumstances of the case.[3] Absent evidence that parents may have been contributorily negligent, the instruction on the possibility of such contributory negligence on the part of the parents is improper and reversible error.[4]

In some cases, recovery has been denied to parents who have been found negligent in the supervision of their children. When the failure of supervision was found to be the proximate cause of the child's death, recovery was barred in an action for wrongful death of the child.[5] In those jurisdictions utilizing the doctrine of comparative negligence, the parents' failure to properly supervise the child will reduce the recovery against a negligent tortfeasor based on the degree to which the lack of supervision contributed to the child's death.

The final question in this area is whether one parent's negligence will be imputed to the other parent to preclude recovery by either of the parents in the negligent death of their child. Some courts hold that the negligence of one parent is imputed to the other parent. One court has held that the negligence of the mother was imputed to the father to preclude recovery by either parent even though the father was out of the United States at the time of the accident.[6] However, other courts have held that unless both parents are actively supervising their child, one parent's negligence will not preclude recovery by the non-negligent parent.[7]

Once the issue of liability has been determined, the lawyer must decide whether the parents can withstand the emotional trauma of the actual litigation process. Most psychiatrists or psychologists will verify that parents carry intense guilt feelings and deep emotional scars from their involvement in events contributing to the death of their child. Guilt feelings are present in all child death cases, even when there has been no breakdown in the custodial supervision of the child by the parents. These guilt feelings, subliminal, subconscious, or overt, are manifested in a wide variety of behavior. The lawyer should determine the family's emotional stability before subjecting them to depositions, interrogatories, courtroom cross-examination and the defense of their own contributory negligence.

## An Overview of Damage Awards and Death Statutes

The practitioner's challenge in a child death case is to recover an award for damages commensurate with the loss suffered by the parents. Historically, the damage awards in child death cases have been unconscionably low. The first step in reversing this trend is a careful analysis of the provisions in the local jurisdiction's wrongful death statute. The language of the statute governs who is entitled to bring the action, the nature of the pleadings, and, in some cases, the maximum limit on damages allowed. To a large extent, the statute also governs what elements of emotional suffering, if any, can be included in jury instructions and/or oral argument.

Death statutes are classified into two categories: Loss to Survivors, and Loss to Estate. The former contemplates an award of damages to the plaintiffs, and damages are measured by the anticipated pecuniary or economic contributions which the decedent would have made to the survivors had he/she lived. Under a strict interpretation of such a statute, damages are restricted to pecuniary loss and the plaintiff-survivors are required to establish a minimum level of proof that they either were receiving or, in all probability, would have received contributions from the decedent child. The actual measure of damages is the size of the would-be contributions that were lost. In some states the Loss to Survivors statute contains certain elements of emotional grief and suffering which can be included in the damages awarded to the plaintiffs.

A Loss to Estate statute provides for a single award to the estate based on the economic value of the decedent's life. The damages are measured by the decedent's probable future earnings or his earning capacity. Individual beneficiaries need not show the size, nor the probability, of contributions which they may have received from the decedent. Since the majority of wrongful death statutes in the United States are of the Loss to Survivors type, this article will deal with those statutes in the analysis of how to present the issue of damages.

## How to Present Damages Even in the Absence of Actual Pecuniary Loss

The critical question in any child death damage presentation is whether the statute or local case law limits damages to demonstrable pecuniary loss, and precludes any award for emotional grief and suffering on the

part of the parent. If so, the realities of the modern social and family structure virtually preclude large damage awards. Children are rarely wage
earners before their middle teen years. Most often the decedent had no
wage or earning record available, and had not demonstrated a discernible
preference or proclivity for a field of employment or training.

What does the practitioner do when non-speculative proof is unavailable to establish actual pecuniary loss? First, the inequities of such
statutes are readily apparent and have been widely criticized by numerous legal scholars. As a result, most trial judges will be somewhat sympathetic to the overwhelming trend in modern evidence law to allow great
latitude in the presentation of evidence that is somewhat speculative in
nature.[8] Second, when the admissibility of certain evidence is ruled on (at
a pre-trial conference, a motion *in limine*, an evidentiary argument, or as a
last resort in a formal offer of proof), the following capsuled history and
argument should be made in court.

In the latter stages of the development of the common law in
England, courts did not allow an action for damages in the wrongful
death of a person. The harshness of this rule was modified in 1846 by remedial legislation popularly known as Lord Campbell's Act. The Act provided simply that a jury could award damages for the benefit of certain
relatives in proportion to the injury resulting from the death. In its original form, Lord Campbell's Act contained no limitation restricting damages to pecuniary loss. Subsequent English civil cases grafted on restrictions that limited damages to a showing of the actual pecuniary loss
suffered by the survivors. In drafting wrongful death statutes in the United
States, most state legislatures based their statutes on Lord Campbell's Act,
also restricting damages to pecuniary loss. However, the fallacy in this historical setting is that,

1) Lord Campbell's Act was, in itself, remedial legislation and was
   but the first step in a jurisprudential effort to cure a terrible legal
   inequity that existed at the common law.
2) The damage concept instituted by case law following Lord
   Campbell's Act originated when children were considered as
   chattels, a source of potential supplemental income to the family,
   and were put to work at ages 5 through 10 as pawns in the Industrial Revolution. The case law was, in fact, reflecting the economic
   reality of the times. That precedent, however, has no relevance to
   a modern legal setting which protects children through child labor laws.
3) Many years ago courts limited the damages to pecuniary loss because it was thought that ordinary juries were not competent to

analyze such intangible items as pain, suffering, mental anguish and the like. Juries now routinely analyze these very difficult concepts in every form of personal injury case, and *remittiturs* are always available to control any excess that may shock the judicial conscience.

The inherent inequities in wrongful death statutes which trace their origins to Lord Campbell's Act may have been slowly modified by state legislatures, and many states now allow awards for non-pecuniary loss. Some states such as Nevada, Florida and others have recognized the real loss in such cases and allow parents the specific statutory right to recover for emotional grief and suffering over the death of one of their children.[9] Most other wrongful death statutes, which have been modified, allow for the recovery of damages that are "just, fair, and equitable" or they allow damages for the loss of "care, comfort, society and companionship," but do not allow a specific award for emotional grief and suffering. In interpreting statutes of the latter variety, some courts have held that the emotional grief and suffering on the part of the parents can be argued even though the statute does not specifically permit it.[10]

Even if the local court interprets the wrongful death statute strictly, most statutes now include an award for damages for the loss of "society." It is this word the jury instructions should focus on. The United States Supreme Court has given a broad definition to the term "society" and it involves a wide spectrum of human emotions and feelings. In *Sea-Land Services, Inc. v. Gaudet*, 414 U.S. 573 (1974), the Supreme Court stated, "[t]he term "society" embraces a broad range of mutual benefits each family member receives from the others' continued existence, including love, affection, care, attention, companionship, comfort, and protection." That definition provides wide latitude for skillful counsel to roam within in demonstrating the unique emotional loss suffered by parents and other family members when a child in that family is negligently killed.

A relatively new theory known as the negligent infliction of emotional distress should always be explored and utilized in appropriate cases when drafting the pleadings in a wrongful death case. This theory can serve as an alternative theory of recovery where the wrongful death statute precludes any award for emotional grief and suffering on the part of the parents. It may also be used as a separate cause of action in the original wrongful death complaint. Recent decisions indicate that in order to recover under this theory the following elements must be present:

1) Death or serious physical injury;
2) Intimate family relationship between plaintiffs and injured or deceased person;

3) Observation of death or injury at the scene of the accident or very shortly thereafter;

4) The onset of symptomatology related to severe emotional distress after the observance of the accident or injury.

This cause of action is relatively new in its development and originally a "zone of danger" test was developed in the case of *Dillon v. Legg,* 69 Cal.Rptr. 72, 441 P.2d 912 (Cal. 1968), which required that the person seeking recovery for emotional distress had to be physically in danger from the defendant's negligent actions which resulted in the death of the deceased. Many courts since the decision in *Dillon v. Legg,* have extended this theory to eliminate the "zone of danger" test, and have allowed recovery as long as the plaintiff actually witnessed the death of the deceased.[11]

### Checklist of Information You Will Need to Prepare a Strong Case

The initial preparation of the damage case should begin with a sensitive and detailed interview of the parents and family of the deceased child. A wide ranging assortment of bits and pieces of the child's life insofar as they are available needs to be gathered and put into evidentiary form. The following is only a sample checklist of things to ask for and inquire about:

1. Birth certificates
2. Baby pictures
3. Family photos
4. Awards from such activities as Pop Warner football, Little League baseball, Little League soccer, boys clubs, YMCA, Campfire Girls, summer camp, Cub Scouts, etc.
5. Scholastic achievements from grade school and high school
6. Athletic achievements in varsity competition
7. Special skills participation such as debate, student newspaper, music, band, 4-H Club, Glee Club, etc.
8. Positions held as a result of school elections.
9. Craft skills or interesting hobbies such as shop class projects, etc.
10. Participation in church or related activities
11. Health records from family physicians or pediatricians
12. Evidence of plans which the parents had for the child such as family Bible inscriptions, private diary entries, infant savings accounts, sentimental mementos such as grade school Valentines which have been secretly saved or Mother's Day cards created by hand.

## How to Create for the Jury a Vivid Image of the Deceased Child

The preparation of the evidence in such cases, however, demands a great deal more than a mere collection of data, pictures and information. The goal at trial is to create a living mental image of the deceased child so that the loss of the child can become more than just an abstract sense of the loss of a human life, but rather an actual absence in the lives of the parents that a jury can viscerally perceive. To create that image and to make it live, the practitioner must do something that is both difficult and uncomfortable. I strongly recommend that the practitioner visit the home where the child lived and take some time to see the room where the child slept and carefully catalog every detail in the room from stuffed animals to pictures on the wall to articles hidden under the bed. Brothers and sisters should be taken out for a hamburger or a walk around the block and in a relaxed atmosphere asked to discuss their memories of the deceased. Such conversations may be awkward, but they reveal glimpses and mental images of the deceased that cannot be obtained in any other fashion. When appropriate, interview teachers and even best friends outside the confines of the law office. In the case of a high school student, I think one of the great sources of background information is the high school yearbook and the comments of friends and classmates that fill its pages. The suggestions listed above are by no means complete. They are merely guidelines which can be expanded with ingenuity and insight to adequately present the background of each child.

The actual theme for the presentation of damages is presented in the opening statement to the jury. This theme should be considered carefully and referred to consistently throughout the trial. The various aspects of the child's achievements should be presented by non-family members whenever possible. Preferably, the parents should be the last witnesses and their direct examination should be short and succinct.

## 3 Sample Final Arguments to Help You Win an Adequate Award

The final argument is often the key to damages in a child death case, and great care must be paid to the drafting of jury instructions so that every available area of damage is explored in oral argument. Although it is preferable not to have the entire family present during every phase of the trial, they should be seated together and clearly visible to the jury for the final argument. The facts on liability should be reviewed first in some detail. Then the issue of damages should be presented. Each lawyer has a personal style but, as a general rule, the deep emotional issues need not be vigorously hammered home in a loud tone. The emotional loss to the parents should be stated in a quiet, emotional, well-rehearsed manner.

The defense attorney will no doubt hammer away from jury selection to final argument that the jury should not render a verdict for the plaintiffs out of sympathy alone. A specific jury instruction on that very point will be read by the court and will undoubtedly be referred to repeatedly by defense counsel. One way to counter that argument is as follows:

Ladies and Gentlemen

I should like to remind you that it was the careless, negligent, and thoughtless act of the defendant which crushed out the life of little John Jones as he was on his way to school one early September morning. His defense attorney now stands before you and asks that you not render a verdict in favor of the plaintiffs based on sympathy alone. I can tell you on behalf of the parents of this little boy that they are not seeking sympathy in this courtroom today, they are seeking what the legal system of this country guarantees to them, justice. They received all the sympathy they could ever want on the day that their little son was killed. They received another avalanche of sympathy the day that his funeral was held and his body was buried. They are going to receive countless expressions of sympathy in the future every Mother's Day, every Christmas, every Thanksgiving, every family picnic or family reunion. They will receive from their own family circle all the sympathy that they need or want or can endure. They do not stand before you this day and ask for sympathy, they ask for justice, and they are doing so in the only way that our system of law in a civilized society allows—here—in a courtroom—before a jury—with people chosen from the community in which they live.

In most child death cases, emphasis is placed on the child's relations to his family and parents, demonstrating when possible that the child was a good member of the family, a good student and a fine citizen of the community. But how do you argue damages for the death of a problem child or teenager who had been in trouble with the law, or had run away from home, or was on drugs? These cases do not automatically lose their value. It is important whenever possible to impanel jurors who are parents, because most parents will sympathize with the problems of raising a difficult child. Perhaps these jurors have had problems with their own children, or maybe they are silently grateful because somehow they were spared similar child rearing difficulties. There are two illustrative Bible stories that can always be argued, regardless of the circumstances, without offending anyone's religious views. The stories are David and Goliath in the Old Testament and the Prodigal Son in the 15th Chapter of Luke in the New Testament. The latter story illustrates the point we want to make. The argument can be stated something like this:

Ladies and Gentlemen:

I would like to repeat for you today a story that was told almost 2,000 years ago. I do not tell you the story for its religious significance, but rather for its truth as a statement of human values, and because it applies to Mr. & Mrs. Jones with respect to the death of their son, John.

In Chapter 15 of Luke, in the New Testament, we are told about a man who had two sons. One was righteous and stayed home and did what his father wanted him to do, and the other expended all of his fortune in riotous living, and went away into other lands and, in effect, broke his father's heart. The day came when the son realized the folly of his ways and returned to the land of his father. He sought to be a servant in his father's field. He was no doubt surprised, as was the other son, at the father's reaction of great joy when the Prodigal Son returned. In fact, the greatest joy that that father probably ever felt during his lifetime, since the birth of the son that went astray, was the joy he felt when he saw that his son had returned. That is a feeling that only a parent who has known the anguish of a difficult child can truly know and appreciate.

In the case at bar, ladies and gentlemen, Mr. & Mrs. Jones have suffered the anguish during their lifetime of having a child not turn out in accordance with their expectations. That is not an uncommon human drama. However, always remember that there is no such thing as a worthless child. One of the saving graces that binds the civilized world together is the realization that parental love is not measured out in a quid pro quo equation. Parents do not measure out a specified amount of love, support, care and concern based upon an equivalent return of such feelings by their children. What is uncommon and equally unjust about the case you have been asked to decide is that these parents have been stripped of the right to enjoy perhaps the greatest joy they will ever know and that is the joy of having a child return.

I ask you for a moment to consider what a difference there would have been in this story 2,000 years ago if that son had been accidentally and negligently killed on his way back to his father's home. That father who had suffered so much would never have experienced the joy in seeing his son return and would not have been able to explain that lesson to his other son. That is the exact position that Mr. & Mrs. Jones were placed in when the defendant carelessly took the life of their son. In the normal course of events they were entitled by law to have the opportunity to grow old and to have their children grow up and develop and perhaps return to a relationship that was more in keeping with the dreams and hopes that all parents have for all children.

The sense of loss, the sense of grief, in this case is perhaps more acute than a normal case, for these people not only raised a child, but for years they nurtured a dream and a hope of expectations in the future. And it was not only their son that was lost through the negligence of the defendant, the hopes and dreams of a closer relationship in the future was crushed as well.

One of the great problems faced by any practitioner is the challenge of translating parental grief and suffering into a viable monetary equation. The question keeps returning, how do you measure the economic value of a child? The most memorable way I have ever seen to answer that question is contained in a brief discussion between the two men in the book *Remembrance Rock* by Carl Sandburg. I have taken the basic idea and changed it slightly for a more modern context, and have argued the point in the following manner.

Ladies and Gentlemen:

I have placed before you today, one of the most difficult tasks that any juror can face, and that is the task of trying to award my clients a specific sum of money based upon the grief and suffering they have endured for the loss of their child. You may come to ask yourselves how does one measure the value of a small child. I would suggest in coming to an appropriate award of damages that you consider the following thought: In your imagination, please conceive of a large room in which is placed a good measure of the wealth of this world. The room contain the most precious paintings, the rarest art objects, gold, silver, diamonds, the rarest gems in all the world, the most beautiful antiques, the rarest books, the gathered treasures of untold kingdoms. In the midst of all this wealth and splendor place a tiny, screaming infant wrapped in a blanket, unaware of who he is or where he is, and then by someone's callous negligence have the room lit on fire so that it is an inferno, and allow any human being who has a conscience and who is worthy of the name parent to stand at the door and be given just enough time to dash into the room and save one thing. Invariably, the person will instantly pass over the wealth of the world to gather up in his arms the child and carry it to safety. If you were to ask him why, he would always give the same answer—because the child lives. It is this quality of life, whether in a baby prince in a palace or in the lowliest urchin in a tenement slum, that in the final analysis is the gift that is most prized by the society in which we live.

Ladies and Gentlemen, your verdict in this case will evaluate for these parents the value of the life that was so carelessly taken from them.

## Notes

1. *Goodfellow v. Coggburn,* 560 P.2d 873 (Idaho, 1977)

2. *Latimer v. City of Clovis,* 495 P.2d 788 (N.M. App. 1972)
   *Talley v. J & L Oil Co., Inc.,* 579 P.2d 706 (Kan. 1978)

3. *Perleberg v. General Tire & Rubber Company,* 221 N.W.2d 729 (N.D. 1974) *Smith v. Americania Motor Lodge, et al.,* 39 Cal. App. 3d 1, 113 Cal. Rptr. 771 (1974)

4. *Bickley v. Farmer,* 211 S.E.2d 66 (Va. 1975)

5. *Alves v. Adler Built Industries, Inc.,* 366 So.2d 802 (Fla. App. 1979)

6. *Martinez v. Rodriguez,* 215 So.2d 305 (Fla. 1968)

7. *Wright v. Standard Oil Company,* 319 F. Supp. 1364 (N.D. Miss. 1970)

8. 22 AM. JUR.2d, Death §147

9. N.R.S. 41.085(4) F.S.A. 768.21(4)

10. *City of Tuscon v. Wondergem,* 66 P.2d 383 (Arizona, 1970)

11. *Portee v. Jaffee,* 417 A.2d 521 (N.J. 1980)
    *Dave Snelling Lincoln-Mercury v. Simon,* 508 S.W.2d 923 (Tex. App. 1974)

# Gerry Spence on the Karen Silkwood Trial

## An interview with Gerald L. Spence

Gerald L. Spence graduated from the University of Wyoming Law School in 1952 and served as County and Prosecuting Attorney in Fremont County, Wyoming. He is now senior partner in the Jackson, Wyoming law firm of Spence, Moriarity & Schuster. He is a member of the Board of Editors of *Trial Diplomacy Journal*.

*Karen Silkwood died in 1974 attempting to expose unsafe conditions in Oklahoma's Kerr-McGee plutonium plant. In May of 1979, a jury in Oklahoma City handed down a $10.5 million verdict against Kerr-McGee Corporation on behalf of the Karen Silkwood estate.*

### A Profile of an Extraordinary Case

EDITOR: Could you give us some of the background of the Karen Silkwood case, preparatory to talking about the techniques you used in that trial?

SPENCE: The Karen Silkwood case was the first case tried anywhere in the world that dealt with the question: what is the liability of people who play around with plutonium and radioactive materials, in the event that material escapes their custody and control, and contaminates people outside the facility in which the handler deals with the nuclear material. I call that distinction to your attention, because if somebody receives injuries while they are working, presumably they are covered by workman's compensation, and although Karen Silkwood was an employee of Kerr-McGee, she was not injured as a result of the employment, nor was she injured on the premises. Her contamination by plutonium was an offsite contamination not covered by workman's compensation; and it was therefore the first case brought by a citizen against a handler of radioactive materials.

Because it was the first case, it had a great deal of significance from the standpoint of determining the liability of such a company, what the law would be, what the defenses might be, what kinds of government standards might be defenses, and whether or not government standards would in fact be defenses. That whole gamut of inquiry was covered in what was the longest trial in the Oklahoma Federal Court System. It was a trial that consumed approximately three months of time, and it resulted in the largest verdict at that time in the United States, a verdict of ten and a half million dollars—ten million dollars in punitive damages, and half a million dollars for the nine days of suffering and torment that Karen Silkwood went through before she died, believing that she would die in the future of cancer.

The case dealt with a number of other firsts. It dealt with a definition by a jury of what an injury is. In this case there wasn't any kind of evidence of what is called a *medical* injury. That is, a doctor couldn't see the injuries that Karen Silkwood had received from plutonium by any known medical tests, or by any kind of x-rays, or by any kind of micro-examination. There was not any empirical, demonstrative evidence of her injury. But under the law, she had to be injured physically before she could recover for mental pain and suffering. So it was necessary to establish the question as to whether or not she had received injury. This case stood for the proposition that injury can indeed be demonstrated by the expert testimony of such people as Dr. Gofman and others who had *opinions* as to her injury, and as to the *probability* that she would die of cancer.

Some of the testimony that was received in this case were statements by Gofman to this effect: "Karen Silkwood was unalterably married to cancer"—although cancer couldn't be demonstrated. And then these experts were able to show that there was microscopic damage to cells, to the DNA, to the basic nucleus of the cell, which isn't observable to the human eye but is known to medical science; and that in their opinion had she survived the automobile accident, she would have died of cancer years later.

There were some legal goodies about the Karen Silkwood case that made it an extraordinary case to try; and it is a case that will result in Karen Silkwood becoming a modern day heroine. Karen Silkwood represents the ordinary, average human being, without any political base, without any political power, who was weak, who had no connections, who had no money, who had no position. She typified the average American citizen who says, "There's nothing I can do to change all of this." But along the way she recognized that people in the uranium business, and particularly in the plutonium plant where she worked, weren't being advised, and didn't know of dangers that they were facing. She complained about young boys, nineteen- and twenty-year-old boys, who were playing with materials as if it were dirt, and who were being exposed to radiation in quantities that she felt were surely detrimental to their health, and they didn't know better. She discovered such frightening things as missing plutonium from the plant, in quantities as much as forty pounds, which it was said is enough to make ten bombs the size of those used in Nagasaki and Hiroshima. She discovered the rather shameful game that the government and industry were using to try to account for the missing plutonium: silly number games that made no sense, and that offered no solution to the missing plutonium, excepting in the mysteries of their formulas. She discovered, much as in "The China Syndrome," the fact that the photomicrographs taken of the fuel rods that were being manufactured there at the plant for use in the breeder-reactor in Hanover, Washington, x-rays needed for quality control, were being doctored. And that the flaws in the photomicrographs were being covered with black marker pencil.

And she had decided, although she hadn't commenced in any way as a union zealot, that the only way to deal with these problems was through union activity. She became very active in the union, and she had with the union personnel planned to reveal many of these facts to the public through the *New York Times*. She had in fact set up a date with a gentleman by the name of Dave Burnham of the *New York Times*, to meet him in Oklahoma City, and to deliver to him physical data to show and to prove the allegations that she had made.

The last she was seen was fifteen minutes before her death, on her way to meet David Burnham. She had the testimony, and a folder was under her arm—presumably the photomicrographs, files full of documents bearing the Kerr-McGee insignia, and other materials, that filled a rather large manila folder—and she told the woman as she was leaving that she was on her way to meet David Burnham with the goods that were necessary to prove her case against Kerr-McGee. Fifteen minutes later she was found dead in a ditch, and there is evidence that she was struck from behind, that it wasn't an ordinary automobile accident. And the papers that she carried with her were never discovered after the date of the wreck.

So those were the background facts that lent some kind of interest to the case, although the question of how she came to her death was never a part of the trial and was never permitted by the court to be gone into.

### Selecting a Jury of Six Independent Thinkers

EDITOR: Now I'd like to ask you about the techniques you used in the trial. Let's start with jury selection.

SPENCE: This was a federal trial, I think, tried in the highest form of modern trial tradition by a federal judge who was quite willing to leave behind the old, staid ideas of federal trial procedure and to try something new in the federal court. Judge Theis, who himself was a trial attorney, permitted a limited voir dire by the attorneys in the case. This isn't, as you probably know, standard in federal courts—there are very few federal judges who permit a trial attorney to voir dire at all in the federal courts. In this case, Judge Theis voir dired the jury to his satisfaction, and then permitted the attorneys to make limited inquiry of the jury.

EDITOR: Did you have any pre-conceived ideas about what kind of jury you wanted or did not want?

SPENCE: There were certain obvious kinds of people that any attorney wouldn't want to have on the jury. The jury of course was voir dired carefully with respect to their attitudes toward nuclear energy, and toward their relationship with Kerr-McGee and the employees of Kerr-McGee. But generally what we wanted was a jury out of the heartland of America. I wanted a jury that didn't have any conflict *within itself*. I wanted jurors who, in other words, could get along among themselves. I wanted a jury that didn't have a whole series of preconceived ideas. I wanted a jury that would act, that had the strength to act, the courage to act, because this was a special kind of case. It was a case in which the whole future of the human species might indeed be at stake. And so I wanted a courageous jury.

This jury, which must act as a single entity, needed to be made up of people from different walks of life, and indeed it was. It was a jury of three men and three women. It was a jury that I think represented pretty much a cross section of America. There was a retired woman school teacher— thoughtful, strong, positive in her attitudes. There was a young architectural engineer. There was a young male who was a foreman of a sort of labor crew for a utility company. There was a middle-aged lady who worked as a clerk for the state government in the highway department. There was a young-to-middle-aged housewife. There was a telephone repairman.

These six people didn't have any conflict with each other. I tried not to permit a sexual conflict to develop: there weren't any raving beauties in the women, and there weren't any Romeos in the men. They were people who could sit together and keep their minds on their business. There weren't any people there that would have any natural conflict with me. The women were the kind of women you could sit down and have an afternoon's conversation with—open, interested, inquiring people. The men were the kind of people you would like to spend an afternoon fishing with—there wasn't any macho problem of control, of one man being strong and threatening others. There wasn't any problem or conflict that I could see between myself and the other men on the jury.

Those were the principal things that I was looking for in a long trial. People who could sit comfortably and consider carefully what was about to happen to this country from the standpoint of the nuclear question.

EDITOR: Did you look for a juror with a social conscience?

SPENCE: Of course I wanted jurors with social consciences. However, by the time that would be revealed very strongly, the defendants would be able to recognize that this juror had a strong social conscience, and would undoubtedly take the juror off. It is necessary to have sort of a sense about jurors, and be able to look for that sort of thing in a person without really strongly revealing it in the questioning.

For example, people who talk a great deal about the organizations that they belong to—their belonging to the chamber of commerce, their belonging to church organizations, their dedication to the Boy Scouts, their involvement in such things as the Kiwanis Clubs—surprisingly indicate to me people who have a very limited social conscience. And I don't really want those people on a jury in a case of this kind. Those are the kinds of people that permit society to dictate as to what their conscience should be, and as to what their conduct should be. I wanted independent thinkers, people who would rather go fishing than go to church on Sunday; people that would have a sense of themselves, rather than people who were looking to others to proclaim a sense of themselves.

### The All-Important Opening Statement

EDITOR: What did you try to accomplish in your opening statement in this case?

SPENCE: The opening statement in this case, as in every case, is perhaps the most important single presentation an attorney gives to a jury. It's the most important of all because it gives a jury its first taste of the attorney, and its first taste of his case; and first impressions are the most important impressions. They are the most important impressions that we have of people, and they're the most lasting. And they're extremely important in a jury trial.

And so it is important for the attorney in an opening to lay out the case, I think, in exquisite detail. Usually the court doesn't limit trial attorneys in the opening statements as they do in the closing statement. Time isn't as pressing. People are more relaxed, and the opening statement seems to just sort of flow, and lay out the contentions and the issues of the lawyer's case. It is then, for the first time, that he can make sense to the jury of what his case is all about, and prepare the jury to receive the evidence, and prepare the jury to see the justice of his case. And it is that time when the jury really gets a sense of whether or not the case has any merit, and whether or not the attorney is a meritorious person—whether or not the attorney can be trusted, whether or not they can, to say it another way, *buy* the case, whether they feel comfortable with it. And if the attorney does a good job in the opening statement, the rest of the trial becomes easier: the evidence flows into place, fits into the places where it's supposed to fit, and makes sense. The opening statement becomes really a skeleton upon which the meat of the case is placed.

So the opening statement is extremely important, and it was done carefully in this case. The opening statement in this case took maybe four hours, and involved several recesses. It was laid out carefully in a narrative form, as if I were telling the jury a story in an interesting and exciting way; a story that they could buy into and become a part of, and felt a *need* to become a part of. This is what happens in the opening statement, and this is what we did in the Silkwood case.

EDITOR: Did you think the jury would have any problem with the fact that Karen Silkwood was dead, and her death was not related to the injuries for which you were seeking damages?

SPENCE: From the standpoint of a typical personal injury case, viewed on a scale of one to ten, where ten is the most profitable and winnable kind of case that attorneys want to take, and one is the least, there were things about this case that would rate it as a one, instead of a ten. It was a case in which the client was dead. There wasn't any plaintiff there to present to the jury, except a sort of empty chair, and we weren't suing for her death. The facts that covered her death and that were so mysterious were excluded by the court. And what we are asking for was pain and suffering and mental trauma of a woman who died of causes that weren't a part of the trial. So here we were asking a jury to give us hundreds of thousands of dollars for her mental suffering; and it wasn't a long period of mental suffering, it was a period of eight or nine days. To go to a jury and say, "Give me hundreds of thousands of dollars, Mr. and Mrs. Jury, for my dead client; not for her death, but for her suffering before she died," you know, is a hard thing for an attorney to do, and it's a hard matter to discuss and to make real to a jury. So that was one of its basic weaknesses.

EDITOR: How did you try to overcome that, in the opening statement?

SPENCE: The opening statement, of course, was used to put the issue in perspective. It became clear in the course of the trial that there were other issues that were equally important, the issues of punitive and exemplary damages, which made the case exciting and compelling to the jury. We dealt out a good deal of our energies in that area.

### Using Medical Experts to Prove a Hard-to-Detect Injury

EDITOR: How did you use medical experts to prove there was an injury?

SPENCE: The answer to that question starts with just a tiny bit of scientific background, that any of us can understand, and which the jury thoroughly understood.

Our bodies are made of billions of cells. Inside each cell, in the nucleus, is a tiny but exquisite little library that tells the cell when to live, when to die, when to divide itself and how, and in what manner to grow. And if it weren't for that special knowledge that is contained in every cell, our eye cells wouldn't know whether to become eyes, or wouldn't know whether to become five eyes or twenty eyes or two-ton eyes, or when to stop growing. And our noses would grow like Pinocchio's, and we would grow until we covered the landscape, like algae grow in the sea. These highly refined cells, these beautifully knowledgeable cells of ours, have the secret of life, every one of them, in this little library that's called the DNA.

Now, alpha particles are known to attack cells and to kill cells. If they kill a few cells, well that's quite all right, because we are capable of reproducing others. And as a matter of fact, that's how we kill cancer—by killing the cancer cell. But when the alpha particle from radiation doesn't kill the cell but only knocks out the library, the cell has indeed suffered injury, has it not? At that point, that library is no longer there to tell the cell when to quit growing, and a cancer is formed. And fifteen years later that unhappy little shadow appears in your lung's x-ray; or it appears as a lump in your wife's breast; or you have funny sensations in your gut and in your bowel. And fifteen or twenty years later after that first insult was done to the library of that single cell, that cell has continued to multiply itself without restriction, and finally it presents itself as a troublesome cancer which may or may not be controllable.

Now, how do you prove that? Nobody sees it. Nobody can show it empirically. And so the nuclear industry has been going around saying things like this: "There has never been a human being who was shown to have been killed from cancer caused by a particular nuclear exposure." Because we can't *show* that initial cell injury, because you can't *see* the injury to the DNA—you can't even see the DNA. Since you can't see the injury to the DNA, they have been able to say that nobody has been able to prove that an injury to the cell causes cancer, or that exposure to radiation causes cancer. And there have been such ridiculous statements, and almost criminally misleading statements, as, "More people died in Teddy Kennedy's car than have died from plutonium exposure or radiation."

In the course of this trial, the defendants made the very bad mistake of attempting to mislead the jury by having expert after expert make this gross statement, that there has never been shown any kind of cancer resulting from any exposure to radiation in the business.

The other side of the coin is that every reputable expert in the world knows, and has known for years, that exposure to radiation causes cancer, and that hundreds of thousands of people in this world have died as a result of radiation from fallout from the bombs, from nuclear testing. It's common knowledge that radiation causes cancer; it's as common knowledge among scientists as the fact that a virus causes a cold. It's the trickery in the wording of the issue that has caused the problem, and has confused the public.

And so we were required to rely on expert witnesses who said such things as: For fifty years we have known that people who were exposed to radiation in the pitchblende mines in Yugoslavia died like flies from lung cancer. Pitchblende is simply a form of uranium. For years we have known that the poor little ladies who were the radium dial painters, who painted the numbers on our wrist watches, simply died like flies. They took the tips of their little brushes and stuck them in their mouths to make them pointed, and then they painted radium on the dial of the watch so that we could see at night what time it was. And the price of that luxury was to die. They died of all kinds of cancer. Early experiments with plutonium in dogs showed that they died in almost 100% of the cases, many of them in their old age, but all of them from cancer. And it is a fact that low exposure to radiation over long periods of time is as deadly as high exposure over short periods of time.

This kind of testimony was given by such experts as Dr. John Gofman, from the University of California at Berkeley, who was the first man to isolate a milligram of plutonium. And it then became a question for the jury to determine which of the experts were most credible.

## Cross-Examination: The Key to Victory

EDITOR: Were there any particular techniques of cross examination that were key to winning this case?

SPENCE: I think cross-examination *was* the key to winning the case. It was a case in which the defendants, Kerr-McGee, called over twenty experts, and any one of those experts, had the cross-examination failed, could have resulted in turning the tide for Kerr-McGee. It even got to the point where the case maybe turned upon the successful cross-examination of their last expert, Dr. Voelz from Los Alamos. He was their star witness, and they of course saved him for last.

Cross-examination enabled the jury to weigh the respective credibility of the experts. The jury had to say, "Dr. Gofman says that Karen Silkwood was married to cancer. Dr. Voelz said she wasn't injured and there wasn't any evidence that she would ever die of cancer. Who do you believe?"

Dr. Gofman says that Karen Silkwood was the victim of a company that was grossly negligent; and one of our other witnesses said that Kerr-McGee was more than grossly or willfully and wantonly negligent—they were "callous."

Dr. Voelz and the other witnesses for the defense said that Kerr-McGee was careful; that they complied with government standards; that government standards were reasonable. Dr. Carl Morgan, the father of the field of health physics, said that the standards were as much as two to four hundred times too lax. Dr. Voelz, on behalf of Kerr-McGee, and others, said that the standards were adequate, if not too stringent.

Now, here were reputable men of science on both sides taking opposite positions. The question is, which witness is credible? And that is ultimately revealed through the skill of the cross examiner.

I think the *imperative* of successful cross-examination is preparation. I had attorneys who would meet with me every morning. Sometimes they had spent the entire previous day preparing the facts, that is, sort of cataloging the facts that had been gathered over months and months relative to each of the witnesses that were being called. We would usually have twenty-four hours notice of a witness being called. And these attorneys would meet with me early in the morning before the trial began— sometimes 6:00, sometimes 7:00 in the morning—and would feed me the information that was necessary to prepare me for the cross-examination.

Through appropriate discovery we had the files of their principal employees, who had been in charge of the plant. From the files we were able to discover that one of their principal witnesses, who sat as their representative throughout the entirety of the trial, was a man who had a fine record in college, but his degree was in poultry farming. We found out that those who were in charge of the fabrication of the plant, the building of the plant, the design of the plant, were people who had really never had any experience in designing a plutonium plant before. One of them had worked for a company that made paints. One of the individuals in charge of the plant had simply been an employee that they received in a trade from another company when Kerr McGee bought the other company up—a man who was now in charge of a plutonium plant who had never really dealt with plutonium before he came there to become in charge of it. The man who was in charge of security had never had any experience in security, but was a retired Air Force colonel whose only experience was in maintenance.

It was this kind of attack relative to the experiences and qualifications of many of their experts that was made. But I think one of the important things that was revealed in the cross-examination was just how comfortably industry and government were in bed together in this case, as they are in almost every segment of American industry. The cross-examination revealed, as we pulled back the bed sheets, a rather interesting configuration of the government and the nuclear industry in a sado-masochistic relationship. They were sado-masochistic lovers. They sort of hated each other. They sort of whipped and beat each other. But when the chips were down they were still lovers, and they were still there in bed together, and still supporting each other in the process of the trial. The skillful revelation of those facts had a great deal to do with the undermining of the credibility of both the government and Kerr-McGee.

For example, Dr. Voelz is the highest man up the totem pole at Los Alamos, which is a program financed completely by the government, contracted through the University of California. That program, with Dr. Voelz at the head of it—Dr. Voelz is an M.D.—dealt with experiments in the environment, experiments and research with respect to radiation in human beings; some twelve programs involving literally thousands of people, and hundreds of scientists. He was the top man. The government's man. He was a man who had been put through school by the government, who had been a part of the Atomic Energy Commission's scholarship program, who had worked for government or for government-financed programs all of his life, and finally had achieved the pinnacle of power in these programs. And it was interesting, I'm sure, to the jury, and it was interesting to us, to see Kerr-McGee reach out and pluck that top man off as their own private plum, and bring him back into the courtroom as their own expert, paid by them as their witness in that case, to testify to a jury on their behalf as their private consultant.

It was interesting to see that this man had also consulted with Karen Silkwood. Here she was in the grave, her lips sealed by death. And here was the man with whom she had consulted about such personal things as whether she could have babies, now testifying against her cause three or four years later.

Let me show you the kind of cross-examination that might occur in the event that we were cross-examining someone like Mr. Keppler, the head of District Three, who was in charge of inspecting what Kerr-McGee was doing here with this dangerous stuff called plutonium:

Q: How many violations of your regulations do you suppose that Kerr-McGee has committed in its operation here?

A: Oh, maybe 75.

Q: What, you mean to say 75 violations?

A: Yes.

Q: Would it be fair to say that Kerr-McGee was cited some 75 times for those violations? And you did cite them for those violations?

A: Yes.

Q: And that's sort of like the highway patrolman who stops a citizen on the highway for having violated a traffic ordinance, and gives the citizen a citation, isn't that true?

A: Yes.

Q: It's that kind of citation, isn't it?

A: Yes.

Q: And after the first citation was given, I suppose you gave them sort of a warning, didn't you?

A: Yes.

Q: And after the second violation came along, you warned them further, didn't you?

A: Yes.

Q: And after the third, you warned them further, did you not?

A: Yes.

Q: And after the fourth, you were still warning them, weren't you?

A: Yes.

Q: And after the twenty-fifth you were still warning them, weren't you?

A: Yes.

Q: And after the fiftieth, you were still warning them, weren't you? And after 75 violations, it is fair to say that you never once fined them a penny, isn't that true?

And the answer is yes.

That is substantially the kind of cross-examination that revealed the kinds of close relationships that existed between government and industry. The facts in the case under cross-examination revealed that there were over 500 exposures of human beings to plutonium at the plant and many of these were exposed to a much greater extent than Karen Silkwood was. And the government, despite the fact that many of the great scientific minds of this country disagreed vehemently, was still mouthing the same kinds of platitudes that I have already made reference to—that there has never been a showing of any cancer having been caused by plutonium. This is, of course, the very same thing that the cigarette industry has said for years and years, and still says—that there has never been a case where it has been proven that exposure to any given cigarettes or tobacco caused any given cancer.

Let me give you another example. They called in a radiologist who treated cancer by x-ray therapy. Now this doctor had never seen Karen Silkwood, and had no previous experience in research and radiation outside the very limited field of x-ray therapy. This doctor was called to tell the jury that he had examined Karen Silkwood's x-rays after her exposure, and that they were perfectly normal; that he had examined her blood samples and that they were normal; her urine samples were normal; and that there was no showing of any kind of medical injury having occurred to Karen Silkwood.

Now that doctor knew, just as I knew, and every reasonable medical expert in the country knew, that that testimony was misleading to a jury, because it would lead to the conclusion that there wasn't now, nor ever would be, anything wrong with Karen Silkwood, and this was a groundless lawsuit. The cross-examination should go something like this:

Q: Doctor, if Karen Silkwood was injured by radiation to the extent that she would have cancer in fifteen or twenty years, developing from this exposure, that wouldn't be seen in an x-ray, would it?

A: No.

Q: You couldn't see any kind of radiation injury excepting the grossest kind, that is, excepting where people are actually burned. You cannot see the kind of injury we are talking about here, in x-rays, can you?

A: No.

Q: The injury isn't revealed in ordinary medical tests, is it?

A: No.

Q: You know that, don't you?

A: Yes.

Q: You knew that when you told the jury that there wasn't any evidence of it, didn't you?

A: Yes

This is the kind of cross-examination that can be used successfully to reveal the word games that go on here. I would give you one more quick example, if you would like one.

How about the missing 40 pounds of plutonium? What happened to it? First of all, we got involved in a word game right off, because the defense counsel did not like my calling it "missing." He wanted me to call it "unaccounted for." Then they said, well, the missing 40 pounds of plutonium is in the pipes. This stuff goes through thousands of feet of pipes and it's clinging to the pipes, and that's where it is. Just like, you know, milk clings to the glass and it makes the glass dirty, that's where it is. And so they wash the pipes. And they wash the pipes not once, they washed them not for two days, not a week, but they washed the pipes for six weeks, until the pipes started to disintegrate. They washed them with acid, and finally they still couldn't find the missing plutonium, and so they called in what the government and industry often call in when they are in trouble, and that is the mathematician.

Now, the mathematicians, you know, can come up with formulas that are plus and minus certain figures. They are very difficult formulas to understand, and they are put on the board; and I can't understand them, the jury can't understand them, nobody can understand them. Ah, but if on cross-examination I ask them a simple question like this: "I weigh 230 pounds. Now applying your formula, your plus or minus formula, how much do I weigh?"

Well, his answer was, "You weigh between 160 and 370 pounds," or something like that.

The mathematician was trying to show that the 40 pounds of plutonium was within a margin of error that was acceptable, and we showed that when you plugged your weight into that formula, the margin of error was outrageous.

## Controlling the Witness on Cross Examination

EDITOR: On cross-examination, did you attack the experts as aggressively as you do right now?

SPENCE: It depends on the expert. I handle cross-examination like the good fisherman handles a trout at the end of a line. I control the trout. The trout doesn't control me. If I let the trout and the line go, the trout will go downstream and break my line, or he'll get it all twisted up in some brush, or he'll jump out of the water and shake the fly out of his mouth. And so it is necessary in cross-examination to keep the line taut. On the other hand, if you pull the trout out, and just jerk him out over your shoulder, the line will break and you will lose him as well.

The cross-examination of a witness is very much like that. You have to deal with each witness differently. If the witness is gentle and compassionate, and seems open, you would hardly attack that kind of a witness aggressively, until such time as he commences to become evasive. You tighten the line and pull the witness in with the correct questions; at which time either he supports your position, or he starts to wiggle and to become evasive and hostile. And when the witness becomes hostile, then you yourself can become aggressive and hostile.

But if you attack a witness and the jury likes the witness, the result is the jury ends up disliking you, and your cross-examination has been a failure. So the answer to your question is that one has to deal with the witness as he develops on the witness stand.

EDITOR: Once you get an admission from a witness on cross-examination that is in your favor, do you stop there or try to get more?

SPENCE: Well, I think there is a certain skill in knowing when to stop and there is a certain skill in taking the admission. Too often I see attorneys take admissions that are damning to their opponent's case, but the witness lets it come out very quietly and gently in the cross-examination, and it just slips by the jury's ears as nothing, although the words are strong and important words as they are printed in the record. It is important that the attorney have sufficient presence to know whether or not the admission is understood and felt and appreciated by the jury. That's handled with the way the attorney responds to it—for example, an exclamation mark that comes after the answer: "You say so and so and so and so?"—said with his eyes wide open and a kind of incredulous look on his face, which causes the jury to listen and to understand.

On the other hand, once having gotten the admission, one has to be careful that the witness doesn't have a chance, as you approach him the second time, to undermine that with further explanations.

### Damages and Final Argument

EDITOR: How much did you ask for in damages?

SPENCE: They started out with a request for $10,000, just a jurisdictional amount. Then it was amended a number of times. By the time the trial started it was $10,000,000 in punitive damages. And then during the course of the trial, I asked the judge to further amend it. At the time of the final arguments I was asking the jury for something like $70,000,000 in punitive damages, which represented two weeks in gross earnings of Kerr-McGee. And so all I really asked them for was a two-week paycheck.

Closing arguments in that case took a whole day. And we spent half a day each side, arguing.

EDITOR: In the final argument, did you urge the jurors to be pioneers, or to be courageous?

SPENCE: I tried in the final argument of the case to call the jury's attention to *their* presence, to who *they* were, to have them develop a sense of their position in history, and to understand the importance of what was really happening in the case. And I think they had a concept of that. I think that the jurors early on in the trial understood that this case was one of the important cases in the history of our country. It's been perhaps the most important case that has ever been tried in America, and maybe in English jurisprudence. Take, for example, such cases as the Scopes trial, where the issue was whether or not man could talk about monkeys and his beginnings, and whether there should be a freedom of expression, and of education. Indeed, those were important issues, and they were tried by important lawyers such as Clarence Darrow and William Jennings Bryan.

But this case dealt with the very issue of the survival of the race. And the question as to whether or not we as human beings have enough intelligence to survive.

# Effective Appellate Advocacy

## Alfred L. Scanlan

Alfred L. Scanlan is a member of the Washington, DC, law firm of Shea & Gardner. As an attorney he has participated in more than 250 appeals, including more than 60 Supreme Court cases. As a judge of the Court of Special Appeals of Maryland (1972-1973) he sat on several hundred appeals, both civil and criminal. Scanlan has lectured and written widely on the subject of appellate advocacy.

**Many experienced trial lawyers have rarely had occasion to write a brief in the true sense. They may be fully able to compose effective trial memoranda and workman-like statements in support of pre- or post-trial motions, but they have not been called on to think through the writing and filing of the type of brief required for an effective appeal.**

### Preparing Your Ultimate Tool of Persuasion

Before starting to write the brief, read (or at least review) and then index the record. If there are several issues to be dealt with in the appeal, it is advisable to have a topical index of the record as well as a chronological one. A topical index serves three distinct purposes:

    1. It assists counsel to accurately designate the portions of the record on which the parties rely in their briefs.

    2. It is helpful in writing the brief, especially in composing the statement of facts, the critical portion of the brief.

    3. It is often useful as a memory refresher in preparing an oral argument which is scheduled a number of months after the brief has been filed.

    It is important to carefully review the applicable appellate rules pertaining to form, content, length, and even the color of the cover page, of the brief that you plan to file. Remember that the brief is of singular importance in most appellate courts. When an appellate judge first reads the brief, he gets his initial feel for the case and begins to develop that which Judge Hutcheson once called his "judicial hunch" as to how the case should come out. The importance of the brief has increased in recent years because of the tendency of federal and state appellate courts to cut back on the number of cases which are afforded oral argument. Thus, despite the importance of oral argument, the brief is a critical document, and so far as most appeals are concerned, is the ultimate tool of persuasion.

### How to Write the Statement of Facts

The statement of facts should be in as complete and polished a form as possible before you move on to write the remainder of the brief. In drafting the statement of facts, an attorney should attempt to observe what John W. Davis* once referred to as the "three C's"—chronology, candor, and clarity.

**1. Chronology:** Tell the court the story as it occurred, not in the order in which the witnesses testified, or in which the facts were put on record. When you can, make use of the opinions or findings below in setting out the material facts.

**2. Candor:** In composing the statement of facts, above all be accurate. Demonstrate that accuracy with citations to the record for every material fact stated. Grasp the nettles firmly; don't let your opponent be the first to advise the court of a material fact which is adverse to your case. As Mr. Justice Rutledge once put it:

> Do not try to dodge or minimize the facts which are against you. If you can't win without doing this—and it is seldom you can by doing it—your case should not be appealed ... [F]ew things add strength to the argument as do candid and full admissions.

Do not argue, editorialize, or snipe at the appellee, his counsel, or his witnesses. Personalities have no place at all in an appellate brief; argument and opinion should be reserved for the section of the brief devoted to argument.

---

*Vice-presidential candidate in 1924, onetime solicitor general, and leading authority on the Supreme Court.

**3. Clarity:** If the statement of facts is on the long side, use subheadings to hold the attention of the court. Short paragraphs are to be preferred. A final bit of advice for appellee's counsel: if there were inaccuracies and material omissions in the appellant's statement of facts, write your own—you have the privilege.

Finally, remember the basic goal of drafting the statement of facts: to write a statement of facts so that an appellate court will be inclined to decide the case in your favor when it has finished reading your statement.

## How to Draft Effectively "Loaded" Questions

When drafting the questions to be presented, bear in mind that this is your first opportunity to indulge—very subtly—in the art of persuasion. By this I mean that while you should draft the questions in a manner which is informative, clear, accurate and fair, they should also be pregnant with the answer you would like the court to give. This is "loading" the question—inserting key facts which will subtly suggest the answer that you desire.

A question should be informative; it should state in a nutshell what the case is about. Do not rest with general statements such as, "Did the trial court err in excluding the appellant's evidence of self-defense?" The question should also be sound in syntax and grammar. Above all, it should be clear, especially after you have finished loading it.

As an example of an effectively loaded but nonetheless informative and fairly-stated question, I refer to a question prepared by a partner of mine in a federal criminal case:

> Whether evidence supported the conviction of aiding and abetting transportation of narcotics discovered in an automobile in which the appellant was a passenger where the testimony showed that he did not know that narcotics were in the car and that he had not assisted the owner and driver in any way.

## Tips for Writing a Clear, Strong Argument

Do not start writing that part of the brief devoted to argument until you have completed your statement of facts and concluded your legal research. After all, there are deficiencies in any key index system, and as a consequence, recent relevant decisions are often overlooked in the preparation of a brief.

Prepare an outline before starting to write your argument. Write the brief consecutively, i.e., don't start writing the draft of a third section until you have finished the drafts of the first and second sections.

Always have someone else, preferably a partner or an associate, read your final draft. If any portion of it is unclear to the reader, revise it. In polishing your final draft, delete awkward sentences and hyperbole. Carefully check your citations, quotes and references to the record and shepardize all significant case citations. Remember that there's no need to clutter the brief with excessive citations; one or two cases supporting a particular point are sufficient. However, be sure the cases that you do cite support the point for which they've been summoned.

Counsel for the appellant should not hesitate to assign weak contentions to footnotes, or to abandon them completely. Argue your strongest points first. By this I mean not the points with which you are infatuated, but those which you as a lawyer objectively feel that an appellate court is most likely to be taken with.

Distinguish your opponent's leading cases. Don't take the "ostrich" attitude to your adversary's authorities. Argumentative headings and subheadings can also be helpful, especially when the argument can be divided into a number of sections and subsections. If the section on argument is on the long side, it is wise to prepare a summary of the argument. This may be an introductory section to precede the argument itself. However, don't write the summary until you have finished the brief in its final form. That way, the summary of argument will not go off on a frolic of its own. Its purpose is to succinctly and accurately inform the court of the arguments that are to follow.

Finally, some special advice for appellee's counsel. Don't let the appellant mark out the playing field for you. Resist preparing an appellee's brief that is merely a point-by-point refutation of arguments in the order set in the appellant's brief. Actually, it is a good idea for appellee's counsel to have at least a rough outline of his brief even before he receives the appellant's brief.

### Effective Oral Argument

Opinions differ as to the importance of oral argument in the conduct of an appeal. Mr. Justice Brennan, for example, has said, "My whole notion of what a case is about crystalizes at oral argument." Others—and this is probably the more widely held view—feel that you can lose your case with a bad oral argument, but it is difficult to win it with a strong one.

Nevertheless, to assure a fully effective presentation of any appeal, oral argument is important and cannot be neglected.

As in all aspects of the law, counsel should prepare carefully for oral argument. Re-read all of the briefs and all of the important cases, including those of your opponent. The pertinent cases should be shepardized and otherwise brought up to date. It is helpful to have index tabs to the major points in the various briefs, and to significant references to the record. You might also consider rehearsing your oral argument before your associates. My own personal preference is to prepare a detailed outline and go over it in my mind many times before the actual argument.

At oral argument, counsel for the appellant should introduce himself and indicate what portion of his time he desires to observe for rebuttal, unless that has been previously communicated to the court through the clerk. At the outset, appellant's counsel should let the court know how the case reached it. This is especially true in the case of an argument before the Supreme Court.

Try to have a short paragraph in your mind which sums up the essence of your case, and state that somewhere during the course of your oral argument, preferably either at the outset or at the conclusion.

It is usually appropriate for counsel for the appellant to give a very brief statement of the facts which are critical to the argued issues. But since most appellate judges now read the briefs before hearing oral argument, and if the facts have been fully and fairly stated in appellant's brief, there is no need to spend too much time restating the facts in oral argument.

After giving a brief description of the order of argument which you intend to follow, as counsel for the appellant you should plunge into your main arguments. Go for the jugular; avoid any rehash of your brief. Address only the major points—oral argument is an exercise in persuasion, not an oral treatise. Don't bog down in giving detailed facts or an extended analysis of pertinent cases. All of that should have been accomplished in the brief.

It goes without saying that a lawyer should never read his argument to the court. This is completely unprofessional. Avoid racing through your argument, or speaking in a monotone. Above all, answer questions put to you by members of the court at the time when these questions are asked; don't postpone answering until late in your argument. Questions from the judges indicate their interest in the argument and furnish the appellate advocate with the opportunity to clarify, explain, and persuade. They should be welcomed, not feared or avoided.

I advise against distracting mannerisms, such as waving a pencil or a pair of eyeglasses. Have your notes on the lectern and use them when you must. Don't try the Harry Houdini trick of speaking without any notes at all. Apart from the frailty of human memory—even that of a well-prepared appellate advocate—there is the hazard that the court might become more interested in seeing if you can pull off the trick than in listening to the actual argument.

Be flexible in oral argument. Be ready to change emphasis, shift oratorical gears, and even abandon points of argument if the court's attitude appears to justify it.

There is no one particular style of oral argument that is most effective. Some lawyers speak quietly and carefully; others have a tendency toward a more bombastic presentation. No one style is recommended—only that with which you're most comfortable. Be yourself. If you've prepared your case and know that of your opponent as well, your message will get through to the court.

# INDEX